New Currents in Soviet-Type Economies: A Reader

GEORGE R. FEIWEL

Professor of Economics
The University of Tennessee

INTERNATIONAL TEXTBOOK COMPANY
Scranton, Pennsylvania

Preface

It was not long ago that, in order to grasp the essentials of Soviet-type economies, a student could probably profit most by studying the Soviet case which not only had a longer history, but also served as a prototype which was unimaginatively transplanted after World War II to the East European countries that came under the Soviet sphere of influence. A mark of the dramatic changes taking place is that the designation "Soviet-type" economies can no longer be applied to the varieties of solutions with which these economies are experimenting. Whereas about a decade ago, a uniform so-called road to socialism was still followed, today differentiated approaches are being sought and tried.

It would seem that the winds of change often blow from different directions. The Soviets, not infrequently, are the followers rather than the initiators of change. Indeed, in many respects, East European economic revisionism is more interesting, imaginative, daring, and far-reaching than the Soviet brand. For all these reasons, a study of the changing economic scene in the Soviet Union together with Eastern Europe seems to be more instructive. It might offer the student a broader outlook on the logic of the reforms and the changes yet to come.

Indeed, to better comprehend the problems involved, and to understand the workings of the system under various conditions, a study of the first renegade from the Soviet bloc, Yugoslavia—the country of "permanent reform"—and a study of the Chinese brand of Communism would be very much in order. But then it would also be necessary to include a survey of economic planning in mixed economies and all this would require another volume.

I am indebted to all the authors whose contributions are reproduced here. The publisher's cooperation and good will are appreciated. Special thanks are due to David J. Gabriel and John A. Wargo for their assistance. I am particularly grateful to Professors John M. Montias and Jan M. Michal for having undertaken to contribute unpublished papers, especially at a time when they were preoccupied with other endeavors. Sincere thanks are also due to Professor George J. Staller for sending me his excellent paper which, unfortunately, was received too late for inclusion. Professors Gregory Grossman, Alexander Erlich, and Joseph S. Berliner were good enough to review this compilation. Their excellent suggestions are gratefully appreciated. It goes without saying that the choice of material was not easy and I alone bear the responsibility for it.

GEORGE R. FEIWEL

Knoxville, Tennessee
June, 1968

Contents

Growth, Scarcity, and Reform Movements
in Soviet-Type Economies . . . 1

Part I

The Anatomy of the Soviet-Type
Command Economy . . . 11

Part II

The Winds of Economic Change . . . 221

Growth, Scarcity, and Reform Movements in Soviet-Type Economies

Alterations in working arrangements for resource allocation taking place in the Soviet and East European economies are being watched and analyzed with considerable interest, for they not only are of significance to the future economic performance of these countries, but they may be the precursors ushering in liberalization and greater freedom in other domains of public and social life. It is probably not an exaggeration to advance that humanity at large has a stake in their success.

As the Communist world celebrates the fiftieth anniversary of the October Revolution, it can look back with satisfaction at its accomplishments in rapidly industrializing essentially agricultural countries, at a notable record of accelerated growth in countries (Czechoslovakia and East Germany), which were relatively industrialized at the outset and in creating the second largest industrial power. But the impressive achievements had their price in terms of the population's welfare, the massive inputs of resources, abstracting from the huge sacrifices that cannot be assessed in terms of economics.

In evaluating Soviet or East European economic performance at least two vantage points could be chosen: 1) how well the goals postulated by the regime's leaders have been achieved, and 2) the extent to which consumers' preferences have been respected.[1] According to the second standard, the performance of the Soviet-type economy is inordinately poor to the extent that consumers' welfare is disregarded and consumers' preferences as to allocation between current and future consumption are violated. However, a strong argument can be built to prove that these were not the objectives set by the regime's leaders and that conformity to the second standard is not an appropriate criterion for evaluating performance. But if we are to

---

[1] I am purposely abstracting here from international comparisons. Cf. A. Bergson, *The Economics of Soviet Planning* (New Haven: Yale University Press, 1964), pp. 340–58.

abide by the first standard only, it may be argued that the performance is less impressive than it seems at face value if we can establish that the system did not utilize resources to their best advantage in achieving the leadership's aims, or could have utilized them to better advantage under different working arrangements and/or with an alternative growth strategy. However, this proposition's quantitative effect is particularly difficult to assess. Nevertheless, Western research points to this contention and one can even find support to this effect in Soviet writings.

Although the leaders' goals cannot always be precisely assessed, at least since the beginning of the 1930's, Soviet leadership has been preoccupied with superrapid industrialization within the limits of the population's endurance, with overriding stress on heavy industry and defense potential. The development pattern focused on attaining tangible and immediate results in terms of impressive growth rates, rather than on achieving higher sustained growth for a longer span of time. To the extent that the leadership viewed development of heavy industry as the key link in its growth strategy, it would probably not be too far-fetched to say that the population's welfare was considered de facto, if not de jure, rather a constraint than an aim, and as such was subordinated to the growth of heavy industry. Apart from political repercussions, living standards obviously influence labor productivity, a relationship which for many years was markedly underestimated. It is refreshing to note that the distinguished Soviet mathematical economist A. L. Vainshtein recently argued that "a considerable and uninterrupted decline in industrial labor productivity serves as a strong warning that within the next few years the share of investment in national income should not increase. Therefore, in perspective planning of the development of the U.S.S.R. economy, it is necessary to maintain, or even somewhat reduce, the share of investment in national income." Concurrently a reduction of the share of consumption in national income causes a considerable slowdown in the dynamics of industrial labor productivity.[2]

To be sure the central planner did not willfully attempt to overrule consumers' preferences in all matters; if the "wrong" output was often produced it was not always because it was desired by the planner. Although the planner was not entirely indifferent to consumers' preferences, they were not determining factors even in the sphere where they would not have infringed on the planner's priorities. A considerable handicap was the lack of rules or mechanism for ensuring that increases in consumers' demand would invariably elicit increases in the flow of output in the required quantity and composition.

The system of priorities reigned supreme. Those responsible for eco-

[2]A. L. Vainshtein, *Ekonomika i matematicheskie metody*, No. 1 (1967), pp. 26–27.

nomic decision-making committed the bulk of resources to heavy industry, skimming the cream from resources for capital formation in those branches, and creating an acute imbalance among various sectors of the economy and branches of industry. The disproportions resulting from relative overinvestment in chosen branches, accompanied by severe underinvestment in complementary branches, generated hypertensions, aggravated by planning without reserves, the inefficient system of rationing of resources, the faulty price structure, and the incentive system. The development of agriculture was sacrificed to the chosen growth strategy, weakening the raw materials base. Output of consumer goods, services, and housing were neglected. New industrial giants were built to work side by side with backward and obsolete factories operating at exorbitant costs. Managers and workers were exhorted to maximize physical output at almost any cost. Capital dilapidated in nonpriority areas and was not being systematically replaced.

By instilling the plan overfulfilment "cult" the planner came more and more to rely on the additional forthcoming flow of output, without realizing that the uneven overfulfilment was as likely to cause disproportions as the underfulfilment. Reliance on overfulfilment intensified the tautness in planning. Disproportions not only were created at the planning stage by over-developing some branches in relation to others, but were magnified at the execution stage by shifting the meager appropriated resources from nonpriority to priority areas to compensate for errors in planning, deficiencies in fulfilment, changing policies, and desiderata, etc. Agriculture and the consumer goods' sectors served, in fact, as shock absorbers; they were considered as maneuverable variables within wide limits to be satisfied with leftovers.

The chosen growth strategy rested on the firm conviction that high growth rates could be maintained and accelerated predominantly by additional commitment of resources to capital formation in chosen branches. The distribution of national income to consumption, investment, defense, administration, education, etc. was determined entirely by authoritarian political decision which the consumer could not influence. As long as the additional growth from additional investment was respectable and the standard of living did not provoke political unrest, the question of optimum share of investment in national income was neglected. The goals of the highest attainable rate of growth was equated with the highest sustainable rate of investment. To be sure the optimum share of investment is not easy to determine. The point in question is that such a highly politicized economy was not conducive to searching for criteria to approach such a level.

As is known, production is subject to the law of variable proportions and the returns to investment may be liable to diminishing marginal productivity as the size of investment is increased. The higher rate of growth would not always result from a higher rate of investment and, indeed, as a rule, in the U.S.S.R. national product grew at a slower rate than the capital stock.

Taking into account the adverse conditions under which they were laboring, the Soviets attained most impressive and unprecedented growth rates. These rates were primarily achieved through extensive use of investment, manpower, and natural resources, helped by the advantages of backwardness, ample borrowing, and assimilation of foreign technology and know-how, and possibilities to accord precedence to a relatively small number of basic industries. But in the U.S.S.R. and some East European countries the opportunities for further extensive growth abated in time, as the reservoir of manpower from which the industrial labor force could be drawn neared exhaustion, and the cost of the additional labor force became prohibitive in terms of the opportunity cost of the output that would have had to be forgone, and the palpable incentives in terms of the additional consumer goods and housing that would have had to be offered. As the opportunities of borrowing techniques on an ever increasing scale diminish, and as the impact of diminishing marginal productivity of investment becomes more intense, a larger commitment of resources to investment is required to produce the same high rates of growth as before. Concurrently increasing growth rates would require a more than proportionate increase of investment. The policy of ever-increasing growth rates cannot be pursued ad infinitum with this growth strategy as it would require an ever-increasing reduction of the share of national income devoted to consumption (even though its absolute size may rise). Such a policy seems inconceivable for many reasons: the increasing exigencies of the consumers, adverse effects on productivity, the Yugoslav example, remarkabe improvement of Western living standards and lesser Communist isolation, etc. As the economy becomes more complex, with increasingly intricate interrelationships, the spectrum of priorities widens, impinging on one another, limiting maneuverability, and rendering choices more difficult.

As these problems become more acute, the shift toward intensive use of resources can hardly be avoided. As Communist economic growth rates slow down, while the capitalist economies generally evince remarkable prosperity, pressures mount and the traditional tools for coping with the problems do not produce the desired effects or even contribute to deterioration of performance, the growth strategy and planning system are subjected to searching scrutiny. A very interesting phenomenon may be noted: Wherever the growth rates fell sharpest (or stagnation had set in as, for example, in Czechoslovakia), the reform cries were loudest, and the envisaged departures from the traditional approach seemed most pronounced.

For example, in cases like Poland where the 1956 intellectual debate had spent itself, producing a new economic model which remained at the blue-print stage, the present reforms are merely timid half-measures, because the growth rates are still respectable. The moderate reform movement in Rumania indicates that the potency, nature, and speed of reforms depend largely on the economy's recent growth performance and its immediate prospects. With the slowdown it becomes evident that the dynamics of growth rates is considerably affected and could largely be improved by combatting waste and improving the system's overall efficiency. No doubt, major corrections of inefficiency would be a palpable source of additional growth.

It is beyond dispute that the traditional system is flagrantly inefficient in allocating resources among alternative uses. Although modern capitalism also suffers from resource misallocation, there is a good indication that the malady is by no means on as grand a scale as in Soviet-type economies. The inefficiencies requiring correction are mainly of a twofold nature: 1) visible waste from squandering of resources, and 2) hidden waste from misallocation to inferior uses. The prima facie test of the hidden waste is obvious when by reallocating resources and/or producing an alternative composition of output a larger or more satisfactory output (from the users' or planner's standpoint) can be obtained.

The issue as to what extent the Soviet-type economy is conducive to innovation (dynamic or intertemporal efficiency) is perhaps a more complex one. The deterioration of capital-output ratios can be arrested by introducing new techniques and organizational know-how which would drastically reduce the quantity of capital required per unit of output, or generally produce considerable shifts in the production function. But no sufficient incentives are offered to generate innovations at the enterprise level; they are generally foisted from above, and the system does not benefit from the creativity when such efforts are undertaken by agents of economic change in pursuit of entrepreneurial profit. Whatever the advantages of centrally imposed technical progress, and undoubtedly there are a number, it is capable only of exploiting a fraction of the potential endeavor in this field, but fails in harnessing participants in the economic process at all levels. In addition, the system features built-in disincentives against technical progress in enterprises by urging and rewarding current results only. It is especially noteworthy that none of the reforms have successfully grappled with the problem of awakening a spark of entrepreneurial spirit.

The planning system that evolved in the Soviet Union since the 1930's, and was later unimaginatively transplanted to Eastern Europe, was designed to facilitate a massive, swift, and expedient mobilization and redirection of resources to selected areas, and to tightly control economic processes. Among other problems, the planner faced forceful overcoming of the population's preferences for current consumption and the peasants' unwillingness to carry a considerable share of the cost of industrialization. Enforcement through command, rather than through economic measures of inducement, was the predominant method adopted. In view of the tasks to be carried out, the solution was not without its merits. It may be recalled that the regime faced a serious problem in the dearth of qualified politically acceptable managerial personnel; so that both the inexperienced party men and the experienced hostile managers had to be directed from the center, and the execution had to be controlled by relatively simple methods.

The aim in constructing such a plan is to achieve an internal consistency or accounting balance between requirements and availabilities. But even if it should achieve consistency, the plan is not necessarily optimal, as it may not satisfy the conditions of economic efficiency, i.e., it may not be the one that best fulfils the objectives, subject to existing constraints (e.g., the one that maximizes the results in terms of the means used). Primarily, physical units are used to balance requirements against availabilities at the plan-construction stage, and the equilibrating mechanism, using prices performing an allocative function, is not incorporated into the system. Prices serve as calculatory devices for aggregating heterogeneous quantities. Prices are not designed as indexes of scarcities and cannot serve as choice coefficients. Hence they cannot be used for selecting production methods, and for comparing effects with costs. Profit or profitability (whether computed as profit to cost or as a return on capital) may indicate spurious results if used as measures of efficiency or guides for resource allocation, for we are dealing here with accounting as distinct from economic, categories. It is so not only because of fallacious costing methods and manner of determining the markup, but mainly in view of the arbitrary value scale. A plan so constructed has to revert to commands for implementation. Incentives (in the form of premiums—additions to salaries) are used to support commands, but not to replace them, for the primary objective is to implement the plan and not to verify or improve it during execution. Use of prices that have been formed independent of the plan, and that do not reflect its embodied scarcities, as choice coefficients steering plan execution, would usually 1) produce results other than those desired by the planner, 2) create undue disturbances and imbalances, and 3) undermine the overall consistency, without assurance that they would lead to efficient choices. Hence the overdeveloped system of management by administrative methods, exertion of pressures, political appeals, and exhortations is a logical outgrowth of the system.

There is an inevitable proliferation of commands, with the propensity to overcentralize decisions. The lower echelons suffer from inertia and lack of initiative, stultifying activity. Due to its visible adverse effects, overcentralization is often followed by some decentralizing measures to allow executants more discretion in choosing how to fulfil the plan. Economic levers are sometimes reverted to produce this or that effect. But since they are often arbitrary by design and do not spring from concerted action, with over-all conditions remaining hostile to guidance by economic instruments, the changes may prove impotent or in outright violation of the system's workability. This is often the fate of half-measure reforms, followed shortly by recentralization.

When attempts are made to shift to a more intensive pattern of development, economic efficiency comes to the fore because considerable and sustained improvement of performance can be achieved by a more economical use or combination of inputs so as to produce the largest and most desirable composition of output. Once again, whose preference the plan will reflect is a fundamental question. The trend seems to be to leave the planner with the crucial decisions, but to take increasing cognizance of consumer preferences, at least to the extent that they do not impinge on planners' priorities. But no matter whose aim, or how extensive the integration of aims reflected in the plan, only when economic efficiency conditions are satisfied, can the economic performance of the system be markedly improved and the reform measures produce consequential and sustained results.

The scope and extent of reforms differ considerably from country to country. The measures taken to alter the working arrangement in the Soviet Union and Poland are probably the most conservative, in terms of retaining the crucial features of the command economy, in comparison to reform proposals of their profit-oriented schools, and the ferment in economic thought, in view of their failure to incorporate the more significant attributes of market socialism, and, of course, in relation to their neighbors' envisaged reforms. Perhaps the Czechoslovak, and largely the Hungarian reforms are the most radical modifications of the traditional system, although they too fall short of market socialism. Contrary to the monolithic approach of the bloc in the early 1950's the present diversity of solutions is noteworthy and warrants careful study. But no matter how significant the variations, there are so far no distinct signs of a major breakthrough to solutions as radical as the Yugoslav blend of the plan and the market.

It is in this context that there is a key flaw in the reform movements. Prices are not being significantly overhauled. Enterprises are increasingly urged to calculate without giving them the means for doing so effectively. Without prices approaching scarcity, decentralization measures contain the seeds of recentralization. When the planner finds that "wrong" choices are increasingly made, resources dissipated to users other than intended, pressures mount, central allocation of resources increases, and the entire system tends to return to the expedient, but inefficient, methods of the command economy. To be sure, those results are likely to occur, irrespective of the reformers' sincerity and good will.

If, as seems to be the case, there is no major relaxation of the overcommitment of resources to heavy industry with persisting taut planning without reserves and room for maneuverability, the powerful pressures generated in the economy are likely to impede the reform movement and add fuel to the recentralization trend. The reform movement may yet be succesful in reducing visible waste, but unless supported by other far-reaching measures, it does not seem to be destined to have a considerable impact on improving allocative efficiency to do away with hidden waste. Granted the general framework of the socialist planned economy, to be effective the reforms requires, *inter alia,* a basic rethinking and revision of the growth strategy and of the methods of plan construction and execution, with prices reflecting or approaching scarcity, rules for efficient production, and sufficiently potent incentives for innovation and risk-taking.

Among other impediments, the reform movements face the inbred inertia and often hostility of the party and economic bureaucracy and even the enterprises' management and workers. It should not be assumed that the new, more efficient, and businesslike ways are overly appealing to the manager who has learned his trade and was successful in dealing with the set of problems that confronted him under the traditional system. The worker may not be too enthusiastic about increased demands on his performance and the sharper wage differentiation in relation to performance. He may be quite complacent about the status quo. All over the world the bureaucracy never rushes into anything new. Moreover, in this case it stands to lose much of its power and prestige.

There are some indications of considerable differences at the top Party echelons as to the nature, scope, and directions of reforms. A good deal of conservative bias is injected into the final versions of the reform. Although it would seem that drastic concurrent changes on a broad front are required to assure successful reforms the steps taken are hesitant, cautious, and diffused over a long period of time. To say this, it is not to understate the regimes formidable tasks which are complicated by dangers and overwhelming difficulties that would beset such a broad undertaking, but it is to stress that the often understandable prudence is likely to undermine reform implementation or debilitate its impact.

Although economic thought in the U.S.S.R. and particularly in Eastern Europe can boast of many feats during the last decade, a considerable effort is yet required to rid economics of some obsolete and often harmful dogmas. At the centenary of Marx's *Das Kapital*, it would not be amiss to recall his warning that at the gates to science, as at the gates to hell the inscription should read:

Qui si convien lasciare ogni sospetto:
Ogni vilta convien che qui sia morta.[3]

No matter how great or small the contribution of Marxist economics may be in illuminating the processes of capitalism in motion, it seems beyond dispute, that Marxist economics is inferior in providing tools for solving the resource allocation problem. Resistance against the apparatus of modern economics is giving way to a gradual acceptance of its analytical tools, with recognition that this tool box can be advantageously used in tackling the scarcity problem in any social system. To the extent that economic theory affects economic realities and policies, this development is indeed encouraging.

[3]"Here all mistrust must be abandoned; And here must perish every craven thought." With these words, borrowed from Dante, Marx concluded the preface of *A Contribution to a Critique of Political Economy*, published in 1859.

part I

The Anatomy of
the Soviet-Type
Command Economy

In order to comprehend the changes taking place in Soviet-type economies, a firm grasp of the fundamentals of the traditional system is required. The Soviet command economy has evolved as a result of a deliberate growth strategy embarked on in the early 1930's. To understand the functioning of the traditional system, one must constantly bear in mind the interdependence between the regime leaders' obsession with superrapid economic growth and the tools used to carry it out.

Perhaps some acquaintance with the milestones in the development of the Soviet economic system is necessary. There is an introduction to the subject of Soviet development in Robert W. Campbell, *Soviet Economic Power* (New York: Houghton Mifflin Co., 1966), Chapter 2. An overall view in given by Harry Schwartz, *Russia's Soviet Economy* (New York: Prentice Hall, 1954), Chapter 4. Alexander Gerschenkron, "Russia: Patterns of Economic Development," *Economic Backwardness in Historical Perspective* (New York: Frederick A. Praeger Inc., 1965) is well worth consulting. Naum Jasny, *Soviet Industrialization, 1928–52* (Chicago: Chicago University Press, 1961) is very critical. For a more sympathetic view see M. H. Dobb, *Soviet Economic Development Since 1917* (New York: International Publishers, 1966). A recent contribution is Anatole G. Mazour, *Soviet Economic Development* (Princeton: D. Van Nostrand, 1967).

An insight into Soviet growth strategy can best be gained through the study of the great controversy during the 1920's, the "golden age" of Soviet economics. A superb exposition and analysis of the controversy can be found in Alexander Erlich, *The Soviet Industrialization Debate, 1924–1928* (Cambridge, Mass.: Harvard University Press, 1960). Professor Nicolas Spulber has edited some of the most significant contributions to the controversy, *Foundations of Soviet Strategy for Economic Growth*

(Bloomington: University of Indiana Press, 1964). His instructive commentary on the debate may be found in the companion volume, *Soviet Strategy for Economic Growth* (Bloomington: University of Indiana Press, 1964). What was perhaps one of the most significant contributions to the debate was recently translated into English and is highly recommended reading, E. Preobrazhensky, *New Economics* (New York: Oxford University Press, 1965). Feldman's growth model has been succinctly analyzed by Evsei Domar, *Essays in the Theory of Economic Growth* (New York: Oxford University Press, 1957), Essay No. 9. Z. Fallenbuchl's "Investment Policy for Economic Development," *Canadian Journal of Economics*, No. 1, 1963, provides a clear analysis of the Communist experience.

The evaluation of Soviet growth performance has a rich literature. Professor Abram Bergson's monumental book, *The Real National Income of Soviet Russia Since 1928* (Cambridge, Mass.: Harvard University Press, 1961) should be consulted by any serious student as well as the volume edited by Abram Bergson and Simon Kuznets, *Economic Trends in the Soviet Union* (Cambridge, Mass.: Harvard University Press, 1963). Professor Robert W. Campbell has summarized some of the other contributions in *Soviet Studies* (July, 1964). The student should also refer to G. Warren Nutter, *Growth of Industrial Production in the Soviet Union* (Princeton, N. J.: Princeton University Press, 1962). For recent data on Soviet economic trends see Stanley H. Cohn, "Soviet Growth Retardation," *New Directions in the Soviet Economy*, U. S. Congress, Joint Economic Committee (Washington, D. C.: U.S. Government Printing Office, 1966). Alexander Erlich's "Development Strategy and Planning: The Soviet Experience," *National Economic Planning*, Max F. Milikan (ed.) (New York: Columbia University Press, 1967) is a most thoughtful paper. The reader should also consult Professor Bergson's comments in the same volume.

Professor Wiles' provocative inaugural lecture at the London School of Economics, "The Political and Social Prerequisites for a Soviet-Type Economy," *Economica* (Feb. 1967), is particularly worthy of notice. The problems of growth in Eastern Europe were treated, inter alia, in Nicolas Spulber, *The Economics of Communist Eastern Europe* (New York: John Wiley and Sons, 1957); in *The State and Economic Development in Eastern Europe* (New York: Random House, 1966); Alfred Zauberman, *Industrial Progress in Poland, Czechoslovakia and East Germany 1937–1962* (New York; Oxford University Press, 1964) and Frederic L. Pryor and George J. Staller, "The Dollar Values of the Gross National Products in Eastern Europe 1955," *Economics of Planning*, Vol. 6, No. 1 (1966). Thad P. Alton and Associates have published a number of monographs estimating national product in Czechoslovakia, Poland, and Hungary; and one on Bulgaria is forthcoming (New York: Columbia University Press).

The literature on the functioning of the Soviet-type economy is vast. Perhaps a good road for a novice to follow is to start with the aforementioned Campbell book to be followed by Alec Nove, *The Soviet Economy* (New York: Frederick A. Praeger, Inc., 1966). I have found that students are apt to grasp the *modus operandi* better through a careful reading of Joseph S. Berliner, *Factory and Manager in the USSR* (Cambridge, Mass.: Harvard University Press, 1957). For a more recent survey of Soviet management see David Granick, *The Red Executive* (Garden City: Doubleday, 1960). Professor Bergson's *The Economics of Soviet Planning* is a very solid and rewarding, even if at times difficult, study. P. J. D. Wiles, *The Political Economy of Communism* (Cambridge, Mass, : Harvard University Press, 1962) is full of insight. Gregory Grossman, "Notes for a Theory of the Command Economy," *Soviet Studies* (October, 1963) is a very lucid exposition of the traditional system and is well worth the effort required to read. David Granick, "An Organizational Model of Soviet Industrial Planning," *The Journal of Political Economy* (April, 1959) offers an interesting model of Soviet industrial organization. See also the stimulating paper by Professor Egon Neubergen, "Central Planning & Its Legacies," The Rand Corporation (Dec. 1966), this will be published in proceedings of a conference on International Trade and Central Planning, Allan A. Brown and Egon Neubergen (eds.) (Berkeley: University of California Press, 1968). The study of the supply system by Professor Herbert S. Levine, "The Centralized Planning of Supply in Soviet Industry," in U. S. Congress, Joint Economic Committee, *Comparisons of the United States and Soviet Economies* (Washington, D. C.: U. S. Government Printing Office, 1959) affords a lucid insight into Soviet operational planning. Gregory Grossman (ed.), *Value and Plan* (Berkeley: University of California Press, 1960) contains a number of significant contributions on the functioning of the economy. On the problem of resource allocation see Stanislaw Wellisz, *The Economies of the Soviet Bloc* (New York: McGraw Hill, 1964) which contains a particularly good section on the consumer. There are a number of useful articles dealing with specific subjects reprinted by Morris Bornstein and Daniel R. Fusfeld, (eds.) *The Soviet Economy* (Homewood, Ill.: Richard D. Irwin, Inc., 1966), Franklyn D. Holzman (ed.) *Readings on the Soviet Economy* (Chicago: Rand McNally, 1961), and Harry G. Shaffer (ed.) *The Soviet Economy* (New York: Appleton-Century-Crofts, 1963). There is a number of significant monographs on specific topics which could be consulted with profit. For example, Abram Bergson, *The Structure of Soviet Wages* (Cambridge, Mass.: Harvard University Press, 1944), Janet Chapman, *Real Wages in Soviet Russia Since 1928* (Cambridge, Mass.: Harvard University Press, 1963), Emily Clark Brown, *Soviet Trade Unions and Labor Relations* (Cambridge, Mass.: Harvard University Press, 1966), Franklyn D. Holzman, *Soviet Taxation* (Cambridge, Mass., Harvard University Press,

1955), Michael C. Kaser, *COMECON* (New York: Oxford University Press, 1967), Frederic L. Pryor, *The Communist Foreign Trade System* —(Cambridge, Mass.: MIT Press, 1963), Holland Hunter, *Soviet Transportation Policy* (Cambridge, Mass.: Harvard University Press, 1957), Gregory Grossman, *Soviet Statistics of Physical Output of Industrial Commodities* (Princeton: Princeton University Press, 1960), Marshall I. Goldman, *Soviet Marketing* (New York: The Free Press, 1963), R. W. Davies, *The Development of the Soviet Budgetary System* (Cambridge: Cambridge University Press, 1958), Hans Hirsch, *Quantity Planning and Price Planning*, (Philadelphia: University of Pennsylvania Press, 1961), and Stanislaw Swianiewicz, *Forced Labour and Economic Development* (London: Oxford University Press, 1965). Specific references on East European countries can be found in Part II.

1. GROWTH STRATEGY AND PERFORMANCE

*THE ROLE OF PLANNING IN SOCIALIST ECONOMY**

Oskar Lange†

Economic planning, or more precisely, the planning of economic development is an essential feature of socialism. It expresses the fact that socialist economy does not develop in an elemental way but that its development is guided and directed by the conscious will of organised society. Planning is the means of subjecting the operation of economic laws and the economic development of society to the direction of human will.

The experience of the construction of socialism in various countries indicates that the establishment of planned economy is one of the first achievements of the socialist revolution. It precedes the full development of socialist relations of production, though it requires a certain minimum of such relations. In the transitional period, when non-socialist modes of production still play an important role, the economy becomes already subject to planned direction of its development. This is made possible by the existence in the economy of a large socialist secor which controls, as one frequently says, the "commanding outposts" of economic life. This is the minimum requirement of establishing planned economy.

*Reprinted from "The Political Economy of Socialism," Institute of Social Studies, *Publications on Social Change*, No. 16 (The Hague: 1957), pp. 16–23, by permission of The Institute of Social Studies and Vitgenerij Van Keulen, N. V.

†The late Dr. Oskar Lange was Professor of Economics at the University of Warsaw and Deputy Chairman, State Council of the Polish People's Republic. His publications in English include: *The Economic Theory of Socialism* (1938), *Price Flexibility and Employment* (1944), *The Working Principles of the Soviet Economy* (1944), *Introduction to Econometrics* (1962), *Political Economy* (1963), and *Wholes and Parts* (1963).

Economic planning starts with the direct intervention of the State in economic relations. This intervention has for its objectives the liquidation of capitalist relations of production and the control of the non-socialist sectors of economy which still remain. The basis which makes control of the non-socialist sectors possible, is the existence of a socialist sector, particularly that part of the socialist sector which is nationalised (i.e. state-owned), and which controls the commanding outposts of the economy.

In this first, transitional phase the new revolutionary State is not neutral with regard to the various sectors of economy. It consciously utilizes the nationalized socialist sector as an instrument of controlling the development of the whole economy. The means it utilizes consist of economic instruments which result from the existence of the nationalized sector comprising the decisive controlling part of the economy, and also of intervention by political force, i.e. non-economic force. In the first revolutionary period intervention into economic processes by political force plays a decisive role.

In the first period of development of a socialist economy both the planning of economic development and the day-to-day management of the socialist sector is highly centralized.

There may be some doubts, how far this represents a universal necessity. For instance, in Poland, we had some discussions whether the passing through such a period of highly centralized planning and management was a historical necessity or a great political mistake. Personally I hold the view that it was a historical necessity.

It seems to me that, first, the very process of the social revolution which liquidates one social system and establishes another, requires centralized disposal of resources by the new revolutionary State, and consequently centralized management and planning. This holds, in my opinion, for any socialist revolution.

In underdeveloped countries, there has to be added a further consideration. Socialist industrialisation and particularly very rapid industrialisation, which was necessary in the first socialist countries, particularly in the Soviet Union, as a political requirement of national defence and of the solution of all kinds of political and social problems, due to backwardness, requires centralized disposal of resources. Thus the very process of transformation of the social system and in addition, in underdeveloped countries, the need of rapid industrialisation, impose the necessity of high centralization of planning and management.

The process of rapid industrialisation requires such centralized disposal of resources for two reasons. First, it is necessary to concentrate all resources on certain objectives and avoid dissipation of resources on other objectives which would divert resources from the purpose of rapid industrialisation. This is one of the reasons which leads to highly centralized planning and management and also to the allocation of resources by means of administrative establishment of priorities. The second reason why rapid industrialisation demands centralized planning and management is the lack and weakness of industrial cadres. With the rapid growth of industry the cadres are new and inexperienced. Such old cadres which had some experiences in management of industry and other economic activities are frequently politically alien to the socialist objectives. In consequence high centralization of managerial decisions becomes necessary.

Thus the first period of planning and management in a socialist economy, at least according to our present experience, has always been characterised by administrative management and administrative allocation of resources on the basis of priorities centrally established. Economic incentives are in this period replaced by moral and political appeals to the workers, by appeals to their patriotism and socialist consciousness. This is, so to speak, a highly politicalised economy, both with regards to the means of planning and management and the incentives it utilizes.

I think that, essentially, it can be described as a sui generis war economy. Such methods of war economy are not peculiar to socialism because they are also used in capitalist countries in war time. They were developed in the first and the second world war. In capitalist countries similar methods were used during the war, namely concentration of all resources on one basic purpose, which is the production of war material, centralization of disposal of resources in order to avoid leakages of resources to what was considered non-essential utilisation (everything which was not connected with the prosecution of the war). Allocation of resources by administrative decision according to administratively established priorities and wide-scale use of political incentives to maintain the productivity and discipline of labour through patriotic appeals were characteristic of war economy. This was the case in all capitalist countries during the war.

It shows clearly that such methods of centralized planning and management are not peculiar to socialism, that they are rather certain techniques of war economy. The difficulty starts when these methods of war economy are identified with the essence of socialism and considered as being essential to socialism.

One of the methods of war economy, which most of the socialist countries used at one stage or another, are compulsory deliveries by peasants of part of their produce. Many comrades in my country feel rather upset by the present programme of our government of abolishing such deliveries. They fear that this implies giving up some socialist principle. I usually answer them by asking whether they remember who in Poland first introduced compulsory deliveries by peasants. Such deliveries were first introduced during the first world war by the occupation army of Kaiser Wilhelm the Second, whom I do not think anybody regards as a champion of socialism. These methods cannot be considered as an essential aspect of socialism, they are simply methods of war economy necessary in a revolutionary period of transition.

The fate and history of these methods is a classical example of the dialectical character of the development of socialist society. Methods, which are necessary and useful in the period of social revolution and of intensive industrialisation, become an obstacle to further economic progress when they are perpetuated beyond their historic justification. They become obstacles because they are characterised by lack of flexibility. They are rigid, they lead therefore to easte of resources resulting from this inflexibility, they require a wasteful bureaucratic apparatus and make it difficult to adjust production to the needs of the population. However, it seems that the greatest obstacle to further progress results from the lack of proper economic incentives in this bureaucratic centralistic type of management. This hampers proper economic utilisation of resources, encourages waste and also hinders technical progress.

Therefore, the moment, when socialist society starts to overcome these centralistic, bureaucratic methods of administrative planning and management, indicates, so to speak, that the new socialist society matures. Yesterday we spoke in the discussion about the period of transition—when it ends and how it should be defined. I would not want to enter into this problem here and make this a final definition of the period of transition. But I might say, that the substitution for the methods of administrative and centralized management and development of new methods based on the utilisation of economic laws indicates the end of the period of transition and the beginning of the functioning of an established socialist economy. I would not say that this is the only aspect of the problem of the period of transition, but it is certainly an important aspect of it.

The period of centralized planning and management, as I said, is the result partly of the necessities of the revolutionary transformation of society and, in underdeveloped countries, also of the needs of rapid industrialisation. In studying this period a certain important sociological factor has to be taken into account, whch is the weakness of the working class in an underdeveloped country. It seems to me that it is on the basis of this weakness of the working class, under conditions of underdevelopment that the bureaucratic state machine gains great importance, and phenomena like that of the "cult of personality" develop. It, so to speak, in a way substitutes the spontaneous activity of the working class.

But here again the dialectics of the processes of construction of socialism becomes apparent. The centralistic methods are successful in achieving rapid industrialisation and, as a consequence, cause a rapid growth of the working class. The working class grows in numbers as well as in consciousness and political maturity. Next to the growth of the working class another important sociological element appears. This is the growth of a new socialist intelligentzia which largely comes from the ranks of the workers and peasants. When it becomes clear that the highly centralized administrative and bureaucratic methods of management create obstacles to further progress also a part of the political and state apparatus becomes convinced that a change of methods of administration and management is needed. Thus new social forces mature which require and also make possible a change of these methods.

This, precisely is the basic difference between the development of socialist society and a society which is based on antagonistic class relations. There is no ruling class which may oppose these changes. There may be, as I said yesterday, certain strata or groups, which have a vested interest in the old methods and create obstacles, but these obstacles can never become of such importance as to make impossible the changes required by new historical circumstances.

This was very clear, if you take, for instance, the experience of Poland, where the industrialisation by means of centralized administrative planning and management has led to a great increase of the working class. Our working class is now more than three times what it was before the war. The working class has got experience in large industrial establishments. It was at first to a large extent of peasant origin and that, of course, weighed on its psychology. But that was only a transitional phase. Industrialisation and the social revolution have created a new intelligentzia—largely coming from workers and peasants. All that led to a maturation of the forces of the new socialist society. In consequence we got such a phenomenon as the great movement of workers councils demanding selfgovernment of workers in industry, the general demand to change the methods of management of the national economy. The Party has accepted these demands of the people and given them organised expression.

Changes in the methods of planning and the management of the economy are taking place today practically in all socialist countries. Forms, contents are different, but all these changes imply a certain decentralization or deconcentration of management of the economy. I do not want to enter into a description of what is happening in the various socialist countries. I shall rather present to you what I personally believe is the proper formulation of the role and methods of planning in a socialist economy.

First, it must be stated that in a socialist society planning of the economy is active planning. Some of the economists in Poland use the term "directive planning" but this term is ambiguous, therefore I shall rather use the term "active planning." By this I mean that planning does not consist only of coordination of the activities of various branches of the national economy. It is something more, namely it is an active determination of the main lines of development of the national economy. Otherwise, if planning were mere coordination, the development of socialist economy would be elemental, it would not really be directed by the will of organised society. If economic development is no to be elemental but is to be directed by organised society, then planning must be active economic planning.

Two problems arise with regard to active economic planning. First: What is its scope, what activities in the economy have to be planned? And second: what are the methods of securing the realisation of the plan?

The active character of planning does not require that the plan goes into each detail of economic life. We actually had a period in the socialist countries, may be with the exception of China, which already started at a later level and profited of the experience of other socialist countries—when the output of even the least important commodity was planned. There was the famous joke in Poland—really it was not a joke, but it was true—that the production of pickled cucumbers is in the national economic plan. Another case which was not a joke either but was a fact—was that the State Planning Commission made a plan of the number of hares which will be shot during year by hunters. At the same time, you could not get, for instance, buttons or hairpins for ladies, simply because they had been forgotten the national economic plan.

Active planning and effective direction of the development of the national economy is quite possible without planning such details. Even more, planning such details hampers really effective direction of the national economy. Actually I think it may be said that putting such details in the national economic plan had nothing to do with planning. It was a part of the high centralization of day to day management of the economy by means of administrative measures. This is a different thing than planning.

However, the national economic plan which is to determine the development of the national economy must include at least two things. First, the division of national income between accumulation and consumption. Second, the distribution of investments among the different branches of the economy. The first determines the general rate of economy growth, the second determines the direction of the development.

Unless these two things are in the plan there is no active guidance of the development of the national economy. This is, therefore, the minimum requirement of the plan. In addition, the plan may or may not include the targets of the production of certain basis commodities, like basis raw materials, basis means of prodution, and so on. These are technical problems and not fundamental problems.

These are the fundamental aspects of the plan which determine the pace and the direction of development of the economy. In addition to these, economic planning must be concerned with coordination of the activities of the various branches of the economy. First of all, with coordination of the financial aspects of the plan and of the real aspects of the plan, in particular coordination of the total purchasing power at the disposal of the population and the amounts of consumer goods which are provided for individual distribution. The plan must also in some way and by some means be interested in the coordination of the output of the various branches of the national economy. Otherwise, the determination of the directions of development established by the plan may become impossible to realise. If there is no proper coordination between the output of the various branches of economy, investments may not be possible to be realised, because the necessary investment goods are not produced. All kinds of bottlenecks appear and cause difficulties, which may make it impossible to carry out the investment plan. So much about the content of the plan.

The second problem is that of the methods of securing the realisation of the plan. Here, we have basically two possible methods. One of administrative orders and administrative allocation of resources. The various units in the socialist economy are ordered to do certain things, for instance to produce that and that much of something. The resources which are necessary for that purpose, both material and financial resources, are allocated in an administrative way. This was the traditional method of realising the plan in the past period. The second method consists in the use of what we call "economic means," namely of setting up a system of incentives which induces people to do exactly the things which are required by the plan. It seems to me, that in an effective planning of a socialist economy, both methods have to be used, though in different proportions.

Preference should be gven to the use of economic means. Administrative methods should be limited to such fields where, for some reason or other, economic means are ineffective. Such situations, where economic means are not effective, always do exist. They exist, of course, particularly in periods of very great changes, because economic means are rather subtle instruments responding to "normal" changes in the situation, and frequently breaking down when very fundamental or revolutionary changes are needed. In such cases the use of administrative means must be accepted. Even in capitalist economy, in situations of profound changes, the State uses in its economic policy measures of administrative control because the normal kind of economic means are not sufficient to provoke the responses which are necessary.

The fundamental decisions of the plan concerning the division of national income between accumulation and consumption and concerning the basic directions of investments are really of a political character, the means of implementations must partly be administrative. The decision of the plan concerning the rate of accumulation is basically realised by administrative measures. Part of the national income produced is not paid out in the form of individual incomes, part of the profits of the socialist enterprises are held back by the State and this is an administrative measure. So are also all forms of taxation of enterprises and individuals. The basic directions of investments, for instance the decision to build an electric power plant, are usually not made as a reaction to market situations, but are made as basic decisions of economic policy. Though in this case the realisation of the decisions may make use of all kinds of economic instruments.

We may ask in what sense the economic plans must take account of economic laws. Even when the realisation of the plan is achieved by administrative measures the plan must observe the general economic laws concerning the proportions necessary in the process of production and reproduction. For instance, if the plan provides for an increase of the production of steel, it must provide for a certain additional output of coal which is needed to produce the additional steel. *Any* kind of planning has to take care of such objective kinds of relationships.

There are also other economic laws which must be observed by the plan. These are the laws which result from the operation of economic incentives under the circumstances created by the plan. The process of realisation of the plan sets into motion definite economic incentives to which the people react in a certain way which can be calculated. Even in the period of administrative planning certain economic incentives were operative and their consequences had to be taken into account. In this period, however, economic means were only subsidiary in relation to administrative means. I would say that now the situation has to change in the sense that the economic means are the rule and administrative means become subsidiary to the economic means. Thus the plan has to observe the laws of production and reproduction; and in so far as the realisation is based on the use of economic means, i.e. the operation of economic laws, it also has to consider these laws.

STALIN'S VIEWS ON SOVIET ECONOMIC DEVELOPMENT*
— · — · — · — · — · — · — · — · — · — · — .

Alexander Erlich†

I

On s'engage, et puis on voit: this phrase borrowed from Napoleon was used by Lenin more than once to describe the position of his party after

*Reprinted by permission of the publishers from Ernest J. Simmons, (ed.) *Continuity and Change in Russian and Soviet Thought* (Cambridge, Mass.: Harvard University Press), pp. 81–99. Copyright 1955 by the President and Fellows of Harvard College.

†Dr. Alexander Erlich is Professor of Economics, Columbia University. His publications include: *The Soviet Industrialization Debate, 1924–1928* (1960) and "Development Strategy and Planning: The Soviet Experience" in Max F. Millikan (ed.) *National Economic Planning* (1967).

November 1917.[1] With regard to the issues of economic policy the interval between getting involved and seeing, or even looking, was rather
protracted. During the first few years the pressure of external events was
so overwhelming as to leave virtually no room for choice. The spontaneous
seizures of factories by the workers in early 1918 and the exigencies of the
Civil War forced upon the reluctant Lenin and his collaborators the policy
of "War Communism." With similar inevitability the swelling tide of
popular unrest climaxed by the Kronstadt revolt and by the peasant up-
risings of Central Russia imposed the retreat toward the NEP. And in both
cases there was always the great expectation that the European revolution
would link up before long with its Russian bridgehead and assist the
Soviet republic with equipment, industrial consumers' goods, and organizing ability. In 1924 the situation was entirely different. Chances of a
quick rescue from the West, which had already been declining at the time
of the transition to the NEP, had now passed. The discontent of the peasants, moreover, was no longer restrained by the fear of the "White"
counterrevolution: they had just forced the regime off the "War Communist" path, and they were grimly awaiting the results of this victory.
Under such circumstances the policy could no longer consist of spasmodic
responses to catastrophes and of fervent hopes for the future. Only positive
action directed toward improvement in the wretched living standards of
the population could stabilize the regime; only forceful economic development aimed at enlargement of the productive capacity of the country
could provide a durable basis for such action and make the Soviet Union a
viable state. But how could this be done, how could these two objectives
be reconciled in conditions of a backward, war-ravaged country in the
thick of a great egalitarian upheaval? This was a question to which the
"old books" provided no answer.[2]

[1]The author acknowledges gratefully the support of the Russian Research Center of
Harvard University in the preparation of this study. He is also indebted to Professor Alexander Gerschenkron and Dr. Joseph S. Berliner for valuable suggestions.
    [2]It goes without saying that the men who faced this question approached it with some
definite, preconceived ideas. All of them were emphatic in recognizing the need for rapid
economic development and in taking the latter to be synonymous with industrialization; in
this respect they were faithfully following the line of Russian Marxism of the prerevolutionary
era. They sharply deviated from the traditional approach by accepting Lenin's view that a
proletarian party which succeeded in rising to political power in a backward country had a
clear duty not to leave the task of industrialization to the bourgeoisie but to put itself in charge
after dislodging the propertied classes from their positions of control. But this amendment,
which came in response to the massive *faits accomplis* of the first revolutionary years, could
not by itself make the original doctrine grind out solutions which would provide a clear-cut
directive for action. The Marxian theory, to be sure, helped to bring sharply into focus some
phenomena and relationships which were of relevance for the impending decisions, like advantages of large-scale production, capital-consuming and labor-displacing effects of technological progress, importance of the relative size of investment and consumers'-goods industries. It was equally categorical in assigning to the transformation of property relationships
the key role in the process of social change. But it provided no criterion for optimal solutions

Bukharin, who was at that time the leading economic theorist of the Party, felt that the solution was clearly at hand. It was contained, according to him, in continuing the NEP as conceived by Lenin and as elaborated on in his famous *O prodnaloge*. The vicious circle of idle industrial capacity in the cities and the supply strikes in the villages was to be broken by lifting restrictive measures which had hitherto inhibited the peasant's willingness to produce a surplus above his bare needs or at any rate to part with it. Transformation of the wholesale requisitioning into a limited "tax in kind"; opening the channels of trade through which the nontaxable part of peasant surplus could be profitably sold; denationalization and encouragement of small-scale industry which would not need, because of the nature of its plant, any protracted reconditioning in order to start producing goods demanded by the peasants—these were the key devices which were expected to unfreeze the productive energies of agriculture and make increased supplies of foodstuffs and raw materials flow into the nearly empty pipelines of the urban economy. The part of this flow which would reach the large-scale industrial sector would set some of its idle wheels turning and make possible a counterflow of manufactured products to the goods-starved village, thus providing the latter with an additional incentive to increase its marketings. A genuine process of cumulative growth would be set in motion hereby. The logic of the reasoning seemed compelling, and even more impressive was the impact of facts: between 1920 and 1924 the output of large-scale industry increased more than threefold.

Could this upward trend be relied upon to start off a process of long-range expansion and set the pattern for it? Lenin was never explicit about it: but his strong emphasis on the need of attracting foreign investment seemed to indicate some doubts whether the policy of "developing trade at all costs" would be sufficient to do the job. Bukharin, writing three years later, betrayed no such qualms. He enthusiastically proceeded to sharpen up Lenin's analysis by praising the high allocative efficiency of the market mechanism, denouncing the tendencies toward "monopolistic parasitism" in the nationalized industry, and sounding solemn warnings against "applied Tuganism" (*prikladnaia Tugan-Baranovshchina*), which postulated the possibility of expansion of productive capacity without proportionate increase in effective demand on the part of the final consumer. This disproportion, in his view, had been ultimately responsible for the downfall of

---

within each of these areas, or more particularly, for appropriate speed at which the transition from the existing state of affairs to a more satisfactory one should take place. Moreover, even determined efforts toward establishing such optimum conditions would not change the situation to any substantial extent. They could, at best, lead to a more clear-cut formulation of existing alternatives and, consequently, to elimination of some minor errors and inconsistencies from the judgments: but this would not eliminate the need for choosing nor reduce the formidable risks and uncertainties attendant upon the final decision and due to the nature of the problems involved.

tsarism as well as for the Soviet "scissor crisis" of 1923. In order to prevent this from happening again, a consistent policy of "small profit margins and large turnover" was called for. Nor was this all: Bukharin outlined an elaborate system of institutional arrangements serving the same purpose. Marketing and credit coöperation in agriculture were, in his opinion, the most desirable devices for enlarging the peasant demand for industrial goods. But he had some words of appreciation also for the village kulak whose relentless drive to raise his output and to expand his demand made him, like Goethe's Mephisto, *ein Teil von jener Kraft, die stets das Boese will und stets das Gute schafft.* In the long run, this stratum was expected to be gradually squeezed out under the joint pressure of the proletarian state and the growing coöperative movement among the peasants.

It was the last-mentioned aspect of Bukharin's conception that evoked particularly violent attacks. The conciliatory attitude toward the village rich could not but arouse most deeply the Left Wing of the Party, which had considered the compromise with the individualist peasantry a bitter, if temporarily unavoidable, sacrifice and which was pushing toward resumption of the offensive against propertied classes both on the domestic and on the international scene. But spokesmen of this group, with Preobrazhenskii as its leading economist, did not leave things at that; they penetrated to the core of Bukharin's reasoning and denounced his extrapolation of past experience into the future as a typical "psychology of the restoration period." They were explicit, if rather brief, in dealing with long-range issues like modernization of industry, opening up areas with untapped natural resources, absorption of agricultural surplus population, the importance of what we would call today "social overheads" like transportation and the power system (as well as of industrial development in general) for the efficiency of peasant farming, and, last but not least, the requirements of national defense. They were equally specific in emphasizing some of the basic characteristics of modern productive technology which made its adoption a costly proposition. But the crux of their argument lay in pointing to definite short-term features of the situation of the Soviet economy which made it imperative to move toward these long-range objectives at a high speed in spite of the high cost involved. According to Preobrazhenskii and his friends, people who rejoiced in record-breaking rates of increase in industrial growth up to 1925 lived in a fool's paradise. The expansion at small cost was easy as long as the large reserves of unutilized capacity existed; but with every leap forward in industrial output the time at which future increases would require investment in additional productive facilities was drawing closer. To wait with such investment until that stage, however, would be dangerous. The replacement of a large part of equipment actually in service had been due, but not carried out, in the period of Civil War and in the early years of the NEP. Yet while such a life-extension was possible for a while, each passing year would increase the probability of breakdown of overaged equipment; and this would imply a shrinkage in the capital stock of the economy unless the replacement activities were drastically stepped up. Another powerful source of increased pressure for expansion of capacity lay in the redistribution of income along egalitarian lines which was brought about by the Revolution and which expressed itself in a steep increase in the share of consumption in income. At the same time the large-scale import of capital which had played an important role in the economic development of pre-revolutionary Russia was now reduced to a trickle.

But the very circumstances which called for rapid expansion created a grave danger for the stability of the economy. The limitations of resources permitted the required increase in investment to develop only by keeping down the levels of current consumption, while the low real income and the egalitarian mode of its distribution made it more than unlikely that this restriction in consumers' spending would take place voluntarily. Such a situation, if left uncontrolled, would mean a "goods famine," more specifically, a shortage of industrial consumers' goods; and since the Russian peasant then enjoyed, in Preobrazhenskii's words, "a much greater freedom [than before the Revolution] in the choice of the time and of the terms at which to dispose of his own surpluses because of the decrease in 'forced sales,' "[3] he would be likely to respond to an unfavorable turn in the terms of trade by cutting down his marketable surplus and thus administering a crippling blow to the industrial economy. The way out of this deadlock was to be sought in compulsory saving, with monopoly of foreign trade and price manipulation at home as its main tools; the first would secure high priority for capital goods in Russian imports, the second was expected to contain the pressure of consumers' demand at home against the existing industrial capacity by keeping the prices of industrial commodities higher than they would be under conditions of a free unrestricted market. As a result, the capital stock of the society would be permitted to increase up to a level at which the demand for high current output of consumers' goods and requirements of further expansion of productive capacity could be met simultaneously and not to the exclusion of each other. In the planning of this initial increase, moreover, particular care had to be exercised to keep its inflationary potentialities to a minimum: the largest volume of capital outlays would fall into the initial year of the Plan, when large reserves of the old capacity could provide a cushion for the unstabilizing effect of newly started construction projects, and then gradually taper off

---

[3]"Ekonomicheskie zametki," *Pravda,* December 15, 1925. The notion of "forced sales" referred to the part of the produce sold by the peasant in order to meet such obligations as taxes or (in prerevolutionary Russia) payments to the landlords.

in the following years during which these reserves would approach exhaustion.

This last-mentioned point caused little interest at the time of its enunciation; it was, incidentally, brought up not in the actual debate but in a rather technical proposal of a committee of experts known by its initials as *OSVOK*.[4] But the proposals for compulsory saving (bracketed by Preobrazhenskii under the anxiety-provoking name of "primitive socialist accumulation") did call forth an immediate reaction; indeed, they proved an ideal target for attack. The representatives of the Bukharin group were quick to point out that a policy recommended by the Leftists would in its immediate effects greatly increase the tensions which its long-range consequences were expected to alleviate. The policy of monopolistic price manipulation would make the peasants worse off; they would be certain to resist this deterioration by using all the devices Preobrazhenskii and his friends had so eloquently described; and the possibility of steering through the economic and political trouble caused by such a policy toward the time at which the new investment would smooth the waves by starting to deliver the goods could be asserted merely as an act of faith.[5]

II

The assertion that Stalin's interventions in the debate of 1924–1927 did not break the impasse would be an understatement. Indeed, his pronouncements on controversial issues of economic policy in these years exhibit such a definite tendency against sin and in favor of eating one's cake and having it too that it appears at first almost hopeless to distill out of them a clear view not only of the nature of the problems, but also of the attitude of the man. But after a closer examination of the record, there can be no doubt that Stalin's statement at the Fourteenth Party Congress: "we are, and we shall be, for Burkharin,"[6] provides a substantially correct description of his position at that time. True, in certain respects he sounded a somewhat different note. He showed a strong inclination to indulge, on every propitious occasion, in exalting the glories of the coming industrialization; moreover, the aspect of the future developments which received the fondest attention on his part was the possibility of making Russia a self-contained unit, economically independent of the outside world—"a country

[4]Abbreviation for *Osoboe soveshchanie po vosproizvodstvu osnovnogo kapitala promyshlennosti SSSR.*

[5]For a more detailed account of the controversy, see Maurice Dobb, *Soviet Economic Development Since 1917* (New York, 1948), ch. viii; *The Soviet Industrialization Debate, 1924–1928* (Cambridge, Mass., 1960).

[6]*XIV s"ezd vsesoiuznoi kommunisticheskoi partii (b). Stenograficheskii otchët* (Moscow-Leningrad, 1926), p. 494. In Volume VII of Stalin's collected works containing the text of this speech the words "and we shall be" be" are omitted.

which can produce by its own efforts the necessary equipment."[7] He started to emphasize the need for intensive reconstruction of Soviet industry earlier than Bukharin did; and in the same speech in which he dramatically refused to give "Bukharin's blood" to the opposition, he did not hesitate to disassociate himself from the "get rich" slogan.[8] But neither these nor similar instances could alter the fact that on issues which were relevant for actual policy the agreement was practically complete. When Stalin was applauding the removal of "administrative obstacles preventing the rise in the peasant welfare" as "an operation [which] undoubtedly facilitates any accumulation, private capitalist as well as socialist,"[9] or when he denounced on an earlier occasion any attempt to fan the class struggle in the village as "empty chatter," while praising peasant coöperation as a road toward socialist transformation of agriculture,[10] he was talking like a Bukharinite pure and simple; his wailings about "get rich" sounded, in view of this, very much like the famous admonition given to Eduard Bernstein, the father of German "revisionism," by one of his senior friends: "Such things should be done but not said." The identity of position on the larger issue of relationships between industry and agriculture was equally evident. Although Stalin did not invoke the ghost of Tugan-Baranovskii (he was at that time somewhat chary of incursions into the field of theory), he believed firmly that "our industry, which provides the foundation of socialism and of our power, is based on the internal, on the peasant market."[11]

The last point, to be sure, did not jibe very well with his other declared objectives: if industry had to be oriented primarily toward the satisfaction of peasant needs, it would be impossible to spare an adequate amount of resources for a large-scale effort toward reconstruction of industry, particularly if this should be done with a view of future self-sufficiency in the sphere of capital-goods production. But to proclaim long-term goals was one thing, and to rush toward them at a high speed was another. Stalin in these days showed no inclination toward the latter. In the same speech in which he extolled the virtues of economic independence, he readily admitted that large-scale imports of foreign machinery were, at least for the time being, indispensable for the development of the Soviet economy; and in his polemics against Trotsky at a somewhat later date, he went to considerable lengths in order to emphasize that the Soviet Union would not

---

[7] I. V. Stalin, *Sochineniia* (Moscow, 1947), VII, 355.

[8] *Ibid.*, p. 382.

[9] *Ibid.*, p. 153.

[10] *Ibid.*, pp. 123, 125.

[11] *Ibid.*, p. 29. How seriously Stalin took this idea can be seen from the fact that in the immediately following sentence he expressed grave concern about the situation in which Russia would find itself after her industry had "outgrown" the internal market and had to compete for the foreign markets with the advanced capitalist countries.

endanger her economic sovereignty by trading extensively with the capitalist world—first of all because the dependence involved would be a two-way affair and, secondly, because nationalization of large-scale industry and banking as well as state monopoly of foreign trade would provide powerful safeguards against any attempt at foreign encroachments.[12] His attitude toward the problem of the rate of industrial development was characterized by similar circumspection. At one point he would attempt to sidetrack the issue by injecting a larger one and by insisting that a reconstruction of fixed capital in industry would not solve the problem of building socialism in Russia as long as agriculture had not been transformed along collectivist lines.[13] On another occasion, he praised glowingly the rapid increase in output of the Soviet metal industry as proof that "the proletariat . . . can construct with its own efforts a new industry and a new society,"[14] without mentioning the obvious fact that this increase had been so rapid precisely because it had been based on increased utilization of the old industrial capacity and *not* on the creation of the new. But when he actually came to grips with the problem in his report to the Fourteenth Congress, he left no doubts as to his real attitude:

> In order to switch from maximal utilization of everything we had in industry to the policy of constructing a new industry on a new technological basis, on the basis of the construction of new plants, large capital outlays are needed. But since we are suffering from a considerable capital shortage, the further development of our industry will proceed, in all probability, not at such a fast rate as it has until now. The situation with regard to agriculture is different. It cannot be said that all the potentialities of agriculture are already exhausted. Agriculture, in distinction from industry, can move for some time at a fast rate also on its present technological basis. Even the simple rise in cultural level of the peasant, even such a simple thing as cleaning the seeds could raise the gross output of agriculture by 10 to 15 per cent. . . . That's why the further development of agriculture does not yet face the technological obstacles our industry has to face. . . .[15]

[12]"Our country depends on other countries just as other countries depend on our national economy; but this does not mean yet that our country has lost, or is going to lose, its sovereignty [*samostoiatel'nost'*], . . . that it will become a little screw [sic] of the international capitalist economy" (*ibid.*, IX, 132–133). Contrary to what may be the first impression, this passage is not incompatible either with the above-quoted statements or with Stalin's well-known pronouncements of later years. It does, however, provide an additional indication that Stalin's real long-term goal was superiority and not insularity. Such a policy, and more particularly the high rate of economic growth implied in it, did in fact make it rational to develop the domestic capital goods industry on a substantial scale since the demand for the services of this industry was known to be large and sustained and a sizable initial stock was already in existence; but it would also call for making extensive use of the advantages of international division of labor. Still, in the middle twenties, all this sounded rather academic because, as will be shown presently, the decision in favor of the high rate of growth had not yet been made.

[13]*Ibid.*, VII, 200.

[14]*Ibid.*, p. 131.

[15]*Ibid.*, pp. 315–316.

Stalin could not be more frank in formulating the basic problem which was, as we have seen, at the core of the whole discussion: the very same factors—limited productive capacity and low levels of income—that called for expansion in Soviet industry were putting obstacles in its way. In the paragraph quoted the emphasis was clearly on the obstacles. Still, when the arch-moderate Shanin applauded heartily, he must have done so with a twinkle in his eye: in fact the Fourteenth Party Congress did signalize the transition from "filling-in" to reconstruction—but reconstruction on a limited scale and in a cautious mood. Although the volume of capital outlays increased substantially in the years 1926 and 1927, the Leftists led by Preobrazhenskii and Trotsky immediately opened fire. The new investment program, they claimed, was neither here nor there; it was too limited to secure an increase in capacity large enough to stabilize the situation in a not too distant future, too ambitious not to cause inflationary disturbances now in view of the absence of drastic taxation measures.

In the face of these attacks, and of actual difficulties which did not fail to materialize, something more than a sober and judicious description of the two horns of the dilemma was called for. A characteristic division of labor developed at this point. Bukharin and Rykov, who were the guiding spirits of the new line, were wrestling with large, clear-cut issues—the relation between heavy and light industry, the limits for investment in time-consuming projects, the possibility of absorbing the surplus labor in production lines with low capital requirements—in a desperate search for solutions which would make the adopted policy work. Stalin followed a different procedure. He visibly tried to avoid sharply delineated problems; instead, he let his argument seesaw from bold statements of principles to sobering but comfortably loose observations on present-day realities, and he switched from obtuse mystique to gruff common sense. Rapid industrialization? Yes, indeed! More than that: it should be kept in mind that "not every development of industry constitutes industrialization" and that "the focal point of industrialization, its basis, consists of development of heavy industry (fuel, metals, etc.) and of eventual development of production of the means of production, development of domestic machine-building."[16] But right on the heels of such proclamations there would come a caustic remark about those who "sometimes forget that it is impossible to make plans either for industry as a whole or for some 'large and all-embracing' enterprise without a certain minimum of means, without a certain minimum of reserves,"[17] and a warning that "an industry which breaks itself away from the national economy as a whole and loses its connection with it cannot be the guiding force of the national economy."[18] Could the Soviet

[16]*Ibid.*, VIII, 120.
[17]*Ibid.*, p. 131.
[18]*Ibid.*, p. 132.

economy in its present shape afford a rate of economic development which would exceed that of the capitalist countries? Of course! The capitalist countries had based their expansion on exploitation of colonies, military conquest, or foreign loans. But the Soviet Union expropriated the capitalists and the landlords, nationalized strategic areas of the economy, and repudiated the tsarist foreign debts. This circumstance enabled here to provide a sufficient volume of accumulation without having recourse to any of these devices.[19] Furthermore, it permitted this accumulation to unfold alongside of "a steady improvement in the material conditions of the working masses, including the bulk of the peasantry . . . as contrasted with the capitalist methods of industrialization based on the growing misery of millions of working people."[20] No specific reasons for any of these assertions were given. However, the most elaborate of such attempts at solution by definition concluded by admitting that the socialist principles along which the Soviet economy was organized offered merely a *possibility* of achieving the appropriate level of accumulation, but no more than that; and the concrete proposals for policy which followed were in their sum total excruciatingly modest not only in comparison with the grandiloquent claims that preceded them but also, and more significantly, with regard to the size of the investment programs they were supposed to sustain.[21]

All this looked very much like trying to buy a second-hand Ford for the price of a discarded piece of junk while pretending that a brand-new Packard was being obtained. True, there was another line of defense: to play down the importance of recurrent spells of "goods famine" and to present them as transient phenomena. Although Stalin tried this device occasionally, it was obviously a tenuous argument to use, particularly since the assertion that "quick development of our industry is the surest way to eliminate the goods famine"[22] sounded too much like conceding a point to the Left opposition. It was therefore only logical for him to shift the battleground to the territory of the adversaries, to concentrate on the crucial weak spot in their position and to pound relentlessly upon it:

> The oppositionist bloc assumed a conflict between industry and agriculture and is headed toward breaking industry away from agriculture. It

[19]*Ibid.*, pp. 122–125.

[20]*Ibid.*, p. 287.

[21]They include 1) improved incentives for peasant saving; 2) reduction in retail prices of industrial goods; 3) orderly amortization policies; 4) building up export reserves; 5) creation of budgetary surplus (*ibid.*, pp. 126–129). In other contexts elimination of waste and inefficiency in economic and political administration receives the top billing (*ibid.*, IX, 196 and joint declaration by Stalin, Rykov, and Kuibyshev in *Pravda*, August 17, 1926). Some of these measures, while pointing in the right direction, could hardly be expected to have much effect in the immediate future, and others involved putting the cart before the horse, e.g., price reductions not preceded by substantial expansion in productive capacity.

[22]Stalin, *Sochineniia*, IX, 120.

does not realize and it does not admit that it is impossible to develop industry while neglecting the interests of agriculture and hurting these interests in a rude fashion. It does not understand that if industry is the guiding force of the national economy, the agricultural economy represents in turn the basis on which our industry is able to develop . . .

. . . The Party cannot and will not tolerate [a situation in which] the opposition continues to undermine the basis of the alliance of workers and peasants by spreading the idea of an increase in wholesale prices and in the burden of taxation upon the peasantry, by attempting to "construe" the relationships between proletariat and peasantry not as relationships of economic *cooperation* but as relationships of exploitation of the peasantry by the proletarian state. The Party cannot and will not tolerate this.[23]

At the Fifteenth Party Congress, which carried out this solemn vow by expelling the Left-wingers, Stalin was surveying the field once more. He displayed again the full array of the familiar arguments: praise for the growth of the Soviet industrial output at a rate which, while declining continuously since 1924–1925, was still showing "a record percentage which no large capitalist country in the world has ever shown";[24] reaffirmation of faith in the superiority which the Soviet system possessed with regard to capitalism in its ability to accumulate and which should make it possible to increase the industrial output by roughly 75 per cent during the coming five years in spite of the exhaustion of the capacity reserves; strong emphasis on the possibility of developing "in an atmosphere of constant *rapproachement* between city and village, between proletariat and peasantry,"[25] as one of the greatest advantages of Soviet industry. His backhanded remarks about what he termed the "shadowy aspects" of the Soviet economy ("elements" of goods famine, lack of reserves, etc.) contained no specific proposals for remedy but carried a clear implication that if people on the spot would apply themselves to their tasks with more energy, all would be well. There was, however, no complacency in his remarks on agriculture, and here indeed something new was added: in view of the slowness of agricultural development, Stalin declared, the task of the Party would now consist in bringing about "a gradual transition of pulverized peasant farms to the level of combined large-scale holdings, to the social collective cultivation of land on the basis of the intensification and mechanization of agriculture."[26] He was careful not to give any hint as to the anticipated speed of this movement, and, in an enunciation antedating by a few weeks his report to the Fifteenth Congress, he was explicit in emphasizing that it would take a long time to collectivize the bulk of the

[23]*Ibid.*, pp. 288, 352–353.
[24]*Ibid.*, X, 300.
[25]*Ibid.*, pp. 301–302.
[26]*Ibid.*, p. 309.

peasantry because such an undertaking would require "huge finances" which the Soviet state did not yet have.[27] Still, his statement was surprising: but events which were even then fast advancing were to provide *ex post* a clue to it.

III

The beginning of 1928 saw large consignments of the Leftist "super-industrializers" move toward places of exile in Siberia and Central Asia. But at the same time their dire predictions were coming true. For the first time since the "scissors crisis" of 1923 the peasant bolted the regime. By January 1928 the amount of collected grain fell by roughly one-third as compared with the same period of the preceding year. During the following few months it rose again only to drop in the spring; and the emergency methods by which the temporary increase was enforced stirred up once more the feelings of bitterness and resistance which had been dormant in the villages during the seven years of the NEP. The crisis of the system was there—the first crisis Stalin had to cope with as the undisputed leader of the Party and of the state. During the eighteen months that followed, Stalin was no longer arguing, as before, against opponents who had been isolated and outmaneuvered before they began to fight; he was reappraising a policy which had promoted his rise to power and which seemed now to explode in his face. It is therefore not surprising that his pronouncements of that period differ significantly from those of the earlier years. They certainly contain their due share of crudeness, obfuscation, and outright distortion; but at the same time they show flashes of astonishing frankness and incisiveness clearly due to realization that everything was at stake and that the time of muddling through was over.

The prime task consisted, understandably enough, in providing the explanation of the agricultural debacle. One can clearly distinguish several parallel lines of attack in Stalin's statements on the subject. The first of them was already indicated in his report to the Fifteenth Congress when he mentioned the low productivity of small-scale peasant agriculture and its low marketable surplus as a serious obstacle for the rapid industrial development of the country. This proposition was in itself neither new nor controversial, provided that the "obstacle" was taken to be a retarding factor rather than an insuperable barrier. It was a breath-taking jump to conclusions, however, when Stalin went on to claim that "there is no other way out" except for collectivization. In the audience to which he was addressing himself there were, to be sure, no doubts as to the superiority of the large-size units in agricultural economy. But it was generally understood that there was still a wide range of opportunities for increases in the

[27] *Ibid.*, p. 225.

productivity of peasant farming which would not call for large-scale mechanized equipment and for drastic expansion in the size of the productive
unit; and it was agreed that the extensive application of the latter category
of improvements should be postponed, in view of the high capital requirements involved, until after the capital-goods industry had been sufficiently
expanded. Consequently, while the idea of collectivization of agriculture as
a long-range objective held a place of honor in the Party program of 1919
and was repeatedly invoked after that, particularly in the pronouncements
of the Left, no one had thus far suggested putting it into effect on a large
scale within the next few years in order to solve difficulties facing the
Soviet economy at the end of the "restoration period." In fact, Stalin
himself seemed to take quite an edge off his argument and to hark back
to his earlier views when he admitted the existence of considerable reserves for improvement within the framework of the small-scale economy,[28] and as late as April 1929 he still kept insisting that "the individual
farming of poor and middle peasants plays and will play the predominant
role in supplying industry with food and raw material in the immediate
future."[29] But, and most important, the whole point seemed to have no
direct bearing on the concrete issue under consideration. By the end of
1927 and at the beginning of 1928 the Russian peasants had not less but
more grain at their disposal than in the preceding years; still, they were
willing to sell less of it than in the years of bad harvest. The reference to
the low productivity of small-scale farming, even if reduced to sensible
proportions, was definitely too "long run" to provide an explanation for
this phenomenon.

The second line of argument was succinctly summed up in the phrase
"as long as the kulak exists, the sabotage of grain collections will exist
too."[30] This point, made in Stalin's speech in January 1928 and repeated
by him with increasing vehemence ever after, was certainly straightfor-
ward enough; still it raised more questions than it answered. The fact of
formidable kulak resistance did not fit very well, to begin with, into the
rosy picture of the Soviet village Stalin had been unfolding before his
listeners only slightly more than a year earlier when he proudly referred
to the steadily increasing proportion of middle peasants in the agricultural
population and asserted, with a long quotation from Lenin on hand to
bear him out, that nobody but panic-stricken people could see a danger in
the growth of "small private capital" in the villages because this growth

---

[28]"There is every indication that we could increase the yield of the peasant farms by
15–20 per cent within a few years. We have now in use about 5 million hoes. The substitution
of ploughs for them could alone result in a most substantial increase in the output of grain in
the country, not to speak of supplying the peasant farms with a certain minimum of fertilizer,
improved seeds, small machinery and the like" (*ibid.*, XI, 92).

[29]*Ibid.*, XII, 59.

[30]*Ibid.*, XI, 4–5.

"is being compensated and overcompensated by such decisive facts as the development of our industry, which strengthens the positions of the proletariat and of the socialist forms of the economy."[31] True, in this case also there were, at first, important qualifications which softened the impact of the shock: stern warning against any talk about "dekulakization" as "counterrevolutionary chatter," condemnation of the excessive zeal in applying reprisals, and announcement of moderate increases in prices of agricultural products.[32] But after all this had been said and done, it was still to be explained why the kulak was so successful in his criminal endeavor—more particularly, why he was able, as Stalin reluctantly acknowledged, to carry along with him the "middle peasants" who were supplying the bulk of the marketable surplus at that time.[33]

Stalin had a clear answer to this as well as to all other questions the previous explanations had left unanswered; between the "low-productivity" argument and the cloak-and-dagger theory of the kulaks' plot he had a third line of reasoning which hit the nail straight on the head. It was less publicized than the former two and for good reasons: it amounted to a clear and unqualified admission of a complete impasse. Stalin no longer tried to play down the impact of the goods famine; he stressed instead that the shortage of industrial goods on the peasant market, aggravated by an increase in peasant earnings in the preceding period, had hit not merely the kulaks but the peasants as a whole and had made them strike back by cutting the grain deliveries.[34] He spelled out more fully than ever before the connection between the goods famine and the discontinuous increase in the volume of investment:

> Industrial reconstruction means the transfer of resources from the field of production of articles of consumption to the field of production of means of production . . . But what does it mean? It means that money is being invested in the construction of new enterprises, that the number of new towns and new consumers is increasing while, on the other hand, the new enterprises will begin to turn out additional masses of commodities only in three or four years' time. It is obvious that this does not help to overcome the goods famine.[35]

He rounded out the picture when he dropped his usual double talk and shocked his colleagues of the Central Committee by revealing his views on the true sources of accumulation in the Soviet economy:

> The peasantry pays to the state not only the normal taxes, direct and indirect, but it *overpays,* first of all, on the relatively high prices of indus-

[31]*Ibid.,* VIII, 291–292.
[32]*Ibid.,* XI, 15, 124–125.
[33]*Ibid.,* p. 12.
[34]*Ibid.,* p. 14.
[35]*Ibid.,* p. 267.

trial goods, and is being more or less *underpaid* on the relatively low prices of agricultural products . . . This is something like a "tribute" [*nechto vrode "dani"*], something like a supertax we are temporarily compelled to impose in order to maintain and to develop further the present tempo of development of industry, to secure the industry for the whole country, to raise the well-being of the village still further, and to abolish entirely this supertax, these "scissors" between the city and the village.[36]

All this sounded very much like a somewhat awkward rephrasing of Preobrazhenskii's "law of primitive socialist accumulation." The crucial task at that time of the day, however, was not to restate an old diagnosis but to construe a "tribute"-collecting device that would work: and this was exactly what Stalin did. The collective farm, in which decisions about size and disposal of the marketable surplus were made not by individual farmers but by management carrying out the orders of the state, was to serve as a high-powered tool for enforcing the necessary rate of saving in the most literal sense of the standard Marxian definition: it could make the peasants "sell without purchasing" to a much greater extent than they would have done if left to themselves. Here was the decisive point. Still, Stalin was undoubtedly right in not being too ostentatious about it and in holding on firmly to the two other arguments referred to above in spite of their inadequacy. To proclaim in so many words that collectivization was needed in order to squeeze out the peasants in a most effective way would clearly be a poor tactic; it was much smarter to present the collective farm as an indispensable vehicle for modernizing Soviet agriculture and for drastically increasing its productivity. In view of everything Stalin had to say about the impact of the "goods famine" on the peasantry as a whole and about the inevitability of the "supertax," the diatribes against kulak sabotage could not be taken very seriously. They could, nevertheless, be of appreciable help in whipping up emotions against an alternative solution which was advanced at that time by Stalin's former comrades-in-arms. The representatives of the Bukharin-Rykov group did not propose to revise the investment plans below the fairly impressive levels set by the Party leadership at the end of 1927. They believed, however, that in order to carry out these plans it was not necessary to abandon support for individual peasant farming and to renounce the policy of no interference with the growth of large-scale kulak farms while curbing the non-productive and exploitative activities of their owners. On the contrary, although by that time the controversy had already been quite muffled, and it was difficult to ascertain what exactly the leaders of the Right Wing were prepared to do, the general tenor of their pronouncements, as well as occasional statements of second-string representatives

---

[36]*Ibid.*, p. 159 (italics in original). It may be worth noting that this speech, which led to the final break between Stalin and the Bukharin-Rykov group, was not published until 1949.

and "fellow travelers" of this group, indicated a willingness to go to greater lengths than ever before toward placating the peasants in general and the kulaks in particular, in order to provide them with incentives for increasing the marketable surplus and the volume of voluntary saving in an effort to contain the mounting inflationary pressures.

Stalin never earnestly tried to assail the economic logic of this position. He never attempted to prove that it was impossible for socialized industry and kulak farming to operate smoothly within one economic system, although he made a few obiter dicta to that effect. Neither did he care to show (which would be a more serious point) that an investment policy, sustained to a considerable extent by the peasants' free decision to restrict their consumption, would tend to be rather narrow in scope and susceptible to rude shocks as a result of such uncontrollable events as drought or changes in international terms of trade. Instead, he asked: "What is meant by not hindering kulak farming? It means setting the kulak free. And what is meant by setting the kulak free? It means giving him power."[37] Taken literally, this seemed to be one of the dubious syllogisms Stalin was notoriously fond of whenever a weak case was to be defended. It is quite conceivable, however, that in this particular instance he believed every word he said; and, what is vastly more important, there can be no doubt that the consistent application of the Rightist recipe would be fraught with gravest political dangers. The efforts to enlist voluntary support of the peasantry for the industrialization developing at considerable speed would require a veritable tightrope performance on the part of the Soviet rulers. In order to maintain the precarious balance and to steer clear of trouble at every sharper turning of the road, the regime would have to combine compulsory control measures with additional concessions; and since there was little room for compromise in the economic sphere, it could become well-nigh indispensable to explore a new line of approach and to attempt to earn the good will of the upper strata of the peasantry by opening up for them avenues of political influence even if confined, at first, to the level of local government. There was nothing either in the logic of things or, for that matter, in the tenets of the accepted doctrine to warrant the conclusion that such a situation, if permitted to endure, would inevitably result in "giving power to the kulaks" and in restoring capitalism. But it is quite probable that under the impact of initial concessions and of further maneuvering the system of authoritarian dictatorship would have become increasingly permeated by elements of political pluralism and of quasi-democratic give-and-take. The vacillating and conciliatory attitude which, judging by Stalin's own testimony,[38] was shown by the lower echelons of the Party hierarchy and governmental apparatus, during

[37] *Ibid.*, p. 275.
[38] *Ibid.*, pp. 3–4, 235.

the critical months of 1928, underlined the gravity of the situation. The choice was clear: either a deep retreat and the gradual erosion of the dictatorial system or an all-out attack aimed at total destruction of the adversary's capability to resist.

Stalin's pronouncements since early 1928 showed beyond possibility of doubt that he had decided in favor of the second alternative. The transition from theory to action, however, was all but a masterminded advance toward a well-defined goal. Stalin evidently planned at first to move in the agricultural field by stages; his repeated declarations about the predominant role of individual farming for many years to come, as well as his condemnations of "dekulakization" and readiness to meet the restive peasantry part of the way by granting price increases, can be taken as a clear indication of this. And the impression of caution and groping for solution is still further reinforced when the position on issues of agricultural policy is viewed in a broader context. There was, undoubtedly, a perceptible change of emphasis in Stalin's declarations on questions of industrialization policy after January 1928. He no longer spoke about Soviet industry as "the most large scale and most concentrated in the world," as he had at the Fifteenth Party Congress.[39] Instead, he denounced its "terrible backwardness" and sounded a call for catching up with the West as a condition for survival: the old aim of "economic independence" was now transformed into "superiority" and further dramatized by the stress upon the element of tempo at which the catching up was to take place. And while all this talk was still couched in most general terms, the language of the drafts of the First Five-Year Plan, which were at that time being prepared by the official governmental agencies and which reflected in their successive versions the changes of the official policy, was much more outspoken: during the whole period between the Fifteenth Party Congress and adoption of the final draft of the First Five-Year Plan in the spring of 1929 there was a clear upward trend in all the crucial indicators of the "tempo"—rate of growth in industrial output, volume of investment and its increase over time, share of heavy industry in the total capital outlays. But at the same time there was strong evidence that the momentous implications of the new policy were not yet fully grasped. Stalin was, no doubt, most persistent in stressing that industry and agriculture were interdependent, the first constituting a "leading link," and the second being a "basis." Still, whenever he went beyond these generalities, he pointed out that industry would have to expand and to reëquip itself in order to start reëquipping agriculture; in fact this was, in his view, one of the strongest forces pushing for speedy industrialization.[40] The implication was clear: the bulk of the reorganization of agriculture was to take place *after* the

[39]*Ibid.*, X, 301.
[40]*Ibid.*, XI, 252–253.

completion of a cycle of intensive industrial expansion and not *simultane-ously* with it. Moreover, although Stalin kept extolling the superiority of "*smytchka* through metal" over "*smytchka* through textile," he could not refrain from remarking wistfully that it would be very fine indeed "to shower the village with all kinds of goods in order to extract from the village the maximum amount of agricultural products" and from leaving at least a strong implication that the attainment of such a happy state of affairs was one of the major objectives of the industrialization drive.[41] Stalin was merely hinting at these diverse points, but they were spelled out fully in the targets of the First Five-Year Plan: more than doubling of the fixed capital of the whole nonagricultural sector over the quinquennium, increase in output of industrial consumers' goods by 40 per cent, and no more than an 18 per cent share of the collective farms in the marketable output of agriculture.

No doubt, if the planned sizes of the first two items of the blueprint had been mutually consistent, the comparatively moderate targets for the third would be appropriate. But they were not; moreover, in view of Stalin's own statements about the causes of the "goods famine," the high target for consumers' goods could be to him only a pious wish, if not plain eyewash. As a result, there was an awkward dilemma. From the standpoint of reducing the pressures on the facilities of the capital goods industry, a postponement of full-dress collectivization seemed wise. But the function of collective farms consisted, first and foremost, in providing the technique for imposing the required volume of compulsory saving, and since the astronomic rate of planned expansion in fixed capital would inevitably entail, at the very least in the first years of the Plan, a drastic cut in consumption levels, such a technique was desperately needed from the very beginning of the process. How could the conflict be resolved? The answer was not slow in coming. Before the Plan was two months old the moderate targets in the agricultural field mentioned above went overboard, because Stalin had reversed himself; in response to the repeated and more dismal failure of the grain collections, all-out collectivization was sweeping the country.

Up to this point the whole development looked like some sort of cumulative process gone mad. To begin with, there was a "goods famine" generated by expanding industry and throwing agriculture into a crisis, with an incipient collectivization drive as a result. Then, there was the perspective of an extremely rapid transformation of agriculture imparting additional impetus to plans of industrial expansion and pushing them to lengths which would disbalance agriculture more than ever and, finally,

[41]*Ibid.*, p. 40.

the sudden burst of all-out collectivization spread disruption in the social fabric of the country-side and left in its wake the wholesale slaughter of livestock by rebellious peasants. But after reaching what seemed to be the stage of explosion, the fluctuations began to subside as the new device went to work. Collective farming pulled the Plan over the hump because it did what an agriculture based on individual ownership would never have done, even if confronted with an equally formidable display of terror and repression: amidst mass starvation, in the face of contracting agricultural output and an appalling shortage in industrial consumers' goods, the new set-up secured an iron ration of food sufficient to keep alive the workers of rapidly growing industry, and provided an export surplus big enough to finance record-breaking importations of foreign machinery. The feat was achieved to a large extent on the basis of old, decrepit equipment; the capital-goods industry was permitted to make huge forward strides in its own expansion before being called upon to supply the collective farms with technology which would correspond to their size. The moral of the story was clear: if a half-completed structure of collective farming and a capital-goods industry still in the throes of acute growing pains succeeded in making possible economic expansion at an unparalleled rate, there was every reason to maintain this pattern of development after these two key elements had been firmly established and to continue using up at a high rate the opportunities for investment in enlarged productive potential and increased power, with the satisfaction of consumers' needs firmly relegated to the rear.

Such was, in fact, the conclusion Stalin had drawn. But while the practical consequences of this decision were momentous, little would be gained by discussing his running comments on them in any detail. There is no doubt that after 1929 Stalin was more assertive than ever before in proclaiming his long-range goals and in exhorting to further efforts. All his earlier pronouncements on the need of catching up with the West look pallid in comparison with his famous "we-do-not-want-to-be-beaten" speech.[42] Although the successes of the five-year plans failed to improve the quality of their architect's theorizing, it was only natural that in the process of directing Soviet industrialization he sharpened some of his earlier notions of its distinctive features and made a few new observations: his remarks on short-term profit considerations as an inadequate guide for developing new areas of economy, and on Russia's advantage in not being weighted down in her attempts to adapt new technology by the massive stock of old-type equipment already in existence are cases in point.[43]

[42]*Ibid.*, XIII, 29–42, esp. 38–40.

[43]*Ibid.*, pp. 192–93 and *Voprosy leninizma*, 11th ed. (Moscow, 1947), p. 575.

And he displayed to the full his uncanny ability to change tactics and re-cast arguments in the face of unexpected difficulties.[44] For all these new touches and variations, however there was no longer any real change either in the structure of the system or in the views of its builder. He summed up his ideas once more shortly after the war when he contrasted the "capital-ist" pattern of industrialization, putting the development of consumers'-goods output first, and the "socialist" pattern starting with the expansion of heavy industries.[45] And he restated the same position in a more gener-alized way a few years later when he answered one of his last self-addressed questions: "What does it mean to give up the preponderance of the produc-tion of the means of production [over production of consumers' goods]? This means to destroy the possibility of the uninterrupted growth of the national economy."[46] Bukharin would have called it *prikladnaia Tugan-Baranovshchina*. Indeed, this it was: "applied Tuganism" harnessed to the service of a totalitarian state.

---

[44]His "Golovokruzhenie ot uspekhov" (Stalin, *Sochineniia*, XII, 191–199), which put a temporary halt to the forced collectivization, is, to be sure, the best-known example of this. It may be worth while, however, to quote a similar instance from a different area. In 1930, with reports from industrial battlefields claiming big victories, Stalin allowed himself another brief spell of "dizziness with sucess": he called for raising the 1933 target for pig iron from 10 to 15–17 million tons and used abusive language against the "Trotskyite theory of the leveling-off curve of growth" (*ibid.*, pp. 331, 349–352). In 1933, however, when the actual level of pig iron output fell far short of the initial target and the rate of over-all industrial expansion slumped heavily, he did not hesitate to move more than halfway toward this much-detested theory: he argued then that the rate of growth in output had shown a decline as a result of the transition from the "period of restoration" to the "period of reconstruction," and went on to say that there was nothing sinsiter about it (*ibid.*, 183–185). But in the following years the rate of increase went up again, if not quite to the level of the preceding period, and the unholy distinction between "restoration" and "reconstruction" disappeared from Stalin's vocabulary.

[45]Speech to the voters of the Stalin electoral district of Moscow, *Pravda*, February 10, 1946.

[46]I. Stalin, *Ekonomicheskie problemy sotsializma v SSSR* (Moscow, 1952), p. 24. It goes without saying that this is much too strong a condition. An "uninterrupted growth of the na-tional economy" is secured whenever the volume of investment exceeds the amount needed to maintain the capital equipment at a level sufficient to keep the income per head of growing population constant. This requirement might indeed involve a "preponderance [for example, more rapid tempo of growth] of the production of the means of production" if at least one of the following assumptions could be taken to hold: (1) abnormally high rate of wear and tear due either to low durability of the average piece of machinery or to the unusually large share of old-vintage equipment in the existing capital stock; (2) necessity to provide productive fa-cilities for a discontinuously large increase in the total labor force in order to offset the pres-sure of increasing population on the income-per-capital levels; (3) the capital-goods industry exposed to these pressures being adapted in its capacity to a very limited volume of net capital construction over and above the "normal" replacement levels. It would certainly be bold to argue that any of these assumptions actually prevailed in the Soviet economy of 1952. But it would be even more drastic to assume that when Stalin said "uninterrupted growth" he meant precisely this, and nothing else.

THIRTY YEARS OF SOVIET INDUSTRIALISATION*
— · — · — · — · — · — · — · — · — · — · — ·

Gregory Grossman†

Just thirty years ago, in October 1928, the First Five-Year Plan was launched. For three decades the resources of a vast country, the energies of large and talented population, and the capacity of a most elaborate and centralised organisation, have been mobilised as no country has been mobilised before, for the attainment of supremacy in the twin fields of industrial power and military might. The avowed goal—to 'catch up with and overtake America' in per capita output—is now being daily proclaimed to be within easy reach; but even in the early years of the Plan Era, when it was only dimly seen, the eyes of the leaders were already fixed upon it.

Clear though the objective has been, it is not easy to measure the distance traversed by the Soviet economy in the three decades. There are, first, the facade of propaganda and the curtain of secrecy to contend with. Although incomparably more statistical information has been published in the last few years than in the preceding twenty (but still less than before that), the data are far from satisfactory for purposes of careful analysis. Important gaps in information remain; much of the data are difficult to interpret for lack of explanation of their derivation; and many statistics are of questionable reliability or are even known seriously to distort what they purport to reflect. The last refers particularly to summary measures of economic growth.[1]

A second difficulty arises from the character of Soviet economic growth, namely, its great unevenness. In some areas progress has been exceedingly rapid, in others there has been very little growth or none at all, and in some respects there has even been retrogression. The economically efficient and inefficient, the technically advanced and backward, are constantly found side by side, often under the same roof. While to a certain extent this unevenness of development was unintended, generally it is the result of consciously adopted and pursued priorities; in any case it makes a balanced appraisal more difficult.

*Reprinted by permission from *Soviet Survey*, Vol. 26 (October–December, 1958), pp. 15–21 (excerpts).

†Dr. Gregory Grossman is Professor of Economics, University of California, Berkeley. His publications include: *Soviet Statistics of Physical Output of Industrial Commodities* (1960), *Value and Plan* (ed.) (1960), *Economic Systems* (1967), and "Gold and the Sword: Money in the Soviet Command Economy" in Henry Rosovsky (ed). *Industrialization in Two Systems* (1966).

[1] The reader will find further discussion of the problems raised by the recently published Soviet statistical handbook in Naum Jasny's *The Soviet 1956 Statistical Handbook; a commentary* (Michigan University Press, 1957), and in Alec Nove's article in *Soviet Studies* (Glasgow), January 1957.

Thirdly, and closely linked, is the 'index number problem,' which makes its appearance whenever we ask—as we inevitably do—such comprehensive questions as: How much has total industrial production increased? Was there any improvement in levels of consumption, and if so, to what extent? How rapidly has the national income grown? etc. The answers to such questions depend on the relative importance, *i.e.* the 'weights' assigned to the individual components while aggregating (combining) them. Since there is usually a number of possible weighting systems, each with a logic and rationale of its own, as well as a number of mathematical formulae to employ, different answers to the same question may be obtained depending on the method. And the more uneven the growth among the individual components, the greater the likelihood that the answers will differ significantly.

In terms of total industrial production the Soviet Union has moved up from fifth place in 1928 (after the USA, Germany, Britain, and France, and before Italy) to second place today, although on a *per capita* basis it ranks—now as then—considerably lower than on an over-all basis. In 1928, Soviet industry produced approximately one tenth as much as American industry. Lately, taking the American recession year together with the preceding peak, the ratio has been perhaps 40–50 per cent. However, the ratio varies greatly from branch to branch: for example, with regard to machinery and munitions it is doubtless considerably higher. Today, as contrasted with three decades ago, the Soviet Union produces about the same range of industrial articles (though in different proportions) as do the more advanced western countries, and in many instances the levels of technology are also similar. Labour productivity in Soviet industry, on a man-hour basis, is substantially less than half the American level, but probably compares quite favourably with the levels in the major countries of Western Europe.

But what has been the 'tempo' of Soviet industrial growth? Western economists have analysed the official Soviet index of industrial production, and have generally concluded that because of various faults in its construction it greatly overstates the actual growth of Soviet industrial output.[2] For this reason several attempts at constructing a more reliable index of Soviet industrial production have been made in the West, based on the available information on the output of commodities in physical terms. One such recomputation, quite comprehensive in coverage and ex-

---

[2] Soviet economists themselves admit the upward bias of the official index, at least when they are engaged in serious discussion among themselves and not in defending the official position; cf. the proceedings of a conference published by the Institute of Economics, Academy of Sciences of the USSR, as *Voprosy metodologii izucheniia i izmereniia proizvoditelnosti truda* (Moscow, 1956), *passim*.

TABLE 1

SOVIET INDUSTRIAL PRODUCTION,[4] 1928—100

	1937	1940	1948	1950	1955	1956	1957 (as % of 1956)
Total							
Official Index	446	646	761	1,119	2,069	2,290	110
Shimkin's Index	274	294	294	434	715	773	
Producers and Military Goods							
Official Index	652	1,000	1,299	2,049	3,895	4,339	111
Shimkin's Index	426	452	536	781	1,290	1,400	
Consumer Goods							
Official Index	311	415	409	510	899	984	108
Shimkin's Index	171	183	128	197	323	344	

tending through 1956, was recently undertaken by D. B. Shimkin and his associates, and although methodologically this index differs from the official one, it is nonetheless interesting to examine the two side by side.[3] See Table 1.

Thus according to Shimkin's estimate there was a 7.7-fold increase in total industrial production between 1928 and 1956,[5] or only one-third as much as the official claim. The well-known policy of 'primacy of heavy industry' stands out in sharp relief in our table. In terms of Shimkin's index, the output of producers' and military goods increased 14-fold from 1928 to 1956; of manufactured consumers' goods—3.4-fold; however, since 1950 the two components have been growing at an equal pace.

To calculate the average annual rate of Soviet industrial growth we cannot simply consider the growth to have taken place over the 28 years that separate 1956 from 1928. First, we must eliminate the eight years (1941–1948) that elapsed until the pre-war (1940) level of industrial production was re-attained. Secondly, although *recovery* in this sense was achieved by 1948, reconstruction of damaged capacity continued on a substantial scale at least until the end of 1950, and indeed (as can be computed from our table) industrial output rose during 1949 and 1950 at about twice

[3]D. B. Shimkin and F. A. Leedy, 'Soviet Industrial Growth,' *Automotive Industries*, 1 January, 1958, p. 51. Shimkin's index is weighted (following Hodgman's pioneering work) by 1934 values-added. The official index on the other hand is a 'gross' one, *i.e.* it aggregates the values of output (at supposedly constant prices) of individual enterprises.

[4]Soviet definition of industry, which includes mining, power generation, logging, and fishing. Territorial coverage corresponds to the boundaries of the respective years.

[5]All such estimates of course are less than perfect. Shimkin's results however agree quite well, allowing for differences in method and coverage, with the results of other recomputations.

the annual rate that obtained in the more 'normal' years. Surely the expansion of industrial production while reconstruction is still proceeding cannot be equated with 'normal' growth, and therefore we count these two years as four. This gives us altogether 22 'effective years' of growth of industrial production, and the average annual rates implicit in Shimkin's series therefore are: 9.7 per cent for total industrial output, 12.7 per cent for producers' and military goods, and 5.8 per cent for consumers' goods.[6]

It would be wrong to think of Soviet industrialisation under the Plans as a smooth and steady process. The heroic period—heroic in the scale of its feats, sacrifices, and errors—was surely the years 1929 through 1936, when the rate of growth of industrial output averaged 12 or more per cent per annum (and well over this during the last four years of the period). It was in those years that the basic institutional framework of the Soviet economy was established, and the basic locational pattern laid. The next four years, 1937 through 1940, stand in sharp contrast. Years of the Great Purge and of intensified preparations for war, they show an average rate of growth (annexations apart) of probably only a few per cent a year, although the exact record is obscured by territorial change. During the last five years covered by Shimkin's index, 1952 through 1956, industrial output seems to have increased at an average rate of just about nine per cent per year. Some slowing down apparently took place in 1957, and, as we shall presently see, the Soviet planners apparently expect considerable retardation over the next ten to fifteen years.

If the long period rate of industrial growth implicit in Shimkin's index —9.7 per cent per year over 22 'effective' years—is approximately correct, then the tempo of Soviet industrial expansion has certainly been extremely high, though not entirely without precedent or parallel among non-communist countries. Over even somewhat longer periods, South Africa (1911–1940) averaged 9 or more per cent, and Japan (1910–1937)—8.5 per cent per year. Over shorter spans of time, Sweden equalled, and (significantly) Russia herself approached, the long-term Soviet rate in the late eighties and in the nineties of the last century.[7] Political and institutional differences for the moment apart, the uniqueness of the Soviet industrialisation record therefore lies not so much in the rate of growth, or even the length of the period over which it has been so far sustained, as in that it occurred

---

[6]Strictly speaking, a small downward adjustment in these rates should also be made to take account of the annexation of industrial capacity at the beginning and at the end of the Second World War. We omit it for the sake of simplicity and statistical 'conservatism.'

[7]For the underlying statistics see League of Nations, *Industrialisation and Foreign Trade* (Geneva, 1945), pp. 130ff.; Alexander Gerschenkron. 'The Rate of Industrial Growth in Russia Since 1885,' *Jour. of Econ. History*, Supplement VII, 1947, pp. 146 and 156; and Wm. W. Lockwood, *The Economic Development of Japan* (Princeton 1954), p. 117. The Russian rate during 1890–1900 was over eight per cent per year.

simultaneously with a huge peacetime military programme, and benefited relatively little from capital inflow from abroad (taking the period as a whole).

This observation also applies to the total national product, whose growth had also been very rapid, although (over the long period) obviously not nearly as rapid as that of industry. While sectors closely linked with the industrialisation programme, such as transportation and construction, have more or less kept pace with industrial expansion, and the military sector of course grew rapidly too, agriculture and the various activities directly serving the consumer (housing, retail trade, and even education and medical care) expanded much more slowly. Agriculture, in particular, lagged badly; even with the considerable upswing that occurred after Stalin's death, it is very doubtful that agricultural production, and especially food production (for there was a shift to industrial crops), is much above the level of three decades ago in relation to the country's population.

Rapid urbanisation in a peasant country, involving as it does a radical change in the mode of life, warps our statistical yardsticks and renders any over-all judgment on trends in *per capita* consumption very difficult. (The share of the urban in the total population was 18 per cent in 1928 and is approaching 45 per cent now.) Urban consumption levels, taken separately, are probably moderately better than in 1928, though this is due not so much (if at all) to higher real wages as to the reduction in the number of dependants per wage earner. However, the composition of urban consumption has shifted greatly: housing, clothing, and foodstuffs of high nutritive value are in lower or approximately equal supply per person, while there has been a marked increase in the availability of the more 'modern' manufactured consumers' goods. So far as the peasants are concerned, the virtual silence of Soviet statistics with regard to their income, consumption, or even numbers, in itself suggests (to put it mildly) no great advance since the pre-collectivisation level.

There is no miracle or mystery about the speed of Soviet economic expansion. At the same time, to attribute it—as does the quasi-mystical Kremlin cliché—to the 'socialist law of proportional, planned development of the national economy' is to ignore several elements of at least equal importance. It would do even greater violence to reason to assume that any underdeveloped country today can reach the front rank of industrial powers in a generation or so by faithfully following the Soviet formula for industrialisation.

In 1928, Russia had a much more favourable heritage than the typical underdeveloped country enjoys today. Although *per capita* income and industrial production were low by European (but certainly not by Asian) standards, and the population was still mostly illiterate and some 80 per cent agricultural, Russia already possessed (as we have noted earlier) the fifth largest industrial complex in the world, including a substantial heavy industry. The relation of population to natural resources—not even excluding the least adequate of these, agricultural resources—was much better than in most countries that stand at the threshold of industrialisation today. She had a relatively small but well-qualified supply of scientific and technical skill, and—within its limits—a brilliant tradition in these fields. (The Academy of Sciences was already over 200 years old.) The railway system, which for over half a century had been in the van of economic development, was small in relation to the country's vast territory, but large enough to serve as a basis for much further industrial growth. And, finally, Russia had had a centuries-long history of centralism, authoritarianism, elitism and economic leadership by the state—which the new régime was quick to adopt, adapt, perfect, and pervert.

The three chief ingredients of the Soviet industrialisation formula have been the technology of the West, the country's natural resources, and the underemployed manpower of the village. There is of course nothing distinctly Soviet about them—these are the obvious ingredients of industrialisation in any backward, overpopulated agrarian society—although the lavish scale on which all three have been drawn is worthy of note. Rather, the Soviet experience is distinguished by 1) close centralised controls over the physical 'surplus' of agriculture and over the 'reserve army' of the rural underemployed, both implemented primarily through the collective farm system; 2) a readiness to depress consumption sharply and to keep it low until a large investment and defence potential has been created; 3) channeling the human and material resources so mobilised into the rapid expansion of heavy industry, construction, and supporting activities, and into the creation of associated technical skills; 4) once a large investment potential has been created, using a part of it to raise consumption while retaining most of it to expand heavy industry, *i.e. to enlarge the capacity for further growth* (to the extent that these resources are not diverted to military use); 5) political coercion and terror to maintain the collective farm system and low consumption levels; 6) constant over-commitment of resources, oriented towards a severe system of priorities and a succession of 'campaigns'; 7) assignment of physical targets to producers, from the lowly worker up to the minister, and inducing the fulfilment of the targets by administrative pressure, propaganda, and especially by means of an elaborate system of material incentives; 8) continuous pressure from above in the face of resistance from below, for such 'progressive' measures as cost reduction, rise in labour productivity, and the introduction of new techniques and products.

The 'socialist law of development' pales before the authoritarian principles of its implementation.

Certain demographic aspects of Soviet industrialisation that have received inadequate notice should not be overlooked. Considering the territorial annexations which added over 20 million people, and the high rate of natural increase in 'normal' years, the total population has increased relatively little in the past three decades; from about 152 million in mid-1928 to some 206 million in mid-1958, or by 36 per cent. The explanation of course lies with the two great demographic disasters: one associated with the collectivisation crisis of the early 'thirties, and the other with the War and the hard years immediately thereafter. Superimposed on both was the human toll of the forced labour camps. The population loss—in the sense of the difference between the number that would have obtained at the end of the period had the 'normal' yearly increment of about three million held good, and the number actually on hand—may be placed at over 10 million in the former case and over 40 million in the latter. (Not all of these were deaths, of course; a large part were, so to say, non-births.)

The human tragedy of these events, and the economic damage involved in the loss of life can be left to the imagination. But it would be incorrect to assume that there was no short-run benefit to rapid industrialisation in these demographic catastrophes. In fact there was such benefit on two scores: in the reduction of the surplus agrarian population, and in a shift in the age structure of the total population.

It is not unreasonable to assume that nearly the whole impact of the population deficit caused by the two disasters fell on the village. The town population could not have grown much more than it actually did (from 28 million on the eve of the First Plan to 70 million by the end of 1950), at least without diverting large additional capital resources from pre-war industrialisation or post-war reconstruction to town-building. It would be too much to contend that the presence of an additional 10 million persons in agriculture in the 'thirties, or of (say) an additional 40–50 million after the War, many of working age, would not have had a positive effect on agricultural output; especially since it was primarily young adult males that were leaving the village for economic, military, or educational purposes. But one wonders—remembering the shortage of draft power and other non-labour limitations to agricultural production at the time—whether the presence of these additional millions of consumers in the village would not have claimed more of the country's resources than their contribution as producers would have added. More concretely, with 50 (or 40, or 30) million more people in the village after the War, could the rate of extraction of agricultural 'surplus' have been as high as it was? If not: Could recovery in urban living standards from the post-war low in 1946 have been as fast as it was? Could there have been as large an urban population, and hence as rapid reconstruction and further economic growth, as there was in the late 'forties and the 'fifties?[8]

The deficit of births during the War is also largely responsible for the higher ratio of the population of working age to the total population, and a correspondingly lower dependency ratio,[9] in the post-war years just elapsed.

Remembering that a low dependency ratio means not only fewer children to feed, clothe, and educate, but also more mothers released for work outside the home, we may well ask whether as large a proportion of resources could have been devoted to reconstruction and further growth as has been since the War, had the number of children been more nearly 'normal?' Or, alternatively and also plausibly, whether average consumption levels would not now be substantially lower than they actually are?

The unborn children and the drastic excision of a large part of the agrarian overpopulation under tragic circumstances were a loan extended by time to the Soviet industrialisation drive. The loan is falling due. The children of the 'forties have begun to enter the labour force, and until the mid-sixties it will expand very little. Agriculture, charged with new urgent tasks, no longer can release millions of men; at least not quickly and cheaply, although over the longer run and with sufficient material investment it may still do so. Organisational reforms, such as the transfer of tractors and other machinery from the machine-tractor stations to the collective farms, may help, and even more radical institutional reforms may help more. 'Underemployed' elsewhere, in administration, in the forced labour camps, even in the armed forces (we are told), are being transferred to more productive work.

History is recalling other loans at the same time. Urban housing, which (aside from heavy war destruction) has been severely overcrowded and badly undermaintained for nearly thirty years, is now claiming a larger share of resources.[10] Similarly, the transportation network—so far essentially the pre-revolutionary rail net—is due for large-scale re-equip-

---

[8] It follows from the argument in this paragraph that the two demographic disasters explain a substantial part of the sharp rise in the statistical urbanisation ratio. If both the total and the rural population of the USSR were now, say, 50 million larger than they are, the urban population would comprise not about 45 per cent of the total as it does, but about 35 per cent.

[9] From Shimkin's estimates (*loc. cit.*, Table IV, p. 59) of the size of the working-age population—which he defines as males 15–59, and females 15–54—the following percentages of working-age population in the total population and dependency ratios (persons in the other age groups per person of working age) can be computed: 1926—55, 0.82; 1937—56, 0.785; 1950—60, 0.67; 1955—62.5, 0.6. For lack of precise data on age distribution for all years except 1926, these figures can be only approximate, but the trend is not in doubt.

[10] The slogan is to eliminate the housing shortage in 10 to 12 years (*Pravda*, 2 August, 1957), whatever this may mean.

ment, modernisation, and extension to sustain further industrial growth.

Such are some of the major retarding factors; serious as they are, the outlook is not one-sided. The Soviet economy still has quite a bit of slack to take up and quite a few technological gaps to bridge, not to mention the new frontiers that technology is unfolding and will continue to unfold. The recently announced programme to expand greatly the production of plastics and synthetics is a case in point, as it is also an important attempt to by-pass the inadequacies of the agricultural base (*e.g.* fibres). Automation is the subject of an intense campaign and great expectations for overcoming the labour shortage rest on it. Soviet theoretical and experimental work in this field is proceeding apace, although the widespread adoption of automation faces some characteristic Soviet obstacles, such as managerial conservatism, irregularity and undependability of materials supply, poor maintenance of equipment and insufficient standardisation of components. And lastly, the rapidly growing supply of Soviet scientific and technical manpower is certainly another favourable factor, and a well-known one.

Interesting questions can be raised about the longer-run effects of the reorganisation of industrial management introduced by Khrushchev in mid-1957, which created over a hundred regional authorities, in the place of a score of ministries each in charge of an industry. The expectation that the reform will tend to promote regional autarky has already been fully borne out. No less significant from a dynamic point of view is the fact that the reform has affected the communication pattern within branches of industry. While before such growth-inducing and growth-promoting organisations as research, development, and design institutes in a given industry were under the same ministry as the corresponding producing enterprises, now the former as well as the latter are administratively dispersed, with indications that the collaboration necessary for technical advance may at times suffer. Secondly, the ministerial channels through which pressure for cost reduction, new techniques, etc. (our point 8 on page 46) in each industry was transmitted to an exerted upon the enterprises no longer exist. It remains to be seen whether the new administrative set-up, in which regional problems take precedence over those of any particular branch of production, can fully replace the old one in this respect.

But in any assessment of growth prospects the largest unknown of all is the diversion of resources to military use, which during the 'fifties has probably been approximately of the same order of magnitude as *net* investment (*i.e.* net addition to the capital plant). It is clear that their substantial re-channeling to benefit investment could considerably, and favourably, influence the rate of economic growth. This fact cannot be emphasised too strongly.

SOVIET ECONOMIC PERFORMANCE*
— · — · — · — · — · — · — · — · —
Angus Maddison†

I. Favourable Factors

A. *Investment*

High Level of Investment. A major reason for the fast pace of Russian growth is the high rate of investment. Soviet investment in the 1950's was about 28 per cent of G.N.P., when ruble prices are adjusted to conform more closely to the Western price system. This is a good deal higher than in any Western country except Norway and Japan in the 1950's, it is much higher than in developing countries and it is very much higher than the historical experience of Western countries. It would seem from the evidence available that the Russians did not increase the rate of investment appreciably in the 1950's. This could be interpreted as a reflection of popular pressure for increased private consumption, but because of the relative easing in defence expenditures and communal consumption, there was in fact a very large increase in private consumption per capita in the 1950's, and one might therefore conclude that the Soviet authorities felt that they were already pressing investment to the point where further increases would yield sharply diminishing returns.

There are several reasons why one would expect the Soviet authorities to push investment further than in a capitalist country:

1. The nature of the Russian pricing system, the absence of interest rates and rent, reduce the apparent cost of investment.

2. Except when the immediate political situation is desperate, the Soviet authorities would be willing to sacrifice a bigger amount of present consumption for a given increase in future output than would be the case in the West, because they are keen on catching up with the West. They are therefore content with a somewhat lower return on investment at the margin.

3. The major advantage of the Soviet planning process is the reduction of the uncertainty of investment decisions. The co-ordination of all investment decisions eliminates some of the problems which investors have in a private enterprise economy where entrepreneurs face the risk that other enterprises will duplicate their investment and create surplus capacity, or, conversely, that they will refrain from taking the complementary

*Reprinted by permission from *Banca Nazionale Del Lavoro Quarterly Review* (March 1965), pp. 19–51 (excerpts). All footnotes deleted.

—— †Angus Maddison is an Economist at the Development Centre, Organization for Economic Cooperation and Development. His publications include: *Economic Growth in The West* (1964), and *The Contribution of Foreign Skills, Training and Technical Assistance to Economic Development* (1965).

decisions which will determine whether or not their own view of the future is actually realised. Centralised planning makes it possible to assess future demand and productive opportunities more clearly and enables the overall investment level to be raised because of a genuine reduction of risks. This advantage of the Soviet system can be reproduced to a large extent under capitalism by planning of the French type, but in fact France is the only Western country to have made substantial efforts in this direction.

4. Soviet planners do not worry about fluctuations in the overall level of demand in the economy. Western investors still have to weigh business cycle risks, although these have been greatly reduced by government policies for maintaining high and stable demand and entrepreneurs now have a much more buoyant view in capitalist countries than in prewar years.

The first two influences we have mentioned will tend to raise investment for reasons which are not particularly rational. The other two influences will tend to raise both investment and its productivity as compared with Western countries. We should now inquire whether there are any other factors which tend to enhance the capacity of the economy to absorb profitably a high rate of investment.

Natural Resource Context. The U.S.S.R. has a wider range of natural resources than is the case in any West European country, but this is unlikely to make investment more profitable, for there are offsetting disadvantages in the more severe climate which increases construction costs (just as it does in Canada, Sweden and Norway). In transport, too, Russia suffers from vast distances, bad weather, poor ports and water communications as well as from a deliberate policy of industrial dispersion.

Standardised Output and Size of Market. One advantage which the U.S.S.R. has over the West is standardisation. This brings some losses of consumer satisfaction, but for intermediate and capital goods there is probably a substantially greater economy deriving from standardised runs than in Western countries, e.g. nearly all new Russian housing consists of massive standardised apartment blocks to which industrialised techniques are applied. This may reduce capital cost to some extent and helps in other ways to raise productivity. This tendency to economies of scale is further helped by the size of the Russian market which is bigger than that of all other European countries.

Intensity of Capital Use. The Soviet Union could economise on capital by using shift-working to a much greater extent than the West, as it could presumably more easily overcome the social obstacles to intensifying use of capital in this way. In fact, it does not seem that shift-working in manufacturing is any more widespread in the Soviet Union than in Western countries. However, in transport the capital stock is used much more intensively than in the West. "Soviet railroads now carry nearly four times as much goods per track mile as the American and the disparity is greater still in passenger traffic." There are seldom empty seats on Russian passenger transport—either air, rail or subway. Soviet policy has been to keep private automobile transport to negligible proportions, and this has helped to economise on the need for roads.

Replacement. Up to about 1955, it was Soviet policy to scrap equipment only when it was worn out. Industrial equipment therefore had a longer life in the Soviet Union than in Western countries. This happened both because of the smaller pressure to change consumer goods for stylistic

TABLE 1

BREAKDOWN OF GROSS DOMESTIC FIXED INVESTMENT BY SECTOR 1960
(per cent of total fixed investment)

Country	Agriculture	Industry	Transport & Communications	Housing	Other
France..............	6.1	38.5	15.4	25.3	14.7
Germany	6.5	36.8	14.5	22.5	19.7
Italy...............	12.1	29.5	16.8	24.8	16.8
U.K.	3.7	39.4	13.1†	19.7‡	24.3†
U.S.	4.0	25.6	7.4	27.4	35.6
U.S.S.R.*..........	15.1	38.6	8.4	22.2	15.7

* 1958–62.
† Road investment included under other.
‡ Including legal fees, stamp duties, etc.
SOURCE: Western countries from *Statistics of National Accounts 1950–61*, O.E.C.D., Paris, 1964; U.S.S.R. from *Narodnoe Khoziastvo, op. cit.*, p. 434.

reasons and because the previously abundant supply of labour made productivity considerations less important than in the West. Since 1955 there has been much greater emphasis on the need for increased labour productivity, and equipment is now scrapped when it is considered technologically obsolete. For this reason a higher proportion of new investment is now required for replacement, but the ratio of replacement to total gross capital formation is probably smaller than in the West, both because the Soviet capital stock is newer, and the rate of new capital formation is higher. See Table 1.

Structure of Investment. The impact of investment on growth may be enhanced by reducing the amount which goes to housing, for housing is very costly in relation to the flow of income which it yields. In the years 1928 to 1950 Soviet investment was concentrated heavily on industry, and housing was given much lower priority than in Western countries. More recently, the structure of Soviet investment has become much more similar to that in the West. From 1958 to 1962 about 22 per cent of investment went to housing and about 38.6 per cent to industry. This is rather like the situation in the major countries of Western Europe.

The major structural differences between the Soviet Union and Western Europe are that the Russian investment in agriculture was twice as high a proportion of total investment, and investment in transport was only half as high. The high level of investment in agriculture reflects the greater importance of agriculture in Russian than in Western G.N.P. but it is also a reflection of the high cost of output increases in this sector. Russian agricultural output rose faster than that of the West in the 1950's but productivity rose more slowly than in most Western countries. In transport the relatively lower Russian effort reflects the savings made by a much more intensive use of capacity.

Capital Widening. A good deal of Russian investment in prewar years went into capital widening, i.e., providing extra workers with equipment.

TABLE 2

PERCENT INCREASE IN EMPLOYMENT 1950–60

Belgium	4.1	Netherlands	12.8
Denmark	10.5	Norway	2.3
France	3.8	United Kingdom	6.3
Germany	24.4	Canada	20.8
Italy	18.9	U.S.A.	14.0
Japan	25.0	U.S.S.R.	17.4

SOURCE: A. Maddison, *Economic Growth in the West*, p. 6.

It is always possible to do this without running into diminishing returns for it does not involve a change in factor proportions as is the case with productivity-raising investment. Between 1950 and 1960, Russian employment increased by 17.4 per cent which was higher than in several Western countries, but smaller than in Japan, Germany, Canada and Italy. Thus this factor contributed to lowering the Soviet capital-output ratio relative to some Western countries, but not relative to the fastest growing ones. See Table 2.

Capital Deepening. The fundamental source of economic growth is increased productivity. The return on investment which is devoted to raising productivity (i.e. capital deepening) will depend on the level of productivity at which the economy is currently operating. The Soviet productivity level is below that in Western Europe and very much below that of the United States, which means that the U.S.S.R. should find it profitable to push the rate of investment a little further than Western Europe and a good deal further than the U.S.A. because it is exploiting a range of technology which is already known. Some sectors of Soviet industry such as chemicals, automobiles or textiles are much more backward than Western Europe so it can be expected that the recoupment of the backlog will be a source of rapid growth in future. The lower productivity level in agriculture would also provide an opportunity for future rapid growth if it were not frustrated by political and institutional obstacles.

The return on investment destined to raise productivity will also depend on the rate of increase in productivity which is to be achieved. There will be more and more sharply decreasing returns, the further the process is pushed. There will be increasing human and administrative strains in adapting production processes, work habits, skills and managerial capacities to more modern technologies. The U.S.S.R. has mitigated some of these problems by its gigantic effort in training and research which have increased the capacity to absorb high rates of investment, but the Russian system is not altogether weighted in favour of progress. Planning controls and targets may inhibit new processes or introduction of new products. The lack of a pricing system which reflects relative scarcities may lead to waste of resources, as happened in the over-development of hydropower. Mistaken policies may sometimes be carried further than in Western countries because of the reliance on campaigns and controls instead of market competition and initiative of individual firms.

Conclusion on Investment. The factors and policies we have examined may have presented the U.S.S.R. with a somewhat more favourable schedule of returns on new investment in the 1950's than in most West European countries. However, there were no great recovery elements in Russian growth in the 1950's which were not available in Western Europe, nor was the situation as favourable to investment as it was in Germany or Italy. The main difference between the Western and Soviet situation is that in the U.S.S.R. investment was pushed further, and because of this the U.S.S.R. may have obtained a lower return at the margin than in Western Europe. There is, of course, no way of measuring empirically the schedule of potential returns on investment which any country faces. All we can do is look at the *ex post* results of investment decisions and this will reflect the total impact of all the influences we have described. For various reasons which I have analysed at length in my book, *Economic Growth in the West,* it is not possible to judge from *ex post* figures how far a country has pushed its capital deepening investment into the area of diminishing returns. Within a certain range, an increase in gross investment will appear to produce increasing returns because of the lower relative burden of replacement in a high investment economy. The incremental gross capital output ratio (I.C.O.R.) in the U.S.S.R. in the 1950's was lower than in most Western countries but higher than in Japan Germany and Italy. With investment at 28 per cent of G.N.P. and a G.N.P. growth rate of 6.8 per cent, the I.C.O.R. (including stocks) was about 4.1 compared with 3.2 in Germany and Japan, 3.5 in Italy, 4.3 in France, 5.9 in the U.K. and 5.8 in the U.S.

B. Training

The Soviet Union has made a very large investment in education, and was the first country to plan its education systematically to promote economic growth. This has greatly increased the skills available and technical and managerial capacity to use new investment effectively. The education effort is the major reason why it has been possible to get a reasonable pay-off on such a high rate of investment.

The rate of spending on communal services—mainly health and education—rose from 4.6 per cent of G.N.P. in 1928 to 10.5 per cent in 1937. Between 1920 and 1939 illiteracy was eliminated amongst the population aged less than 50, and the literacy level is now equivalent to that in the developed countries of Europe. The level of educational attainment amongst the population as a whole is probably still below that in Western Europe, and school enrolment amongst those aged 5–19 is also below that in all the major industrial countries of the West. However, in secondary technical education and in higher education the Soviet effort is bigger than in Western Europe, and the stock of people with higher education is at least comparable with that in Western Europe. In some key professions such as engineering and medicine the Soviet stock of skills is superior to that of Western Europe.

The impressive thing about the skills of the Russian labour force is not that they are markedly superior to those of Western Europe, but that they have grown so quickly. At the time of the Russian revolution, the technical capacity of the labour force was relatively less than in present day India. By 1950 it was something like that of present day Greece, but by 1962 it was somewhat better than that of the U.K.

High Level Manpower. In 1913 the number of people with higher education in the labour force was 136,000, by 1950 it had reached 1,443,000 and by 1962 4,050,000. In 1959, about 3.8 per cent of the Soviet labour force had higher education as compared with 2.9 in France (1954), 3.0 per cent in Italy (1961), 3.7 per cent in Japan (1960), and 11.3 per cent in the U.S. (1960). From 1950 to 1959, the U.S.S.R. tripled its stock of engineers and agronomists from 402,000 to 1,209,000. In the same period the increase of engineers and agronomists was less than 6 per cent in France; Italy had the fastest rise in Western Europe, but the increase was only 95 per cent. Engineers and agronomists were 1.2 per cent of the Soviet labour force in 1959 as compared with 1 per cent in the U.K., 0.9 per cent in Italy and 0.8 per cent in France. The proportion of engineers and agronomists in the Russian labour force is thus higher than in any West European country, but lower than the 1.7 per cent in the U.S.A.

The sectoral distribution of employment of people with higher education in the U.S.S.R. is broadly similar to that in Western Europe. Less than 0.3 per cent of the labour force in agriculture has had higher education, about 2.5 per cent in industry, and about 8.7 per cent in services. However, the U.S.S.R. has very few people with higher education in trade and distributive services—only about 0.15 per cent of the labour force in this sector has higher education. This is in sharp contrast with the West which attaches greater importance to salesmanship, advertising and consumer satisfaction. In Russia less than 2 per cent of the high level labour force are in this service sector compared with over 20 per cent in the U.S.A. However, the rate of increase of high level manpower in this sector has been higher than any other in Russia in the past few years.

It is interesting to note that higher educational attainments in the Asiatic parts of Russia are not significantly lower than in European Russia. 83 per cent of the Russian population now lives in Europe, and 85 per cent of the people with higher education live there. The ratio of people active in the labour force with higher education to total population is 1.9 per cent in European Russian and 1.6 per cent in Asiatic Russia.

In 1960 enrolment in higher education in the U.S.S.R. was 11.5 per cent of the age group 20–24, as compared with 8.3 per cent in France, 5.8 per cent in the U.K., 5.3 per cent in Germany and 4.1 per cent in Italy. However, more than half the 2,944,000 Russians enrolled in higher education in 1962–63 were part-time students. 374,000 of these were in evening classes, and 1,283,000 were taking correspondence courses. The part-time students and correspondence students are allowed a fair amount of time off work to pursue their studies, but drop-out rates for these students are higher than in Western Europe (though lower than in the U.S.), so that the Soviet advantage over Western Europe was smaller in terms of new graduates than in terms of student enrolment. The proportion of Soviet graduates in science and medicine is no higher than in Western Europe. However, the Soviet education system is more highly specialised than in the West, and much more closely linked to manpower needs. There are only 40 universities in the U.S.S.R. but about 700 other specialised institutions of higher education. There were only 249,000 university students in 1960–61 or only about a tenth of those in higher education.

Middle Level Manpower. As far as middle level manpower is concerned, the Russian effort has been even larger than at the higher level. In 1913 the number of middle level technicians active in the labour force was 54,000. By 1952 the figure was 2,227,000, and by 1962 5,906,000. Thus the increase since 1913 was 97 fold, as compared with a 26 fold increase for high level personnel. Before the revolution, Russia suffered from the same shortage of middle level technicians as many developing countries today. The ratio of middle to high level personnel was about 0.4 in 1913, in 1962 it was 1.5.

Middle level technicians are trained in semi-professional secondary schools (technicums) which provide very intensive highly specialised courses. Up till 1950 they ran 4 year courses but they are now shorter. In recent years they have had an enrolment of about 1,800,000 students aged 14 to 30. Instruction hours are about 40 a week. There are also part-time evening courses for students already working. The total graduations from these schools were 7,600,000 between 1928 and 1960, of which 2.7 millions were engineering-industrial technicians, 1.1 millions agricultural, 0.6 million socio-economic, 1.7 millions educational or cultural, and 1.5 millions health-medical personnel.

One notable feature of the Soviet labour force is the high participation rate for women. In the U.S.S.R. 48 per cent of the labour force are women, compared with about a third in Western Europe. About 53 per cent of the labour force with higher education are women and 63 per cent of those with semi-professional jobs. There is therefore less wastage of women's education than there is in the West.

Another indication of the massive educational effort in Russia is the output of books. About four times as many titles are published as in the U.S. or U.K., and the output of volumes per head of population is much higher. Public library facilities and their stock of books are much better in the U.S.S.R. than in Western Europe. In Moscow the Lenin Library has 22 million books and there are two libraries in Leningrad each with 15 million volumes.

The Russians have not hesitated to change wage differentials to make the acquisitions of new skills attractive and they have not, of course, been restrained in this by trade unions. Their policy in this respect has varied a good deal, but they have enjoyed more freedom of action than the West. Their system has inculcated a respect for manual effort and technical skills which is absent in many developing countries.

C. Research and Development

The economy of the U.S.S.R. works well below the level of best practice technology as exemplified by the technological leader—the United States. The Soviet aim has always been to catch up with the United States. It has not been interested simply in reaching the intermediate level of Western Europe. In fact in many parts of industry its present technical level is abreast or beyond that of Western Europe. Its lower overall level is due primarily to the large size of its lagging agriculture. In view of these goals a good deal of its scientific programme has been devoted to catching up with the most advanced part of the industrial world, and in some fields such as atomic and space technology, the U.S.S.R. is in a leading position. Russian scientists have won a number of Nobel prizes, and their contributions in fields such as physics and medicine have been outstanding. It is extremely expensive to be in a pioneering position where you are attacking the frontiers of knowledge for the benefit of the world as a whole. On purely economic grounds the size of the Russian research effort is hardly justifiable. The reasons for it are both military and ideological. Marxist theory is based on a rejection of religion and a materialist conception of reality which places heavy emphasis on science. For this reason Soviet scientists have a very high prestige, high pay and great resources for their work, in fundamental as well as applied science. In some fields politics have interfered with academic freedom to the detriment of science. This is particularly true in the social sciences. The economic repercussions of this have probably been greatest in agriculture, where economic performance has been poorest, where politicians have hoped for miracles, and where Lysenko has dominated the scene. Soviet achievements in agricultural research seem to have been less successful than those in smaller countries such as Mexico, Israel or Japan which have had better returns on a smaller expenditure which was aimed to solve practical economic problems. In some respects Soviet technology is simpler than that of the West, simpler machine tools, lathes, tractors, cars that work on cruder petrol, etc., and may therefore in some lines be marginally more useful to developing countries, but Soviet scientific research has not made any major contribution in devising a technology appropriate for countries which are poor in capital. It has always been dominated by the aspiration for the technical optimum.

Therefore a good deal of Russian scientific effort has been devoted to the progress of the world as a whole rather than to solving specifically Russian economic problems. It is, however, more centrally directed than Western science, because of the powerful role of the Academy of Sciences, and in many military fields has been able to produce quick results when heavily concentrated.

According to E.C.E., Soviet expenditure on research and development was 2.5 per cent of G.N.P. in 1960, a figure surpassed only by the U.S.A. However, Russian research in the 1950's appears to have absorbed

TABLE 3

RESEARCH AND DEVELOPMENT EXPENDITURE AS SHARE OF G.N.P.

Country	1950	1955	1960
U.S.A.	1.0	1.4	2.8
U.S.S.R.*	1.2	1.5	2.5
U.K.		1.7	2.5
Germany (F.R.).................		0.8	1.3
France.........................			1.1†

*Share of net material product.
†There may be some understatement here, arising from the fact that the fiscal treatment of private research outlays is less favourable in France than elsewhere.
SOURCE: E.C.E., *Some Factors in Economic Growth in Europe During the 1950's,* Geneva, 1964, Chapter V, p. 5.

an even bigger share of G.N.P. than in the U.S.A. A good deal of this research was for military purposes. In France, 40 per cent of research outlays have been for military purposes. In the U.K., the defence departments financed 59.1 per cent of research in 1955 and 38.7 per cent in 1961. It seems likely that the defence proportion in the U.S.S.R. has been at least as high as in the U.K. and France. See Table 3.

In 1962, the U.S.S.R. had 4,476 scientific institutes of which 1,911 were research establishments. For 1959, the E.C.E. Gives the following figures on the comparative number of personnel engaged on civilian scientific research:

TABLE 4
Scientists and Engineers Engaged in Civilian Research in 1959

U.S.	U.S.S.R.	U.K.
327,000	318,000	98,000

Source: E.C.E., *Op. cit.*, Chapter V, p. 12.

It seems clear that the Soviet scientific effort is relatively bigger than that of any European country except the U.K. See Table 4.

A major drawback of Russian science and technology is its isolation from the Western effort. There are very few foreign technicians working in Russia. Those who come are mostly engaged in installing machinery purchased in the West, and there are very few working under contract as there were in the 1920s. In Western countries there is a good deal of foreign private investment which helps to diffuse new technologies as well as a very free interchange of scientists. But the proportion of Russians who study abroad is very small indeed—about 300 in 1960 as compared with many thousands of Western graduate students.

The Russians have done a great deal to combat this isolation and to adapt foreign technology. They have no legal constraints such as royalty, copyright, patent or licensing arrangements to inhibit them from copying the West, and they will where necessary pay for licenses. Similarly their firms do not hide trade secrets from each other.

In addition they have an abstracting service which digests 400,000 foreign scientific papers a year. This effort is an important reason for their capacity to adapt new technology and to maintain such high levels of investment without sharply diminishing returns.

D. Structural Change

Most of the Russian output increase in the 1950's was due to the rise in productivity, whereas the bulk of the output gains from 1928 to 1950 were due to the increase in employment. In the 1950's Soviet productivity growth was faster than that of all Western countries, whereas from 1928 to 1950 it was generally lower.

Less than a quarter of the Russian output growth in the 1950's was in services and more than three-quarters of it was attributable to the commodity producing sectors of the economy. This was a somewhat higher proportion than in most West European countries, and much higher than in the U.S. where services accounted for 60 per cent of the output increase in the 1950's. This concentration on commodity production was favourable to productivity growth because productivity rose faster there than in services. However, the Russians had a bigger relative increase in agricultural output where their productivity gains were slower than in industry.

In analysing the impact of structural change on productivity growth, the important thing is the switch of employment between sectors with a low *level* of productivity to those with a higher *level*. This is more significant than the impact of employment movements between sectors with different *rates* of productivity growth. In fact the differences between productivity levels in the major sectors are much wider in the U.S.S.R. than in Western countries, so that a given change in employment structure will have a bigger impact on output there than it would in a Western country. If the Russian employment structure had remained as it was in 1950 without affecting productivity developments within sectors, then Russian output in 1960 would have been 9.5 per cent lower. This is larger than the impact of structural change in Western countries—if we make the same assumptions for Italy, the 1960 output would have been 7.5 per cent lower, German output 6.8 per cent lower, French output 6.3 per cent lower, U. S. output 1.7 per cent lower, and U.K. output 0.1 per cent lower.

Although the impact of structural change was bigger in the U.S.S.R., the change in Russian employment structure was not as favourable to productivity growth as that in Western Europe. The impact of the Soviet change was larger simply because of the stark contrast between productivity in the backward agricultural sector and modern industry. If the U.S.S.R. had had the same change in employment structure as Germany (but had retained its own in-sector productivity characteristics), its 1960 output would have been 2.4 per cent higher than it actually was; if it had followed the French pattern its output would have been 16.1 per cent higher.

Thus structural changes contributed to Soviet growth in the 1950's, but not on a substantially greater scale than in continental Western Europe. If the Soviet Union manages to release a significant amount of labour from agriculture, structural factors could well play a greater role in the future than in the 1950's.

E. Disarmament

According to the estimates of Bergson, the U.S.S.R. devoted 13 per cent of its G.N.P. to its military effort in 1955. This ratio is one which is subject to error as it involves estimates of magnitudes which are military secrets. It is, however, a field in which Western experts have done a great deal of research, and there is little reason to think that it is very much out of line. At the end of the 1950's the figure was probably a little lower than this.

If we assume that there were an arms freeze in the course of the 1960's, in which the absolute size of Soviet military expenditure remained unchanged, then the Soviet Union would have extra resources available which during the 1960's would average around 3 per cent of G.N.P.

It is difficult to say where the extra resources would go, but we can safely dismiss the hypothesis that a fall in military demand would simply lead to unemployment. Some of the resources released would be of a type which could be switched to space programmes, and others would be highly suitable for building up consumer durable output for which there would be a very ready demand, e.g. transistor radios and automobiles. It is also possible that the Soviet authorities would find it profitable to increase the rate of investment. This is already high, but could be pushed higher. After all, the Japanese rate of gross investment in the early 1960's was as high as 40 per cent of G.N.P. If we assume that half of the resources released by an arms freeze were devoted to investment, and that the return on investment remained the same, then the rate of growth would be increased by about half a per cent a year, e.g. from about 6.5 to 7.0 per cent in the 1960's. My own hunch is that the organisational difficulties in agriculture and in the service sector, and some of the organisational problems of running an overplanned economy will not make it profitable to push investment much higher than present levels, and that the consumer would therefore probably claim a sizeable part of the resources released from an arms freeze.

F. Foreign Trade

The Russian economy improved resource allocation in the 1950's through increased international trade. Total trade rose faster than output, but trade with non-bloc countries rose about three times as fast as output. This was a move away from the extreme autarky which had been developed between 1917 and 1953. The earlier period was dominated by feelings of insecurity which are no longer appropriate to a country with hydrogen bombs, and in a world where communism is a well established political system adopted by thirteen other countries. A narrowly autarkic system would not be consistent with the belief in the possibility of peaceful coexistence and of co-operation with the new neutralist world created with the end of colonialism. In fact the foreign trade of the Russian economy is now as big as that of the U.S. relative to G.N.P., so that one might well expect the trade ratio to have reached a peak, particularly as the U.S.S.R. is a larger country than the U.S.A. However, the U.S.S.R. is less well endowed with the wide variety of natural resources which the U.S. enjoys; it is contiguous to a large number of other countries unlike the U.S.; it is at an earlier stage of development in which commodity output (i.e. tradable output) is a much higher proportion of G.N.P. than in the U.S.— the U.S. once traded 7 per cent of its G.N.P.; the Soviet economy's range of comparative advantage in different industries is wider than in most countries as a result of past policies and the nature of its institutions— such as collectivisation. There is therefore every reason to expect that the U.S.S.R. could still find it profitable to expand considerably the proportion of output which is traded. In particular it would seem highly attractive to export capital goods and import more consumer goods, raw materials, tropical foodstuffs, and cereals. In many respects its technology is such that it has a natural complementarity with the underdeveloped countries. An increased foreign trade ratio would lead to additional uncertainty in the economy, and is for this reason unappealing to Soviet planners, but this can be tempered by long term trading agreements and many underdeveloped countries welcome the type of long term trading arrangements which the U.S.S.R. likes to make. Some of the problems of expanding trade are technical. In a country which has practised autarky for so long, the knowledge of foreign markets may be inadequate, particularly for consumer goods. Arrangements for credit may not be easy and the non-convertibility of its currency is also a handicap. But none of these points can be expected to prove a serious obstacle to more rational trading policies.

II. Unfavourable Factors

A. Centralised Controls and Inefficient Price Mechanism

The Soviet economy is one in which all means of production are publicly owned, and where private enterprise is virtually non-existent apart from the small private plots of members of state and collective farms. Private house ownership is largely confined to the countryside. The extent of public ownership is more extreme than in other communist countries in some of which agriculture is still to a good extent in the hands of peasant farmers—such as Poland or Yugoslavia—or where small shopkeepers and traders still exist. Unlike Western economies there is no pluralistic interplay of countervailing pressure groups in the economy. Because the government wields power directly, it has no need of an elaborate tax system to redistribute income. It can directly determine what it feels to be equitable or economically useful. Similarly it does not need to compensate fluctuations in private activity by monetary and fiscal policy. It does not have to worry about the maintenance of enough private demand to maintain full employment as do Western governments. It does not have to appease the interests of tráde unions or employers, and is much less sensitive to regional pressure groups than most countries. The system relies on very detailed government controls to allocate resources according to the priorities of the planning authorities. Soviet policy has always preferred economic enterprises to be run on a giant scale so that they would be easier to administer from the centre. There are, of course, some very real economies of scale to be obtained from large enterprises. Gigantomania probably does little damage to efficiency in industry, but it hurts agriculture, and did very great damage to handicrafts, small repair shops, etc. Because of these direct controls over all economic activity the administrative burden of running the U.S.S.R. is higher than that of a Western country, and a good deal of the state's economic discipline is reinforced by the activities of the communist party. This group is no longer particularly enthusiastic and dedicated, as in the early days of the Soviet regime, nor is it brutally coercive as in the days of Stalin, but it is bureaucratic and heavy handed. The efficiency of the system can be very high in key sectors, but in those with lower priority it is bumbling and unsatisfactory. Hence the different sectors tend to move in uneven leaps as campaigns are directed to make good deficiencies arising from previous neglect.

One of the major disadvantages of this system of resource allocation is its inflexibility in responding to sophisticated consumer tastes and meeting changes in demand. The output criteria of enterprises are fixed in terms of planned targets and these may predominate over the consumers' needs. As the economy becomes more complex it becomes more difficult to take rational decisions centrally, Nails will be big if the plan target is in terms of weight, and small if the target is fixed in number of nails. Therefore the number of directives to be given is very large. In many cases managers have devised semi-legal substitutes for the price mechanism, and there have been substantial administrative changes since 1957 in an attempt to decentralise decision making, but these do not seem to have been highly successful. In recent years there has been a considerable development of econometric models and data processing but these tools have not yet made a major contribution to the efficiency of economic policy.

A major defect in the Soviet economic system is the inefficiency of the price mechanism as a device for allocating sources and as an indicator of scarcity relations. There is a reluctance to use rent or interest payments as a device for rationing the use of scarce resources, because under capitalism these payments are a reward to property owners. There is still a strong utopian strain in Soviet thought in spite of Marx's rejection of Utopian socialism as unscientific. Marxist politicians tend to assume that human wants are satiable or that technology will be revolutionised to a degree where certain goods will become free. They retain an austere and techno- logically obsolete view of what constitutes a decent standard of personal consumption. As a result some scarce items such as accommodation and public transport are sold at ridiculously low prices, and availability of automobiles is restricted to such a degree that their use for private trans- portation is regarded as almost immoral.

The consumer suffers a good deal because of the failure of prices to re- flect the state of supply and demand and this also impedes the efficiency of production. As the standard of living rises, the state also finds itself with the problem of inventories of unsaleable products. At the beginning of 1965 the chairman of the state committee on commerce drew attention to in- ventories in the garment industry of 270 million rubles. There have been increasing complaints from Soviet experts that lack of an interest rate leads to misallocation between investment projects or that absence of rents for scarce natural resources has led to squandering of mineral wealth or wasteful use of land in farming or as between farming and build- ing uses. When the detailed directives of the plan are not clear or con- sistent the price relationships do not help to reinforce the plan objectives by pushing resources in the right direction, because the price structure has not been designed to perform an allocatory function.

The Soviet economy therefore suffers from two major defects—over- centralised planning, and an inefficient price system. These defects of the Soviet system are not a necessary feature of all communist economies, just as the genuine advantages of planning need not be denied to capitalist economies.

In Yugoslavia, enterprises have much more autonomy than in the U.S.S.R. Prices are fixed much more like those in a Western economy and managerial decisions can be made largely in response to market forces. This is also true of peasant agriculture in Yugoslavia. As a result the Yugoslav planning authorities are largely concerned with "global proportions," and their task is closer to that of French planners who like to define their system as "indicative" as opposed to the "imperative" planning of the U.S.S.R.

Soviet economists have been increasingly critical of the usefulness of such heavy reliance on direct controls as a mechanism for allocating resources. The official reluctance for change is due not merely to conser- vatism but to reluctance to decentralise political and economic power. Very recently, it would seem that the protagonists of market forces (led by Pro- fessor Liberman of Kharkov University) have gained ground. After an experiment with a few factories, a decree of January 1965 has changed the system for 400 consumer goods factories. From April 1st these factories will respond to orders from retail outlets rather than from the central planning authorities, and they too can pass on orders to raw material suppliers. In this way consumer demand can make its impact much more directly than ever before.

The major adverse effect of the Soviet system of resource allocation has not been on production as measured statistically, but on consumer satisfactions. The consumer gets rather poor quality goods as a result of extreme standardisation, inadequate design and the emphasis on quantitative rather than qualitative production targets. He also suffers because of the tendency to regard service industries as unproductive. Soviet shops show little disposition to attract customers, to carry out market research, to select the goods consumers prefer, or to provide them with sophisticated services. They do not display their goods well, advertise, or provide packaging or delivery services, and their facilities for consumer credit are limited. There is evidence of some improvement. Queues are not particularly obvious nowadays, except those outside churches, and the increase in workers in distribution has been substantial.

The Soviet consumer is isolated from the outside world because of lack of foreign films, books or newspapers, but the stylistic isolation has been mitigated by the influence of foreign tourists and broadcasting which have affected tastes in some directions, such as clothing styles for men, hair styles for some women and tastes in pop music. In respect of the theatre, museums, libraries and circus, the Russian public gets a much better deal than that in the West. There are more of these facilities than in Western countries, they are cheaper and better; nevertheless the system of resource allocation adds unnecessarily to the drabness of Soviet consumption.

B. Agriculture

In most Western countries, agricultural productivity grew rapidly in the 1950's and the abundant supply of agricultural products made it possible for large numbers of people to move from agriculture to higher productivity occupations elsewhere. In the Soviet Union, agricultural productivity grew very much faster in the 1950's than in earlier decades, but agricultural products remained in short supply and very little labour was released from agriculture. The U.S.S.R. devoted relatively more of her investment to agriculture than did Western countries. Russian agriculture in the 1950's also went through a phase unparalleled elsewhere, in that about a third was added to the total acreage of arable land. The Russian productivity achievement was therefore achieved at greater cost than in the West. There was a marked slackening in agricultural growth after 1958. Between 1952 and 1958 agricultural output rose 7.4 per cent a year, but from 1958 to 1962 it rose only 1.7 per cent a year and in 1963 it fell. The difference was partly due to weather, partly because the impact of earlier policy changes had worn off. See Table 5.

TABLE 5

AGRICULTURAL INPUTS IN 1961-62

Country	Hectares of Arable Land per Head of Population	Consumption of Fertilisers— Kg. per Hectare of Arable Land	Tractors per 100 Hectares of Arable Land
Canada	2.25	10	1.3
France................	0.46	122	3.7
Germany (F.R.)........	0.15	304	11.8
Italy	0.31	57	2.0
Japan	0.06	270	0.2
U.K.	0.14	194	5.7
U.S.A.	0.99	45	2.5
U.S.S.R.	1.04	12	0.6

SOURCE: F.A.O., *Production Yearbook*, 1963, Rome.

The absolute level of output per man is much lower in the U.S.S.R. than in Western Europe in spite of more abundant land. The lower level of productivity is only partly due to adverse climate. The stock of capital in agriculture is much smaller in the U.S.S.R. than in Western Europe—the supply of tractors is only about a tenth of that in the U. K. or a twentieth of that in Germany per unit of arable land. Inputs of fertiliser are even further behind those in Western Europe. But the major reason for the lag in Russian agriculture has been bad economic policy.

There have been five major problems hindering the productivity of Russian agriculture:

1. The process of change from peasant ownership to collective farms was extremely costly and did lasting damage.

2. The management units have been inefficient with excessively large collectives, quarter hectare private plots, and machine tractor stations which separated control of equipment from the farm enterprise.

3. The use of centralised directives and absence of efficient market prices have been particularly inappropriate in agriculture.

4. The peasantry has in fact been an exploited class. The effective taxation of peasants has been pushed to lengths which have been a disincentive to production.

5. Agricultural research and extension has been inefficient. The political desire for miracles has encouraged charlatans, and vast experiments

have been undertaken without adequate preparation or progress in producing appropriate seeds, etc.

The process by which the Soviet state achieved collectivisation involved very considerable brutality and suffering as well as severe damage to the capital stock and productivity of agriculture. The peasantry was hostile to collectivisation, destroyed frame buildings and equipment and slaughtered livestock on a tremendous scale. Livestock production in 1933 was less than half of that in 1928, and the 1928 level was not achieved again till 1953. As a result, a good deal of the investment in Russian agriculture up to the 1950's simply went to replace losses of draft power due to the slaughtering of the early collectivisation period. Similarly, inputs of fertilisers had to make good losses from animal manure. Much of the managerial talent in Russian agriculture was also liquidated with the kulaks. Peasant hostility to collectives has meant that management had often to be entrusted to party officials who did not always enjoy the confidence of the peasants, and who were not always good managers.

The system of agricultural organisation in Russia is highly unfavourable to productivity and is the major weakness of the Russian economic system. As a fundamental change in organisation is unlikely for political reasons, it seems likely that this will remain as a major factor retarding economic growth. In several types of agriculture the most efficient production unit is relatively small. This is particularly true of dairy farming, and rearing of certain kinds of livestock. The giant sized Russian farms are probably quite efficient in certain crops, but even here they put a severe strain on managerial capacity. The productivity of the private plots is much higher than that of the collectives. These are about ¼ or ½ a hectare per family and in 1961 they occupied 3.2 per cent of the sown area. However, they produced 63 per cent of the potatoes, 46 percent of the vegetables, 41 per cent of the meat, 47 per cent of the milk and 87 per cent of the eggs.

It is much more difficult to run agriculture efficiently on the basis of centralised directives than is the case in industry. The pace of work varies greatly throughout the year, and techniques of production have to be responsive to local variations in soil and climate. It is therefore extremely difficult to subject this sector to factory production methods and disciplines or to centralised control. Nevertheless the process of consolidation of collective farms into bigger units was continued in the 1950's, when the number of farms were reduced three quarters. It is easier to exercise central control if farming units are very big, but to run these large farms successfully it is necessary to have very large inputs of machinery and highly skilled management, which are very scarce resources.

Productive incentives were hampered by the fact that peasant incomes were depressed well below the level of urban workers. The State paid farmers low prices for compulsory deliveries, and taxed income from private plots heavily. The *trudoden* system of wage payment on collective farms by which the proceeds of the enterprise were allocated between farm members meant that rural incomes were very uncertain, were paid annually and largely in kind. The rewards for effort varied considerably from one farm to another according to their endowment in terms of soil and climate. There was no system of differential rents to correct for these variations, though some crude attempt to do this was made in fixing the delivery quotas. Capital goods purchased by collective farms were more expensive than those for state farms, and, until recently, farm workers were not entitled to social security benefits. As income was largely in kind, farmers had to engage in very wasteful marketing activities to raise cash. Their efforts to increase their income by developing their private plots were frustrated by severe controls as well as heavy taxes. Their tax burdens also tended to be arbitrary in their incidence. Apart from these factors which kept income low, peasants suffer because social and educational facilities are poor, shops and their merchandise, transport facilities and entertainment are inferior to those in the cities.

The original justification for squeezing the income of the farm population was to finance the increase in investment of the economy. At the present stage of development, it is no longer necessary for them to bear this burden. Even in the first five year plan period this policy was not justified in the extreme degree to which it was applied. The simultaneous attempt to squeeze the consumption of the farm population and to seize their property reduced the rate of growth of the economy because of its adverse effects on agricultural output. A smaller squeeze would have reduced output less, and would have reduced the need for tractors to replace slaughtered farm animals. Moreover a greater monetisation of farm income and a greater reliance on tax policy rather than compulsory deliveries would have mitigated some of the wastes of the clumsy system of payment in kind which has clogged agricultural production and markets.

The Soviet attitude to agricultural ownership and control was based on ideological principles which were pushed ruthlessly in spite of their obvious economic disadvantages. All communist countries have had trouble with agriculture, and some of them have retreated sharply from these policies, e.g. Yugoslavia and Poland. In Russia the system has now existed for such a long period that there would probably be economic losses in moving back completely to peasant proprietorship, and the commitment to collectivisation is in any case much greater ideologically than in other communist countries. The Soviet government is seeking to overcome these problems by developing agriculture in a highly mechanised way with large scale units as in the U.S.A. There has already been a substantial concentration of collective farms in larger units and a growing importance of state farms whose members are wage earners. Russia has better possibilities for extensive agriculture than other communist countries because of its enormous size relative to population. However, a highly capitalised agriculture is a wasteful substitute for better economic incentives to the abundant supply of agricultural labour.

The agricultural situation improved greatly from 1953 to 1958 for several reasons. In the first place the relative incomes of the farm population were raised by the reduction of taxes in cash and kind on private activities, farm prices were raised, and in 1958 the complex multiple price system for deliveries at or beyond quota was abandoned in favour of a single price system with area variations. More recently social security has been extended to farmers. However, the basis of farm income is still somewhat arbitrary and uncertain, and restrictions still remain on the private activities of peasants. After 1958, the abolition of the M.T.S. imposed heavy financial burdens on farmers who had to purchase their equipment at a time when bad weather reduced income from crops.

There was a major increase in the farm area by the opening up of the virgin lands, particularly in Kazakhstan, so that the ploughed area increased by about 42 million hectares between 1954 and 1960. This had a considerable once-for-all effect in raising output, but had increased the impact of weather fluctuations on total agricultural output, has increased the problems of erosion and has posed a whole series of new technical problems.

There has been a considerable switch to maize production to provide feed for livestock. The area under corn rose from 4.3 million hectares in 1954 to 37 million in 1962. It was hoped that this would contribute greatly to productivity by using hybrid maize as developed in the United States. This programme has helped to raise output but it has been difficult to develop a type of corn well adapted to Russian conditions. In 1961 Khrushchev started a campaign to plough up grass and fallow and grow corn, sugar beets, peas and field beans instead. This gave a short-run boost to output but was challenged by scientists because of the risk to soil fertility. Nevertheless Krushchev planned to plough up 41 million hectares.

The policies of increasing acreage and increasing farm incentives had a major effect in increasing farm output up to 1958. Since then progress has been very slow in spite of the relatively high rate of investment. The poor performance since 1958 was only partly due to bad weather. It was also poor because the earlier policy changes were inadequate. The extension of the cultivated area had a once-for-all effect, the policy for increasing and stabilising farm income did not go far enough and the control apparatus remained too heavy handed.

As far as the future is concerned, it seems that agriculture will remain a major obstacle to faster Russian growth. The level of income and food production per head is lower than in Western Europe, so that the future demand for farm products will continue to be substantial—with an elasticity smaller than in the past, but higher than in Western Europe.

The organisational problems of agriculture are likely to remain a serious handicap. There is still pressure to increase the size of farms, to run the farm economy on the basis of centralised directives and to hamper production on the small private plots. In spite of the abolition of M.T.S., centralised direction was reinforced in 1961 and 1962. There is still a good deal of party interference with farm management. None of these tendencies seems likely to be radically changed.

In the longer run, the production problem for many crops will probably be eased if large amounts of fertilisers and farm machinery can be provided to highly capitalised state farms where workers are paid regular wages, and organised in fair sized towns with reasonable social amenities and shopping facilities. But improved livestock production will require more freedom and better marketing arrangements for private plots. The Soviet state will need to give collective farmers a higher and steadier income. In fact this seems quite feasible now that the savings ratio of the economy is so high and farmers are only a third of the total population.

III. Future Growth Potential

The major reasons why the Russian economy did better than most Western countries in the 1950's was that it had a higher rate of investment, it made a large scale effort to produce the new skills required for economic growth and it made some improvements in agricultural policy. There were some recovery elements in growth in the 1950's but these were not greater than in Western Europe, and the structural pattern of output change and of investment was only a little more favourable to growth than developments in the West. Growth was also helped in the U.S.S.R. as in Western Europe by the reduction in the relative burden of defence, and the improved allocation of resources through trade. Because of the decline in the defence burden, and the fact that share of investment and government expenditure did not increase, the consumer was able to enjoy the fruits of economic progress on a scale unparalleled in Soviet history. The increase in labour input was smaller in the 1950's in the U.S.S.R. than in all major industrial Western countries in terms of man hours. The rate of productivity growth was not paralleled elsewhere. At the end of the 1950's and the beginning of the 1960's, Soviet growth slowed down because of difficulties in agriculture, deficiencies in the planning mechanism, and the reduction in working hours.

The future rate of growth will be affected by the inputs of new investment, labour, and the skills of labour. It will also be affected by the pattern of output, which in its turn will depend on the structure of demand (to a considerable extent this is simply a reflection of the government's preferences as to resource use). The effectiveness of these inputs will be affected by the constraints imposed by the quality of natural resources, the existing economic structure and level of development, and the rate of technological progress. Growth will be affected by institutional and administrative constraints on economic efficiency, and by relations with the outside world. We have tried to analyse the interplay of these forces in explaining past growth, and some of our views of the future have already been stated or are implicit in what has already been said.

The increase in employment in the 1950's was at an annual rate of 1.6 per cent. The population of working age is likely to increase a little faster in the next decade than in the last, so that one might expect the growth of labour supply to be as favourable to future growth as that of the 1950's. In the 1950's, working hours fell considerably from 48 to 41 per week, i.e. by about 15 per cent. A good part of the fall in working hours took place in 1960, toward the end of the year. It therefore had little impact on the growth of G.N.P. in the period 1950–60. Consequently the increase in output per man hour recorded in our Table 5 is very large for 1950–60, but somewhat misleading. The cost of such a large fall in working hours was not reflected in output until after 1960, and is probably a major reason for the slowdown in the early 1960's. Further reductions in working hours are likely to have an even bigger proportional impact on output. A good deal of wasted time was probably eliminated in the reduction to 41 hours, whereas this would not be the case if weekly hours were reduced, e.g. to 35 as was once stated to be the official aim for 1964–68. The facilities for enjoyment of leisure are somewhat limited in the U.S.S.R., and annual holidays are already rather long, so that it would seem irrational to sacrifice output gains for increases in leisure in the 1960's. It therefore seems unlikely that working hours will fall nearly as drastically in the 1960's as they did in the 1950's—a figure of 5 per cent seems more likely than 15 per cent of the 1950's. We might therefore expect total labour input to increase at something like 1.3 per cent a year over the next decade, as compared with around zero in the 1950's.

In the 1950's, Soviet output per man rose by 5.1 per cent a year, and output per man hour by 6.8 per cent. For the reasons given above, the output per man hour figure was influenced by special factors, and it would not seem reasonable to expect output per man hour to grow at much more than 5 per cent a year. This would mean a total G.N.P. growth of around 6.5 per cent a year.

However, it does not make sense simply to extrapolate past trends. We must see whether the factors likely to affect productivity will be different in the 1960's from those in the 1950's. This, of course, involves a judgement on many factors, some of which are imponderable, and others largely political.

It seems likely that the rate of non-residential investment will be at least as high in the 1960's as in the 1950's, though there are some grounds for thinking that the return on investment in the 1950's was a little more favourable than can be expected in future. The level of investment in Japan is higher than in the U.S.S.R., marginally so in the 1950's, but much higher in 1960–63 at about 40 per cent of G.N.P.. The high Japanese investment rate is a major factor in its high growth rate, and the U.S.S.R. may also try to devote a bigger share of its resources to investment. The profitability of a given degree of capital deepening depends on the level of productivity at which the economy is operating, and as the Japanese level is below that of the U.S.S.R., the Soviet possibilities may be more limited than those of Japan. A more serious constraint on the profitability of a major increase in the investment rate is that it would put a considerable strain on the planning mechanism to make resources flexible enough for a higher rate of growth.

In housing and in transport the Soviet capital stock is much more tightly stretched than in Western countries. In the years before the 1950's the U.S.S.R. was able to neglect these two kinds of investment to the benefit of sectors more closely geared to the growth of output. In the case of housing, this policy was changed in the 1950's, and the proportion of investment going to housing was no different from that in Germany. There may be some further increase in the share of investment going to housing, but this seems unlikely to be of major proportions as the rate of construction is already high. In the case of transport, the investment effort of the U.S.S.R. in the 1950's was proportionately much lower than that of Western Europe. This lower investment was partly due to a more rational use of resources in the U.S.S.R. which has avoided some of the competitive waste of the West. However, it seems doubtful if the U.S.S.R. can continue to economise on transport to the same degree in future. Farm efficiency depends to a sizeable extent on improvements in farm-to-market roads, and the Soviet consumption standard has got to a level where there will be increasing pressure for the use of private automobiles. For this reason there may be some slight increase in the capital output ratio in future.

Another factor which may make for a slightly higher investment output ratio in future is the higher proportion of gross investment required for replacement. Until the mid-1950's equipment was not scrapped in the U.S.S.R. until it was physically worn out. It is now scrapped when obsolete. This change in practice had already started in the 1950's, so that it involves no great change from the present situation. It will however, probably raise the burden of replacement somewhat as compared with the average for the 1950's.

As far as training is concerned the Russian effort can hardly expand at the same pace as in the past, if only because the present effort is so large. But the stock of people with economically useful skills will continue to increase rapidly as the people entering the labour force will be much better trained than the existing average. Human resources may be a bottleneck to growth in sectors like distribution and farm management, but here again, a large effort can readily be mounted if skills prove to be the bottleneck.

The research activities of the U.S.S.R. are likely to be directed to similar purposes as in the past. Some reduction in military research would probably result in a higher concentration on space research, aeronautics and other fields at the frontiers of knowledge, which are likely to advance the technology of the world as a whole rather than the economic growth of the U.S.S.R. Applied research on new industrial problems of chemicals has already been undertaken on a large scale. Research on agriculture may have a higher pay-off in future if it is given greater freedom, and research on consumer demand should certainly have a high payoff.

There is still considerable scope for productivity gains arising from structural change. Russian agriculture has a very low productivity; improvements there could release a great deal of labour for higher productivity sectors. The scope is bigger than in Western countries, as 38 per cent of the Soviet labour force is still in agriculture as compared with an average of less than half this for Western Europe. Even if agriculture does not reduce its labour force much in absolute terms, its share of the labour force will continue to decline, and that of industry will increase. On the other hand, there may well be a bigger expansion in services in the 1960's than the 1950's. The level of productivity in services is much higher than in agriculture, but it is lower than in industry, so that a bigger proportionate switch to this sector will somewhat dampen the benefits of structural change.

We should now consider how productivity is likely to move within each sector. There is reason to believe than the U.S.S.R. should still continue to get the same kind of return on industrial investment as in the past. Like Western Europe it is still working well below the fringe of best practice technology, the rate of investment in this sector is likely to remain high, and the effort to improve technical skills will also be intense. The level of development in industry is more uneven than in Western Europe, and there are sectors such as chemicals, textiles, and footwear where there is scope for large improvement by copying the West. If it is decided to make automobiles available to Soviet consumers on a large scale, the scope for productivity gains should be particularly large in this industry and its subsidiaries.

The performance of Soviet agriculture in the 1950's was much better than in earlier years, but this involved a major investment effort and a very large extension of the area of cultivation. Agriculture is likely to remain the major problem sector and the extension of cultivation to marginal areas has brought new risks of substantial crop fluctuations. Future growth will probably be slower than in the early 1950's, but should be better than from 1958–63. In future, there will be no scope for massive increases in the area cultivated, and main reliance will have to be placed on better incentives to farmers, more investment and fertilisers. It seems unlikely that there will be any move away from collectivisation, but even a moderate increase in the size of private plots would have very favourable effects on productivity.

It is likely that consumer income will continue to rise rapidly and the Soviet consumer will put up increasing pressure for better goods and sales resistance to inferior ones. This pressure has already led to changes in official policy towards production of consumer goods. It also seems likely that an increasing proportion of Russian income will go on services. The distributive services have been neglected and need vast improvement— better display of goods, more space for trying out goods, more variety, market research, advertising, and consumer credit. Restaurants, cafés and bars need great expansion and there are vast needs for improved repair services. Service facilities for automobiles are almost non-existent and will need enormous expansion if car ownership starts on any scale. Pressure in these directions is bound to rise as Soviet consumers increase their incomes. Many of the consumer service which need expansion are of a type where the private entrepreneurship of the West gives it distinct organisational advantages over the rather bureaucratic and centralised Soviet system. Progress in providing these services will probably also be impeded by lingering official prejudices against "unproductive" activities and "luxury" consumption. However, there is no reason to believe that productivity growth within the service sector will be slower in future than in the past. It may well be faster, once it is realised that progress in these fields is necessary. A major reason for poor performance in these sectors is that almost no high level manpower or managerial talent has been put into meeting these needs. If policy is changed in this respect good results can be anticipated.

Further progress towards improved allocation of resources through international trade seems likely, and some better degree of multilateralisation of the payments system, but it is unlikely that the Soviet authorities will want to continue to make the large scale imports of food products which would obviously be in line with their comparative cost situation. They would probably regard such dependence as strategically risky, and as too public an acknowledgement of the failure of their agricultural policies.

In any case the relative expansion of trade is unlikely to be any faster than in the 1950's so that any impact it has in helping growth should simply continue the influence already present then.

Finally, it seems that the Soviet authorities are trying to increase the efficiency of resource allocation by greater freedom to enterprises, and are moving towards a price system which reflects relative scarcities.

On balance, therefore, it seems likely that Soviet growth policies may prove sufficiently flexible to push the economy above the growth path of the early 1960's, though they may not bring it back to the growth rates of the 1950's.

POSTWAR ECONOMIC GROWTH IN EASTERN EUROPE*
— · — · — · — · — · — · — · — · — · — · — · —

Maurice Ernst†

A Comparison With Western Europe

This paper uses comparisons with Western Europe to evaluate postwar economic growth in Eastern Europe. Three main aspects of comparative economic growth are examined: the growth of production; the increase in personal consumption; and the efficiency in the use of inputs. In addition, the relative influence of external factors on economic growth in the two areas is considered. The method of analysis is statistical—a comparison of various measures of economic growth and of the measurable factors which may have influenced this growth. Its purpose, however, is to provide evidence on a very intangible question—the relative performance of the market-type economic system of Western Europe and of the Soviet-type "command economy" of Eastern Europe.

An evaluation of economic performance founded on international comparisons can be highly artificial since governments or populations may set for themselves standards for growth or efficiency that differ greatly from those of other countries. In the case of Eastern and Western Europe, however, both history and geography give inter-country comparisons considerable importance for national governments and stimulate people to look across the border for standards of consumption. Moreover, even in the absence of direct comparisons and influence, technological and sociological trends on both sides of the border tend to be similar enough to make international comparisons meaningful.

The comparison in this study is limited to six Eastern European coun-

*Reprinted from U.S. Congress, Joint Economic Committee, *New Directions in The Soviet Economy* (Washington, D.C.: U.S. Government Printing Office, 1966) pp. 875–916 (excerpts).

†Dr. Maurice Ernst is Economist with the Central Intelligence Agency. His publications include: "Overstatement of Industrial Growth in Poland," *Quarterly Journal of Economics*, No. 4, 1965.

tries—Bulgaria, Czechoslovakia, East Germany, Hungary, Poland, and
Rumania—and nine Western European countries—Austria, Belgium, Denmark, West Germany, France, Greece, Italy, Netherlands, and Norway.
The selection was based partly on the availability of appropriate statistics—
which excluded such countries as Albania and Spain. A second criterion was
a reasonable degree of similarity in economic system among the two groups,
which excluded Yugoslavia because its system is a blend of state planning,
decentralized state administration, and the market mechanism. A third
criterion was to include only countries which met either defeat or occupation during World War II and thus suffered some economic retardation.
For many reasons—some evident, some subtle, and some that are not
yet clear—victors, such as the United Kingdom, and neutrals, such as
Sweden, have had a very different pattern of growth than the defeated or
occupied countries. They emerged from the war with increased production
and have since tended to grow more slowly.

The main statistical findings of this study are the following:

1. Over the postwar period as a whole, the growth of production has
been rapid in Eastern Europe, but no more so than in Western Europe. In
recent years it has been slower in Eastern Europe than in Western Europe.

2. The improvement in per capita consumption and probably also in
general consumer welfare has been much smaller in Eastern Europe than
in Western Europe.

3. By the main statistical indications, economic growth has been less
efficient in Eastern than in Western Europe—it has taken larger investment
expenditures to obtain similar rates of growth. Lower efficiency, indeed,
is a major cause of the relatively slow rise in consumption in Eastern
Europe.

The causes of these differences in economic performance are complex
and include a great many factors unique to individual countries of Eastern
and Western Europe. But the advantage of the Western over the Eastern
countries in the measures of economic performance appears large and
general enough to suggest important common causes, notably the effects of
the separate institutional development of these two areas—Western Europe under capitalist institutions with broad access to the world market;
Eastern Europe under Soviet-type institutions with close ties with the
U.S.S.R.

Soviet exploitation of Eastern Europe, in contrast to large U.S. aid to
Western Europe probably was largely responsible for the slower recovery
of the Eastern European economies after World War II, but neither this
factor, nor the trends in the volume and terms of trade appear to explain
the recent economic slowdown in Eastern Europe or that area's postwar
disadvantage in economic efficiency. This is not to say that membership

in the Soviet bloc did not have far-reaching effects for economic growth and efficiency, but rather that the external influences on each country's economy of applying Soviet-type policies and institutions are inseparable from the internal effects. These policies and institutions embrace among other things the method and principles of detailed state planning, the method of economic administration through a vast state bureaucracy, the relegation of the market mechanism to a minor role, and the collectivization of agriculture. In the author's opinion, such institutions and the associated policies were mainly responsible for the relatively poor performance of Eastern Europe.

I. Characteristics of the Eastern European Economies

Excluding East Germany and the Bohemia-Moravia section of Czechoslovakia, which historically has been part of Central Europe, Eastern Europe has always been a relatively undeveloped region. Before World War II agriculture was the predominant economic activity, although there were islands of urban and industrial development. Peasants, by and large, were poor, eating mainly self-produced crops and buying little besides the most essential items. The industrial workers were much better off than the peasants, but there were few industrial jobs. In Poland, Rumania and Bulgaria, more people were employed in handicraft shops than in factories. Outside East Germany and Czechoslovakia, the main industries were textiles, leather and food processing (throughout the area), coal mining (Poland), oil extraction (mainly in Rumania), and nuclei of the metallurgical, metal-working and chemical industries. East Germany and Czechoslovakia were highly industrialized, but lacked a strong heavy industrial base, having concentrated on the manufacture of finished products.

Although postwar industrialization has raised considerably per capita GNP's in Eastern Europe, these remain considerably lower than those in most of Western Europe. In 1963, per capita GNP in Czechoslovakia and East Germany was less than three-quarters of that in West Germany and about halfway between the West German and Italian levels. Hungary and Poland were in an intermediate position, with per capita GNP's less than half of the West German level and falling between Italy and Greece. Bulgaria and Rumania were in the rear, at about the level of Greece. The combined GNP of these six Eastern European countries was about 10 percent smaller than that of West Germany and came to roughly one-third of the combined GNP's of the EEC countries or the U.S.S.R. The six countries range in size from Poland—the largest—whose GNP is about half that of Italy, to Bulgaria—the smallest—whose GNP is about four-fifths of Norway's.

Two alternative sets of figures for GNP and per capita GNP in Eastern and Western European countries are shown in Table 1. The GNP's of

TABLE 1

COMPARISONS OF GNP AND GNP PER CAPITA
IN SELECTED EUROPEAN COUNTRIES IN 1964
(1963 U.S. dollars)

Country	Using Official Exchange Rates for Western Countries		Using Calculated Exchange Rates for Western Countries	
	Total GNP, billion dollars	Per capita GNP dollars*	Total GNP, billion dollars	Per capita GNP, dollars*
Eastern Europe				
Bulgaria........................	4.9	600	5.6	690
Czechoslovakia	18.0	1,280	20.7	1,470
East Germany	21.0	1,220	24.1	1,400
Hungary.....				
Hungary........................	9.0	880	10.3	1,020
Poland	24.1	770	27.7	890
Rumania	11.2	590	12.9	680
Total above	88.1	880	101.3	1,020
Western Europe				
Austria........................	8.1	1,120	9.3	1,290
Belgium	14.6	1,560	17.7	1,890
Denmark	8.6	1,820	10.1	2,130
France.........................	83.6	1,730	97.0	2,010
West Germany..................	100.2	1,720	115.2	1,980
Greece.........................	4.7	550	5.9	690
Italy..........................	46.3	910	57.9	1,140
Netherlands	15.6	1,290	20.7	1,710
Norway	6.0	1,610	6.9	1,870
Total above	287.7	1,420	340.7	1,680

*Rounded figures.

the Eastern European countries were estimated through direct comparisons with West Germany by means of calculated exchange rates and quantity indexes. The relatives so obtained were applied to two estimates of the dollar value of GNP in West Germany—one with the official exchange rate, the other with a calculated exchange rate obtained from a study for the OEEC.

The ranking of the Eastern European countries as to industrial production per capita is similar to that for GNP per capita, although, as might be expected, the differences among countries are greater. Estimates of the relative levels of industrial production, total and per capita, are shown in Table 2. My estimates are nearly identical to those made by the Council for Mutual Economic Assistance (CMEA).

TABLE 2

Comparisons of Industrial Production, 1961
(Total Eastern Europe equals 100.)

Country	My Estimate		CEMA Estimate* Total
	Total	Per capita	
East Germany	28	165	28
Poland	26	90	27
Czechoslovakia	23	165	23
Rumania	11	80	12
Hungary	8	60	7
Bulgaria	4	50	3
Total Eastern Europe	100	100	100
West Germany	123	220	....
U.S.S.R.	....	....	262

*See *Planowane Hospodarstvi*, No. 4, Apr. 1, 1964.

The differences among Eastern Europe countries and between them and Western Europe are more pronounced for per capita GNP and industrial production than for the sectoral distribution of GNP at factor cost, which is shown in Table 3. The contribution of agriculture to GNP is considerably larger in most of the Eastern European countries than in nearly all the Western European countries—which was to be expected—and the

TABLE 3

Percentage Distribution of GNP at Factor Cost, 1960

Country	Percent of GNP Originating in—		
	Industry and construction	Agriculture and forestry	Other sectors (services)
Bulgaria	39	29	32
Czechoslovakia	52	15	33
East Germany	54	9	37
Hungary	40	24	36
Poland	41	31	28
Austria	55	13	32
Belgium	45	8	47
Denmark	42	18	40
France	49	10	41
West Germany	55	7	38
Greece	28	28	44
Italy	48	19	33
Netherlands	44	12	44
Norway	39	11	50

contribution of services (all sectors other than industry and construction and agriculture and forestry) is smaller. The contribution of industry to GNP on the average is only slightly smaller in Eastern Europe than in most of Western Europe, in spite of the fact that the relative volume of industrial output is much smaller. This may be due to high relative costs of industrial production in Eastern Europe, particularly in such countries as Bulgaria and Poland, although differences in the method of calculating factor costs may also have strong effects on the sector shares.

II. Statistics and Methods

Comparisons of economic growth and performance require comparable statistics and until recently such statistics did not exist for Eastern Europe. In recent years, however, a great deal of work has been done to recalculate economic aggregates and indexes for Eastern Europe using Western-type methods. Much of this work has been a product or an outgrowth of the "Project on National Income in East-Central Europe" at Columbia University, under the direction of Thad Alton, who has published three monographs and a number of occasional papers. The statistical analysis of this paper for Eastern Europe is based predominantly on these recalculated series.

The official series (on national income, industrial production, and so forth) differ considerably in concept and method from the recalculated series and tend to show considerably higher rates of economic growth. Although very sound analysis of trends in the individual countries can be based on judicious use of official statistics (as for example in the ECE's Economic Survey of Europe and Economic Bulletin for Europe), the same is not true of international comparisons. Moreover, the differences in methodology between Eastern and Western countries are such that rule-of-thumb adjustments (for example, to achieve greater comparability of coverage) rarely suffice—complete recalculations are usually necessary. The differences in methodology can indeed be crucial to an evaluation of comparative economic performance. For example, the United Nations Economic Commission for Europe in an otherwise very thorough and competent study[1] draw what I believe are wholly incorrect conclusions as to the relative productivity of investment in Eastern and Western Europe by relying on official series, with adjustments, for both sets of countries. According to the ECE, returns to investment during the 1950's were probably not greater in market economies than in planned economies. The use of recalculated series for the Eastern countries makes it clear that returns to investment were in fact considerably greater in market than in planned economies.

[1]UN/ECE, "Economic Survey of Europe in 1961," pt. II. "Some Factors in Economic Growth in Europe During the 1950's" (especially ch. II, p. 30).

Official Eastern European measures of the growth of national income are not comparable to Western-type measures for three main reasons. First, the Marxist concept of national income excludes so-called nonproductive services (that is, direct governmental and private services and often also passenger transportation). In postwar Europe the output of direct services generally has grown more slowly than the output of goods so that their exclusion has tended to raise the rate of growth of national income. Second, market prices—the basis of valuation for national income in Eastern Europe—differ drastically from factor costs in these countries. This is because of the absence of explicit charges for the use of capital and land and the collection of the resulting savings in accounting costs by the Government in the form of the turnover tax. The turnover tax is levied mainly on industry, whose weight in national income is thereby increased, at the expense mainly of that of agriculture. Since industry usually is the most dynamic sector the rate of growth of national income is raised. Third, the method of calculating the growth of individual sectors of the national income differs from that used in the West. Although some of the Eastern European indexes of income originating in industry and other sectors give reasonable results, others do not, and little is known about them.

Official indexes of gross industrial production in Eastern Europe in my opinion overstate considerably the rate of growth. The main reason is that industrial production indexes in Communist countries are not just measures of the results of industrial activity, but also are devices for the direction of industry and the establishment of producers' incentives. Industrial managers, whose success often depended on fulfilling a plan for gross industrial production, had every incentive to produce an assortment of goods and to negotiate prices that would show the best results for the smallest effort. Although there were a multiplicity of controls designed to specify assortment and fix prices, these controls rarely prevented an inflation of the gross production index.[2]

III. Growth of Production

A. *Gross National Product*

Postwar economic growth has been rapid in both Eastern and Western Europe[3] (see Table 4). In Western Europe total GNP in 1964 was about double the 1950 level and two and a half times the prewar level; in Eastern Europe, total GNP in 1964 was double both the 1950 and the prewar level. Economic recovery from the effects of World War II was more rapid

---

[2]These points are developed further in Maurice Ernst, "Overstatement of Industrial Growth in Poland," *Quarterly Journal Of Economics*, November 1965.

[3]That is, the six Eastern European countries and the nine Western European countries listed earlier.

TABLE 4

GROWTH OF GNP, PREWAR TO 1964

Country	Indexes, 1955 = 100					Annual Percentage Increases*			
	Prewar	1950	1955	1960	1964	1951–55	1956–60	1961–64	1951–64
Bulgaria	68	75	100	142	168	5.9	7.3	4.3	5.9
Czechoslovakia	79	84	100	137	145	3.6	6.6	1.3	4.0
East Germany..........	84	71	100	127	141	7.2	4.9	2.7	5.1
Hungary	80	76	100	123	147	5.5	4.2	4.6	4.8
Poland................	72	79	100	127	155	4.8	5.0	5.0	4.9
Rumania..............	66	66	100	119	144	8.6	3.5	4.9	5.7
Total Eastern Europe...	76	76	100	128	148	5.7	5.2	3.6	4.9
Unweighted average....						5.9	5.2	3.8	5.1
Austria	62	74	100	129	151	6.1	5.2	4.2	5.2
Belgium..............	67	84	100	112	133	3.6	2.3	4.3	3.3
Denmark	68	91	100	127	157	2.0	4.9	5.5	4.0
France................	66	80	100	126	155	4.4	4.8	5.3	4.8
West Germany†	51	65	100	135	163	9.1	6.2	4.8	6.8
Greece................	93	71	100	131	183	7.0	5.6	8.7	7.0
Italy	71	75	100	133	165	6.0	5.9	5.5	5.8
Netherlands...........	58	76	100	122	146	5.6	4.1	4.5	4.7
Norway...............	62	84	100	117	143	3.6	3.2	5.1	3.9
Total Western Europe ..	62	75	100	129	157	5.9	5.2	5.1	5.4
Unweighted average....						5.3	4.7	5.2	5.0

* Calculated from unrounded data.
† Excluding the Saar.

in Western Europe than in Eastern Europe. By 1950, the western economies were well beyond prewar levels, except in the case of Greece, where
the effects of the civil war were felt for years. By contrast, GNP fell short
of prewar levels in East Germany by 15 percent and in Hungary by 5 percent, just reached this level in Rumania, and showed a significant rise in
Poland only because the change in boundaries greatly increased that country's economic potential—in postwar boundaries Polish GNP in 1950 was
at least 10 to 15 percent lower than in 1937.

After 1950, the Western European economies combined grew somewhat faster than the Eastern European economies combined, mainly
because of the large weight and usually rapid growth of West Germany.
If we compare average growth rates with each country having equal weight,
the rates in the east are about the same as those in the west.

The growth rates in Eastern Europe vary inversely with per capita
GNP, East Germany being an exception because of its delayed recovery—
after 1955, East German growth is the slowest in the area. In Western
Europe, growth rates range widely, from around 7 percent (Greece and
West Germany) to 3.3 percent (Belgium), with no clear pattern.

There have been marked changes in growth rates over the years. On the average, growth in both Eastern and Western Europe was only a little slower in the second half than in the first half of the 1950's. An acceleration of growth in Czechoslovakia and Bulgaria was more than offset by a deceleration in East Germany, where postwar recovery finally had ended, in Hungary, as a result of the 1956 revolt, and in Rumania, mainly because of poor results in agriculture. Since 1960, however, growth in Eastern Europe has slowed considerably, while there has been little change in the Western rates. The sharp slowdown in Eastern Europe is due almost entirely to the severe economic recession in Czechoslovakia and a cut of nearly one-half in the East German growth rate in comparison with 1956–60. Czechoslovakia sustained one of the highest growth rates in Europe during the late 1950's and in 1960. Growth slowed a little in 1961 and considerably in 1962. Then GNP fell nearly 3 percent in 1963 and did not rise in 1964; no other industrial country has had a more severe economic recession since World War II. The East German slowdown came at least a year earlier, under the strain of the Berlin crises and the sudden collectivization of agriculture, but it was not as severe as that in Czechoslovakia, annual growth having been fairly steady since 1962. Among the other eastern countries, the sharp decline in Bulgarian growth reflects mainly the economic consolidation following an extremely rapid expansion during the "great leap" of 1959–60 and the increased rate of growth in Rumania is influenced by the fact that 1960 was a bad agricultural year. Growth accelerated slightly in Hungary and decelerated slightly in Poland. Polish growth has been remarkably stable since 1950. In Western Europe growth rates increased during 1961–64 in six countries out of nine and decreased substantially only in West Germany, which fell from first to sixth place among the nine countries.

Some of the ranking of growth rates, although not the broad relationships between the Eastern and Western countries, are changed if we compare the growth of per capita GNP's (Table 5). The largest difference is for Poland, where boundary changes, war losses and migration after the war caused a large decline in population. By 1950, Polish GNP per capita was about 50 percent above prewar levels (in the old boundaries) although total GNP had risen only 10 percent. In Czechoslovakia also, where the expulsion of the Sudeten Germans reduced the population, per capita GNP had increased almost one-third from 1937 to 1950 with a 7 percent growth in total GNP. During the early postwar years East Germany gained some population, although much less than West Germany, as a result of the expulsion of Germans from the areas acquired by Poland. Between 1950 and 1962, however, the East German population declined steadily because of its unfavorable age structure and the flight to West Germany, while the West German population grew rapidly. In consequence, the growth of East German GNP per capita is about the same as that of

TABLE 5

GROWTH OF GNP AND GNP PER CAPITA

Country	Percentage Increases					
	Prewar to 1964			1950 to 1964		
	GNP	Popu- lation	GNP per capita	GNP	Popu- lation	GNP per capita
Bulgaria	148	21	105	123	12	99
Czechoslovakia	84	−3	105	73	13	53
East Germany	69	6	59	100	−6	113
Hungary..................	83	10	66	93	8	78
Poland	116	−10	140	96	25	56
Romania	117	21	79	117	16	87
Total above	94	3	88	94	13	72
Austria...................	146	6	132	103	4	95
Belgium	97	12	76	58	9	45
Denmark	129	24	84	73	10	57
France....................	136	15	105	93	16	66
West Germany.............	219	39	129	151	17	114
Greece....................	97	20	64	157	12	129
Italy......................	132	17	98	121	9	103
Netherlands	150	39	80	92	20	60
Norway	128	27	80	70	13	50
Total above	155	23	107	110	15	83

Sources for population: U.S. Bureau of Census and OECD statistics.

West Germany for the postwar period (it is much smaller in comparison with prewar) in spite of a lag of one-third in the growth of total GNP. On a per capita basis, Hungarian growth is about average among European countries while Polish growth is one of the lowest.

B. Pattern of Economic Growth

Industrialization has been the dominant form of economic growth in Eastern Europe. As shown in Table 6, industry and construction account for about 70 percent of the postwar increase in GNP in East Germany and Czechoslovakia and for nearly 60 percent even in so undeveloped a country as Bulgaria (twice as high a share as in Greece). The role of agriculture in total growth ranged from small (10 percent or so) to negative and the role of services ranged from a quarter to a third. The contribution of industry and construction to total economic growth was smaller in six out of nine of the listed Western European Countries than in any of the eastern coun-

TABLE 6
COMPOSITION OF THE GROWTH OF GNP AT FACTOR COST, 1951–64
(percent of increment in GNP)

Country	Industry, Including Construction	Agriculture, Including Forestry	Services
Bulgaria*	59	9	32
Czechoslovakia	68	−2	34
East Germany†	72	0	28
Hungary	59	9	32
Poland	66	11	23
Austria	62	7	31
Belgium‡	53	3	44
Denmark	48	8	44
France	55	5	40
West Germany	63	3	34
Greece*	30	22	48
Italy	65	11	24
Netherlands	51	3	46
Norway	40	−1	61

* 1951–63.
† 1951–62.
‡ 1956–64.

tries in spite of a generally higher initial level of industrial development, while the contribution of services was generally much larger.

1. *Industrial production.*[4] Industrial production has increased more rapidly in Eastern Europe than in Western Europe over the entire postwar period, and at about the same rate as in Western Europe since 1960, as shown in Table 7. All of the eastern countries, except East Germany, had easily surpassed prewar levels by 1950 and since then annual rates of growth have averaged around 8 percent in Eastern Europe compared with 6 or 7 percent in Western Europe. As in the case of GNP, however, industrial growth in the Eastern countries has slowed down since 1960, largely because of the recession in Czechoslovakia, where industrial production in 1964 was below the 1962 level, and a fall of nearly one-half in the rate of growth in East Germany.

Rates of industrial growth in both Eastern and Western Europe have been inversely related to the level of economic development and there is little difference in rates of growth among countries at similar levels of economic development. For example, the three least developed countries, Bulgaria, Rumania, and Greece have been at or near the top in industrial growth rates, with Greece lagging somewhat behind the other two be-

---

[4] Industrial production is here defined to include construction and all handicraft production.

Growth Strategy and Performance

TABLE 7

GROWTH OF INDUSTRIAL PRODUCTION* PREWAR TO 1964

Country	Indexes, 1955 = 100					Annual Percentage Increases			
	Prewar	1950	1955	1960	1964	1951–55	1956–60	1961–64	1961–64
Bulgaria	40	67	100	183	250	8.4	12.7	8.2	9.9
Czechoslovakia	69	80	100	155	167	4.6	9.1	1.9	5.4
East Germany........	80	59	100	141	166	11.2	7.2	4.1	7.7
Hungary.............	57	65	100	131	179	9.0	5.5	8.2	7.5
Poland..............	53	63	100	148	196	9.6	8.1	7.3	8.4
Rumania	49	69	100	157	244	7.6	9.4	11.7	9.4
Total above	64	67	100	148	185	8.5	8.1	5.8	7.6
Unweighted average..	....	.....	.....	.....	.....	8.4	8.6	6.9	8.0
Austria	47	69	100	134	159	7.8	6.0	4.3	6.2
Belgium	63	80	100	110	139	4.5	1.8	6.1	4.0
Denmark	59	90	100	130	168	2.0	5.5	6.5	4.5
France..............	65	79	100	131	166	4.9	5.6	6.1	5.5
West Germany	51	56	100	138	170	12.1	6.6	5.5	8.2
Greece..............	60	67	100	150	200	8.2	8.5	7.4	8.1
Italy	48	60	100	150	199	10.6	8.4	7.3	8.9
Netherlands.........	52	75	100	130	158	5.9	5.5	4.9	5.5
Norway.............	50	82	100	114	141	4.1	2.7	5.5	4.0
Total above	55	67	100	135	170	8.3	6.2	5.9	6.8
Unweighted average..	....	.....	.....	.....	.....	6.7	5.6	5.8	6.1

*Includes construction for post war years, except Rumania and East Germany. Excludes construction for prewar years.

cause of its more balanced economic development; in the next group, Poland and Hungary have lagged slightly behind Italy; and in the more advanced group, growth in Czechoslovakia has been about the same as that in France and Netherlands. Eastern and Western Germany have been exceptions, both being industrialized countries with high growth rates until recent years, and West Germany has had the edge.

2. *Agricultural production.*[5] In contrast to industrial production, which grew quickly in all the Eastern European countries, agricultural production in the area has barely surpassed the prewar level, while it is more than 50 percent above this level in Western Europe. A substantial lag in Eastern European agriculture in comparison with Western Europe developed in the early postwar years and the lag increased during the postwar period. Only in Poland, Rumania, and Bulgaria did production in the early 1960's exceed the average for 1934–38, and most of the Polish gain is due to boundary changes. The more developed countries did much worse. Production in East Germany was 20 percent, and in Czechoslovakia nearly 10 percent, below the prewar level, and in neither of these countries has there been an upward trend since the early 1950's (see Table 8).

[5]Agricultural production refers to the contribution of agriculture, forestry, and fishing to the GNP in constant prices.

TABLE 8

TRENDS IN AGRICULTURAL PRODUCTION
(Indexes: 1950–53 average equals 100.)

Country	Prewar	1960–63 Average	Country	Prewar	1960–63 Average
Bulgaria	96	107	Belgium	75	131
Czechoslovakia	114	105	Denmark	77	117
East Germany	122	98	France	89	134
Hungary	120	118	West Germany	88	119
Poland	95	126	Italy	85	125
Rumania	112	144	Netherlands	77	123
Austria	106	129	Norway	85	96

NOTES: Western Europe:

1950–53 to 1960–63.—GNP originating in agriculture and forestry in constant prices.

Prewar to 1950–53.—Agricultural output, excluding forestry (total agricultural production less the use of self-produced materials).

3. *Services.* This residual category of GNP is a composite of transportation, trade, and direct services, such as housing, personal services, and government services. Rates of growth vary a great deal among these components and, for individual components, among countries. By and

TABLE 9

TRENDS IN THE OUTPUT OF SERVICES* 1951–64

Country	Annual Percentage Increases	Ratio of Rate of Growth of Services to Rate of Growth of GNP (in percent)
Bulgaria	5.9†	98
Czechoslovakia	4,2	105
East Germany	3.8‡	69
Hungary	4.4	92
Poland	3.9	80
Unweighted average	4.4	....
Austria	4.8	92
Belgium	3.0§	100
Denmark	4.4	110
France	4.7	98
West Germany	5.9	87
Greece	5.5†	81
Italy	4.6	79
Netherlands	4.4†	98
Norway	5.0†	135
Unweighted average	4.7	....

* All sectors of GNP except industry, construction, agriculture, and forestry.

† 1951–63.

‡ 1951–62.

§ 1956–63.

large, the output of transportation, communications, and trade, approximately kept up with the total output of goods during the postwar period. In the case of direct services, government services increased much faster than direct private services and housing in the Eastern European countries—indeed, the output of many personal services declined. In the Western countries the differences are in the same direction but less marked. These differences in both areas are offsetting, and production of services rose at about the same rate as GNP in almost all of the countries covered (see Table 9).

IV. Trends in Consumption and Consumer Welfare

The Eastern European consumer has not benefited in proportion to the growth of production. In the Western European countries, the growth of personal consumption since World War II and since prewar years has almost kept up with the growth of GNP. In the Eastern European countries for which reliable consumption statistics are available (they are not for Bulgaria and Rumania), the growth in personal consumption was much slower than that of GNP (Table 10). The most extreme difference is in Czechoslovakia, where personal consumption grew about half as fast as GNP, the discrepancy being most marked during the early postwar years. In East Germany on the other hand, consumption grew much faster than GNP in the early 1950's and almost as fast as GNP in the late 1950's. The reason was the open border with West Germany, which forced the East German regime to keep living conditions as close to those in West Germany as possible. The closing of the border in 1961 made this competition

TABLE 10

GROWTH OF PERSONAL CONSUMPTION IN RELATION TO THAT OF GNP

Country	Ratios of Growth Rates (in percent)				
	1951–55	1956–60	1961–64	1951–64	Prewar to 1964
Czechoslovakia	31	55	136	55	43
East Germany	160	90	22	114	79
Hungary	36	100	89	71	52
Poland	85	84	76	84	76
Austria	100	100	112	104	94
Denmark	75	76	102	85	81
France	111	83	114	102	78
West Germany	88	105	106	97	100
Italy	75	76	133	91	100
Netherlands	62	98	142	94	....
Norway	67	94	80	79	....

unnecessary at a time when the slowdown in overall economic growth made it more impractical. Consequently, there was almost no increase in East German consumption between 1961 and 1964. The postwar pattern of growth of consumption in Hungary clearly shows some causes and effects of the 1956 revolt. During the early 1950's the growth of consumption was less than 40 percent of that of GNP; since 1955 consumption and GNP have grown at about the same rates. In Poland, the stability of the ratios in table 10 hides some considerable fluctuations in consumption policy within the periods shown—consumption was sacrificed during 1951–53; favored during the "new course" of 1954, the disorders of 1956 and the period of consolidation of Gomulka's power in 1957; and again given a low priority after 1957.

The effects of Communist policies and priorities on comparative changes in per capita consumption are shown in Table 11. The increases in

TABLE 11

GROWTH OF PERSONAL CONSUMPTION PER CAPITA

Country	Percentage Increases		
	Prewar to 1964	1950 to 1964	1960 to 1964
Czechoslovakia	35	20	5
East Germany	43	134	3
Hungary	24	47	16
Poland	97	39	10
Austria	119	100	17
Denmark	58	43	19
France	76	67	18
West Germany	127	110	16
Italy	100	88	29
Netherlands	....	52	20
Norway	....	36	14

per capita consumption are much smaller in Eastern Europe than in Western Europe whether we consider the period since prewar years, since the early postwar years, or since 1960. Unusual circumstances explain the two exceptions—the changes in boundaries and the decline in population explain the large improvement in Poland since prewar days; and the late recovery and open border until 1961 explain the rapid postwar increase in East Germany. The only substantial increase in recent years among the Eastern countries, although a moderate one by Western standards, was in Hungary, a fact that has been noted by many travelers.

Lags of this sort in the growth of consumption inevitably had dramatic effects on relative consumption levels. Table 12 compares per capita

TABLE 12

COMPARATIVE LEVELS OF PERSONAL CONSUMPTION PER CAPITA

Country	Prewar*	1950	1955	1960	1964
West Germany	100	100	100	100	100
Austria	81	82	79	78	79
Czechoslovakia	95	100	71	63	57
East Germany	95	54	68	68	60
Hungary	87	69	52	49	48
Poland	45	60	48	42	40

*1936 for West Germany and East Germany; 1937 for Poland and Czechoslovakia; 1938 for the other countries.

consumption levels in East Germany, Czechoslovakia, Hungary and Poland with those in West Germany and Austria—of all the countries considered, those which have the closest historical, social, and cultural ties, and so for which comparisons are most relevant to the governments and populations involved. Before World War II, East Germany was roughly at parity with West Germany, with Czechoslovakia not far behind.[6] Since the war, personal consumption in East Germany and Czechoslovakia have fallen to around 60 percent of the West German level. These two countries also lost a clear lead over Austria, which they now trail by a wide margin; and Hungary, which before the war probably was at about the Austrian level was some 40 percent below the Austrian level in 1964 and not much above that of Poland. These contrasts have been evident to travelers for some time but until recently the necessary statistics were not available.

The contrast between the Eastern and the Western European countries in the growth of personal consumption is certainly large enough to warrant some definite judgments on relative changes in consumer welfare in spite of probable inaccuracies in the calculations and the fact that many other things besides the average volume of personal consumption affect welfare. Among the influences on consumer welfare that the personal consumption statistics do not reflect, some probably favor Western Europe, others Eastern Europe. For example, the range of choice among products and models has been considerably narrower in Eastern Europe than in Western Europe. Recurring shortages of many products and the consequent need to queue up for hours, possibly to go home emptyhanded, also has been a negative feature of the Eastern European scene. On the positive side has been the large increase in the supply of free, or nearly free, social services, such as educational and health services and recreation, which,

[6]If prewar consumption were known for the same year—for example, 1938—in all the countries, consumption in both parts of Germany would be higher than in table 12 relative to that in Czechoslovakia and Hungary.

in contrast to personal consumption, probably was at least as rapid in Eastern as in Western Europe (although to make certain of this would take additional research).

Most difficult of all to evaluate are the changes in the distribution of income among various socioeconomic groups. This is still largely an unexplored subject on which available information is very scarce. My general impressions on Eastern Europe, based mainly on Polish data, are the following. Among the various socioeconomic groups the peasants since prewar days have had the largest increase in per capita consumption. The main reason has been a shortage of agricultural products, caused originally by the disruptions of World War II, and later sustained by the inadequate growth of agricultural production. The Communist governments tried at various times to depress the farmers' terms of trade, with some success, particularly where they had strengthened their control over agriculture as a result of collectivization. But success was only temporary; farm incomes had to be raised to stimulate food production. Semiskilled and unskilled blue-collar workers also saw a considerable improvement in their standard of living, particularly those who formerly had been peasants.

These groups of workers gained from what appears to have been a general reduction in wage differentials due both to egalitarian Socialist ideology and the easy overfulfillment of work norms. They also were the main beneficiaries of the low prices of necessities, such as bread, and the rationing of housing at nominal rent levels. On the other hand, the skilled blue-collar workers often suffered from these changes and the white-collar workers lost the favored economic and social status that they had had before the war. The prewar middle class, of course, fared worst of all, and the relative and absolute position of managerial and professional people generally declined, although with some exceptions. According to a Polish estimate,[7] which places the overall increase in per capita consumption from 1937 (old boundaries) to 1960 at 100–115 percent, the increase in per capita consumption of farm families was more than double that of nonfarm families—125–150 percent compared with 60 percent (the increase resulting from the shift of population from farm to city also is substantial). The increase in nonfarm consumption was due only in part to a rise in real monthly wages (30 percent). Other factors were the near elimination of unemployment, an increase in the number of breadwinners per family and a large increase in moonlighting. Considering that the workweek lengthened and that the above Polish estimates probably have some upward bias (the Polish figure for the percentage increase in total consumption is 25–40 percent above the estimate used in the present study)

7Leszek Zienkowski, *Dochod Narodowy Polski 1937-60* (Warsaw, 1963), pp. 199–201.

it is quite likely that the choice of weights largely determines whether average real wages increased or declined. In any case, real wages, and probably also per capita consumption, of some social groups certainly are still lower than before World War II, and in 1956—the time of the Poznan riot and the near revolution in Warsaw—most groups of older workers had ample reason to believe that they were worse off than before the war.

Although the other Eastern European countries probably experienced less dramatic changes in income distribution than Poland, they also had much smaller increases in average per capita consumption. The net effect on the real incomes of the less privileged groups, in comparison with prewar years, consequently, was probably similar to that in Poland.

V. The Cost of Economic Growth

A low productivity of investment has been the major cause of the lag in the growth of consumption in Eastern Europe. Eastern European countries used a considerably larger proportion of their GNP for investment than Western European countries to achieve similar rates of growth in output. The productivity of investment was lower in Eastern Europe in spite of several favorable factors, including a more rapid increase in industrial employment, a distribution of investments that favored industry at the expense of the more capital-intensive service sectors, and relatively smaller needs for the replacement of fixed assets. A strong case can be made, therefore, for attributing the low productivity of investments in the Eastern countries to the economic policies and institutions that have characterized communism of the Soviet type.

A. Volume and Distribution of Investment

In both Eastern and Western Europe the key factor in postwar economic growth has been the large and rapidly rising level of investments. The share of gross fixed investment in GNP at factor cost increased steadily in nearly all Eastern and Western European countries during the entire postwar period, as shown in Table 13. Typically the Western European shares rose from 20 percent or less in the early 1950's to near 25 percent in the early 1960's, while those in Eastern Europe (excluding East Germany) went from the low 20's to near 30 percent. In East Germany the high priority given to raising consumption during the 1950's and the heavy reparations payments to the U.S.S.R. until about 1957 (see Sec. VI), greatly limited investment, which was low even by Western European standards. Since the ending of reparations, and especially since the raising of the Berlin wall, investments have increased rapidly, becoming a respectable share of GNP.

Much more striking are the differences in the distribution of invest-

TABLE 13
Size and Distribution of Gross Fixed Investment

Country	Years	As a Percent of GNP*				As a Percent of Total Investment†		
		Total invest-ment	Invest-ment in industry‡	Invest-ment in agricul-ture§	Invest-ment in services	Invest-ment in industry	Invest-ment in agricul-ture	Invest-ment in services
Eastern Europe								
Bulgaria	1950–54	23.7	10.6	4.1	9.0	45	17	38
	1955–59	27.7	12.1	7.6	8.0	44	27	29
	1960–63	41.5	19.3	11.2	11.0	47	27	26
Czechoslovakia...	1950–54	23.5	10.6	2.3	10.6	45	10	45
	1955–59	27.3	11.4	4.3	11.6	42	16	42
	1960–63	27.7	12.9	4.4	10.4	46	16	38
East Germany....	1950–54	14.5	5.8	1.8	6.9	40	12	48
	1955–59	19.4	8.3	2.2	8.9	43	11	46
	1960–63	23.6	11.4	2.9	9.3	48	13	39
Hungary	1950–54	25.9	12.2	3.6	10.1	47	14	39
	1955–59	24.2	11.0	3.9	9.3	46	16	38
	1960–63	27.2	12.0	5.3	9.9	44	19	37
Poland..........	1950–54	21.1	9.9	2.0	9.2	47	10	43
	1955–59	25.1	11.0	3.2	10.9	44	13	43
	1960–63	28.1	12.5	3.4	12.2	45	12	43
Western Europe								
Austria	1950–54	20.1	7.2	2.5	10.4	36	12	52
	1955–59	23.1	7.8	3.2	12.1	34	14	52
	1960–63	24.1	....	....	....	....	....	....
Belgium..........	1955–59	17.1	5.5	.8	10.8	32	5	63
	1960–63	19.1	6.7	.6	11.8	35	3	62
Denmark	1950–54	17.2	3.1‖	2.6	11.5	18‖	15	67
	1955–59	18.6	3.2‖	1.9	13.5	17‖	10	73
	1960–63	22.5	4.6‖	2.2	15.7	21‖	10	69
France..........	1950–54	18.1	....	....	....	....	....	....
	1955–59	20.3	7.4 **	1.6 **	11.3 **	36 **	8 **	56 **
	1960–63	21.7	8.5¶	1.3	11.9¶	39¶	6¶	55¶
West Germany ...	1950–54	21.1	7.9	1.3	11.9	38	6	56
	1955–59	24.3	9.2	.9	14.2	38	4	58
	1960–63	26.4	10.3	1.5	14.6	39	6	55
Greece..........	1950–54	15.9	4.3	1.6	10.0	27	10	63
	1955–59	19.2	3.5	2.0	13.7	19	10	71
	1960–63	28.9	....	....	....	....	....	....
Italy	1950–54	19.7	6.8	2.6	10.3	35	13	52
	1955–59	22.4	6.7	2.7	13.0	30	12	58
	1960–63	25.6	8.5	2.6	14.5	33	10	57
Netherlands......	1950–54	21.5	6.9	1.2	13.4	32	5	63
	1955–59	24.4	7.5	1.0	15.9	31	4	65
	1960–63	24.7	7.9	1.0	15.8	32	4	64

*Percent at estimated factor cost in constant prices.
†Distribution at constant market prices.
‡Includes construction.
§Includes forestry.
‖ Excludes construction and handicrafts.
¶Calculated from the distribution in current prices.
**1956–59.

ments. Investment in industry (including construction) and agriculture (including forestry) took a much larger share of total investment in Eastern Europe than in Western Europe; investment in services, a correspondingly much lower share. The Eastern European countries put a remarkably uniform 45 percent of investments into industry and construction, while few of the Western shares, even in the most industrialized countries, approached 40 percent and one (Greece) was as low as 20 percent, less than half that of Bulgaria. The share of agriculture in total investment is much greater in Eastern than in Western Europe not only in absolute terms but also in comparing countries where the relative importance of agriculture in the economy is similar (for example, Bulgaria and Greece; East and West Germany; Czechoslovakia and France). Moreover, in the East the share of agriculture in investment has been rising while the contribution of agriculture to GNP has been falling. In one Eastern European country, Poland, agricultural investments have not been high by Western standards considering the large size of the agricultural sector; but as will be seen later, the exception proves the rule—Poland is the only Eastern country which has not collectivized agriculture.

As a result of the higher share both of total investment in GNP and of industry and agriculture in total investment, investment in these sectors took a much larger share of GNP in the East than in the West, as shown also in Table 13.

The counterpart of the high investment in industry and agriculture in Eastern countries is the low investment in services—transportation, trade, housing, and so forth. Typically, the share of services in total investment has been around 40 percent in the East, compared with 60 percent in the West, although with wide variation among individual Western countries. An adequate breakdown of investment in services is lacking, but it appears that the East invested relatively less than the West both in "tertiary" sectors like transportation and trade and in social overhead like housing.

B. Productivity of Investment

The estimates of the growth of output and of gross fixed investment provide measures of the productivity of investment. In accordance with usual practice, the reciprocal of the productivity of investment—the ratio of gross fixed investment to the increment in output—was used.[8]

[8]For the economy as a whole, these were obtained as the ratios of the percentages of gross fixed investment in GNP at factor cost to the average annual percentage increase in GNP. For the three main sectors of GNP (industry and construction, agriculture and forestry, and services), the ratios are the average shares in GNP of the sector's investment to the rate of growth in the sector's output, the latter being weighted by the average share of the sector's contribution to GNP. For all periods, the increase in output is lagged 1 year behind gross fixed investment—for example, average annual investment in 1950–54 is related to the average rate of growth in output during 1951–55.

We will call this ratio the investment cost ratio (or just investment costs) instead of the more usual, but cumbersome term, incremental capital-output ratio.

The investment cost calculations, the results of which are summarized in Table 14, reveal some important differences between the Eastern and Western European countries. Investment costs in Eastern Europe were higher than in Western Europe—on the average by some 25 percent for the total economy, by 40 percent for industry, and by a great deal in agriculture. Only for services were the ratios similar in the two areas. Very few Western investment ratios exceed those in any of the Eastern countries and the differences between the most comparable countries of the two groups are very large. For example, the Bulgarian ratios exceed those in Greece by 75 percent for the total economy and by more than 100 percent for industry; Czechoslovak investment costs are two-thirds more than those of France for the total economy and more than double the French in industry; Hungarian and Polish overall ratios respectively are only 25 percent

TABLE 14

COMPARATIVE INVESTMENT COSTS, 1951–64

Country	Gross Fixed Investment Per Unit of Increase in Output*			
	GNP	Industry	Agriculture	Services
Bulgaria..............................	5.1	3.8	33.6	4.7
Czechoslovakia.........................	6.7	4.4	40.0	7.8
East Germany†..........................	6.1	3.5	‡	7.2
Hungary	5.3	4.0	9.6	6.1
Poland	5.0	3.4	3.6	9.5
Unweighted average	5.6	3.8	....	7.1
Austria................................	4.3	2.1	7.6	7.1
Belgium†..............................	5.9	4.7	3.6	7.7
Denmark..............................	4.9	1.9	5.5	8.0
France	4.1	2.8	4.5	5.7
West Germany†	4.6	2.9	8.3	8.6
Greece	3.0	1.8	n.a.	5.5
Italy..................................	3.9	2.0	5.3	7.8
Netherlands	5.0	3.2	4.4	6.5
Unweighted average	4.5	2.7	5.6	.7.1

* Increase in output lagged 1 year behind gross fixed investment.
† 1956–64.
‡ Decline in output.

Note: Norway is excluded because its investment statistics have a broader coverage than those of other countries (they include all kinds of repair expenditures).

above those of Austria and Italy, but in industry the difference is 100 percent and two-thirds. Investment costs in agriculture were astronomical in Bulgaria, Czechoslovakia, and East Germany (in the latter country, net agricultural output declined), and were higher in Hungary than in any of the listed countries of Western Europe. However, Poland with its predominantly private agriculture, had a low ratio, even by Western European standards.

Investment costs have tended to be higher in Eastern Europe than in Western Europe during the entire postwar period, but the difference has been growing in recent years, as shown in Table 15. The astronomical

TABLE 15

CHANGES IN INVESTMENT COSTS

Country	Gross Fixed Investment per Unit of Increase in Output*					
	Total economy			Industry		
	1951–55	1956–60	1961–64	1951–55	1956–60	1961–64
Bulgaria.............	4.0	3.8	7.7	4.3	2.6	5.5
Czechoslovakia......	6.5	4.1	25.2	5.1	2.6	12.2
East Germany.......	2.0	4.0	8.7	1.1	2.3	5.0
Hungary	4.7	5.8	6.0	3.8	5.2	3.6
Poland.............	4.4	5.0	5.8	3.2	3.6	3.4
Austria.............	3.3	4.4	5.7	1.8	2.4	....
Belgium............	....	7.4	4.4	....	6.7	2.8
Denmark...........	8.6	3.8	4.4	3.8	1.4	1.7
France	4.1	4.2	4.2	....	2.7	2.8
West Germany	2.3	3.9	5.5	1.3	2.5	3.4
Greece	2.3	3.4	3.3	2.2	1.5	....
Italy	3.3	3.8	4.6	1.7	1.8	2.4
Netherlands.........	3.8	5.9	5.7	2.8	3.2	3.6

* Increase in output lagged 1 year behind gross fixed investment.

cost ratios for Czechoslovakia during 1961–64 reflect the near stagnation of output in the face of a high level of investment, and the ratio in East Germany has become the second highest among the listed European countries, after having been the lowest during the early 1950's when a considerable amount of unused productive capacity still remained because of the delayed recovery from the effects of the war.

C. Factors in Investment Costs

The wide differences in investment costs are the key to a comparative analysis of the determinants of economic growth in Eastern and Western Europe. The remainder of this section will deal with some of the factors that may have caused these differences in investment costs—the growth and distribution of labor inputs; the sectoral and branch distribution of investment; the options and policies regarding replacement of fixed assets; and a number of pertinent institutional factors and policies in industry and agriculture.

1. *Labor inputs.* The overall rate and pattern of growth of employment was similar in the two parts of Europe, as shown in Table 16.[9] In both

TABLE 16

GROWTH OF EMPLOYMENT AND OUTPUT PER EMPLOYEE, 1951–62*

(annual percentage increases)

Country	Employment†			Output per Employee‡		
	Total labor force§	Industry	Agriculture	Total	Industry	Agriculture
Bulgaria	0.5	5.2	− 1.3	5.6	4.7	2.0
Czechoslovakia	1.0	3.1	− 3.2	4.2	3.2	3.7
East Germany.........	0	− .1	− 3.0	5.5	8.4	2.8
Hungary..............	1.2	4.6	− 2.1	3.4	2.8	3.8
Poland...............	1.1	3.5	− .8	3.6	5.1	3.1
Rumania	1.0	3.6	− .2	4.7	5.2	3.9
Unweighted average...	1.0	3.3	− 1.8	4.5	4.9	3.2
Belgium	3	.4	− 3.5	2.8	3.1	6.2
Denmark	1.3	2.0	− 1.6	2.5	2.1	3.2
France ‖	.2	1.1	− 3.5	4.8	4.6	6.5
West Germany........	1.5	3.1	− 3.0	5.6	5.0	4.8
Italy ‖	.7	4.5	− 3.0	4.8	4.1	5.3
Netherlands..........	1.1	1.3	− 1.8	3.4	4.1	3.9
Unweighted average...	.	2.1	− 2.7	4.0	3.8	5.0

* Industry includes construction (except in East Germany and Rumania); agriculture includes forestry.

† 1951–62 unless otherwise specified.

‡ For Total and for Industry, 1951–62 unless otherwise specified; for agriculture, calculated from increases in output from the 1959–53 average to the 1960–63 average.

§ Includes the unemployed and the military.

‖ 1956–62.

SOURCES: Eastern Europe, U.S. Bureau of Census; except for employment in construction. Employment in construction from various statistical yearbooks of individual countries. Western Europe: OECD Manpower Statistics, 1950–1962.

Eastern and Western Europe, the growth of the total labor force was less than one quarter as fast as the growth of output per person, and it is possible that there was no increase at all in the total number of hours worked in several countries. In industry both employment and output per worker in-

[9]Comparable employment statistics are more scarce than comparable production statistics. Those shown in Table 16 cover the 1951–62 period for most countries, but shorter periods for a few countries.

creased faster in the Eastern than in the Western countries, but on the average the difference was greater for employment (two-thirds) than for output per worker (one-third). Agricultural employment declined in all the countries of both areas but on the average the decline was more rapid in the West, and consequently the advantage of the West was greater for output per worker in agriculture than for agricultural output. These averages disguise some wide differences among countries—particularly the contrast between East German growth, which resulted entirely from increased labor productivity, and West German growth, which was supported by the fastest increase in employment among the countries listed. Nevertheless it appears that somewhat less substituting of capital for labor was necessary in most of the Eastern countries than in the Western countries to achieve a given rate of growth in output. A definite judgment on the relative role of labor inputs in Eastern and Western Europe must await a much more thorough study of the use of labor and also of education, training, and other influences on the quality of the labor force. But it is probable that the effect of labor inputs on relative investment costs was at worst neutral, and most probably tended to keep costs in the East lower than those in the West.

2. *Sectoral and branch distribution of investment.* The relatively high investment costs in Eastern Europe clearly are not due to the sectoral distribution of investments. Indeed, the opposite is true—the sectoral distribution of investment in the East was intended to keep, and should have kept, overall investment costs lower than in the West. The reason is evident from Table 14—investment costs are higher in services, into which the Eastern countries put a relatively small share of investments, than in the economy as a whole, and much higher than in industry (almost double in the Eastern countries and two and a half times in the Western countries).

The Eastern countries followed the strategy of maximizing expenditures in the construction of new factories (or major expansion of old factories) by minimizing expenditures on the modernization of railroads, the construction of a modern road network, the expansion of warehouse space, and the satisfaction of consumer demand for housing. This strategy could be sustained for some years because to a point the use of capacity in these services is quite elastic. It was hoped that the extra boost given to industrial production by concentrating investments in industry would be sufficient to allow the backlog of investment demands in services to be made up eventually without strain on the economy. These hopes were disappointed, however. We have seen that agriculture took a large part of investment with little yield (for reasons to be described later), and the expected advantage in industrial production did not materialize because of the relatively low yield of industrial investments. Moreover, the possibilities for squeezing more output from existing capacity in services have been running out and in recent years industrial growth has been hindered with increasing frequency by a lack of freight cars (notably in Czechoslovakia), while great waste of agricultural products has resulted from the lack of storage facilities and adequate farm-to-market roads. In the future, the need to make up for the deficiencies caused by the shortsighted policies of the past probably will raise overall investment costs and hence limit the possible rate of economic growth.

It is unlikely that these conclusions on the effect of the distribution of investment on investment costs would be greatly changed if more detailed comparative data on investment allocations were available. Within industry, the Eastern countries probably put a greater emphasis than the Western countries on some capital-intensive branches, like steel and cement, and less emphasis on some labor-intensive branches, like textiles. On the other hand, chemicals and petroleum refining, which are both highly capital-intensive, probably were developed more intensively in the West.

3. *Replacement and maintenance of fixed assets.* Eastern Europe had another advantage over Western Europe that should have tended to hold down its investment costs—the fact that replacement needs took a smaller part of its gross investment. There are no comparable data on capital stock for Eastern and Western European countries, but it is probable that Eastern countries, being in general less developed, had lower average capital-output ratios than the Western countries both before World War II and in the early postwar years. It is also likely that the average age of capital was somewhat less in the East than in the West because the industrial revolution had started later. For both these reasons a smaller share of GNP is likely to have been needed in the East than in the West to cover replacement needs for capital. Moreover, since investment was a higher share of GNP in the East than in the West, the share of replacement needs in investment would have been smaller even if their share in GNP was the same. Thus it is probably safe to assume that net investment correctly measured—that is, gross investment, less the expenditures required to maintain the productive capacity and efficiency of the existing capital stock—was a considerably larger share of gross investment in Eastern Europe than in Western Europe. This means, of course, that investment costs in the East were relatively even higher measured with net investments than with gross investments.

In practice, the Eastern European countries appear to have tried to maximize the increase in productive capacity by minimizing retirements, relying on repairs to maintain the productivity of existing assets. Again the intention was to hold down investment costs. The few available data on actual retirements of fixed assets indicate that retirement rates in Eastern countries were extremely low. For example, they were less than 1 percent of productive fixed assets per year in Czechoslovakia during most of the 1950's.[10] Actually, this policy probably had the opposite effect from that which was intended—in the end, it probably increased investment costs. Expenditures on repairs, both capital repairs, which are included in the present investment statistics, and current repairs, which are not included, were high but insufficient, leading to frequent breakdowns of equipment (the tractor standing idle for lack of spare parts is as common a scene in Eastern Europe as in the U.S.S.R.), which in turn created unused capacity and caused a loss in efficiency. Moreover, the strong bias against retiring existing assets, long after they had become obsolete, caused some of the most productive investment opportunities to be unused.

4. *Other factors affecting investment costs.* We have seen that the growth of employment, the broad sectoral distribution of investment, and the maintenance and replacement needs for fixed assets all should have helped the Eastern European countries to keep investment costs below those in Western countries. The influence of external factors is discussed in the next section. Here we will consider from an internal point of view the effect of such factors as the introduction and use of new technology, and the planning and management of production.

In general, the relative backwardness of the Eastern European countries should have given them opportunities for a more rapid technological transformation than in Western Europe (such an advantage has often been attributed to the U.S.S.R. relative to the United States). In addition, the relatively larger gross investments and probably much larger net investments in Eastern Europe provided relatively greater means to take advantage of these opportunities. Among Western countries, high shares of investment in GNP usually have been accompanied not only by a rapid growth of GNP but also by low investment costs.[11] Large investment not only can mean a large injection of new technology, but also opportunities for introducing economies of scale in new and old plants. However, the relatively small size of the Eastern European economies tends to limit the possible economies of scale. There could be offsetting opportunities in foreign trade, but these opportunities probably were less favorable in Eastern than in Western Europe.

There is no way of measuring the actual development of technology in Eastern and Western Europe. One gains the impression that new technology in Eastern Europe was inferior to that in Western Europe, partly for lack of effort, partly because of bad planning and management, and

---

[10]K. Novotny, "Vyvoj zakladnich fondu v letech 1948–1957," *Statisticky Obzor,* No. 1, 1959, p. 15.

[11]See, for example, Angus Maddison, *Economic Growth in the West* (New York, 20th Century Fund, 1964), p. 77 and United Nations, Economic Commission for Europe, "Economic Survey of Europe in 1961, pt. 2, "Some Factors in Economic Growth in Europe During the 1950's" ch. II, p. 20.

partly because of lack of access to the best Western and Soviet technology (technology in the Communist bloc was generally inferior to that in the West). Any technological disadvantage for Eastern Europe was bound to have the most serious effects on the industrialized countries, East Germany and Czechoslovakia. But technological lags are by no means the only explanation for the high investment costs in Eastern countries. Bad planning and management were also important, and indeed, contributed to the technological lags.

An important source of inefficiency was the insistence on investing at rates which strained the capacity of the construction and machinery industries. The result was unduly high costs and long periods of construction for new plants[12] and an accumulation of unfinished projects well beyond what is probably usual in the West. The value of unfinished investments in Czechoslovakia, East Germany, and Hungary has amounted to about 1 year's gross fixed investment.[13]

In industry, the bulk of investments went for new plants, often in previously undeveloped sites, leaving insufficient investments for an efficient modernization of existing plants. (We have already discussed a similar bias in regard to replacement.) The main recipients of investments in new plants were of course the least developed industrial branches and those where there was the least flexibility in the utilization of existing capacity. Most basic industrial branches—at first, metallurgy, and later electric power, fuels, chemicals, and construction materials—had a great deal of new plant construction because they were initially relatively less developed than the branches producing finished goods and there was continuously an incipient shortage of industrial materials. Many new branches of the machinery industry also were built. Existing machinery plants and nearly all of light industry, however, received very little investment; their management was always under strong pressure to squeeze more output from existing equipment and what improvements there were entailed the installation of a few new machines, leaving production processes unchanged.

Moreover, new plants in the East often were run at well below full capacity and produced at high unit cost for a long time after they had been commissioned.[14] This was probably due partly to inexperience, at least in the less industrialized Eastern countries, but the principal cause was certainly poor planning of the plants and poor coordination of the construction of complementary facilities and of supplies and components.

[12]See, for example, Andrzej Karpinski *Zagadnienia socjalistycznej industrializacji Polski* (Warsaw, 1958), pp. 89–92.

[13]United Nations, Economic Commission for Europe, "Economic Survey of Europe," 1962, pt. 1, pp. I, 20–23.

[14]According to Karpinski, op. cit., pp. 206–216, in 1955 nearly all the major industrial plants built during 1949–55 in Poland produced for some time at higher unit costs than the old plants, in spite of considerably greater capitalization and an advantage in technology.

There are also plenty of indications that bad management led both to unused capacity—for example, the well-known "storing" of foundry capacity by machinery plants to protect themselves against possible shortages of parts—and to unnecessarily high costs of production, which in turn held down the possibilities for increasing output. The institutional roots of such problems are well known; they will be taken up briefly in the concluding section.

The principal cause of the extremely high investment costs in agriculture already has been mentioned. The collectivization of agriculture, and before that the threat of collectivization and the discrimination against private farmers increased the demand for investment while they held down the growth of agricultural output. Collectivization increased the demand for investment in several ways: by creating a need for common livestock shelters and other "overhead" expenditures which do not necessarily raise production; by hastening the flight of labor from agriculture and hence the need for machinery to replace the labor; by tending to reduce the effective input of the remaining farmworkers, at least those who work on collective land and livestock, and so again increasing the need for mechanization. At the same time collectivization tended to depress output because of reduced incentives for farmers to work hard, carefully, and skillfully. Complaints are often heard from Eastern Europe that mechanization and other farm investments were inadequate. This inadequacy, however, is largely a reflection of the inefficiency of agricultural institutions in using available capital.

Inefficiency in the system of economic planning and management in Eastern Europe has been prevalent during the entire postwar period and was probably worse during the early 1950's than today. Recently, however, it has been more apparent because it has become more of an obstacle to economic growth. Until around 1960, although plans for the cost of investment projects, the growth of labor productivity, and the reduction of unit costs of production were rarely fulfilled, production goals nevertheless were often achieved by mobilizing so-called hidden reserves.

There were many such reserves; mobilizing labor from the farm and the kitchen for use in industry; keeping obsolete equipment in production; making increased use of existing productive capacity in railroads, warehouses, and plants in low priority industries; and taking advantage of easy opportunities for the rationalization of production after industry had been nationalized. The Government's ability to pass on the burden of inefficiency to the consumer, was another kind of "hidden reserve," for investment could be raised rapidly enough to generate high rates of growth in output in spite of high investment costs. Among the burdens passed to the consumer were the poor quality, assortment, and design of consumer goods. When increased consumer resistance and increased strain in the supply of raw materials were manifested during the mid-1950's, most of the Governments had to temporarily lower or stabilize the share of investment in GNP, raise consumption and concentrate on straightening out the "disproportions" which had developed in the economy. New intensive investment drives were launched during the late 1950's, however, causing "reserves" once again to be used up at a rapid rate, and these drives were to continue during the early 1960's. Collectivization of agriculture, which accelerated between 1958 and 1961, made matters worse. By about 1960 the reserves had nearly run out in the more industrialized countries, East Germany and Czechoslovakia. Agriculture had run short of labor, most housewives were already working, the strain on the railroad system had become excessive, and in many branches of the machinery and light industries equipment and processes were too obsolete to produce in accordance with modern technical specifications. At the same time, both domestic and foreign customers were becoming increasingly discriminating and large inventories of unsalable goods accumulated. With the lack of production reserves and the greatly reduced possibilities for dumping low-quality products on domestic or foreign consumers, the inefficiency of the system of planning and management was bound to force a sharp slowdown in economic growth.

VI. External Factors

The foregoing analysis indicates that economic performance in Eastern Europe was decidedly inferior to that in Western Europe. Production grew no more rapidly in the East than in the West; consumption increased much more slowly; and by all indications, economic growth was achieved less efficiently. It remains to be seen to what extent the East's inferiority in performance can be attributed to external disadvantages, for example, to Soviet impositions in contrast to U. S. aid, less favorable price terms, or more limited access to foreign goods and technology. We will deal first with quantifiable aspects of external economic relations—comparative trends in the volume of imports; foreign aid and impositions; and the terms of trade—and then evaluate the effects of these factors on economic performance and consider also nonquantifiable factors, such as the broad foreign economic environment.

A. *Statistical Evidence*

1. *Trends in the volume of imports.* Except in East Germany, trends in the volume of imports were at least as favorable to economic growth in Eastern Europe as in Western Europe. Imports grew very rapidly in both areas, as shown in Table 17. Until the early 1960's annual rates of growth in the volume of imports (that is, the value of imports in constant prices) were in excess of 10 percent in nearly all the Eastern European countries,

TABLE 17

GROWTH OF IMPORTS IN CONSTANT PRICES

Country	Indexes: 1955 = 100				
	Prewar*	1950	1955	1960	1964
Bulgaria	58	73	100	262	447
Czechoslovakia	58	64	100	189	258
East Germany	†371˙	37	100	194	233
Hungary	47	58	100	187	291
Poland	38	72	100	164	233
Rumania	48	54	100	148	272
Total above	137	59	100	185	262
(Excluding East Germany)	49	65	100	......	......
Austria	60	61	100	167	233
Belgium‡	66	75	100	141	207
Denmark	§	80	100	155	222
France	73	73	100	143	229
West Germany	†78	47	100	146	214
Italy	46	64	100	199	297
Netherlands	59	72	100	146	211
Norway	65	71	100	143	194
Total above	§	64	100	152	224

*East Germany and West Germany, 1936; Poland and Czechoslovakia, 1937; Bulgaria, 1939; all other countries, 1938.
†Includes interregional trade between East Germany and West Germany.
‡Includes Luxembourg.
§Not available.

and for the most part were below 10 percent in Western Europe. During the early 1960's the growth of imports has slowed in Eastern Europe and accelerated in Western Europe. The post-1950 expansion began from levels which were already above those of the late 1930's in all the countries covered, except East and West Germany. The exception for the two Germanys is due to the inclusion of estimates of interzonal trade in the prewar statistics. Interzonal trade had been far more important to East Germany than to West Germany, a factor which largely explains why the volume of imports in 1950 was only about 10 percent of that of 1936 in East Germany, while it was 60 percent in West Germany.

In nearly all of Europe imports grew much more rapidly than GNP, as shown in Table 18. Traditionally, dependence on imports had been greater in Western Europe than in Eastern Europe, largely because most of the Western countries were more industrialized. The prewar ratios of imports in GNP had been surpassed by 1950 in all of Eastern Europe, except East Germany, but had not been in Western Europe, except in Italy and West Germany. Since 1950 the ratio of imports to GNP has risen steadily in every country and the difference between Western Europe and Eastern Europe has narrowed further. By 1964 the smaller Eastern Euro-

TABLE 18

RELATION OF IMPORTS TO PRODUCTION

Country	Imports as a Percent of GNP (from values in constant 1963 dollars)					Import Index as a Percent of Industrial Production Index— 1955 = 100			
	Prewar	1950	1955	1960	1964	Prewar	1950	1960	1964
Bulgaria............	8	9	9	17	24	146	109	143	178
Czechoslovakia.....	6	6	8	12	15	84	80	122	155
East Germany	*37	4	8	13	14	*464	63	137	141
Hungary	5	6	8	13	17	82	90	143	163
Poland	3	6	6	8	10	72	114	111	119
Rumania	4	5	6	8	12	98	78	96	112
Austria............	15	12	15	20	23	127	89	125	147
Belgium†..........	25	23	25	32	40	106	94	129	149
Denmark..........	‡	19	21	26	30	‡	88	119	132
France	9	7	8	9	12	113	93	109	138
West Germany	*18	8	12	12	15	*153	83	106	125
Italy	5	7	8	12	15	96	105	133	149
Netherlands	31	26	30	36	44	115	97	112	133
Norway	25	20	24	29	33	130	87	125	137

*Includes interregional trade between East and West Germany.
†Includes Luxembourg in imports.
‡Not available.

Note—Prewar imports are in prewar boundaries while prewar GNP and industrial production are in postwar boundaries for Bulgaria, Czechoslovakia and Rumania. In comparable boundaries the prewar ratios of imports to GNP and industrial production should be somewhat higher than in the table in Bulgaria, slightly lower in Czechoslovakia, and considerably lower in Rumania.

pean countries (Bulgaria and Hungary) had achieved higher import ratios than the larger Western European countries and much higher ratios than before World War II. The Bulgarian experience is especially noteworthy, the import ratio having increased from 9 to 24 percent in less than a decade. The Polish and Rumanian ratios, however, continue to be much lower than those in Western Europe—a reflection of the relatively rich resources of these countries in relation to their degree of industrialization. The contrast between East and West Germany remains striking— the ratio of imports to GNP is only one-quarter of the prewar ratio in East Germany while it has almost recovered to the prewar level in West Germany.

Imports grew not only in relation to GNP, but also in relation to industrial production in all the listed countries, except the two Germanies, as also shown in Table 18. Industrial production recovered from the war faster than did imports in most countries of both areas, but then lagged behind imports during the post-1950 expansion. Surprisingly, imports in the Eastern countries, except Poland, rose faster than industrial production even between 1950 and 1955, a period when all of the countries were try-

ing to become more self-sufficient. Apparently, rapid and broad industrialization created a derived demand for imports so large that it swamped the
effects of import substitution.

2. *Foreign aid and impositions.* Unquestionably the postwar balance
on economic aid and impositions has been highly unfavorable to Eastern
Europe and highly favorable to Western Europe. The Eastern European
countries had to make large net payments to the U.S.S.R. for reparations
and other reasons and these net payments were concentrated in the early
postwar years, when they were most burdensome. By contrast Western
Europe was a large net recipient of U. S. aid and most of this aid was obtained early, when it was most needed. The following discussion of
foreign aid and impositions and of international capital movements will
treat these complex subjects only in very general terms, for a detailed
treatment would require a number of specialized studies.

No reliable estimate exists of Soviet takings from Eastern Europe, but
an order of magnitude of $15 to $20 billion in postwar prices probably is
reasonable to cover dismantlings, reparations, and occupation costs. The
bulk of this amount (probably some $10 to $15 billion) was taken from
East Germany between World War II and the mid-1950's (10 to 15 percent
of East German GNP). Another half billion dollars at least is accounted for
by deliveries of coal by Poland to the U.S.S.R. at nominal prices. Soviet
removals of fixed assets and current production on reparations account
from Hungary and Rumania also were substantial, although much smaller
than those from East Germany. There were also Soviet takings from the
jointly owned but Soviet-controlled companies in Hungary, Rumania, and
Bulgaria. The great bulk of all these Soviet impositions came between
World War II and 1953, and the burden on the Eastern European economies probably declined steadily over this period. In comparison with
Soviet impositions, Soviet economic aid to Eastern Europe (which was
entirely in the form of credits, although repayment obligations for some
of these were waived), was small—in the order of $4 billion, not much over
1 billion of which was extended before 1956. For its part, Eastern Europe
extended some $2 billion in credit to non-Communist developing countries,
all after 1955, and about $1 billion to other Communist countries.

The large unrequited Eastern European exports to the U.S.S.R. make
a striking contrast with the even larger net receipt of U.S. aid by Western
Europe. Total U.S. economic aid to the nine Western European countries
treated in this paper came to nearly $19 billion for 1946–64 (excluding
UNRRA aid), $16 billion of which had been disbursed by the end of 1962.
(The United States also extended one half billion dollars of aid to Eastern
Europe, consisting mainly of Public Law 480 credits to Poland after 1956.)
For the 1946–52 period, U.S. economic aid on the average amounted to
some 2 percent annually of the combined GNP's of the nine Western

European countries (about the average proportion for France, West Germany, and Italy; a considerably larger proportion for Greece and Austria; and smaller proportions for the other countries). These figures exclude some $13 billion of U.S. military aid, which was disbursed mainly after 1952. They also exclude private long-term U.S. investments in Western Europe, which have exceeded the flow of official and private aid from the Western European countries to the developing countries. Both U.S. private investments in Western Europe and Western European aid to developing countries have become important only since the mid-1950's.

To conclude, the balance of aid, impositions and credits was highly unfavorable to Eastern Europe for the postwar period as a whole, but the disadvantage for Eastern Europe (and the advantage for Western Europe) was concentrated in the early postwar years. Since the mid-1950's, both Eastern and Western Europe appear to have been net importers of long-term capital.

3. *The net terms of trade.* Rough estimates of trends in the "net terms of trade" (the ratio of the export price index to the import price index) are shown in Table 19 for Bulgaria, Czechoslovakia, Poland, these three countries combined, and, by way of comparison, the EEC countries. The move-

TABLE 19

NET TERMS OF TRADE*

Country	Indexes: 1964 equals 100				
	Prewar	1950	1955	1960	1964
Bulgaria	168	....	111	99	100
Czechoslovakia	102	109	95	98	100
Poland	70	78	97	95	100
Above countries together	95	87	98	97	100
EEC Countries	96	87	89	96	100

*Ratio of export price index to import price index.

ment of the "net terms of trade" is nearly the same for the two groups of countries, except that the changes were more favorable to the Eastern group between 1950 and 1955 and more favorable to the Western group between 1955 and 1960. But there were wide differences in trends among Eastern countries. Czechoslovakia suffered a marked worsening in its net terms of trade in the early 1950's, which it has not yet made up, while Poland's terms of trade improved substantially from prewar years to 1950 and again from 1950 to 1955. These opposite trends between 1950 and 1955 may have been due to the stabilization of prices in intrabloc trade at levels which favored primary producers, like Poland, but hurt importers of foods and industrial materials, like Czechoslovakia. In addition, there was a strong European market for coal, Poland's principal export of the early 1950's. The drastic fluctuations of Bulgaria's terms of trade appear to be due mainly to price fluctuations for tobacco, until recently Bulgaria's predominant export. There is no information on the terms of trade of the other Eastern European countries—the combined price indexes for Bulgaria, Czechoslovakia and Poland were used to calculate price and quantum indexes in Hungary and Rumania. But although the information is very spotty, it appears to indicate that trends in the terms of trade in the East were not greatly different from those in the West.

These findings on trends in the net terms of trade appear to be consistent with evidence on the pricing of Eastern European trade with the U.S.S.R. and the West, which can be summarized as follows:

1. Soviet foreign trade statistics show that the U.S.S.R. charges Eastern Europe higher prices and pays Eastern Europe lower prices than it charges and pays for the same commodities in its trade with Western Europe.[15] The evidence is convincing for Soviet exports, which consist mainly of materials and foods with fairly definite prices, but much less so for Soviet imports because most of these consist of manufactures, for which meaningful price data are lacking.

2. Eastern European trade statistics show that the Eastern European countries obtain higher prices from the U.S.S.R. (and each other) than from the West for their exports of the same commodities. Comparisons of import prices are inconclusive. Corroborating evidence comes from Western trade statistics, which seems to indicate that Western countries pay the Eastern European countries less for the same goods than in their trade with other Western countries.[16] It would appear, then, that 1) the U.S.S.R. has better terms of trade with Eastern Europe than with the West; and 2) that Eastern European countries also have better terms of trade with the U.S.S.R. (and each other) than with the West. In other words, Eastern Europe appears to be discriminated against, on the one hand by the U.S.S.R. and on the other by Western Europe. There is nothing inherently inconsistent about this. A plausible explanation is that pricing in intrabloc trade actually was based, as Soviet and Eastern European sources often state, on world market prices—that is the actual prices used in world commodity markets or in contracts between large Western

[15]Horst Mendershausen, "Terms of Trade Between the Soviet Union and Smaller Communist Countries, 1955–57," "The Review of Economics and Statistics," No. 2, May 1959. "The Terms of Soviet-Satellite Trade: A Broadened Analysis." ibid., May 1960.

[16]Franklyn Holzman, "Soviet Foreign Trade Pricing and the Question of Discrimination," "Review of Economics and Statistics," May 1962. "More on Soviet Bloc Trade Discrimination," "Soviet Studies," July 1965. Frederic Pryor, "The Communist Foreign Trade System" (Cambridge, Mass., 1963), ch. V.

firms. The prices obtained in the West by the Eastern European countries were usually much less favorable to these countries than the "world market prices." This is especially true of Eastern European manufactured goods, which suffer in world markets from tariff barriers, lack of publicity, reliable trade contacts and adequate servicing facilities, and from inflexibility in the planning and management of foreign trade. Exports of raw materials and foods fare better, but even these tend to receive lower prices than average because they are often sold in small lots and at the wrong time. The basing of prices in intrabloc trade on actual world market prices (with many modifications, including a tendency to stabilize the prices of raw materials for a number of years) would tend to create similar trends in the terms of trade as in Western Europe. This, as we have seen, is what the statistics appear to show.

B. Evaluation

What conclusions can be drawn from the statistical analysis as to the relative influence of external factors on the economic development of Eastern and Western Europe? It seems certain that Soviet impositions in the early postwar years and the unwillingness or inability of the Soviet Union to make up for the loss of interzonal trade had a great deal to do with the severe lag of the East German economy behind that of West Germany. The enormous structural adjustments forced upon an economy whose imports in 1950 were only about 10 percent of the prewar level can be imagined. East Germany had to develop a substantial steel industry, production of nearly all types of heavy machinery and transportation equipment, and many other industrial branches. Some of this forced structural change was bound to involve a loss of efficiency in the allocation of resources—certainly initially, and probably also in the long run. In addition the lack of imported materials for many years held down the utilization of existing plant capacity and the growth of labor productivity. This massive readjustment had to take place simultaneously with an outflow of uncompensated exports to the U.S.S.R. that cut deeply into investment possibilities. Economic recovery from the effects of the war had hardly begun in 1950 and during the early 1950's, with the U.S.S.R. taking 10 to 15 percent of GNP and with heavy pressure to improve living conditions rapidly, East Germany could not undertake a large investment program. As was shown earlier, investments reached a respectable share of GNP in East Germany only in the late 1950's, after reparations had ceased. By contrast, West Germany adjusted very easily to its separation from East Germany because interzonal trade had been a much smaller part of West German than of East German trade, the West German economy was much larger and more balanced, and there were broader trade opportunities abroad and larger receipts of U.S. aid.

The evidence that measurable external factors were seriously disadvantageous is far less clear for the other Eastern European countries than for East Germany. The quantitative growth of imports was certainly more than adequate to sustain a rapid growth of output. Changes in the net terms of trade appear to have been generally similar in Eastern and Western Europe. In the early postwar years Hungary and Rumania paid substantial reparations, and the other Eastern European countries, unlike the Western European countries, were not net recipients of aid, but since 1955 the Eastern European disadvantage in this regard probably has been small.

To conclude, the measurable factors probably account fully for the severe lag in East German growth until the mid-1950's. It is reasonable to suppose that they were largely responsible also for the lags of most other Eastern European countries behind Western Europe during the early postwar years of economic recovery and growth. Hungary and Rumania, the two countries which, after East Germany, were probably most affected by Soviet impositions, were the latest to regain prewar levels. After Poland and both parts of Germany these countries also suffered the most war damage. Except in East Germany, where Soviet impositions affected mainly investment, the main impact of these impositions (or the lack of aid) probably was on consumption. But these external factors do not explain the decline in rates of growth in recent years nor the high investment costs in all the Eastern European countries during the postwar period.

The preceding analysis, since it deals only with measurable external factors, leaves out a highly important difference between Eastern and Western Europe—the general foreign economic environment. This difference, however, is both external and internal, and it is most appropriately treated as an aspect of the broad institutional and policy framework of the two areas. Membership in the Soviet bloc entailed among other things the adoption of Soviet-type economic policies and institutions and it is pointless to speculate about the extent to which Soviet pressure or the willing emulation of things Soviet by local Communist parties were responsible.

The application of Soviet-type policies and institutions in Eastern Europe had interrelated effects on the domestic use of resources and on foreign trade opportunities. Trade opportunities were to some extent limited by Western controls, but Soviet and Eastern European policies were much more important limitations.

For the individual Eastern European country, materials, foods, and machinery were almost always in short supply—they could rarely be imported in the desired quantities and qualities. Consequently it was necessary to develop high-cost mineral resources, raise expenditures in agricul ture to the point of small return, and overdiversify manufacturing production. Shortages of industrial materials were especially severe in the early and mid-1950's. In recent years availability of foodstuffs and technology have been increasing problems. Inability to import the most advanced or appropriate technology kept labor costs and often also investment costs higher than they might have been. This disadvantage was especially burdensome for the more developed countries, East Germany and Czechoslovakia, which depended on advanced technology to maintain their lead in productivity. Moreover, the cost of doing without first-rate technology has increased in recent years as East Germany and Czechoslovakia have exhausted the opportunities for tapping "reserves" of unused productive capacity and labor and as all of the Eastern European countries have faced more exacting customers abroad.

Some of the overdiversification and development of high-cost production during the early 1950's can be traced to a form of Soviet exploitation— the levying of requirements on Eastern Europe for a wide variety of machines and other goods, without regard for prior experience, factor endowments, or economies of scale. East Germany and Czechoslovakia suffered most from such Soviet policies. Since the mid-1950's, however, the U.S.S.R. has greatly increased its support for Eastern European economic development. The Soviet share of Eastern Europe's total imports has remained at about 40 percent since 1950, but since 1955 the U.S.S.R. has supplied a growing share of Eastern European imports of industrial materials, some of which it produced at high marginal cost, and has provided considerable amounts of grain in spite of domestic shortages. Moreover, the U.S.S.R. has tried, although with little success, to bring about a more rational allocation of resources in Eastern Europe through intrabloc coordination of economic plans and specialization in production, thereby reversing previous policies.

At least since the mid-1950's, the external difficulties of the Eastern European countries appear to be largely symptoms of ailments which have affected all Communist countries. Shortages of materials were caused by excessively rapid increases in production of finished goods, by lack of coordination of national investment programs, and by inefficiency in the use of materials. Shortages of foods were due mainly to collectivization and to other policies depressing farmers' incentives. Lagging technology was the result of a system of economic incentives which rewarded increased production at any cost and penalized innovation and careful consideration of customers' interests. Uncertainty in deliveries of imported goods and components and the lack of flexibility in adapting import schedules to changing domestic needs reflected the general rigidity of management in foreign trade as well as the domestic economy.

VII. Internal and External Policies

One after the other, the Eastern European regimes have become aware of the poor performance of their economies, and have been groping for more effective economic policies and more efficient forms of planning and management. The revolution in Hungary and the near revolt in Poland in 1956 brought home the necessity for change to the regimes of these countries earlier than to those of the other Eastern European countries. Although the consumer-oriented priorities adopted at the time in both countries and the partial decentralization of management in Poland were short lived, economic policies have been much more moderate and flexible since 1956 than before, and this early adjustment to realities is one of the reasons why the rate of growth of the Polish and Hungarian economies has not declined. The Czechoslovak and East German regimes, however, in spite of rapidly declining economic "reserves," tried to maintain or accelerate economic growth, relying heavily on Communist Party activists to create the necessary stimulus, and in 1959–60 the Bulgarian regime went so far as to try a "great leap" somewhat on the Chinese model. It was the sharp slowdown of economic growth in East Germany in 1961, in Czechoslovakia in 1962, and in Bulgaria in the aftermath of the "great leap" of 1959–60, that brought home the need for economic reform in these countries and this example has created new pressure for reform in Poland and Hungary. Only Rumania, which has achieved increased rates of industrial growth since 1958, has been generally satisfied with the old system of economic planning and management.

Improvements in economic performance have been sought both through internal economic reform and through external assistance and international economic cooperation.

FLUCTUATIONS AND TREND IN THE RATE OF ECONOMIC GROWTH IN SOME SOCIALIST COUNTRIES*

— · — · — · — · — · — · — · — · — · — · —

Josef Goldmann†

In this paper an attempt is made quantitatively to analyse the economic effects of the traditional system of economic planning and management in a period of transition from "extensive" to "intensive" development.

The guiding idea of the research, reported upon below, is as follows: The traditional system was adequate to conditions of "extensive" development and speedy industrialization under which it originated in the Soviet

*Reprinted by permission from *Economics of Planning*, Vol. 4, No. 2 (1964), pp. 88–98.

†Dr. Josef Goldmann is Economist with the Economic Institute, Academy of Sciences, Prague, Czechoslovakia.

Union. Given the major objectives of economic policy—dictated by the Soviet Union's international isolation and economic backwardness at that time—and taking into account its ample resources both natural and man-power—maximization of output rather than minimization of input had to become the overriding consideration.

To some extent analogous conditions—including under-use of output-capacity, some free or potential man-power resources, and the internal impact of acute international tension—prevailed in Czechoslovakia, Poland, Hungary and the GDR at the time when economic planning was fully introduced in these countries about 1950. To the extent, however, that the possibilities of further "extensive" growth became exhausted, and changing conditions rendered the need for such growth less and less imperative, the necessity arose of changing over to "intensive" development. A conflict developed between the given system of economic planning and management on the one hand and the economic conditions under which it is supposed to function, on the other.

The higher the level of economic development already attained, and the more complex the process of extended socialist reproduction, the more outdated, necessarily will become the traditional system with its detailed output targets, centrally determined and compulsorily imposed, and its corresponding technique of factor allocation. It is a well-known fact that the traditional system makes possible and even induces "spurious" production of goods that are not in demand, excessive growth of stocks and uncompleted construction, and fails to secure minimization of factor input or to stimulate technical advance, thus inducing what has come to be known in Czechoslovakia as "extensive" growth.

Planners are increasingly coming to the conclusion that it would be wrong to take the centralized model as the only one that corresponds to the requirements of planned control of a socialist economy, while the de-centralized model, giving greater scope to the play of market forces, would be conceived as a retreat to the methods of capitalism. Refuting ideas about the alleged incompatibility of the plan and the market, it might be useful to go back to the arguments and results of those economic discussions in the Soviet Union of the twenties, which to the detriment of economic theory and practice were brought to an abrupt close by the so-called cult of personality.

Analysis of the dynamics of industrial production and investment activity in Czechoslovakia, Poland, the GDR and Hungary supplies the following results:

1. The rate of growth of industrial production shows relatively regular fluctuations, with maximum increments of output in the years 1951–1952 and 1959–1960, and minimum increments in the years 1953–1955 and 1961–1963. In 1963 there actually was a fall in industrial production in

TABLE 1

RATE OF GROWTH OF INDUSTRIAL OUTPUT
IN CZECHOSLOVAKIA, GDR, POLAND AND HUNGARY
(Annual Increments, Per Cent)

	1950	1951	1952	1953	1954	1955	1956	1957
Czechoslovakia	14,5	14,7	16,7	8,7	4,0	11,5	9,5	9,4
GDR	28,5	22,4	15,6	12,4	11,0	8,1	6,0	7,9
Poland	28,3	22,1	18,0	19,0	11,1	10,2	8,8	10,0
Hungary	28,8	25,8	23,3	11,1	5,0	9,4	−9,2	11,6

	1958	1959	1960	1961	1962	1963	1964 plan
Czechoslovakia	10,3	10,8	11,9	8,9	6,2	−0,4	3,6
GDR	11,0	12,0	8,4	6,6	5,5	5	5
Poland	9,4	8,6	10,7	9,8	8,2	5	6,3
Hungary	10,9	11,9	12,6	11,1	7,9	7	7

Czechoslovakia (see Table 1). These fluctuations are still more pronounced if the analysis is confined to producers goods (see Table 2).

2. In the period investigated, fluctuations in investment activity are even greater than those in the rate of growth of industrial output. Both, inter-country synchronization and the amplitude of oscillation are rather striking. (See Figure 1.)

TABLE 2

RATE OF GROWTH OF INDUSTRIAL OUTPUT IN CZECHOSLOVAKIA AND POLAND,
FOR PRODUCES (A) AND FOR CONSUMERS' GOODS (B)

		1950	1951	1952	1953	1954	1955	1956	1957
Czechoslovakia—	"A"	16,0	18,0	24,2	12,3	3,7	8,8	10,9	9,9
	"B"	15,0	9,2	11,2	4,4	5,4	13,1	8,1	10,3
Poland	—"A"	27,0	25,0	22,4	19,6	13,1	11,1	10,9	7,8
	"B"	25	19,0	14,3	15,4	9,6	11,6	7,3	12,1

		1958	1959	1960	1961	1962	1963	1964 plan
Czechoslovakia—	"A"	11,5	13,2	13,0	9,2	7,3	−0,4	5,7*
	"B"	10,9	7,6	9,9	8,3	4,7	−0,4	2,9†
Poland	—"A"	8,7	13,4	13,6	11,7	9,9	7	7
	"B"	10,8	5,1	8,2	8,2	6,3	1,6	5,7

* "Basic" branches of industry
† Manufacturing industries

FIGURE 1

Rate of Growth of Investment in Czechoslovakia , Poland
and Hungary, 1950—1964

[Annual increments, per cent, real prices (except for Hungary)]

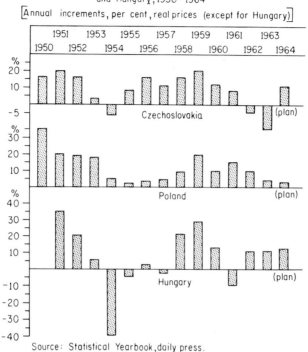

Source: Statistical Yearbook, daily press.

FIGURE 2

Long-Run Decline in the Rate of Growth

(moving averages on a seven-year base)

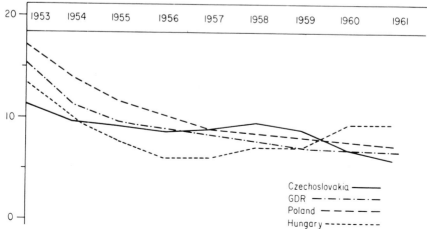

3. Taking the period under review as a whole, a slight falling trend in the rate of growth of industrial output is observed. (See Figure 2, based on 7-year sliding averages.)

The share of industry in the formation of national income (64, 52, 64 and 60 per cent, respectively, in the order of countries given above) and the significance of foreign trade were taken as the criteria for selection of the four countries mentioned. Comparable data on the share of industry in national income for the Soviet Union, Rumania and Yugoslavia are 63, 46 and 47 per cent, leaving aside the problems of the somewhat specific price structure common to all the countries concerned.

I. Fluctuations

Rapid development in the early fifties was due to the socialization of the means of production and the transition to economic planning, releasing considerable reserves of output capacity, man-power, and labour productivity. These, of course, were factors operating once-for-all; the mechanism of fluctuations in the growth rate may be described as follows.

As shown by Professor Michal Kalecki, in a relatively small, industrially developed socialist country there is a tendency for the raw material base to lag behind the growth of manufacturing industries whenever the rate of growth exceeds a certain optimum level (given the traditional methods of economic planning and management). Such development is due to a tendency for underfulfilment of production (and investment) plans in the extracting and basic materials industries and for overfulfilment of such plans in the higher-stage manufacturing industries, resulting in the formation of what has come to be known as the raw-material barrier.

This in turn will bring about additional inbalances in the foreign trade balance. The foreign trade barrier, likewise, is bound to slow down economic growth, particularly in a relatively small country with limited domestic raw-material resources.

In the given context, agriculture is playing a similar role as the basic industries mentioned above, in view of the economic and social factors making for slow growth in this industry. Thus, the relatively slow development of agriculture will cause additional strain and disproportions whenever the overall growth rate exceeds the optimum level. (The term optimum rate is used here to stand for the maximum rate that can be sustained under given conditions, including resources available, degree of proportionality at the given phase, social and institutional factors, etc.)

The loss of proportionality, ensuing from a rate of growth in excess of the optimum level, will be intensified in its results by the well-known effect of overinvestment, induced or necessitated by the selected rate of growth. Overinvestment, consequently, is not an independent cause of the decline in the rate of growth, but one of the factors accompanying excessive growth.

The disproportions and acute economic difficulties, ensuing from an above-optimum rate of growth, can only be overcome by slowing down the pace of economic development. This breathing period will continue until new investment projects, initiated in the preceding period, predominantly in the "basic" industries, will successively mature and go into operation. As a result of both, the slow-down in growth and the contribution of new output facilities, the supply situation will gradually improve. Thus, conditions will be set up which—through a certain voluntarism inherent in the traditional system—will permit such a quasi-cycle to restart again.

Historically, the fluctuations in the growth rate in the four countries under review developed as follows: The success in the period of postwar reconstruction, of economic planning as it was initially conceived, and the gradual release of large output and labour-productivity reserves in those years, in conjunction with the deterioration of the international situation, resulted in 1950–1951 in the revision of current plans (or plan projects). This led to a considerable rise in the rate of economic growth far beyond the optimum level. The economic difficulties and disproportions, following from such development, could not be overcome but by remarkable cut in the rate of growth and in the volume of investment (1953–1954). The radical economic measures of that period were not so much due to political changes; they were, in fact, the unavoidable outcome of the preceding economic development. Making possible the solution of the disproportions inherited from the preceding period, they simultaneously set up the indispensable preconditions for the implementation of the "New Deal" after Stalin's death.

Following a gradual recovery beginning from 1954, a new period of very rapid development started about 1958. At that time many investment projects, initiated in the early fifties, particularly in the 'basic' industries, were successively completed and put into full operation, (see Table 3), playing a decisive part in overcoming or substantially alleviating the economic disproportions that had brought about the fall in the rate of growth in 1953 and 1954. All available data show that 1958, similarly as the years 1950–1951, was one of the most successful years in the history of economic planning. However, these objective conditions, in conjunction with certain subjectiviste tendencies inherent in the traditional model of economic planning and management, gave rise to a new wave of industrialization and a new investment drive, culminating about 1959–1960. For reasons mentioned above, such development necessarily caused—or aggravated—disproportions, such as already once before had made their appearance in 1953–1954, and induced a similar, though far steeper decline in the rate of growth of industrial production in the period 1961–1963. While in Czecho-

TABLE 3
INVESTMENT PROJECTS, COMPLETED IN CZECHOSLOVAKIA, 1948–1963

	Unit	1948–1955 Yearly average	1950–1955 Yearly average	1956	1957	1958	1959	1960	1961	1962	1963
Thermal power stations	MW	145		155	196	245	556	342	300	241	456
Coal mines (deep and open cast) Hard coal	1000 t.	890		1509	90	75	400	2055	1461	—	1209
Brown coal	"	1140		660	2360	3830	1960	3210	2660	4830	310
Blast furnaces	"	215		—	—	450	—	505	—	550	—
Open-hearth furnaces	"	135		—	—	690	300	690	—	400	300
New basic assets in industry (million Kčs, 1962 prices)			7,2	8,2	10,6	10,8	15,9	15,8	15,7	17,1	17,9

SOURCE: *Statistical Yearbook of Czechoslovakia,* 1962, p. 138; 1963, p. 141; 1964, p. 147.

slovakia there even was a fall in output in the latter year, a turning point seems to have been reached already in Hungary and some consolidation is apparently taking place in the other three countries.

As to the interrelations between objective and subjective factors in the genesis of quasi-cyclical movement in the rate of growth, the following conclusion may be drawn from the analysis given above: Deceleration is objectively unavoidable. Disproportions, once they have been allowed to develop rather far, in a planning system, reacting only indirectly and with some time-lag to market signals, cannot be overcome otherwise than by reducing the rate of growth.

Things are more complicated as far as acceleration is concerned. Certain subjectiviste, voluntaristic tendencies towards maximizing the rate of growth assert themselves continuously. However, it is only under conditions as prevailed about 1950 or 1959 (conditions such as in the latter year may re-occur cyclically), that voluntarism in planning has an exceptionally wide field of action. The process of acceleration, though ensuing from subjective—and subjectiviste—decision-making, nevertheless has its specific objective foundation.

The fluctuations in the rate of growth, analysed above, obviously differ in principle from cyclical development under capitalism. While a fall in output is quite exceptional under socialism, it occurs more or less regularly in capitalist countries, at least in the most developed ones. Moreover, the trade cycle follows necessarily from the very essence of the capitalist system and can only be mitigated by State intervention. On the other hand, fluctuations in the rate of growth are not inherent to the socialist order, but ensue from insufficient knowledge of the economic laws of socialism and from shortcomings in their application. Selection of optimum rates of growth (coupled with a thorough overhaul of the system of economic planning and management) would contribute to the prevention of disproportions that otherwise might again arise in the future, thus securing more regular and—in the long run—more rapid economic growth.

II. Trend

The falling trend in the rate of growth is exhibited in Figure 2, where sliding averages on a 7-years basis have been applied in order to iron out the fluctuations observed. Moreover, more exact analysis, using the method of least squares, reveals a tendency for the rate of growth of industrial output to be reduced by 0.7 per cent per annum, taking Czechoslovakia in the 1950–1964 period.

It might be argued that deceleration was due to the combined effect of such accidental factors as the successive exhaustion of output-capacity, man-power and labour-productivity reserves, released by socialization and economic planning; the impact of "economic maturity" on the rate of growth; and the gradual elimination of the inflationary effect on the global output index of industrial production. More detailed analysis, however, shows that only a minor part of the deceleration that is observed can be explained in terms of the three factors mentioned.

Hence, the question arises: How is it possible that the high share of accumulation, and the considerable lead of the rate of growth for the output of means of production as compared with the production of consumers' goods which prevailed practically throughout the whole period did not secure the expected effect? Far from resulting in an acceleration—or at least stabilisation—of the mean rate of growth, they did not even prevent a notable deceleration.

Statistical data that are available give an interesting, though necessarily approximative picture of three main escape canals through which parts of the global social product (as this term is used in the socialist countries) are "falling out" of the reproduction process. Reference should be made to Tables 4, 5, and 6 on the long-run rise of stocks, uncompleted construction and (relative) materials input in the countries under investigation. These three factors, in conjunction with a deterioration in the real terms

TABLE 4

RISE IN STOCKS, UNCOMPLETED CONSTRUCTION AND (RELATIVE) MATERIALS INPUT, CZECHOSLOVAKIA 1956–1963 (BILLION Kčs)

	1956	1957	1958	1959	1960	1961	1962	1963
Increase in uncompleted construction	3	1	4	1	5	5	5	
Rise in stocks	3	4	7	4	1	8	8	8
Accumulation, total	16	21	26	27	28	35	32	22
National income	133	141	149	152	163	172	175	173
Rise in (relative) materials input	—	0	1	6	8	11	13	17

SOURCE: Statistical yearbooks and other official publications.

Editor's Note: Compared to Table 12, p. 68, of Goldmann & Kouba *Hospodarsky Rust v CSSR* (Prague: 1967), the first row should read 3, 1, 4, 1, 5, 9, 9, 6; the second row should read: 3, 4, 7, 4, 1, 10, 9, – 1; and the remaining data are the same. The reasons for the discrepancy seem to be: 1) transposition, and 2) revised figures from 1961 to 1963.

TABLE 5

RISE IN STOCKS AND (RELATIVE) MATERIALS INPUT, POLAND 1956–1962 (BILLION ZLOTY)

	1956	1957	1958	1959	1960	1961	1962
Rise in stocks	14	26	24	21	27	32	21
Accumulation, total	51	74	78	87	90	102	101
National income	257	301	321	346	375	411	426
Rise in (relative) materials input	—	1	5	9	31	50	61

SOURCE: Statistical yearbooks and other official publications.

TABLE 6

RISE IN STOCKS AND UNCOMPLETED CONSTRUCTION,
HUNGARY 1955–1962 (BILLION FORINT)

	1955	1956	1957	1958	1959	1960	1961	1962
Rise in stocks	8,9	−5,5	16,9	4,4	8,0	9,5	13,1	16
Increase in uncompleted construction	−0,5	1,3	0,3	0,6	10,0	2,0	1,4	
Accumulation	19,1	3,5	26,1	15,9	27,3	35,9	37,5	43

SOURCE: Statistical yearbooks and other official publications.

of trade—due to a differential development in labour productivity, result-ing in price differentials between (Czechoslovak) home and foreing mar-kets,—e. g. in Czechoslovakia, are of a sufficient quantitative effect to be taken as the immediate causes of deceleration. It would not be too difficult to demonstrate that industrial output and national income would rise more rapidly if stocks and uncompleted constructions were at the much lower indispensable level and only rose roughly in proportion to the change in national income while relative factor inputs were declining instead of increasing.

The question now arises as to whether the genesis of the three escape canals is due to structural factors or may be explained in terms of the func-tioning of the traditional system of economic planning and control. As shown by Professor Wlodzimierz Brus, the main drawbacks of the tradi-tional model, particularly under modern conditions, are inflexibility, exces-sive factor input, insufficient stimuli for technical advance, in addition to alienation and the growth of bureaucracy. Hence, it can be easily demon-strated that the genesis of the first two escape canals (excessive growth of stocks and uncompleted construction) can be fully accounted for by model factors while the relative rise of factor input is to some—and perhaps to a large extent—likewise the result of model as distinct from structural fac-tors.

The above arguments lead to the conclusion that the long-term de-cline of the rate of growth is primarily and directly due to the effects of the traditional system of planning and management under conditions of the transition from "extensive" to "intensive" development. Only to a far lesser extent can it be taken as its indirect result, with the economic struc-ture, as it was brought about by economic planning and mangement in the past years, forming the intermediate link.

In terms of the Kalecki model of economic growth under socialism, the fact that production relations, conceived as including the given model of economic planning and management, are increasingly lagging behind the development of production forces, results in significant changes in the strategic parameters of the growth model. While the coefficient "u", representing "non-investment" factors of growth, is declining, the capital coefficient "k" is rising, with a resulting decline in the rate of growth.

Referring to conditions in Czechoslovakia, this argument makes possible a further, necessarily still tentative conclusion relating to the main ways of overcoming some unfavourable results of economic development so far, and to the relative significance of each of them. Even if at the expense of large investments, the structural changes, envisaged by the recommendations of previous analyses, were to be brought about rapidly, this would by no means remove the antistimuli to economic efficiency which are inherent in the traditional system. On the contrary, if as a first step a thorough reform of the traditional system were to be carried out, with a view to consistent decentralisation of economic decisionmaking in favour of the enterprise level, the escape canals analysed above would turn into additional resources. Thus it might be far easier to find the means for implementing the structural changes that are required. In fact those means would not have to be obtained, directly or indirectly, in the sphere of consumption—nor outside the country.

Moreover, at the present phase of development, the mechanism, making for fluctuations in the rate of growth, apparently sets up conditions for somewhat accelerated growth in the next few years. The transition to the decentralized model, more adequate to the present stage of development and fully gearing the economic interest of the enterprise and its workers to the economic interest of society, might thus be carried out under more favourable conditions. Securing the more consistent application of the principle of the economic calculus, of rationality in economic decisionmaking both at the micro- and macro-economic levels, it might open up new sources of economic growth.

2. THE FUNCTIONING OF THE ECONOMY

*SOURCES OF SOVIET ECONOMIC INEFFICIENCY**
— · — · — · — · — · — · — · — · — ·
Abram Bergson†

If the inquiry has thus far shed light on economic efficiency, this has been done chiefly by elaboration of sources of economic inefficiency. To try now, therefore, to summarize findings in this regard, these related but

*Reprinted by permission of Yale University Press from *The Economics of Soviet Planning*, pp. 329–40. Copyright 1964 by Yale University.

†Dr. Abram Bergson is Professor of Economics at Harvard University, and Director, Russian Research Center, Harvard University. His publications include: *The Structure of Soviet Wages* (1944), *Soviet Economic Growth* (ed.) (1953), *The Real National Income of Soviet Russia Since 1928* (1961), *Economic Trends in The Soviet Union* (edited with Simon Kuznets, 1963), *Essays in Normative Economics* (1966), and *Planning and the Market in The USSR: the 1960's* (with Alexander Balinky, John N. Hazard, and Peter Wiles, 1967).

distinct features appear to be the more consequential sources of Soviet economic inefficiency:

Value Theory. In the U.S.S.R. the system's directors have never considered themselves bound by the labor theory of value, and even the preferred status of the labor theory as the only analysis of value that might overtly be espoused has lately begun to erode. But the labor theory has been influential and, in diminished degree, still is. As a result, economic efficiency has been impaired in diverse ways. By far the most outstanding is that where the choice of technology is in question, and here the labor theory is no longer as influential as it once was, for, as we have seen, an interest-like criterion once considered as dubious in this light has recently received quasi-official sanction. Yet Soviet project appraisal continues to have its limitations, and for these the labor theory probably is partly responsible. Under Soviet conditions, any resultant misuse of capital has been particularly costly because of the relative scarcity of this factor.

Working arrangements for nonlabor primary factors other than capital, particularly mineral resources and farm land, have as yet been little explored. But the labor theory should have had an important adverse effect here as well. More generally, at least until recently, the labor theory has been construed not as it might be in the light of contemporary Western analysis but much as it was long ago by Marx. Most importantly, it has been construed without the benefit of the fundamental notion of marginal value.[1] Almost inevitably, then, the very concept of an economic optimum that is integral to economic rationality has been understood only imperfectly. One wonders, therefore, whether in consequence decision making has not been adversely affected in some measure almost everywhere.

I refer to dubious principles of resource use the application of which has been a corollary of adherence to the labor theory. Another closely related source of inefficiency is dubious principles of price formation of similar origin, and resultant miscalculations where alternatives are appraised in monetary terms. I shall refer below to limitations of ruble prices as a source of inefficiency, and shall consider there those due to the labor theory.

Where there has been a departure from the labor theory, the alternative, at least implicitly, has sometimes been contemporary Western theory, but not always, for the alternative to the labor theory has often been no theory. And this too must have been a source of waste, for given the aversion to principle, arbitrariness was unavoidable. Such arbitrariness, however, is not easily disentangled from that originating in the feature to which I now come.

Administrative Burden on Superior Agencies. Contrary to a prevalent impression, responsibilities for resource use have been delegated to a sig-

[1]For further discussion, through from different standpoints, see Oscar Lange and Fred M. Taylor, *On the Economic Theory of Socialism* (Minneapolis, 1938), appendix; and P. J. D. Wiles, *The Political Economy of Communism* (Oxford, 1962), ch. 3.

nificant extent in the U.S.S.R., even to the lowest level of the vast administrative apparatus which determines resource use—that is, to the management of individual enterprises. The fact remains, however, that economic decision making has been notably centralized.

Another source of inefficiency is found in this feature, for in seeking to carry out the onerous responsibilities which they bear, superior agencies at all levels have often found themselves without the information needed for adequate and timely appraisal of alternatives, or if such information is at their disposal, without the capacity to process and digest it sufficiently for such appraisal. Consequently, decisions again and again have had to be arbitrary, and resources again and again to be misused. This has been so not only when decisions called for positive action, but also when either purposefully or by default there has only been inaction.

Since prices are largely fixed by superior agencies, the arbitrariness necessarily has been a further cause, in addition to the labor theory, of limitations of ruble prices, and hence of miscalculations in monetary terms. But the arbitrariness also affects resource use more or less directly. Recall, for example, the difficulty, because of the sheer complexity of the task, in coordinating plan targets to assure that the projected mix of products is a desired one; the need of superior agencies to negotiate with inferior ones about targets for activities about which the former can only be partially informed; the inadequate and frequently erroneous data on the basis of which alternative technologies are appraised; and the deficient information on consumers' demand, although there probably is no impelling concern to allocate resources closely in accord with such demand anyhow.

In this study I have dealt only in part with decision making at superior levels, but among spheres where they play a cardinal role two chief ones passed by are determination of the volume and allocation of materials supply when capacity is variable, and determination of the volume and allocation of supplies of investment goods. Difficulties encountered in respect of materials supply can only have been compounded by the need to fix capacity concomitantly, and obviously also have their parallel in the case of investment goods. Gosplan no doubt has worn "steel blinkers," as Khrushchev has charged,[2] but it has not been alone in this practice, and among superior agencies generally one need not inquire far to become aware that blinkers of other materials have also been worn. This habit must originate variously, but it can only be reinforced by the fact that, even if only arbitrarily, it simplifies a most formidable task. Given centralized decision making, the task of superior agencies would have been inordinate in any case, but in the U.S.S.R. it must have been even more so because of the transient nature of organizational arrangements generally.

[2]*Current Digest* (December 19, 1962), p. 9.

Price Formation. The extent to which ruble prices diverge from "scarcity values" perhaps is sometimes overstated, but prices must differ markedly from scarcity values where, as in the U.S.S.R., the tendency is to fix them in accord with average rather than marginal cost and with only limited concern for the current state of demand. Moreover, average cost has been calculated without any allowance for interest on fixed capital or any systematic charge for rents on extractive branches, although very recently the latter lacuna may have been filled after a fashion. And these fixed prices have been changed only infrequently.

I refer primarily to prices of basic industrial goods, but for processed foods and manufactures the only important novelty is the turnover tax with its widely varying rates. This tax brought prices of processed foods and manufactures closer to clearing levels than they otherwise would have been, but they hardly have corresponded to them, while any systematic relation to cost, either marginal or average, is difficult to perceive. We have explored the prices of other goods only unevenly, but circumstances generally could not have been very different from those described.

While such divergencies from scarcity values originate in the labor theory and the inordinate task of superior agencies, these are not the sole causes. Most importantly, while ruble prices have suffered from the labor theory, they have not benefited where the alternative has been no theory.

Whatever their cause, the divergencies have also contributed to the inefficiency. Thus, while the price system has suffered because of the inordinate task of superior agencies, this task has only been the greater because of the deficiencies in the price system itself. For being aware of these deficiencies, administrators have felt impelled to compile and digest even more information than might otherwise be needed, information not only of a summary monetary sort but of a detailed physical sort. And it is but another facet of the same phenomenon that deficiencies in ruble prices have been a cause as well as an effect of flexibility in regard to value theory, for principles of economic calculation usually have to be expressed in monetary terms. Given the deficiencies in ruble prices, the system's directors have only been the more hesitant to commit themselves to such principles. Thus, to refer again to the treatment of choices of technology, while application of an interest-like criterion here has been opposed on ideological grounds, that it entails monetary calculations has been an additional stumbling block. And now that an interest-like criterion has been sanctioned, the authoritative source of this endorsement still asks that project makers consider not only monetary data but also pertinent "physical indicators."

But, however much they consider physical aspects, superior agencies must still rely on monetary calculations in some degree, and the deficiencies in ruble prices become at this point a source of inefficiency more clearly in their own right, for manifestly the authorities must often have been led into miscalculations on this basis.

Not only at higher levels have monetary calculations been a basis for decisions. Under the *khozraschet* system, decisions have been affected generally. And where they have, they must again and again have been distorted.

In sum, the ruble price system fails to perform the function which, the primers teach, a good price system should—to convey reliable information on prevailing scarcities. This must be by no means the least of the causes of economic waste in the U.S.S.R.

Success Criteria. This feature is in a sense a corollary of the one just considered, for the chronic difficulties the government has experienced in formulating success criteria have had various causes, but a principal one has been the limitations of ruble prices. Given these, it could not be easy to summarize in any meaningful way the results of managerial activity. At any rate, the government has not found it so, and here, too, there has been inefficiency. Managerial malpractices in concealing reserves, in violating quality standards, or in departing from the assortment plan sometimes may have permitted the system to function more effectively than it otherwise could, but they must still have been economically wasteful.

Success criteria have had to be formulated for managerial personnel both in the enterprise and at higher levels. I have focused on the former, but in engaging in dubious practices enterprise managers have often had the acquiescence if not active support of their superiors, and these too have had their foibles. Futhermore, at high levels as well as low, the dubious success criteria have been more deleterious in an environment where typically there has been a sellers' market for materials, and where materials procurement has been hazardous. Of course, such a market in a sense is but the obverse of the divergencies of prices from scarcity values.

Thus the phenomenon, curious in a planned economy, of managerial striving for self-sufficiency. This has been manifest in the enterprise in efforts to acquire excess stocks of scarce materials. It has been manifest in both the enterprise and at higher levels in the endeavor to acquire auxiliary services, to limit specialization and the like. A principal aim of the reorganization of industry in 1957 was to inhibit such practices, but departmentalism has sometimes been eliminated only to be succeeded by localism. In the *glavki*, which are subordinate to regional councils, departmentalism itself probably has not been liquidated.[3]

In order to buttress more formal success criteria, the government has

---

[3]On managerial interest in "self-sufficiency" in the U.S.S.R., see David Granick, "Organization and Technology in Soviet Metalworking," *American Economic Review, 47S* (1957), 631–42; Nove, *The Soviet Economy,* pp. 196 ff.

also relied on priorities. As revealed by the system's directors, these are supposed to guide decision makers generally, and decision makers often observe them. But as an instrument of control priorities are inherently blunt, and even choices made in their light must frequently be dubious. This must be so generally, but the distortion is only magnified where the priorities are implemented through the famous "campaign" form of administration. As the Russians themselves acknowledge the campaign, whatever its merits, has its limitations as a method of allocating resources.

The system's directors nevertheless have still had reasons to rely on priorities as an instrument of control. But one must have been that alternative controls of a relatively sensitive kind often have to be in monetary terms. Hence here again divergencies of ruble prices from scarcity values have been a factor, for because of such divergencies monetary controls also have their limitations.

We also find here still another reason for the onerous burden of responsibility on superior agencies: the limitations of success criteria have made all the more difficult delegation of responsibility.

Collective Farm Agriculture. While I have referred primarily to non-farm sectors, the sources of inefficiency described are found also in agriculture. The economic ills of this sector, however, no doubt have been to some extent special. This has been true particularly of the collective farm component. Even in industry incentive arrangements have had their limitations: Because of the onerous sales taxes wage rates on the margin must have tended to inhibit exertion, acquisition of skills, and assumption of responsibility. But in collective farm agriculture incentive arrangements have been especially unfavorable. The collective farmer like the industrial worker has been able to gain by using his talents productively, but as a residual claimant his reward has not been very impelling.

As a cooperative organization the collective farm supposedly has enjoyed a special relation to the government and party bureaucracy, but these authorities have not hesitated to intervene in the management of the farm, and arbitrary decision making by superior agencies cannot have been any less costly here than elsewhere. The extraordinary reforms in crop schemes, imposed with little regard to local circumstances, are only the most dramatic instances of a pervasive phenomenon. Then, too, overlapping of responsibility has been a source of difficulty generally, but especially so where the actuality of control has had to be cloaked with the symbols of autonomy.

In complex ways not easy to summarize, deficiencies in working arrangements must sometimes have been the more deleterious simply because agriculture has been the sector affected. Thus, despite all controls, the collective farmer must retain a greater measure of discretion over his productive activity than the factory worker. Hence weak incentives are the more important in the former case. Detailed circumstances of time and place must be considered in administration anywhere, but they become the more consequential in a sector where weather can be a decisive factor, and where a major input, land, is almost infinitely varied in character. If overburdened superior agencies disregard such circumstances, therefore, the costs must be especially great in agriculture.

Autarky. I have had little to say about foreign trade, but I should be remiss if I did not refer to the Soviet policy of self-sufficiency. Under this policy, since 1928 Russia's exports have averaged but 1 to 2 per cent of her national income. Exports of the United States, during the period 1869–1913, averaged 6 to 7 per cent of total output; and while trade lately has been less important, exports in 1960 still amounted to 3.8 per cent of output.[4]

The relatively limited Soviet participation in trade may in part reflect factors other than the Soviet policy of self-sufficiency, and may have been a source of economic gains as well as losses. But the policy has been carried notably far, and the losses probably have been preponderant. Autarky, therefore, has been another source of economic inefficiency, and perhaps an important one.

We cannot always know the ends that the system's directors have pursued, but the foregoing aspects I believe have all been sources of economic inefficiency even from their own standpoint, for waste occurs equally in the light of diverse preferences. The inefficiency, it is true, has often been greater than it might otherwise have been because of the intense concern for growth. But it hardly is proper to conclude from this that the system's directors have been unconcerned about the inefficiency. But for the inefficiency, growth might have been even more rapid.[5]

Where the working arrangements have been inefficient, the system's directors have frequently had reasons to value them apart from their material consequences. They have had ideological reasons, political reasons, and presumably personal reasons. Nevertheless, even from their standpoint the reasons may not always have been very good ones, and

---

[4]Holzman, "Foreign Trade," in Bergson and Kuznets, eds., *Economic Trends in the Soviet Union,* pp. 290, 313.

[5]I am not sure I fully grasp Peter Wiles' very provocative arguments concerning "choice versus growth" (*Political Economy of Communism,* ch. XI), but it must be agreed that growth in the U.S.S.R. has had to be purchased in some degree at the expense of efficiency. Some sacrifice of efficiency has been unavoidable, since lump sum taxes that do not impair incentives are not feasible. There has thus been no way in which required investments could have been financed without some adverse effect on resource use. Then, too, when an economy expands, schedules of "costs" and "demand" (however conceived) shift, and with this an optimum must be more difficult to approach than when there is no expansion and schedules of costs and demand are unchanged. That the difficulty is also materially greater the more rapid the expansion is not so clear but may be true.

where they have been, the implication in part is only that, as with politicians anywhere, the system's directors have sometimes been constrained in their choices. But no doubt the working arrangements have often been immediately satisfying to them. Hence they should have felt compensated in some measure for the inefficiency.

Households must value the working arrangements differently, however, and from their standpoint the inefficiency is the more pronounced. Thus where consumers' welfare is the standard all the sources of inefficiency that have been listed remain so, and we must add another: the divergence of planners' from household preferences. This perhaps is not quite so great as is sometimes supposed, for the failure to conform to household preferences must often be unintentional, and therefore would represent a misallocation from the standpoint of both the system's directors and the households. But obviously household preferences have been supplanted in consequential ways. Most outstanding is that where choices are made between present and future. But household preferences have frequently been overridden also in respect to consumption structure, and with the elaboration of the new "rational norms" this practice threatens to become pervasive. Sometimes the system's directors must not have overridden but merely have been indifferent to household preferences. To the households the difference cannot have been material.

Even in terms of their own economic ends, the system's directors should perhaps have been more attentive to household preferences than they have been,[6] but the fact remains that such preferences have been violated. Where consumers' welfare is the standard, this has not been the least important source of inefficiency in the U.S.S.R.

When planners' preferences are the standard, it sometimes is assumed that there can be no economic inefficiency to speak of in the U.S.S.R. The system's directors necessarily act to assure that resources use conforms to their desires. Hence only when consumers' welfare is the standard is there economic waste. This is far from true, for even from the standpoint of the system's directors, resource use has its limitations, but no doubt the limitations are compounded from the standpoint of households.[7]

---

[6]*Ibid.* p. 8.

[7]I said in the text that all the sources of economic inefficiency are such even where planners' preferences are taken as the standard. Strictly speaking, this would be so for autarky only if the system's directors should value a product in the same way regardless of origin, particularly whether domestic or foreign. This manifestly is not so, and while such differences in valuation as have prevailed have ultimately been political and military in origin, in accord with the usage adopted in this essay resource allocation reflecting such a difference would conform to planners' preferences, hence not represent a source of economic inefficiency from this standpoint, From the standpoint of household preferences, however, economic inefficiency still results.

PRINCIPLES OF SOVIET PLANNING*

George R. Feiwel†

Since the 1930's economic planning was used as a tool of the state's direct intervention in determining the direction, speed, choice of methods, and instruments in mustering and organizing resources for rapid industrialization. The decisive role played by central decision-making, representing the political leadership's aims, pervades the entire process of planning both with regard to selection of goals and methods for constructing the central plan and the choice of strategies and means for implementing and controlling it, with a highly centralized operational management of current production decisions. The planning functions are tightly interwoven with those of day-to-day operational management, and administration is often equated with planning. Although with varying intensity and stress, administrative measures, commands, and direct distribution of resources are characteristics of the system.

Accelerated industrialization is assumed to require a swift, massive and expedient redirection of resources which is considered best accomplished through centralized disposal and direct intervention, rather than through inducement and use of economic levers. Centralization of economic activity evolved as a strategic device for mobilizing and concentrating resources on selected crucial targets, preventing their dispersion on other objectives, and imposing the central planner's will on producers and consumers. In this process tensions on resources build up due to the rapidity, scope, and efficacy of the structural change, accentuated by taut planning with insufficient proviso for reserves, making the system acutely sensitive to even minor bottlenecks. The system is void of a mechanism of adjustment to eliminate the bottlenecks created.

The central planner aims at maximizing output in priority areas, given the production and consumption constraints. Consistency is sought to assure the plan's internal balance between output and requirements. Since the plan must take into account the production potential, processes, and requirements of producing enterprises, the planner relies on the information that the lower units generate. Because the information supplied influences plan targets, and hence the size of rewards for meeting and overfulfilling them, there are built-in pressures for the lower units to distort the information to advance their purposes. To compensate, the central planner arbitrarily increases the output targets

*Reprinted by permission from *The Soviet Quest for Economic Efficiency,* (New York: Frederick A. Praeger Inc., 1967) pp. 66–78. All footnotes deleted.

†Dr. George R. Feiwel is Professor of Economics, The University of Tennessee. His publications include: *Cost: The Various Meanings of the Concept* (1964), *The Economics of a Socialist Enterprise* (1965) and *New Economic Patterns in Czechoslovakia* (forthcoming).

and decreases the inputs allotted; often as a result of bargaining with the lower echelons. Hence the units which are less able to resist the pressures get the high quotas with less resources. The pressures built up from above and below tend to render information flowing up much less reflective of actual potential and requirements. The commands emanating from above are based less and less on information. The significant consequences are that the degree of plan fulfilment and particularly overfulfilment varies nonuniformly, contributing to interruptions of interenterprise flows, and the unbalancing of the laboriously contrived attempt at internal consistency of the plan.

Although the stress on particular features and institutional arrangements shifts in time, in broad contours the characteristics of Soviet central planning of industry, as it developed, may, at the expense of oversimplification, be reduced to the following salient points:

1. The operational plan is imperative, of binding nature, and enforced as law. In contrast to plans of a forecasting nature, it is addressed to specific units to fix their responsibility for its fulfilment, specifies concrete assignments, and the totality of working arrangements with which these objectives are to be reached. Planning so conceived requires a widespread and costly apparatus for gathering, processing, and transmitting information and commands, and for controlling their execution. Although there are several organizational strata, arranged in hierarchical order of subordination, the central decision-maker (central planner) and the executant (enterprise) could be singled out as the dramatis personae because the intermediary echelons are essentially channels for processing and transmitting commands and information. However, the latter are not passive agents and simple transmission belts, for their role is to aggregate the reported data flowing upwards and disaggregate the commands emanating from the top, tampering with both in the process. Being vitally interested in the lower units' fulfilment of the plans assigned to them, the central planner has established for the enterprises and intermediary echelons performance criteria on the basis of which he judges their activity and rewards them. These are usually linked with and support the cardinal plan targets (e.g., gross output). *Nolens volens* the central planner has established for these lower units certain goals whose attainment is usually recompensed with premiums, and other less tangible rewards. The lower units' endeavors to attain these goals with minimum effort will color the information which serves the planner as one of the cogent starting points in plan construction. The commands issued at the center will similarly be distorted in their disaggregation by intermediary echelons. Hence both the intermediary levels and the enterprise are in a way able to influence the plan assignments addressed to them.

2. The central planner is the economy's supreme policy-maker on key decisions. However, what constitutes the main decisions may vary with time and circumstances. Decentralization in this context refers essentially to allowing the lower echelons to decide on how best to implement the plan. Plan construction remains the central planner's prerogative. The lower units' scope of decision-making is constrained by regulations and commands, and it is within this scope only that they *de jure* may exercise their powers, whereas *de facto* they do so to a much larger extent, not only because they benefit from the degree of aggregation of the data, but also because, *inter alia,* the remoteness of the central agencies and the time element involved in processing decisions, make it practically impossible to regulate centrally the enterprise's minutest tasks. The imperfect central knowledge of the executants' positions is the planner's weakness and the enterprise's strength. Deficiencies and inconsistencies of commands, performance criteria, value parameters, reward system, and methods of calculation, enable managers to map their course of action and exercise discretion and initiative to a much larger extent than it appears at first glance. Management has evolved ways and means to adapt to the system, maximizing benefits under given constraints. In addition, the central planner's realization that overcentralization leads to inertia and lack of initiative in the executants awaiting decisions from above, has at times been instrumental in vesting the enterprise's management with greater prerogatives in deciding how to execute the plan better. In general, emasculation of discretionary power and

> . . . elimination of any spontaneity in a subordinate position is in reality much rarer than one might assume from popular speech which uses very freely such terms and phrases as 'compulsion,' 'no other choice,' 'absolute necessity,' and so on. Even in the most cruel and oppressive states of subordination, there usually exists a considerable measure of personal freedom.

The centralized pattern relies on commands and constraints for fulfilling the plan, with economic parameters (prices, interest rates, taxes, credit, etc.) not designed as tools for transmitting impulses for plan implementation and resource allocation, but rather predominantly as calculatory devices. In a perfectly centralized model, all decisions would be made at the top and the administration of the economy would be conducted solely on the basis of transmitted commands. The fundamental behavioral rule of the pure command economy would be, therefore, execution of orders received, without support of rewards and incentives to comply. Such a perfectly centralized model is unworkable, not only because the decision-making process is protracted, rigid, costly, wasteful, etc., but also because it ignores the material interest and aspirations of executants, without motivating them and using their initiative. The various degrees of decentralization result from combining use of commands and parameters in operational management of the economy, and by supporting commands with incentives inducing their fulfilment. The predominance of commands over parameters, or vice-versa, characterizes the degree of centralization or decentralization in plan execution. However, a symbiosis of commands and parameters is not a mark of a mutually consistent system. Parameters are made to perform functions for which they were not designed and they are not redesigned for the new functions with which they are vested. The problem of administrating the economy is indissolubly linked with the rationale behind the type of economic calculation used for the construction and execution of the plan.

3. The Soviet planning procedure relies on determination of priorities (leading links) by the regime's leaders, with crucial targets for key intermediate and final products singled out. The point of departure in plan construction is a set of exogenously predetermined targets for intermediate and final products. To *start* economic planning by target setting is, as Professor Frisch has shown, to wander in the fog. To assure optimum use of resources, rational planning must take as its starting point and retain at all times a basic distinction between the preferences of the regime's leaders who are steering the economy (the selectively free form of the preference function) and the fundamental data describing the structure of the economy (those things that the planner cannot alter and must consider as data). Frisch argues that the construction of the preference function must be absolutely free of the notion of target setting and should be approached in what he calls the "Santa Claus spirit." The pertinent question, to be addressed to the policy-makers to get the necessary information for constructing their preference function, is—"would you have this or would you rather have that *if you had a free choice?*" Frisch challenges the view that the preference function should reflect a set of quantity targets which is to become the focal point in plan construction. If this were so, the preference function would have little relevance since the policy-makers are unable to account for the "infinite variety of *structural* aspects which will determine whether a given set of quantity targets is *feasible* or not, and if feasible, whether it is optimal or not. Feasibility can only be adequately analyzed by a number of scientific specialists." The ultimate goal of plan construction is to arrive at and end up with a constellation of quantity targets for the development of the economy, but to start with such a set, is to put the cart before the horse.

4. It is considered the unquestionable prerogative of the central planner to make the major decisions with respect to the direction and tempo of economic development, the share of national income to be diverted to capital formation, defense, and the size of the individual and

collective consumption funds. The central planner is not guided by consumers' time preferences. In the main, the central planner decides on the
allocation of investments to particular sectors of the economy and
branches of industry on the basis of priorities, singling out the key investment projects; promulgates and enforces a general policy on the manner
of carrying out investments; and establishes the methodological procedures for selecting investment variants according to their capital intensity
(choice of technology). The central planner allows a varying scope of
decision-making on inconsequential investments of limited or local nature
to lower units, within the investment limits imposed on them centrally.

5. The central planner decides the size (rate), methods, and composition of production. The degree of specificity depends on the priority of
the industry and relative scope left to decentralization measures in execution. In general, the central planner decides on the physical quantity of
output to be produced, aggregated in more or less broad groups depending on the scarcity and significance of the products for predetermined
priorities. He determines the major types and sources of procurement and
allocates supplies to specific uses, with considerable constraints on substitution of centrally allocated factors. He regulates and establishes the terms
of employment for specific skills. He decides on the implementation of
new processes and introduction of new crucial products. In principle, the
cardinal microeconomic decisions as to what, how much, how, where,
when, and for whom to produce are not made by the producing enterprise which largely performs only executing functions. The consumer generally enjoys freedom of choice but not consumer sovereignty. He can
react, but not decidedly influence planners' production decisions.

6. Given the politically determined priorities, the state of constraints,
and lacking the mechanism of a market for producer goods, the major task
of the central planning agencies is to construct an internally consistent and
feasible plan. The problem of maintaining a balance, or what Professor
Grossman calls coordinative planning has always been at the forefront of
the planner's attention. To achieve this end the planner elaborates a network of balances, generally in physical terms, of products and their uses,
so that total output of a product is equated with the quantities which all
users must receive to carry out their tasks. The method of planning by
balances is a primitive version of input-output analysis, to trace interindus-
trial and intersectoral flows. While sharing many shortcomings with input-output, the method of balances is also hindered by the use of noncumu-
lative input coefficients, the crudity of measures to eradicate imbalances
and resolve shortages, and above all, the absence of a mechanism for reducing them. In plan construction, calculation is performed predominantly in physical units and prices used for aggregating heterogeneous output, rather than as coefficients of economic choice, (choice of investment

and foreign trade variants excluded). There is a lack of economic verification of the plan, with little evidence of adherence to any rational economic efficiency rules or choice criteria. At best a plan so constructed may evince a degree of internal consistency, but it will not provide an optimal solution, i.e., a solution that would yield the maximum value of the objective function; the intended and measurable quantity to be maximized subject to exogenous and evolved constraints. Technical input coefficients are viewed as independent structural constants. No mechanism for verifying production methods is available because the latter are treated as external to the system.

Prices are arbitrarily set, essentially for reducing heterogeneous output to a common denominator. Generally they cannot be used for verifying the economic rationality of production in the lower units as essentially no efficiency test was applied in choosing production variants during plan construction. Since prices were not used for equilibrating the plan, they cannot guide efficient choice of plan executants. It follows from the logic of the scheme that to safeguard the laboriously contrived balance of the plan, its execution may require a system of detailed commands to transmit the orders to executants, rather than use of value parameters which were not designed with that purpose in mind. When these parameters are used in the process of plan implementation, they lose their attributes of passive calculatory devices. Their relative structure becomes a focal point to plan executants, as the degree of plan fulfilment (hence the rewards received) hinges on price ratios. A device which was originally designed for aggregating output becomes an indicator guiding the enterprise (subject to choice constraints) in its output composition and choice of inputs. When commands are supported by incentives to execute the plan, and value parameters are used as relevant measures, a contradiction between the various tools of plan implementation may develop and work at cross purposes with each other. Therefore, there is a built-in proclivity for perpetuating commands, enforcing adherence to plan targets, rationing supplies, setting norms and limits, and exerting pressures to observe them. The degree of enforcement of these measures depends on their relative importance from the central planner's standpoint. Given the proclivity (and perhaps necessity) for centralization to implement the goals of super-rapid industrialization, the functioning of a centralized economy will evince, *inter alia*, inappropriate adaptation of the lower units to the orders transmitted. To remedy the situation the central planner often reacts by intensifying the degree of centralization.

7. To facilitate control, fix responsibility for plan execution, and expedite operations, the enterprise is a legal entity endowed with a stock of fixed and working capital, with the state the powerful owner and management the recipient and executant of orders. Essentially the enterprise

should be a self-supporting unit, covering its expenditures for current operations from its receipts. A budget constraint is imposed on it to induce parsimony. Since prices incorporate only an insignificant markup on planned costs, the excess of planned revenue over expenditures should be positive but minimal; large enough to constitute a source for incentives and decentralized funds—even though they have not been substantial enough in the past to be of real incentive value—and to keep the enterprise solvent, but small enough to constrain waste. The mere possession of financial resources by the enterprise does not entitle it to decide on their uses, lacking, therefore, a fundamental precondition for financial autonomy. Although the composition of assets and destination of funds are strictly regulated, even at times of most acute centralization the planner has not succeeded in regulating the minutest transactions. It may be argued that leaving financial resources at the enterprise's disposal, even granted the constraints, goes against the grain of a centralized system for there is always the danger that the enterprise may engage in undertakings incompatible with those mapped out by the central plan. To circumscribe the enterprise's opportunity for maneuvering financial resources, the state not only siphons off the substantial share of profits, institutes strict limits and special funds, but transactions are also partially financed by the bank—an additional controlling agency that has a decisive say on the use of the credits it grants. Moreover, excess funds are often confiscated and shortages replenished from the state budget, killing incentive for parsimony and accumulation of funds.

8. Within the state sector money plays a passive and subordinate role, facilitates recording, reporting, and control of activity, without directly affecting economic decisions. Economic quantities measured in monetary terms are used merely for expressing and summarizing inputs, output, and financial results *ex post facto*, after the targets and resources have been determined by the superiors. Conceptually, the financial plan is merely a monetary recalculation of targets and means in natura. Nevertheless, there is often a lack of harmony between the actual financial and production plans, contributing the disproportions in plan execution. It follows from planning by material balances that the system distrusts profit or any other composite (synthetic) measure of activity as a performance criterion and favors particularly the easily ascertainable gross output measure. From the standpoint of material balances it is imperative to know which output targets have been met or overfulfilled and which inputs have been saved or substituted in the process. The benefits from larger output, substitution, or savings, etc., even if monetarily equivalent, are considered to be nonadditive and may not be of the same order of magnitude on the planner's scale of preferences.

In the labor and consumer goods markets, money does play an active role in directly affecting economic choices for the wage earner to select his place and type of work and the consumer to spend his income as he chooses, circumscribed, however, by what the central planner decides to offer and at what terms. Wage differentials are insufficient to compensate skills, managerial abilities, and responsibility. Entrepreneurial activity is not rewarded sufficiently and there is little incentive for its development.

9. The system features operational, current planning, limiting the time horizon imposed by the plan on the factory manager. Hence the latter is chiefly preoccupied with fulfilling his current assignments, because he will be rewarded for current performance. This is, of course, subject to looking ahead into the following plan period, and executing the current plan to an extent warranting receipt of premiums, but not entailing sharp increases of future assignments. The observable motive for maximization of current income, in the form of salaries and premiums—the variable portion of income—reinforced by the low level of consumption, further limits management's time horizon and influences calculation in terms of current production results. The problem is intensified by a chronic large turnover of management and workers. The most unfavorable repercussions from management's limited time horizon are the brakes and disincentives it creates for technical progress. The system is not conducive to innovation, creative activity, and dissemination of technical knowledge at the production level. The reluctance toward technical progress measures is especially severe if their implementation should disrupt current operations and threaten nonfulfilment of the plan. Introduction of technical progress is also inhibited by the special efforts involved and the possible rise in production costs at the initial production stages, without assurance of compensation in the future or the particularly protracted time span until it will materialize. The enterprise's resistance is further intensified by a fear of tightening of norms, automatic increases of assignments in the future, reduction of workers, etc. as a result of implementing technical progress. On the other hand, retention of the status quo does not threaten the enterprise with particularly severe repercussions unless implementation of technical progress has been assigned by superiors and its nonexecution is penalized. The system suffers from the lack of a mechanism for promoting innovation at the lower echelons. Consequently, it is almost entirely foisted from above, and in the process must overcome built-in obstacles against such action.

10. The system places on a pedestal quantitative increase of output and its entire machinery, through various economic, social, and political pressures, is geared toward attainment of this end. Production of larger output is, of course, not synonymous with efficiency, if by reallocating the productive agents a larger output and/or more desirable composition, from the users' standpoint, could be obtained. Fulfilment and overfulfilment

of the output quota, whether or not sold, becomes the performance criterion and yardstick to whose size rewards are related. In addition, the output
target is reinforced by relating to it the size of the wage fund and the
number of workers, Due to the aim of the enterprise's staff to maximize
current income, the size, composition, and labor intensity of output are
subject to further pressures and manipulations,. The quantum in question
is the volume of output produced against that planned, with the built-in
incentive to aim at obtaining the lowest possible plan which could be easily
overfulfilled and the ensuing industry-wide underestimation and under-
utilization of capacity.

The tendency is to produce for the plan rather than for the user. There
is a deeply ingrained sellers' market, where the seller dominates the buyer,
with permanent shortages at the prevailing terms of exchange, no competition among sellers who encounter few difficulties in disposing of their products to constantly hungry buyers. The buyers, as a rule, compete for the
scarce products and are not only willing to accept deliveries which deviate
from the orders placed with respect to time of delivery, prices (when calculated on cost-plus basis by the producer for nonstandard output), assortment of products, quantity, quality, and technical specifications, but also
are willing to engage in "socialists graft" (*blat*). The monopolistic position
of many producers is demonstrated in the selling outlets usually representing the sellers' interests and the buyers' negotiating powers being limited.
The assignment of specific supply sources for many products to specific
buyers intensifies the producers' lack of interest in the market for their
products. Since, generally, production of output, or strictly speaking, the
act of reporting it, is the crucial test of fulfilment of assignments by the
enterprise, its channels for transferring the output are assigned to it, or
assured, and due to the sellers' market, there is, as a rule, no compelling
force to adapt to the study the users' needs. The absence of price competition contributes to deterioration of quality and waste as the enterprise
does not essentially benefit from producing better and cheaper.

THE STRUCTURE AND ORGANIZATION OF THE
SOVIET ECONOMY*
— · — · — · — · — · — · — · — · — · — —

Gregory Grossman

There is hardly an economic problem that preoccupied the Soviet
regime twenty-five years ago which does not preoccupy its successor today,
or indeed has not plagued the economy and its rulers continuously for at
least three decades. The list is a long one; there is no need to recite it

*Reprinted by permission of the publisher and the author from *Slavic Review* (June
1962), pp. 205–220.

fully here. But we may take a look at the more important problems, grouping them in an arbitrary fashion.

1. Problems pertaining to agriculture: its pronounced lag behind the rest of the economy, its sluggish response to many of the remedial measures, the low productivity of labor, the great dispersion of peasant incomes around a relatively low average, the contrasts between the socialized sector and the private plot.

2. Overcentralization and bureaucratization of the whole economy, with attendant delays, inefficiencies, and political problems.

3. Deficiencies of planning: cumbersomeness, great delays in the plans reaching the executants and their frequent revisions; their imperfect internal consistency and balance; poor articulation between production (or investment) planning, supply planning, and financial planning.

4. Inadequate attention to economic efficiency (optimization) in planning and management; related problems in pricing.

5. Chronic and general supply difficulties with regard to producer goods, including equipment; and, as the other side of the coin, poor quality, improper assortment, incomplete assembly, and many other defects of the goods themselves.

6. Obstacles to innovation, whether owing to "friction" in the bureaucratic hierarchies or to resistance from below.

7. "Localism" and "departmentalism" of varying degrees of enlightenment or selfishness; neglect and pilferage of socialist property; self-serving acts of the greatest variety and ingenuity, not to say ubiquity; and widespread deception of superiors.

8. The many ills of the construction industry, such as dispersion of funds and resources among too many projects, building without blueprints, great delays in completion and frequent partial noncompletion (the notorious *nedodelki*), a very large amount of resources frozen in the "unfinished construction" and "uninstalled equipment,"[1] and the generally low quality of the product. When, at the 22nd Party Congress, Mr. Khrushchev characterized the performance of the construction industry as "the problem of problems,"[2] he was merely attaching a new—and since much popularized—label to a decades-old headache.

---

[1] As of January 1, 1961, the volume of unfinished construction was 21.4 billion (new) rubles, and the increment for the preceding year was 2.4 billion rubles (*Экономическая газета*, Sept. 4, 1961, p. 14). The total of construction by the state, centralized and decentralized, in 1960 was 19.3 billion rubles. The amount of uninstalled equipment as of May 1, 1961, on enterprises subordinated to republic Councils of Ministers (accounting for 94 per cent of gross industrial production in the country) was 2.47 billion rubles (*Экономическая газета*, Dec. 18, 1961, p. 7). Total investment in machinery in the state sector during 1960 was about 9.3 billion rubles. 1960 data from *Народное хозяйство СССР в 1960 г.* (Moscow: ЦСУ СССР, 1961), pp. 591–92.

[2] *Правда*, Oct. 18, 1961, p. 6.

9. The consumer's well-known woes: shortages of consumer goods and interruptions in their supply, their poor quality and limited variety, the lack of both service and services, and the ever-present housing shortage.

While a quarter of a century ago one could attribute these difficulties in good measure to the workers' and peasants' "darkness" (as the Russians might say) and to the planners' and managers' greenness, today their children are hardly wanting in the experience, training, education, indoctrination, and tools to do a much better job of it. The persistence of the problems is strong evidence that they are a systemic phenomenon.

Economic systems are best known by the institutions they keep. The undogmatic student nowadays realizes that all classifications are no more than constructs and abstractions, that their function is to be tools of analysis and not its master, and that therefore they ought to be adapted to the object of his study. In examining economic systems from a dynamic standpoint it is useful to look at the factors conditioning their motion in particular phases of their histories, namely, their ideologies (or the ideologies of their governing elites) and the points in economic-historical development marking the beginning of these phases. The latter of course determine the resources on hand, while the ideologies bear on the directions and speed of development, the degree of pressure on the available resources, and the political restraints that might or might not be placed on the single-mindedness of the advance.

Some—notably Alexander Gerschenkron[3]—would argue that the nature and intensity of the ideological commitment to industrialization is related to the country's relative economic backwardness at the beginning of the relevant phase; in other words, that the march of Economic History is not an orderly procession but a grand and inexorable game of catching up. Be that as it may, the USSR can be seen as a special case of a country that despite considerable economic backwardness relative to the other great powers 1) enjoyed a favorable resource endowment and had already had its industrial "take-off" decades earlier (in this regard it is very different from many an underdeveloped country today), 2) has been, for various reasons good or bad, in an enormous hurry to industrialize and to build up its military might, and 3) has had a polity providing few checks on the urgent and single-minded policy of industrialization. It is not necessary to accept the dubious thesis that the actual Soviet pattern of development, including its noneconomic aspects, was the only possible one in order to see that this pattern was a consistent product of the logic of haste under conditions of relative backwardness and (to put it mildly) within a highly au-

---

[3]See particularly his "Economic Backwardness in Historical Perspective" in Bert F. Hoselitz, ed., *The Progress of Underdeveloped Areas* (Chicago, 1952).

thoritarian political milieu. The logic of haste is above all a powerful centralizing force in social affairs. In the Soviet instance "centralism" found a ready and most convenient ally in "socialism," however incompatible with some of the European intellectual roots of socialism the total social mobilization in the Soviet case may have been.

The Soviet—or, more exactly, Stalinist—formula for industrialization is by now well known. One of its cornerstones has been, of course, the collectivization of agriculture, which permitted a large unrequited extraction of agricultural surplus while avoiding (or so it was thought) a large-scale withdrawal of effort by the peasants, as happened during War Communism. The extraction of the agricultural surplus in turn allowed a very high rate of investment out of the national product. Physical resources have been "mobilized" for capital construction by virtue of central planning and a tight control over the allocation of materials and foreign exchange. Western technology has been taken over on a vast scale and injected into the economy from above under constant pressure. A large training program has been conducted. Material benefits and social privileges have been offered in a highly selective and differentiated way in order to stimulate labor to maximum self-improvement and best performance on the job. But direct controls were exercised over labor for a long time, too.

Money, of course, remained in use, but in the production sector more "passively," to control compliance and constrain independence, than "actively," to guide performance.[4] The economy has not only been planned centrally (although all effective national planning is by definition "central," and no planning is entirely centralized), and not only has the volume and distribution of investments been centrally determined, but the economy has also been *centrally managed* by dint of a plethora of production directives and allocation orders *in natura*. It is primarily the last of these three features of central direction, rather than the first two, that sets the Soviet-type economy apart from other planned economies such as the Indian, Norwegian, or Yugoslav, and which has produced such appellations as "command economy" and *Zentralverwaltungswirtschaft*. (The Soviets have no name for their own type of economy except "socialist," which is of course quite imprecise.) A command economy, in contrast to a market economy, allocates resources and attempts to attain balance between requirements and availabilities by means of commands (orders, directives) from the center, rather than by the mutual interaction of many decentralized economic units linked together by a market (price) mechanism. A command economy must also be a planned one in the sense that a certain

[4]On active and passive money in alternative economic systems see, for example, P. J. D. Wiles, "Rationality, the Market, Decentralization, and the Territorial Principle" in G. Grossman, ed., *Value and Plan* (Berkeley and Los Angeles, 1960), esp. pp. 188 ff.

minimal amount of co-ordination between the directives is required lest
the economy break down. While a command economy need not be socialist
—the Nazi war economy is frequently cited in evidence of this—it is difficult to imagine one except in a highly authoritarian milieu. On the other
hand, a market economy can be both planned and socialist, as these words
are commonly understood in the West. The Yugoslav economy, and the
Soviet economy itself during the NEP era, are the most outstanding examples of "market socialism" with central planning.

It is only with reference to the logic of haste under conditions of relative economic backwardness and of political dictatorship that one understands those crucial features of Soviet industrialization (and the later
Chinese industrialization) which go completely counter to Western experience. If in the West industrialization was associated with commercializa-
tion and a great extension of the scope of the market mechanism, Soviet
industrialization, as we have just seen, all but abolished the market mechanism. If in the West there was a parallel monetization of the economy, the
Soviet economy was to a considerable degree demonetized. If in the West,
and even in Tsarist Russia, restrictions on labor mobility were progressively removed and the individual's relation to society tended to shift "from
status to contract," in the Soviet case there was a marked return to restrictions on labor mobility, paternalism of a sort, and even labor adscription
within the new institutional context. The functional role of the three "M's"
of Western industrialization—the market, money, and mobility—are well
known: in brief, they afforded the greatest scope and incentive for innovation, accumulation, and growth under essentially decentralized initiative
and decision-making. *Laissez-faire* is the name we use for the more extreme form of such decentralization. It was only later in the West (at least
in the Anglo-Saxon world) that substantial curbs came to be placed on the
working of the market mechanism, and trade unions came to impart status
privileges to labor as the production ethic gave ground to considerations
of welfare, social justice, and economic stability.

Ideologically rooted in the nineteenth-century revolt against *laissez-
faire* and politically committed to dictatorship as it was, the new Soviet
regime could hardly have been expected to opt for rapid industrialization
within a decentralized framework, not to say with private initiative and
private property in industry. The rate of accumulation, and hence the rate
of growth, and the pattern of investment, and hence the direction of development, could hardly have been left to the despised and dreaded *stik-
hiinost'* (spontaneous and atomized decision-making). But—not to mention
coercion and terror—it is questionable that the (socialist) market mechanism had to be destroyed, the economy partially demonetized, and labor
mobility impaired, to the extent that they were. And it is quite understandable that these three "non-M's" would tend to come into progressively
sharper conflict with the very development of the economy that they orig-

inally were intended to spur—a conflict whose manifestations were repressed by Stalin, but which, together with the closely related problem of agriculture, has dominated the *Problematik* of the post-Stalin era. The fact is that the three "non-M's" clash with some of the most fundamental requirements of a modern economy and society. The lack of a market mechanism, that is, the command principle, obstructs decentralization and thus conflicts with a modern economy's enormous complexity, the need for dispersed initiative to take full advantage of industrialism's productive and growing potential, and the modern consumer's quest for quality and variety of goods and services. Demonetization, albeit partial, stands in the way of effective decentralization and bars the use of a rational calculus even within the framework of the command economy. And lastly, direct controls over labor—trained and educated labor at that—offend against human dignity and the sense of justice. In terms of the historical contrast with the West, the wheel is set for another turn.

Labor

The breaking of the autonomy of the Soviet trade unions at the outset of the Five-Year Plans—more precisely, at the 16th Party Conference in April, 1929—was essential for the consolidation of Stalin's power. Their concern with living standards and distributive justice would have stood in the way of Stalin's industrialization. What followed is well known. Less than a year later began the collectivization drive, a kind of mass enserfment in the name of socialism, an adscription of the peasantry to state-controlled (if not formally state-owned) estates complete with *barshchina* (*corvée*).[5] The impressing of millions into forced labor camps or work at places of banishment was an even harsher kind of adscription, though primarily to industrial and building enterprises. The structure of wages was revised to reward contribution to the industrialization drive above all other considerations.

Toward the end of the first decade of the Plan Era came the notorious measures aimed at limiting the mobility and controlling the activity of free nonpeasant labor: the introduction of labor books on December 20, 1938, penalties against absenteeism and loafing on December 28, 1938, and prohibitions against voluntary quitting and much stiffer penalties against absenteeism on June 26, 1940. In October of the same year appeared decrees empowering authorities to transfer skilled and technical personnel regardless of the individual's wishes and establishing a labor draft (State Labor Reserves) for youths. During the war additional restrictions on labor mobility were decreed in the face of the new and grave emergency.

One must also bear in mind that in all these cases it was the individual's

---

[5] It is said that some peasants deciphered the then initials of the party, VKP(b), as *Vtoroe krepostnoe pravo (bol'shevikov)* ("The Second Serfdom, that of the Bolsheviks").

mobility that was being curbed; the state's freedom to move labor was in no way limited. On the contrary, it was enhanced. Where in the West the individual had to be freed to be drawn into new forms of life in the course of industrialization, in the Soviet Union the conflict between curbs on mobility and industrialization did not appear, at least not at that stage. The adscriber and the industrializer were one and the same.

If we cannot approve these developments on ethical grounds, we can at least understand some of them with reference to the logic of haste operating in the particular milieu. But the controls over labor—and especially the concomitant drop in living standards (including "leisure") and the brutalities of the collectivization drive and of the forced labor camps—had a great and lasting negative impact on two of the regime's prime long-run goals: the re-education of man according to the Communist model, and productivity (particularly in agriculture).

More gradually and less dramatically, but in the long run possibly of no smaller importance, there also appeared a situation in which the life of the individual urban worker or employee—not to mention the peasant on the kolkhoz—became closely tied in very many ways to his immediate employer and the closely-related trade union. The individual came to depend largely on the employer and the trade union for housing, recreation, vacations, medical care, cultural activities, and further technical or professional training. This tended, and still tends, to "pigeon-hole" the individual in society along the lines of his job and profession to a greater extent than is usually the case in other industrial systems. In a sense, the regime has striven to maintain some aspects of a rural social structure as well as a village morality while industrializing and urbanizing at unprecedented speed. Convenient as this may have been for the regime for political, educative, and economic purposes, one wonders how well it accords with a more highly developed, urban, industrial society. Or, alternatively, whether it might not hide the seeds of a certain particularism along economic lines.

The post-Stalin developments with regard to labor are far from consistent. In some respects the direct controls over individuals have been tightened, despite the over-all relaxation of terror in the country. This is especially true of the peasants, by now of course a much smaller proportion of the population. [6] Although criminal prosecution for failure to work the required minimum for the kolkhoz was apparently abandoned in October, 1953, beginning with mid-1954 the minimum itself was sharply increased on a farm-by-farm basis. Certain new sanctions were introduced to enforce compliance with the minimum work norms, the most important of which seems to be the curtailment or complete recapture of the

---

[6]According to the January, 1959, census, *kolkhozniki* engaged in "social production" represented just under one-third of the total active population (excluding that engaged in private subsidiary agriculture).

private plot. But at the same time, in the usual "carrot and stick" fashion, work for the kolkhoz has been made materially much more attractive. The direction (largely through the Komsomol) of many hundreds of thousands for settlement in the "virgin lands," annually for harvesting, and for construction projects in the East, are other instances of retained or even enlarged direct controls over labor. Graduates of various technical and professional schools are apparently also still administratively assigned to their first jobs. And last, but certainly not least, there are now the "anti-parasite laws," adopted by the various republics in somewhat varying form between 1957 and 1961, and aimed against those deemed not to engage in socially useful activities. [7]

On the other side of the ledger the two major developments are 1) the transformation of at least a large part of the forced labor camps into "correctional labor colonies" and apparently a very large reduction in the number of persons undergoing forced labor, and 2) the repeal in April, 1956, of the 1940 decrees pertaining to penalties for absenteeism and the compulsory transfer of workers. The latter, however, apparently merely recognized the *de facto* situation, since the decrees had not been really enforced for quite a number of years. Simultaneously, a thoroughgoing wage and income reform has been carried out, chiefly for the benefit of the lowest paid workers and employees and of pensioners. Its effect has been to reduce very markedly the extent of income inequality in the nonpeasant sector and, with the relative pulling up of the peasants' earnings, in the society as a whole. The fact that the reduction in wage inequality coincided with the abolition of certain direct controls (outside the village) only served to underline how anachronistic the latter had become by the mid-fifties.

Thus, what a Western economist would consider a rather "normal" labor market has emerged (always excepting the kolkhoz sector). True, the total supply of labor in this market is subject to much greater social and political pressure than exists in other industrial systems, as, for instance, through the medium of the anti-parasite laws. [8] Moreover, chiefly because of inertia, labor exchanges have not yet been organized, though the matter is apparently receiving attention on the part of some economists. Although rate setting is still formally a centralized function, the allocative function of Soviet wages is on the whole the same as in any labor market, and in their slow way they tend to move accordingly.

It is therefore not surprising that the factory trade union committees

---

[7] See R. Beermann, "The Parasites Law," *Soviet Studies,* XIII, No. 2, 191–205.

[8] The Program aims at drawing an even higher percentage of women into gainful employment by means of expanded child-care facilities, shortcuts for housework, and higher minimum wages. The anti-parasite laws could presumably be employed to the same end. The drafters of the Program were probably aware that strong countertendencies may be appearing as the housing shortage is alleviated, real incomes of primary breadwinners rise, and the over-all sense of national or social urgency declines.

should be significantly revitalized and should become more actively concerned with questions of fairness as they affect the individual worker. At the same time, the range of these questions is being significantly broadened as mechanization and automation begin to release substantial numbers of workers from their jobs. [9]

But effective trade union independence or local workers' management are something else again. Both imply a degree of pluralism in the society of which there seems to be no sign on the horizon, least of all in the party Program. Workers' management also implies a degree of enterprise autonomy that hardly has a place in the Soviet command economy; it cannot come while management itself, for all its authority in the plant, has hardly any autonomy in relation to the environment.

The party Program is concerned with something quite different, namely, the remaking of man into a "Communist man," that is, into a willing, eager, honest, and highly efficient worker. (Indeed, so eager and willing that the question of autonomy on any level would lose much of its meaning; and we are moreover told that the Communist society will retain the centralized guidance of production.) This is the Program's paramount goal, its center of gravity. In a sense, it is also its most conservative feature: it sets out to change man, not institutions, on the way to "communism." No one will say that the party has set itself an easy target.

Money

During the period of so-called War Communism, under the double impact of the direct emergency and a misguided doctrine, money lost virtually all its usual functions: as a medium of exchange, unit of account, and store of value. One could even say that it disappeared, were it not for its conspicuous presence in hyperinflated denominations. Under the impact of another dire emergency, and after a painful confrontation of doctrine with reality, its usual roles and functions were restored with the NEP. Then, roughly from 1929 on, as the market mechanism was squeezed out and the command principle enthroned in its place, the Soviet economy was again partially demonetized.

In what ways was the Soviet economy under Stalin partially demonetized? True, money retained the traditional functions cited above, but with many important exceptions. Because of the reliance placed on it for wage payment and consumer goods distribution (chiefly for labor-incentive pur-

[9]With regard to this paragraph see particularly the following articles by Emily Clark Brown: "The Local Union in Soviet Industry: Its Relations with Members, Party, and Management," *Industrial and Labor Relations Review,* XIII, No. 2 (Jan., 1960), 192–215, and "A Note on Employment and Unemployment in the Soviet Union in the Light of Technical Progress," *Soviet Studies,* XII, No. 3, 231–40. On the recent wage reform see Walter Galenson, "The Soviet Wage Reform," *Proceedings of the Thirteenth Annual Meeting, Industrial Relations Research Association* (1961), pp. 250–65.

poses), money was most in its own in the relations between the state and the household sector and within the household sector itself. Yet even here there were important exceptions: distribution of income within the kolkhoz, most of which was in kind, the maintenance of forced labor, the rationing of urban housing at nominal rents, self-supply in housing and foodstuffs by both the agricultural and the nonagricultural populations, compulsory road labor by the peasantry, and so forth.

Money as a medium of exchange was also removed, or almost removed, from a considerable number of transactions in the production sector. Kolkhozy paid in kind for the services of MTS equipment, and more by way of tribute than by way of fee at that; the state purchased most foodstuffs from the kolkhozy and their members at "procurement prices" which were not far from zero; with insignificant exceptions,[10] nothing was paid by enterprises for the use of natural resources, or of fixed capital and a large part of working capital; the portion of working capital borrowed from the Bank carried only nominal interest rates; the "charter capital" extended by the state to its enterprises was not only interest-free, but was also nonrepayable; certain intangibles were not legally subject to sale or purchase, for example, patents, licenses (except for fiscal levies on some), "goodwill"; tangible capital assets were also generally not subject to sale after having become part of a state enterprise's "basic fund," and after 1941 even surplus equipment could not be easily disposed of. Finally, the use of money by enterprises was circumscribed in many ways (earmarking, rationing of producer goods) so as to minimize the chance of unauthorized claims against resources.

The function of money as a unit of account was equally seriously impaired. What could not be bought or sold generally carried no price at all (land, natural resources, intangibles, the services of capital as a factor of production in most cases), or was often accounted for at rather unrealistic prices (structures and installed equipment). The system of physical success indicators for management and of physical investment-choice indicators for planners, in itself partly a consequence of the demonetization, tended to reduce the role of money in accounting and calculation even further. The result was to render economic calculation often impossible or extremely difficult, quite apart from the rationality of such price parameters as existed. Agriculture, with its crazy quilt of prices and no prices, was only the most conspicuous example of a situation that cut across the whole economy. (Although the discussion in this and the preceding two paragraphs is in the past tense, much of what is said still applies at this writing.)

It would be difficult to assign a single explanation for the partial de-

---

[10]For instance, the nominal rentals for urban sites and rather low stumpage fees in forestry.

monetization of the Soviet economy after 1929. Certainly ideological and doctrinal factors were quite important. Marxian economic analysis attributes more of a distributive than an allocative importance to "value categories" (price, wage, rent, interest), and with the distribution problem "solved" in the new order, there seemed to be little need for attention to them. This view still finds expression among those Soviet economists who see only a very limited connection between "the law of value" and resource allocation by the planning organs. Also, if certain things, such as land, are not for sale, why have prices for them? Why account for them? "Direct" calculation, that is, calculation in physical terms or in labor time, seemed to bring the economy closer to its ultimate goal of full communism— a tendency that was no doubt reinforced by the technocratic biases in Soviet planning.

Technocracy (though not necessarily under its own name)—whether in the earlier decades in the USSR, in the United States during the Great Depression, or in some underdeveloped countries today—is essentially a response to great economic need, to crisis, in the form of a revolt against conventional methods of problem-solving. It is another expression of the logic of haste. While the technocrat's dismissal of money is irrational, nonetheless long-range planning for a technological and economic revolution of the magnitude of that in the USSR in the thirties must rely a good deal on physical criteria, because value magnitudes become too unstable and unpredictable over time under such conditions.

Further, considerations of social control were doubtless also quite important. Money is a form of social power that may lead resources astray and is subject to only imperfect control by political authority. The considerable demonetization of agriculture under Stalin was thus a way of bringing this sector under the most direct political control for the extraction of its surplus. That this demonetization of agriculture, along with other measures applied to it, turned out to be disastrous for its long-run productivity is another matter. And, as we have already seen, the use of money funds by nonagricultural enterprises was also limited in many ways for control purposes.

The post-Stalin period saw a moderate but significant reversal in this regard, especially in agriculture, where relations between producers and the state were largely remonetized, mainly owing to the abolition of the MTS and the considerable reduction in the multiplicity of prices. Yet the kolkhoz's obligation to sell predetermined amounts of produce to the state remains. The relations between the kolkhoz and its members have also been considerably remonetized, chiefly by virtue of much higher farm prices, though payment in kind against labor days and self-supply are still important.

Outside agriculture the progress in remonetization has been less actual than by way of problem-setting and intellectual debate. The official position under Khrushchev has been the opposite of Stalin's—the role of "value categories" is to increase progressively, and the entry into moneyless communism is to be "dialectical" rather than gradual. (It is very convenient indeed to have both dialectical and smooth—*neuklonnyi*—progress in one's intellectual baggage!) The 1961 party Program reiterates this position, although one searches in vain in the literature of recent years for a clear explanation of just what the increased role of "value categories" is to represent henceforth. The answer is probably not yet available. We may note in passing, however, that questions of money, and gold, [11] still tend to be suffused with considerable mysticism in the Soviet economic mind.

One should take note, though, of the partial resolution along rationalist lines of such an important problem as that of "capital efficiency," that is, of allowing explicitly for the scarcity of capital. The resolution is partial because it only legalizes the use of a surrogate for the interest rate and legitimizes established practice; it fails to answer the crucial question of how such a charge is to be determined in fact. However, there are now those who advocate interest payments by enterprises on the capital invested in them by the state, and even repayment of such capital, various types of rent on natural resources, assignment of capital values to subsoil resources, relative valuation of different parcels of land, and even a consistent and integrated system of rational prices for all scarce goods and resources. [12] The fat is in the fire, but clearly major changes must take time. It seems that at this writing the 1962 reform of wholesale prices is to proceed according to rather conventional principles, that is, the principles that shaped such Soviet reforms from 1936 on. [13]

At stake is of course more than monetization; even more than economic calculation, rational prices, and allocative efficiency. At stake is the whole centralized structure of the Soviet economy, the command economy itself, and ultimately, the location and distribution of power in the society. This brings us to what is, with agriculture, one of the two most topical questions in the Soviet economy, the question of centralization-decentralization.

Overall Organization

The Soviet press and economic literature may still eschew the word "decentralization," but they cannot avoid the thought. Many ideas on the subject are clearly abroad in the land. Managers, who often found the

[11]Note, for example, Khrushchev's point that the USSR might have to pay in gold for any food imports from "capitalist countries" (*Правда*, Dec. 16, 1961, p. 2).

[12]See, for example, Robert W. Campbell, "Marx, Kantorovich, and Novozhilov: *Stoimost'* versus Reality," *Slavic Review*, XX, No. 3 (Oct., 1961), 402–18.

[13]*Экономическая газета*, Sept. 25, 1961, pp. 13–14.

sovnarkhozy easier and faster to deal with than the old ministries and *glavki* but who have in fact gained hardly any additional powers since Stalin's death,[14] seem to be bringing their complaints more into the open again.[15] These are the traditional ones: delays in receiving plans, too many plan revisions, too many authorities, chronic supply difficulties, and—foremost—lack of power at the enterprise level and "petty tutelage" from above. The sovnarkhozy plead for more power as against their superiors, and republic authorities ask for more power vis-à-vis union authorities. Judging by the complaints, the situation has changed little on the whole since 1957, despite considerable optimism on this score at the time.

The complaints are perfectly understandable but should not be dismissed as mere ex parte pleas. The disinterested observer can see great need for decentralization in the Soviet economy, and primarily to the following ends:

1. To permit far greater modernization and innovation on the basis of dispersed initiative. At the moment such attempts run into serious obstacles not only because of management's conservatism but also because decision with regard to the necessary elements—finances, production of equipment, supply of materials, technological policy—is highly centralized, and coordination among them is poor and slow. A kind of "contradiction" has developed between the abundance of skill and talent on the spot and the organizational means for translating this creativity into reality. The much-publicized party and "public" supervisory committees, established mostly after the June, 1959, Plenum of the CC CPSU, can perhaps spur and goad allegedly conservative managers, but can they "fight city hall"?

2. To permit a certain amount of local investment in response to local needs. The argument here is similar. Immediately after the 1957 reorganization there was apparently some thought even in the highest places of turning investment funds over to the sovnarkhozy in lump sums,[16] but manifestations of localism on their part led to progressive re- (not de-) centralization of this function.

3. To permit greater lateral communication within the economy, a type of communication that necessarily suffers in a command economy. This refers to the sensitivity and responsiveness of production and distribution to demand (for both producer and consumer goods). It also refers to that specifically Soviet problem of trilateral communication between the designers, builders, and users of equipment and structures. The vertical communication that today largely substitutes for lateral communication is

---

[14]Reference is primarily to the decree of the Council of Ministers USSR, entitled "On Increasing the Rights of Enterprise Directors," dated August 9, 1955.

[15]E. g., *Экономическая газета*, Oct. 9, 1961, p. 23, and Dec. 18, 1961, pp. 8–12.

[16]See especially Khrushchev's speech before a construction conference on April 12, 1958, printed (with considerable delay) in *Строительная газета*, July 2, 1958.

long and slow, passes through a large number of intermediate levels, and often involves decisions by a considerable number of authorities even at the highest levels. Better lateral connections would presumably also permit improvement in the success indicators for management.

4. To alleviate the unfavorable trend of increasing complexity and burden of planning, checking on plan fulfillment, and collecting data. In the case of Soviet-type planning the main burden of the work (especially in production and supply planning) arises from the need to determine the *interrelations* between goods (factors, products, construction jobs) and between economic units (regions, enterprises). Thus, crudely speaking, the amount of planning work is proportional to the square of the product of the number of goods and the number of economic units. (Of course, in very many instances there are no interrelations between given goods or enterprises. This, however, does not affect our conclusion so long as the proportion of such empty cells in our notional matrix remains roughly constant.) It is clear, therefore, that in the absence of major methodological or organizational changes the burden of planning and related work in such a rapidly expanding economy as the Soviet must be growing very fast. Decentralization would seem to be one of the ways in which the burden of this work might be held down.

The "territorialization" of economic organization after the 1957 reform has by now resulted in a considerably more complicated structure than was probably originally intended. First, two additional territorial levels have been created: in mid-1960 republic sovnarkhozy in the three larger republics (RSFSR, Ukraine, Kazakhstan) to supervise the local sovnarkhozy; and in May, 1961, the so-called Councils for Co-ordination and Planning in seventeen newly-created "large economic regions," each embracing on the average about six of the original economic-administrative regions. [17] Secondly, by the end of 1961 there had been established eleven USSR State Commissions (*Komitety*) for individual branches of industry and for construction.[18] While the CCP's and the Commissions are presumably less concerned with day-to-day operations than with technological and investment policies, nonetheless the channels of communication within the economy must have been substantially lengthened and complicated.

The limits to decentralization in a command economy such as the

---

[17] Экономическая газета, May 28, 1961, p. 2, and *Problems of Communism.* X, No. 5 (Sept.–Oct., 1961), 46–48.

[18] As of December, 1961, there exist the following "branch" State Commissions of the Council of Ministers USSR in industry and construction: automation and machine-building, aviation equipment, defense equipment, radio-electronics, electronic equipment, shipbuilding, chemical industry, ferrous and nonferrous metals, fuels, atomic energy, construction (*Правда*, Dec. 9, 1961, p. 2).

Soviet, however, derive not only from the presumably considerable vested interests that might be arrayed against it. (In connection with the latter point, let us recall that the 1957 reorganization was carried out as part of a major power struggle in the Kremlin.) Such limits also stem from (a) the fact that the lower echelons' objectives do not always coincide with objectives at the top, and (b) from the lower echelons' incomplete information. That is to say, "centralism," to use the Soviet term, serves the crucial functions of safeguarding the regime's values and of assuring balance to the economy. The two have in common, *inter alia*, a certain dependence on the extent to which pressure is put on the economy's resources. The greater the haste and the less slack in the economy, the more the regime strives to prevent any unauthorized use (or non-use) of resources, and, at the same time, the sellers' market becomes more acute and the problem of balance arises more urgently. In short, given its political and economic realities, there is generally a substantial recentralizing tendency in the Soviet system, though it usually operates on a piecemeal basis as individual problems are faced and resolved by taking them away from the jurisdiction of lower authorities.[19]

Short of a renunciation of the command economy in favor of a radically different structure, what courses of action are open to reduce the costs of centralization or to decentralize without the disadvantages just mentioned? The one attracting high attention at the moment in the USSR (and, by reflection, abroad) is the use of mathematical techniques, primarily input-output matrices, in conjunction with modern computational equipment, to speed up the construction of plans and to permit the preparation of alternative plans. Academician V. S. Nemchinov, a leader in this new trend among Soviet economists, has propounded the more elaborate notion of "economic cybernetics" which would combine the high-speed plan-construction techniques with high-speed, continuous transmission of information to the planning center and of directives from it.[20] This is not the place to analyze at length the promise that input-output or economic cybernetics offer to the Soviet economy. It must be borne in mind, however, that the matrix would have to be very large to supplant the present set of material balances at the Gosplan USSR level alone; in planning for 1962, Gosplan USSR employed over 14,000 material balances. Even if a matrix of this size were constructed and successfully utilized, and if similar tables were employed at other levels, many of the present difficulties of the Soviet economy—sellers' market, faulty success indicators, faulty prices,

---

[19]A noticeable recentralizing trend is proceeding at the time of this writing (end of 1961), affecting particularly "plan indicators," research, investment, and the construction industry. See, for example, *Правда*, Dec. 7, 1961, p. 4, and *Экономическая газета*. Oct. 9, 1961, p. 9, Nov. 27, 1961, p. 28, Dec. 18, 1961, pp. 4 and 7–8.

[20]*Экономическая газета*, Oct. 23, 1961, pp. 21–23.

and so forth—need not be completely remedied. Nor are the planners very like to automate entirely their delicate functions (and work themselves out of their own jobs besides).

Secondly, some sectors might be taken out of the command-economy structure and linked to the rest of the economy by means of a price nexus as, for example, is already the case with the household sector. Steps in this direction have also been taken since Stalin's death (e.g., in 1955 and 1958) with regard to the collective farm sector. It was expected that collective farms would determine their production programs with reference to the prices posted by the state. But delivery quotas were never abolished, and because of the constant pressure from the top, the kolkhozy have been subjected to rather detailed control and guidance by local authorities.[21] Thus, the price mechanism has not been given a chance to be decisive. At any rate, agriculture can be potentially so "separated out" because of its rather small use of current inputs from the rest of the economy. Where the flow of current inputs is much more important in relation to output, the given sector's reciprocal relation with the rest of the economy is greater, and therefore its "separation" by means of the price mechanism is not likely to be viewed with much favor so long as the command principle remains dominant.

Thirdly, a way of meeting some of the problems of the sellers' market is to merge enterprises with their suppliers, thus transforming the problems into intra-enterprise ones and thereby facilitating their solution, as was done in Czechoslovakia in 1958.[22] This was also done for years in the USSR in a relatively small number of conspicuous cases (the so-called *kombinaty*). Recently, a merger movement among industrial enterprises was started in the Ukraine.[23] The development bears watching, although the motives in this instance seem to be mixed: many of the mergers are horizontal, having been formed to amalgamate what are regarded to be uneconomically small units.

A more topical issue than greater enterprise self-sufficiency is regional autarky. There is a strong bias under Soviet conditions in this direction, for regional autarky may appeal both to the local interests, by easing supply problems, and to central authorities, by reducing planning complexities. In other words, it shortens the lines of communication, and over time may ease the problem of assuring balance. But of course in the short run it is likely to increase supply difficulties elsewhere, and in the long run may also amount to an uneconomic allocation of resources. An important reason for the creation of the "large economic regions" seems to be the

---

[21]For recent confirmation see Khrushchev's speech, *Правда*, Dec. 25, 1961, p. 1.
[22]See Jan M. Michal, *Central Planning in Czechoslovakia* (Stanford, 1960), pp. 53ff.
[23]*Экономическая газета*, Dec. 4, 1961, p. 7.

countering of autarkic tendencies on the part of the local sovnarkhozy;[24] yet, autarkic development of the large economic regions may now be stimulated.

In sum, imbalance is avoided or reduced in the command economy through greater centralization or by permitting more regional or sectoral self-sufficiency. Overcentralization is avoided by risking imbalance or allowing autarky. And the suppression of autarky is bought at the cost of a high degree of centralization, or alternatively, of imbalance. We may therefore speak of the command economy's "triangle of hazards," the vertices of which are the three conditions named. (See Figure 1.) Moving away from one fault brings the economy closer, though not necessarily in equal degree, to the other two.

FIGURE 1

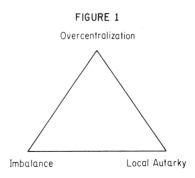

The most recent recentralizing trend[25] is probably a response to a multiplicity of factors: the heightened pressure on resources[26] brought about by increased defense commitments, lags in construction of new capacity in a number of sectors, and the unsatisfactory performance of agriculture; autarkic moves by the sovnarkhozy; and lags in technological progress (in relation to intentions).

Neither the text of the party Program nor the speeches by Khrushchev and others at the 22nd Party Congress foreshadows any significant departure from the present system of planning and economic administration; on the contrary, they amount to its reaffirmation. And despite the traditional bows in the direction of "the role of local authorities" and "enter-

[24]*Ibid.*, June 23, 1961, p. 2.

[25]See footnote [17].

[26]The budget for 1962 (*Правда*, Dec. 7, 1961) increases defense outlay to 13.4 billion rubles, or nearly 45 per cent above the amount originally budgeted for 1961. It is difficult at the moment to say to what extent this is a "real" increase. Note, however, that planned capital investments are to increase in 1962 by 8.1 per cent, against the 12–13 per cent planned for each of the two preceding years, while noncentralized investments are being reduced in absolute amount in comparison with 1961.

prise initiative," their general tenor suggests, if anything, stronger central controls for the balancing of plans and in investment and technological policy. Perhaps the only important contrary note was struck by Khrushchev when he said, "For the sake of better plan fulfillment it is necessary to give enterprises greater opportunities to dispose of their profits, and to use the latter more amply to stimulate better work by the enterprise's staff and for the enterprise's expansion."[27] It may be noted that this was the only point in the whole part of the speech dealing with planning and organization that elicited applause, according to the official transcript.

THE ROLE OF CENTRAL PLANNING*
— · — · — · — · — · — · — · — · —

Herbert S. Levine[†]

This paper is concerned with the role played by Soviet centralized planning in the growth attained by the Soviet economy. One possible and interesting way of approaching this problem would be through the question: to what extent did the Soviet economy grow because of and to what extent independently of or even in spite of Soviet centralized planning? That is, in the absence of centralized planning as it was developed, even in the absence of the Communist regime, might the Russian economy have grown anyway? This is not a completely meaningless question for the economic history of Russia from the middle of the 1880's to the first World War, with the notably rapid strides in industrialization it exhibited, gives a background to such conjectures.

But we will not pursue this approach. Not because we do not think it is interesting, but because of the analytical difficulties involved. These historical "if games" simply defy meaningful handling. We will instead, pursue the problem through a discussion of the ways in which Soviet centralized planning has affected growth—how it has fostered growth and how, perhaps, it has hampered it.

What is Planning?

To begin, let us first make clear what we mean by the term planning and then what we mean by Soviet centralized planning. In its most general

[27] *Πpae∂a*, Oct. 10, 1961, p. 6.
*Reprinted by permission of the editor, publisher, and the author, from "Growth and Planning in the Soviet Union" in Wayne A. Leeman (ed.) *The Soviet Economy in Theory and Practice* (Columbia, Mo.: University of Missouri, School of Business, and Public Administration, 1964, pp. 67–94. All footnotes deleted.
†Dr. Herbert S. Levine is Associate Professor of Economics, University of Pennsylvania. His publications include: *The Centralized Planning of Supply in Soviet Industry* (1959), and "Pressure and Planning in the Soviet Economy" in Henry Rosovsky (ed.) *Industrialization in Two Systems* (1966).

sense, economic planning is the working out of a description of a desired state of the economy at some future date, and the use of active instrumentalities to bring about this state of the economy. The key elements here are: "the working out," "desired state of the economy" and "use of active instrumentalities."

In Soviet planning practice, the economic plan is worked out centrally. The policy to be embodied in the plan is set by the Soviet political leaders and is communicated by them to the central planners who work out the details of the plan. In this process, the central planners employ a two way system of communication with the intermediate planning and administrative bodies in the economy and the basic producing units. Instructions reflecting the desires of the leaders flow down from the center and information reflecting production possibilities flows up from the periphery and is coordinated by the planners at the center. It is the task of the central planners to construct a plan which embodies, at the highest possible level permitted by the real production possibilities, the state of the economy desired by the political leaders.

What is the Soviet political leaders' desired state of the economy? What is the aim of Soviet planning? According to Marx the aim of planning was to eradicate the exploitation of the working class, to eliminate the disharmony, the disproportions which arise from the anarchy of the capitalist system and the economic crises this and other factors cause, and to foster the further growth of the economy after capitalism has ceased to perform its positive growth function. Other 19th and early 20th century socialists stressed the social justice and welfare aims of planning. While the more recent socialist writings of the 1930's (e.g. Lange) speak of the aim of planning as being the achievement of the optimum (more in the static than dynamic sense) allocation of resources that is described by the model of the perfectly competitive economy.

All of these writers assumed to one degree or another, that the planning they spoke of would be used in a mature, relatively "overdeveloped" economy. However, when planning began to be used in the Soviet Union, the Russian economy was still relatively underdeveloped and in fact planning was begun in order to change this situation. Therefore, contrary to these previous writings, the aim of Soviet planning has been growth—not harmonious performance or current welfare or static optimum. Furthermore, after extensive debate in the mid-twenties, the Soviet leaders decided that this growth had to proceed at an extremely rapid rate. All the pressure of the planning mechanism was devoted to the attainment of the fastest possible pace of economic development. Each sector of the economy was encouraged to grow as fast as it could and pressure was put on lagging sectors to catch up. The disharmonious performance of the economy which resulted from such planning has been characterized by some Western analysts as a failure of Soviet planning. They have said that it is as bad for a sector of the economy to run ahead of the plan as it is for it to run behind, in the same sense that it is as bad for a train to run ahead of schedule as it is to run behind. Now it is true that it would be quite disconcerting if one appeared at a train station at 7:45, planning to take an 8:00 train only to be told that the glorious engineer of the 8:00 train overfulfilled his plan and left the station at 7:30. However, the analogy is not a useful one because the aim of Soviet planning is not to accommodate the people in Soviet society, it is not to "pick up the most passengers." It is to get the economy to its destination of a highly industrialized economy as rapidly as possible even if this means that many "passengers" suffer.

This desire for rapid growth which required drastic structural change in the economy, compressed into a short period of time, has had a direct effect on the "active instrumentalities" used by the Soviets to implement their plans. In the choice between indirect and direct methods of control, a question arises about the usefulness of the indirect method, the price system with its marginal price calculations, when the aim is to change the entire face of the economy and change it rapidly. How useful, it can be asked, is the price mechanism in accomplishing politically determined goals when the society is declared to be (as if) in a state of war and the economy in a state of full mobilization? Under such circumstances, the price system is felt by many to work too slowly. It is also not clear that it works at all effectively. For the parameters needed to make decision at the margin are, in such situations, themselves variables and uncertainty runs rampant. When concentration is on the rapid development of new industries, new products, new regional complexes, close marginal calculations are difficult to make. Furthermore, many of these decisions are better made in concert rather than being made by individual decision makers who are unable to take external economies into account.

As a consequence, the Soviet leaders, having decided on a program of forced draft industrialization, also decided to accomplish the program through reliance primarily on nonprice methods of plan construction and control. Price-type calculation did not play an important role in plan construction. And plans were implemented through a command system in which output targets and input limits, essentially in physical terms were communicated through an administrative hierarchy, and considerable monetary and nonmonetary incentive rewards were paid for the fulfillment and overfulfillment of the tasks assigned.

Soviet Planning, Structural Change, and Resources Supply

Having presented this brief sketch of the aims and methods of Soviet centralized planning, we can now proceed to the question of the role of planning in Soviet growth. It is our contention that Soviet centralized planning has had its main positive impact on Soviet growth through the changes it has wrought in the output structure of the economy, and in the availability of productive resources. The impact has been on a macro level rather than a micro level. Centralized planning and control, with the force of the dictatorship behind it, has been used more as a powerful blunt instrument to effect large "macro" changes than as a fine instrument to effect "micro" efficiencies.

Let us look at some of the evidence which pertains to this contention. As regards the output structure of the economy, the impact of Soviet centralized planning is evident in the data presented in Table 1. At the

TABLE 1

SHARE OF INDUSTRY AND CONSTRUCTION IN NATIONAL PRODUCT
(percent)

	USSR	USA
1869/1879		21
1899/1908		26
1928	28	34*
1937	35	34
1950	38	40
1958	49	37
1962	53	37

* 1929

Sources and Notes: USSR—1928 and 1937, from O. Hoeffding, *Soviet National Income and Product in 1928*, p. 85 (these data are in current prices); 1950–1962, calculated on basis of data in JEC, *Annual Economic Indicators for the USSR* (1964) pp. 93–94, without imputation of agricultural rent (these are in 1955 prices).

USA (all data from Department of Commerce publications in current prices)— 1869/1879 and 1899/1908, from *Historical Statistics of the United States from Colonial Times to 1957*, p. 140; 1929–1950, *National Income, 1951 Edition*, p. 158; *Survey of Current Business,* July 1960, p. 13; 1962, *Survey of Current Business,* July 1963, p. 17. Except for 1869/79 and 1899/08, industry includes forestry, fisheries and utilities (electric and gas) so as to correspond to Soviet statistical practice. The omission of these categories in the two early periods is not thought to have a significant effect.

start of the plan period in 1928, the share of the two highest priority sectors, industry and construction, in total national product was 28%. In the course of the initial nine years of intensive economic change and growth, the share of industry and construction rose to 35%. It then continued to rise, so that by 1962 the share of these two sectors in total output reached 53%. The power of Soviet centralized planning to force the change in output structure desired by the political leaders is clear when the Soviet record is compared with that of the United States. In the thirty year period of our early industrialization at the end of the last century, the change in our structure of output was nowhere near as great as the Soviet's in the plan era. The share of industry and construction rose only from 21% in the decade 1869/1879 to 26% in the decade 1899/1908. And presently, the share of industry and construction in our total output is under 40%, far less than in the Soviet economy.

A further illustration of the power of centralized planning to force desired changes in output structure is seen in the structural changes within industrial output itself. Soviet planners have stressed the output of producers' goods in preference to consumers' goods. While it is generally true that economies in the process of industrialization show an increase in the share of producers' goods in gross industrial output, the Soviets have shown a very rapid growth in the share of producers' goods and have pushed this share to an extremely high level.

The data in Table 2 show that the Soviets began the plan era with the share of producers' goods at 40% and by 1962 had increased this share to

TABLE 2

SHARES OF PRODUCERS' GOODS AND CONSUMERS' GOODS
IN SOVIET GROSS INDUSTRIAL OUTPUT
(percent)

	Producers' Goods	Consumers' Goods
1928	40	60
1937	58	42
1950	69	31
1958	72	28
1962	74	26

Source: Ts. S.U., *Narodnoe Khoziaistvo SSSR v 1962g.*, p. 120.

74%. Comparable data for the United States are difficult to get but some rough calculations based upon information in a number of "input-output" tables tend to show that in 1919, 1929 and 1939, the share of producers' goods in U.S. gross industrial output was about 50%, while in 1947 it was in the neighborhood of 60%.

Soviet centralized planning has also demonstrated its power to foster economic growth by its ability to increase the supply of productive factors —capital and labor—in terms of both quantity and quality. The Soviet data in Table 3 illustrate how the real resources devoted to capital formation have been a growing proportion of national product since the inception of centralized planning. The American data fail to exhibit any great change in our early period of growth; in the recent period the trend, if anything, appears to be downward.

TABLE 3

GROWTH OF THE SHARE OF GROSS INVESTMENT
IN GROSS NATIONAL PRODUCT
(percent)

USSR		USA	
(in 1950 ruble factor cost)		(in 1929 dollars)	
1928	14	1869/78	23
1937	27	1879/88	22
1950	28	1889/98	25
1958	33	1899/1908	23
1962	36	(in 1954 dollars)	
		1929	24
		1948	20
		1957	19

Sources and Notes: USSR—1928–1950, A. Bergson, *The Real National Income of Soviet Russia Since 1928*, p. 237. 1958 and 1962, projected from the 1955 figure given in Bergson, *ibid.*, and the following: the growth of gross investment and GNP (without imputation of agricultural rent).

This increase in the proportion of real output going to capital formation, augmented by the fact that in a newly developing economy a large part of gross investment goes directly into net additions to capital stock rather than replacement of worn-out capital, has been a significant factor in fostering growth. But in addition to this quantitative increase in capital, there has been a qualitative increase, in the sense that advanced foreign technology has been borrowed and adapted for new capital projects and capital has been directed into areas where it would most foster growth. The figures in Table 4 show that Soviet central planners have directed a much

TABLE 4

SHARES OF GROSS INVESTMENT GOING TO INDUSTRY AND HOUSING,
TRADE AND SERVICES
(percent)

	USSR		USA	
	1928–1937	1953–1959	1880–1912	1953–1959
Industry	39	40	19	27
Housing, trade and services	24	35	52	61

Sources and Notes: USSR—1928–1937, N. Kaplan in Bergson (ed), *Soviet Economic Growth*, p. 52 (simple average of figures for 1928/29–1932 and 1933–1937); 1953–1959, S. Cohn in JEC, *Dimensions of Soviet Economic Power*, p. 83 (simple average of 1953 and 1959).

USA—1880–1912, Kaplan, *op. cit.*, p. 54; 1953–1959, Cohn, *op. cit.*, p. 83 (simple average of 1953 and 1959).

greater proportion of their investment into machines and factories for industry and a much lower proportion into housing, trade and services than has been true in the United States. In this way the Soviets get more of increase in total national product per unit increase in capital stock than we do (in technical terms their incremental output-capital ratio is higher than ours).

Turning to the development of the labor force in high priority sectors, we again see evidence of the power of Soviet centralized control to foster high speed industrialization. The figures in Table 5 show that the average annual rate of growth of the Russian nonagricultural labor force in the period 1928–1959 was higher than that in the United States in 1870–1900.

TABLE 5
AVERAGE ANNUAL RATE OF GROWTH IN
NON-AGRICULTURAL LABOR FORCE
(percent)

USSR		USA	
1928–1959*	4.9	1870–1900	3.7
1928–1937	8.6	1880–1980	4.3
1950–1959	3.0	1930–1960	1.8
		1950–1960	2.6

*Excludes World War II; period considered to be 27 years long.

Source: W. Eason in Bergson and Kuznets (eds), *Economic Trends in the Soviet Union*, pp. 76–77.

And this was so despite the fact that immigrants were swarming into America in that period and our population doubled, whereas in the Soviet Union in the period 1928–1959 population grew by only 40%. Moreover, in the Soviet Union in its period of intense industrial development, 1928–1937, the Soviet nonagricultural labor force grew at an extremely high rate, twice what we experienced in our fastest growing decade since 1870 (the decade 1880–1890).

How did the Soviet central planners effectuate such increases in the labor force in the high priority, growth producing sectors? Looking specifically at the increase in the industrial labor force, the data in Table 6 show that in the period 1928–1962, while the industrial labor force increased almost 350%, the total population increased by less than 50%. However, within this 50% increase of the total population, the regime was able to achieve over a 300% increase in the urban population. This resulted in a 12% drop in the rural population. Between the years 1928–1937, the urban population in Russia grew by almost 20 million people, which in terms of the rate of total population growth in that period meant roughly

TABLE 6

INDEXES OF INDUSTRIAL LABOR FORCE AND POPULATION IN USSR

	Industrial Labor Force (1928 = 100)	Total Population (1928 = 100)	Urban Population (1928 = 100)	Rural Population (1928 = 100)	Percent Urban (%)
1928	100	100	100	100	18
1937	193	109	169	96	28
1950	267	119	251	89	39
1958	379	137	346	89	47
1962	440	147	405	88	51

Sources: Industrial Labor Force: Powell in *Economic Trends*, p. 188; extended by *Nar. Khoz. v 1962*, pp. 118, 132. Population: Eason in *Economic Trends*, pp. 72–73; *Nar. Khoz, v 1962*, pp. 7–8.

that there was a net migration of over 15 million people from the country-side to the cities in those nine years alone! In 1928, the Soviet Union had about the same proportion of its total population in urban centers as did the United States in 1860, but after 1928, the growth of Soviet urbanization was twice as rapid as that in the United States after 1860. Furthermore, while the use of child labor in industry decreased, the Soviets were able to increase substantially the participation of women in the industrial labor force, primarily by keeping real wages low, making it necessary for more members of a family to be wage earners. Women comprised 28% of the industrial labor force in 1929 and 46% in 1962. Use of female members of urban families in the industrial labor force was of particular advantage in that it reduced the need for investment in urban housing.

The centralized control of agriculture played an important part where the regime, through the power it exerted over the peasantry by means of collectivization of agriculture, was able to move these great numbers of workers from farms to factories and was also able to move the food necessary to feed them.

These developments in the growth of the labor force in high priority sectors reflect the power of Soviet central planners to accomplish massive economic changes by means which include both force and effective incentives.

The Soviets have put much effort into improving the quality of the labor force through a substantial increase in education generally and through the development of a system of technical schools and on-the-job training. The increase in labor skills coupled with the new additions to the capital stock have led to a significant increase in the level of technology. Part of the impact of these educational efforts is seen in Table 7.

Further indication of the role played in education by economic priorities is to be found in the fact that during the period 1926–1960, 57% of all graduates of higher education in the USSR were in the fields of engineer-

TABLE 7

PROPORTION OF TOTAL LABOR FORCE IN USSR
SEVEN OR MORE YEARS OF EDUCATION
(percent)

1926	3
1939	12
1959	40

Source: N. DeWitt in *Dimensions of Soviet Economic Power*, p. 244; Eason in *Economic Trends;* pp. 72–73.

ing and science, whereas in the U.S. this proportion was 24%. Finally, there may be some disrespectful souls who might say that the clearest indication of the devotion of Soviet education to the real needs of economic growth is to be found in the fact that while 17% of those in the United States who received bachelor's degrees or first professional degrees in 1960 were in the category which included economics (economics, management and law), the Soviets kept this proportion down to 7%!

Soviet Planning and Economic Efficiency

In view of what has been said, can we conclude that Soviet centralized planning has been an unadulterated success in fostering the political leaders' goal of maximum possible economic growth? The answer is, of course, no. There are a number of weaknesses in the system which limit the ability of the economy to grow. Though it is true that the effect of these deficiencies is often reduced by the operation of the command system of communication and the constant statistical reporting which enables the planners to make changes rapidly when they are called for and redirect actively into high priority channels, the deficiencies still remain and have their effect. First of all, since the Soviet system of output and input valuation and plan construction methodology is quite poor, Soviet plans are far from optimum (in both the static and dynamic sense). Thus resources are wasted and output is less than it might have been. What is more, plans are quite frequently not even feasible. That is they are internally inconsistent, unbalanced and therefore unfulfillable. This too leads to losses in potential output.

Secondly, the Soviet economy suffers from many ills of overcentralization. The planners at the center are not familiar enough with the details of the real situation at the periphery. This leads to losses from unsuitable production assignments at the enterprise level, lack of consistency among different types of commands (outputs, inputs, deliveries, finances, etc.) given to the enterprise by different superior planning bodies, multiplicity of paper work and red-tape hindrances to production.

Thirdly, there is a whole set of deficiencies related to the workings of the incentive mechanism, a mechanism which was set up to reward the successful fulfillment and overfulfillment of assigned targets. The system undoubtedly has its virtues, but it also has its vices. For example, it has led enterprise managers, in successful periods when large increases in output could be achieved, to temper their rates of plan overfulfillment because this year's accomplishments become next year's plan. The operation of this "ratchet principle" has also led managers to shy away from innovational activity. The benefits to them are short-lived and the risks often great. Furthermore, while managers are given a number of targets to fulfill, mostly the physical output target has been the dominant one. The pressure to fulfill this target which builds up under the Soviet incentive system has led to many actions inimical to growth: hiding of productive reserves, statistical falsification, low quality output, changes in output mix through emphasis of easy to produce items and the wastes associated with the difficulty of getting a useful designation of the unit of output for many products and processes (e.g., production of very heavy machines when the unit of output is in terms of tons). The pressure to fulfill output targets has also led to a serious amount of supply unreliability and has led managers generally to ignore the needs of the enterprises and people who use their products. Thus, for example, a product is often produced in large numbers more because it is easy to produce than that it is useful to the purchaser. Or to the extent that there is innovation, it is more often that a manager will improve his own production techniques rather than improve his product to make it more useful to his customer.

The knowledge that deficiencies exist is helpful to our analysis, but not sufficient. What we would like to know is how important have these deficiencies of Soviet centralized planning been? By how much have they reduced output and growth? It should be borne in mind that, *purely in arithmetic terms*, the presence of inefficiencies which reduces yearly output below the maximum level, does not necessarily reduce the rate of growth (in fact, the rate of growth may end up higher than if there were no inefficiencies to begin with). But it does necessarily mean that the sum total of output over the period will be below the maximum attainable and the output in the last year will be less than the potential in the last year. This is so because there might be a steady increase in efficiency causing the percentage of potential output lost each year to fall and thus causing the rate of growth to be higher than if output in each year were at the potential maximum. However, since output in each year will be less than the potential, the sum total will be less than the potential total.

This suggests that the objective of Soviet political leaders is in reality more complex than just maximum rate of growth. It might more appropriately be said to be a desire for a level of output each year as close as possible to the potential maximum—even if this meant a lower rate of growth—assuming these potential maxima to describe in some sense an optimum growth path over time. Our measure of the cost of the inefficiencies of Soviet centralized planning would then be related to the divergence of the actual growth path from this optimum growth path. However, since we do not know what this optimum growth path for the Soviet economy is, we cannot pursue this approach. An alternative approach, perhaps less satisfying but still useful, is to compare the "efficiency" of resource use in the Soviet economy with that in other economies. This has been done in a number of recent studies in terms of the output per unit of aggregate inputs (labor and capital) for the USSR and the USA in a given year (1960), and in terms of the rate of growth of output per unit of aggregate inputs (labor, capital, farm land and livestock herds) for the USSR, USA and other countries in different periods. The former gives us a measure of the relative "static efficiency" of the Soviet and American economies (in 1960) which indicates the costs in terms of output of the deficiencies of Soviet centralized planning in that year compared with the standard of efficient resource use set by the American economy. Unfortunately, however, it also includes the influence of the relative levels of technology, relative "quality" of labor and capital. The second set of studies gives us a measure of the relative "dynamic efficiency" of the Soviet, American and other economies. An increase over time of output per unit of aggregate inputs may be caused by an increase in technology, a direction of new or shifting of old inputs into high productivity or high growth producing sectors and also by an improvement in economic organization, administration and plan construction.

The studies referred to are replete with index number difficulties and since by this point the reader is perhaps weary of such problems, let it suffice for us to indicate the rough contours of the studies' results. The study of "static efficiency" shows that if in 1960 the Soviet output mix had been produced by both the USSR and the USA using the same bundle of inputs, the USA would have produced an output mix approximately 5–20% greater than the USSR. This is a measure of the relative costs of the deficiencies of Soviet centralized planning (and the influence of the relative "quality" of Soviet and American labor and capital) in the year 1960.

The studies of "dynamic efficiency" indicate that while the Soviet rate of growth of output per unit of aggregate inputs during the Soviet's intense period of economic change, 1928–1937, probably was lower than the American rate during the last three decades of the 19th century, the Soviet rate during the entire period 1928–1958 (excluding World War II) was roughly comparable to ours in the period at the end of the last century. And the Soviet rate in the period 1950–1958 was considerably higher than ours in that period and in fact high enough to put her among the leaders along with Japan and West Germany.

These studies (especially with regard to static efficiency) are quite speculative and not too much weight should be placed on them. However, they do suggest that the loss in static efficiency suffered by the Soviet economy, while not as high perhaps as many think is not completely insignificant. And also, the Soviet ability to improve its efficiency (and its technology) over time, except perhaps for the period 1928–1937, has been comparable to the best in the non-Communist world.

Conclusion

We have tried to demonstrate in this paper that the Soviet record of economic growth has been impressive and in terms of the objectives of Soviet political leaders, which have not rated human welfare very highly, it has been quite successful. Further, we have tried to show that the main impact of Soviet centralized planning on Soviet economic growth has been felt in the ability of the central planners to force structural change in outputs and inputs on the economy. This has been reflected in the more rapid growth of industry and construction relative to total national product and within industry by the relatively more rapid growth of producers' goods in comparison with consumers' goods. And it has been reflected in the rapid increase in the quantity and quality of capital and labor. Finally, we have argued that Soviet central planners were not so effective in fostering growth in the realm of micro resource allocation, that is, they were not too successful in getting the economy in a given year with its given resources to produce an output close to its potential maximum. However, we have also argued that they have been relatively successful in achieving dynamic efficiency. The growth of outputs per unit of aggregate inputs in the Soviet economy has generally been equal to that of the leading capitalist economies.

Before closing, a short epilogue on the current situation regarding Soviet growth and planning. As our data have shown, the rate of growth since 1958 has been lower than in previous periods. While we have said that it is still too early to be sure that this will be a permanent downturn, we have pointed out that there are certain aspects of the current situation which create difficulties for maintaining rates of growth at past levels. The Soviet economy is now more mature. The products it produces are more sophisticated and differentiated and cannot as easily be produced or as rapidly run off the production line. The economy is more complex; the interrelations within it more extensively entwined. All this makes planning more difficult.

In addition, the main tasks facing the central planners are not what they used to be. The major structural changes in economic output have already been accomplished. Labor can no longer be as easily drawn into the high priority sectors. What is more, it is no longer as clear which the high priority sectors are. The situation calls for planning techniques which will be able to calculate relative values and relative costs and make close decisions on the basis of close calculations. The brute force methods of Soviet centralized planning of the past are no longer as appropriate as they once were.

As a result of this, pressures are building up and will continue to build up among Soviet planners, administrators and economists to modify the system of centralized planning. To many outside, and inside, the Soviet Union, the road to take is obvious. What is needed is more decentralization, more decision-making power at the periphery, improvement and extended use of the price mechanism.

While all this has been transpiring something else new has come upon the Soviet scene—the computer and with it a veritable rampage of work on the use of mathematical methods in economics and planning. Much of this work supports the drive toward decentralization. But also much of it opens entirely new horizons for improvement in the effectiveness of centralized planning. The possibilities offered by the application of cybernetic systems to Soviet planning—the computerization of data collection and processing, of centralized problem solving and control—are sufficiently large as to make the future course of Soviet planning no longer obvious.

That there will be significant changes is almost certain. That there will be a movement toward more decentralized techniques is also most likely true. But how much? And what will be the role and future form of centralized planning? The answers to these questions are not very clear.

*MANAGERIAL INCENTIVES AND DECISIONMAKING: A COMPARISON OF THE UNITED STATES AND THE THE SOVIET UNION**

— · — · — · — · — · — · — · — · — · — · — · —

Joseph S. Berliner†

Summary

The rewards in income and prestige in the United States and Soviet economies are such that a larger proportion of the best young people in the U.S.S.R. turn to careers in heavy industry, science, and higher education, whereas in the United States a larger proportion of the best talent flows into such fields as heavy or light (consumer goods) industry, finance,

*Reprinted from U.S. Congress, Joint Economic Committee, *Comparisons of the United States and Soviet Economies* (Washington, D. C.: U.S. Government Printing Office 1959), pp. 349–76. All footnotes have been deleted.

†Dr. Joseph S. Berliner is Professor of Economics at Brandeis University. His publications include: *Factory and Manager in the USSR*, (1957), *Soviet Economic Aid* (1958), and "The Economics of Overtaking and Surpassing" in Henry Rosovsky (ed), *Industrialization in Two Systems* (1966).

commerce and trade, law, medicine, etc. Higher education, particularly technical, is more of a prerequisite for the attainment of a top business career in the Soviet Union than in the United States.

The principal managerial incentive in Soviet industry is the bonus paid for overfulfillment of plan targets. The incentive system is successful in the sense that it elicits a high level of managerial effort and performance. But it has the unintended consequence of causing managers to engage in a wide variety of practices that are contrary to the interests of the state. Managers systematically conceal their true production capacity from the planners, produce unplanned types of products, and falsify the volume and quality of production. In the procurement of materials and supplies they tend to order larger quantities than they need, hoard scarce materials, and employ unauthorized special agents who use influence and gifts to ease management's procurement problems. The incentive system causes managers to shy away from innovations that upset the smooth working of the firm.

Since American managers operate in a different economic environment, their problems and therefore their practices differ from those of Soviet managers. But in those aspects of economic life in which the U.S. economy approximates the operating conditions of the Soviet economy, American managers develop forms of behavior similar to those of Soviet managers. The separation of management and ownership characteristic of the modern corporation leads to conflicts of interest between managers and stockholder-owners, and management's pursuit of its own interest leads to activities similar to those of the Soviet manager striving to defend his interests against those of the owner-state. The spread of legislation constricting the freedom of operation of the American firm leads to the evasion of laws and regulations characteristic of the Soviet economy, though on a larger scale there. Finally, under wartime conditions the burgeoning of Government controls and the dominant role of the Government as customer alters the operating conditions of the U.S. economy in such ways that it closely approximates some of the normal operating conditions of the Soviet economy. The change is accompanied by black-market operations, hoarding, quality deterioration, and the use of influence, practices which are normal in the peacetime Soviet economy.

Chapter 1. Managerial Incentives and Recruitment

The most important decision a manager has to make is made before he ever becomes a manager; namely, the decision to prepare for a managerial career. The factors influencing this decision are of vital importance for our industrial society. Imagine the consequences if no one aspired to become a manager, or if young people chose management only as a last resort, or if other careers were so attractive that management got only the last pickings of each year's crop of youngsters. It might therefore be appropriate to begin with some reflections on the incentives that the United States and the U.S.S.R. offer their young people to choose a managerial career rather than some other.

The factors motivating young people to choose one or another occupation are probably not vastly different in the two countries. Family tradition is often decisive; many a youngster chooses a career simply because he wishes to be like his father (or mother). Special talents such as those of the artist, or early conceived deep interests, like the boy who must be a scientist, account for the career choices of some others. But most teenagers have no clear idea of what they would like to be. It is with respect to these youths that it is most interesting to speculate upon the incentive-pulls that the two systems offer for the choice of one career or another.

Education and Career Choice

The role of higher education in career choice is different in the two nations. Higher education is very much more of a prerequisite for the prestigeful and high income occupations in the U.S.S.R. than in the United States. To be sure, the person with a high school education or less has an increasingly difficult time entering the managerial ladder of the large American corporation. But in such fields as trade, commerce, construction and in small business in general, the opportunities are still vast for a financially successful career. College, and education in general, is not of decisive importance. And the brute fact is that a college diploma can always be obtained somewhere in the United States, with very little effort or ability, by just about anyone who can pay the tuition and write a semi-literate paragraph. Those who don't aspire to a managerial position or who fail to make the grade can, as workingmen, nevertheless enjoy a standard of living that is the envy of the world. The point is that the young American who is not inclined toward academic work need not feel that he is out of the competition for our society's best rewards.

This is not true in the U.S.S.R. A number of conversations with young Soviet people have convinced me that to be "worker" is something devoutly to be shunned by most young people who have reached the high school level. There are at least two reasons for this attitude, which seems so anomalous in a "worker's state." The first is the enormously high prestige that Russian (and European) culture has always placed upon the "intelligent," the learned man, the man who works with his mind instead of his hands. The Soviet regime has striven hard to make manual labor respectable, and it undoubtedly has succeeded in endowing the worker with a social position relatively much higher than before the revolution. But the young person who has reached the educational level at which he can choose between being a worker or an "intelligent" would, other things being equal, choose the latter without question.

Other things are not equal, however. In particular, the income possibilities of a worker are far smaller than those of a college graduate, and this is the second reason for the desperate, and sometimes pathetic, drive for a higher education. Of course, a person must have reached the high school level before he can even begin to think about choosing between the career of a worker or an "intelligent." The steady annual expansion in the high school population has had the effect of presenting ever-increasing numbers of young people with the choice, and few of them would freely choose to be workers. If the expansion of the school population had continued, giving more and more young people the opportunity to avoid being workers, it would have raised serious problems for the recruitment of the labor force. The radical reform of the educational system by Khrushchev was undoubtedly motivated, in part, by the wish to avoid that problem.

Thus, the undesirability of a career as a worker has intensified the desire for higher education. Add to this the fact that there is no private enterprise, no small business in which a man could pull himself out of a worker's status and reach a position of prestige and income comparable to the self-made American businessman. I do not wish to state that the door is completely closed. By dint of hard work, ability, and certain other qualities, a Soviet citizen without the college diploma can from time to time rise to an important position in some economic hierarchy. But his chances are about as good as those of an equivalent person in a progressive American corporation. And the young person evaluating the importance of higher education understands this.

Finally, the Russian teenager who decides he has to get a college diploma has very few easy ways out. He can't buy his way into college, as the American student can if he has the money. There are no private colleges that can set whatever standards they wish. To be sure there are instances of bribery or influence, but they are certainly the exception. If the Soviet student wants a college diploma very badly, he has to work hard to gain admission and to be graduated. The very intensity of the drive for education, and the competition of many applicants for the limited number of admissions, permits the high schools and colleges to maintain high standards of performance. Moreover the colleges are financially independent of student tuitions: not only are there no tuitions but most of the students earn stipends. The consequence is that the typical Soviet student works harder and has to meet higher standards of performance than the typical American student. The standards are different in the two countries, of course, because of differences in the philosophy of education. But there is no doubt that study is a much more serious business for the young Soviet student than for the American.

One final note on education and incentives. The quality of the managerial (and technical) manpower of a nation depends on the proportion of the population comprising the pool from which the managers are drawn. That is, if half the population were for some reason excluded from the pool, the quality of the managers would be lower than if the whole population comprised the pool. Both nations suffer in this respect from the fact that rural educational facilities are poorer than urban, which reduces the pool of the potential college group. Since the Soviet rural population is larger percentagewise than that of the United States, and since their rural educational facilities are probably relatively worse than ours, they suffer more than we from this loss. But there are other ways in which our pool is curtailed more than the Soviet. First is the fact that the private cost of education keeps a substantial portion of our talented young people in the lower income groups out of college. I admit that this fact puzzles me. With our network of free State universities and with a fairly abundant scholarship program, I don't fully understand why any competent student who really desired it could not get a college education. It is my impression, however, that systematic studies generally show that we are losing an unfortunate number of young people to higher education for financial reasons. If this is so, we are worse off than the Soviets in this respect, for their education is absolutely free, and most students of any merit earn stipends besides. Lower income young Soviet people may nevertheless be unable to go off to college if the family needs their earnings. A young Soviet woman told me, in reply to my question, that this was why she never went on to college. She is not a very good illustration of my point, however, for she went on to say that she really wasn't very smart anyhow.

The second group that is largely lost from America's pool of potential managerial manpower is the Negro and some other racial minorities. It may well be that the proportion of college graduates among some of the Soviet national minorities is smaller than for the Slavic nationalities; I have seen no data on this. But I would doubt that their loss from racial discrimination is as large as ours.

The third and largest group lost from our pool comprises exactly half our population—the female half. Sex discrimination certainly exists in the Soviet economy, probably more in management than in science and technology. But undoubtedly the female population enlarges the pool of technical and managerial manpower much more in the U.S.S.R. than in the United States. The difference in the role of women in the two countries must, I think enter into the balance I am trying to strike, but it is not a subject on which I would recommend that your committee consider writing corrective legislation. For one thing it is not perfectly clear which way sex discrimination works in the United States. Women discriminate against working about as much as jobs discriminate against women.

Let me summarize briefly this discussion of the relationship of education to career choice. Education, and particularly higher education, is more important in the U.S.S.R. than in the United States as the gateway to a prestigious and highly remunerative career. Competition is keener for higher education, the cost of education to the individual is less, and the standards of admission and performance are higher in the U.S.S.R. Both nations lose part of the potential pool of managerial talent, the U.S.S.R because of its large rural population, the United States because of financial burdens and racial and sex discrimination.

Competition Among Careers

How does a managerial career compare with the attractiveness of other careers in the two nations? The young American not dedicated to some particular field, but motivated by a roughly equal desire for prestige and money, might select some field such as law, medicine, business, or engineering. He would decidedly not go into education or science. An equivalent young Soviet person would make a somewhat different choice. He would certainly not select law, which has been assigned a most humble role in Soviet society. Nor would he select medicine, for while the prestige is high, the income is low. On the other hand, higher education or science would be an excellent choice. The very title of "Professor" or "Scientific worker" would assure him one of the highest places of honor in the society. And an outstanding career in either of those fields would assure him an income ranking in the upper 10 percent or perhaps even 5 percent (data are hard to come by) of the population. The difference in the economic and social position of the scientist and teacher in the two countries is of fundamental importance in the matter of career recruitment.

The American who decides to choose a career in the business world has a much wider range of choice than his Soviet counterpart. A great variety of fields offer roughly equivalent rewards in prestige and incomes: advertising, accounting, finance, commerce, trade, sales, light manufacturing, heavy industry. Of all these fields, it is only the latter that would exert a great pull on the young Soviet person. For 40 years the Government and party have hammered home the central role of heavy industry, children are instilled with an admiration of technology, and heavy industry has been endowed with an aura of glamour that exceeds even our American fascination with technology. The ideological cards are stacked, in varying degree, against all other branches of the economy. In keeping with the ideology, the prestige and income possibilities in heavy industry are decidedly greater than in the other branches.

Not only will the student be attracted to heavy industry, but he is likely to choose engineering as his path of entry into whatever branch of heavy industry he selects. He would be attracted to engineering for the educational reasons discussed above. Engineering is, moreover, the most direct line of approach to a managerial career.

The Soviet engineering graduate will find his first job opportunities rather different from those of his American counterpart. If he is at the top of his class, the best offers will come from the research institutes, with top starting salaries and opportunities for graduate work. The poorer students will find lower paying jobs in industry. In the United States the situation is quite the reverse. The most successful students will be snapped up by recruiters from the large corporations, with the best starting salary offers. Some of the top students will, to be sure, spurn the attractive job offers and go on to further graduate work, but I suspect that many of those who go immediately into graduate work are the men who didn't get the good job offers. To be sure, many of the top American students who join the corporations are put immediately into research and development, but as many of them will be working on new passenger car or dishwasher design as will be working on electronic development and automation technique. The Soviet researcher is more likely to be working on the latter than the former.

The young Soviet engineer who goes into industry starts at the bottom of the managerial ladder, as chief of a production shop, or the design or maintenance departments of the enterprise. As new job opportunities develop, he faces the choice of continuing in direct production or taking one of the staff jobs in the enterprise, such as the planning department. If he stays in production proper, his career path may lead to chief engineer of an enterprise or to one of the higher economic agencies. If he moves into staff work, his career may lead to the directorship of an enterprise or of one of the higher organs. Either career leads to the pinnacle of Soviet management.

The paths that are least likely to lead to top management are finance or sales. I would guess the proportion of top management in the United States who started in such fields as finance and sales is much larger than in the U.S.S.R. There are no "colleges of business administration" in the Soviet Union. The ambitious youngster who wants to work for the top of the Soviet business world studies engineering, not personnel and marketing.

Summarizing, industry in the United States has to compete with a wide variety of other branches of economic activity for its share of the best potential managerial talent. In the U.S.S.R. the values and the rewards are concentrated in relatively fewer fields, and industry is far more attractive than most others. Science and higher education which scarcely compete with industry in the United States, is a strong competitor of industry in the U.S.S.R. Among the various branches of industry, in the United States the light and consumer goods industries compete very effectively for both managerial and engineering talent. In the U.S.S.R. light and consumer goods industries are much less attractive than heavy industry. And finally the nature of industrial recruitment is such that technical education is much more important as part of the training of a would-be manager in the U.S.S.R. than in the United States.

My conclusion is that heavy industry, science and higher education attract, by and large, a better and more competent crop of young people in the U.S.S.R. than in the United States. Moreover, the competition for education is keener in the U.S.S.R., so that they get a more rigorously trained (trained in different ways, to be sure) corps of managerial, engineering, scientific and university personnel. On the other hand, such branches of the economy as sales, advertising, finance, trade and commerce, light industry, and law attract a much more competent group of people in the United States than in the U.S.S.R. Most of the outstanding people in these fields in the United States would, if they were Soviet citizens, have enjoyed successful careers in heavy industry, science, technology, or higher education. There is, after all, nothing startling in this conclusion. It is but another way of saying that each society gets what it pays for.

Chapter 2. Managerial Incentives and Decision Making

Material Incentives

The incentives that attract people into management are not necessarily the same incentives that motivate managers to do their jobs and do them well. What are the goals of the manager? What are the considerations that impel him to make one decision rather than the other?

The moving force of our economic system is the pursuit of private gain. The worker chooses the higher paying job, the businessman accepts the more profitable contract, the investor buys the higher interest security. The usual exceptions must of course be made; the laws must be obeyed, public opinion may sometimes require that one decision be made rather than another, people make wrong decisions, a short-run loss may be accepted for a longer term gain. But by and large—"other things being equal," as the economist likes to say—it is private gain that determines economic decision.

The Soviets have at various times experimented with other forms of incentive, for it did not at first seem quite appropriate that a Socialist economy should stress private gain. But practicality won out over dogma, and private gain has for the last 25 years been the keystone of the managerial incentive system. To be sure, we still find references to various social incentives such as Communist enthusiasm. But we are also reminded that while enthusiasm is well and good, communism, as Lenin used to say, must be built "not directly on enthusiasm but with the aid of enthusiasm born out of the great revolution; [communism must be built] on private interest, on personal incentive, on businesslike accounting." Moreover, the incentive of private gain will be with us for a long time. According to the eminent labor economist E. Manevich, it will not disappear until the day of general overabundance arrives, until the differences between country and city are eliminated, and until the differences between mental and manual labor vanish. We are safe in saying that for the next several decades at least, private gain will be the central economic incentive in both economic systems.

The form that material incentives take is of some importance. For the American businessman it is clearly profit. If you ask why did he take on this contract rather than that, why did he order this machine rather than that, why did he ship by truck rather than train, the answer would normally be, "because it's cheaper that way," or what comes to the same thing, "because he would make more money that way."

For the private businessman managing his own business, profit is clearly the guide to his actions. But most American business is not managed in this way. The men who actually run the firm are salaried managers, hired by the stockholders' representative body, the board of directors. The profit of the business does not belong to the manager but to the stockholder-owners. The fact is that the private interest of the manager need not necessarily coincide with that of the stockholder. In order to bring the manager's private interest into closer coincidence with that of the owners, most corporations have instituted some kind of bonus system, on the assumption that if the manager has a direct stake in the profit of the enterprise, his decisions are more likely to be those that will earn more profit.

In fashioning an incentive system for its managers, the Soviet Government faced a problem similar to that of the American corporation. For all Soviet enterprises are run by salaried managers. If the Soviet manager's income consisted solely of his salary, it was conceivable that his private interest would not coincide at all points with the interest of the Government. Accordingly a considerable variety of supplementary bonuses are available to the managerial staff. The bonuses are designed to motivate managers to make those decisions that the Government considers to be in its own interest.

The amount of income earned in the form of bonuses is substantial. In 1947, the last year for which detailed data are available to me, the managerial personnel of the iron and steel industry earned bonuses averaging 51.4 percent of their basic income. In the food industry at the low end, the percentage was 21 percent. Since these are averages, many individual managers earned considerably more than this. Bonuses of this magnitude must be a potent incentive indeed.

But incentive for what? This is surely the crucial question. For we can readily imagine an incentive which was extremely successful in motivating action, but action of an undesirable kind. The test of an incentive is therefore not only its motivating power, but the extent to which it leads to the desired kind of decision.

Before proceeding to the relationship of incentives to decision making, let me clarify the sense in which I use the term incentive. By incentive I mean that consideration which explains why one decision was made rather than another. If a young person decides to find employment in the electrical machinery industry rather than in the furniture industry, the difference in basic salaries in the two industries may well have been the decisive consideration. In this case salary is the effective incentive. But once in the job, the salary does not vary according to whether one operating decision is made rather than another. When the manager decides to put one order into production ahead of another, or to substitute on material for another, it is not his salary he is thinking about. It is usually the size of the month's bonus that will depend on the decision taken. It is in this sense that the bonus is the principal incentive in the operational decisions of the Soviet enterprise.

Production Decisions

Two generations ago people debated the question of whether a Socialist economy could possibly work. History removed that question from the agenda. The last generation changed the question to whether the Soviet economy could work at all efficiently. That question has also been answered. These hearings would not otherwise be taking place. My discussion takes for granted that the Soviet economy is reasonably efficient, and that the question at issue is how efficient.

There is little doubt that the system of managerial incentives, broadly viewed, has created a corps of managers dedicated to their work and responsive to the production demands made upon them. Like their American counterparts, they are deeply involved in their work, they worry about production quotas, they demand results from their labor force. As hired managers, they are aware that if their performance is not satisfactory, there are always other persons spoiling for a chance at their jobs. I have no way of knowing whether the intensity of managerial life is greater in the U.S.S.R. than in the United States; in both countries there are variations from industry to industry. But there are two reasons why industrial life probably proceeds at a faster tempo in the U.S.S.R. than here. The first is that the absence of free trade unions makes it difficult for workers to resist pressure for intense operation. The second is that industry is under constant exhortation from Government and party for ever-increasing levels of production.

But the question as indicated above is not whether management is motivated to work hard. It is rather whether the incentive system motivates them to do what the state wishes them to do; whether, in other words, they get as much mileage out of their effort as they might get.

One of the most interesting conclusions of the study of Soviet managerial incentives is that the bonus system is directly responsible for motivating management to make a variety of decisions contrary to the intent and the interests of the state. The decisions to be described go far back in the history of the Soviet economy, and have resisted countless efforts by the Government to eliminate them. Most of them have survived the great organizational changes in industrial organization of the past several years. They are clearly deeply rooted in the soil of Soviet economic organization.

First, consider the matter of the reporting of information. In a planned economy it is vital that the central planners have as accurate information as possible about the productive capacity of enterprises. The bonus system, however, acts as a prevailing motivation for managers to understate their real production capacity. The reason is that the most important of the bonuses available to managers depends on the extent to which the production target of the enterprise is overfulfilled. If the manager honestly reports his full production capacity, and if for some reason something goes wrong in the course of the month, then he and his staff will lose that month's bonus. It is safer therefore to report a smaller capacity than really exists, in order that the production target will be kept low enough to allow for emergencies. The Russians call this "insurance" or "security." The consequence is that the planners can never be sure that their plans are based on accurate figures. The Government is aware of the problem: "This is fully understandable," writes a Soviet economist, "because the lower the plan, the greater the opportunity to fulfill and overfulfill it * * *."

Because the higher state agencies cannot trust management's reporting of its productive capacity, various techniques have been fashioned for setting targets high enough to force the firms to operate as close as possible to capacity. One of these techniques is the arbitrary increase of targets over last year's production. As a prominent state planning commission economist put it, "they take as the base magnitude the level of production achieved during the preceding period and raise it by some percentage or other." Sometimes this technique helps flush out the manager's "hidden reserves," but in other cases the arbitrary increase in targets leads to impossibly high tasks. Indeed, the spirit of planning is reflected in the systematic use of high targets as a device for keeping managers working at as fast a tempo as possible. In the past targets have been set so high (deliberately, one suspects) that one-third of all enterprises failed to fulfill their annual plans. There is some evidence that in the last year or two this policy of deliberate overplanning has been modified, and we are told that in the first half of 1958 only 19 percent of all enterprises failed to fulfill their plans. This still represents one out of five enterprises, and indicates that the high level of plan targets remains a dominant fact of life for the Soviet manager. The intense pace of plant operation has its distinct advantage from the state's point of view: it elicits from management a high level of effort that might not be forthcoming if the plans were set at a more modest level. But the price paid by the state is the manager's effort to defend his enterprise by concealing his full capacity.

When the target has been set, the manager's bonus depends on the success with which he fulfills it. Most of the firm's production does indeed follow the lines laid down in the plan. But when the end of the month rolls around and, as often happens, production is far short of meeting the month's target, then managers turn to a host of timetested techniques of meeting—or seeming to meet—the targets. In certain types of production, such as metals, the target is expressed in tons; in such cases the manager might order his shops to curtail the production of relatively lightweight products (special and quality metals) and to throw more men and materials into the production of the heavier products. In textile production we read that the practice of setting targets in "running meters" (that is, in measures of length, without regard to width) causes managers to overproduce narrow-width cloth and underproduce broad width. In firms with a considerable variety of products, the production targets are expressed in value units—so many millions of rubles of production. In such cases managers tend to overproduce those products that have high fixed prices (all prices are fixed): they may deliberately use more expensive materials in order to drive up the value of production. These are some of an endless variety of ways in which managers "violate the planned assortment of production"—to use the official expression of disapproval.

How widespread are these practices? We really don't know. From time to time individual managers are publicly excoriated for such practices, and figures are published to show how widely the planned assortment of production had been departed from. But these may well be extreme cases, and it would be unwise to generalize from them. Occasionally, however, the results of special studies are published, and they give us some idea of the magnitude of the problem. The State planning commission recently released the results of a survey of the production practices of 63 enterprises. Of the total production by these enterprises in excess of the plan targets, only 43 percent consisted of the basic products normally produced by them; 26.5 percent consisted of "products not included in the plan when it was originally confirmed," 20 percent consisted of "other production," and 7 percent consisted not of finished products but of an increase in semifabricated parts and goods-in-process. While these data are not precisely in the form in which we would want them, they do provide a good indication of managers' tendency to produce those products that are best from their own enterprises' point of view, rather than those products that the State would most wish to have produced.

Two other consequences of the bonus system (and the pressure of high targets) should be noted. One is the simple falsification of reported production. "Thus, for example," we read in a Soviet article, "if the plan is fulfilled 99 per cent, the managerial and engineering personnel receive no bonus. But if the enterprise fulfills the plan 100 percent, they receive bonuses of from 15 to 37 percent of their salary." Quite a lot of money hinges on that last percentage of production, and it is no wonder that management may succumb to the temptation to "fudge" the report a bit in order to earn the bonus. Again, the techniques of covering up for falsely reported production are myriad. To cite only one, production is "borrowed" from next month. That is, production that is expected to occur next month is reported as having been produced this month. If things go well next month, the "borrowed" output is "repaid"; if not the manager may get into trouble.

More serious than falsification, however, is the deterioration of the quality of production. The poor quality of much of Soviet consumer goods production is well known. In other types of production the danger of detection is greater, and quality standards are less readily violated. But the explanation of management's tendency to shave on quality is the same: the high production targets are so often not attainable, and the manager wants to keep his job. Much of the quality shaving is of a kind that is not easily detected: fewer stitches in the garment, fewer screws in the piece, greener lumber in the building, more impurities in the metal. But if the pressure is keen enough, more extreme forms of quality deterioration will be adopted.

Summarizing, the bonus system is an effective device for eliciting a high level of managerial effort, but in the context of excessively high production targets, it induces management to make certain types of decisions that are contrary to the intent of the State. The production of unplanned products, the concealment of production capacity, the falsification of reports and the deterioration of quality are the unintended consequences of the system of managerial incentives.

Procurement Decisions

The high level of production targets is but half the problem facing the Soviet manager. The other half is the perpetual shortage of materials and supplies. In order to get the greatest possible production from the available stocks of materials and supplies, the State employs a variety of devices to minimize the use of materials in production and inventory. Undoubtedly these devices have served to control wasteful use of resources, and they have also helped channel the flow of resources in the direction most desired by the State. But they have been self-defeating to some extent for they have forced managers to make certain kinds of decisions which frustrate the intent of the State.

The core of the matter is that managers simply don't trust the planning system to provide them with the supplies and materials they need in the right quantity and quality, and at the right time. The recent decentralization of industrial organization may have improved matters somewhat, but the evidence we have indicates that supply problems are still the most troublesome feature of managerial life. Moreover, the reasons are similar to those we used to read about before decentralization. For all important materials the manager must still obtain an allocation order from his home office (usually the Council of the National Economy of his district), which must in turn get the allocation order from the republican or all-union planning commission.

Thus, we still read of the "existing complicated system of obtaining allocation orders, under which every enterprise must submit detailed requisitions to Moscow a long time before the new planning quarter is to begin." Because plans are not always finally set at the time the planning period is to begin, enterprises sometimes start with "advance allocations," that is, temporary allotments of resources designed to keep them operating until the final allocation orders are available. Decentralization of the economy was supposed to have made it easier for neighboring enterprises to sell to each other without having to go through Moscow. But central purchasing agencies still exist, and agencies anywhere must find something to do. Thus the Chief Purchasing and Marketing Administration located in the republic capitals (Moscow, for example) still insist on being the middleman in purchase and sale contracts between enterprises even when the latter are located in the same outlying city (such as Sverdlovsk). Perhaps even more serious than the complex supply planning system is the large percentage of enterprise that regularly fail to fulfill their plans, or fulfill them by producing the wrong products or substandard products. Since the production of these enterprises constitute the planned supplies of other enterprises, the supplies of the latter are delayed or simply not available. Perhaps enough has been said to explain why "managers of enterprises did not have confidence in the possibility of getting their materials on time and having them delivered to the factory by the supply depot's trucks."

What does the manager do to make sure he gets his supplies? Just as he "secures" his production plan by attempting to conceal the existence of some production capacity, so he "secures" the flow of supplies in various ways. He overorders, in the hope that if he doesn't get all he ordered, he may at least get as much as he needs. He also orders excessively large amounts of some supplies in order to be able to buy directly from the producer, instead of having to go through the maze of jobbing depots. A survey of 15 Moscow enterprises showed a 10.4 percent overordering of metals for just this reason. Sometimes management's boldest efforts to obtain supplies are unsuccessful: "* * * over 300,000 construction workers undergo work stoppages daily because of the absence of materials at the workplace." In other cases their padded requisitions are accepted and they receive more than they need of some materials. The consequence is the piling up of hoards of supplies of all kinds, one of the most enduring problems of Soviet industrial organization. The Government has waged a long-standing war against hoarding. One of the weapons by which it attempts to hold hoarding within bounds is through the use of quotas of working capital; that is, for its annual production program the enterprise is allowed to keep on hand at any one time no more than so many tons of coal, so many board feet of lumber, so many rubles worth of inventory. These quotas must be negotiated between enterprise and government, and the enterprise's interest demands that they be set as high as possible. The mutual attempt at outguessing the other leads to a familiar bureaucratic game: "* * * enterprises try to 'justify' and obtain as large quotas of working capital as possible. The financial agencies, aware of this, strive on the other hand to reduce the quotas of working capital." This kind of planning is hardly calculated to lead to the establishment of the optimal quotas. It is more likely that some quotas will be too large and some too small.

The most interesting of the techniques used by managers to "secure" their supply of materials is the employment of special supply expediters called tolkachi, or "pushers." The table of organization does not provide for this occupation, yet so great is the need that firms manage somehow to employ these people. The chief job of the expediter is to make sure that his enterprise gets the materials it needs and when it needs them. Accordingly he spends most of his time on the road, visiting his enterprise's suppliers, handing out little gifts here and there to assure that his orders are well-handled, picking up supplies of one kind or another that his firm may be able to use or trade for other goods. Much of their activity is associated with the black market, that is, obtaining materials for which no allocation order has been issued. This may be done either by wrangling an allocation order out of a reluctant government official by one means or another, or persuading an approachable enterprise official to sell him the things he needs without an allocation order.

Some tolkachi take up permanent residence in the city in which the chief suppliers are located, and only occasionally return to their home firms for consultations. To keep the record clean, they are carried on the books as "senior buyer," or "supply agent." If they are known to be particularly adept at their jobs, they may be asked by other firms to represent them. Nothing is known of their incomes, but there is no doubt that they earn many times their base pay. And they fully earn it, both because of the vital nature of their work, and because the risks they take make them vulnerable to prosecution.

How widespread is the use of these expediters? Again, we catch only occasional hints of their prevalence. The most recent outburst against them reports that the number of tolkachi who annually visit the typical large enterprise runs into the thousands of rubles. These, however, are only the reported expenses. More often than not their expenses are not reported as such but are concealed under such rubics as "exchange of technical information," or "contract negotiations." Our latest informant, who is a senior investigator for the state control commission of the U.S.S.R., is of the opinion that despite continued official criticisms of the use of expediters, their number has acutally been increasing. One of the reasons he adduces is interesting. In 1956, along with a wave of measures designed to give more freedom to plant managers, an order was issued relieving managers of the need to report in detail on all minor expenditures. Travel expenditures were among the items exempted. The measure had the unintended effect of encouraging the increased use of expediters.

The economic effect of the use of expediters is difficult to assess. There is no doubt that they are of vital importance to individual enterprises, but from the national point of view much of their activity involves merely the transfer to one fortunate enterprise of resources that otherwise would have gone to another. Since the higher priority enterprises have less need for expediters, the chances are that the net effect of their activity is to cause more resources to flow to lower priority enterprises at the expense of higher priority ones. On the credit side, however, their wide knowledge of sources of supply, of who has what to sell, is of some importance, and they do arrange for the movement of supplies that otherwise would have lain idle in one plant while another had need for it. In short the expediter possesses a certain kind of knowledge that may be as important to economic organization as the knowledge of the engineer or the machinist. The planning system is able to direct the bulk of the nation's resources with reasonable effectiveness, but substantial quantities of materials and equipment elude the main stream of planning. How to get these resources back into the system is a problem that has exercised Soviet economists for a long time.

In summary, the incentives that motivate managers to strive for the fulfillment of their production targets are the same incentives that motivate them to evade the regulations of the planning system. Because of the tightness of the supply system, which is deliberately engineered by the state, managers are compelled to defend their enterprises' position by over-ordering supplies, by hoarding materials and equipment, and by employing expediters whose function is it to keep the enterprise supplied with materials at all costs, legal or otherwise. The very planning system that serves to channel most of the nation's resources in directions desired by the state, serves also to misdirect a substantial volume of resources toward uses that are contrary to the wishes of the state.

Investment Decisions

If one were to ask what feature of the Soviet economic system accounts most of all for the rapid rate of growth, the answer would undoubtedly be the high rate of capital formation. The question at issue is whether it is as high as it might be, other things being equal. An examination of the system of managerial incentives will provide part, though by no means all, of the answer to this central question.

Management has a direct interest in obtaining new capital. It adds to productive capacity, and it is good for the record to show steady increases in production. Moreover fixed capital is provided to the enterprise as a free grant by the state, with no interest charge. The problem, therefore, has not been one of inducing management to accept more machines; it has rather been one of dissuading management from ordering too many machines. Far back in Soviet economic history one can find expressions of the problem similar to that recently uttered by Khrushchev in connection with the dissolution of the agricultural machine-tractor stations:

> The machine-tractor stations accept any machine whether they need it or not. They don't grow flax, but they take flax-growing equipment. They don't grow cabbage, but they take cabbage-planting machines. Consequently many machines are not used for years and hundreds of millions of rubles worth of state resources are frozen.

The reason enterprises accept any piece of equipment they can get their hands on is similar to that discussed above in connection with materials hoarding. One can never tell when he may need just that kind of machine and not be able to obtain it. If one has a chance to get it now, order it by all means. It may come in handy some day for trading in return for something one might be able to use more readily. And above all, there is no charge for holding the equipment; there is no interest payment, and if the machine is not used there is no depreciation charge either. Hence there is everything to gain and nothing to lose by holding on to as much machinery and equipment as one can obtain.

How to induce managers to take a less cavalier view of capital has been a longstanding concern of economists. They look with some nostalgia at the effectiveness of the profit motive under capitalism in this respect. An eminent Soviet economist put it this way recently:

> In order to increase his profit as much as possible, the capitalist strives to use his equipment to the fullest extent possible, and in no case will he buy a machine that he doesn't need at the moment, since every surplus machine slows down the turnover of his capital and reduces his profit. For the same reason he strives to keep his inventories down to the very minimum and to market his finished products as quickly as possible.

Recent economic literature contains a number of suggestions of ways in which Soviet managers might be induced to order only that amount of capital needed for production purposes. One of the more interesting is a proposal advanced by the author quoted above. He suggests that profit be calculated not as a ratio to total production costs (as has always been done), but as a ratio to value of invested capital. In this way the enterprise with too much idle capital will show a lower rate of profit, and profit is one of the principal indicators of overall performance. The suggestion is interesting because it proposes that return on capital be used as a criterion of performance, a rather "bourgeois" notion. It should not, however, be thought that the proposal envisages reliance on the "profit motive" as we know it. Profit is an important indicator of the efficiency of plant operation, but the firm does not "own" its profit, although it shares in the profit in a minor way. As a personal incentive, profit is relatively unimportant in Soviet industry, certainly by comparison with the bonus.

If the incentive system motivates managers to overorder and hoard equipment, the situation is quite the reverse with respect to technological innovation. Concern over managerial resistance to innovation is of long standing, but it has come to the fore in recent years in connection with increased emphasis on automation and modernization of plant and equipment. The reasons for managers' tendency to drag their feet in introducing new products or production techniques are well understood by Soviet economists:

> The explanation is, first of all, that the introduction of new technology involves certain risks and requires a considerable expenditure of time; secondly, after new technology has been introduced, more difficult plan targets are set and consequently there is less opportunity for fulfilling them and receiving bonuses.

When a manager has a well-running plant, when the workers have learned their jobs and have become experienced in using the existing equipment, he is reluctant to upset the cart by trying something new. A new production line means trouble. Production bugs have to be eliminated, workers have to be retrained, time is lost, and spoilage is high. The chances are that plans will be underfulfilled and the precious bonuses lost, particularly in view of the tendency for plan targets to be raised to the rated capacity of the new equipment. It is courting disaster to try new things. If the old machines are wearing out, it is safer to repair or even rebuild them rather than introduce the more complicated new models. Outlays on the rebuilding of old machines often exceed the price of a new modern machine.

There is another reason why managers shy away from innovation. Even if the potential gains from new technology are great, it usually takes a number of years before they are realized. But it is Soviet policy to shift managers around from plant to plant every few years. Therefore managers have a strictly short-run point of view. Why take on all the headaches of introducing a new line when one is not likely to be around to enjoy whatever benefits may eventually accrue? Capital investment policy is by its very nature a matter of long-term planning, and therefore does not commend itself to the short-run horizon of management.

How does the state combat managerial resistance to innovation? One technique is direct pressure. Pressure exerted on and by their own superiors explains much of the innovation that does occur. Enterprise managers may drag their feet for a long time, but when the direct order comes down that the new automatic line must be installed in the next 6 months, it is eventually acted upon. Pressure is also exerted through the Communist Party; if the party officials in the enterprise are under direct orders from Moscow that automation must be accelerated, they are in a position to force the manager to move faster than he otherwise might. Such pressures are important, although it must be noted in passing that both the manager's bosses and the local party people often try to shield the enterprise from such pressures. They are as dependent for their careers upon successful plan fulfillment as are the plant managers themselves.

Direct orders from above are one way of getting management to innovate. But innovation would proceed more rapidly if managers could be made to wish to innovate, instead of waiting until they are forced into it. The literature of the past few years is full of suggestions on how this can be accomplished. It is suggested, for example, that attractively high prices be set on new machines, in order to stimulate the producers of those machines to put them into production more rapidly. While this measure might ease the financial strain on the innovating firm, it will not remove the risk that the production plan may be sacrificed. And production is much more vital to the success of the enterprise than finance.

More to the point are the suggestions that the bonus system be employed as an incentive for innovation. Soviet economists seem to have enormous confidence in bonuses as a device for getting management to wish to do what the State wishes them to do. But how to adapt the bonus system to this purpose is more difficult. In the course of years a variety of special bonuses have been introduced for one purpose or another, in addition to the major bonus that comes from fulfillment of the production plan. There are special bonuses available for economizing certain critical materials, for reducing the volume of goods in process, for conserving fuel, for increasing labor productivity, for keeping the plant clean, for reducing the volume of spoilage, for operating the plant without stoppages, for winning Socialist competitions, and many others.

This dilution of the bonus system may actually weaken its power as an incentive. If the special bonuses are small, they will not be very effective. If they are large they may detract effort from what is, after all, the main objective of the state: fulfillment of the production plan. For it is interesting to note the evidence that the relative size of the bonus for this or that special purpose often determines the manager's decision to concentrate on this or that objective. There are two types of innovation: relatively small measures such as organizational improvements or inexpensive alterations, and the more dramatic large-scale changes in production techniques. The former are included in the overall enterprise plan each year, under the name of the plan or organizational and technical measures (Orgtekhplan). It happens that there are certain bonuses available for the design and introduction of the large-scale innovations, but none for the fulfillment of the Orgtekhplan. The consequence is that research and managerial personnel concentrate on the large items, and pay little attention to the small ones, even though the latter could result in great savings with relatively little cost and effort. Thus the very potency of the bonus as an incentive militates against its use for too many special purposes which may compete with each other.

To conclude this discussion, the unreliability of the supply system and the absence of a charge for the use of capital motivates management to order more fixed capital than they need and to hoard machines and equipment. This tendency deflects a certain amount of currently produced capital goods from being put directly into production in their best uses. On the other hand, the incentive system discourages management from taking the risks associated with innovation. Direct orders from above lead to a substantial volume of innovation, and in many cases management may consider certain forms of innovation to be to their interest. The provision of special bonuses for innovation, if they were large enough to compete with the production plan bonus, might help provide an incentive for innovation, and much of the current discussion in the Soviet Union seems to point to this as the next phase.

Chapter 3.   Some Comparative Observations

The preceding chapter has shown that Soviet managers are motivated to make a variety of decisions that are contrary to the interest of the state. Since the state's interest is paramount in the Soviet scheme of things, we may properly conclude that the incentive and decision making system is "relatively inefficient," or "less than perfectly efficient." Let me caution the reader once more against inferring from this that Soviet managers do not do a good job. They do. There is no doubt that their system works well. If I have chosen to concentrate on the "pathology" of Soviet management, the purpose was not to create the impression of ineffectiveness, but to illuminate the gap that every economy shows between the actual and the ideal.

A comparison of Soviet and American management will help drive the point home. No one doubts that American management does a good job. But it would be fatuous to allege that it operates with perfect efficiency. An exploration of the inevitable gap between the actual and the ideal in the case of American management will help to place the corresponding gap in the U.S.S.R. in proper perspective.

A comparison of Soviet and American management is difficult for a curious reason; namely, we don't know enough about the more intimate aspects of American managerial practice. A moment's thought will make the reason clear. The American firm is a private enterprise in the full sense of the word. Its internal affairs are no one's business but its own. No one has the right to pry except with special causes. To be sure, the laws of the land have, over the years, required enterprises to disclose more and more of their private affairs to public and governmental perusal. But large sectors of the enterprise's internal operations are protected from the eyes of curious outsiders.

One of the most striking differences in the conduct of American and Soviet management is precisely in this matter of privacy. The Soviet enterprise is a public enterprise in the fullest sense of the word. It has no right to conceal its operations from any officially recognized agent of the state. And a great range of such agents have been deliberately endowed by the state with the obligation of keeping close watch on management and disclosing any irregularities or sources of inefficiency that come to their attention. These agents include the "home office" of the firm (the regional economic council, or formerly the ministry), the state bank, the local governmental body, the central government's State Control Commission, the Finance Department (the tax collector), the local Communist Party boss and his staff, the party secretary of the enterprise itself, and indeed just about anyone in the enterprise who enjoys the extracurricular activity of attending meetings to discuss the affairs of the enterprise (the aktiv).

If we can imagine an American business executive suddenly placed in charge of a Soviet firm, it is this public character of the enterprise which above all would drive him to distraction. It means that any government official can at any time demand to examine any aspect of the firm's operations he wishes to, that at any time he can be called on the carpet by the local party boss to explain a charge made by an irate customer, that any member of his staff (perhaps bucking for his job) can write a letter to Pravda exposing him for having made an irregular deal on some supplies, that any scatterbrained worker who wants to "get his picture in the papers" can rise at a public meeting that the director is obliged to attend, and compel the director to explain why he hasn't yet installed the new assembly line. The point is that the result of this authorized prying often finds its way into the published Soviet economic and political literature, which gives us an insight into the more intimate operations of the Soviet firm that we cannot have in the case of the American firm. But in view of this committee's expressed interest in comparisons of the United States and Soviet economies, I have attempted certain comparisons below which appear to be highly suggestive.

Managers and Owners

The original form of modern business organization was the small firm in which the owner was also the manager. The owner-manager was responsible to no one but himself for his business decisions, and his interest as manager could not conflict with his interest as owner. The development of the modern giant corporation, however, had led to that separation of management and ownership first elaborated in the work of Berle and Means. Under the new conditions the private interests of the hired managers (and the controlling group) need no longer coincide at all points with the interests of the stockholder-owners. This is precisely the relationship between the hired Soviet manager and the owner-state.

Berle and Means concluded from their study that "the controlling group, even if they own a large block of stock, can serve their own pockets better by profiting at the expense of the company than by making profits for it." This is precisely what Soviet managers do when they produce unplanned commodities that are advantageous to their firms but not to the State, when they overorder and hoard commodities, and when they resist innovation. Because of the differences between the two economic systems, we should expect that the precise forms that the owner-manager conflict takes would be different in the U.S.S.R. and the United States. In the United States they are to be found in such decisions as the awarding of subcontracts, the accounting of profit in such way as to benefit the claims of the controlling group, the awarding of bonuses and other benefits to management, and in dividend payment policy. As in the Soviet enterprise, the accountant is of crucial importance in handling the books of the enterprise in such way as make the best possible case for the manager; it is he, for example, who figures out the best way to distract the state's attention from the large expenditures on talkachi. The accounting techniques are, of course, different in the United States; they involve "the charging or the failure to deduct depreciation; charging to capital expenses which properly should be charged against income account; including nonrecurrent profits as income though their real place is in surplus; and the creation of 'hidden reserves'."

A major difference between the Soviet firm and the American firm is that in the last analysis profit remains the criterion of managerial performance in the latter, whereas the Soviet manager is evaluated by a number of criteria that are sometimes mutually exclusive. Both systems have attempted to bring managerial interests into harmony with owner interests by some sort of profit-sharing system. In the Soviet case, it is clear that profit plays a very minor role, compared with bonuses, as a managerial incentive. In the United States the manager shares directly in profit to a very limited extent, and often follows other goals in his decisions. "The executive not infrequently tends to look upon the stockholders as outsiders whose complaints and demand for dividends are necessary evils * * *" concluded one American student of management. In like fashion, the Soviet manager often begins to feel like the "boss" and resents the intrusion into "his" affairs by the state, which after all is the owner. I have described above some of the ways in which the Soviet manager promotes the interest of "his" enterprise by means contrary to the interests of the owner-state. In the American corporation the forms are somewhat different. "* * * profits are reinvested in the business for the sake of bigness and to protect the company, and the interests of the stockholders may be given second place to the business leader's conception of what is best for the firm itself." Executives manifest a "general unwillingness to liquidate unsuccessful enterprises" and thus put themselves out of jobs, however consistent liquidation might be with the interests of the stockholders. The dramatic growth of corporate self-financing in recent years has strengthened the power of management to expand their own enterprises without having to go through the "test of the marketplace" for capital.

It was observed earlier that the desire for "security" and for what the Russians call a "quiet life" motivates a wide variety of managerial decisions such as concealing production capacity and resisting technological innovation that might rock the boat. Students of American management have also noted the change from the adventurous business tycoons of earlier days to a more professionalized managerial climate in which "greater emphasis is placed on education, training, and a scientific approach, and less on rugged, venturesome, and frequently heedless individualism. The desire for security seems to have increased, and the concomitant of a growing emphasis on security is a diminishing desire for adventure for its own sake." There is indeed a remarkable parallel to this development in the change in the character of Soviet managers. There would have been a great affinity between the industrial empire builders of 19th century America and the Soviet directors of the first two decades of the Soviet regime. Those directors were often men of little education who came out of the romantic conflict of revolution, who dreamed great dreams of building an industrial nation and who created an ethos of bold plans and adventurous undertakings. The old Commissar of Heavy Industry, Sergei Ordzhonikidze, would have understood the spirit of the iron-monger, Andrew Carnegie, and the man who built the great ZIL auto-motive works (now named after him) had the drives and the dreams of the bicycle mechanic Henry Ford.

Time, and Stalin's purges, removed most of those oldtimers and their place has now been taken by Soviet-educated young men born not of revolution but of bureaucracy. Organizations seem to develop "organiza-tion men" types, whether the organization happen to be communist or capitalist. An American reporter visiting with a group of Communist intellectuals reports that one of them had badgered him with questions about David Reisman's book, "The Lonely Crowd." "The Communist had read Reisman's book and had been fascinated by it—not, he said, because of its application to life in the United States but because of what he maintained was its extraordinary relevance to the present conditions of life in the Soviet Union." It is not, on reflection, very surprising that the job of running an industrial bureaucracy should place a common stamp on men of otherwise different backgrounds. The same would probably apply to the running of a large city or a large university.

Managers and the Laws

We have found that the Soviet manager is often compelled to evade regulations or even break laws. Part of the explanation is simply that there are so many laws. If a Chicago manufacturer fails to ship an order to a New York firm, and ships it instead to another Chicago firm, he has nothing to fear but the ire of the New York firm. But if a Kiev manu-facturer fails to ship an order to a Moscow firm and ships it instead to another Kiev firm, he has injured a state enterprise and is subject to administrative action, a fine, or even criminal prosecution. If an Ameri-can firm sells a substandard generator, he may lose money or his business. But if a Soviet firm sells a substandard generator, the director may go to prison. Thus, even if Soviet managers acted exactly as American managers do, we should expect to find more illegal or evasive activity in the Soviet Union than in the United States.

With the growing complexity of our society, more and more legisla-tion is enacted to protect the public from potential abuses. With the growth of such legislation, managers find their activities more and more circumscribed by laws and regulations. The Soviet manager apparently treats such legislation rather lightly when it conflicts with the interests of his firm (and his career and pocketbook). How does American management react when confronted by a spreading web of restrictive legislation?

It is not easy to find out very much about American managerial practice in this respect. Unlike the Soviet press, which throws its pages open to reports of the irregular activities of managers in order to warn others, the American press is likely to shy away from this kind of reporting. Moreover the private nature of American business keeps this sort of activity from coming to light as easily as it might in Soviet industry. Nor is it the sort of thing that businessmen are inclined to talk about very readily. If it is true that a businessman would more readily be interviewed on his private sex life than on his private business activity, then we should require the late Dr. Kinsey to help provide the answers to the extent of unlawful or quasi-lawful business activity.

Prof. E. H. Sutherland, the eminent American criminologist and sociologist, made a bold attempt to investigate the phenomenon he refers to as "white collar crime." His study is based on the decisions of a limited number of courts and administrative commissions against the 70 largest industrial-type corporations in the country. In the period 1935 to 1944 these 70 corporations were convicted 585 times for such practices as restraint of trade, misrepresentation in advertising, patent and copyright infringements, unfair labor practices, granting of rebates, and a few others. The average was 8.5 convictions per corporation. These data provide some idea of the extensiveness of such practices but they clearly understate the magnitude for a variety of technical reasons. Sutherland's conclusion is that "a great deal of scattered and unorganized material indicates that white collar crimes are very prevalent."

The point I wish to make is that when American management finds itself in a position approximating that of Soviet management they tend to react in ways similar to those of their Soviet counterparts. Sutherland's unique study notes many aspects of American managerial practice that are astonishingly similar to those one might find in the literature on Soviet management. "These crimes are not discreet and inadvertent violations of technical regulations. They are deliberate and have a relatively consistent unity." It is in precisely this way that the Soviet manager deliberately misappropriates earmarked funds or decides to shave on the quality of production. There is evidence that the Soviet manager, aware of the fact that "everybody does it" and that the investigating agencies have restricted budgets, counts on the law of averages (and his own superior shrewdness) to get away with it. So a member of Federal Trade Commission wrote that "about the only thing that keeps a businessman off the wrong end of a Federal indictment or administrative agency's complaint is the fact that, under the hit-or-miss methods of prosecution, the law of averages hasn't made him a partner to a suit," and "Samuel Insull is reported to have remarked during his trial that he had only done what all other businessmen were doing."

Similarities in managerial practice are paralleled by similarities in attitude to such violations, and toward the administrative agencies enforcing the laws and regulations. The Soviet manager does not think it is "wrong" to use influence to obtain materials unlawfully, or to fudge his reports to the Government. Success is the important thing, and if you are successful you can get away with all sorts of violations. There is evidence that the Soviet manager feels contemptuous of government planners and of party hacks who try to tell him how to run his business but who themselves had "never met a payroll." Sutherland's picture of American Management's attitudes resemble constraints of the same kind.

> The businessman who violates the laws which are designed to regulate business does not customarily lose status among his business associates. Although a few members of the industry may think less of him, others admire him * * *. Businessmen customarily regard government personnel as politicians and bureaucrats, and the persons authorized to investigate business practices as "snoopers."

In the first chapter of this paper, it was pointed out that a managerial career carries a great deal of prestige in the Soviet Union and attracts a large number of the better students. These youngsters have been raised in Soviet schools and have absorbed the incessant propaganda of the Communist regime. Many of them enter industry as green novices fresh from school, filled with high ideals about building the socialist fatherland and working for the common welfare. One wonders about the process by which the naive, idealistic young Komsomol member is transformed into the hard-headed manager who knows all the angles for survival in the Soviet business world. Numerous incidents such as the following provide a key to the answer. A young Soviet chemist had been assigned to the quality control department of his enterprise. He was quite pleased with himself when his test showed that a sample of production, which had previously been declared acceptable by his laboratory chief, turned out to contain an excess of phosphorus. He reported the "error" and expected to get a bonus for it. Instead, his boss obtained a new sample, gave it to an outside chemist for analysis, and submitted a report showing that the batch of production was acceptable after all. The young chemist protested, was transferred to another shop, and was finally fired on trumped-up charges.

What happens to such young people? Some never quite get the point and remain ordinary engineers in the plants. Others learn to adapt themselves after a few buffetings and when they decide to play the game according to the real ground-rules, begin to rise in the managerial hierarchy.

It is interesting to note that Sutherland's interviews with American businessmen turned up accounts rather similar to that narrated above. His explanation of the process by which the naive American youngster is initiated into the business of selling used cars, settling insurance claims, covering up irregularities in clients' accounts—indeed, toning down the results of chemical analysis—helps explain the process of transformation of the young Komsomol member:

> In many cases he is ordered by the manager to do things which he regards as unethical or illegal, while in other cases he learns from others who have the same rank as his own how they make a success. He learns specific techniques of violating the law, together with definitions of situations in which those techniques may be used. Also he develops a general ideology. This ideology grows in part out of the specific practices and is in the nature of generalization from concrete experiences, but in part it is transmitted as a generalization by phrases such as "we are not in business for our health," "business is business," and "no business was ever built on the beatitudes." These generalizations * * * assist the neophyte in business to accept the illegal practices and provide rationalizations for them.

Summarizing, the economic world in which the Soviet manager operates compels him to engage in a variety of illegal or evasive practices. Since the Soviet business world is enmeshed in a much greater web of laws and regulations than the American, the Soviet manager finds his interest in conflict with the laws and regulations more often than his American counterpart. But when American managers' interests conflict with the laws, they too are prepared to take the chance of violating them. Both American and Soviet managers justify their actions by an attitude of contempt for governmental controls and investigating personnel, and by a hardheaded view that "business is business" and "everybody does it." Young people in both systems who wish to achieve managerial prominence have to learn to play the game according to the rules, or disqualify themselves from the tough competition for the top.

Managers and Overfull Employment

Many of the peculiarities of Soviet management spring from the fact that the economic system works under conditions of perpetual overfull employment. By "overfull" employment I mean a condition in which there are not merely as many jobs as employables (as under full employment), but the demand for labor far exceeds the available supply. The same applies to other factors of production: materials, equipment, and commodities in general are demanded in far greater volume than the current rates of production. The ability of the Soviet Government to maintain, through the planning system, a condition of permanent overfull employment is one of the greatest economic assets of the regime. We err when we interpret evidence of shortages in the Soviet economy as signs of economic weakness; they are rather indications that the economic engine is racing with the throttle wide open.

But just as an engine does not work at its maximum efficiency when it is working at its maximum capacity, so the Soviet economy pays a certain price for the advantages of overfull employment. It is the perpetual shortages of supplies that account in large measure for the losses due to overordering and hoarding. The hunger for goods by both firms and consumers encourages the deterioration of quality. The "sea of ink" associated with materials allocations, price fixing, priorities, and all the rigamarole of a controlled economy nurtures the spread of the tolkach and the use of influence for personal gain.

The normally functioning American economy does not confront our managers with this kind of problem. Hoarding makes no sense when materials are in adequate supply. Competition and consumer resistance force the quality of production up to standard. The role of influence is narrowly circumscribed when the bureaucratic machinery of Government controls is removed. The biggest problem of American managers under normal conditions is marketing, not purchasing. The energy spent by the Soviet firm on obtaining materials is spent by the American firm on selling and advertising.

Thus, the major differences between the practice of American and Soviet management are to be ascribed to the differences in the economic environment. The interesting question is, How do American managers behave when placed in an environment that approximates that of the Soviet manager? The obvious test case is war. During World War II the national emergency forced us into a state of overfull employment. Along with this came the total immersion of Government into economic life, with a great burgeoning of materials allocation, price fixing, cost-plus contracting, and a prevailing shortage of supplies.

It is interesting to note that the rate of growth of production during the war rose to levels rivaling the current rates of Soviet economic growth. The implication of this fact is important; it means that there is no magic in the Soviet economic system. Our economy could grow as rapidly as the Soviet economy does if our people would consent to being pushed around as totally as the Soviet people are.

But like the Soviet economy, we paid for our high rate of production in various forms of waste. One of the first consequences of the introduction of materials controls was the rise of the black market. The only full-scale study of the black market, to my knowledge, confirmed what many people felt to be the case at the time:

> During the war at least a million cases of black market violations were dealt with by the Government. Illegal profits ran into billions of dol-

lars. Business interests and Government vied with one another in estimating the seriousness of the black market; business estimates, curiously, often being higher than those of the Government. Such extensive conniving in the black market in illegal prices and rationed commodities took place among so many businessmen, ordinary criminals, and even the average citizen that serious questions might be raised as to the moral fiber of the American people.

To understand the position of the Soviet manager, we must realize that the American black market flourished at a time when the Nation was fighting for its life and public indignation acted as a restraint. But if the economic controls that led to violations could not be justified by a national emergency, they would be thought of as just irritating obstacles, as so many hurdles that the resourceful manager must overcome as part of the risks of the game. There is good evidence that the Soviet manager takes just this amoral attitude toward economic controls, and it is therefore quite understandable that the evasion of controls would be more widespread.

The high quality of American production in normal times is a byword in international markets. But the effect of the economy of shortages was similar to that in the Soviet economy. One of the techniques used by Soviet managers is to present lower quality merchandise as of higher quality, and to sell it at the higher price. In the United States during the war—

> Upgrading was one of the most difficult violations to detect, particularly where no professional investigator was available who could appraise the grade or where there were no State or Federal grades stamped on the commodity.

The reports of Government investigators read like some of the indignant letters of complaint we read in the Soviet press; men's shorts made of cheesecloth, water-resistant baby's pants which permit a third of a glass of water to leak through after one laundering—

> If you pick up a board by both ends without breaking it in the middle, it's No. 1 Select.

testified an American businessman.

One of the features of Soviet managerial life which helps protect the manager is the feeling of "mutual support" among various officials whose fortunes depend on the success of the enterprise. The Communist Party secretary doesn't report the manipulations of a successful director because the party benefits from the success of the enterprise; the people in the "home office" (the Ministry or the Council of the National Economy) are reluctant to fire a director who violates the laws in order to get the materials his plant needs, for while the next director may be more lawabiding, he may not succeed in fulfilling his plan. This tendency to maintain a solid front against authority is a source of great irritation to the Government, which periodically inveighs against it but has not been able to eradicate it. A similar sense of common front prevailed among groups of businessmen.

> Nothing better illustrates the degree of organization and consensus among businessmen then their reluctance to testify against each other * * *. Some businessmen felt that the trade would disapprove of behavior that might undermine the solid front against the Government as well as interfere with supplies.

One of the major differences in the position of management in the two countries is the nature of the penalty for failure. Under ordinary conditions the unsuccessful manager loses his job. But the Soviet manager faces many more situations in which the action necessary to get the job done carries with it the threat of criminal action. Indeed, whenever the Soviet Government has found some managerial practice too damaging to its interests and too intractable to the normal sanctions, it has turned to the criminal courts. Immediately after the death of Stalin the punishment for economic transgressions was relaxed, but the new regime has not been able to continue operating without the courts. One of the severest economic problems following the decentralization of industry was the tendency toward "localism": that is, each economic region tended to favor the plants in its "own" region, and would discriminate against plants in other regions. When all exhortation failed, the Government had to turn to the law. Today, a manager who fails to honor the orders of plants outside his own region is subject to "administrative action, fines, or even criminal punishment."

Financial penalties, such as fines, have rarely proved successful as restraints on Soviet managerial behavior. American managers seem to have reacted the same way to the fines imposed for black-market violations. "They don't hurt anybody." "It just comes out of profits, like a tax." "They make so much money on the black market they can afford to pay steep fines." But imprisonment was another matter. "Jail is the only way; nobody wants to go to jail." "A jail sentence is dishonorable; it jeopardizes the reputation." This would not be quite the same in the case of the Soviet manager. At least during Stalin's lifetime some of the best people served their time in jail, and it definitely did not destroy their reputation among their neighbors; although the neighbors might be wary of associating with them. One has the impression that large numbers of Soviet managers feel the chances are fair that some day they will do their stretch, hopefully for a minor transgression.

The wartime economy of shortages injects the government into business life not only as an agency of control but also as the largest customer of many firms. In the Soviet case we have noted the importance of the tolkach, the expediter, the peddler of influence. We might note in passing that the economic system of Nazi Germany, in which government had also assumed a dominant role, also gave rise to this chap. The Germans called him the "contact man." As described by an American student of the German economy:

> To influence the powerful agencies of control, however, he [the German businessman] has good use for what might suitably be called a private relations department. Under the Nazi system of control of business by an absolute government, the contact man, or graft, or both, take the place of the public relations executive.
>
> The contact man is primarily a political figure. His job is to pull wires. He knows the influential members of the all-pervading Nazi Party in a position to bring pressure successfully to bear upon the men in charge of controlling agencies. * * *. Two types of contact man are known to be used: one is an independent agent whom the businessman hires, or attempts to hire, whenever necessary; the other is carried on the payroll of the business in a more or less permanent capacity.

The words might well have been written about the Soviet economy. In that sector of the U.S. economy in which Government plays a dominant role as customer, the symbols of the mink coat or Dixon-Yates, depending upon one's political persuasion, come to mind. "Washington," wrote Senator Paul Douglas, "is indeed full of lawyers and 'representatives' whose primary commodity is 'influence'." The techniques of the American influence-peddler differ little from those of his colleagues in the Soviet or Nazi economy. Gifts and quid pro quo favors are standard among Soviet tolkachi. Another way in which Soviet enterprises manage to exert influence is to have one of "their" men placed in other organizations that can be of use, rather like the unusually high employability in industry of retired military personnel. During the war the problem was particularly acute because of our Government's desperate need for skilled managerial personnel, many of whom were on loan from corporations with which the Government placed contracts. But the use of influence is not confined to Government-business relations, as Senator Douglas pointed out in his critical defense of the ethics of Government personnel:

> As a matter of fact, the abuses which have been exposed and properly denounced in the field of Government are quite widespread practices in private business. Thus the "padding" of expense accounts is so common that they are often referred to as "swindle sheets." Purchasing agents and buyers frequently exact toll from those who seek to sell to them, and their Christmas presents and other perquisites appreciably increase their income. Business managers and directors think nothing of awarding contracts, insurance, and underwriting privileges on the basis of friendship and relationship rather than the quality and prices of the goods and services supplied. All this is taken as a matter of course in private business, although it obviously increases costs and intercepts gains which should go to stockholders and consumers.

While gifts, payoffs, and bribery play their role in the Soviet scheme of things, the subtler and much more pervasive technique of influence is known as "blat." To have good blat with someone means that one has an "in"; one can always count on him for a favor because of friendship or family ties or some other relationship of confidence. Blat may be used to obtain everything from a new apartment to a carload of coal. The prominent British observer, Edward Crankshaw, has called blat the most significant word in contemporary Russia. The way in which the American equivalent of blat is cultivated is described in one final quotation from Senator Douglas:

> Today the corruption of public officials by private interests takes a more subtle form. The enticer does not generally pay money directly to the public representative. He tries instead by a series of favors to put the public official under such feeling of personal obligation that the latter gradually loses his sense of mission to the public and comes to feel that his first loyalties are to his private benefactors and patrons. What happens is a gradual shifting of a man's loyalties from the community to those who have been doing him favors. His final decisions are, therefore, made in response to private friendships and loyalties rather than to the public good.

Summarizing, many of the differences between Soviet and United States managerial behavior spring from differences in the economic climate in which they operate. The stress on quality and appearance, the drive for innovation and technological development, and the interest in cost reduction reflect the force of competition and the buyer's market. Such similarities as have been observed in managerial behavior, spring from features of the economic environment that are common to the two systems, such as large-scale organization and the intrusion of Government into the economy. Under wartime conditions our economy takes on more of the features of normal Soviet economic life, and the consequence is that our managers adopt more of the normal practices of Soviet management.

THE NATURE OF PRICES*
— · — · — · — · — ·
George R. Feiwel

Decision making, the choice between alternative courses of action, is the core of economics, the science of administration of scarce resources in human society. Economic efficiency can almost never be based on technological considerations alone. To govern production (optimum combination of factors and output composition) an economic dimension is necessary,

*Reprinted by permission from *The Economics of a Socialist Enterprise* (New York: Frederick A. Praeger Inc., 1965) pp. 43–45. All footnotes have been deleted.

a criterion or choice indicator, a sufficient summary measure of all opportunities forgone. Such an indicator "cannot be derived from any property possessed by that particular thing, but which reflects, or in which is condensed, its significance is view of the whole means-end structure. It is the presence of the value scale that is the *differentia specifica* of the economic, as distinct from the technological, problem. As Schumpeter points out, an economic dimension, a phenomenon basic to efficient functioning of any society, "at all times and under all circumstances, finds expression in coefficients of choice which are fundamentally the same thing as prices in capitalist society." To select between alternatives an economic unit must have at its disposal reliable information: the choice coefficients on which to base its decision. The role of prices as signals and summary measures to convey such information is lucidly summarized by Koopmans:

> . . . price is regarded as a label, a signal, a piece of information that is attached to the good or service traded. This information expresses simultaneously the ultimate usefulness to consumers of this good, and the foregone usefulness of other goods or services that could have been produced alternatively from the resources absorbed in making this good. Choices about methods of production and about amounts to be produced are based on this information; if these choices are to be good choices, the information used has to be accurate.

Indeed it is the allocative function of prices as guides for resource allocation that renders prices indispensable for rational economic calculation. It is particularly in solving the allocative problem that Marxist economics is most deficient. There is virtually no Marxist micro-economics. Prices must be used in the planning process to afford economic calculation aiming not only at consistency but at finding optimum solutions. The control function of prices—as a common denominator for aggregating heterogeneous physical quantities in value terms and performing the control and evaluative functions, in an auditing sense—will be a serious impediment for the use of prices as tools of economic calculation. Even in a highly centralized economy the questions "what, how, how much, and for whom to produce efficiently" must be resolved on the basis of rational prices. Three sets of data are required for a determinable solution of the allocative problem: 1) preference function, which may reflect consumer or planner preferences, 2) choice indicator, and 3) production function. If the data under (1) and (3) are given, (2) can be determined. Hence it is claimed that a socialist economy can operate with rational prices without a market in an institutional sense.

In Soviet-type economies price is a derivative of cost. The constituents of price are cost elements which themselves are not independent variables. The production cost of a given good cannot be said to be price determining since the constituting cost elements are determined by prices. In these economies planners allocate productive agents and then set prices. Hence there is a basic flaw in the system as prices cannot be set rationally unless the productive agents were beforehand allocated efficiently to their various uses. Under such circumstances the *conditio sine qua non* for setting rational prices would be that the prior allocation of productive agents satisfies the efficiency test. However, this condition is not fulfilled. The fundamental weakness of an economy where the predetermined production quota and appropriate input allocations are largely based on physical planning is evident in the inability of economic verification of production decisions. Without such verification there are no criteria for determining rational costs for measuring the whole range of alternatives forgone at the margin. Without rational coefficients of choice there can be no economic calculation:

> The Pharaohs—wrote Lord Robbins—did not need a price system for the erection of the pyramids. But at what sacrifice of other goods its products would be secured, at what economic, as distinct from the technical, efficiency it functioned, could not be ascertained.

THE DUAL PRICE SYSTEM: THE POLISH EXPERIENCE*

· — · — · — · — · — · — · — · — · — · — ·

George R. Feiwel

Consumers' prices are to achieve equilibrium between aggregate planned expenditures on individual consumption, largely a function of the total wage fund, and planned output (and imports) of consumer goods. The objective is not only to equate aggregate supply with aggregate demand but the structure of relative prices should be so devised as to equate consumers' demand with the available supply of each consumer good. Hence, in principle, the state has to set such relative retail price ratios as to equate supply and demand for each commodity reckoning with substitution, complementarily, and income effects. For the system to be efficient it must embody an equilibrating mechanism with flexible prices should any of the magnitudes diverge from the plan. In theory excess demand is a signal for an upward price adjustment discouraging consumption and encouraging production. And in practice? Retail prices are seldom changed. They are not designed to reckon the interdependencies of related products and largely aim at balancing total supply with total demand. Even if prices were originally set to balance supply and demand for a commodity, they are now obsolete in view of the shift parameters. Hence disequilibrium prevails for particular goods.

*Reprinted by permission from *The Economics of a Socialist Enterprise* (New York: Frederick A. Praeger Inc., 1965) pp. 58–64. All footnotes deleted.

By stabilizing prices for necessities the state aims at counteracting inflation. The stability of consumers' prices is considered one of the basic aims, since upward movements have direct repercussions on wage levels and structure, rendering cost calculation, planning, and auditing intricate and arduous. Price stability, in such conditions, induces increased consumption and discourages production of deficit products.

Viewing the entire socialist industry as a gigantic combine of successive production phases, Turetski, as far back as 1929, pointed out that "the prices of producer goods, under those circumstances, maintain only a calculatory, purely conventional meaning." The role of producers' prices as tools facilitating accounting calculation was emphasized by Stalin:

> Why . . . do we speak of the value of means of production, their cost of production, their price, etc.? . . . this is needed for purposes of calculation and settlement, for determining whether enterprises are paying or running at a loss, for checking and controlling the enterprises.

The function of producers' prices is closely tied in with business calculation. The necessity of enforcing stringent control over the firm's activity has given rise to the phenomenon of business calculation. The budget constraint is imposed on the enterprise. It induces economy by requiring the firm to carry out operations within the state-determined targets, covering its expenditures from its receipts. The latter should not exceed the payments, depriving the firm of surplus funds which it might use for unplanned ventures. This is one of the reasons for setting producers' prices at costs plus only a slight margin of profit.

Prices of consumer goods include not only their own cost of production and accumulation, but also the accumulation of producer goods used in their production. The total accumulation (surplus product) is realized almost entirely in the prices of consumer goods which considerably exceed costs, whereas the prices of producer goods gravitate around, and often below, costs. In the past the disparity between those two in the U.S.S.R. was such that Turetski reported in 1959 that a crude estimate by Soviet economists indicated that should the prices of producer goods reflect value, they would have to be doubled.

While prices of consumer goods ought to balance supply and demand, this is deemed unnecessary for prices of producer goods since they can only be procured by socialized firms on the basis of their plans and no real market for producer goods exists. The major producer goods are distributed centrally on the basis of the material and technical procurement plans.

In principle, producers' prices are set on the planned average production costs of a branch of industry producing a given good. In Fiszel's words:

> The law of value requires the basis for the proportions of prices of means of production to be the socially necessary labor inputs for pro-

duction of specific products, expressed in the average cost of production. This signifies that prices of specific goods should generally remain in the same ratios as costs.

Deviations of prices from costs are sanctioned to allow for the relative technical "use value," to enhance or limit usage in view of relative shortages or surpluses, or to alleviate the balance of payments and other policy reasons. At times the majority of producers' prices fall below costs and the firms must be subsidized by the state. The dual level of prices often features deficits of many producer goods, whereas consumer goods may be exceedingly "profitable." One of the reasons for deficits is the increase in wages unwarranted by an increase in labor productivity. This results in higher costs exceeding the meager profit. Wage increases occur between price changes. When prices are changed and profitability restored another increase in wages causes the return of deficits. For reasons of control and financial expendiency deficits tend to be focused on materials which originate in the early stages of the production phase (minerals, raw materials, etc.). Planning and financial control are facilitated by concentrating subsidies on fewer items of major importance. The infrequency of price changes and the recurring shifts in the production function, quality of inputs used, changing wage level and structure, as well as many other factors aggravate deficits.

The obsoleteness of prices is intensified with time. Demands for a price reform increase but the planner resists since any price reform reduces his control over the firms, necessitates recalculation of plans for comparability purposes, and involves innumerable repercussions as price changes are interdependent. During the ensuing price reform, prices are set up allowing only a meager margin of profit on planned costs. Planned cost is usually based on overoptimistic assumptions as to the increase in labor productivity. In view of an intensive exploitation of resources and the accomplishment of increased output through conversion of peasants into industrial workers, undue overtime, etc., labor productivity falls short of expectations. Since the wage rate is the least stable variable, its proposed changes are kept secret even from the price fixing officials to avoid unrest and speculation on the consumer market.

In Poland the divergence between costs and prices of producer goods markedly increased during the Six-Year Plan. Prices of producer goods, however, remained virtually unchanged. Tracing the history of pricing in the U.S.S.R., Kondrashev pointed out that already during the first Soviet Five-Year Plan costs exceeded prices notwithstanding the restriction on money wages through payments in kind. The 1936 price reform did not produce the desired results. Heavy industry suffered deficits after a year due to increased costs. This was followed by annually increasing deficits. The prices remained unchanged until 1941 regardless of marked increases in costs. Kondrashev's conclusion is most instructive pointing to the similarity with the Polish pre-1960 experience:

> During several revisions of producers' prices the planning authorities have committed one and the same error: disregarding the future they predetermined too low a level of costs, consequently, at the same time, the planned price.

The foremost argument in favor of low producers' prices is that they stimulate technical progress by reducing the relative cost of capital assets. The second argument is that low producers' prices facilitate economic calculation since they confront only a part of value added by labor (excluding surplus product) with only a part of labor embodied in the means of production. The third argument maintains that low prices facilitate planning and levying turnover tax by concentrating the bulk of accumulation in relatively few industries. It seems that here again financial expediency outweighs economic arguments.

Contrary to claims that low producers' prices facilitate economic calculation, the opposite may be claimed: the dual price system distorts calculation. The artificially reduced price level of producer goods in relation to consumer goods hampers the analysis of processes in the national economy. The share of the branches of industry producing producer goods is actually greater, and that of light and food industries lower than represented by the national income calculated at prices based on costs. The parts of national income diverted to consumption and accumulation are similarly distorted. In comparison with total output produced, the part of output consumed is reported larger than it actually is. The dual price system hampers calculation of economic efficiency in the planning and analysis of relative efficiency of investments. Since producers' prices are low, the share of material inputs in total costs appears to be low, facilitating the introduction of technical improvements of actually low efficiency but resulting in considerable savings on wage payments. The reasoning that low prices of capital assets foster technical progress rests on fallacious premises. The firm is largely indifferent to the cost of capital goods since the planner distributes investments among enterprises with the monetary equivalent allotted from the state funds. No matter what price the state imputes to the capital asset the monetary equivalent is paid out. As a result of low prices of capital assets smaller depreciation charges will mean lower costs to the firms, lowering simultaneously the price of the product based on cost. Furthermore, low producers' prices apply also to material inputs, which has very little to do with technical progress but much to do with waste, as management tends to substitute materials for labor whenever possible. Since some of the basic raw materials are imported, or may be exported, the ensuing harm to the economy is enormous.

Producers' prices are deficient as coefficients of choice distort cost calculations, are not summaries of alternatives forgone at the margin, abstract from current scarcity relations, and the supply or demand for an input is largely not a *function* of its price. In allocating producer goods and eradicating shortages, the central planner relies on "balancing" conducted mainly in physical units without reverting to the allocative function of prices.

Recently Wakar and Zielinski concentrated on the question of the present system of allocating resources, and on improving the efficiency of this system with the handicap of irrational prices. They emphatically point out that effective functioning of the economy does not depend primarily on the degree of decentralization but on the types of economic calculation adopted, distinguishing, in pure form, direct and indirect (or market-type) calculations. Zielinski maintains that there are three alternative ways of achieving rational prices: 1) determination by free interplay of supply and demand, 2) Lange's trial and error solution, and 3) shadow prices. In his view (1) is unacceptable due to deficiency of market prices for choosing optimal investments, market failures, etc.; (3) would be more compatible with the present institutional framework than (2) and more acceptable to the central planner as it would not necessarily require decentralization of decision making and could be used in conjunction with commands. The type of economic calculation adopted prejudges whether value parameters or commands are the most suitable tools for fulfilling the plan.

Under the prevailing method of direct calculation, the central planner largely reckons and coordinates directly in physical magnitudes (hence the name). Prices perform, or ought to perform, the aggregation function only, and there is no mechanism for verifying the technical production coefficients. Hence transmission of minute commands is the only logical solution. The central planner basically operates with three sets of data: 1) the available capital, human, and natural resources, 2) the desired output, reflecting his preferences, and 3) technical input coefficients as independent structural constants. The transformation of (1) into (2) is constrained by the size of (3). At the stage of plan construction what has been "chosen *in natura* must, in turn, be chosen by the means of prices." The planner sets prices, wages, interest, etc. but he is not guided by them, and reaches his own solutions without reverting to prices as coefficients of choice. The aim is to produce an internally consistent plan, but the problem of economic efficiency of production is almost disregarded. The methods of production are chosen on the basis of prevailing techniques or "progressive engineering" mechanically transplanted from more advanced countries. Since the substitution effect is eliminated in plan construction, it should logically be eliminated in plan implementation. Passive prices perform this function admirably. Activating prices would bring about factors' substitution, therefore alterations in technical coefficients with the inevitable consequence of demolishing the laboriously achieved internal consistency of the plan. At the executing stage of the plan prices, as a constituent part of the premium system, do influence managerial behavior. Hence they are called to perform a function for which they were not designed. This causes undesirable effects which bring about, *inter alia*, bottlenecks and disproportions that must be mitigated by central commands and allocations restraining managerial actions.

From the fundamental weakness of direct calculation it would follow that this type of calculation should be abandoned, or if retained, practical consequences must be drawn from its very nature. The plan should be executed by a conglomeration of integrated minute commands. Prices that were not designed for transmitting information must not be activated to perform such a role. Hence the role of prices in plan execution is strictly defined by the nature of economic calculation employed in planning. Indeed the question may be raised: Should functions other than accounting be assigned to producers' prices, and does not the central planner defeat his own purpose by activating prices?

PRICING OF PRODUCER GOODS: FACTORY PRICES IN POLAND*

— · — · — · — · — · — · —

George R. Feiwel

From their very inception (1954) factory prices were mainly used for computing turnover tax and settlement between producers and foreign trade centrals. The ministries were to set factory prices on the basis of planned average production costs in a branch of industry plus a markup not exceeding 5 per cent of costs. Factory prices were to be equal to transfer prices less turnover tax, or in the absence of the latter, coincide with transfer prices whether or not they covered costs plus markup. Not only did factory prices not ensure profit, but they maintained deficits. With the aim of enhancing the usefulness of factory prices their 1960 reform featured: 1) Factory prices are always equal to average cost plus profit, irrespective of the level of the corresponding transfer prices, thus ensuring profit to the producers. 2) The percentage of profit may be calculated either on total costs, costs of processing, direct labor, or transfer price. 3) The rate of profit may be set so as to promote or curtail production. 4) The factory price may be changed once a year when profit exceeds the upper limit imposed or when transfer prices of inputs are increased.

*Reprinted by permission from *The Economics of a Socialist Enterprise* (New York: Frederick A. Praeger Inc., 1965), pp. 80–88. All footnotes deleted.

The most recent regulations governing factory prices reinforce their influence on product mix by allowing wider variations of the rate of profit to encourage or discourage flow and composition of output. For example to promote production of goods "of substantially improved technical attributes, construction, or quality" their factory prices may include up to 50 per cent profit for the first year or, in exceptional cases, for two years. The upper limit of profit for producer goods was specified as 10 per cent, leaving the PC (Planning Commission) in conjunction with the MF (Ministry of Finance) and SPC (State Price Commission) the prerogative of manipulating the upper limit. This revision also condones levying turnover tax when the factory prices of producer goods are lower than the corresponding transfer prices.

The revisions of official regulations indicate that the trend is to vest factory prices with an economic incentive function. This issue has been raised on several occasions in literature before the first shaky steps were taken in the 1960's to attack the problem. Of late it is increasingly stressed that factory prices should perform three major functions: 1) to serve as economic incentives, 2) to measure output and 3) to serve as tools for financial calculations and settlements with the budget and foreign trade centrals.

In a nutshell the argument for factory prices to perform the incentive function is: if some choice is left to the firms (or associations) the planner needs a tool for influencing his subordinates. Transfer prices could not serve as such a tool because their increase or reduction to discourage or encourage quantity demanded, would, *ceteris paribus*, promote or curtail quantity produced. This may not be the result intended by the planner. Transfer prices, primarily designed to influence the buyer, often deviate from average costs to take into account the technical relationship of substitutes, policy considerations to restrict or enhance the use of a particular factor due to its relative scarcity, relation to import prices, price ratios on foreign markets, and other considerations deemed beneficial for policy reasons. Consequently, when revenue is reckoned in transfer prices, the rate of accumulation or deficit varies substantially, and not necessarily in the same direction as the state intends to influence the producer. Hence factory prices are required to influence the producers' product mix in the direction desired by the state.

As early as 1960 Stankiewicz proposed the use of factory prices with a uniform rate of profit neutralizing the producers' behavior towards assortments, rendering them all equally attractive to produce. Lately Kalecki went a step further. He suggested varying the rate of profit for different branches of industry or large groups of products according to central preferences. This would still leave the enterprises of those branches neutral towards their product mix since the rate of profit would remain uniform for the goods produced in that branch. Furthermore, through an appropriate determination of factory prices, it is possible, when desired, to influence the producers' output composition and flow by varying the rate of profit on individual goods to stimulate or contract production.

Hence the pricing system rests on the separation of the prices for the buyer (transfer price), for whom they constitute elements of costs of production and investments, from the prices for the producer (factory prices), for whom they constitute revenue covering production costs and profit. Consequently "if the main purpose of transfer prices is to shape demand . . . the purpose of factory prices is to form a basis for a possibly objective evaluation of activity of enterprises and associations, as well as limit the restraints in adaptation of production to needs."

Transfer prices which include widely divergent rates of accumulation or deficit are heterogeneous and do not present a clear picture of the cost of total output. The rationale behind the second function of factory prices, i.e., output measurement, is to have a uniform standard for measuring production based on supply conditions only. Such a standard can be obtained only by eliminating the influence of demand conditions from transfer prices.

Factory prices perform their third function in facilitating levy of turnover tax, the difference between the factory price and the corresponding transfer price. They are the basis for budget subsidies when transfer prices fall below average costs plus profit. They are also the prices at which producers sell their goods to the foreign trade centrals. The third group of functions is the one for which factory prices were primarily designed and is still the one for which they are most commonly used.

How well do factory prices perform these three functions simultaneously? Firstly, let us consider the problem of the upper limit of profit in factory prices. When the rate of profit actually attained exceeds the upper limit allowed, a new lower factory price is set. The lowering of the factory price was considered a necessity to keep enterprises on a budget constraint and to prompt them into a constant "fight and struggle for cost reduction." This stand is highly questionable. Given the existing price system, the firm will not be interested in cost reduction that will provoke a reduction of the factory price jeopardizing profit. This would be so because the new rate of profit would be lower than the one actually attained, since it is the excess of the actual rate of profit over the allowed limit that has brought about the decrease in factory price. Reduction of costs, if followed by a proportionate reduction in the factory price, would simply mean a transfer of the enterprise's savings to the state budget at the detriment of the producer who will be entitled to a smaller amount of profit than he otherwise would had the factory price not been decreased. Analyzing the responses received Dudzinski writes:

> Lately enterprises and associations repeatedly claim that the principle of decreasing factory prices minimizes their interest in cost reduction. Since every year as costs are reduced the factory price is to be re-

duced to a level safeguarding the stable 5 to 7 per cent margin of profit, the enterprise's efforts to increase profit in this manner are turned against it. The principle of a yearly limitation of profit through factory prices cannot be reconciled with that of interesting enterprises and associations with the economic results of their activity.

Firms will report relatively high profits only when they are "conservative" in cost reduction. It is advantageous for them to reduce costs only up to the point beyond which factory prices would be reduced. But the firms are guided by a range rather than a point. They assume a safety margin and as a precautionary measure are not interested in cost reduction that will endanger the safety margin.

Nevertheless the prevailing current practice largely counteracts the built-in tendency against cost reduction beyond a given point. The firm's performance is primarily judged on accumulation, the difference between transfer price and respective cost. Since the enterprise is evaluated on the basis of the transfer price rather than the factory price, the latter does not perform in practice its role of economic incentive.

The claim that factory prices measure output in homogeneous terms adequately since they reflect cost of production with uniform rates of profit and show the relative contribution of each output, firm, or branch of industry to total output, stems from the reasoning that "when a dual price system is maintained prices of the means of production and means of consumption can be reduced to a 'common denominator' only if factory prices are used." This reasoning seems to be sensible enough since transfer prices of producer and consumer goods are incomparable magnitudes. Yet it seems questionable whether output and relative contribution to output can be measured by reverting solely to supply prices. The fact that output was produced and cost incurred is not sufficient evidence that a contribution which will benefit society has been made as it lacks the buyer's seal of approval. Notwithstanding this criticism, the cost data on which factory prices are based are not indications of true cost. Barring the limitations of cost data, discussed in the following chapter, it is generally admitted that the cost data used as a basis for factory prices during the 1960 reform were the crudest of approximations.

When establishing factory prices, costs were calculated by using precomputed indexes established centrally on the basis of general and very rough computations. The factory price catalogs were prepared hastily using 1958 and partly 1959 costs. It is not surprising that after the reform the rate of profit on many items proved to be very high and in most cases varied considerably. Sztyber reports that the 1962 actual rates ranged from deficits to profits exceeding 30 per cent. For example, the estimated and reported rates of profit in 1960 for the several branches of light industry were: cotton industry 6.3 and 11.6, wool 1.9 and 8.3, silk 4.2 and 7.7, felt 3.6 and 14.9, button and haberdashery 3.8 and 13.4, and leather industry 4.3

and 6.9 per cent. In many cases the rate of profit, depending on the assortment and the branch of industry, exceeded 10 per cent by 1961. In the chemical and heavy industries it gravitated around 12 to 20 per cent. In the machine building industry by 1961 70 per cent of total output had factory prices with a rate of profit exceeding 10 per cent, 10 per cent of output was unprofitable, whereas only 20 per cent of output was profitable in the range of 5 to 7 per cent. Although the profit included in factory prices as a result of their 1960 revision is greatly differentiated "in a majority of cases it is largely accidental and exhibits no correlation to existing preferences (from the market, technical progress, export, etc., standpoints)."

It is especially in view of the practical difficulties in cost determination that Struminski attacks the proposals aiming at reinforcing the use of factory prices. As a result of this deficiency the actual profit realized departs from the postulated rate of profit rendering central manipulation of this rate futile. If factory prices remain constant for a number of years their shortcomings are magnified. But their annual revision on a large scale cannot, according to Struminski, be accomplished accurately. Hence the usefulness of factory prices as economic incentives and to aggregate output collapses.

A price which reflects supply conditions only, based on a fallacious definition and computation of costs, cannot perform satisfactorily the function of economic incentive, and it is even doubtful whether it performs the function of aggregating output adequately. If factory prices are to function as economic incentives the rates of profit must be differentiated. But if they are to serve as tools for aggregating output the rates of profit should be uniform. Hence factory prices cannot simultaneously be economic incentives and tools for measuring output given their present formation.

Until now the factory price system has fulfilled primarily the settlement functions. In view of the limited role and functions of these prices it was concluded that keeping this system exclusively for settlement purposes cannot be substantiated since it is extremely labor cosuming. Recently a commission under the chairmanship of M. Kalecki was called by the chairman of the PC to study and report on the uses of factory prices in planning and the financial system. In a nutshell the proposals, which are now being considered, were:

1. To relate the incentive system to profit instead of accumulation rendering producers sensitive to factory prices. The latter will be employed, together with the rate of profit therein, to stimulate or contract flow of production. Transfer prices will be used to induce or discourage buyers' demand. For example, to promote technical progress transfer prices of newly produced goods could include low turnover tax, or none at all, and factory prices include a high rate of profit to promote both demand

and production. The turnover tax on outdated products could be raised and factory prices decreased to discourage both demand and output. This would be equivalent to introducing separate prices for buyers and producers. It is claimed that under conditions of a more or less deeply ingrained sellers' market, separate prices for buyers and sellers are preferable. Kalecki argues that in cases of increased demand for a particular good a price exceeding average cost would have to be set to limit usage. However, it does not follow that the same price should regulate the producers' behavior because they may be operating at full capacity and the additional cost would be prohibitive. Moreover, there may not be sufficient reasons for investment expenditures as costs may be incommensurate with returns.

2. Factory prices should also be used to aggregate output. The turnover tax included in transfer prices being widely differentiated, aggregation in transfer prices affords management a wider field for product mix manipulations. Furthermore, factory prices should be the basis for calculating cost reduction when the latter is computed as the share of costs in value of total output. In this case again factory prices, where the rate of profit is less differentiated, narrow down management's field of manipulation.

3. Due to the importance of the size and relations of the rate of profit on different products, the following principles should be observed when establishing those rates: a) The standard rates of profit should vary for different branches of industry or large product groups in view of central preferences to promote increase of output or cost reduction. The magnitude of profit increments (z) in relation to costs depends on: cost reduction (k) and increase of output (p). With a given rate of profit (m), this may be represented as:

$$z = k + pm$$

Consequently, the higher the rate of profit, the greater is the influence exerted on the increment of profit by increase of output, and a smaller influence by cost reduction. Where increase of production is preferred the rate of profit should be higher. Conversely, where cost reduction is the target, the rate of profit should be lower. For example, if in the textile industry premiums are based on accumulation, the increase of production is rewarded more than cost reduction. The situation should be reversed. This industry suffers from shortages of imported materials and incentives for saving of materials are needed. Hence the rate of profit should be lower than the accumulation to stimulate cost reduction. b) The rate of profit in factory prices should be increased to promote production of goods in short supply and decreased to curtail the output in cases of oversupply. c) To discourage production of material intensive goods, the rate of profit should be set on value added (or a standard approximating value added by eliminating material costs from total costs). d) Factory prices should not, as a rule, be subject to change during a five-year plan as a result of cost reduction. This should induce enterprises to reduce costs since they will benefit from such action.

4. Factory prices should still serve for computing the turnover tax due the state budget as well as the amount of subsidy owed an enterprise in cases where the factory price is higher than the transfer price.

5. When transfer prices are changed during the course of a five-year plan, the factory prices should be recalculated to allow for the increased production costs.

6. In view of the limited scope foreseen for the 1965 revision of producers' prices new factory prices could be introduced simultaneously or one year later. When calculating the new factory prices the planned cost reductions should be considered. If a substantial revision of transfer prices should take place in the future, the factory prices should be changed only one or two years later to afford full cognizance of the mutual interdependence of prices and costs.

The IV Congress of the Polish United Workers Party reiterated the stability and regidity of transfer prices, acknowledging simultaneously the need for flexibility. It promulgated that the flexibility element could be introduced through a wider application of factory prices. However, the process of revising factory prices has in itself a built-in rigidity. The adjustments of output to stimuli introduced by factory prices and the required adaptation feature most of the shortcomings that Hayek so clearly conceived. Without questioning the nature of profit determined, it is doubtful whether a markup on cost fallaciously determined is a measure of some significance since cost reduction may be achieved, *inter alia*, at the expense of capital intensive processes for which no cost is imputed. Scrutinizing the proposal and Kalecki's arguments, the deficiency of computations based on average instead of marginal costs becomes more apparent, and indeed the sacrifice for not following a sort of Lange-Lerner Rule is evident.

Apart from all other limitations and deficiencies, one may have strong reservations about a wide use of factory prices since they undoubtedly widen the rift between the producer and the market for his products. The producer is rendered insensitive to any stimuli but those originating within the four walls of the PC, or those inadvertently created by calculatory errors which may be undesirable from both the consumers' and planner's standpoints.

BANKING AND CREDIT IN EASTERN EUROPE:
THE STANDARD SYSTEM*

— · — · — · — · — · — · — · — · — ·

George Garvy†

Before turning to more specific consideration of the new role assigned to credit and the cost of money and capital, we must look at their place in an economic system that tried to reduce the function of money to that of an accounting unit (or to abolish it altogether, as in the Soviet Union in the early twenties), to make the distribution of credit a by-product of the administrative allocation of resources and products, and to make capital a free good. This system, which I have discussed elsewhere in some detail, emerged in the Soviet Union after the credit and banking reforms of 1930–32, and was adopted by the other countries of Eastern Europe when communist governments were established there after World War II. I shall refer to it as the "standard system."

The system required a specific structure of banking organizations which represents a distinctive characteristic of the economies of Eastern Europe (though some parallels can be found in underdeveloped countries). It is highly centralized, dominated by a single institution that combines central-bank functions with those performed elsewhere by a network of commercial banks. I shall refer to this all-encompassing state bank as the monobank. In some countries—but not in the Soviet Union—there is a separate Agricultural Bank and in most a Foreign Trade Bank. With the exception of Czechoslovakia, all the countries have an Investment Bank, which extends credit to the construction industry but otherwise serves merely as a distributing agent for allocating nonreturnable grants of budgetary funds to finance fixed investment. The countries of Eastern Europe know no credit-granting institutions other than the official banks; no financial assets except money, government savings bonds, and deposits in the single savings bank system; and no financial markets.

The monobank services, with insignificant exceptions, only the social-ized sector of the economy. The credit available to the private sector in in-dustry and trade is an altogether trifling part of total credit extended. Since direct lending between economic units is prohibited (though this does not prevent *de facto* indebtedness to suppliers, incurred by delaying pay-

*Reprinted by permission from "Banking and Credit in the Framework of New Eco-nomic Policies in Eastern Europe," *Banca Nazionale del Lavoro Quarterly Review* (Sept. 1966), pp. 8–18. All footnotes deleted.

†Dr. George Garvy is Senior Economist with the Federal Reserve Bank of New York. His publications include: *Deposit Velocity and its Significance* (1959), *Debits and Clearings Statistics and Their Use* (1959), *Financing Small Business* (ed.), (1958) "The Role of the State Bank in Soviet Planning" in Jane Degras (ed.) *Soviet Planning* (1964), and *Money Banking, and Credit in Eastern Europe* (1966).

ments) the monobank is virtually the sole souce of credit to the economy. In addition it is the bank of issue and it performs a number of other functions, such as collecting all budgetary revenue, paying out all expenditures at all levels of government and supervising the financial performance of socialized enterprises.

The difference between the monobank and both the central and the commercial banks of the noncommunist countries is reflected in the structure of the monobank's balance sheet. The assets side consists mainly of loans to the various segments of the economy (in some countries including a relatively small amount of housing loans to individuals). It contains an undisclosed amount of gold and foreign exchange, but no government or private securities. Liabilities consist of currency issue and free balances of enterprises, government units, specialized banks, and the savings bank system; the balances of the savings bank system are substantial in countries where it makes no loans (Soviet Union, Bulgaria).

In the countries of Eastern Europe, currency and deposit money are not interchangeable. Currency alone serves as a medium of payment for the population. The monobank has the responsibility of not putting into circulation an amount of currency that would increase the flow of purchasing power to the population in excess of the economy's ability to deliver consumer goods and provide services. With fixed prices, such excess, when it nevertheless occurs, results in the disappearance of goods from the shelves and the formation of queues at the stores, which until quite recently were a familiar sight in Eastern Europe. The monobank exercises rigid control over currency circulation to avoid hoarding and unauthorized spending. Thus, for instance, stores must each day deposit all receipts with the monobank. Detailed cash circulation plans are prepared, which are coordinated with the credit plans within which all banks operate. All payments within the socialized sectors—among enterprises and between them and the budget—are made through transfers on the books of the monobank. To facilitate control, each enterprise is required to keep its accounts with a single monobank office—one in whose territory it is located—and it obtains all its credit accommodations from that office. For the same reason the specific method of settling payments is determined by regulation rather than by negotiation between the interested parties. The separation of payments flows into two circuits (currency and deposits) also facilitates planning and control. Obviously, the two flows are interrelated, and both kinds of money are expanded in the same way—through credit creation.

Ownership of money does not give an absolute command over resources, and the absolute order to the bank to make payment from an existing balance is unknown; deposit transfers are made and cash paid out only on the basis of supporting documents. Individual enterprises can make expenditures only in strict conformity with applicable economic plans, and the monobank has wide powers to make sure that payments are effected only for authorized purposes. Particularly detailed and rigid controls are applied to withdrawals of currency for payroll purposes. They are still rigidly applied in the Soviet Union, but in some other countries, notably Poland, monobank control of the wage fund has proved largely ineffective, and it has been given up altogether in Hungary.

In what sense, then, can one speak of credit policy in the countries of Eastern Europe prior to the introduction of reforms which are the subject of the final section of this article? Treatises and textbooks in Eastern Europe typically deal almost exclusively with the practical problems of controlling monetary circulation, crediting production and trade, and financing capital investment, without discussing the role of monetary policy as such, or its relationship to fiscal policy. In the writings of Soviet economists, who so far have been setting the tone in the other countries of Eastern Europe as well, one would look in vain for an explicit discussion of monetary policy. The authoritative Soviet *Financial-Credit Dictionary* contains no entry for it. Credit policy is defined as "a system of measures in the area of credit, designed to secure the economic interests of the ruling class"; what it is in a socialist economy is not defined, but a short review of its tasks is prefaced by the statement that "In the Soviet Union credit policy corresponds to the tasks that the government places before the country in each phase of the construction of socialism and communism." "Credit restrictions" are described as "limitations or reductions in the volume of credit, which are put into effect by capitalist banks and the bourgeois state," and "credit expansion" is "enlargement of credit, put into effect by capitalist banks and the bourgeois state, which exceeds the growth of production, stimulates over-production and the coming about of economic crises." Similarly, banking officials of the countries of Eastern Europe, in their published speeches and articles, typically focus on how the monobank can best implement the economic plan or party decisions. Such statements clearly reflect the implementary nature of the monobank's activities and characteristically treat the monetary aspects of those activities (credit, currency circulation) on the same footing as routine operations (mutual offsets of transfer payments) or control functions (control over payroll disbursements).

Soviet-type command economies expect to maintain equilibrium conditions and achieve their growth objectives through proper overall planning of material resources, and not through indirect means of influencing aggregate demand and its structure. The allocation of resources is determined by the economic plans, which specify for each enterprise, or group of enterprises, the kinds and sources of inputs and the channels through which output is to be distributed. Consumer prices as well as transfer prices among state enterprises are set by authority and are changed infrequently. Equilibrium between supply and monetary demand for consumer goods and services is attained by production, price, and wage decisions taken by the planning authorities. Deviations from planned magnitudes, whether arising on the side of production or distribution, are dealt with through administrative intervention rather than through the market mechanism. Adjustments needed to maintain equilibrium are made by the various economic planning and administrative agencies, not by the monetary authorities.

From its very origin, financial planning in the Soviet Union has been derivative. Monetary flows are planned as the counterpart of physical flows, and adjusted to changes in such flows. Thus, monetary and credit policies, subordinated to achievement of the real goals of the economic plans, are concerned primarily with assuring the efficiency of currency circulation and of the payments mechanism and with facilitating the economic performance of enterprises. Given the institutional arrangements centered on the monobank and its policy goals, most of the monetary tools typically used by the central banks of the noncommunist countries are irrelevant in Eastern Europe. Such changes in the allocation of credit as have occurred in the various countries have resulted from administrative decision, embodied in financial plans, rather than achieved (or attempted) by application of the monetary tools typically used by the central banks of the noncommunist countries. Under the standard system, interest is merely a service charge intended to meet operating costs, and rates tend to be uniform for all loans, irrespective of purpose. The low level of interest rates reflects the view that interest has no place in a socialist economy and that it is tainted by similarity to a particularly objectionable type of "parasite income" in capitalist countries. Even the increased differentiation of interest rates during the last decade merely reflects judgments as to how the cost of credit should be related to costs of products and distribution; it does not reflect decisions as to how much credit should be used and where—questions that are settled by the economic plans.

The basic function of credit in the countries of Eastern Europe is to supplement the working capital with which state-owned enterprises are endowed. Except in agriculture, the role of credit in fixed capital formation is very minor, although in recent years a certain amount of long-term credit has become available for private and cooperative home construction.

Since the overriding goal of all economic activity in centrally planned economies is fulfillment of production targets stipulated in physical terms, credit is provided whenever it can help to meet those targets ("fulfill the plan"). Thus access to official banking institutions does not depend on profitability or creditworthiness. Indeed, economic plans may provide for some government-owned enterprises to operate at a loss, either temporarily or permanently: the authorities may decide not to recover all production costs during the run-in period of a new facility, or they may wish to subsidize socially-desirable production. Because producers' prices are not equilibrium prices and do not reflect relative scarcities, but are set by the authorities on the basis of considerations that are complex and not necessarily consistent (in particular when several different agencies set prices of materials entering into the cost of a given final product), situations may arise wherein an enterprise operates quite efficiently in terms of physical and technical indicators and yet shows a deficit.

The amount of short-term credit extended in the Eastern European countries is large in relation to output. In the Soviet Union the aggregate amount of loans extended during 1964 was 524 billion rubles ($575 billion) as compared with a national income of slightly less than 190 billion rubles. Under the standard system, short-term crediting performs three basic functions: it reduces the need for working capital by automatically financing peak working capital needs (mostly through inventory credits); it assures prompt replacement of working capital after completion of production (through automatic crediting of collection float); and it provides an added means for controlling not only the finances but all aspects of the activities of each borrowing enterprise.

The bulk of short-term credit to enterprises is intended for the financing of inventories. In each country the precise proportion of inventory to be credit-financed is stipulated for each industry (often in great detail for individual types of raw and auxiliary materials) by higher-level administrative authorities, with proper provision for seasonal variations where appropriate. Much of the discussion about credit in Eastern Europe revolves around the determination of the proper share of bank loans in the financing of various types of inventories. Since 1956 there has been a gradual backing-away, at least outside the Soviet Union, from excessive details and rigidity in setting inventory-production ratios ("norms") and determining the share of credit in their financing. In fact, Poland and Czechoslovakia have now given enterprises the right to determine their own norms (which originally were stipulated, and in the Soviet Union still are, by the ministries and other administrative units in charge of the various industries), and more limited moves in this direction have been made in other countries of Eastern Europe.

Despite the bank's efforts—and despite the all-encompassing planning and the absence of cyclical fluctuations—chronic overaccumulation of inventories plagues all communist economies, more severely at some times than at others. Production bottlenecks and unbalanced inventories of raw materials result in a damming-up of goods in process. And, because of lack of market guidance, inventories of finished consumer goods tend to be high and to include a large proportion of wrong sizes and models not in demand; in recent years this problem has been aggravated by consumers' rejection of goods of poor quality and unfashionable design. Thus, although the volume of inventory credit is planned in accordance with rigid ratios, additional credit needs, not stipulated in financial plans, arise whenever there are disruptions in the planned flow of materials and finished products or consumer reluctance to purchase the goods offered.

The second main use of short-term credit is for bridging the collection gap. All deliveries must be paid for promptly upon presentation of shipping documents, but the monobank grants loans to producers for the—usually short—period during which the payment documents are in process of collection. This system amounts to an automatic restoration of the seller's working capital without putting additional pressure on the buyer to discharge his obligation promptly.

As for the control function of short-term credit, this amounts under the standard system to a continuous and detailed audit by the monobank of the enterprises' physical and financial performance. Until the emergence of new trends in recent years, the bank and its customers were involved in a web of impersonal accounting relationships, embracing uniform and rigid rules, few alternatives, a minimum of flexibility, and supervision that reached into the minute details of an enterprise's activities—including the regularity with which it discharged its current financial obligations (maintained a sufficient balance to pay bills and loans when due). The monobank's main criterion for measuring performance of its borrowers was the meeting of production, inventory, unit cost and profit targets as stipulated in the economic plans.

In comparison with short-term financing of the state-owned sector, all other types of credit are considerably less significant. Agriculture is still the most important single economic sector in most of the countries of Eastern Europe, but the amount of credit, both long- and short-term, made available to it by the banking system is relatively small. Short-term lending to collective (cooperative) farms is usually geared to the cash outlays needed for seasonal production and to the amount of produce sold to state agencies in charge of purchasing farm output for urban consumption (and export). Since each collective farm is an independent entity, its working funds do not benefit from infusions or reallocations by higher-echelon authorities, and bank credit is the only means of overcoming seasonal and other shortages of working capital. Long-term credit is extended to collective farms to supplement their own resources for investment in farm equipment and livestock; because of the relatively backward farm technology that still characterizes Eastern European economies, there is considerable unfulfilled need for investment funds in agriculture. Independent farmers, where they have survived in significant numbers, as in Poland, also receive both long- and short-term credit, usually on the basis of contracts committing them to sell their output to the state purchasing agencies; more limited availability of credit and less favorable terms have been widely used as means of inducing them to join collective farms.

Unsatisfactory financial performance of enterprises, evidenced most often by delays in paying bills and repaying loans and by operating losses that necessitate additions to working capital, has from the beginning posed a serious problem in communist economies. Because of the priority attached to uninterrupted production, the monobank has had to find ways of stretching the rules in order to extend overdue loans—frequently advancing funds under a different heading to repay the original advance. As a last resort, budgetary funds were normally forthcoming to replenish working capital of an enterprise. Penalty rates of interest and similar disciplinary measures had little effect in improving economic performance, and since they merely reduced the amount of the enterprise's profits their cost was ultimately borne by the national budget. Even the application of "financial sanctions" required high-level decisions and usually such sanctions could not be imposed by bank officials on the firing line (who in any case had little interest in doing so). One of the issues currently debated in several countries of Eastern Europe is how to make the monobank directly interested in the profitability of the enterprises to which it extends credit.

While in the area of short-term credit there is at least a superficial similarity between arrangements in the West and in the East, differences in the channels through which investment funds flow are considerable. In the communist countries the national budget is the most important funnel for all payment flows within the socialized sector and between economic sectors. It also fulfills a significant redistributive function, particularly between agriculture and industry and among industries and regions (and transfers are made from it to the lower units of government, which have only minor direct sources of income). About half the national income of each country flows through the budget, a much larger proportion than in the Western countries. Expenditures for the economy, mostly for investment in fixed capital, typically account for about one third of total expenditures. The private sector, which does not benefit from budgetary expenditures, is very small in all the countries, probably nowhere exceeding 5 per cent of total nonfarm output; in the Soviet Union all production except that of artisan cooperatives is carried out by state enterprises and collective farms.

Almost the entire surplus of state-owned enterprises' receipts over direct production costs is channeled into the national budget, in the form of profit levies and turnover taxes (differentiated by products and designed to raise prices for each product sufficiently to prevent effective demand from exceeding available supplies). For instance, such payments accounted in 1961 for 68 per cent of total receipts in the Soviet budget. The relatively minor part of profits retained by enterprises is used to augment enterprise welfare funds and to provide fringe benefits and cash bonuses to the staff.

Under this system, decisions on the division of current output, like all other macroeconomic decisions, are embodied in the central budget. It includes, in effect, a central pool of investment funds from which new industries are created, existing enterprises are enlarged, and working capital needs of a growing economy are met. Enlargement of working capital of individual enterprises (and replacement of capital impaired by operating losses), if it does not occur through monobank loans or through retention of a portion of profits, is effected through grants from the national budget. The main difference is that working capital obtained in the form of credit is onerous, while budgetary grants are free.

Any unit's working capital judged excessive by the supervisory authority (usually a ministry) may be transferred to some other state enterprise. This administrative redistribution of working capital, which has been resorted to more systematically in some countries than in others, contributes toward diminishing the concern of enterprise managers with the proper management of such capital. There is little incentive to build up "owned" funds when these are continuously at the end of a string that can be pulled by the various supervisory administrations. And, indeed, under the standard system the dividing line between the "owned" and borrowed working capital of a given enterprise is without real significance either from an operating point of view or with regard to its effect on the performance record of an enterprise.

For a diagnosis of the drawbacks in the standard system, one no longer need rely on the efforts of a generation of Western students who have endeavored to extract from fragmentary statistics and the muted criticism of insiders a realistic picture of the inner workings of a command economy. The verdict is on the table: it is spread in the recent resolutions of the policy bodies of the communist parties of Eastern Europe.

The bill of particulars can be reduced to a few main propositions. The financing of fixed capital investment from budgetary resources on a non-returnable grant basis involved considerable misallocation of resources and costly delays in the completion of construction projects. Failure to include the cost of capital among factor costs resulted in wasteful use of capital, the most precious resource in all developing countries; it also led to distortions of prices for producer and consumer goods and to crass disparities between domestic and foreign prices. Gearing all rewards to the fulfillment of goals specified mainly or exclusively in real terms resulted in a disregard of consumer preferences and a lack of incentives to maximize profits. The extension of credit on the basis of uniform, centrally determined criteria designed to facilitate the fulfillment of production plans rather than to influence the allocation of real resources resulted in almost automatic credit availability and hence, again, encouraged wasteful use of resources. Excessively detailed statistical reporting produced reams of data that made it possible to calculate the degree of "plan fulfillment," in terms of hundreds of separate indicators, but did not generate impulses to trigger adjustment processes.

part II

The Winds of
Economic Change

It is not easy to trace the origin of economic reforms in Soviet-type economies. They are probably all caused by combinations of factors. Deterioration of growth performance, changes in factors endowment, the growing complexity of the economy, striking inefficiency, rejuvenation of economics, greater freedom of expression, and the rise of the consumer were among the factors which, with different intensity and in various combinations, have made the search for economic rationality not only an intellectual revolution, which might have remained in the realm of thought, but also a pragmatic movement which has encroached on the state's economic policy. Thus the reform movement has broken out of the walls of universities and research institutes into the party's Politburo meetings. The problem of reforms is not really one of whether or not the system will be altered, but what will be the direction, scope, timetable, and manner of implementation of the alteration. These in each case are the significant unknowns. We can only tentatively evaluate the initial steps.

A good background to the value controversy can be found in Alfred Zauberman, "The Soviet Debate on the Law of Value and Price Formation," *Value and Plan*, G. Grossman (ed.). The two translations from the original Russian, L. V. Kantorovich's *The Best Use of Economic Resources* (Cambridge: Harvard University Press, 1965) and *The Use of Mathematics in Economics,* V. S. Nemchinov (ed.) (Edinburgh: Oliver & Boyd, 1964) should be examined by the serious student. The reader might also wish to look into the intriguing review of Kantorovich's book by Professor Robert Dorfman in *American Economic Review* (Sept. 1966). A good, but rather technical, exposition of Kantorovich's views is presented by Benjamin Ward, "Kantorovich on Economic Calculation," *The Journal of Political Economy*, (Dec. 1960). Dr. Alfred Zauberman has written a number of most instructive articles in *Soviet Studies* on planometrics. See in particular the July 1960 and July 1962 issues. There is also a good exposition of the essentials of planometrics in John M. Montias, "Central Planning in Soviet-Type Economies: An Introduction to Basic

Problems," *The Soviet Economy in Theory and Practice*, Wayne A. Leeman (ed.), (Columbia, Mo.: University of Missouri, School of Business
and Public Administration, 1964). There is a stimulating article by Egon
Neuberger, "Libermanism, Computopia, and the Visible Hand," *American Economic Review* (May 1966). See also Joseph Berliner's comments
in the same issue. Professor Ragnar Frisch's lecture at the Soviet Academy
of Sciences published in *Economics of Planning*, No. 2 (1966) could be
read with profit. On the perplexing problems of welfare criteria in a
socialist economy see Abram Bergson, *Essays in Normative Economics*
(Cambridge: Harvard University Press, 1966), Essays No. 9 and 10;
Michael C. Kaser, "Welfare Criteria in Soviet Planning," *Soviet Planning,*
Jane Degras (ed.) (New York: Frederick A. Praeger Inc., 1964); Jan
Drewnowski, "The Economic Theory of Socialism: A Suggestion for
Reconsideration," *The Journal of Political Economy* (Aug. 1961); Jan
Tinbergen, "The Significance of Welfare Economics for Socialism,"
and Joan Robinson, "Consumer's Sovereignty in a Planned Economy,"
On Political Economy and Econometrics: Essays in Honour of Oskar Lange
(Warsaw: Polish Scientific Publishers, 1964); Alastair McAuley, "Ration-
ality and Central Planning," *Soviet Studies* (Jan. 1967), and Alfred Zau-
berman, "On the Objective Function for the Soviet Economy," *Economica,*
(Aug. 1965).

Some of the Soviet literature on the Liberman discussion and the
reforms, previously translated in *Problems of Economics*, has been com-
piled by Myron Sharpe (ed.), *Planning, Profit and Incentives in the
USSR*, 2 vols (White Plains, N.Y.: International Arts and Sciences
Press, 1966). For a background and preliminary evaluation by Western
scholars see Alexander Balinky, Abram Bergson, John N. Hazard, and
Peter Wiles, *Planning and the Market in the U.S.S.R: The 1960's* (New
Brunswick: Rutgers University Press, 1967); Eugene Zaleski, *Planning
Reforms in the Soviet Union, 1962–1966* (Chapel Hill: The University
of North Carolina Press, 1967), and George R. Feiwel, *The Soviet
Quest for Economic Efficiency* (New York: Frederick A. Praeger Inc.,
1967). The subject was discussed in a number of articles: *inter alia*, Rush V.
Greenslade, "The Soviet Economic System in Transition"; John P. Hardt,
Dimitri M. Gallik, and Vladimir G. Treml, "Institutional Stagnation and
Changing Economic Strategy in the Soviet Union"; in U.S. Congress,
Joint Economic Committee, *New Directions in the Soviet Economy*
(Washington, D. C.: U.S. Government Printing Office, 1966); Marshall
I. Goldman, "Economic Controversy in the Soviet Union," *Foreign
Affairs* (Apr. 1963); and "Economic Revolution in the Soviet Union,"
Foreign Affairs (Jan. 1967); Leon Smolinski, "What Next in Soviet
Planning?" *Foreign Affairs* (July 1964); Harry G. Shaffer, "Soviet Eco-
nomic Growth and the Growth of Soviet Economic Rationality," *The Anti-*

och Review, (Summer 1966); Alfred Zauberman, "Liberman's Rules of the Game for Soviet Industry," *Slavic Review* (Dec. 1963); and Alec Nove, "The Liberman Proposals," *Survey* (Apr. 1963).

The subject of economic reforms in Eastern Europe was allotted much space for the last few years in *East Europe*, and *Eastern European Economics* has translated some of the articles from various East European countries. The third international conference of the CESES, Centro Studie Ricerche su Problemi Economico-Sociali held in Florence, Italy in September 1966 has dealt with prices and finance in Eastern Europe. The papers are to be edited by Dr. Renato Mieli, Director of the CESES.

The various aspects of the interesting Polish case have been treated in Thad P. Alton, *Polish Postwar Economy* (New York: Columbia University Press, 1955); John M. Montias, *Central Planning in Poland* (New Haven: Yale University Press, 1962); and George R. Feiwel, *The Economics of a Socialist Enterprise* (New York: Frederick A. Praeger Inc., 1965). Jan M. Michal's *Central Planning in Czechoslovakia* (Stanford: Stanford University Press, 1960) provides a background to the Czechoslovak scene. Boris Pesek, *Gross National Product of Czechoslovakia in Monetary and Real Terms, 1946–58* (Chicago: The University of Chicago Press, 1965), and George Staller, "Czechoslovak Industrial Growth: 1948–1959," *American Economic Review* (June 1962) are well worth consulting. There are also several articles on the Czechoslovak reforms: Harry G. Shaffer, "The Enterprise Director and the New Economic Model in Czechoslovakia," *The Journal of Industrial Economics* (Nov. 1966); V. Holesovsky, "Czechoslovakia's New Economic Model," *Problems of Communism* (Sept.–Oct. 1965); Jan M. Michal, "The New Economic Model"; John M. Montias, "Economic Reforms in Perspective," *Survey*, (Apr. 1966); and John M. Montias, "A Plan for All Seasons," *Survey* (Apr. 1964). The reader may also wish to refer to G. R. Feiwel's *New Economic Patterns in Czechoslovakia* (New York: Frederick A. Praeger, Inc., forthcoming). For a Czechoslovak point of view see Ota Sik, *Economic Planning and Management in Czechoslovakia* (Prague: Orbis, 1965). Bela Balassa's *The Hungarian Experience in Economic Planning* (New Haven: Yale University Press, 1959) provides a very good background and analysis of planning during the essentially prereform period, and J. Kornai's *Overcentralization in Economic Administration* (translated from Hungarian) (New York: Oxford University Press, 1959) is a lucid exposition of the incentive system and constraints imposed on management. On the East German case, see James R. Elliott and Anthony E. Scaperlanda, "East Germany's Liberman-type Reforms in Perspective," *The Association for Comparative Economics* (mimeographed: 1966); Heinz Kohler, *Economic Integration in the Soviet Bloc, with an East German Case Study* (New York: Frederick A. Praeger, Inc., 1966); Wolfgang F. Stolper, *The Structure of the East*

German Economy (Cambridge: Harvard University Press, 1960); and Gustav Stolper, Karl Hauser, and Knut Borchardt, *The German Economy 1870 to the Present* (New York: Harcourt Brace and World, 1967), Chapter 8. For an illuminating analysis of the Rumanian economy see Professor John M. Montias' forthcoming *Economic Development of Communist Rumania* (Cambridge: M.I.T. Press, in print).

1. VALUE, OPTIMALITY, AND PREFERENCES

SOVIET PRICE THEORY AND POLICY*

Morris Bornstein †

Summary

In the Soviet Union, as in all modern, complex economies, prices play an important part in the guidance of economic activity. However, their role in the Soviet economy is different both from their role in a capitalist market economy and from their role in the Socialist market economy described in the theoretical models of Lange, Taylor, and Lerner. In the Soviet economy (and in the Soviet-type economies of Eastern Europe and Communist China), prices are not an autonomous force determining production, resource allocation, and consumption. Instead, prices are manipulated by the central authorities as one of various instruments intended to accomplish their planned goals.

Following a summary view of the various functions of prices in the Soviet economy, this paper deals in turn with the three major subsystems of the Soviet price system: industrial wholesale prices, agricultural procurement prices, and retail prices. The discussion focuses on current pricing practices, theoretical controversies among Soviet economists about price reforms, and pending changes in price policies. Because of space limitations, and in order to avoid duplication with other contributions to this compendium, certain types of prices—such as wages, transportation rates, and foreign trade prices—are not considered here. The paper also does not treat in any depth such aspects as the historical evolution of the price system in the 1930's and 1940's, narrowly technical aspects (such as the construction of price lists), or minor types of prices (such as those which collective farms charge their members).

*Reprinted from U.S. Congress, Joint Economic Committee, *New Directions in the Soviet Economy* (Washington D. C.: U.S. Government Printing Office, 1966) pp. 65–94. All footnotes deleted.

†Dr. Morris Bornstein is Professor of Economics, University of Michigan and Director of its Center for Russian and East European studies. His publications include: *Comparative Economic Systems* (ed. 1965), and *The Soviet Economy* (ed. with Daniel R. Fusfeld, 1962, 1966).

Chapter I. Role of Prices in the Soviet Economy

The functions of the Soviet price system may be classified under three very broad headings: control and evaluation, allocation, and income distribution.

Control and Evaluation

Prices are used by the central planners to secure compliance by enterprise managers with the plans elaborated by the former, and to evaluate the performance of the managers in the execution of their assigned tasks. Although resource allocation is determined by the planners largely in physical terms, it is necessary for them to express complex input and output targets for the enterprise in value terms in order to have a common denominator for physically dissimilar units of raw materials, labor, and capital goods. Thus the enterprise plan contains targets for the value of output, sales, cost, profits, tax payments, etc.

Allocation

Although physical allocation by administrative commands predominates in the Soviet economy, prices do influence the allocation of resources, and thus the pattern of production, in various ways.

1. At the central planning level, prices are used to construct macroeconomic balances, such as national product and intersectoral accounts, and capital-output ratios to supplement the basic physical planning tools. In addition, the relative pricing of substitutes may have some influence on the selection of technological coefficients for physical planning, as the planners substitute more abundant for scarcer materials during the successive iterations of the balancing process. Finally, project designers use value calculations in choosing among alternative variants of a given-output investment project and in assessing the benefits of modernization or innovation.

2. It is impossible for the central authorities to specify in complete detail the inputs and outputs of each enterprise. As a result, managers have a limited range of choice regarding both inputs and outputs. The relative prices of inputs and outputs influence the choices which managers make in trying to increase the value of output, sales, and profits.

3. Prices affect both the total supply of labor and its distribution. The state relies on low real wages, resulting from the relationship of money wages and consumer prices, to evoke a high rate of participation of the population in the labor force. Wage differences, in turn, are the principal means of securing the distribution of the labor force (by skill, industry, enterprise, and geographical location) desired by the planners.

4. In the collective farm sector, the central authorities use prices,

along with delivery quotas, to influence the allocation of resources to certain crops and products in preference to others. (In addition, prices are used, along with delivery quotas, to stimulate total output, but in this case the aim is primarily to raise the productivity of given resources engaged in agriculture, by increasing real compensation and thus incentives.)

Income Distribution

In the Soviet economy, the basis of income distribution is the "socialist" principle of unequal monetary compensation according to labor services rendered, rather than the "communist" principle of distribution according to need; and the promise of unequal monetary compensation is the basis of production incentives. The wage (i.e., price) system—together with transfer payments and income taxes—determines the distribution of (disposable) money income. The Soviet Government endeavors to make the distribution of real income less unequal than the distribution of money income by two chief methods. One is a broad program of "free" health and education services financed from general budget revenues. The second is to fix relatively low prices for mass consumption goods and relatively high prices for luxury goods by means of differentiated turnover taxes. The distribution of real income is also made less unequal than the distribution of money income through the administrative allocation of housing and through the informal rationing of queues and empty shelves when retail prices are fixed below the market-clearing level.

Chapter II. Industrial Wholesale Prices

Nature and Trends

Industrial wholesale prices are those at which goods are transferred or evaluated within the state sector of the Soviet economy. The term covers prices of producer goods, including raw materials, semifabricates, and machinery, as well as manufactured consumer goods. It excludes prices at which agricultural products are obtained by the state from collective farms but includes prices at which procurement agencies sell agricultural products to state enterprises for processing or to trade organizations for retail sale without further processing. It also excludes foreign trade prices, although it includes the prices at which foreign trade organizations buy from and sell to Soviet enterprises. Since 1958, collective farms have been permitted to buy various producer goods at wholesale prices, rather than at retail prices, as previously.

The Soviet industrial wholesale price system is composed of three types of prices. The enterprise wholesale price (*optovaia tsena predpriatia*) is the price at which a producing enterprise sells its output. The industry (i.e., branch of industry) wholesale price (optovaia tsena promyshlennosti) is paid by the state-enterprise buyer and includes, in addition to the enterprise wholesale price, 1) the turnover tax, if any, on the product; 2) the markup of the branch sales organization; and 3) transportation charges if these are borne by the sales organization rather than the buyer. Finally, a settlement or accounting price (raschetnaia tsena) is used in some branches where production costs diverge widely, notably the extractive branches. Individual enterprises or groups of enterprises receive different settlement prices, rather than a single, uniform enterprise wholesale price, from the branch sales organization. The latter, however, sells to customers of the branch at a single industry wholesale price.

Enterprise wholesale prices are composed of the planned branch average cost of production (*sebestoimost'*) and a profit markup. The former has no exact equivalent in Western cost accounting. It includes direct and indirect labor, materials (including fuel and power), depreciation allowances, and various overhead expenses. Although interest payments for short-term bank loans are included, both rent and interest on capital are excluded. The profit markup is supposed to provide a "normal" profit, for the branch as a whole, of 5 to 10 percent, calculated in relation to *sebestoimost'*. This profit markup is not intended to allocate resources among alternative uses, but rather is to provide a source of "net income" (chisty dokhod) or accumulation to the state, to serve as an instrument of financial control, and to promote the "businesslike" operation of Soviet enterprises.

Another source of accumulation is the turnover tax, which is levied primarily on consumer goods and included in the wholesale prices of the light and food industries, and thereby in retail prices. As a result, there is a great disparity between producer and consumer goods in the relationship between their "costs" and their wholesale prices. In 1964, for example, in heavy industry, production and marketing costs accounted for 81.6 percent of the value of output in industry wholesale prices; profit, 11.5 percent; and turnover taxes, 6.9 percent. In contrast, the corresponding figures for the light and food industry branches were 66.5, 8.2, and 25.3 percent.

The main trends in Soviet industrial wholesale prices from 1949 to 1964 are shown in Tables 1 and 2. In the price reform of January 1, 1949, heavy industry prices were raised sharply (on the average by 58 percent above the 1948 level) to eliminate most subsidies and to remove the turnover tax from all producer goods except electric power, natural gas, and petroleum products. As a result of subsequent cost reductions, heavy industry prices were later reduced through comprehensive price revisions in 1950, 1952, and 1955, and through more limited adjustments in particular industries since 1958. Changes since 1958 include reductions in the prices of electric power, machinery, and petroleum products, and a sharp

TABLE 1

INDEXES OF SOVIET INDUSTRIAL PRICES: ENTERPRISE WHOLESALE PRICES
(EXCLUDING TURNOVER TAX), SELECTED YEARS, 1950–64
(1949 = 100)

Commodity Group	1950	1952	1955	1958	1962	1963	1964
All industrial production	83	72	68	67	71	71	71
Heavy industry	80	68	61	58	57	57	57
Chemical industry	84	76	67	67	67	67	67
Ferrous metallurgy	71	63	60	60	60	60	60
Coal industry......................	100	91	84	84	84	84	84
Petroleum refining.................	85	72	65	65	63	63	63
Electric power.....................	92	82	74	70	61	60	60
Machine building and metalworking..	76	60	52	45	44	43	42
Timber industry	85	85	85	107	107	107	107
Cellulose and paper industry	81	68	65	65	65	65	65
Construction materials industry	82	67	57	57	57	57	57
Light and food industry	91	82	86	93	110	112	112
Light industry	91	83	80	80	81	83	83
Food industry	91	81	91	104	135	137	137

SOURCES: Nar. khoz. 62, p. 144; Nar. khoz. 63, p. 136; Nar. khoz. 64, p. 154.

increase in timber prices. In the case of electric power, turnover taxes
were approximately doubled in 1961, reducing enterprise wholesale
prices (Table 1) while leaving industry wholesale prices (Table 2) unchanged.

TABLE 2

INDEXES OF SOVIET INDUSTRIAL PRICES: INDUSTRY WHOLESALE PRICES
(INCLUDING TURNOVER TAX), SELECTED YEARS, 1950–64
(1949 = 100)

Commodity Group	1950	1952	1955	1958	1962	1963	1964
All industrial production	80	69	61	60	61	61	61
Heavy industry	80	68	61	59	59	59	58
Chemical industry	84	76	67	67	67	67	67
Ferrous metallurgy	71	64	60	60	60	60	60
Coal industry......................	100	91	84	84	84	84	84
Petroleum refining.................	85	72	65	72	66	66	66
Electric power.....................	92	82	74	70	70	70	70
Machine building and metalworking..	76	61	52	45	45	45	45
Timber industry	85	85	85	107	107	107	107
Cellulose and paper industry	81	68	65	65	65	65	65
Construction materials industry	79	67	57	57	57	57	57
Light and food industry	80	70	59	61	61	61	62
Light industry	88	88	70	70	70	70	70
Food industry	77	62	54	57	59	59	59

SOURCES: Nar. khoz. 62, p. 145; Nar. khoz. 63, p. 137; Nar. khoz. 64, p. 155.

In the food industry, enterprise wholesale prices (Table 1) have been raised several times since 1952 to cover higher costs from successive increases in agricultural procurement prices. Industry wholesale prices (Table 2) do not show a corresponding rise, however, because these cost increases have been largely offset by reductions in turnover taxes, intended to prevent the higher agricultural procurement prices from affecting industry wholesale prices and thus retail prices.

Price-Reform Discussion

In the lengthy discussion on price reform which began in 1956, Soviet economists have criticized the industrial price system on various counts and have advanced different proposals for price reform.

Criticisms

The chief criticism include the following:

1. Many Soviet economists believe that producer goods prices do not properly reflect their "values," in the Marxian sense of the term. In Marxian value theory it is possible for the actual prices of commodities, whether determined by market forces or administratively, to differ ("deviate") from their values, which in a long-run, "normal" sense are regarded as determined by the amount of past and present socially necessary labor embodied in them. ("Socially necessasary" labor is the amount used with average skill, intensity of work, and conditions of production.) According to Marxian value theory, the value (*stoimost'* in Russian) of a commodity is regarded as composed of three parts: (a) the value of past labor embodied in the materials and that portion of plant and equipment (as measured by depreciation charges) used up in producing the commodity; (b) the value of current labor for which workers receive compensation in the form of wages; and (c) the value of current labor for which workers are not compensated ("surplus value" or "surplus product"). In Marxian terminology, these components of value are designated respectively c for constant capital, v for variable capital, and m (or s) for *mehrwert* (or surplus value or product).

In applying this value $= c + v + m$ formula to the Soviet economy, Soviet economists usually take *sebestoimost'* as equivalent to the sum of c and v, and they regard the sum of total profits and turnover taxes as equal to total surplus product or aggregate m. One criticism of industrial price formation is that, because (as noted above) prices of producer goods contain significantly less profits and turnover taxes (m) in relation to sebestoimost' ($c + v$) than do prices of consumer goods, producer goods as a group are "priced below their value." In addition, this criticism asserts, because surplus value is not properly distributed in the prices of different commodities, relative prices of producer goods do not correspond to their relative values. That is, both the level and the structure of producer goods prices are held to deviate from their Marxian value.

2. In turn, because producer goods prices fail to correspond to their values, either in some aggregate sense or relative to each other, they furnish unreliable guides for choices by planners and enterprise managers. If relative prices are not correct, then incorrect choices will be made regarding alternative inputs and outputs. Because producer goods as a group are considered underpriced relative to consumer goods, in the calculation of production expenses both materials and machinery are undervalued relative to labor—whose wage rates are related to the price level of consumer goods—leading to the unjustified substitution of materials and machinery for labor. Similarly, the shortcomings of producer goods prices distort the comparisons of internal and external prices on imports and exports which are made in planning foreign trade.

3. The defects of industrial wholesale prices impede the effective use of value targets in the control and evaluation of enterprise operations. For example, they cause differences in the level or rate of profits (or losses) which are unrelated to the performance of enterprises or their contribution to the economy.

4. Soviet economists agree that this scheme of industrial pricing causes part of the value created in producer goods branches of industry to be "realized" in the prices of consumer goods. Thus, the calculation of various macroeconomic relationships using these prices does not give an accurate picture of the structure and development of the economy. For instance, the share of heavy industry is understated in the distribution of national income by sector of origin, while the share of accumulation (i.e., investment) is understated relative to consumption in the distribution of national product.

Reform Proposals

On the issue of what reforms should be made in the industrial price system, Soviet economists are divided into three main schools: a traditionalist school, a surplus product markup school, and an opportunity cost school.

1. *Traditionalist school.* One group upholds the essentials of the traditional scheme of industrial price formation but suggests relatively modest adjustments in order to improve the structure of producer goods prices without altering their level significantly. It believes that the use of prices as instruments of economic control requires many deviations of price from "value," in order to promote the efficient operation of enterprises, recognize supply and demand factors in certain cases, promote or discourage consumption of certain goods, etc. The traditionalists see no justification for a large increase in the overall level of producer goods

prices to incorporate more "surplus product" in them. Instead, they stress selective adjustments in the structure of producer goods prices to eliminate losses and excessive profits, establish the "correct" price relationships between substitutes, encourage the introduction of new models of machinery, etc.

2. *Surplus product markup school.* Another group of Soviet economists favors pricing on the basis of "value" by adding a uniform, proportional surplus product (m) markup to *sebestoimost'* ($c + v$) to derive a price equal to value (i.e., to the sum of $c+v+m$). They propose to rise the level of wholesale prices of producer goods without altering the general level of wholesale prices (or retail prices) of consumer goods. This would be accomplished by a partial shift of surplus product (profits and turnover taxes) from consumer goods prices to producer goods prices in order to raise the latter relative to the former.

The members of this school differ among themselves, however, on the manner in which surplus product should be distributed in the prices of goods. One view favors using labor cost as the base to which the markup would be applied; a second, *sebestoimost'*; a third, capital; and the fourth, a combination of labor cost and capital. Each of these will be discussed briefly in turn.

(*a*) The most orthodox position advocates relating the surplus product markup to labor cost—i.e., the wage bill—in order to obtain prices that are truly based on "labor value" (*trudovaia stoimost'*). It proposes a uniform surplus product markup related to the wage bill, according to the following formula:

$$p = c + v + v \frac{M}{V} = c + v \left(1 + \frac{M}{V}\right) \tag{1}$$

where p represents the price of a commodity, c the branch average materials costs (including also depreciation charges) per unit of the commodity, v the branch average wage cost per unit of the commodity, M the total surplus value to be distributed among goods, and V the total wage bill for workers engaged in "material production." The prices of the material inputs (and capital equipment to be depreciated) in c would themselves be calculated in the same way.

(*b*) Another formula relates the markup to total *sebestoimost'* ($c + v$) rather and to labor cost (v) alone. With p, c, v, M, and V defined as before and C representing the total materials cost (including also depreciation) of aggregate "material production,"

$$p = c + v + (c + v) \frac{M}{C + V} = (c + v) \left(1 + \frac{M}{C + V}\right) \tag{2}$$

This formula resembles the traditional price-setting practice in relating the surplus product markup to *sebestoimost'*, but it differs from it in calling for the uniform application of the same percentage markup to all producer and consumer goods.

(c) A third position relates the markup to capital. With p, c, v, and M defined as before and k representing the average amounts of fixed and working capital per unit of the commodity and K the total fixed and working capital used in "material production," the corresponding formula is

$$p = c + v + k \frac{M}{K} \qquad (3)$$

The supporters of this position hold that the magnitude of surplus product depends not only on the quantity of live labor used in production but also on its productivity, which in turn depends on the capital with which it is equipped. They believe that capital investment should be reflected in prices in order to promote the economization of capital in choices between more and less capital-intensive goods and methods of production. Likewise, enterprises should pay capital charges to the State, because such charges would lead them to request less fixed and working capital and to use more effectively the capital they have.

(d) A fourth position, which has evolved in the past few years, offers a compromise between the first and third formulas, by relating part of the surplus product markup to labor cost and part to capital. According to this position, with p, c, v, k, and K defined as before and M_1 representing the part of surplus value to be distributed in proportion to the wage bill and M_2 the part of surplus value to be distributed in proportion to capital,

$$p = c + v \left(1 + \frac{M_1}{V}\right) + k \frac{M_2}{K} \qquad (4)$$

It is suggested that M_1 correspond to the portion of the total "surplus product" devoted to "social-cultural expenditures" (health, education, and social welfare measures) and that M_2 correspond to the portion devoted to investment, defense, and general administration. In some variants of the formula, an additional price-forming element D is added to include differential rent on natural resources. Also, some proponents favor a single rate for the capital charge M_2/K, while others prefer a charge differentiated by branches of industry according to the structure of capital and the rate of return of capital. It should be noted that all of these formulas are cost-oriented, neglecting demand as a basic element in value and price. They do not recognize a connection between value and allocation. The allocation of resources would still be accomplished by directives in physical terms, supplemented by selected divergences of price from the "value" result yielded by the particular formula—for example, in order to secure the correct relative price structure for substitute fuels or machines.

3. *Opportunity cost school.* The members of this school, in contrast, advocate, explicitly or implicitly, efficiency prices which reflect relative scarcities and include capital and rent charges. These prices would, ideally, be the shadow prices obtained from the formulation of an "optimum" plan by input-output and other mathematical programming techniques. Such an optimum plan would achieve as fully and as efficiently as possible a set of final output goals specified by the political leadership. The members of this school recognize that such a plan, and its shadow prices, cannot be formulated at present, because of the absence of the necessary detailed information on many millions of economic relationships and the lack of the necessary data processing and computing facilities to handle this information if it did exist. However, they believe that is is still possible at present to improve the existing price system by incorporating, if only imperfectly, some of the features of the ideal prices of the optimum plan.

The advocates of this approach—particularly V. V. Novozhilov and L. V. Kantorovich—have been attacked on the ground that they reject the Marxian labor theory of value by recognizing land and capital as factors of production, relating value to scarcity, and using the "notorious" bourgeois marginal analysis. However, Novozhilov and Kantorovich steadfastly deny any deviation from Marxian value theory, asserting that their prices are different from capitalist prices, that land and capital are considered only insofar as they affect the productivity of labor, etc.

Pending Changes

1961–64 Price Revision

The July 1960 Plenum of the Central Committee of the CPSU called for a revision of heavy industry prices and freight rates during 1961–62, with the aim of introducing the new prices in 1963. The main features of the revision, as disclosed while the work was in progress, indicated that it would conform to the views of the traditionalist school.

The principal objective was to adjust prices and costs (i.e., *sebestoimost'*) in heavy industry to provide a "normal" level of profitability, in relation to *sebestoimost'*, of about 9 percent. The general level of wholesale prices for heavy industry was to remain virtually unchanged, being reduced by only about 3 percent. However, the structure of heavy industry prices was to be altered markedly, by price increases in most extractive branches and price reductions in the secondary branches, such as machine building and chemicals. The revision thus sought to recognize and ratify wage and cost increases in the extractive branches, on the one hand, and productivity gains and cost reductions in the manufacturing branches, on the other, since the last general price revision in 1955. In some cases (e.g., coal and petroleum), relative prices of substitutes were to be changed to adjust demands on the part of users to the planned supplies. The effects of the producer goods price revision in other sectors of the price system—such as wholesale prices of consumer goods, agricultural procurement prices, and retail prices—were to be negligible.

Work on the price revision was not completed on schedule, however, because of the huge volume and great complexity of the work. One source estimates that the total volume of price lists amounted to 38,400 printed pages, containing several million prices. By the end of 1962, price lists had been completed for raw materials and fuels, chemicals, construction materials, and electric power, but not for machine building, in which, because of technological developments, some 40 percent of the entries in the price lists were new items. Nevertheless, it appears that by late 1963 or early 1964 the new price lists were ready, as instructions were issued in June 1964 to recalculate the 1964 plan and budget in the new prices, as a basis for calculating the 1966 plan and budget and the 5-year plan for 1966–70 in the new prices.

On the basis of the new heavy industry prices, a revision of wholesale prices on the output of the light and food industries was undertaken in 1964. It affected about 85 percent of light industry output but only about 30 percent of food industry output, because wholesale prices on many food products had already been adjusted in response to the successive increases in agricultural procurement prices since 1953. Thus, the revision affected all segments of the textile, knitwear, and leather and rubber footwear industries, but not bread products, meat, fish, butter, sugar, tobacco, or canned vegetables. One aim of the revision was to adjust prices for changes in production costs (including the cost of heavy industry inputs, such as synthetic fibers from the chemical industry). Another objective was to reduce the large variations in the profitability of different items within the same product categories (e.g., different types of clothing or footwear), and thus to curb the tendency of enterprises to "violate the assortment plan" by producing more of the "advantageous" and less of the "disadvantageous" items than called for in the plan. A third goal was to reduce the number of enterprises operating at a loss. Finally, the revision was supposed to simplify price lists by eliminating out-of-date items and low-quality goods not in demand. The revision was not to lead to any increase in the level of retail prices.

The actual promulgation of the new heavy industry price lists was successively postponed, however. According to S. G. Stoliarov, Chief of the Department of Price Statistics of the Central Statistical Administration, one reason was the opposition of critics of the traditional scheme of price formation, particularly those who favored the surplus product markup approach instead. After the ouster of Khrushchev in October 1964, the adoption of new prices was delayed while the new leadership formulated its economic program, including the decisions on economic planning and management announced in Kosygin's speech to the Central Committee on September 27, 1965.

1966–67 Price Reform

According to this speech, the Soviet Government plans to introduce by the beginning of 1968 a number of important changes: 1) Sales and profitability, rather than total output, will be the principal enterprise performance indicators. 2) Enterprises will receive somewhat greater freedom in determining the composition of their output and inputs. 3) To economize on capital, enterprises will be required to pay interest on their fixed and working capital, their profitability will be calculated in relation to capital rather than cost, and new investment will be financed in large part from bank credits instead of budget grants. 4) Enterprises will retain a larger share of their profits for investment and the payment of bonuses to both workers and management. 5) The regional economic councils created in 1957 will be replaced by ministries for the different branches of industry.

Kosygin called for a revision of industrial prices to implement the new scheme of planning and management, indicating the following guidelines for price reform:

1. "Prices should to the greatest degree reflect socially necessary labor costs and must cover the costs of production and distribution and insure the receipt of profits by each normally operating enterprise."

2. From the sale of its output, the normally operating enterprise should receive enough profit to make payments on its assets and other payments into the budget, build up incentive funds, and expand its capital.

3. Enterprise payments to the budget of a percentage charge on fixed and working capital are not to be in addition to previous payments to the budget but rather are to replace in part payments made in the form of profits taxes and turnover taxes, whose share in enterprise payments to the budget will be reduced.

4. Prices should also take into account the quality, durability, and reliability of products and "the economic effect" obtained by consumers.

5. Industrial wholesale price revisions should not result in a change in retail prices.

A State Price Committee (SPC), under U.S.S.R Gosplan, was established to prepare, by the beginning of 1966, recommendations on the main features of a system of wholesale prices, "proceeding from the necessity of bringing prices closer to the level of socially necessary labor costs. These prices should assure the achievement of the indicated measures for improving planning and economic incentives for enterprises." Recognizing that the actual calculation of new prices and preparation of new price lists would require much more time, Kosygin called for the introduction of new prices in 1967–68, or possibly earlier in certain parts of industry.

According to the chairman of the SPC, V. Sitnin, the main features of the new industrial wholesale prices will be as follows:

1. Prices will be based on average branch *sebestoimost'*, rather than marginal cost, and planned losses will still be possible in those enterprises whose costs are much above the branch average.

2. Profitability will be calculated in relation to fixed and working capital. Profit rates will be high enough to cover investment for expansion, payments to the budget equal to 5–6 percent of capital, and contributions to incentive funds. The average rate of profitability for industry as a whole is estimated at approximately 12–15 percent, but rates will vary by branch of industry. (The uniform surplus product markup approach is specifically rejected by Sitnin). For example, in heavy industry, in order to cover costs in the coal industry and at the same time secure the proper relative prices for substitute fuels, accumulation (in the form of both profits and turnover taxes) must be higher in the petroleum and gas industries than in the coal industry. In light industry, accumulation (particularly in the form of turnover taxes) will be higher on alcoholic beverages and tobacco than meat.

3. In the extractive industries two methods will be used to deal with large differences in costs due to natural conditions. In some cases, group settlement prices will be used, as at present. In others, enterprises in more favorable natural conditions will make fixed rent payments.

4. Greater use is to be made of increments to prices to *reflect quality and durability features.*

5. The revision of industrial wholesale prices is not to raise the level of retail prices or to alter their structure significantly. Also, it is not to modify significantly the prices on industrial producer goods sold to agriculture, in order not to affect the terms of trade for agriculture established by the March 1965 and other agricultural measures taken by the post-Khrushchev leadership.

The actual revision of individual prices along these lines is now underway. It is expected that new wholesale prices will be adopted in the textile industry on October 1, 1966; in the footwear industry on January 1, 1967;

in machine building, metallurgy, chemicals, and electric power on July 1, 1967; and in all remaining branches by January 1, 1968, when the change-over to the new scheme of economic planning and management is to be completed. So far, however, detailed information on the new prices has not been published.

Nevertheless, on the basis of the information available to date, it appears that the new wholesale prices will to a large extent follow tradi-tional lines, rather than those recommended by either the surplus product markup school or the opportunity cost school. Although the new prices are to include a capital charge, the 5–6 percent rate chosen is neither the M/K rate *recommended by surplus product markup formula number (3),* nor the kind of scarcity charge for capital advocated by the oppor-tunity cost school. Instead, the capital charge seems to be intended, in the words of one Soviet economist, "not as a price-forming factor but as a form of redistribution of profit."

In other respects, the principles underlying the new prices appear to differ little from those used (in 1955) in preparation of the existing prices and those followed in the 1961–64 revision. The new prices are to be based on average cost rather than marginal cost. They attempt to provide a "normal" level of profitability (defined in a new way, to be sure) to the normally operating enterprise fulfilling its plan. With the exception of relative prices of some substitutes (e.g., fuels), however, they are not intended to be scarcity prices capable of allocating resources in the most efficient way. It is questionable, therefore, whether the new prices will contribute much to improving the choices which enterprise managers, exercising their expanded decisionmaking powers, will make regarding current inputs and outputs and investment. Nor are they likely to enhance the ability of higher administrative authorities to evaluate enterprise performance. Rather, it appears that the reform of industrial prices is not as bold as would be required to carry out successfully the changes in planning, management, and incentives which it is supposed to help im-plement.

Chapter III. Agricultural Procurement Prices

Agricultural procurement prices are those at which collective and state farms sell to state procurement agencies. Collective farm market prices, at which agricultural producers sell to households, are analyzed in the following section on retail prices.

Nature and Trends

Collective Farm Prices

In setting procurement prices for collective farms, the Soviet Govern-ment has pursued two conflicting objectives: 1) to fix the terms of trade for the collective farm peasantry so as to make it bear a large share of the burden of industrialization, and 2) to provide incentives to produce. The former objective clearly dominated during the Stalin era. Since 1953, the latter has been more characteristic of collective farm price policy.

The terms of trade and real income of the peasantry depend on the relationship between agricultural procurement prices paid to the collective farms, on the one hand, and prices paid by collective farms for material inputs and prices paid by collective farmers for consumer goods, on the other. The terms of trade for the peasantry were extremely unfavorable during the Stalin era. Procurement prices for grain remained almost unchanged from 1929 to 1953. Livestock prices doubled from 1929 to 1940 but remained unaltered from 1940 to 1953. Over the same period, retail prices (at which collective farms also bought many of their industrial inputs) rose many fold. In 1952, the level of retail prices was 10 times the 1940 level. Grain and livestock production was very unprofitable, and the price of potatoes did not even cover the cost of delivery to the city. For technical crops, such as cotton, sugarbeets, and tobacco, the situation was more favorable, as procurement price increases after 1940 had kept pace with increases in the prices of consumer goods and industrial inputs.

One of the first steps taken by Stalin's successors in 1953 was to embark on a broad program to increase agricultural output, involving changes in planning and administration, delivery obligations, taxes, investment, and prices. The changes in agricultural procurement prices included a large increase in the general level of prices, regional differentiation of prices, a revision in the relative price structure in favor of food crops, a greater effort to relate prices to costs, and the unification of multiple prices into single procurement prices for each crop. Major price increases were made in 1953, 1956, 1958, 1962, 1963, and 1965. Table 3 shows the trend of collective farm procurement prices from 1952 to 1962. More recent data unfortunately are not available.

In 1953 the Government increased sharply both obligatory delivery prices (tseny obiazatel'nykh postavok) and state purchase prices (tseny gosudarstvennykh zakupok). The former applied to the delivery quotas fixed for each farm, and the latter to additional sales to the state above the quota. Although the state purchase prices were higher than obligatory delivery prices, they were still below collective farm market prices, and hence sales at state purchase prices were in most cases not voluntary but compulsory. In addition to increasing both types of prices, the Government further raised average realized prices on vegetables and potatoes by reducing obligatory delivery quotas, thereby releasing more of their output for sale at the higher state purchase and collective farm market prices. In 1956, procurement prices were again increased, and in some cases the differential between the basic and the higher incentive price was reduced.

Prices were again changed in 1958, when multiple pricing was replaced by a single state purchase price for each product. Concurrently, the machine-tractor stations (MTS's) were abolished and their machinery sold to the collective farms. For the first time, prices of all crops were revised

TABLE 3

INDEXES OF SOVIET AGRICULTURAL PROCUREMENT PRICES, SELECTED YEARS, 1953–62*

(1952 = 100)

Commodity group	1953	1954	1955	1956	1958	1962†
All agricultural products........	154	207	209	251	296	332
Grain‡	236	739	553	634	695	843
Technical crops§	115	111	117	147	143	143
Sunflowers..................	528	626	987	928	774	848
Fruits ‖	119	135	138	192	179	167
Potatoes	316	369	368	814	789	1,043
Cattle.......................	385	579	585	665	1,175	1,523
Milk........................	202	289	303	334	404	434
Eggs........................	126	135	152	155	297	339
Wool	107	146	158	246	352	346

*Average state procurement-purchase prices on agricultural products procured from collective farms and private plots.
†Preliminary data.
‡Wheat, rye, barley, oats, maize, millet, buckwheat, and rice.
§Raw cotton, flax fiber, hemp fiber, sugarbeets, and tobacco.
‖ Including wine grapes.

SOURCE: Stoliarov 63, p. 106.

at the same time—providing an opportunity for a comprehensive adjustment of relative prices. However, the new prices could not be accurately related to costs (even if this had been intended) because of a lack of appropriate cost data. For decades, as long as average procurement prices were extremely low, reference to costs was politically inexpedient, and collective farms did not calculate their production costs. The notion was even widely accepted that the concept of cost was not applicable to collective farms. Only in 1955 did the state begin to investigate the level and structure of collective farm costs, and only in 1958 did farms begin to calculate their costs. The 1958 prices were therefore not based on costs. Instead they were set on the principle that the total bill to the state for procurements from the collective farms should not exceed the previous bill for procurements plus the bill for MTS operations and investment. Thus, basically, the existing terms of trade between the agricultural and industrial sectors were left unchanged; as one Soviet economist put it, "only the channels of exchange were altered."

In the case of livestock products, it was not intended that the 1958 prices should cover costs. Instead it was "supposed" that collective farm losses on livestock products would be covered from earnings on grain, sunflowers, and other crops. The ratio of prices to costs in 1960, for example, was 155 percent for grain (excluding corn), but only 65–67 percent for meat and eggs and 86 percent for milk. This relative price-cost structure provided little incentive to collective farms to increase livestock production, and they instead emphasized the more profitable plant crops. In 1962, the Government raised purchase prices on cattle and poultry by an average of 35 percent. It also took the politically unpopular step of raising retail prices of meat products by an average of 30 percent and of butter by 25 percent. However, despite the substantial increase in livestock prices, they still failed to cover costs. As Table 4 shows, the average 1963

TABLE 4

SOVIET COLLECTIVE FARMS: AVERAGE 1961–63 PRODUCTION COSTS* AND
AVERAGE 1963 PURCHASE PRICES OF SELECTED COMMODITIES

Commodity	Average 1961–63 production cost (rubles per ton)	Average 1963 purchase price (rubles per ton)	Ratio of average 1963 price to average 1961–63 cost (percent)
Grain†	45	86	191
Potatoes	43	72	167
Sugarbeets	18	29	161
Raw cotton	243	399	164
Milk	147	122	83
Cattle‡	967	781	81
Pigs‡	1,319	1,004	76
Sheep‡	543	538	99
Wool	2,545	3,797	149

Sebestoimost', including collective farm labor costs valued at state farm labor norms and wage rates.
† Excluding corn.
‡ Weight gain.
SOURCE: Khlebnik v 65, p. 39.

purchase prices for milk, cattle, and pigs were well below their respective average 1961–63 production costs. Moreover, in many regions the price-cost discrepancy was greater than the national averages in Table 4. (The table also reflects the impact of price increases in 1963 on cotton, sugarbeets, beans and peas, and potatoes.)

In 1965, as part of the broad Brezhnev-Kosygin agricultural program, prices for milk, livestock, and grain were raised, and above-quota premium prices were reestablished for wheat and rye, cotton, and sunflowers. Data are not yet available to permit a precise assessment of the magnitude of the price increases and the resulting price-cost relationships for 1965. It appears, however, that the milk and livestock price increase will go a long way toward eliminating losses on these products on farms of average efficiency. They may even make livestock products profitable for collective (and state) farms as a whole. In the case of grain, prices should cover costs in the main producing areas, though not on high-cost farms in the marginal areas. The increases in prices for technical crops should further stimulate their output.

In addition to these changes since 1953 in the level and structure of procurement prices, the terms of trade of collective farm agriculture have been improved through reductions in the prices of industrial inputs and in the prices of consumer goods sold to the peasantry. Until 1958, machinery, trucks, spare parts, and fuel were available to collective farms only at retail prices, while state farms bought these goods at much lower wholesale prices. In 1958, uniform wholesale prices for state and collective farms were established on trucks, machinery, and spare parts. But this concession was offset, at least in part, by an unpublicized increase in the same year in the wholesale prices of farm machinery and spare parts and in the retail price of gasoline. This measure was reversed in 1961, when the Government reduced retail prices on gasoline and wholesale prices on trucks, machinery, and spare parts. In 1962 it authorized collective farms to buy construction materials at wholesale, rather than retail, prices. Prices of trucks, farm machinery, and spare parts were again reduced at the beginning of 1966.

Though no precise calculations are available, it is evident that successive increases in agricultural procurement prices, together with adjustments in prices of industrial inputs and of consumer goods, have markedly improved the collective farm peasantry's terms of trade since 1953. The general price increases from 1953 to 1958 helped, in conjunction with other measures, to bring about a large increase in agricultural output. Subsequent price increases have been more selective, focusing on lagging commodities, particularly livestock products. It is by no means clear, however, that the 1965 price increases, whose magnitude was limited by the decision not to raise retail prices, will be sufficient to cover costs (including reasonable compensation for collective farm labor) and make livestock production profitable.

State Farm Prices

State farm delivery prices (sdatochnye tseny sovkhozov) are essentially different in nature from the prices paid to collective farms. State farms are "factories in the field" similar to state enterprises in industry, transportation, trade, etc. Their employees receive money wages on a piece-rate basis, and they calculate cost of production (*sebestoimost'*) in essentially the same way as other state enterprises. If—as has commonly been the case—sales revenue fails to cover *sebestoimost'*, the deficit is met by redistributions of profits within the state farm network or by operating subsidies from the budget. (In addition, investment has been financed by budget grants.) Because state farm costs are reimbursed by the combination of delivery prices and subsidies, the failure of prices to cover costs does not restrain output. In contrast, for the collective farms, prices are the sole source of compensation for production expenses and productive effort.

Until 1954, state farm prices were based on (but were lower than) the corresponding state purchase prices for collective farms. As these prices did not cover production costs, a subsidy was planned for each type of state farm output. In 1954, with the announced objective of eliminating subsidies, state farm delivery prices were raised and differentiated by geographic zones. The new prices were supposed to yield an overall profit of 7.7 percent on *sebestoimost'*, although it was expected that livestock would still be produced at a loss, to be covered from earnings on crops. But, as Table 5 shows, by 1956 the overall profit rate was only 5.6 percent, and by 1958 crop profits failed to cover livestock losses, resulting in an overall loss rate of 1 percent. By 1960, net losses of the state farm system

TABLE 5

SOVIET STATE FARMS: PROFITABILITY* OF SELECTED COMMODITIES,
SELECTED YEARS, 1956–64
(in percent)

Commodity group	1956	1958	1961	1962	1963	1964†
All products	5.6	− 1.0	− 4.8	− 6.2	− 12.6	3.9
Crops	38.9	15.6	19.1	24.0	17.5	27.5
Grain	44.9	18.4	13.9	23.5	4.5	19.6
Raw cotton	12.0	− 20.0	13.7	− .6	18.8	15.9
Sunflowers	82.7	110.9	102.2	121.4	100.0	107.4
Sugarbeets	27.9	20.8	18.8	9.1	.1	30.7
Potatoes	13.5	10.1	4.4	1.0	13.0	16.2
Livestock products	− 14.6	− 11.8	− 15.2	− 17.7	− 22.6	− 7.9
Milk	− 12.5	− 5.8	− 16.9	− 25.3	− 29.2	− 17.8
Cattle	− 42.1	− 36.5	− 20.1	− 15.3	− 23.7	− 7.4
Pigs	− 13.7	− 15.8	− 29.2	− 28.2	− 35.7	− 11.1
Sheep	− 23.2	− 9.4	15.2	6.5	5.5	12.0
Poultry	− 38.0	− 40.5	− 43.6	− 30.3	− 26.1	− 22.8
Eggs	19.2	8.7	− 9.1	− 4.8	− 4.1	− 1.2
Wool	7.3	5.0	37.3	11.1	13.4	23.2

*Profitability $= \dfrac{\text{Sales revenue} - sebestoimost'}{Sebestoimost'}$ Minus sign means loss.

†Plan.

SOURCE: Semenov 65, p. 25.

covered by budget subsidies amounted to 600 million rubles (in terms of "new" rubles after the 1961 monetary reform). To eliminate these subsidies, the Government in 1961 reduced the state farms' input prices and raised their output prices. State farm costs were cut by about 300 million rubles per year through a reduction of prices on machinery, spare parts, and fuel. State farm revenues were augmented by 500 million rubles through higher prices for livestock products, grain, sugar beets, and fruits. In 1962, state farm livestock prices were raised again, concurrently with the increase in collective farm livestock prices. However, as Table 5 shows, the new prices still failed to cover costs for cattle, pigs, poultry, and eggs. In 1963, along with collective farm prices, state farm prices were raised on cotton, sugarbeets, and certain vegetables.

The state farms also benefited from price increases under the new agricultural measures announced in 1965, although their prices remain below collective farm prices by 10 percent on meat, 15 percent on wool, 17 percent on cotton, 39 percent on grain, and 55 percent on sunflowers. The new state farm prices are expected to provide a profit of 5–10 percent on livestock and at least 30 percent on grain. At the new prices, the profitability of total state farm output in 1965 is planned at 21.1 percent (in relation to *sebestoimost'*). However, even if the new prices can provide this level of profitability, they would still fall short of enabling the state farms to join other state enterprises in shifting to the method of operation envisioned in Kosygin's September 1965 speech. To do this, the state farms would have to earn profits sufficient to make payments on their capital, establish incentive funds, and finance most of their investment programs. According to one estimate, the state farms would have required a profitability rate of 48.6 percent (on *sebestoimost'*) simply to finance the investment program planned for them in 1965—excluding any payments on capital or contributions to incentive funds. The new state farm prices thus apparently aim only at covering operating costs (for all farms taken together), rather than at putting state farms on the same financial footing as other state enterprises. To accomplish the latter would require a much larger increase in state farm prices—which would conflict with the traditional policy of setting state farm prices at or below collective farm prices.

Price Reform Discussion

Beginning in 1958, defects in agricultural procurement prices have been criticized and suggestions for improvement advanced at scholarly conferences and in Soviet economic journals and newspapers. The agricultural price reform discussion has been more cautious than the industrial price reform discussion, because agricultural price changes are politically sensitive measures which directly affect the distribution of income between the rural and urban populations. Changes in industrial prices, in contrast, primarily affect financial relationships within the state sector.

Criticisms

The principal criticisms concern price-cost relationships for different products, defects in geographical differentiation of prices, and the failure of prices to promote a rational pattern of specialization.

1. One criticism is that both the level and the structure of procurement prices have been set without adequate regard for production costs (including reasonable compensation for the labor of collective farm members). As a result, incentives to expand collective output are lacking, and collective farmers instead devote as much effort as possible to their private plots. On the one hand, more accurate calculations of costs are needed. On the other, the Government should fix prices so as to make the production of each product profitable, rather than expecting profits on plant products to compensate losses on livestock products.

2. Prices of individual crops are differentiated geographically in an effort to skim off differential rents arising from more favorable natural conditions. However, the variation in prices is not as great as the variation in costs in the different zones. As a result, the profitability of a given crop varies greatly from zone to zone. For some crops, such as potatoes, flax, and wool, prices are not differentiated geographically, even though they are produced in different areas with widely varying costs. In addition, there are large differences in costs and profitability within price zones, some of which cover a very large area. For example, grain price zone IV stretches from the shores of the Arctic into southern Siberia, comprising an area 10.3 times that of France, with extreme variations in soil, rainfall, temperature, and length of growing season. One consequence of these defects in price zoning is large differences in the incomes of collective farmers in different regions, and even in the same region, due to natural conditions, rather than to differences in equipment, productive effort, or managerial skill. Another consequence is that the state does not obtain the maximum results from a given total expenditure on agricultural procurements. By increasing prices in some zones and reducing them in others, the state could secure a net increase in the volume of procurements without any increase in total procurement expenditures.

3. Many collective and state farms operate at low profitability or losses because they are required, by their delivery plans, to produce products for which they are not suited. It is not unusual for collective farms to receive procurement plans for 15 or 20 different products, some of which they are expected to produce at a loss. Often the quotas exceed the farm's capabilities, forcing it to request loans in kind for seeding or planting purposes. In part, the lack of rational specialization is the result of the low level of agricultural production: the state is afraid to reduce or elimi-

nate delivery plans from low-yield areas lest it lose badly needed supplies. On the other hand, the requirement that farms produce and deliver products for which they are not suited prevents them from specializing in those crops on which their yields would be much higher.

Reform Proposals

Various proposals have been advanced to deal with shortcomings in the level, structure, and regional differentiation of agricultural procurement prices. They include the following: 1) basing prices on marginal rather than average costs; 2) revising the boundaries of price zones; 3) using instruments other than price differences to take differential rent; and 4) varying prices in accordance with harvest fluctuations.

1. At present, the zone price of a product is supposed to be based on the average cost of production in that zone. As a result, collective farms with higher than average costs for the zone have difficulty covering expenses, and the incomes of their members are correspondingly low. The supporters of marginal cost pricing argue that if the state requires a farm to produce and deliver a commodity, the state should pay the farm a price adequate to cover costs (including reasonable compensation for the labor of its members) and provide a profit for expansion. Although a few members of the marginal cost school favor basing price on the national marginal cost of the product, most accept the principle of zonal price differentiation and urge instead that price be based on the marginal cost of the zone. More precisely, they advocate basing the price on the cost of production of farms with the worst land in the zone (in terms of fertility and location) but with average conditions of production in regard to mechanization, labor productivity, and managerial efficiency. The differential rent accruing to farms with better land would be taken by taxation.

Prices based on marginal costs would, of course, mean a much higher bill for state procurements—double, or for some products or zones even triple, the bill with prices based on zonal average costs. However, there need not be a corresponding increase in wholesale and retail prices. As noted, additional tax revenues would be collected on the differential rent of farms on inframarginal land. These revenues would be allocated to subsidies to the light and food industries and the trade network intended to keep wholesale and retail prices below the level of procurement prices. Opponents of this approach object that it is undesirable to set retail prices below procurement prices, as this situation encourages farms to buy agricultural products at retail prices in order to resell them to the state at procurement prices. Critics also point out that it would be difficult to determine the correct amount of differential rent to be taken through taxation from all but the highest cost farms.

2. Suggestions for improving price zoning include the following: The number of zones should be increased to make them more homogeneous

and to reduce intrazonal differences in cost and profitability. For example, the number of zones for grain in the RSFSR should be increased from 8 to 16 or 18. Zone prices should be introduced for such crops as potatoes, flax, and wool. The revision of zone boundaries should consider both natural factors (such as soil, temperature, precipitation, topography, etc.) and economic factors (such as the structure of output, extent of mechanization, income per acre and per man-day, etc.). Price zoning should promote rational specialization through higher profitability for crops in the zones most suited to them, but prices should be high enough to cover costs and provide a profit even in the less suitable areas.

3. Even with improvements in the delineation of price zones, intrazonal differences in cost and profit would continue to exist. To take some of the differential rent of farms with better than average, or better than marginal, land in the zone, income taxes and/or land taxes are recommended. An income tax has been levied on collective farms for a number of years, not only to take differential rent but also to exert control over the fulfillment of production and financial plans. However, the tax has been levied on gross income (including labor-day distributions to members) rather than on net income, and with virtually no progression in rates. Reform proposals have recommended using net rather than gross income as the base, and introducing a progressive scale of rates. In 1965, the base was shifted to net income, and an element of progression was introduced through the exemption from taxation of the first 15 percent of net income. An alternative, or supplementary, method of taking rent is direct money rent payments varying with the quality of the land. However, this method requires a land cadaster, which is not likely to be available for many years.

4. Another reform proposal is that, instead of keeping prices stable despite variations in harvests, the Government raise them temporarily when harvests are especially poor. Under this proposal, in bad harvest years both agricultural procurement prices and state retail prices would be increased. The 1958 agricultural price revision was supposed to have introduced flexible procurement prices varying with harvests, but in practice flexibility operated in only one direction: prices were reduced for very good harvests but not raised for bad harvests.

The 1965 agricultural price revisions reflect these reform proposals only to a very limited extent. Prices are still based on zonal average costs, except in the case of grain procurements in the main grain areas, where the new prices seem to be related to cost conditions on farms located on the least favorable land. While some price zone boundaries were altered, there was no comprehensive revision based on a careful study of natural and manmade factors affecting costs. The nature of the collective farm income tax was significantly improved, but it is still an imperfect instrument for taking differential rent—inferior to explicit rental payments, which are precluded by the absence of a land cadaster. Prices are not to vary inversely with the size of the harvest. Rather, the reintroduction of premium prices for above-plan deliveries of wheat, rye, cotton, and sunflowers will make their average realized prices higher when harvests are good.

On balance then, the 1965 price changes appear to be another desirable, but still relatively modest, step on the road to guiding Soviet agriculture through prices and monetary incentives, rather than administrative commands. Soviet agriculture still lacks sound prices capable of securing rational specialization of production through decentralized decisions of farm managers. Moreover, it is important to recognize that although higher prices, properly related to costs, can stimulate production, the development of Soviet agriculture also requires a steady and adequate flow of industrial inputs (including investment goods) at reasonable prices and on reasonable credit terms, as well as adequate and guaranteed remuneration for farm members.

Chapter IV. Retail Prices

Nature and Trends

There are two principal types of retail prices at which goods are sold to households in the Soviet Union: state retail prices and collective farm market prices.

State Retail Prices

The state retail price (gosudarstvennaia roznichnaia tsena) is charged by state retail stores, consumer cooperative stores, and state and cooperative service establishments, such as restaurants, laundries, theaters, etc. The consumer cooperatives, which operate primarily in the rural areas, are closely supervised by the state, which determines their number, size, location, etc.; allocates goods to them; and establishes sales plans for them. Of total state, cooperative, and urban collective farm market sales in 1964, the respective percentage shares of the three types were 68, 28.1 and 3.9.

State retail prices supposedly are fixed with the aim of clearing the market both in aggregate terms and for each commodity. In aggregate terms, the objective is to set the general level of state retail prices so that total retail sales at that price level will absorb the money income which the population is expected to want to spend at state and cooperative retail outlets. For individual goods, the objective is to fix the price of each at a level which equates planned supply and expected demand.

The general level of retail prices depends upon both tax and wage policies. The Soviet Government relies primarily on price-increasing taxes, namely the turnover and profits taxes, to finance investment, military programs, and social services. As a result, the general retail price level is higher than it would be if direct taxes on households were used to a greater extent. Planned increases in private consumption can be distributed among households by reducing retail prices or by increasing money incomes (or by a combination of the two). The first method distributes the increase in consumption among the population as a whole, while the second is more selective. With stable retail prices, money incomes of different segments of the population can be increased by different degrees (and at different times) to provide selective incentives for increased production and for occupational and geographical shifts.

The first method was used from 1948 to 1954, when retail prices were reduced each spring. As Table 6 shows, since 1954 the state retail price level has been relatively stable, although there have been adjustments in the prices of individual goods. In addition to a moderate rise in the general wage level, there have been selective increases in the money incomes of

TABLE 6

INDEXES OF SOVIET STATE RETAIL PRICES, SELECTED YEARS, 1952–64
(1950 = 100)

Commodity group	1952	1955	1958	1962	1963	1964
All commodities	87	74	76	76	76	76
Food	82	70	73	75	75	75
Meat	74	60	66	78	85	85
Fish	88	79	77	76	76	76
Butter	74	64	65	76	83	83
Vegetable oil	84	65	65	65	65	65
Sugar	91	80	80	77	75	75
Bread and bread products	73	60	59	59	59	59
Potatoes	*	*	92	100	112	110
Vegetables	*	*	88	84	90	83
Alcoholic beverages	88	78	94	94	94	94
Nonfood commodities	95	81	80	79	78	78
Cotton fabrics	98	71	71	71	71	71
Woolen fabrics	97	92	92	89	89	89
Silk fabrics	99	91	89	80	77	77
Clothing	98	90	90	86	86	86
Knit goods	99	88	87	87	87	87
Leather footwear	98	81	81	82	83	83
Rubber footwear	99	76	75	76	76	76
Tobacco products	87	82	81	82	82	82
Watches	86	82	79	54	54	49
Bicycles	87	78	78	60	60	60

*Not available.

SOURCES: Nar. khoz. 58, p. 771; Nar. khoz. 61, p. 654; Nar. khoz. 62, p. 533; Nar. khoz. 63, p. 540; Nar. khoz. 64, p. 647.

particular segments of the population, through increases in agricultural procurement prices, pensions, minimum wages, and the wages of selected occupations (miners, teachers, etc.).

Under planners' sovereignty in the U.S.S.R., the basic method of eliminating a disequilibrium in the market for a particular good is to adjust demand to supply, in contrast to the adjustment of supply to demand which characterizes the response under consumers' sovereignty. The latter kind of adjustment occurs in the U.S.S.R. only to a limited extent when, in response to evidence in the form of shortages or surpluses at the prevailing prices, planners modify the composition (types, models, etc.) of the output of the various kinds of consumer goods which can be produced with the resources which they have allocated to those lines of production.

On some goods, retail prices are set with other objectives which conflict with the aim of clearing the market. One such additional objective, stemming from administrative considerations, is to avoid changing prices very often. This objective clearly conflicts with the aim of balancing demand with supply.

Another objective is to make the distribution of real income less unequal than the distribution of money income. To do this, the Government fixes the lower prices for mass consumption goods (such as basic foodstuffs) which predominate in the budgets of lower income groups, and higher prices for goods (e.g., consumer durables and luxury foodstuffs) which are relatively more important in the budgets of higher income groups. In pursuit of this objective, prices of some food products, such as meat, have been deliberately set below the equilibrium level (even below the corresponding agricultural procurement prices in some cases), as persistent shortages attest. In this way, the informal rationing of queues and empty shelves helps to modify the distribution of real income from the initial distribution of money income.

Relative prices are also used to pursue other objectives of social policy. For example, low prices are set on books in order to promote indoctrination and education, and on children's apparel in order to aid large families, while high prices are intended to curb the consumption of vodka.

The turnover tax, which provides about 40 percent of total budget revenue, is the principal device used by planners to secure the desired level and structure of retail prices. The principal components of the state retail price are 1) the enterprise wholesale price (or the agricultural procurement price plus the markup of the procurement agency), 2) the turnover tax, 3) the wholesale trade margin, and 4) the retail trade margin. In addition, there are transportation charges. The wholesale and retail margins are intended to cover expenses and provide a profit at the respective stages. The respective shares of enterprise wholesale prices, turnover taxes, and the two trade margins in the total value of state retail sales in recent years may be estimated very roughly at 50, 40, and 10 percent. Their relative importance in the prices of individual goods differs markedly, however, precisely because the turnover tax is used to fix the retail price at the desired level.

The turnover tax thus serves as a cushion which separates the retail prices paid by households and the wholesale prices received by producing enterprises in industry and agriculture. It permits the planners to alter consumer prices without changing producer prices correspondingly, and vice versa. Retail price reductions need not be accompanied by wholesale price reductions, and wholesale price increases need not be followed by retail price increases. The turnover tax separates not only the levels but also the structures of consumer and producer prices, since the different rates of taxation on different goods cause their relative retail prices to differ from their relative wholesale prices. For most goods the turnover tax is set as a specific ruble amount, and there are separate wholesale and retail price lists. For a limited group of goods, chiefly intended for local markets, the turnover tax is levied as a percentage of the enterprise wholesale price. These goods include some types of haberdashery, household items, and recreational and educational items. For certain nonfood consumer goods, the turnover tax is calculated as a percentage of the retail price. This scheme is used for consumer goods produced by the paper, chemical, and radio industries, as well as for sewn and fur items.

Collective Farm Market Prices

The collective farm market price (tsena kolkhoznogo rynka) of goods is determined by supply and demand in the individual collective farm markets, varying from market to market and from day to day in the same market. There are about 8,000 collective farm markets, approximately half of them in towns of various sizes and half in rural areas. The markets occupy designated trading areas and are equipped with a varying number of stalls, benches, tables, storage bins, meat and milk control points, etc. Sellers are charged a small daily fee for the right to offer their wares. About 700,000 peasants are reported to participate in the markets each day.

Although urban collective farm market sales represented only about 4 percent of total state, cooperative, and urban collective farm market sales in 1964, their importance in Soviet retail trade is greater than this figure suggests. In relation to total trade of the three channels in the same food goods, the collective farm market share in 1964 was 12 percent. In some important cities the collective farm markets account for 20 to 40 percent and more of total sales of major food products.

Collective farm market prices are set by supply and demand, but both supply and demand are strongly influenced by the State. Demand on the collective farm market depends on the extent to which the State retail network is able, with available quantities at the established prices, to satisfy the effective demand of households. The excess purchasing power remaining after household expenditures in the State retail trade sector finds an outlet in the collective farm market. The supply offered by agricultural producers (collective farms, peasants, and urban workers with garden plots) depends on the amount of output they have left after selling to State procurement agencies.

In contrast to the relative stability of State retail prices (see Table 6), collective farm market prices have risen sharply in the last few years as a result of poor harvests and reduced supplies in both State stores and collective farm markets. Table 7 shows the trend of collective farm market

TABLE 7

INDEXES OF SOVIET COLLECTIVE FARM MARKET PRICES,
SELECTED YEARS, 1958–64*
(1950 = 100)

Commodity group	1958	1960	1963	1964
All Commodities, including cattle	109	108	131	138
All commodities, excluding cattle	107	107	129	135
Bread products	67	64	100	119
Grains	67	62	89	111
Flour	53	49	91	120
Groats	63	63	97	105
Potatoes	119	119	170	159
Vegetables	131	119	158	161
Cabbage	146	148	193	190
Onions	124	91	130	162
Fruits	118	115	124	118
Vegetable oil	70	67	68	75
Meat and meat products	105	109	121	151
Beef	126	127	148	171
Pork	88	92	100	123
Poultry	120	129	146	186
Milk and dairy products	92	96	116	125
Milk	84	88	108	114
Butter	87	86	102	131
Eggs	96	96	112	123
Cattle	132	126	150	184

* Based on data for 251 large cities.
SOURCE: Nar. khoz. 64, p. 659.

prices during recent years. According to one estimate, toward the end of 1962 collective farm market prices exceeded State retail prices on the same items by about 60 percent on the average. Comparable data are not available for a more recent period, but it is clear that the difference is now much greater, because of the rise in collective farm market prices in the face of stable State retail prices.

Price Reform Discussion

At scholarly conferences and in the economic literature of the last few years, Soviet economists have criticized a number of aspects of retail price formation and have advanced suggestions for changes.

Criticisms

Among the criticisms of retail prices are the following: 1) prices diverge from a market-clearing level; 2) prices are set without adequate study of demand; 3) rural price differentials are unjustified; and 4) price-lists are outdated and too complex.

1. For decades, many state retail prices have been too low, and demand has exceeded supply, giving rise to shortages and queues. Among the causes responsible are the effort to modify income distribution in favor of lower income groups, underfulfillment of ambitious production plans, and the failure to meet assortment plans. In addition, local shortages often exist because of errors in the distribution of goods by the trade network. A general situation of excess demand was even justified by Stalin on the ground that it was a "law" of socialism that demand should outstrip supply. This position has now been condemned as theoretically unsound and undesirable in practice. Nevertheless, prices remain below the market-clearing level for various goods, particularly meat and certain consumer durables, and for certain services, notably housing.

While there are shortages of these goods, at the same time there are large excess inventories of yard goods, clothing, footwear, cameras, bicycles, watches, and sewing machines. In part, these surpluses are due to overpricing, but they also are due to poor estimates of demand and to the failure to adjust production to changes in consumer tastes. Thus, sharp price cuts on sewing machines and outmoded clothing failed to liquidate excess stocks.

2. If it is intended to strive for market-clearing prices, then accurate estimates of current and future demand are essential. But such studies of consumer demand are lacking. Only in the last few years has serious attention been devoted to demand studies, and work on the subject is still relatively primitive. In particular, demand estimates are too aggregrative, covering excessively broad categories of goods and very large geographic areas, and neglecting differences in the demands of different income groups. There has been little application of mathematical techniques to the analysis of retail trade problems.

3. Since 1949, prices on various goods in rural areas have exceeded

urban prices for the same items by about 7 percent. This differential has been justified on the ground that marketing and transportation costs are higher for rural trade. However, the price differential tends to divert peasant purchases from rural to urban retail outlets, and to encourage "speculation," i.e., resale of goods bought in the city to other peasants at higher prices.

4. Many retail price lists are out of date. Retail price lists on some goods, especially fabrics and sewn goods, were fixed in 1954 on the basis of 1939–40 prices. In 1963, the RSFSR price list on sewn goods contained 100,000 prices, of which about one-fourth pertained to items long since removed from production. Retail price lists are so numerous and so complex that only a small group of specialists understands them. For example, there are over 90,000 price lists for clothing and over 7,000 for footwear.

Reform Proposals

Various suggestions to improve retail prices have been advanced, including 1) more intensive study of demand, 2) greater flexibility of prices, 3) more decentralization of price fixing, and 4) wider use of the two-price-list scheme.

1. As a basis for improved price-setting, consumer demand studies should be intensified. In particular, attention should be devoted to income as well as price elasticities of demand, rural versus urban demand, and the long-term evolution of demand and prices. The work of the various research institutes studying different aspects of demand should be more closely coordinated.

2. Price flexibility should be increased in various ways: Clothing and footwear prices should be raised more often and more quickly on fashionable items in high demand, and reduced on slow-moving, out-of-style items. To adjust production to sales, wholesale prices of producers should be varied in the same direction as retail prices. Seasonal prices, now used for a limited number of food products (such as eggs, fruits, and vegetables), should also be applied to yard goods, clothing, and footwear. When harvests are poor, both retail and agricultural procurement prices should be raised.

3. Since 1957, the union republic and regional authorities have been responsible for fixing retail prices on a group of goods accounting for about 45 percent of retail sales. This group includes sausage and confectionery articles, eggs, milk, sewn goods, furniture, toys, and non-alcoholic beverages. The central authorities in Moscow set prices on the remainder of retail trade, including such important goods as bread, meat, fish, butter, cloth, footwear, knit goods, tobacco, vodka, and most consumer durables. It has been suggested that further decentralization of price-fixing is desirable, in order to increase price flexibility and bring prices closer to a

market-clearing level. In particular, it has been proposed that producing enterprises, in conjunction with the trade network, fix prices on new items, in line with prices on analogous existing items.

4. In the case of sewn goods, china and earthenware, glass articles, and pots and pans, it is proposed that the two-price-list scheme be adopted instead of the present arrangement of levying the turnover tax as a percentage of the retail price. When the tax is levied as a uniform percentage of the retail price for an entire class of goods, the relative structure of retail prices also determines the relative structure of enterprise wholesale prices. In many instances, items which are more complex and more expensive to manufacture do not have correspondingly higher retail and wholesale prices. As a result, the profitability of different items to the producing enterprise varies, and it is inclined to depart from its assortment plan by producing more of the "advantageous" items and less of the "disadvantageous" items. By adopting the two-price-list scheme—that is, by fixing the turnover tax as a specific ruble amount for each item—the Government could adjust the wholesale price structure independently of the retail price structure and thus reduce or eliminate differences in the profitability of producing different items in the assortment. To adopt this scheme in the case of clothing, however, it would be necessary to shift the turnover tax, now levied on the cloth rather than on the finished garment, to the final product.

Recent Changes

Recent measures in the sphere of retail price formation show a limited response to these criticisms and recommendations. For example, in 1965 the State Committee on Trade of the U.S.S.R Counsil of Ministers was instructed to establish an All-Union Scientific Research Institute to study the demand for consumer goods and the problems of trade fluctuations, with branches in the union republics. Organizations to study demand have been created in trade organizations, republic ministries of trade, and at various levels of the consumer cooperative system.

In 1963 a scheme of temporary prices was established under which temporarily high prices are set for new fabrics, clothing, footwear, and furniture in high demand. At the end of 1 year (or sooner if the demand declines), prices are reduced to their "permanent" level. The temporary surcharge of 10 to 15 percent applies to enterprise wholesale prices as well as to retail prices, because the enterprise wholesale prices of these goods are set as a percentage of their retail prices. This scheme has been criticized because of lengthy delays in setting the new prices, which are fixed at the republic level. Another criticism is that the resulting enterprise wholesale prices do not always make the new goods as profitable to produce as the older items which they replace, causing the enterprise's profits to fall.

In the now famous Bolshevichka-Maiak experiment, the pricing of new goods was decentralized to the enterprise level. The RSFSR Ministry of Trade authorized the factory and its retail outlets jointly to establish retail prices on new garments, on the basis of prices of existing goods but with due recognition of demand factors and additional costs incurred in producing the new garments. Because there is no turnover tax on clothing, enterprise wholesale prices were increased in the same proportion as retail prices. However, the factories found that the new models were less profitable to produce than the old ones, and their profits declined. While price setting (on new goods) was decentralized to the enterprise level during this experiment, when the scheme was extended to a large part of the light and food industry in 1965, enterprises were not given the right to fix prices on new products, and this right was taken away from the two experimental firms. This retreat from decentralized price setting was not publicized or explained in connection with the announcement of the "success" of the experiment and its extension to other enterprises.

Other developments in retail pricing worthy of brief mention are the elimination of the rural price differential and the revision of long-neglected prices on services. As part of the effort to improve the peasantry's terms of trade, beginning in 1959 the rural price differential was successively eliminated on a number of products, and it is to be abolished completely in 1966. During 1962–65, a comprehensive revision of prices on personal services (laundry, haircuts, clothing, shoe and appliance repairs, etc.) was conducted in the Ukraine, and it is apparently to serve as a guide to similar revisions in other areas.

These measures indicate a new interest on the part of the Soviet Government in setting better retail prices—an interest stimulated by the dramatic buildup of unsold goods, after a long period of excess demand conditions when improper relative prices could be tolerated. However, the Government has been reluctant to move toward more flexible prices responsive to supply and demand conditions. The use of temporary prices has been limited, and the decentralization of price fixing to the enterprise level, tried in the Bolshevichka-Maiak experiment, has been rescinded. In sum, it appears that the central authorities are much more concerned about retail prices than ever before, but they are hesitant to surrender control over retail prices to the enterprise and through it to the market.

Chapter V. Conclusion

Soviet economists, planners, and political leaders have been devoting growing attention to prices as the Soviet economy slowly moves toward a greater role for market forces and money flows, rather than administrative commands in physical terms, in guiding production and resource allocation. A broad critical discussion of industrial prices, at scholarly conferences and in the economic press, began in 1956. Similar, though more cautious, discussions of agricultural and retail prices started a few years later. These discussions have exposed many defects in the price system and have produced a wide variety of suggestions for improvements, ranging from minor technical revisions to sweeping changes of a basic character.

It is clear that the highest levels of the Communist Party and the Government are now concerned with price problems. Yet the central authorities have shown great reluctance to embark on major reforms in the price system in order to secure prices which reflect scarcity and can allocate resources efficiently. One reason, surely, is resistance to such reforms by members of the planning and administrative bureaucracy, who are used to, and comfortable with, command economy methods which do not depend on sound prices. They have a personal stake in the preservation of the traditional approach to resource allocation. They also genuinely distrust moves toward reliance on market forces and scarcity prices, fearing that they inevitably will bring inflation, on the one hand, and unemployment, on the other.

Because the political leadership and the central planners are unwilling to surrender control over the economy to consumers' sovereignty, they hesitate to let flexible scarcity prices determine output, allocate resources, and distribute income. Thus, it is not surprising that, despite the changes in enterprise performance indicators, managerial powers, and incentives, in Kosygin's "new economic model" price setting remains centralized, and, according to the information available so far, will largely follow traditional patterns. As a result, the planners will continue to be faced with the impossible task of regulating the 8 to 9 million prices in the Soviet economy.

*HOW TO RATIONALIZE A COMMAND ECONOMY: INPUT/OUTPUT**

— · — · — · — · — · — · — · — · — · — · — .

P. J. D. Wiles†

Input/output achieves the same thing at the method of balances, only far better: by simultaneous equations, and the special mathematics of matrices, rather than by tedious iteration. From the present equilibrium of all material balances we can discover how to move to a new equilibrium

---

*Reprinted from *The Political Economy of Communism* (Cambridge: Harvard University Press 1962), pp. 197–203. All footnotes deleted.

†Peter Wiles is Professor of Economics, The London School of Economics and Political Science. His publications include: *Price, Cost and Output* (1963, 1965), *The Political Economy of Communism* (1962), and *Communist Economics* (in print).

of all balances which incorporates both the desired extra quantity of, say, steel and all the infinite regress of consequential changes. When the Russians began to take an interest in this improvement N. Nemchinov claimed that Wassily Leontief's first glimmerings of input/output derived from his study of Soviet planning problems, and were published in *Planovoye Khozyaistvo,* December 1925 ('The Balance of the National Economy of U.S.S.R.: A Methodological Critique of the Work of the Central Statistical Administration'). Such a claim is almost essential if input/output is to be accepted by the ideologues, but it is unfortunately quite untrue. For Leontief was then already in Germany, and his article is a translation of one he published in *Weltwirtschaftliches Archiv* in October 1925. Nor does it deal at all with input/output, since the crucial element of solving a large number of simultaneous equations is wholly missing. We can at most say that the author, owing to his Soviet experience, had already developed interests which later led him to his discovery. In his first published venture with many simultaneous equations was an article in the *Review of Economics and Statistics,* August 1936: 'Quantitative Input/Output Relations in the Economic System of the United States.' *This* is the article correctly cited in the standard textbook as having originated the technique; and certainly from then on input/output was at home in the West, while in the East the seed had fallen on stony ground.

Now input/output is itself a very crude tool, sharing many crucial disadvantages with the method of balances itself. *First,* both assume fixed coefficients: so many tons of steel require so many tons of coke, neither more nor less. In real life an increase in steel output raises the price of coke, perhaps more rapidly than that of labour or blast-furnaces; so it would be best to economize in coke more severely than in labour or furnaces, thus altering the input/output coefficients. And this is but a poor and crude example of the infinitely many subtle readjustments any economy, command or market, makes to a given change.

Secondly, input/output does not tell us whether it would be a good idea to have more steel in the first place, rather than more of something else. The giving of such information has always been the privilege of the price mechanism; and so it remained even after input/output itself was in full flower. For both it and the method of balances tell us only what plans, what relative outputs are consistent with each other. There are infinitely many such self-consistent bills of goods, and neither method gives us any idea at all whether any one such 'bill' or 'mix' is better than another. Clearly we are better off with a device that tells us something about this latter and more important question, even at the cost of some material inconsistency. With high-speed computers, however, this is perhaps not very serious: one can propose a very large number of 'bills' of final output at random, and find oneself left with a fair number that the matrix has proved technically possible, between which one may then exercise choice. The criteria of choice, though, must be separately determined and applied. They have no connection with the matrix and its mathematics.

Thirdly, one cannot deduce a single, determinate bill of outputs from a list of available factors. This clearly follows from the fact that each factor can make many products, in contrast to the assumption that each product requires only one set of factors (fixed input coefficients). Without information as to demand one is powerless here.

Finally, it is most significant that the method will grind out the same answer *whatever* prices are used, since it is basically a set of physical relationships. If a ton of steel requires two tons of coke then we can put the prices of steel and coke at 50 to 1 or 1 to 50; so long as they are constant over the operation they will tell us the same answer in tons. Indeed money is not necessary at all for an input/output table: it might just as well be made in tons or square feet, or even a mixture of money, tons and square feet. For so long as each commodity is measured in the same unit throughout there will be valid fixed coefficients that yield the same answer as a table based on rational prices. A technique that is insensitive even to astronomically ridiculous prices is not of much use. I cannot but think that the mathematical charm of this device has led many grossly to overstate its utility.

But for Soviet-type purposes it would have been extremely suitable! Soviet-type prices *are* ridiculous, Soviet-type planning *is* conducted with fixed input/output coefficients and in physical terms. With the method of balances alone, this kind of planning was arbitrary and difficult, with input/output it could be arbitrary and easy. The technique would have merely been the coping-stone on the method of balances, enabling each material balance to be brought into harmony with all the others in the most elegant and convenient way—and all to produce a quite arbitrary set of outputs by a rather arbitrary allocation of inputs. As previously, there would have been no indication that this was the best set of final products, nor that this was the best way to produce it. It would merely have had the virtue of not contradicting itself.

In fact input/output has not yet (1961) been put to serious practical use in either Poland or U.S.S.R. That is, no current plans have yet been derived from it, though in Poland at least it has been used, with a very few rows and columns, to give planners an idea of what the economy would look like if certain large changes were made.

Has it any more practical uses? It surely has. Coherence or feasibility is not at all a small virtue in a plan. It lowers administrative cost, and ensures the punctual arrival of the document by reducing the amount of objections to it. In a book on a rather abstract level, the tremendous fact that plans are always unpunctual has been under-emphasized. Yet in real life it is one of the greatest problems. Provisionally, the director extrapolates from what he did in the last quarter, but this may not be what the centre really requires. Moreover where there is imperfect feasibility there are bottlenecks, and a bottleneck in one input means a superfluity of another. Therefore perfect feasibility means a fuller employment of resources, and more output. Again it means less 'planner's tension', or at least a more rationally distributed tension.

In conclusion input/output has an interesting relation to the curious Marxist habit of beginning the plan with intermediate products. We already saw the psychological or ideological reasons for this in Chap. 3, Sec. 6c: the labour theory of value derives value up from factors, not down from products. Now strictly such an attitude would tempt us to begin with labour and capital targets, and work forward from them. It is perhaps a measure of the folly of beginning with factors at all that Communists do not do this; instead they set themselves intermediate product targets, and use these as determinants of their plans. Improper to say 'as determinants of their matrices', because proper matrices are hardly yet in use. But a system of material balances has determinants in just the same sense.

Now what is the effect of this? If all final products were also intermediate products (as are some agricultural commodities) then to fix all the latter would also be to fix the final product mix, since the whole includes the part; and the whole system would be determinate. But this is far indeed from being the case. To fix intermediate products is merely to determine the requirements of less fabricated intermediate products, and of the ultimate factors of production. It hardly helps at all to determine final products, since although it puts some mixtures out of court it leaves infinitely many still possible. The essence of input/output is the not wholly ridiculous assumption that each input can make many kinds of output, whereas each output needs a fixed bill of inputs. Therefore determinacy can only begin with final outputs, not somewhere in the middle of the chain of production: a steel target is only in a very restricted sense a determinant.

But whatever the usefulness of this method, it was not in fact a native product. Ironically, in addition to not inventing a system that would have suited them very well, the Russians did invent an inportant refinement of it that introduces the price mechanism. It is possible by a further considerable complication of the mathematics to meet the objections voiced above to input/output, and by means of prices to discover, not merely the many self-consistent solutions, but also the one optimal solution to the problem of how to use the economy's resources. This is 'linear programming' or 'activity analysis'. Much of it was developed by the Leningrad mathematician L. V. Kantorovich in 1939. But, as before, the seed fell on stony ground, and it was left to two Americans, Koopmans and Dantzig, to develop the whole technique quite independently some years later.

The use of prices, and the making of rational choices, is of the essence of activity analysis. Basically it is just a practical technique for making multi-dimensional production-possibility surfaces and indifferences surfaces. However abstractly mathematical, it rigorously entails a quite different attitude to economics from input/output. Arbitrary allocations and meaningless prices are ruled out by the very procedures. Now Leontief's first, path-breaking book on input/output (*Studies on the Structure of the American Economy*, 1941) began to circulate among Soviet economists in an unpublished Russian translation in 1955 or 1956. But already by that time input/output had become inextricable from its more sophisticated successor, and in fact the two techniques have been taken over together and are taught and applied together. A slightly different chronological sequence, and input/output would have been an indisputably Russian achievement, so well evolved by, say, the end of the NEP that Stalin would have accepted it as a 'creative development of Marxist economic science'— which is not far from what it is. Then in 1955 activity analysis, with its chatter of prices and rational choice and optimum solutions, would have been an evil, formalistic, subjectivistic bourgeois perversion. Which again is not far from what it is. For it strikes at the root of Marxism: placing, just as would perfect competition and perfect central adjustment, prices on land and capital as well as labour, dealing in marginal not average magnitudes, striking down the arbitrary power of political authority to decide investments without due thought. It is a corrosive acid indeed that the fissure in the monolith has admitted; though not more corrosive than the rather different acid Tito admitted in 1950.

Kantorovich's original contribution was not especially 'deleterious'. For he began with a purely local, seemingly only technical, problem—of the optimum allocation of the existing scarce resources (i.e. equipment) available to a particular engineering factory. Given its production plan and its sortament, how could the factory so use its machines as to over-fulfil that plan, keeping to the proportions laid down in the sortament? Not Stalin himself could object to calculations of that sort. Doubtless Kantorovich had no notion of what an explosive mixture he was handling.

The real difficulties begin when the scarcity problem is seen to apply (a) outside the enterprise and (b) to the goals for final outputs laid down in the plan. Take (a) first. If we consider more than one enterprise together then they must both have the same shadow prices, and be prepared to exchange. This means that the central plan must enforce the same shadow prices on all, and must adapt its own requirements of intermediate goods to those prices. This means a sharp change in methodology, though hardly in institutions. It means, as we saw in Chap. 6, Sec. 12 in connexion with the old rate of interest controversy, that all decisions except as to final outputs must be subjected to the price mechanism. Neither planner nor politician can any more arbitrarily say what he likes, and in particular the old Marxist habit of beginning with quantitative goals for major producers' goods must be abandoned (Chap. 3, Sec. 6).

In his second book Kantorovich is much bolder and advocates all these things. But he still rigorously accepts the planners' final output pattern, and explicitly condemns consumer's sovereignty. He must thus be described as an advocate of perfect computation under ICM, deriving his shadow prices from the factor-scarcities induced by the plan. The outputs, incidentally, are in all his models imposed upon the enterprise by the planner along with the shadow prices, though there appears to be some independence as to sortament.

MARX, KANTOROVICH, AND NOVOZHILOV: STOIMOST' VERSUS REALITY*

— · — · — · — · — · — · — · — · — · —

Robert W. Campbell†

Like other aspects of Soviet life, economics has been revivified by Stalin's death. The most visible part of its reawakening has been an extensive discussion of, and experimentation with, institutional arrangements, though even questions of strategy and basic policy have also been exposed to an unwonted amount of free discussion. The real measure of this freedom, however, is that the search for theoretical clarification, which inevitably accompanies discussion of practical issues, has been allowed to develop in a way not permitted since the late twenties. One aspect of this dramatic change is the controversy which has developed around the use of mathematics in economics. After long aversion to any introduction of mathematical reasoning into analysis of economic relationships, the Russians are now thinking about the possible usefulness of input-output techniques in balancing supply and demand in price planning and about the application of linear programming to enterprise planning, and have begun to resort to mathematical models to explore the abstract essence of practical problems.

The expectation was that mathematical economics could be borrowed

*Reprinted by permission of the publisher and the author from *Slavic Review* (Oct. 3 1961), pp. 402–418. All footnotes deleted.

†Dr. Robert W. Campbell is Professor of Economics, and Director of the Russian and East European Institute, Indiana University. His publications include: *Soviet Economic Power* (1960, 1966), *Accounting in Soviet Planning and Management* (1963), and "On the Theory of Economic Administration," *Industrialization in Two Systems* (1966), Henry Rosovsky, (ed.).

from the capitalist world just as implements and techniques are. One of the common themes in the post-Stalin discovery of what economists in the capitalist world have been up to is the need to sort out the usable from the nonusable, and to purge mathematical methods of their bourgeois interpretations before they are applied in the Soviet economy. As one might expect, hopes for such an antiseptic transfusion are likely to be disappointed, and even the beginning of Soviet work on mathematical techniques has led to a search for clarification of the theory of value. Mathematics and computers in themselves are ideologically neutral; but the mathematization of any science implies measurement, and in economics the unit of measurement is value. Hence, as one of the participants in the controversy has said, understanding how to measure value is basic to all practical problems of calculation. But progress toward an improved explanation of value and an understanding of its connection with the problem of allocation will require Soviet economists to free themselves from the limitations of Marxist theory. In fact this emancipation has nearly been accomplished already in the writings of two of the participants in the discussion of the use of mathematical methods in economics, L. V. Kantorovich and V. V. Novozhilov. Thus apart from its manifest content, the term "mathematical methods in economics," which is bandied about so freely by Soviet economists, has also become a euphemism for a new theory of value. The present article describes this search for a new theory of value.

Deficiencies of the Labor Theory of Value

As an introduction we must review briefly the divergent histories of the mainstream of world economic theory and Marxism. The basic theory of economics has come of age only in about the last half century. In this period the bits and pieces, the partial insights of earlier years, have been integrated into a unified general theory. Marxist economics, on the other hand, has spent this period marking time in a blind alley, to use a favorite Soviet metaphor. Marxist value theory broke away from the tradition that prevailed in the time of Ricardo, and has missed out on the great scientific success of generalization and unification which has taken place in Western value theory since then.

The nature of this achievement can be explained as follows. One of the central preoccupations of economics has always been what determines price. Movements of foreign exchange rates, the distribution of income among social classes, changes in the general price level, and so on, all involve questions of relative prices, how much one thing is worth in terms of others. Hence the search for a general explanation (i.e., theory) of value has always occupied the center of the stage. The practical questions that economists have struggled to unravel have always led back to this as the basic theoretical problem to be solved. During most of the nineteenth century no consistent and satisfactory explanation was offered. There were cost theories and utility theories, to mention only one dichotomy, and any one theorist might well try to embrace several different theories and use them in different parts of his book for different problems. Ricardo, for instance, has two theories of value—one for the value of land, and another very different one for the value of everything else. The reconciliation of all these conflicting partial explanations into a unified general theory of value came only in the late nineteenth century with the concept of general equilibrium and the reduction of all explanations to the common denominator of utility by the writers of the utility school.

In the process, it also came to be understood that the explanation of value is only one aspect of the central problem of economics. The question of relative prices is inextricably intertwined with the explanation of relative quantities. Indeed the reconciliation and integration of all the conflicting parts of value theory as it had previously existed was made possible only by widening the perspective to take in the question of what determines the proportions among different kinds of output along with the question of what determines value. One reflection of this new insight into the problem of value was the formulation of a new definition of economics, the one commonly used today, as the theory of allocation of scarce resources among competing ends. The definition slights the value aspect of the problem, but its rapid adoption was a response to the profound insight that economic theory must explain not only value but also quantities and the interdependence of both these sets of magnitudes.

It was this achievement that the Marxists and their Soviet intellectual heirs missed out on. The Russians retain, through Marx, ideas about value extant at the time of Ricardo. Marx took the theory of value as it then existed, and compounded from some of its confusions a theory of the dynamics of the capitalist system. (It might be more accurate to describe the process the other way round: Marx had the conclusions and was trying to show how they flowed rigorously and inevitably from the theory of value then generally accepted. With the benefit of hind sight we may look back on his effort as a *reductio ad absurdum* technique for proving the deficiencies of Ricardian value theory.) Thus the bondage of a Marxist heritage in economic theory is not so much that the Marxist view is simply wrong in one particular (i.e., that it assumes that value is created only by labor) as that it does not comprehend the basic problem of economic theory; it has not achieved a full understanding of what a valid economic theory must illuminate. That achievement came in the mainstream of world economic theorizing only after Marxism has already taken the turning to enter the blind alley mentioned above.

This isolation of Marxist economic thinkers from the rest of the intellectual community has not been natural or easy to maintain. Marxist groups have had to wage a constant struggle to preserve the sanctified shortcomings of their economic doctrine against the encroachments of greater sophistication, but they have considered it important to do so because of the central place that the labor theory of value holds in the Marxist theory of the transition from capitalism to socialism. The stagnation of economic theorizing within the Marxist tradition of economic thought has resulted in an irony often commented on. The Soviet planned economy, in which the efficient allocation of resources to achieve competing goals is a constant preoccupation, has muddled through with no body of theory to explain the implications of actual and potential choices. It must seek its guidance in a theory which not only misunderstands value but but which does not even envisage the question of value as having any connection with rational allocation.

This is a supremely unsatisfactory situation, full of tension. As explained above, in the market economy the notion of describing an optimal allocation of all society's resources was essentially an abstract construct, imagined in the process of integrating all the bits and pieces of economics into a theory of choice and value. The social necessity for such an allocation among the competing ends is not self-evident to the individuals in Western society, where the allocation results from the impersonal operation of the price system. In the Soviet economy, on the other hand, the allocation of all society's resources among alternative uses is a highly visible and operational process, which calls out for some sort of theoretical conceptions to clarify and inform the manipulation of it. At the same time a strong motive to find a unified theory of economics grows out of preoccupation with questions of measuring cost and value. Despite central planning there is still a tremendous need in the Soviet system for decentralized calculation of benefits and gains among alternatives, and these calculations must always be cast in terms of some common denominator of value. At the micro-economic level the Russians are engaged in a quest for what they call "effectiveness," but their efforts to calculate effectiveness always founder on the inadequacy of their understanding of value and how it is related to the problem of choice in its allocation aspects. This is clearly an unstable situation; the practice of planning calls for theoretical guidance which Marxist value theory is incapable of providing. Economic theory bears the same relation to planning that physics does to engineering. It provides a model of concepts and interrelations that makes it possible to comprehend the dependence of consequences on other variables as a prelude to manipulation. When Soviet planners seek such insight in Marx, they are not likely to find anything relevant, or if they find something on the subject, it is likely to be misleading. What is needed is some way of seeing the process whole—a vision that makes clear the interdependence of the problem of allocation and the problem of value.

Failing to find such a vision in Marx, practical planners in the Soviet Union are continually trying to make one up for themselves. There are innumerable instances in which planners in some corner of the economy are rediscovering some of the basic ways of economic reasoning, figuring out for themselves some of the basic ideas of value and allocation. It was surely inevitable, for instance, that electrical engineers and mining engineers would come to realize that the condition for efficient allocation of a program among production units working in parallel is equality of marginal cost. Those who are called on every day to decide how far to carry the substitution of capital for labor in designing production facilities quickly come to realize that there must be a limit, and common-sense considerations soon suggest what the nature of that limit is. The difficulty is that these creative responses by individual thinkers have never coalesced into a general theory of allocation and value on the scale of the entire national economy, and that is what is needed. The failure to achieve such unification has been due partly to the fact that the theorists to whom this responsibility is allotted in a modern specialized society were hobbled by Marxism, and such generalization would inevitably contradict some of the Marxist simplicities. Moreover, the task of generalization and integration is probably more difficult than the development of partial theories and explanations.

The seminal works on the problem of value and allocation by V. V. Novozhilov and L. V. Kantorovich originated in precisely the way we have described, as efforts to deal with partial problems of calculation. Novozhilov is an economist who at one point tried his hand at the problem of rational criteria for investment choice, with which Soviet economists have long struggled. In trying to set out conditions for maximizing the effectiveness of investment expenditures, he found that no answer could be given except as part of the answer to a larger question of criteria for the effective allocation of *all* resources. Kantorovich, who is really a mathematician rather than an economist, was drawn to the problem when he was asked to solve a highly specific parochial, and actually insignificant problem of allocation, But in bringing to bear the broad vision of a mathematician upon this problem of allocation within a limited framework, he discovered concepts and operations for clarifying the whole problem of value and resource allocation on a national economic scale. In making these advances, both men inevitably came into conflict with the labor theory of value as developed by Marx, and this is the revolutionary and controversial feature of their work.

The Objectively Determined Valuations of Kantorovich

The development of Kantorovich's thought can be briefly summarized as follows. In the late thirties, the Plywood Trust in Leningrad asked the help of the Institute of Mathematics and Mechanics of Leningrad State University for help in solving a production-scheduling problem. The Trust had several different kinds of machines for stripping logs for plywood, and the machines had different productivities, in terms of volume of logs handled, depending on what kind of logs were to be handled. The proportions among the different kinds of logs to be worked on the machines were given, and the problem was to assign the different kinds of logs among different machines so as to make possible the maximum throughput per unit of time, or in other words to maximize the productivity of the machines. Kantorovich was asked to help find the solution to this problem.

It is logical enough to appeal to a mathematician for help in such a problem. There is a whole branch of mathematics concerned with just the problem of finding *maxima* and *minima* of interrelated variables under specified conditions. But when the problem of the logs and machines was formulated as the maximization of a function subject to certain conditions, it was not the kind of problem that could be solved by the traditional methods of analysis. This did not mean that it was insoluble but that some practically usable technique for finding the solution had to be worked out, and this is what Kantorovich did. His method involved a modification of the use of Lagrange multipliers of traditional analysis to the needs of the problem as he had formulated it. The multipliers could be found by an iterative process, and once found they could be used to find the solution of the problem. That he happened to stumble on this technique for solving the problem was purely an accident. The whole class of linear programming problems, as this kind of problem later came to be called, were rediscovered in the United States, but were solved here at first by a different approach called the "simplex method." That Kantorovich happened on this particular technique, however, was of great significance, since the multipliers he employed turned out to have the same significance as prices in Western value theory, and his trial-and-error search for them an analogue of the process of price determination in a market economy. At the time, Kantorovich thought of these multipliers as simply an intermediate step in the process of finding the set of variables he was interested in, that is, the allocation of log types among machines to maximize throughput. He did note that the multipliers had some significance in relation to the problem: they represented certain tradeoff possibilities that one might wish to consider in making decisions about the allocation involved. However, it seems quite clear that he did not then realize the broad significance of these multipliers as indexes of value.

As is widely known, this discovery was almost completely neglected in the Soviet Union. Such a fate is somewhat difficult to understand. Besides solving the specific problem of the Plywood Trust, Kantorovich had remarked that a great variety of production planning problems could be cast in the same form and hence would be amenable to solution by the same means. Moreover, he made no little effort to pave the way for the widespread application of linear programming to practical problems. The original publication contains a classic defense of abstract theorizing in the form of a rebuttal to all the objections that he supposed "practical" people would make to the mystifications of a mere mathematician. He also took pains to describe a wide variety of situations faced every day by Soviet planners where his method could provide useful guidance; and the Institute sponsored several conferences to bring together mathematicians and planning personnel to explore the feasibility of such practical applications.

Nevertheless, Kantorovich never suceeded in arousing much interest, although he apparently continued to work on linear programming. There is a short list of articles on the subject, which appeared during the forties, but it seems doubtful if more than a handful of Soviet economists had even heard of Kantorovich up to the early fifties.

In the meantime, linear programming was rediscovered independently in the United States a short while after Kantorovich's original paper. In sharp contrast to the Soviet history, it quickly found wide application in practical problems of production planning in the United States, and was also quickly reconciled with and assimilated by the body of traditional economic theory. Ironically, one can find in the extensive literature outside the Soviet Union practical applications illustrating all those potential uses which Kantorovich had pointed out in his pioneer article.

Despite the lack of interest in his discovery, Kantorovich apparently continued to think about its applications and about its general economic significance. When the Soviet infatuation with mathematical methods in economics after Stalin's death had finally made the climate right, Kantorovich was rediscovered as a Soviet pioneer, the original inventor of linear programming. The Academy of Sciences published a full-length book by him entitled *Economic Calculation of the Optimum Utilization of Resources,* in which the method and its implications for value theory and for allocation are explained.

This is a remarkable book. The title itself represents a significant advance, betraying as it does a focus on the problem of the allocation of resources. What distinguishes it from the earlier work is that in it Kantorovich has now fully recognized the significance of his multipliers as indexes of value, and that he has integrated the theory of value and the theory of allocation. This vision is boldly proclaimed by relabeling the multipliers of the earlier work as "objectively determined valuations" (*ob"ektivno obuslovlennye otsenki*). The term is an artful invention. It not only goes as far as one may with propriety in a Marxist society toward saying that these multipliers actually express value, but it also symbolizes the integration of the value problem and the allocation problem. He calls the values "objectively determined" because they are uniquely defined by the conditions of the problem. The allocation of resources which maximizes (or minimizes, depending on the nature of the problem) the variable of interest is consistent with only one set of values for the multipliers. Kantorovich does not use the word *stoimost'* to describe his indexes of value since that term has already been pre-empted by orthodox Marxist value theory. Nevertheless he is perfectly clear on the point that "value" in any meaningful sense is defined by his *otsenki* rather than by *stoimost'*.

The new book contains much else in addition to this basic discovery. Kantorovich has used his method to deal with problems of capital allocation, and he has long sections developing the proposition that the familiar deficiencies of *khozraschet* (which we can define for our purposes here as the technique of administrative decentralization in a centrally planned economy) can be overcome if the objectively determined valuations are substituted for the kind of prices, based on bookkeeping costs, that the Russians now have. His *otsenki* reflect not only the cost aspects of value but also the demand aspects, and their use will therefore discourage those characteristic irrationalities of the Soviet system in which a producer is tempted to do something that looks cheap but is actually a waste of scarce and valuable resources, or to do something that seems very productive but really produces something not vitally needed. In short, Kantorovich has reconstructed most of the significant propositions of the body of production theory previously developed in the West, though in the modern linear programming form rather than in the traditional form which assumed continuous differentiable production functions. And in contrast to the neglect of his earlier work, his ideas are now being widely disseminated not only by the book, but also through articles, papers at conferences and educational programs for training young economists in the new mathematical methods.

Novozhilov's Theory of Value

The second contributor to the renaissance of economic science in the Soviet Union, Novozhilov, also arrived at general conceptions of value by way of a limited problem of resource allocation—the capital allocation problem. The history of that problem cannot be recapitulated in detail here, and the reader is referred to the paper by Grossman. The basis of the controversy over capital allocation was that ideological difficulties were encountered in any attempt to formulate practical rules for deciding how far Soviet designers should go in substituting capital for labor in designing new products, new plants, and new processes. Any workable rules necessarily implied the productivity of capital, a proposition in conflict with the labor theory of value. Moreover, there was a danger of getting involved in the question of the proper division of investment between the consumer-goods and producer-goods industries. The subject was therefore politically as well as ideologically treacherous, and after a short flurry of discussion in the twenties, most economists carefully avoided it. Novozhilov published several papers in which he tried to find an approach that would avoid both these dangers. Actually his basic proposition concerning the theory of value and allocation were developed in these early papers, and his more recent publications contain only restatement, extension to additional problems, and mathematical demonstrations. Nevertheless, we will take as the text for the following discussion one of these more recent papers, "The Measurement of Expenditure and Its Results in the Socialist Economy," published in 1959.

This paper is a wonderful document. It has great appeal to a Western economist as a vicarious rebuttal of all the traditional nonsense of Soviet economists. Novozhilov goes unerringly to the point, with pithy comments on the sterility of the clichés with which Soviet economists treat problems of value and allocation. The following paraphrase of his introduction gives the tone of the whole paper:

> One of the most important problems of our economic science today is the problem of measuring the expenditure and results of socialist production. In fact, that is the main problem. It is natural that much attention is devoted to the methods of economic calculation. There are many books and articles on the subject and not a few conferences have been concerned with the discussion of this question. However, all this huge effort has not yet led to a solution of the problem. The confusion stems from the absence of a correct methodology of measuring expenditure [i.e., the absence of a correct theory of value]. In practice our planners have found it indispensable to make adjustments in the value magnitudes they manipulate in order to avoid absurd conclusions. My objective in this paper is to reconcile theory and practice and to improve the latter through clarification of the theory.

His answer to the problem of how to measure cost is a theory of value based on "opportunity cost." That is, it takes account not only of the labor used in the production of a commodity but also of other resources used, such as land and capital, on the grounds that these are limited in supply, and that their use in the production of one good means that they cannot be used to save on the labor required for the production of some other good.

He begins by formulating the general task of calculation in the socialist economy as one of maximizing the effectiveness of labor, by which he means producing the national output with as little labor expenditure as possible. However, this is not possible just by minimizing the labor cost of producing each component of the total output separately. The problem is that in addition to the direct, obvious labor input into each good there is a second kind of labor expenditure, which he described as "inversely related expenditures of labor" (*zatraty obratnoi sviazi*). This concept is identical with the concept of opportunity costs. These originate in the circumstance that there are some kinds of input that are in short supply in any given planning period. If the labor input into a particular product is minimized by substituting these scarce inputs for direct labor, then the labor cost of outputs elsewhere in the economy will rise in consequence. To reconcile the local efforts to minimize the cost of each good separately with the objective of achieving the minimum labor input for all output taken together, these inversely related costs must be taken into account. To make this possible, it is necessary to have a measure indicating the effectiveness of each scarce input in saving labor. If these costs are known, then they should be taken as the appropriate price tags for such nonlabor inputs in economic calculation. Thus all partial decisions aimed at minimizing costs will take into account not only direct expenditures of labor but also the indirectly related expenditures of labor, and the totality of partial efforts at cost minimization will be consistent with the aim of minimizing the labor input for all output taken together. He later on develops a mathematical proof for these assertions, and before he is done he has shown how the allocation and value problems interact. Value is something that cannot be determined just by accounting; it emerges only from the problem of allocating resources optimally.

All this is perfectly familiar to economists outside the Soviet Union, except for the formulation of the problem as one of minimizing the labor input required to produce an assigned program of total output. The Western economist would formulate the problem as one of finding the values coincident with maximizing the output from given resources. The formal essence of the two problems is identical, but Novozhilov's approach permits him to avoid analyzing what determines the proper assortment of final output, and also expresses all his values (including the inversely related expenditures) in terms of labor inputs, thus preserving an appearance of Marxist orthodoxy.

Armed with a competent conception of value, Novozhilov vanquishes a good share of the problems that confuse the Soviet planner and economist. With a mere flick of this powerful weapon he parts those Gordian knots that Soviet economic theorists have worried fruitlessly for three decades. How can the comparative performance of enterprises in unlike circumstances be compared? Charge for the differential advantages that some enjoy! How stint the importunate demands of project designers for "deficit" good? Price goods not as *stoimost'*, but at their opportunity costs! How maximize the effectiveness of investment resources? Suffer them not to be used except where the returns justify their opportunity costs! How should a socialist society reckon with obsolescence? Novozhilov's answer is not the customary twenty pages of twaddle, but a few short paragraphs directed faultlessly at the essential issues.

Altogether it makes exhilarating reading for a non-Soviet economist, and one suspects that most Soviet students would have the same reaction. This is not to say that Novozhilov never stumbles. His theory of value has the fundamental deficiency of dealing with value only as it reflects production constraints, and when he approaches a problem such as the proper rate of accumulation or the proper choice of output mix, his concept of value is of little help. In these passages, in contrast with other sections of the paper, there are no mathematical formulas, and even his vocabulary— terms like welfare, wants, useful results—becomes fuzzy. It lacks analytical power since it is not infused with meaning drawn from his theory of value. It does not necessarily follow that he does not understand these issues. His vagueness may only reflect discretion.

With so much accomplished, what remains to be done? Have not the Russians overleaped a century of Western thought and made good at last their cultural lag in the science of economics? That would be too sweeping a judgment, as we shall see in a moment, but certainly these two works represent a great achievement. Kantorovich and Novozhilov have shown convincingly that other things besides labor are scarce, and that the problem of value and the problem of allocation are inseparable. They make it clear that value is not something metaphysical, as Marx made it, but that what something is worth is clearly defined as an index of its scarcity in relation to objectives. What are the prospects for the success of this revolution?

The Response of Soviet Economists

It is too early to predict with assurance whether these innovations in the theory of value will be able to make their way into Soviet economic thought and teaching. There are, however, very strong factors favoring their survival. Much damage has been done just in the opportunity allowed for their expression; once Soviet economists have had a chance to ponder them, they can scarcely be rejected except by arbitrary repression. If these innovations are as unorthodox as we have argued, then one might hold that such must be the outcome. But the counter-argument is that heretical though sophisticated value theory may be, it is wonderfully useful, like traditional logic and quantum mechanics. Hence there must be strong pressure on Soviet economists to gain an understanding of it, even though the novices in those secular seminaries, the economics and philosophic faculties of universities, may still be required to learn by rote the old catechism.

In the meantime Soviet economists are not willing to be converted without at least a protest. Kantorovich's book contains a foreword by Academician Nemchinov, expressing strong reservations about some of the implications Kantorovich draws. Similarly the reviews of both men's works in the authoritative economic journals have been unfavorable. However, the most interesting thing about this criticism is that the critics seem to understand very well what Kantorovich and Novozhilov are doing. The new theory has been given competent, if reluctant, sponsors for its debut. They have done their homework well and have thoroughly grasped the logic of the new approach. Their reactions reflect the difficulties of dealing with this threat to orthodoxy. Nemchinov agrees that the objectively determined valuations and the inversely related expenditures are useful concepts, acceptable when kept in their proper place, as techniques for solving particular production problems. The main theme of his protest is that the temptation to find a more general significance in them must be resisted. The novel concepts have nothing to do with value, but are just a special kind of indicator used in a technical problem. Nemchinov is embarrassed by Kantorovich's intransigence in openly labeling his numbers as objectively determined valuations, though he sees perfectly well that this is precisely what they are. In fact he is sufficiently convinced that he equivocates in his denial of their general significance, and in the end does not really deny the possibility of their extension to an economy-wide framework but only says that such applications have not yet been worked out. In evaluating Novozhilov's work he is much comforted that labor remains the *numéraire* for all elements of Novozhilov's measure of value, but is upset by the problem that in Marxist theory rent-like elements (which is one way to describe the opportunity costs) have nothing to do with value but are only a distributive category.

Boiarskii, too, in the review in *Planovoe khoziaistvo* seems to see the truth of Kantorovich's arguments, but also sees that they lead to the wrong conclusions. His review has a schizophrenic air. The first part is devoted to explaining the ideas and praising the practical usefulness of linear programming. But in the second part he says that the book demonstrates the danger of turning a mathematician loose to deal with issues that Marxist economic science has already settled. The real conclusion of his review seems to be that there is nothing wrong with these theories about the proper allocation of resources except they they lead to un-Marxist conclusions about the measurement of value. Boiarskii is never able to explain, however, where Kantorovich got off the track toward something useful and arrived at something harmful.

The review by Kats in *Voprosy ekonomiki* also exudes intellectual distress. He begins with praise, but is then at such a loss to explain what is wrong with the mathematical approach that he is obliged to resort to all sorts of irrelevant and ridiculous criticisms. For instance he complains that it is a weakness to take the composition of output and the amount of resources as given, but as will be explained below, that is one of the ground rules imposed by the Soviet setting. The reasons for the distress are obvious. The only refutation would be to say that the assumptions are wrong or that the mathematics is wrong. For instance, it might be denied that factors other than labor are in short supply or that they can be substituted for labor. (This is indeed the implicit difference between the Marxist conception of value and better ones.) But such a criticism would outrage common sense. It is hard to see how the reviews could be otherwise, of course. Reviewmanship is an exacting art in the Soviet Union, and one of its first rules is to evaluate the conclusions rather than the logic of the argument.

What is really subversive about Kantorovich and Novozhilov is that they are right, and to allow them to propagate their views is to give them the victory. They have formulated the problem, found the solution, derived the corollaries, and all one can do is challenge either their formulations or their mathematics. It is disquieting to good Marxists to see such concepts as rent, returns for capital, and opportunity costs emerge as implications of assumptions with which they cannot quarrel, but this unpleasantness is no refutation. The only protection is to bar mathematicians from the temple. Once they are allowed intercourse with the rest of the intellectual community, they have a tremendous advantage. The veneration of science in the Soviet Union confers great prestige on mathematics, which is after all, the "queen and servant of science." Kantorovich is by all accounts an unassuming, even diffident, man, but shielded by mathematics he has shown no hesitation in pressing his attacks on existing Soviet value theory. At the recent conference on the use of mathematics in economics he replied quite boldly to his critics. Nemchinov in his closing remarks at the conference made a point of rebuking Kantorovich for upsetting the "creative and comradely spirit" of the conference by "underestimating and deprecating the work of Soviet economists." Just what Kantorovich had said to merit this rebuke is not revealed, but is is well known that he considers Soviet economic theory mostly claptrap. At the 1959 annual meeting of the Division of Economics, Philosophy and Law of the Academy of Sciences he expressed the following unflattering opinion of the contribution made by economists to the economic achievements of the USSR:

> How great is the role of economists in these achievements? The accumulation of practical experience in economics and planning has played a definite role here, but this has not been at all generalized by economic science. . . . In the forty-second year of the existence of the socialist state our economic science does not know precisely what the law of

value means in a socialist society or how it should be applied. It does not know what socialist rent is, or whether in general there ought to be some calculations of the effectiveness of capital investment, and if so, just how. We are offered as the latest discovery in the field of economics, for example, the proposition that "the law of value does not govern but only influences," or that "the means of production are not simply commodities but commodities of a particular kind," and so on.

The probable outcome of this co-operation with mathematicians is foreshadowed in one of Nemchinov's remarks in summing up the results of the volume on *The Application of Mathematics in Economic Research.* He warns:

> . . . the chief peril in applying mathematical methods to economics is that the qualitative nature of the economic phenomena being studied falls into oblivion. In the winged expression of V. L. Lenin, directed at idealistic theories in physics and mathematics, the perversion of the role of mathematics both in natural sciences and social sciences is that in these theories matter disappears and only equations remain.

Invoking that lost cause to defend Marxist prejudices against equations conveys a presentiment of defeat.

If our prognosis is right and these innovations are accepted after proper exegesis in Marxist terminology, they will only lead to further trouble. As explained earlier, these theories of value and allocation are still seriously deficient. They take as given some very important variables in the economic system, such as the composition of the final bill of goods and, as one aspect of this, the division of the national output into investment goods and consumption goods. To employ a distinction that played an important role in the development of Western economic thought, Kantorovich's and Novozhilov's theories are *cost* theories of value. In terms of Alfred Marshall's famous metaphor, they still imply that since one blade of the scissors is stationary (that is, that demand is given) it is the action of the other blade (cost or supply) that cuts the paper. They represent an advance over the more primitive labor-cost theory of value that Marx employed, but still fall short of complete generality.

One criticism directed by Soviet writers against Kantorovich's objectively determined valuations is that they are not absolute. One of the factors that "objectively determines" them is the composition of output, which is taken as the starting point. One of the speakers at the conference on mathematical methods in economics pointed out that whether or not the objectively determined valuations mean anything depends on the "correctness" of the output mix postulated as a constraint. He further suggests that maybe mathematical methods could fruitfully be used in illuminating what the correct output mix is. There is great mischief latent in that line of attack. This is indeed a valid criticism of both Kantorovich's and Novozhilov's theories, but their limitation of the problem of allocation to one of efficient production of a predetermined output program is founded on good reasons. To make determination of the correct bill of goods part of the problem involves asking what production is for, and leads directly to the introduction of the subjective category of utility into the analysis. Ideologically, that would be an unforgivable affront.

Novozhilov's approach contains in addition a special snare that will sooner or later cause trouble. His work has a disarming appeal since it seems to conform to the labor theory of value. He starts from the proposition that the problem is to maximize the effectiveness of labor, which sounds unexceptionable to a Marxist. Moreover, all the elements of value, including the inversely related costs, are expressed in terms of units of labor. It thus scrupulously preserves labor as the *numéraire* in which value is measured. But the consistency with the labor theory of value is completely illusory. It makes no sense to formulate the problem as one of minimizing the labor input into a given bill of goods (or to put the same idea another way, of maximizing leisure). The real problem is to maximize leisure and output together. In the Soviet setting, especially, minimizing labor input is a ridiculous goal. Nor can this absurdity be rationalized by claiming that minimizing the labor input is equivalent to maximizing output, since labor saved can be used to expand output. In Novozhilov's method labor is minimized under the condition of using up all the other inputs with which it can be combined. This flaw in the formulation of the nature of the problem is bound to be discovered sooner or later.

Furthermore, it is not difficult to imagine institutional situations in the Soviet economy where anyone trying to apply Novozhilov's method of reasoning will have to take as the point of departure a fixed labor supply and formulate his problem as one of minimizing some other input. For instance, we might realistically pose the problem of agricultural planning as one of finding the minimum capital investment consistent with the size of the agricultural population and the assigned output goal. Or planners in the railroad branch of the economy might be assigned the goal of choosing the patterns of resource use that would minimize fuel inputs, with everything else held constant. In these situations the conformity of Novozhilov's reasoning with the labor theory of value vanishes. In any of these problems the opportunity costs would emerge in terms of the input to be minimized as *numéraire*, and one would end up with a "capital" theory of value or a "fuel" theory of value. These anomalies will never be put right until the bill of goods is entered as part of the variables to be determined, which means resort to the idealistic magnitude utility as part of the explanation.

The reconciliation of two true but contradictory theories (that is, a "fuel" theory of value and the labor theory of value) is only possible when they are recognized as special cases of a general theory under different assumptions; and in the theory of value and allocation this general theory must involve some conception of utility. Utility is the more general, abstract, common denominator into which all other explanations can be translated. The discovery of this general theory and the final collapse of the labor theory of value is by no means only a hypothetical danger. As a matter of fact, the other half of the theory of value—the theory of consumption—has already been worked out and published in the Soviet Union. This is a paper by A. A. Konius in a prestigious volume of essays published by the Academy of Sciences of the USSR in honor of the eightieth birthday of S. G. Strumilin. The theory of consumption is just hanging in the air, waiting to be joined to what Novozhilov and Kantorovich have already done for the theory of production. When someone brings the two together, the rediscovery of Western value theory will be complete.

Konius poses the problem of finding the proper relationship of prices to labor input of different consumer goods for the purpose of minimizing the total labor input for a given level of what he calls vaguely "consumption." Actually the content he gives this vague term makes it identical with the "welfare" or "utility" of Western value theory. Incidentally, Konius' question is not one made up in the quiet of the professor's study but one that has long agitated those who plan the prices of consumer goods in the Soviet Union. The answer given by Western economists to this question appears in every elementary economics textbook as "prices should be proportional both to the marginal rates of substitution and the marginal rates of transformation of the goods in question." Not being accustomed to consulting this kind of source for answers to questions of socialist political economy, Konius enlisted the aid of a professor of mathematics (duly thanked in a footnote) and worked out the answer himself. Not surprisingly, he came to the same conclusion. Neither will it be a surprise to the economist that Konius could demonstrate his proposition only by specifying some assumptions about the nature of the "consumption" he was talking about. Specifically, his proof depends on the postulation of the familiar ordinal utility function or preference surface of Western economics. This assumption is there in the relatively inconspicuous form of some equations, it is true, but it is there.

Conclusion

Konius' case can serve as the thesis for our summary. The search for theoretical clarification of almost any important economic issue will ultimately require the elaboration of normative models regarding allocation of resources and conceptions of value, and these two problems ultimately merge. The rigor and power of mathematics is almost essential for describing and investigating such models, and there is thus great pressure in any science to employ mathematics. It will be difficult for economics to escape this pressure. As one indication, Nesmeyanov, the president of the Academy of Sciences, has admonished economists to make theirs a "real science" by using mathematics and modern computational technology. But when one sits down with a mathematician, as Konius did, to demonstrate a general line of argument, the mathematician's role can only be to check whether the intuitively felt conclusion does or does not follow from the assumptions, or what assumptions might be required to prove it. As the mathematician A. N. Kolmogorov remarked in a speech at the conference on mathematical methods in economics, the advantage of having mathematicians and economists cooperate with each other is that the mathematicians force the economists to define more carefully some of their fuzzy conceptions. If the conclusions are given and the task of economic science is to defend them, as Boiarskii claims in his review of Kantorovich, then it might be better to leave the conceptions fuzzy. But the really novel circumstance in the Soviet Union today is that this is no longer an adequate interpretation of the task of economic science. The planners feel so strongly the need for improvements in calculation and allocation that they must discover a more sophisticated theory of value than that willed them by Marx. It is to this end that they have delivered themselves into the hands of the mathematicians.

BREAKTHROUGH TO ECONOMICS*
· — · — · — · — · — · —

Alfred Zauberman†

A western student who, at the turn of the 1950s, thought he could detect certain signs of a radical change in Soviet economics is being proved right sooner than he could have expected. Few could foretell a few years ago that by the mid-sixties important works in Soviet economics would be published, as they actually are now, without even so much as mentioning the name Marx. The expectations of change were built up on the

*Reprinted by permission from *Survey* (July 1965), pp. 118–124.

†Dr. Alfred Zauberman is Reader, The London School of Economics and Political Science. His publications include: *Economic Imperialism: The Lesson of Eastern Europe* (1955). *Industrial Progress in Poland, Czechoslovakia, and East Germany 1937–1962* (1964). "The Soviet Debate on the Law of Value and Price Formation" in Gregory Crossman (ed) *Value and Plan* (1960), and *Aspects of Planometrics* (1968).

supposition that, once rigorous modes of thinking—through the use of mathematical apparatus—are assimilated, rationalist tendencies must penetrate the ossified economic doctrine and gain momentum, much as they were bound to be resisted by the forces of the old intellectual establishment.

The rise and the rapid career of the mathematical school in Soviet economics have been validly related to the metamorphosis of the Soviet economic milieu: to its growing maturity, complexity, diversification: to the consequent obsolescnece of Gosplan's crude instruments and techniques; and the quest for more modern ones able to cope with it. There again, hardly anybody could have predicted the acuteness and speed with which this problem would confront the leaders, accentuated as it is by a disturbing deceleration-trend in the economy's growth and by the failure of Khrushchevian tinkering with its organisation.

When thinking in terms of decisive individual contributions to the intellectual revolution, one will identify it with the creative and courageous work and untiring efforts of persuasion by Novozhilov and the late Nemchinov, and first and foremost with the conceptual discoveries of Kantorovich (of whom the other, Western, inventor of programming, Dantizig, says: 'If Kantorovich's earlier efforts had been appreciated at the time they were first presented, it is possible that linear programming would be more advanced today').

It is logical that what may be broadly described as the mathematical approach they adopt should be sooner or later recognised as the proper one for the construction of the economic plan. A mathematical programme is concerned to find the optimal solution of a given task, within limits drawn by resource scarcities and employable technologies, and this is precisely what a macro-plan is about. So it was logical that Soviet planning theory and practice, which had been laboriously developing some *partial* efficiency approaches (the search for ways of measuring the efficiency of investment projects is the most important case in point) should be made conscious at the next stage, by the new school, of global efficiency problems. This is precisely what is now happening.

Inevitably, in the first years of the new school, a great deal of effort had to be spent on inculcating the unfamiliar fundamentals and on mitigating their clash with orthodoxy. True, still in 1965, *Voprosy Ekonomiki* feels it worth while lending its pages to a polemic (Kolganov versus Novozhilov) on conformity or otherwise of the mathematicians' price concept with Marxian theory. But essentially the new school has this period behind it—the period of making the teaching palatable to the traditionalist. Rather it is symptomatic of the present climate that in his new, 1964, book Lurie can and does openly criticise Kantorovich for unnecessarily trying to prove, in his classical opus, the agreement of his solving multipliers with the labour-theory price (as Lurie argues—validly, I think—Kantorovich secures this pseudocompatibility by creating an optical illusion: by bringing into his reasoning an artificial *numéraire* of 'averaged' labour). More, it is safe to say that by now the new school has moved well beyond the monumental but rudimentary works of its founders. Broadly speaking it centres more and more on application. It becomes more and more technical. To be sure, it has some impact, if only indirect, on policy and strategic thinking, and one aspect of it may be indicated here. It is the mathematical inter-industry (input-output) analysis that has revealed the very limited meaningfulness of what was during a third of a century, a sacrosanct principle: the 'law of the faster growth of department I as against II (in Marx's dichotomy) or A as against B, heavy as against light industries (though the present writer is inclined to think that it is primarily the change in the economic milieu that has made the 'law' anachronistic and undermined its status). Generally, while focussed on techniques, the work of the new school has, in the usual course of things, a strong and growing impact on theory; it also brings into focus certain theoretical issues which transcend the boundaries of economics proper.

It is not proposed to engage here in any exposition in depth of the increasingly intricate technical issues which clearly dominate Soviet thinking at this stage. But at least one or two hints may be given. The mathematically framed inter-industry analysis is far superior as a tool for checking the coherence of a plan (and to this extent for choice-making) to the crude 'material balance,' Gosplan's main traditional instrument. But the few years of experiment with the Leontief-type input-output matrix have brought into relief its inherent rigidities. The more generalised device, Kantorovich's linear programming construct, has proved to be still more restrictive in empirical work, although it is the achievements rather than the failings that deserve note and appreciation. The work of the Gosplan Institute of Economic Research, culminating in the elaboration of a large-scale inter-industry balance for 1970, is remarkable, and so is the achievement of the Academy's Economics-Mathematics Institute in constructing a dynamic model of such a balance for the calculation of the 1965–70 plan extended into a linear programme. While the limitations encountered in such ambitious work must have bred a good deal of frustration, they have also provided a stimulant to more and more sophisticated inquiries. It is gratifying to see that it is this kind of work—in which requirements of practice push into theoretically important areas of exploration—that absorbs the minds of a pleiad of first-class students. The change from the arid exegetical exercises of the past is indeed striking.

To mention a few of their problems. A good deal of effort is concerned with breaking out of the shackles of linearity, which does not correspond with most of the technical and behavioural relationships with which the planner has to deal in the real world. Hence the effort devoted to non-linear programming. Many of the phenomena with which the planner is daily concerned are quantifiable only as integers: hence the active interest in integer-programming. The assumed constancy of parameters—in particular the constancy of fixed technological coefficients—is one of those rigidities of classical inter-industry and mathematical-programming constructs which depart from reality. Hence the attempt to develop what is known as parametric programming. All these are still very young fields of scientific effort; in hardly any of them has a definitive breakthrough been achieved.

Further, the original classical constructs are static *par excellence*. Obviously, in trying to shape economic life, the planner must be dynamic. Hence the quest for ways of making these constructs dynamic. In this quest, dynamic multi-stage modelling is winning the day. Fortunately, the work of Pontriagin and his team has been made accessible to Western students in English translation—one of the very few among Russian works of this class—and it instantly won their admiration. The story of this work—which relies on the inductive principle, and has a family kinship with, but is independent of, Bellman's dynamic programming—is in many respects symptomatic of what is happening these days in Soviet economics. It has its roots in the pioneering work of Soviet scholars not sufficiently known in the West, especially Feldbaum and Lerner. It was originally conceived as an exercise in pure mathematics, perhaps with an eye to technological application. Only *ex post* was its relevance for controlling economic processes (proceeding stage-wise from a given status towards desired objectives) discerned. It is relevant in particular as a possible means of giving formal shape to continuous—'rolling' or 'sliding' —planning, which has been favoured for some time by the Gosplan and Soviet leaders as a way of coping with the growing intricacy of the country's economic life. To give yet another example: only a few years ago Pugachev was known just as an authority on probabilistic functions. Until the 1960s he did not make any direct contribution to Soviet economics: today he is—and deservedly—one of its leading lights. (Once the implied assumption of the omniscient, all-foreseeing planner is dropped, it becomes essential—in one technical way or another—to tackle probabilistic elements.) This is the kind of penetration by pure mathematics that is fertilising Soviet economics.

These changes were bound to pose the question of rationality—the question, that is, how rationally to relate means to ends in Soviet economic policies. For, it one tries to state the policy-tasks in mathematical form, one has to put down in rigorous terms what it is that one wants to maximise (or minimise). Vague platitudes à la Stalin's fundamental law of socialism would no longer do; nor could the economists accept, when it was spelt out, what had been the *de facto* Soviet strategic aim for decades—growth seemingly for growth's sake. When at least it was forced into a rigorous frame, the inquiry came up against extremely tricky matters of social-political philosophy as well as techniques, which landed it in the hitherto ideologically banned area of welfare economics, complete with the Soviet-Marxian *bête noire,* the concept of marginal utility: more precisely, it is tending to move towards a Bergson-type utility function. When consumption is explicitly set as the ultimate end, a number of questions unfamiliar to Soviet thinking habits are raised, questions as to how to integrate collective (or planner's) and consumer's preferences: how to schedule the optimised consumption-accumulation processes through time, within a given time-horizon; and how to deal with economic processes generating results beyond this horizon. And, to the extent that the planner is the guardian of the unbounded future, how technically to cope with infinity. Important exploratory work in this field is being done by several economists; here Pugachev, Volkonsky, Dudkin, and Girsanov are particularly worthy of mention. In relating questions of techniques at present in focus to changes in the fabric of the economy, the connection between these problems and the change in the Soviet environment have to be noted—the change that favours the shift from the traditional Soviet resource-type to the demand-type of planning.

Further, in trying to give a formal frame to procedures for shaping an efficient path for the country's economy, the planometric school came up against what Bellman calls the 'curse of dimensions'; in the economist's jargon the problem of aggregation. The gist of the aggregation dilemma is how to reconcile the exacting degree of detail required of a plan (to make it realistic) with the limits imposed by manageability at the prevailing level of techniques. For example, how to use a formalised inter-industry system designed for about 130 branches and several hundred commodities (this corresponds to the present state of Soviet matrix construction) in running an economy whose commodity nomenclature has something like 15,000,000 items. This is yet another field in which work, interesting both theoretically and technically, is being done, especially by Gavrilets, though the best one can hope is to find some tolerable way out of what is an insoluble dilemma. (I would take issue with those, in both the West and the East, who argue that this and other weaknesses of formalised planning make it intrinsically less viable than the traditional crude Soviet methods. Surely the troubles of aggregation, of assumed linearities, or of uncertainties, and so on, have been with the Soviet planner for nearly forty years; they only remained unarticulated. Like Molière's Monsieur Jourdain, he has been dealing with them without being conscious of it. More articulation can only give better insight.)

The curse of astronomic dimensions, and a few more troublesome matters mentioned here, immensely complicate the key task of providing the economy with parameters of calculation, prices and rates of interest. It is precisely Kantorovich's merit to have given Soviet economists the concept of a price which corresponds to an efficient allocation of scarce resources (with given policy postulates and objectives), alien to traditional Soviet doctrine. The system of such prices—Kantorovich's multipliers, or, in his terminology, 'objectively conditioned valuations'—would then form the 'dual' of the original efficiency problem, the 'primal'. The two are almost symmetric: as it were, two faces of the same thing; they are indeed, algebraically, a check on each other. Hence the theoretician's precept to the planner: use as convient one of the two to solve the other. The mathematical duality concept is beautiful in its simplicity, but its application in planning—on the scale of the national economy—perplexes the Soviet practician. He knows now that he can get an efficient physical plan if he has a system of efficient prices, and that he can get a system of efficient prices if he has an efficient plan. But what if he has neither? The Soviet mathematical-economics school has not found a satisfying answer to what is empirically the crucial question; and in trying to do so it is divided against itself.

Out of this quandary the idea has emerged and gained ground in recent years in Soviet economics that a practicable solution can be found only in some systematic step-by-step (iterative) procedure of handling information flows and counter-flows, supported by powerful computational methodology and machines. Thus Soviet planometrics has now broadly oriented itself towards cybernetics (ironically, Norbert Wiener thought that one of the fields where his brain-child was unlikely to be helpful was economics), towards the theory of information and control systems and all the other novel disciplines in their neighbourhood. The ultimate stage of development of the economic mechanism is seen as one of a self-regulated, self-teaching system. This is the formative background of the scheme for planning and running the economy officially adopted last year by the *Mezhduvedomstvenny nauchny sovet*, worked out principally, it seems, by Pugachev and Fedorenko. The whole country would be spanned by a giant communication network with some fifty nodal computer-stations, each with a capacity of around $1\frac{1}{2}$ million operations a second, linking up the enterprises and the planning centre horizontally and vertically; a system gathering and processing information and issuing parameters of calculation. The conception is inspired by yet another of Dantzig's famous theoretical discoveries (the 'decomposition principle'), but it is an original and elegant variant (technically formulated as 'aggregation by constraints'). The guiding idea in this variant is to reduce by feedback-planning the load of repetitive rounds (iterations), a load that may in practice be just as heavy as the burden of dimensions from which it was meant to offer deliverance. The approach is one of pragmatically regulating the measure of optimality. That is, it aims at some sufficient approximation, at some second-best *sub*-optimum rather than optimum-optimorum (the theorising planometrician's will-o'-the-wisp, which in any case is beyond reach owing to the imperfections of data, chance disturbance, and so on.) This is to recognise the fact that planning is only an art of the possible. Even then it would be extremely risky for a student to commit himself as to when, and indeed whether, the scheme will prove operational: it is certainly not so at present. Its prospects would be brighter if it proved to be true, as some authorities of Dantzig's calibre believe, that mankind is just now on the threshold of an era of 'computational explosion.'

As the theoretical gropings have crystallised in empirical schemes of the Pugachev-Fedorenko kind, Soviet economics has found itself at a significant cross-roads in its thinking about the feasible and desirable economic mechanism for socialism. The old doctrinaire attitudes have been dropped. In his last published paper Nemchinov warned his readers that in real life differences in economic mechanisms represent only degrees of compromise between the two extremes of a centralized purpose-directed mechanism of management, and a decentralised self-regulating mechanism. The context, incidentally, was French 'indicative' planning as against the Soviet 'normative' type of planning. How far Soviet thought has travelled from the dogma that the Soviet mechanism based on Marxian-Leninist doctrine is a category in itself and has not and cannot have any points of tangency with one peculiar to capitalism!

The implication of Nemchinov's ideas for the moderniser of the Soviet mechanism would seem to be broadly this. You may get efficiency in a socialist economy either by relying on prices provided by a competitive market installed under some kind of indicative planning; or, alternatively, by efficiency-computation; or by some mixture of the two. In his last articles addressed to a wider public, Nemchinov in fact discreetly tried to pave the psychological way to such a marriage. He also gave qualified support to the celebrated Liberman proposals, as did other members of the mathematical school. For to order the manager of a firm to try to get his profits as high as possible does fit perfectly into the mathematician's model of an efficiency-oriented system. There is, however, a serious snag. It stands to reason that maximising profit can lead to efficient choices only if the profit itself is calculated within the frame of efficiency-prices, and it is the weakness of the Liberman proposals, possibly a fatal weakness, that they fail to secure a mechanism (market or computation) which would supply the manager with such prices.

At some stage, as it now appears, some planometricians moved away from Nemchinov in their view of the desired or required mechanism. In its cradle, Soviet planometrics was more or less explicitly wedded to decentralism, but it is not necessarily so today. Indeed, there is a wing in it inclined to draw the full consequences from the logic of a highly automated control regime. This could perhaps be put very roughly in these terms: What is the point in simulating perfect computation by means of inevitably imperfect markets, if this is precisely the job of the computer (assuming you have dependable information and the right mathematical algorithm)? So this wing has turned into one of ultra-centralisers. However, tc do them justice, there is a dialectic in the final consummation of their solution. In his latest work, the architect of the famous original model of market socialism, Oskar Lange, discusses the minimax principle in relation to collective decision-making, and concludes with these words:

> Here we have a mathematical solution to the problem of finding the minimax of elements of some matrix: it can therefore be carried out by a mathematical machine. This opens up to a socialist society the possibility of automation of administrative processes. In agreement with the postulates of socialist democracy, all members of the society would register their preferences (this too could be mechanised), and the decision would be computed by 'electronic brains' on the minimax principle. Such decisions would be the objective logical outcome of valuations by individuals, free from arbitrariness and subjectivism, and from possible distortions by bureaucratic decision-making agencies (*Optymalne Decyzje*, 1964, p. 294).

Lange also hints broadly at the possible significance of automating collective decision-making processes for the issue of the withering away of the state under communism. For Lenin, electricity plus soviets equalled socialism; in the planometrician's ultimate vision electronics minus soviets could equal communism.

PLANNERS' PREFERENCES, PRIORITIES, AND REFORMS*
— · — · — · — · — · — · — · — · — · — · —

Alec Nove†

The object of this paper is to examine some concepts used in discussions of Soviet-type economies, and to relate them to some of the practical issues which are being debated in the Soviet Union in the course of the search for new and more efficient forms of managing the economy.

One such concept, widely used in discussions in the West, is "planners' preferences." These are often contrasted with consumers' preferences, and we are told that Soviet prices could be, or should be, rational

*Reprinted by permission of the publishers and author from *Economic Journal* (June 1966), pp. 267–277.

†Alec Nove is James Bonar Professor of Economics and Director of the Institute of Soviet and East European studies, University of Glasgow. His publications include: *The Soviet Economy* (1961, 1965), *Soviet Economic Strategy* (1959), *Economic Rationality and Soviet Politics* (1964), and *The Soviet Middle East* with J. A. Newth (1967).

in terms of planners' preferences. Some critics refer to the conflict between the two types of preferences said to be inherent in a Soviet-type economy. It would follow that the recent reform discussions, associated with the name of Liberman, represent an attempt to substitute consumers' for planners' preferences, and that therefore this is a change which would challenge the very foundation of the planning system. In my view, this line of thought can lead to confusion.

Let us first examine consumers' goods. What are planners' preferences? Are they represented by the product mix which state industry actually makes available to the consumer? Surely this can not be, for such an assumption is unrealistic on two counts. First, it excludes the possibility of error, of miscalculation, of faulty communication. Secondly, *it treats "the planners" as if they were one body with identical interests, though they are sometimes at odds with one another.* What happens by no means always accords with what the planners wish to happen. The word "wish" has two meanings here. The planners may wish, *i.e.*, order, something, and what actually occurs is not what they intended. Or their "wishes" may indeed have been carried out, but the orders themselves may have been mistaken, in the sense that they were not in accord with the objectives of the planners.

Let us illustrate these propositions with examples taken from the real Soviet world. The product mix actually available, at established prices, is in evident conflict with consumer demand. Stocks in the trading network grow rapidly, the retail trade plan is not fulfilled, there are queues of dissatisfied customers for items in short supply, money savings of the population increase and this last phenomenon is treated by Soviet analysis as a byproduct of the citizens' inability to obtain the goods they need.

What planners did, or could, "prefer" this situation? Their reaction to it shows that they regard it as a consequence of their errors, not of their preferences. Once one rejects the mistaken concept that the planners "prefer" what actually is available, one starts seeking causes. The planners could have misjudged demand. Or deficiencies in the distribution network could have caused the excess stocks to accumulate in one area while people were queuing for these same goods in another area. Or the price system could be clumsy and irrational. Or, quite frequently, a global plan which might be correctly related to aggregate demand is distorted in the process of disaggregation. Thus, a plan to produce a given volume of wool cloth, shoes, women's dresses is fulfilled in detail in such a way that the customers cannot obtain the design, quality or size that they happen to want. This could happen because the plan is expressed in terms of total quantity at a given average cost; or because the financial organs exert pressure to ensure the output of items which, though not in demand, carry a high rate of turnover tax; or because some intermediate authority (region or ministry) is trying to fulfil a plan in terms of gross value of output, and so on. All these various distortions are well known to students of the Soviet economy. All arise either out of ambiguities and contradictions in the plan, or (and) out of conflict and contradictions within the planning system. It is important to emphasize that the planners, or the State, cannot be treated as a single unit with uniform goals and identical interests, and I will return to this point later on.

Peter Wiles once pointed out that in the field of consumers' goods planners have no rational reason to prefer a pattern of output which does not conform to consumer demand.[1] There are, of course, exceptions to this in every country. In Great Britain we tax spirits and cigarettes very heavily, do not tax books, and provide cheap milk and cod-liver oil to mothers. In the Soviet Union spirits are also taxed very heavily, children's clothes are priced low and pop records are taxed more highly than symphonies and folk songs. These examples show that there are some cases where the State does consciously try to stimulate one kind of demand and to restrict other kinds. But Wiles's principle holds over most of the field, and planners' failures to provide the goods that are wanted are mostly unintentional.

Of course, planners prefer to be able to prefer. In other words, they have a vested interest in a decision-making structure that gives them power to make decisions. It is also a social-economic fact that, for various reasons, public authorities in charge of resource allocation often do not seem to care much for the convenience of the citizens. But this is quite another question. It does not mean that the planners prefer any particular bill of goods. They do not consciously desire that the customer be unable to obtain what she wants, though the institutional arrangements are such that she may be unable to do so.

None of the above argument would lose its force if the planners so manipulated prices that they cleared the market of the goods they had decided to produce. This is the situation envisaged by Lange (in 1938), when he wrote:

> One may well imagine a system in which production and the allocation of resources are guided by a preference scale fixed by the Central Planning Board, while the price system is used to distribute the consumers' goods produced. In such a system there is freedom of choice in consumption, but the consumers have no influence whatever on the decisions of the managers of production and of the productive resources. There would be two sets of prices of consumers' goods. One would be the market prices at which the goods are sold to the consumers;

[1] See his *Political Economy of Communism* (Oxford: Blackwell, 1963).

the other, the accounting prices derived from the preference scale fixed by the Central Planning Board.[2]

In such circumstances, too, the bill of goods actually produced could be a consequence of all the distortions already referred to, plus competition between different departments for investment resources, which, since capital has been provided free of charge, is really a form of empire-building in which success results from political "pull" or a well-drafted memorandum. Lange's "preference scale fixed by the Central Planning Board" is a myth, if by this is meant a detailed bill of goods so preferred. In Soviet reality there are very large variations in the difference between "the market price at which goods are sold to the consumer" and the "accounting prices" (*i.e.*, factory prices net of tax). But this, in most cases, is not the consequence of conscious design. Thus, radios, watches and cameras sell close to cost price, while wool textiles and sugar bear high turnover tax rates. This only suggests relative over-investment in radios, watches and cameras, and not anybody's preference scale.

A somewhat similar point could be made in respect of producers' goods. Here it is not disputed that planners make errors. They may choose a higher-cost variant, or issue orders at a level of aggregation which causes subordinate authorities to distort the product mix. The reasons which cause textile factories to produce cloth which is not in demand also cause rolling mills to make excessively heavy metal parts, in this instance to fulfil a plan target expressed in tons. Many production and investment choices are made in ignorance of cost considerations, or by blindly following a primitive and out-of-date input-output ("material balances") table, or because prices are illogical or irrational, or through regional or departmental vested interests. In the case of producer's goods, it is still the rule of the Soviet Union that allocation is by administrative order, at fixed prices, and so any imbalance between authorised demand and available supply must by definition be due to miscalculation. (The sheer scale of the planners' task makes such miscalculations all too common.) Prices, roughly based on average costs of several years ago, have hitherto played a largely passive role, and it seems unreasonable to assign to such prices any very precise economic significance. It is true, as Bergson has pointed out several times, that costs, on which these prices are based, are largely composed (directly or indirectly) of wages, and that, labour being free to move, a labour market exists. To that extent, labour cost as computed through wages has real significance. However, it has always seemed to me to be doubtful if this is a sufficient condition for regarding such prices as rational in any terms. The resource allocation decisions, which cause the

[2]*On the Economic Theory of Socialism,* edited by B. Lippincott (McGraw-Hill paperback edition, 1964), p. 96.

demand for different kinds of labour to change, and thus affect costs, cannot be assumed to conform to planners' preferences, for reasons already abundantly explored. Wiles has argued that planners may be irrational in what they prefer, which is also a legitimate point of view. An example might be the reported preference of Stalin for the great works of Stalin to be visible from the planet Mars. But this, at least, was one despot's notion of the satisfaction of his (despotic) wants, whereas planners' allocation decisions are often due to an inability to define and observe efficiency criteria which they would like to observe, if only they knew what they were.

We must now pass on to another and related question, that of the priority of producers' goods, and of a high rate of investment over current consumption. Whatever may or may not be the planners' view of a desirable product mix of consumers' goods, they do undoubtedly assert the priority of the future as against the present. Indeed, there have been times when the pattern of consumers' goods production was largely pre-determined by the productive capacity already available, or by the supply of domestic raw materials, since virtually all investments and all imports served the expansion of the producers' goods sectors. In the field of foreign trade British controls operated in a not dissimilar way: thus, in 1948 goods were divided into "essential" and "less essential," and we imported raw rubber, cotton, and certain capital goods which could not be made at home, and severely restricted imports of clothing, luxury goods and TV sets. This is undeniably an example of a substitution of "political" choice for market forces, though it is noteworthy that, in Britain then and in Russia now, the price system was so artificial that it could not be used to express or transmit consumers' preferences.

The allocation of resources (domestic and foreign) between current consumption and accumulation to a great extent predetermines the division of actual output between what the Soviet writers call producers' goods and consumers' goods. [3] Obviously, investment must take material forms if it is to be a reality in any economy. (Perhaps one reason for our own chronic balance-of-payments deficits lies in the fact that when investment increases so many of the investment goods are *not* made in this country, thus greatly increasing our propensity to import. But that is another story.) Can we say that in the Soviet Union, in a way fundamentally different to the west, planners—and not the citizens as a whole—decide what proportion of the G.N.P. should be devoted to investment or to communal as against individual consumption?

---

[3] Peter Wiles pointed out, in his above-cited work, that this is the input–output consequence of a high rate of investment and of growth.

Here again, we must avoid excessively sweeping conclusions. There is the repeated assertion in the U.S.S.R. of a special kind of priority for producers' goods, even though the dogmatic assumption that output of such goods *must* grow faster than that of consumers' goods is at last being abandoned. One can indeed establish a Soviet "model" in which the volume of investment is a political decision, wholly financed by forced savings, through the prices of goods sold by the State. This can be contrasted with a western model in which the rate of investment reflects the "time-preference of the community" and the behaviour of individual savers. But this is a little far-fetched. Part of the investment of any western country is state-financed. Much of private investment is in fact financed out of retained profits, *i.e.*, through the prices of goods. A citizen who buys, say, stockings in the Soviet Union is making an involuntary contribution to investment funds through the price he pays. But a British citizen does the same thing too, by contributing to the profits of the company that makes the stockings. It does not seem a tenable proposition to assert that the first is a case of forced saving and the second a manifestation of the free choice of a sovereign consumer. Admittedly, one could treat the company's decision about investment as involving choice between the distribution of the profit as dividend and its re-investment. It is not suggested that the situation in east and west is identical. The institutional arrangements are indeed very different. Therefore, while a conflict between present consumption and future needs exists everywhere, it is resolved differently. However, it is not very realistic to contrast the two systems as if they actually conformed to imaginary models. In fact, there is involuntary saving in both. Although, especially at some periods, the *scale* of forced saving in the Soviet Union was exceptionally great, it is difficult to visualise, *conceptually*, a conflict in this respect between planners' and consumers' preferences peculiar to a Soviet-type economy.

As for the decision concerning the scale of social as against individual consumption, it is hard to discern any difference of principle between the Soviet Union and, say, Great Britain or France. Social services are financed by taxation and compulsory levies of various kinds, in east and west. If in this respect "planners' preferences" contradict "consumers' preferences" they do so in all these countries.

It is also desirable to make clear what is meant by "the final bill of goods," in the context of real or imagined reforms to the Soviet planning system. Planners are criticised—by Wiles and Nemchinov, for instance—for fixing targets for intermediate goods and basic materials and for devising a possible pattern of end-products from them, rather than vice versa. This could well be a valid criticism. However, one should be clear what sort of final bill of goods the critic has in mind. The State as such has, of course, its own claim on resources for its own purposes. These would include, for instance, missiles, submarines, the collected works of Lenin, school desks and smallpox vaccine. All these, except the works of Lenin, are required also by the British State. For the rest, it is either a question of correctly estimating or projecting consumer demand or of finding the best means (machinery, factory buildings, materials, fuels, etc.) to achieve the desired ends. As already pointed out, the planners have no "final bill of goods" in the real world. No doubt planners can and do make estimates which include a pattern of consumption. Even in the Soviet Union, there are studies of income elasticities, designed to aid planners in this task. However, we must distinguish between aggregate long-term projections and operationally valid disaggregation. In the first case we are dealing with, say, textiles or clothing in general. Planners have not, for reasons already analysed, any very clear preference *qua* planners about textiles, but they may proceed intelligently to estimate demand changes and seek to provide for the necessary capacity and inputs. (They do this also, as they must, for basic materials and fuels.) This can form an integral part of a plan for 1970. However, this level of aggregation will not ensure that blue woolen skirts of a given type are available in 1966 in Uzbekistan. Similarly, a global plan for, say, spare parts for farm machinery will not—even if globally correct—ensure the availability of carburettors for a particular type of tractor in any given area at the appropriate time. Plainly, these are quite different kinds of problems. Reformers such as Professor Liberman, and other "decentralisers," are concerned with micro-economic adjustments, and assert that contractual relationships which convey user demand directly to the producer can help to ensure that the right things are produced. The hierarchical planning system which aggregates requirements and issues (necessarily aggregated) instructions to meet them, *i.e.*, the "command economy" of the traditional type, cannot ensure that requirements are rationally met, and this applies to the product mix and to the choice between and supply of inputs. The reformers are thus concerned with blue woolen skirts and carburettors this year, not with clothing and farm machinery in 1970. They are concerned with operational decisions, not with aggregate long-term projections.

The pre-war Lange must be regarded as having been unrealistic when he imagined that prices could be imposed on enterprises. In his words: "The technique of attaining this end is very simple [*sic*]; the central planning board has to fix prices and see to it that all managers of plants, industries and resources do their accounting on the basis of the prices fixed by the central planning board."[4] Would it were simple! It is not surprising

---

[4]*Op. cit.,* p. 81.

that every serious reform proposal, whether it be by Liberman in the Soviet Union of Šik in Czechoslovakia, envisages some price flexibility. The number of prices which would have to be individually determined by the authorities would clearly run into far too many millions to be manageable on a rational basis.

It is in the light of these considerations, too, that one must view the role of computers and of programming. This is a vast and complex subject, which can only be mentioned briefly here.

The computer's value in drafting consistent long-term plans, in speeding up and thus greatly facilitating the process of iteration, is not in dispute. Nor is it to be doubted that computers will be widely used in Soviet planning, as they are in many western firms, to find solutions to particular problems in various sectors of the economy. However, a *system* of centrally directed computers which would permit the retention of *operational* microeconomic control at the centre is surely a fantasy. Or, to be precise, it is a fantasy for many years to come. It is already possible to conceive of a fully cybernetised system in which everything is encompassed. On a less ambitious scale, there are the "two-level planning" experiments of Kornai and Liptak in Hungary. For the immediate future, however, Liberman-style reforms are necessary, and do not conflict with the further development of the computer as an aid to planning; the most eminent of the "mathematicians," Kantorovich, has said this quite clearly.[5] Similarly, Nemchinov, a leading reformer, sought to combine macro-economic "econometric" planning with extensive micro-economic devolution to enterprises, and even competition for orders.[6] All this would imply the dismantlement of part of the existing system of administrative allocation of inputs and of the micro-planning of output.

Therefore proposals for micro-economic decentralisation and for the use of computers to facilitate central planning are being made simultaneously, and sometimes by the same persons. There is no necessary contradiction between them. The reform proposals now being implemented also involve a debate concerning the proper location of decision-making, and this in turn raises issues such as the availability at various levels of the necessary information, the size of management units in different branches of economic activity and so on. One must not be tempted into over-simplification, and contrast an imaginary "command economy" in which super-planners decide everything with an equally imaginary decentralisation of all decision-making to enterprise directors, guided by the profit

---

[5] *Voprosy ekonomiki*, No. 9, 1964, p. 811.

[6] *Kommunist*, No. 5, 1964. This was one of his last articles, as he died later in the year. He performed great services to Soviet economics.

motive. It is evident, if only from the experience of western countries, that there is need for variety, that no single pattern of organisation or of pricing can suit the entire economy. A Soviet enterprise corresponds to a plant. A Soviet enterprise making, say, caustic soda therefore corresponds to a sub-unit of one of the divisions of Imperial Chemical Industries Ltd. Has the manager of such a plant in England any greater decision-making powers than a director of a Soviet enterprise now possesses? This is very doubtful. If it is rational to give such a director freedom to respond autonomously to price-and-profit stimuli in his production and investment programmes, then it would be rational to break up I.C.I. Examples can be multiplied. Thus, it is at the very least not self-evident, if western experience is taken as a guide, that "Liberman" type reforms are universally applicable, or that management at plant level ought always to be given much greater autonomy. No one doubts that the output of, say, clothing factories could be more expeditiously adjusted to requirements by microeconomic decentralisation of management, but even there the Soviet reformers are experimenting with grouping together enterprises to form larger productive units, to which they give the name *firma*, "firm." Similarly, one can envisage a situation in which some prices can be left free to fluctuate under virtually free-market conditions, while others are fixed by ministries. This, for example, is an integral part of recent reforms in Czechoslovakia. This, too, corresponds to western reality, with its mixture of free and "administered" prices, especially if one bears in mind that the analogue to the managing director of I.C.I. is a comrade holding the rank of minister.

Therefore the solution which is being sought will contain elements of market and of administrative planning, of centralisation and decentralisation. It is surely unrealistic to adopt an "either-or" approach; it is simply not true that they (or we) must either adopt the whole free-market system or reassert total "command" planning, neither of which have in fact existed in pure form anywhere. There can be viable positions in between these extremes.

But not all intermediate positions are viable. To find a balance between central macro-economic planning and micro-economic "market" flexibility is a very difficult task, especially as the process must begin in a situation of strains, shortages, irrational prices and long-established administrative "rationing" of inputs. Perhaps the key difficulty concerns the control over investment.

The problem may be best seen by imagining that it is decided that all current production decisions be left to the free play of supply and demand, while the central planners take all the major investment decisions.

The first point to make is that a sizeable part of current output consists of those goods which make a reality of the investment plan. Therefore, if the State controls the bulk of investment and does not directly control the current production programme of enterprises making investment goods there is at least the possibility of something going badly wrong. True, a simplified model can be imagined in which enterprises are neatly divided into those making investment goods and those making consumers' goods, and in which the former can only get orders from the State, as the sole "investor." This, however, is unrealistic on two grounds. First, the enterprises making investment goods, plus those who supply them with inputs, often make consumers' goods, or provide inputs for industries making consumers' goods. This is too obvious to need elaboration. It therefore follows that there could be unbalance and disequilibria which adversely affect the fulfilment of the investment plan.

Secondly, we must now return to the point made earlier, concerning the unreality of imagining the State and the planners to be a unified group with single interests and objectives. In practice, there are many pressure groups. Some are familiar in the west also. Thus, someone is doubtless strongly making a case for necessary expenditures on building more houses, schools, hospitals. In addition, the separate economic departments, ministries, committees, press their own claim. Regional officials (and this includes party officials) argue for "their" projects. [7] Enterprises press for grants to finance extensions or to re-equip the factory. In practice, of course, various subordinate authorities and enterprises do make their own investment plans. These sometimes depend on grants from the (central) budget, or are limited by the Government's insistence on authorising every project over a certain size, and/or by global maxima of investment expenditures. However, enterprises even now have some funds of their own for financing decentralised investments, and the growing practice of allowing the banks to grant credits for this purpose provides another source of funds. All this adds up to an amount which has often been substantially in excess of the financial and material resources available, even after cuts by the central planners. The decisions taken in September 1965 will lead to a substantial increase in decentralised investments.

Soviet writers are conscious of the problem of over-investment, and have been seeking a diagnosis of its causes. Here is one such diagnosis:

> The system of evaluating the performance of productive units, of regional economic councils, of whole sectors, creates excessive demand for investments. Plan indicators of the volume of output, of reduction in costs and of increases in labour productivity can all be more easily fulfilled if more investment resources are received. . . Enterprises which achieve the same labour productivity with a smaller basic capital usually receive absolutely no reward for this. . . It will be possible to reduce the demand for investments if evaluation of economic performance, and

[7] The report of the December 1964 session of the Supreme Soviet, to cite an example, is full of this sort of thing.

material incentives take into account the extent to which additional capital is used. [8]

Other writers have pointed to an underestimation of depreciation and replacement, and also of the actual cost of construction, which "for 475 major construction sites, . . . exceeded estimated costs by 25%." This lack of realism in investment planning "leads to an unjustified expansion of the building programme, which in the last analysis creates overstrain."[9] These are only some of the more recent writings on the subject, and are cited here only to demonstrate that this tendency is known and is causing concern.

It is true that one reason for excessive investment applications is that the money is "free" to the recipient. Under present rules there is no interest levied on basic capital, and a grant from the state budget is non-returnable. If a charge were made, some reduction in the flow of applications might occur. The reforms announced by Kosygin in September 1965 envisage a capital charge, and the bonus system has been altered to encourage enterprises to economise in the use of capital. Outright grants will gradually be replaced by long-term credits. None the less, demand may still be excessive. Yugoslav experience shows that "socialist enterprises" can over-apply for capital, even if they must borrow from a bank, even if there is an interest charge, and indeed even if they have to submit to severe cross-examination on the expected rate of return. The snag is that, while capital for expansion is attractive for the enterprise, its possible inability to repay is not associated with any effective sanctions. The manager can, of course, be dismissed, but by the time the chickens come home to roost he may well have been transferred. The point is by no means a frivolous one. The author of these lines was told both in Prague and in Belgrade that one of the major problems of their systems is how to devise effective (non-criminal) penalties, for instance for overbidding. This makes indirect, "monetary," control hard to operate effectively.

Below the level of the centre it pays everyone to begin as many investment projects as possible, because it strengthens their hand in bidding for another instalment of funds (or a permit to continue) in the year following. This, too, contributes to the notorious *rasplyenie sredstv* ("scattering of resources" over too many investments), the denunciation of which is a regular feature of the Finance Minister's budget speech. Shortages of materials and delays in delivery of equipment also help to prolong the period of construction and the volume of unfinished work. This is one manifestation of over-investment.

[8] K. Popadyuk, *Ekonomicheskaya gazeta,* July 7, 1964, p. 5.

[9] Y. Kvasha and V. Krasovski, *Voprosy ekonomiki,* No. 7, 1965, pp. 3, 4.

So the central planners are under heavy pressure from the lower echelons. But simultaneously they are under pressure from above, because the party leadership aims at maximising the rate of growth. This—as the Czech economist Goldmann has observed in a most original and stimulating article[10]—leads to a recurrent tendency to over-invest, and when critical shortages develop, has sometimes caused a sharp reduction in (in Czechoslovakia even a halting of) growth, which Goldmann treats as a species of business cycle.

The effect of over-investment is to create unplanned shortages, unexpected snags. This leads to repeated amendments of plans, current as well as long term. And it is precisely here that one does see planners' preferences asserting themselves, in a very real way, against consumers' preferences. When unexpected shortages develop, planning officials (and also party officials at various levels) intervene to say whose supplies should be cut off, what investment projects should be halted, who is to be allowed to use scarce rail wagons and so forth. By long-established tradition, they tend to opt for the future against the present, for investment against consumption, for factories rather than housing or schools, and steel and engineering factories rather than textile mills and agriculture. These priorities can be, perhaps are being, modified. But so long as there are chronic shortages and bottlenecks, some priorities there must be. These affect a wide range of producers' goods.

It is the essence of the Liberman type of reform that enterprises must be free to place orders for the inputs they require. Logically, therefore, the input-providers must themselves be free to plan on the basis of their customers' requirements. Thus, market forces, expressing consumer demand, would "permeate" a large part of the economy. As already argued at length, this would not raise issues of principle over the substitution of consumers' for planners' preferences. But it could lead to chaos if the total demand for resources significantly exceeds availabilities. This undoubtedly worries the planners. It is a precondition of the effectiveness of this kind of reform that excess demand be checked, and that known or anticipated shortages become the subject of appropriate production or investment decisions, bearing in mind that there is no capital market which could permit the transfer of investment recovery from one enterprise (or section) to another. Soviet economic officials are accustomed to cope with these problems by allocating resources administratively. They have yet to learn control by what the reformers call "economic means." Yet they must do so if the reforms adopted in September 1965 are to make a decisive difference to planning methods and the performance of the economy.

[10]Reprinted in *Economics of Planning* (Oslo), No. 2, 1964, pp. 99 ff.

2. SOVIET ECONOMIC REFORMS

*THE SOVIET PLANNING PENDULUM**
· — · — · — · — · — · — · — · —

Leon Smolinski and Peter Wiles†

There has been growing recognition in the USSR during recent months that the present planning system is a serious bottleneck which could impede further economic growth and technical progress.

According to an estimate by the well-known mathematician, Glushkov, Vice-President of the Ukrainian Academy of Science, under existing methods the volume of planning tends to increase at least as the square of output. Unless the planning system is drastically reformed, Glushkov predicts that the amount of planning work will have to increase 36-fold by 1980, requiring the services of the whole adult population of the USSR. This is, of course, an oblique way of saying that the output targets on which the whole ambitious program of "building communism" is based will not be met unless new planning methods are adopted.

Academician A. Dorodnitsyn concurs: the task of planning Soviet industrial production is some 1,600 times more complex now that it was in 1928, but planning methods have remained largely unchanged. While anyone knows, he says, that a giant hydroelectric station such as Krasnoyarsk cannot be built with spades, not everyone grasps the fact that "such a complex economy as ours cannot be directed with the aid of abacus, paper and pencil."

An enormous army of employees, exclaims another famous mathematician, Professor L. A. Liusternik, is busy collecting and processing economic data—and the techniques at their disposal are exactly the same as in the Muscovite government offices (*"prikazy"*) of the 17th century, except that the pencil has replaced the quill-pen.

Glushkov's predicted multiplication of planners is inconsistent with the traditional Soviet denials of any such tendency. Published Soviet statistics show an actual decrease of administrative personnel in recent years, but they are not too conclusive: a substantial proportion of data

*Reprinted by permission from *Problems of Communism* (Nov.–Dec. 1963), pp. 21–34.

†Dr. Leon Smolinski is Associate Professor of Economics, Boston College, and Associate, Russian Research Center, Harvard University. His publications include: "The Scale of Soviet Industrial Establishments," *American Economic Review* (May 1962), "What next in Soviet Planning?" *Foreign Affairs* (July 1964), and "The Soviet Economy," *Survey* (April 1966). He is also co-author of *Polish National Income and Product in 1954, 1955, and 1956* (1965). All footnotes deleted.

collection, record-keeping, bookkeeping and other paper work in industry, *e.g.,* is normally performed in shops by foremen and other people classified as production workers. Also, enterprises may find it expedient to report some administrative personnel under other labels. In any event, there is other evidence from Soviet sources that counters the official statistics: according to one recent estimate, 6.1 million were engaged in the administrative apparatus (*apparat upravlenia*) alone, and of these one-third were in statistical and accounting work—a category said to have been on the increase "in recent times." An article published in December 1962 mentions that "the size of the apparatus of planning and control" has increased by roughly 50 percent "within the last seven years." Another source reports that the number of employees of supply organizations, above the enterprise level, increased by some 100,000 during the years 1958-62.

And, according to the Labor Research Institute, the share of engineers, technicians and salaried personnel (*sluzhashchie*) will rise from 13 to 32 percent of the industrial labor force within the next two decades, presumably even after account is taken of the large-scale introduction of electronic computers, accounting machines, etc., during that time.

Stalin's Heritage

The present Soviet planning system came into existence under the first Five-Year Plan, some three decades ago, and reflects the historical situation then prevailing—in particular the reluctance of the central planners to delegate power, and the shortage of competent, politically reliable plant managers.

While the Soviet plant manager is designated as *the* boss (*edinonachalnik*) in his establishment, in fact his relation to Moscow is more like that of a foreman to the production manager in Western enterprise. Specifically, output goals, product assortment and destination and date of delivery of each product are centrally planned. In addition, the manager has to meet centrally fixed targets for the total wage fund, for the number of workers and wage rates paid to them, for production costs, profitability, labor productivity, capital savings, capital investment, and introduction of new technology. Finally, various subordinate targets may be facing him, such as material saving, economy of working capital, socialist competition for fulfilment of particular tasks, mobilization of workers for harvest and sowing campaigns outside his enterprise, and the like.

Even a casual glance at this incomplete list causes wonder. How on earth can a manager function (and in most cases function successfully) under such multiple constraints? And, bearing in mind that there are today some 200,000 industrial establishments in the Soviet Union producing roughly 20,000,000 commodities, how on the other hand can the central planning agencies cope with the prohibitive task of planning and administering all these multiple success indicators for every enterprise?

Concerning the Stalinist past, part of the answer is that the refinements were neglected. A limited number of industries and, within each plan, one success indicator, the output goal, enjoyed an absolute priority in actual practice. If output plans for these industries and establishments were met, this was all that counted: "The (output) plan fulfiller is always right" (*pobeditelei ne sudiat*). Thus, in fact though not on paper, managers were permitted to play, in a somewhat informal manner, the role assigned by the English economist Alfred Marshall to the capitalist entrepreneur: that is, they could to some extent disregard the plans dictating *how* to produce, and combine factors of production in proportions they deemed necessary for success in the overriding consideration, the output goal. Other targets—profitability, production costs, etc.—often played the role of shock absorbers. And, on a nationwide scale, low-priority industries played a somewhat similar role.

As for the central planners, too often they made no attempt to reach the planned targets at the lowest possible cost. Indeed, as pointed out by Professor A. Birman, under Stalin the tendency "to achieve the desired results at any cost, instead of being condemned, was rather encouraged." The planners' whole effort was merely to make their allocation of resources consistent—*i.e.,* to make output goals accord with the inputs provided, whether in a particular enterprise or in a whole industry. And even this elementary consistency was indifferently pursued. Quite regularly more output was demanded than the inputs allowed (so-called "planners' tension," a by-product of which was the stimulus to effort). Plans, quarterly, annual or five-year, were almost never punctual. Innumerable subtle improvements were neglected.

Until recently official descriptions gave no idea of the number of exceptions and loopholes possible in the planning procedure, while at the same time they grossly understated the complexity of the administrative structure. Thus right through the Stalinist period, if latter-day sources are to be trusted, industry of very minor importance, coming under the authority of local soviets, was not in fact "planned" by these soviets but took orders from wholesale organizations—in other words, from the consumer. Similarly, commodities in litte demand and those produced in excess of plan have in recent years, and perhaps for longer, been disposed of through the wholesale organizations for whatever price they would bring. Thus on occasion there is no command economy at all. But on other occasions it burgeons into a nightmarish complexity: the number of intermediate offices with command or consultative status, through whom indents for important materials must pass, is sometimes indefinitely large. A recent source cited the case of a factory whose properly documented indent (*zayavka*) for ballbearings weighed 200 kilograms and was sent to and processed by 14 agencies. Stalin has often been described as Genghis Khan with the telegraph: as creator of the planning system, he figures here as Kafka with an abacus.

In the more rational and self-critical temper of the present day, all these defects and inconsistencies are up for questioning. The low-priority industries and enterprise targets, the old shock absorbers softening the impact of planning errors and miscalculations, have disappeared. In particular, as far as the plant manager is concerned, all success indicators are equally important: if any one of them is not met, the factory fails to get its bonus. This makes the manager's task more difficult than it was under Stalin. So is the planner's.

The Growing Complexity of Planning

As shown by Academician Dorodnitsyn, the number of interrelationships among objects of economic planning grows in proportion to the square of the number of objects themselves. For example, in drawing the plan for the Soviet machine-building industry, which turns out 125 thousand types of commodities, the planner must take account of over 15 billion (or, $125,000 \times 125,000$) relations among these various products. The forthcoming standard industrial classification of *all* industrial products being manufactured in the USSR is to include some 20 million items, which (using the arbitrary rule of squares, which is quite likely an understatement) implies some 4 quadrillion relationships.

Nor is this the end. Dorodnitsyn does not mention explicitly that the complexity of planning grows also with the square of the number of establishments: a single commodity produced in a hundred establishments is likely to involve more calculations and decisions than a hundred commodities produced in one. The number of industrial "census" establishments alone has grown from 30,000 to 200,000 under the Five-Year Plans. It continues to grow rapidly, partly as the result of technical progress which favors vertical disintegration of industry. A formerly "universal" factory, producing all parts and components of a particular machine under one roof splits up and gives rise to narrowly specialized plants engaged in subcontracting. For example, a modern radio-spectrometer, a relatively simple device, consists of 264 components produced by 150 separate factories. But the bureaucratic procedures needed to coordinate the resulting transactions are the same as those used in the coordination of, say, huge shipments made by giant steel mills. No wonder Soviet planners are said to be drowning in "a paper ocean."

Moreover, planning has become more complex not only in the purely quantitative terms of the volume of paper work involved. The demands of modern industry are rising with equal rapidity with respect to the quality of planning—the speed of information flows, the precision of commands, their consistency. The consequences of planning errors and delays become more costly, and some of the traditional Soviet shock absorbers fail to operate under the new conditions. For example, automation makes a factory far more sensitive to shortages of supplies and of spare parts resulting from planning errors. The traditional Soviet remedy of "storming" (*e.g.*, overutilization of capacity during the last ten days of the month to compensate for under-utilization during the first twenty) is inapplicable in an automated plant. The modern trend toward subcontracting has similar effects. The smooth performance of the radio-spectrometer factory just mentioned depends now on the combined successful performance of its 150 suppliers as well as on the accuracy, realism and precision of the central plan which sets in detail the origin and delivery of each shipment.

In practice, of course, the volume of planning done on the central level is not as prohibitive as might appear from these figures. In fact, the Gosplan USSR prepares plans for output of only 18,000 commodities, or less than one-tenth of one percent of the number actually being produced. This is due to the fact that the planners move, for most commodities, on a rather high level of aggregation, leaving the actual product mix within the broad categories (the breakdown by type, size, color, etc.) partly or wholly to decentralized decisions. Even so, the sovnarkhozes (regional economic administrations, about which more later) and factory executives bitterly complain about the needlessly detailed plans, which include salt-cellars, herring plates, ashtrays and plastic collar stays of various varieties on the same footing with tractors and steel, and which—in meat packing, for example—even get down to output targets for such items as raw gall, condensed gall, pancreas (subdivided into salted and frozen), etc.

The Extremes are Better than the Middle

It is thus obvious from the administrative point of view that planning must be decentralized if it is to exist at all. It always has been, and still is: the center draws up a general skeleton and the subordinate bodies put flesh on the bones. The (fluctuating) degree of decentralization, and the structure and nature of the intermediate hierarchy it entails, are matters of high political controversy to which we shall return, but they are of surprisingly little economic interest. Confining ourselves still to economics, it is plain that such technical planning desiderata as consistency and punctuality are compatible with, even possibly favored by, decentralization.

One planning function, however, is very seriously disfavored: the rational allocation of resources. From this point of view decision-making should be *either* central *or* peripheral; a mixture is bad. A simple case is where planning decisions are devolved upon the sovnarkhoz. Suppose that two neighboring sovnarkhozes both use the established criteria of central planning correctly in veiw of the resources and needs of their territories. They will both produce racing bicycles for boys, and compete to sell them in a third sovnarkhoz. Either perfectly centralized planning, or a free market into which no higher body than an enterprise entered, would have resulted in only one sovnarkhoz specializing in such bicycles. The only way in which two independent sovnarkhozes could effect the same result would be for them to establish a perfect inter-sovnarkhoz market and compete in it, like very large firms. In other words, they would have to look beyond the "needs and resources of their own territories" when they made their computations. Or of course they could sacrifice their independence to a central computer.

Whichever solution they adopted, they would have to use it all the time and in exhaustive detail. It would be useless, for instance, to have an inter-sovnarkhoz market in some such broadly defined commodity as "steel," or to accept orders concerning "steel" from the central computer, while filling in the details oneself. For economic life does not consist in making "steel": it means making racing bicycles for boys, or steel tubes for racing bicycles for boys. In such narrow categories are things bought and sold, over immense distances: and in such must they be planned.

The same is true if the subordinate unit we are considering is the enterprise, not the sovnarkhoz. The story of the nails is classic, indeed it is across this *pons asinorum* that the economist enters the field of sovietology. A factory was making nails, and its output target was expressed as a number of nails. In order to avoid excessive centralization all other details were to be settled by the factory. So it made the nails as small as possible. To remedy this the planners re-expressed the target in terms of a weight of nails. So the factory made them as large as possible. Then the planners abandoned decentralization and handed down a plan for kinds of nails, each of a different weight, and a number for each kind. But clearly an alternative improvement would have been to decentralize all decisions in a competitive market.

Now an electronic market is not yet a serious possibility. The masses of information that must be currently, punctually and accurately fed into the computer—essentially the demand and supply curves for all commodities—are simply not available.

Nevertheless, as things are, centralized planning can correct the most obvious irrationalities of decentralized planning. It also has ideology to commend it. Decentralized planning, on the other hand, is administratively far less cumbersome. So it should not surpise us that the pendulum swings, and has always swung, between the two.

The Reform Movement in General

In brief, Soviet economic planning and administration appear to be overcentralized and undercoordinated. While the number and complexity of decisions and choices involved in planning has grown considerably since the 1957 reforms, the apparatus available for their making and implementation appears to have become less operational. The organizational blueprint of the Soviet economy represents at present a crazy quilt of agencies organized according to several principles: territorial (sovnarkhozes, economic regions, republican gosplans); functional (such as state committees dealing with automation, technology, labor, etc.); and production (all-union and republican ministries, state committees in charge of priority industries such as the chemical, and, since November 1962, the Communist Party itself). While the newly created Supreme Council of the National Economy (Vysshii Sovet Narodnovo Khoziaistva) may coordinate the conflicting pulls of these agencies to some extent, the power conferred upon it to intervene at all levels of decision-making may actually tend to compound the confusion rather than eliminate it. No wonder Professor A. Birman, an outspoken critic of the present system of economic administration, proposes, as the first prerequisite of any improvement in its functioning, that:

> . . . first of all one ought to determine, in a precise and concrete manner, the respective functions, rights and mutual relations of all economic agencies: enterprises; regional economic councils (sovnarkhozes); local councils; planning, financial and banking agencies at various levels (local, republican, all union); state committees and ministries. . . . Then, it is absolutely necessary to establish the principle of reciprocal responsibility [in these relations]: Experience has shown that lack of legal responsibility on the part of higher authorities toward the enterprise and lower echelons gives rise to uncoordinated planning and causes great harm to the national economy.

An editorial in *Ekonomicheskaia ga·eta* seconds Birman:

> When a worker breaks a machine component worth one ruble, he is held fully responsible for the damage done. But a planning executive may (and often does) make millions of rubles go with the wind by taking a wrong decision, and no one will bring him to account: this is taken for granted.

There may be some legal and ethical justification for such a measure but one wonders whether it would not work economic havoc. The reluctance to take responsibility and to innovate manifests itself even at present, and making the planners legally responsible for the unpredictable consequences of their decisions might strengthen this tendency; this would hardly be desirable, given the fact that innovation is a crucial determinant of growth in the modern Soviet economy.

A clear-cut delimitation of the various agencies' spheres of activity and responsibility, while necessary and overdue, would at best be a make-shift. There is a widespread demand for more radical reforms, and some of the proposals reach to the very foundations of traditional practices and theories. Since many such schemes have already been discussed in this journal, and a full presentation of others would require too much space, we do not propose to describe them in any detail but shall limit ourselves to a general appraisal of the issues involved.

One might, at first sight, tend to lump all would-be reformers together and contrast them with the opposing bureaucrats. Indeed, there is a common ground on which the reformers all meet. They are dissatisfied with the deficiencies of the traditional system of incentives and success indicators; they are in favor of bringing prices closer to actual factor cost; finally, virtually all of them eulogize electronic computers and have high expectations concerning their potential as a tool of economic planning.

Centralizers and Decentralizers

Apparent similarity conceals, however, deep-seated differences of opinion, especially as regards the degree of centralization.

At one extreme of the spectrum we find proponents of a complete computerization who, as described by Professor A. Birman, would like to trace in economic plans, "each pin, each motion a worker makes," to calculate their effectiveness and plan them in physical terms, preferably without the use of money prices. The approach of reformers of this persuasion would amount to harnessing the computers to the task of preserving and immeasurably strengthening the present centralized system.

Such a person is Professor M. Fedorovich, of the Moscow Engineering Economic Institute named after Ordzhonikidze. He concurs with Glushkov, Dorodnitsyn, and others that the flaw in Soviet planning is its growing inability to receive on time and process a huge flow of information, and on its basis issue accurate and correct commands. But, Fedorovich agrues, this criticism is only valid when applied to the techniques currently being used by the planning agencies, and not to the system of centralized economic planning itself. Let us not decentralize, exclaims the Moscow economist; neither let us adopt any uniform indicator such as profitability, as proposed by Liberman. Instead, let us scrap desk calculators and "put our centralized economic planning on electronic rails so that it can cope with the huge amount of information inputs and of planning calculations."

Eventually, the computers themselves, on the basis of algorithms prepared in advance, will provide each sovnarkhoz and each enterprise with the optimum variant of the plan (so that no human decisions will be needed in selecting that optimum), and then during the planning period the computers will analyze and appraise its fulfillment by sovnarkhozes and by enterprises. Fedorovich envisions a uniform, nationwide cybernetic system of centralized economic planning and control in which an enterprise will play merely the passive role of supplying information and obeying the planners.

Ultimately, the computers are to take over more than just the planning near the top: the lower echelon of the economy is to get dehumanized as well. Within the next two decades, Fedorovich argues, the proliferation of automated factories will further facilitate and strengthen centralized planning. Such factories will be carrying out programs fed into them by computers "without direct interference by human beings," since built-in feedback loops will provide them with the ability to adapt themselves to changing circumstances.

Fedorovich's vision of an electronic Leviathan decontaminated from human frailties should by no means be viewed as an isolated pipe dream. Academician Dorodnitsyn, a highly influential mathematician, appears to follow a similar line of thought when he proposes, for the near future, the use of electronic computers and teletypes for creation of a completely mechanized and automated system of planning, control and administration on the scale of a sovnarkhoz.

Slightly less centralist are the planometricians, such as Kantorovich, the inventor of linear programming. His proposals are consistent with a very far-reaching centralization but differ from the just-mentioned group insofar as they use shadow prices rather than physical efficiency indicators as the criterion of choice. Under full communism, Kantorovich argues,

> . . . society's whole productive activity will be organized like one big factory, and obviously an optimal plan will be drawn for it. In other words, the boundaries of an enterprise will be widened until they coincide with those of the society as a whole.

Meanwhile, however, he permits the central planners to determine the final output pattern, and to sell it off to the consumer as best they can, presumably by the same differentiated structure of turnover taxes and subsidies as is used today. This is his obeisance to political decision in central planning. As to his views on decentralization, Kantorovich thinks it would be rational for sovnarkhozes to do the main computations, within a framework laid down in Moscow. In other words, he falls right into the "steel versus racing bicycles" fallacy discussed above.

A much bigger step toward decentralization is contemplated by E. Liberman who, like Kantorovich, would leave the decision on ends (specifically on the composition and volume of output) with the central planners but decentralize down to the enterprise level decisions on how to attain the ends thus selected, and notably on methods of production.

Only the volume and composition of output, destination and dates of delivery would continue to be centrally planned for each enterprise. Given these constraints, the plant manager would be given just one instruction: to maximize the profitability of his enterprise, computed in relation to its fixed and working capital stock. Profits would become the sole success indicator, replacing the present multiple schizophrenia of often conflicting yardsticks; they would also become the only source of incentive payments. Let central planners set the ends, exclaims Liberman, and leave the enterprise free to decide on means.

A price reform would obviously have to precede such a change, if profits were to be economically meaningful, but Liberman does not seem to be too interested in *how* the planners would go about it. He accepts without reservation the central planners' final output pattern and price structure without spelling out how they should arrive at them.

A more serious defect is that if all enterprises could choose their own inputs, but all their outputs were planned for them, there is an evident contradiction. For the outputs of innumerable enterprises are not consumer but intermediate goods, *i.e.,* the inputs of other enterprises. If Liberman really means what he says, there could be no output targets for such enterprises, *i.e.,* they could hardly be centrally planned at all.

Let us now compare these two men. Kantorovich is a mathematician and an intellectual, interested in the rationality of resource allocation by planners. Liberman is a business economist and a practical man, interested in administrative efficiency and, above all, incentives for managers. He sees the crux of the problem in persuading the manager to *offer* the right plan in the first place—this is what he makes really profitable. Even plan overfulfillment is less important to him. It is no accident that Kantorovich is greatly more centralistic, for our previous section showed that rationality does indeed demand centralization, while administrative efficiency opposes it. Kantorovich's whole approach could be described as enlightened centralism. He goes out of his way to emphasize that his system of planning through linear programming does not aim at profit maximization, at least not at the enterprise level:

> In a socialist enterprise the goal is to obtain an optimum effect for the economy as a whole, *e.g.,* maximum output (*sic*) given the planned amount of resources and supply conditions. This requires a simultaneous maximization of several functions. . . .

Kantorovich contrasts this view with profit maximization, which should involve one function only. Thus his approach differs essentially from Liberman's, who emphatically states that the enterprise should aim at one and only one goal, maximum profitability, and that the addition of even a single extra "success indicator" would vitiate the whole scheme and make him reject it. Kantorovich, on the other hand, warns that one of the reasons why profit maximization cannot be allowed to play a decisive role in a socialist enterprise is that (unlike its capitalist counterpart) it has to heed the effects of its actions on other enterprises' interests. This obviously differs from Liberman's basic principle that "what is profitabile for society as a whole should be profitable for each enterprise." In Western terminology Kantorovich takes account of "external economies," while Liberman minimizes them.

Kantorovich is mainly concerned with the price reform and less so with who is going to apply his optimal valuations: the central planning board in computer analogues of actual markets, or sovnarkhozes acting for the board, or enterprises in actual transactions, or some combination of the three. Liberman, on the other hand, is concerned with just that issue: for him the basic unit that decides resource allocation is the enterprise, and the planners' main task becomes to provide the proper incentives which would make the economy move in the direction desired by planners, through parametric adjustments of enterprises.

Pure Titoism, or the abolition of current central planning, whether in the interests of managers or workers' councils, is not overtly represented among the reformers.

Impact of the Politicians

We now turn to the pure politics of centralization versus decentralization. In doing so we enter an almost totally separate world. In the quarrels about sovnarkhozes *vs.* ministries, army *vs.* party, steel *vs.* chemicals, etc., we are in the realm of the Central Committee. We read *Pravda* not *Voprosy ekonomiki*, Fainsod not Nove. Khrushchev can fill several pages of *Pravda* without mentioning the names of Liberman and Kantorovich. We point to what connections there are between these worlds in our conclusion.

Since December 1956 there have been many organizational changes. Indeed they have followed upon one another so fast as to prove the unimportance of all particular systems. The regime is plainly the complete master of the administrative structure, and changes it virtually at will. Only three elements have hitherto survived all change: the party, the central planning organ and the enterprise. Indeed, of these only the enterprise remains recognizably identical.

There constant changes reveal certain conditions that Khrushchev has been concerned to ensure:

1. that the structures of the party and the state correspond to each other, to facilitate control by the former;
2. that there be as little "bureaucracy" as possible;
3. that the economy remain in some sense centrally planned.

Point (1) has a long history. Even before 1928 the role of the party in the economy was an issue. Trotsky favored a strong and independent state machine; and this is why Lenin accused him of being "too interested in administrative questions." In the NEP period Zinoviev and Kamenev, then on the Left, wanted the party to control the economy. Burkharin, Rykov, Tomsky and the administrators stood for and obtained a somewhat independent state machine. The party was not in fact run by Zinoviev and Kamenev but by Stalin, who was preoccupied with personal aggrandizement and left the state alone. But when by 1929 Stalin had disposed of all his enemies and relaunched central planning, the question presented itself somewhat differently. Both party and state were now the merest transmission belts of dictatorial power but they had, after all, separate functions; should not their hierarchies correspond so that the party might better control the state? The matter was disscussed at the 17th Party Congress in 1934.

From 1919 until 1928 the state economy had been run largely on the *"territoral" principle*: the country was divided into large areas each governed in economic matters by a "council of the national economy" (soviet narodnovo khoziaistva, or sovnarkhoz) which mediated orders received from a Supreme Sovnarkhoz in Moscow. The territorial sovnarkhoz had absolute control over light industry, local transport, construction and agriculture in its area; however, in heavy industry, rail transport and defense output enterprises took their orders directly from an office in the Supreme Sovnarkhoz. Under "war communism" this administrative structure had been a great inconvenience, but under the NEP any overlapping of jurisdiction was tolerable since there was little planning.

In the first and second Five-Year Plans a logical centralization took place, with a general switch to the *"production" principle* hitherto applied only to heavy industry, rails and defense—*i.e.,* a *glavk* (chief committee) in a ministry took over control of the output and distribution of a particular product all over the country. But the party, like any political party, was organized on the "territorial" principle. The extreme discontinuity between the "territorial" party and the "production" state was attacked at both ends.

In 1934, on the suggestion of Kaganovich the "territorial" principle was revived for agriculture and for unimportant "local" industry and construction. These came under, not separate sovnarkhozes, but the regular local government organs. The major republics (except the RSFSR) sprouted gosplans, and certain activities of intermediate importance were declared "union-republican," with control split between Moscow and the republics. At the same time the offices of the Central Committee of the party, previously organized on the *"functional" principle* (personnel, propaganda, and so on), were reshuffled to accord with the "production" principle (heavy industry, light industry, agriculture, etc.).

In 1939 Zhdanov induced Stalin to restore the Central Committee bureaus to their old "functional" pattern, giving two reasons. First, a unitary personnel bureau was necessary so as to put the right party worker in the right job, irrespective of his "production" experience; secondly, there had been too much petty supervision by the party over the economy—the party should not get bogged down, for example, in the search for spare parts. In 1948, however, Stalin—at Malenkov's instance—restored the bureau to the structure of 1934.

Immediately after Stalin's death Malenkov and Beria increased the size and power, and diminished the number, of the ministries in a move to make the state more independent. This tendency was resisted by Khrushchev, working from his base in the Secretariat of the party; at the time he did not raise the issue of party supremacy but merely attacked bureaucracy. During 1954–56 his power—along with that of the party—increased mightily, and agriculture, where politics is always vital and Khrushchev has special expertise, slipped almost irretrievably into his grasp.

However, Khrushchev's secret speech on Stalin's crimes, and its consequences in Poland and Hungary, weakened him so much that there was a veritable "technocratic counterrevolution" in December 1956. The Central Committee met without publishing any speech of his (a rare event): the basis of discussion was a report by two pure technocrats, and the session resulted in a resolution very greatly strengthening the Gosekonomkommissia, the state body that was then the current manager of the economy. The Gosplan, at that time in charge of perspective planning, was left alone, but the Gosekonomkommissia was reinforced to include all the most influential technocrats—not a party *apparatchik* among them—and constituted into a sort of economic cabinet half independent of the Council of Ministers. Power was also decentralized down to individual ministries, republics and other state bodies. Although the party was not directly altered, this was the high point of state independence since the days of Bukharin, Rykov and Tomsky.

In 1957 Khrushchev counterattacked and won—not by tinkering with the CC bureaus or splitting up the ministries but by thoroughly restructuring the state on the "territorial" principle. This was the most revolutionary of all changes hitherto mentioned. The Gosekonomkommissia was reduced in power and renamed. Thirty economic ministries—nearly all of them—were abolished. The sovnarkhozes were revived and put in control of all activities except agriculture, as well as the public utilities and light industry already subordinated to local government. These new sovnarkhozes were much smaller than the old ones; there were about 104 of them, approximately one for each oblast (province). The effect was drastically to emasculate the state machine, and to hand over power in the economy to the party's obkom (province committee) secretary. In short, the small sovnarkhoz was a very different agency from the large sovnarkhoz corresponding to no territorial unit of the party, which logically could escape from party control as easily as could a "production" principle ministry.

Of the obvious administrative inefficiency of this system of multiple economic councils we speak below. Here it is important to see that it sprang from a particular tradition in the Communist movement—the principle that the party, the repository of all dynamism and orthodoxy, must allow no other organ to overshadow it. The opposite view is that the revolution has to settle down and accept expert advice, even to some extent the rule of law. As Lenin complained against Trotsky, so Khrushchev struck down first the security police (Beria), now the state economic machine, and later the army (Zhukov). The view is not necessarily a left-wing one: for Lenin was more moderate than Trotsky, even if Zinoviev stood to the left of Bukharin, and Khrushchev stands perhaps a little to the left of *his* opponents. Nor is the view a Stalinist one: for to Stalin party and state were equally his footballs, and so too were security police and army—the great tyrant did not care through what mechanism he governed. It is no accident that Malenkov and Kaganovich, who in 1948 and 1934 had personally restructured the party to correspond with the state, and who had both borne again and again direct responsibility of a purely state character, violently opposed the reforms of 1957.

The Structure Since 1957

Unlike the earlier sovnarkhozes, these revivals were not meant to bring about decentralization. Decision-making powers granted to them were fairly limited even at the outset and were mainly obtained at plant managers' expense. The sovnarkhozes were to play the part of transmission belts rather than of spark plugs. Nevertheless they were allowed to reallocate supplies and machinery among enterprises and industries, to make some investment decisions, and to reapportion some funds.

The period 1957–62 saw a graduated erosion of these rights. Very soon the sovnarkhozes were accused of using their powers to promote local interests, of neglecting extra-regional delivery plans, of diverting supplies and investment funds into branches serving local needs at the expense of national interests. In a series of decrees, their rights were drastically reduced. On April 24, 1958, and May 22, 1959, they were ordered to give priority to extra-regional deliveries; and on January 22, 1959, their authority to reallocate supplies and investment funds was taken away and vested in the republican councils of ministers and gosplans, an important centralization measure.

The sovnarkhozes' small size may have been a political advantage in 1957, but it was an economic liability. Problems of marketing, automation, regional planning, even large investment projects were beyond their horizon. Centralized agencies created since 1957 were to cut across the sovnarkhozes' boundaries and to assure the coordination of their activities along territorial, functional or industry lines.

Such agencies include the state committees attached to the All-Union Council of Ministers and to the Gosplan, in charge of such nationwide problems as automation or development of a particular high-priority industry. Their number has greatly increased since 1957, and they have increasingly shifted from advisory to planning and decision-making capacity.

The so-called republican sovnarkhozes were established in June and July 1960 in the three largest Soviet republics: Russia, Ukraine, and Kazakhstan. They control the plan fulfillment by the sovnarkhozes of the given republic, coordinate their activity, issue operational orders to them, and have the right to suspend their directives. The creation of the republican sovnarkhozes amounted thus to a further centralization; but in fact they acquired their main powers—such as the allocation of material supplies—not from the sovnarkhozes, which had few powers left to give up in any event, but from the republican gosplans. Interestingly enough, the republican sovnarkhozes' branch subdivisions, the chief industrial administrations, appear to duplicate roughly the functions of the former ministerial glavks abolished in 1957: another step backward in the uneasy effort to reconcile the territorial and production principles of administration.

The republican sovnarkhozes were to serve the purpose of short-term operational planning and administration. The creation of the seventeen "large economic regions" in May 1961 (plus two independent administrative areas, *viz.* Byelorussia and Moldavia) was to facilitate long-range planning and major developmental policies affecting movements of population, shifts in industrial location, development of mineral resources and major agricultural areas, etc. The councils make recommendations to the republican and all-union gosplans, concerning such nationwide problems as optimum location of industry, interregional specialization, and regional planning of capital formation. Their role is not to be affected by the reforms of November 1962.

A vast superstructure of coordinating agencies has thus been imposed upon the base of the sovnarkhozes. But who would coordinate the coordinators? To quote Liberman, "a multitude of authorities have made their appearance, often issuing uncoordinated orders." The main sufferer, as will be shown below, has been the enterprise.

The next major revisions came in 1962. They appeared to express the growing political power of Khrushchev, which was interrupted in the summer by the agricultural crisis (rise in retail food prices, June 1) and the decision to put missiles in Cuba (Raul Castro's visit in July). The withdrawal of the missiles evidently strengthened Khrushchev's hand and enabled him—against some opposition—to reform the party in November much as in March he had reformed the state.

The March reforms affected only the state's organization in agriculture, so they hardly concern us. The agricultural powers of the raion (district) government were transferred to new "territorial kolkhozsovkhoz or sovkhoz-kolkhoz production administrations" (p.a.'s). In November the logical follow-up took place in the party: the party committee at the raion level was abolished, its agricultural concerns going to new p.a. party committees. But if this was logical, other changes in the party structure were strange indeed. The p.a. party committee was set up as a basic party unit whose officers are elected from below: the constituency consists of all party members in the p.a. area concerned with agriculture. Those who live in the countryside, but are concerned with other matters, form the constituency of a different basic party unit covering a still larger area: the zonal industrial-production party committee. The party committees in towns are untouched, and therefore most party members are unaffected. But the oblast (province) committee, or obkom, is divided into two quite independent committees, one for agriculture, one for everything else. Even at republic level the party, united into one committee, nevertheless forms two bureaus with great operational independence.

Though strange, this is perhaps not absurd. For at the same time, the sovnarkhozes were raised to sensible size and their number was reduced in the ratio of $2\frac{1}{2}$ to 1, thus depriving the obkom in any case of much of its function and authority. This particular reform was only a matter of time: that administrative monstrosity, the small sovnarkhoz, had not figured in Khrushchev's original plans, and had clearly been a political gesture to the obkom secretaries, whose support he had needed in 1957. One awaits, of course, the formation of party committees at the level of the new sovnarkhozes. The only new monstrosity is the huge zonal industrial-production party committee, covering selected people in many raions. The oft-proclaimed motive of the November reforms is to give the party greater control over the economy, and the original feature is the basic restructuring of the party on the "production" principle in order to achieve this aim. Khrushchev adduced many data to prove that agricultural preoccupation had been clogging the machinery of the party, and the reform will surely have the paradoxical result of releasing much party energy for industry. Whether industry will benefit thereby is an issue on which we may differ with Khrushchev.

Other changes in November were less important. A separate long-term planning body was retained (previously Gosekonomsoviet, now Gosplan). But current central management (previously Gosplan) was split into an industrial and a construction branch, and all subordinate sovnarkhozes lost control over constucction to new local construction trusts. Thus the "production" principle crept back into the state organization as well as the party. The central industrial body was appropriately named Sovnarkhoz SSSR and given authority over all sovnarkhozes. The new central construction body was formed out of the old state Committee on Construction (Gosstroi), much strengthened. Other less powerful state committees on this and that had been founded since 1957, and more were founded now. This merely confirms common sense: the "production" principle cannot be discarded. Mostly "this" and "that" concerned some branch of production—thus the state committee is the ghost of the old ministry.

The "production" principle achieved one further victory: a special bureau was set up in the Central Committee of the party for chemicals and light industry. This is a characteristically Khrushchevian touch: the full weight of important party officials is thrown behind those branches of industry that interest him most.

In March 1963 still another basic change was effected with the creation of a new Supreme Council of the National Economy of the USSR (hereafter called VSNKh). The VSNKh has charge of industry and construction, and is subordinate only to the Council of Ministers: it has considerable independent power. Directly subordinate to it are the Gosplan, the Sovnarkhoz SSSR and Gosstroi, and the more important state committees (principally defense and technology). The less important state committees are subject to Gosplan and Gosstroi in the cases of industry and construction respectively.

The March reform had at least three purposes: to downgrade the importance of the party vis-à-vis the state, to keep planning centralized, and to enhance the influence of the military. It was in all three respects a blow at Khrushchev, many of whose reforms of the previous November were overturned or outflanked. The VSNKh, of which there had been no hint in November, is in many particulars similar to the strengthened Gosekonomkommissia of December 1956, which Khrushchev personally had struck down in 1957; its first chairman, Dimitri Ustinov, is a figure from the arms industry without much pure party experience. Among other signs that Khrushchev was bested, his new favorite, the chemical industry so much exalted in November, was put under the control of a mere state committee subordinate to Gosplan, not directly under the VSNKh; and the all-union Gosplan and Gosstroi were given explicit authority over republican gosplans and gosstrois, previously denied them. The March meeting itself was not officially a session of the party Central Committee, as in November, but a joint session of the party CC and the Council of Ministers (in both cases plus invitees). No speech by Khrushchev was recorded in connection with the meeting, and *Pravda* give the decisions minimal coverage compared with the immense publicity accorded to Khrushchev in November. Neither *Pravda* nor of course the decrees themselves said one word about party control over the economy.

In sum we return in March 1963 to the situation after December 1956; agriculture remains the bailiwick of Khrushchev and the party, the rest of the economy is in the hands of "statist" technocrats. This is surely not a stable situation now, anymore than it was then.

The Toad Beneath the Harrow

How has the *enterprise* fared through all these vicissitudes? From its viewpoint, the creation of the sovnarkhozes in 1957 was a centralizing measure. It would even have been so apart from all changes in formal rights and duties, simply because a sovnarkhoz is geographically nearer than a ministry, and so can exercise closer control. It was only between Gosplan and the sovnarkhoz as the intermediate body that there was, if anywhere, decentralization. Various rights granted to the plant managers by the Bulganin-inspired decree of August 9, 1955, in the fields of production, financing, and investment decisions were in 1957 largely transferred to the sovnarkhozes.

It was also the enterprise that bore the brunt of the subsequent recentralization measures at upper levels, as the decision-making powers granted to the sovnarkhozes were gradually transferred to republican ministries and gosplans, state committees, etc. The plant manager, who before 1957 had been confronted, as a rule, with just one boss—the minister—now has to satisfy the often conflicting demands of several agencies. Thus, the manager of a telephone equipment factory complains that

> . . . [the plant is] simultaneously directed by the chief administration, the sovnarkhoz, the VSNKh [*i.e.,* the Sovnarkhoz of the RSFSR created in 1961], until recently the Gosplan SSSR, and, in addition, five state committees, two all-union ministries, and so forth. They all believe that the factory should work according to their plans. . . ."

In addition to output and assortment goals, these sundry agencies determine separately the enterprise's planned targets for employment, wage fund, labor productivity, cost reduction, capital saving, investment, and technological innovations. As Liberman puts it:

> . . . a multitude of echelons of command have appeared, issuing orders which often lack coordination. This makes necessary excessive and costly work at alterations and revisions of plans.

But revised targets themselves may be uncoordinated: for example, it has become common practice to raise an enterprise's output goal without granting it additional funds or supplies, and then penalize it for "overspending" by withholding the bonus even though the output plan has been met.

The effectiveness of the bonus payments, the main incentive at the planners' disposal for getting the enterprise interested in plan fulfilment, is greatly weakened under the new conditions. The plant manager, confronted with a growing proliferation of often conflicting plans, orders and directives, has to meet all the planned targets before the enterprise qualifies for the incentive bonus. And even if he meets all the stipulations, the bonus may still be withheld:

> . . . the enterprise's incentive fund may be taken away from it and used for the sovnarkhoz's needs unrelated to the enterprise in question, and no objections are heeded.

No wonder, then, that the number of enterprises and sovnarkhozes failing to meet planned goals has been reported on the increase.

Conclusion

In this welter of cross-currents it is difficult to chart one's way ahead. The *party* will not allow complete decentralization, first on obvious ideological grounds, secondly on the very rational ground that *laissez-faire*, according to all human experience, subserves many goals well but not those of growth and defense. Inclining towards complete centralization, the party will neverthless look askance at it, for that means experts with formulas and computers, or a kind of victory for the state. The party must therefore be reckoned as a force, and probably a decisive one, favoring broadly the status quo.

Between the ruling party group and the higher state officials there is disagreement on the issue of the exact hierarchy of command. In 1953 (consolidation of ministries), 1956 (Gosekonomkommissia) and 1963 (VSNKh) the government officials have come out for a more independent state, which, however, they have each time equated with more centralization than was agreeable to the party. That is, naturally, because they are *higher* state officials: they want an attractive promotions pyramid. But we may doubt whether they would welcome total centralization; for that, with its computers, would cut out human judgment, and substitute junior mathematics graduates for themselves. In fact, the lunatic fringe of extreme centralizers is to be found among *engineers* (Fedorovich), ever and in all countries prone, in their innocence of administration and economics, to technocracy.

Economists cover the whole spectrum of opinion. Doubtless there are some secret Titoists as well as those we have mentioned. These would be theoreticians, as are the centralizers like Kantorovich. The chief moderate decentralizer is a business economist (Liberman), and that is natural too, for like all business economists he is interested in incentives and administrative practicability. Prices and rationality are for intellectuals.

Enterprise managers feel like, indeed are, state officials. They supported these latter in the fight against sovnarkhozes in 1957. But they want considerably more decentralization than higher state officials, because they want power for themselves. Absolute decentralization, however, with the free market that goes with it, threatens every manager of an enterprise that is or hopes to be subsidized. We suspect that the typical manager is rooting for Liberman.

Technical necessity rules out the Fedorovich dream of a computer-run economy for many years to come (there is not as yet the remotest possibility of its being efficiently, let alone rationally, administered); but all other variants are left in play. *Rationality* demands either total centralization or total decentralization. The requirement that *incentives* pull in the proper direction is Liberman's very own problem, and the best solution to it is either his own, or still greater decentralization. The movement towards *full communism* points in just the opposite direction.

No wonder Khrushchev is more interested in foreign policy and agriculture!

ECONOMICS: ROADS AND INROADS*
· — · — · — · — · — · — · —

Robert W. Campbell

This article is being written at a time of confusion and debate in Soviet society over economic theories, policies and institutions. Nikita Khrushchev was an innovator of impressive zeal in Soviet economic life who worked indefatigably to remove some of the more intolerable crudities of the Stalinist approach to running the economy. In his exuberance and naïveté he sometimes made things different without making them better. His successors during the past year have endorsed and even extended some of the changes, such as the rationalization of farm prices, but some others they have judged as misguided and, accordingly, rescinded or revised them. Thus they have moderated his attempted downgrading of steel in favor of plastics and of coal in favor of oil and gas.

Despite all the reforms, the Khrushchev era ended with several important economic issues broached but unresolved, among them the two most fundamental and persistent questions in Soviet economic life: 1) the proper degree of centralization in economic administration and 2) the rela-

*Reprinted by permission from *Problems of Communism* (Nov.–Dec. 1965), pp. 23–23. All footnotes deleted.

tive emphasis to be given to the desire of the population for a better living today as against the use of resources for such goals as high investment, military strength and foreign aid, favored by the party leadership. Because these are questions on which the regime differs sharply with the rest of society, they have always tended to be "ideological" issues, protected from public argument by an armor of official doctrine. Such doctrine usually obscured more than it clarified, but it served the goal of precluding open discussion. During the Khrushchev era, significant breaches were made in this armor as a result of more frank discussion, even though little was changed in either the degree of centralization or in the order of priorities.

Perhaps the most important development of the period was the freedom allowed some unorthodox theoreticians to elaborate new theories of economic decision-making and resource allocation. By ignoring Marxian dogma, these men discovered the connection between prices and economic administration and developed a theory of rational choice in the sphere of resource use. Following the intellectual leadership of L. V. Kantorovich and V. V. Novozhilov, an elite of Soviet economists, mostly young, able and well trained in mathematics, has acquired a sophisticated understanding of what economic efficiency means and how a decentralized system operating on something like market principles could employ prices and profit indicators to assure effective use of resources. This revolution in economic theory has prepared the way for more venturesome consideration of possible institutional changes. though it is still too abstract and esoteric to have had much influence on the current discussion of reform.

The present regime has not yet given any very clear indication of what it would do about the two fundamental issues outlined above. It has, however, given evidence of accepting the new economics by permitting the award of the Lenin prize to Kantorovich, Novozhilov and the official sponsor of the new economic theory, V. S. Nemchinov. On the other hand, no rapid institutional changes can be expected. Premier Kosygin said last March that decisions about reforms in economic administration would be made only after careful thought and preparation, and it is an indication of the unsettled state of mind of the leaders that was innocuous statement was not made public until a month after it had been made. Real decisions about priorities are being embodied in a new Five-Year Plan now being drawn up for 1966–70, but despite a few tantalizing hints thrown out by Kosygin about guidelines for that plan, the priorities it is to embody are still unknown. Since the basic problems involve such difficult choices, it is unlikely that they will be resolved in a clearcut manner at any one point in time. It is more useful, therefore, to concentrate on the underlying issues than to try to guess what changes are likely to occur in the near future.

Diseases of Soviet Planning

The liveliest topic in Soviet economic discussion today is the question of how to reform the planning and supervision of enterprise behavior. The debate has already resulted in the experimental application of schemes which leave more decisions in the hands of enterprise management and rely on profits to measure performance for purposes of incentive payments. This new departure has acquired the label of Libermanism—after one of its most active proponents, Professor Yevsei Liberman—and is often described as a return to the familiar "profit motive" of capitalism. These labels tend to distort and obscure what is really happening, and suggest a more fundamental kind of change than is actually taking place or being considered. To demonstrate this, it will be helpful to describe the kind of problems facing the economists.

The process of making decisions about resource use in the Soviet Union is beset by some notorious maladies. Producers are insensitive to the wishes of their customers regarding quality, variety, convenience and reliability. Enterprises are often encouraged to persist in producing unwanted and unsalable goods by a deranged bonus system. Perfectly obvious desiderata, such as the introduction of more efficient production methods, full utilization of productive capacity, conservation of property and avoidance of waste, seem impossible to achieve because the producers find them disadvantageous to their interests. These diseases are specific to the Soviet system and they are explainable in terms of its basic institutions. To turn a Marxian slogan against its makers, Soviet central planning suffers from a fundamental antagonistic contradiction. According to Soviet ideology, central planning is supposed to guarantee the primacy of the general interest over parochial interests in the economic sphere by subjecting the whole process of production and consumption to central supervision, direction and control. The whole apparatus of this system— state ownership of the means of production, centralized allocation of resources, and detailed plans regulating the activity of each production unit—was intended to replace the anarchy which Marxian socialists professed to see in the market system by a harmonious, consciously coordinated pattern of activity. But this apparatus has developed independent values and rules of behavior. It seems to have a will of its own, often exercised against its supposed masters. Thus the very devices by means of which the vision of a harmonious unity is to be realized—the detailed orders from above, drastic sanctions and material incentives, and the massive bureaucracy of controllers and supervisors—have often not only fostered what is patent folly from any overall point of view but actually interfered with the accomplishment of the leaders' goals. There is a piquant irony in the neatness with which the Marxian idea that property relations can become fetters holding back the growth of production fits the Soviet situation.

Why has the administrative system led to these results? Basically the problem is this. The overseers set for production enterprises numerous targets as well as restrictions and they employ an elaborate system of reporting to determine how well the plan has been fulfilled. "Successful" performance by a production enterprise is a complex phenomenon, but given the tremendous variety of conditions from enterprise to enterprise and the immensity of the control job when a whole national economy is subjected to this kind of procedure, the Soviet controllers have had to content themselves with checking only on a few dimensions of performance. In practice, the Soviet control system has emphasized the volume of output and adherence to cost budgets as criteria of plan fulfilment. Because they have made these or other unidimensional targets the measure of success and because these targets have often been defined in peculiar ways, enterprises have been encouraged to ignore quality, falsify reporting, alter the assigned output mix, balk at innovation, conceal resources and hoard assets. Higher control organs then usually respond by introducing more indicators and targets to which enterprises are made to conform. If the new indicators are backed up by material rewards and sanctions, new evasions on the part of enterprise managers—and new departures from what is desirable from an economy-wide point of view—follow, and this in turn brings a new counterattack from above in the form of more rules, regulations and reporting. As a result, the typical enterprise manager loses interest in making decisions or exercising initiative because his efforts are likely to be frustrated by regulations from above. As the upper-level administrators arrogate more decisions to themselves and interfere more and more with the detailed management of the enterprise, their decisions tend to become more irrational, inconsistent and bureaucratic. This is the famous "petty tutelage" about which Soviet enterprise management has always complained.

In a sense, the behavior of enterprise management in the Soviet Union has always been controlled by the "profit motive." Since the managers are confronted with a system of constraints and incentives which makes some actions profitable to them personally, and others disadvantageous, the rule of survival is to do what the system makes profitable. What is distinctive is the fact that the profitability of an act is measured less by its impact on accounting profit than by its effect on one of the established success indicators. It has been a favorite slogan of socialists that capitalism means "production for profit rather than for use"; yet in the Soviet economy, where gross output has been made the most important success indicator, this slogan, amended to read "production for the sake of production, rather than for use," is equally applicable. And another socialist slogan, which proclaims that in capitalist economies profit is put ahead of the general welfare, can also be converted to fit the Soviet economy once it is recognized that what counts in the Soviet case is not money profit, but "success" as determined by the system of administrative controls.

The case of light industry illustrates best some of the main elements of the problem. Heretofore, clothing producers, for example, worked to fulfill the plan set by their superiors, rather than satisfy the people who were going to consume their output. They took the raw materials the planners sent them, and within the rules and restrictions set for them by the bosses, worked to earn bonuses by producing whatever would be accepted as output under the existing rules. They did not care what happened to this output, but just shipped it off to some warehouse and had no reason to be concerned with the desires of their customers for quality, variety, or novelty.

Efforts have always been made to overcome the deficiencies of the administrative approach by further administrative tinkering: specific irrationalities have been counteracted by redefining the success indicators, by changing the specification of tasks in the plan, by varying the form of reporting. Experiment in these matters is the daily business of the administrative economy, in the same way that there is continuous trial-and-error adjustment of the money supply in a market economy. The novel element in the USSR in the last several years has been the great increase in the frankness with which these problems are discussed by Soviet officials, a more trenchant criticism of the fundamental rationale of central control, and some fairly bold proposals for changing it. This critical and reformist outlook often goes under the label of Libermanism, but the movement for reform should not be treated as a personal crusade on the part of Liberman himself; what is significant is the official encouragement of a wideranging public discussion of the basic issues.

The Liberman Proposals

Liberman put the fundamental problem very pungently when he declared that in principle there should be no conflict under socialism between the interests of society and the interests of the individual enterprise, and that to validate this principle it is necessary to assure that what is useful to society is also advantageous to the firm, and that anything harmful to overall interests be penalized at the enterprise level. Here is where the argument begins—how is this to be done?

Liberman's answer is that the manager ought to have the authority to determine most of the details of his plan, such as the size of his labor force, his budget, choice of inputs, technology, etc. He should be answerable to his superiors not for a host of separate indicators, but only for overall results, and these can best be measured by profit. The interest of management in increasing profit can be assured by making profit the only source of bonuses, and by scaling the amount of bonuses to the rate of profit earned (figured as the ratio of total profit to the total capital under the control of the enterprise). This latter feature would give management an incentive to utilize capacity as fully as possible and to avoid piling up hoards of surplus equipment and inventories. Furthermore, to give the enterprise an interest in continuous improvement, the profit scale would remain in effect for several years, so that rewards for improved work would continue to accrue for a significant period of time. At the present time, better work is usually rewarded with a harder plan in the next period.

Liberman first made these suggestions in the mid-1950's, but he achieved fame only in 1962 when his ideas were set out in an article in *Pravda* (September 9, 1962) with the evident aim of stimulating a wider public discussion of the problems of enterprise planning and control. Many responses to his proposal, both favorable and unfavorable, were published in the central press and many alternative proposals for reform were made. Because this discussion occurred shortly before the November 1962 plenary session of the CPSU Central Committee, many believed that the leadership might be preparing to introduce some real changes in economic administration. In the end, however, no changes were made. The proposals were premature, Khrushchev announced in his final words to the session, and the issue was turned over for further discussion to a special group, the Scientific Council on Khozraschet and Material Stimulation of Production, USSR Academy of Sciences.

Nevertheless, the 1962 discussion revealed a great deal of sympathy for the idea of freeing the managers from petty tutelage, though much disagreement as to how this might be accomplished. Many economists and planning officials feared that the proposals infringed on the principle of planning, which they considered inadmissable. On the other hand, spokesmen for enterprise management supported the general Liberman line, and a great many of the comments received by the press and by the Scientific Council apparently favored even more independence for management than Liberman had proposed. A subsequent review of the discussion revealed that some of the proposals went so far as to divorce the enterprise from the whole idea of national economic planning and to make profit a universal, automatic regulator of enterprise activity.

It is also significant that the argument against Libermanism was conducted less from an ideological than from a practical and technical point of view. In part at least this was undoubtedly the result of a lecture delivered to the party Central Committee (November 1962 Plenum) by

Nikita Khrushchev, in which the former First Secretary pronounced profit a legitimate measure of enterprise performance. He then stated that although socialism did not assign to profit the universal importance it enjoys under capitalism, it does have "in the individual enterprise . . . great significance as an economic index of the effectiveness of its work." Consequently, most of the criticism of Liberman ran in terms of what would happen if certain indicators were not planned from above, how misleading profit would be as a measure of national economic advantage under existing prices, and other such pragmatic considerations.

The strongest argument against the Liberman idea is to be found in the deficiencies of the Soviet price system. Profit can be a reliable measure of the social usefulness of enterprise activity only if the prices of the inputs the firm consumes accurately measure the social cost of its work, and if the prices for its output reflect the value of its contribution to the achievement of overall objectives. The Soviet price system as it exists today certainly does not meet this criterion. The new mathematical economists of the Kantorovich persuasion have developed a thoroughly sound understanding of the principles of rational pricing, and they surely know how prices must be reformed before the use of profit as a measure of enterprise success will be feasible. But it is interesting that this group has had very little to say in the current debate on planning reform. Thus the traditional economists, planners, and managerial officials, who are seriously handicapped by their lack of appreciation of how price is related to profit control of producers, have been most active in the argument, while those who really understand the issue have been curiously silent.

The New Experiments

The Liberman controversy of 1962 was only an episode, and the discussion of possible reforms in administration smoldered on more or less continuously until fanned into vigorous life once again by the announcement of the post-Khrushchev leadership that they intended to take action. Moreover, many of the proposals made in the course of the discussion became the subject of "economic experiments" in a sample of enterprises. This experimental bent is another indication of the weakening of doctrinal imperatives in favor of pragmatic considerations. Some of the experiments have involved a refining of the measurement of output, as in the substitution of the "value added" concept for the formerly used "gross output" in light industry. As of January 1, 1965, all enterprises in light industry were to be using the new system. Similarly, a number of construction projects are being experimentally financed by long-term loans from the Stroibank (to be repaid from profits), rather than by outright grants as is the usual practice.

But the most striking of these experiments has been the attempt to put something like the Liberman idea to work in enterprises of light industry. In July 1964, two clothing manufacturers, the Bolshevichka firm in Moscow and the Maiak firm in Gorky, received permission to work out their own output plan on the basis of orders from retail clothing outlets and to assume control over other factors in their plan, such as the fund and working capital. In addition, their managements obtained the right to manipulate wages within the plant to stimulate regard for quality in production. Success was to be judged by fulfillment of the sales plan the firms had set themselves, and by profit. Bonuses for the officials of the firms were to be paid from profits, and a share of the profits was to be left at the disposal of the enterprise for its own purposes. In order to assure responsiveness to customers' preferences, some flexibility was allowed in price setting and strong financial sanctions were stipulated for failure to make deliveries according to contract. For each day's delay in schedule delivery, the enterprises were to be docked .3 to .4 percent of the value of the undelivered goods, and at the expiration of 20 days, 5 to 6 percent. This year, the program has been extended to an additional 400 firms in the textile, clothing, leather and footwear industries with essentially the same provisions. It was also suggested that the system be tried in some branches of heavy industry, and variations on it have now been reported in mines, food processing, retailing and machine building.

In spite of some measure of success with these recent experiments, the experience with the new system so far does not augur well for the success of applied Libermanism under present conditions. Reports on results under the new rules mention some serious problems and suggest that much more thoroughgoing reforms will have to be put into effect if the new idea is to work. Prices have turned out to be one problem, as might have been expected. To make the producer sensitive to the buyer's desire for something speical, prices must be a negotiable item, but this requirement has been met only partially. The Bolshevichka and Maiak experiment permitted direct negotiation about prices for new items, and special markups for special finishing and trimmings, but in general the prices of their products are still taken from the standard price lists established by higher control organs, and this has caused trouble. The Bolshevichka firm found that on some of its most popular items it incurred losses or made little profit, and the result of the first year's work in both enterprises was a decline in both value of sales and profits compared to earlier periods. The enhanced emphasis on profit as a success measure is not going to make producers interested in catering to buyers' wants if doing so reduces profits.

In view of this basic problem, it is interesting to find in the official magazine of the textile industry a discussion of textile prices which shows no awareness of how the old price structure in the industry will affect the behavior of textile plants under the new system. The author of the article, an official of the Gosplan bureau in charge of price setting, says that existing prices are out of line with present costs (the price list for cotton goods was fixed in 1955 and for woolen goods in 1958), producing big profits in some lines, losses in others. But he seems totally oblivious of what this must mean for the behavior of textile firms transferred to the system of profit incentives. Yet, in some cases, more sensitivity to the price problem has been shown. Thus a Urals producer of bearings has recently been granted permission—by way of quality incentive—to charge higher prices for bearings with a guaranteed life. The Nevskii Machinery Plant in Leningrad has been treated the same way. These price changes, however, have been achieved as a result of decisions taken by higher echelons at the Sovnarkhoz level, not as a result of negotiations between producer and consumer.

The enterprises' freedom of maneuver under the new system is still too restricted to expect much improvement in their work. For one thing, their suppliers have remained under the traditional system of controls. One feature of the Bolschevichka and Maiak experiment was the right granted the two firms to contract for deliveries of clothing to retail outlets on a monthly schedule and in fabrics specified by the customer. But when they turned to textile plants to secure the necessary materials, they could get delivery commitments only on a quarterly basis and found it impossible to obtain the fabric qualities and varieties they needed to fill their orders. The textile firms were still working under the old system on the basis of quarterly output plans, and they cared little about quality or variety. This is surely one of the main reasons for the subsequent extension of the experiment to a larger circle of light industry plants. Unless Libermanism is made universal, however, an interface between the domain of the old system and the new will remain, which will seriously restrict the flexibility of enterprises in the latter sector.

But the really amazing inhibition on the promised freedom in the new domain is footdragging by the bureaucrats. The plant managers under the new system find that their former administrative superiors still prescribe endless detail for them exactly as before, and one fascinating article claims that despite unequivocal instructions in the decrees establishing the new order, the local branch of the Gosbank refused to let the managers of the Bolshevichka and Maiak plants use profits as they saw fit, and that the state arbitration agency refused to allow the financial sanctions for late delivery that were to make suppliers adhere to their promises!

Altogether, the experiment in applied Libermanism has been a less radical departure from tradition than advertised. Moreover, even though the obstacles to change seem to have been bureaucratic rather than doctrinaire, it seems unlikely that the new system will be extended much farther. The willingness to try Libermanism in light industry was conditioned by a special emergency not likely to be duplicated elsewhere in the economy. The last two or three years have seen a frightening build-up of unsold goods precisely in the industries involved in the reform. Stocks of apparel in the retail trade network rose from 1,485 million rubles on January 1, 1959 to 4,133 million rubles worth on January 1, 1964. Many of these goods are said to be unsalable because they are out of fashion and of low quality—second and third grade. There was also a large, though not quite so spectacular, growth in retail stocks of textiles and footwear, at least through the end of 1962. Subsequent trends are not known because, interestingly, in the 1963 Statistical Handbook, data on stocks of goods in retail trade no longer appear. It is known, however, that in 1963 sales of textiles and sewn goods actually declined and that in sales of footwear stagnation had set in. No figures are available yet for 1964, but it is likely that the situation became worse rather than better and that this emboldened the authorities to hasten the extension of the new system to much of the rest of the textile and apparel industry—even though the feasibility and effectiveness of this move was far from proved. The piling up of several billion rubles worth of resources in totally useless output must impress the Soviet leaders as an intolerable waste, especially when so many other resource needs are competing for attention.

The Battle of Priorities

The second issue—the priority to be given to consumption relative to other claims on national resources—has always been the most sensitive question in Soviet economic life. It held a central place in the one period of open debate about economic policy, the industrialization debate of the 1920's, but the outcome of that debate was a decision so adverse to the interests of consumers that the subject could never again be discussed honestly in public; it had become a divisive issue that had the potential for shattering what measure of social consensus there has ever been in Soviet life. The problem was therefore officially laid to rest, embalmed in sterile doctrine and hypocritical slogans and publicly touched upon only obliquely and euphemistically.

Soviet ideologists assert that continuous improvement of the population's welfare constitutes a basic economic law of their society, but this is usually coupled with statements about the priority of the need to build the technical-material base of socialism. They have also rationalized the postponement of improvements in consumption levels by doctrinal references to an "objective necessity" for the output of Sector I, producing the means of production, to grow more rapidly than the output of Sector II, producing goods of consumption. But any discussion of these assertions in operational terms has been notably absent. National income figures on the relative shares devoted to investment, consumption and other end uses have until recently not been published and, one suspects, not even systematically compiled; that would have been too direct, too blunt a revelation of the low priority assigned to consumption. Even today, what information is published on national income allocation is essentially fantasy. If the official figures are to be believed, no part of the Soviet national income is devoted to military purposes.

Because this question of consumption versus other uses of national resources is so explosive, it is ideally suited as an issue for political maneuver within the ranks of the power elite in Soviet society. The favorite method of alluding to it has usually been in terms of the relative rates of growth of "Industry A" versus "Industry B." It has been a part of Soviet economic ideology that the output of Industry A must grow faster than the output of Industry B. This idea is elaborately grounded in Marxian economic theory and it is also supported by numerous pronouncements of Lenin (especially in his pre-revolutionary article "On the So-called Question of Markets").

The distinction between Industry A and Industry B is based on the application to the industrial sector of the Marxian distinction between activities producing the means of production and those producing goods of consumption. Industry A covers the former, Industry B the latter. Great emphasis is placed on this distinction, which invariably appears in Soviet plans and statistical reporting for industry. Yet the question of the relative rates of growth of these two elements in the national output is only vaguely related to the issue of consumption versus other resource use. For one thing, the definition of Industry A and Industry B in Soviet statistical practice differs from the Marxian concepts from which the proposition is drawn. In the real world it turns out that nearly any branch of industry produces both producers' goods and consumer goods. Although we think of the textile industry as a consumer goods industry, much of its output consists of producers' goods. Many products, such as gasoline, for example, can be used either for consumption, as in passenger automobiles, or for further production, as in farm tractors. Moreover, the proposition itself need be true neither in the Marxian growth model, nor in more sophisticated theories of growth. But just because of this unreality, the distinction and its terminology have provided an ideal idiom for referring obliquely to the real problem, and at any time of crisis, such as the Stalin-Malenkov-Khrushchev transition, there is likely to be renewed controversy about relative growth rates of Industry A and Industry B. The last several years of the Khrushchev era and the first year of the new regime have again seen a great deal of discussion in these terms, which implies uncertainty and conflict within the leadership over the relative priority to be given consumption.

What is actually happening to allocational priorities, or what the intentions of the new leadership are, is difficult to discern. But to the extent that evidence on actual resource use is available, it appears that there has been no serious shift from a growth and power orientation toward a consumer-oriented set of priorities, even though numerous policy acts have been so interpreted. In the late 1950's, the government had begun to make loans to citizens for the purchase of consumer durables and for the construction of privately-owned housing, which seemed to indicate encouragement for consumption. But after 1960, the volume of such credit declined sharply.

The introduction of incentives in enterprises of light industry is also interpreted as evidence of a new appreciation of consumer claims. To be sure, the reform is intended to make enterprises producing for household consumption more responsive to the wishes of the population, but as was suggested above, the real concern is to avoid waste within the portion of national resources allocated to consumer goods production; it does not imply greater priority for consumption in overall resources use.

Other indications of a kind of welfare revolution have been seen in such acts as the raising of minimum wages and the extension of the pension system, most recently to collective farmers. But all of these are better interpreted as efforts to improve production efficiency. They represent a rationalization of incentives to encourage more effort on the part of the labor force—a reform of means rather than a shift in the regime's preferences about ends.

Indeed, there has been much evidence in recent years of a repressed inflation in the Soviet economy, which suggests a tendency to cut back on intended consumption goals when over-ambitious commitments being to press against resource limitations. Moves intended to result in higher consumption levels, such as wage increases, increases in farm prices, pension improvements and tax reductions, are not validated by sufficiently large corresponding increases in consumer goods production. The failure of agricultural production to grow appreciably since 1958 has been an important factor in this development, as has also been the refusal of Soviet citizens to buy the obsolete and low-quality goods produced for sale to them. Postponement of the scheduled tax reduction in the early 1960's and the raising of the prices for meat and dairy products in the summer of 1962 were clearly called for by the need to extract excess purchasing power from the population. And frequent comment during the past year that it is important to coordinate fully the monetary demand of the population with the supply of consumer goods attests that the problem remains.

Encroachments of Rationality

Yet despite the lack of any real change in the share of national income allotted to consumption, it is undeniable that there is a new tone in Soviet discussions of overall priorities. Under Khrushchev, there was a much more explicit acknowledgement of the importance of improving the welfare of the Soviet citizen, and the new leadership, to the extent that a change in tone can be distinguished in its pronouncements, appears even more openly committed to the importance of improving living standards. This emphasis is particularly evident in the commentary on the 1965 Plan by the Deputy Chief of Gosplan, in which promises are made to advance the timing of some scheduled wage increases, to increase housing construction and to make special efforts to raise the output of construction goods.

But the most interesting development, which may be symptomatic of a genuine reordering of priorities, ia an attack on the traditional ideological supports for the high investment policy and especially a reevaluation of the "A versus B" doctrine. Khrushchev first called the doctrine into question when in a discussion of growth priorities he declared that is was important to distinguish between different kinds of investment within the means-of-production category. Equipment for new steel mills and equipment for textile factories are both means of production, but the production of textile mill equipment leads directly to increases in consumer goods output, whereas steel mill equipment does not. He asserted that the consumption of the output of Industry A was changing toward items of the textile mill equipment type, so that notwithstanding the continued high priority for Industry A, this now embodied a real promise of an early improvement in the supply of consumer goods. In the past, of course, insistence on priority for Industry A had meant in effect increasing the production of steel to build more steel mills to produce more steel to build more steel mills. In thus digging beneath the surface of the polished cliché, the former Premier prepared the way, whether intentionally or not, for a more intelligent discussion on the consumption-versus-investment issued.

Another form of the same revisionist tendency is the assertion, made frequently of late, that—even admitting the necessity of predominant growth of Industry A over Industry B—the time has come when the divergence between the two growth rates ought to be lessened. More recently, the doctrine has been attacked as altogether false, notably in a series of articles published in *Ekonomicheskaia gazeta* in the spring and summer of this year. On the consumption-investment issue, just as in the argument over profit and prices in the proposed economic reform, discourse in the Soviet Union runs along two completely separate lines. The new mathematical economists have taken up the question in the context of their efforts to construct optimizing economic growth models. These models inevitably stress one central feature of the growth process, namely that consumption can be sacrificed in the present to make available increased consumption in the future via investment. The question of a criterion for choosing an optimal growth rate is inescapable in this kind of theorizing. The obvious and sensible criterion is the preference of the population concerning postponement of some of today's potential consumption to increase that of future years, and this general idea is incorporated in some of the models that have been discussed. So far, there has been no interaction between these two universes of thought. The new economists completely ignore the "A versus B" distinction as meaningless, while the traditional economists and the men of affairs are less interested in the fundamental abstract principles than in chipping away at received doctrine just enough to clear the way for more open discussion. Though limited, this activity is in a way more significant than the more fundamental theorizing of the new economists. Once the ideological obstacles are openly and publicly questioned, an honest discussion becomes possible and the way may be opened for a real debate on allocation priorities.

The adaptation of economic doctrine and practice to changing circumstances is not a new thing in the Soviet Union. There have been numerous instances in the past when an established bit of dogma has had to be ignored or repudiated if those in charge of making economic policy and running the economy were to be free to pursue effectively the primary ends of the regime, such as the goal of pushing the growth rate to the limit or maximizing the economic wherewithal that could be wrung from available resources. Whether the doctrinal point at issue was derived from Marx (as in the idea that an interest rate was inadmissible under socialism) or whether it was invented by the Soviet leadership itself (for example, the now repudiated idea that obsolescence did not exist in the Soviet economy), ideology has seldom been able to maintain itself when it came into obvious conflict with expediency. What is happening today, therefore, is remarkable less for the fact that ideological positions on economic affairs are being subverted than for the fact that the offensive against ideology is now touching on doctrines that are more basic than any that have been involved before, and that it calls into question the fundamental institutions of the Soviet economic system as well as the authority of the party. There is probably some truth in the charge against Liberman and the groups for which he is a spokesman that they are at heart against the principle of central planning. Moreover, the argument about priorities, muted and incoherent though it is, does involve an attack on the right of the party leadership to enforce its preferences over those of the population. This is what makes the encroachments on ideology in economic questions today so portentous.

Postscript

On Septemper 27, a plenary session of the CPSU Central Committee was convened to discuss and approve the long-awaited reforms in economic administration. The changes turn out to be a blend of some elements of the Liberman-style proposals discussed in this article, some other less widely advertised increases in managerial autonomy, and a new round of administrative reshuffling. The central administrative structure is to be organized once again on the sectoral principle, and the territorial economic councils are to be abolished. The lush growth of central planning agencies has also been pruned back somewhat with the abolition of the Supreme Economic Council and the All-Union Economic Council.

The indicators to be planned for the enterprise from above have been decreased and now include volume of sales, output of principal products, wage bill, total profit and the ratio of profit to capital, payments to the budget, centrally planned capital outlay, introduction of new technology, allocations of materials, and disposition of output. Management has gained considerably more authority over personnel matters, especially in establishing incentive systems within the plant. The profit indicator is new and has been given an important role, since significant amounts of profit will be left under the control of the enterprise to be spent for investment, wage incentives, etc. But it is not at all clear to what extent the managerial bonus system will be tied to profit performance alone, as recommended by Liberman. It is also interesting that the reforms do not envisage an extension of the system of direct ties between producers and their customers beyond its present sphere of application. For the moment, inputs are to be made available, and output disposed of, through a central allocation system not noticeably different from that now used.

One far-reaching change will be some decentralization of investment decisions. Enterprises are to have new sources from which they can make investments on their own, and more investment is to be made from repayable bank credit, less from outright grants. The price-reform issue is left unresolved. Its importance for making the profit indicator a meaningful measure of success is acknowledged, but actual price reform has been put off again. The reform scheduled for the end of 1965 will apparently not take place, and an overhaul of the price system is not expected before 1967.

Altogether, the reforms probably mean a certain increase in managerial autonomy and an improved system of incentives, but they are far from the bold move toward decentralization via market techniques that some had expected. With regard to the matter of priorities, the trends described earlier in the text are affirmed in the great emphasis that Kosygin has placed on the need to increase consumer welfare. In his report to the Central Committee he said outright that the share of consumption in national income must be increased.

KOSYGIN, LIBERMAN, AND THE PACE OF SOVIET INDUSTRIAL REFORM*

. — . — . — . — . — . — . — . — . — . — .

Michael Kaser†

The international significance of Evsei Liberman was recently symbolized by his appearance on the cover of *Time* magazine (February 12, 1965), captioned "The Communist Flirtation with Profits." The reforms he has advocated—notably, a profit incentive for enterprise managers and an interest charge for capital—have widely been taken as another sign of the convergence of Eastern European socialism and Western European capitalism. It is, of course, true that while planning is being introduced to more of the Western market economies—the latest example is Britain's first Five-Year Plan—market-type experiments are spreading throughout eastern Europe. Liberman himself has frequently protested that he has never sought to promote such convergence, and the first aim of the present article is to show how far his proposals fall short of free-enterprise capitalism. A second objective presents itself in the context of eastern Europe: both of Liberman's proposed tools—profit criteria and capital charges—are used in the reforms and experiments now under way in Bulgaria, Czechoslovakia, Hungary, Poland, and East Germany.

More restricted experiments along Liberman's lines were begun in the U.S.S.R. in January this year and extended in July; the meeting of the Party Central Committee scheduled to discuss industrial problems is almost certain to introduce further changes. A third purpose of this survey is therefore to examine these developments in the light of the transfer

*Reprinted by permission of the Royal Institute of International Affairs, from *The World Today*, September 1965, pp. 375–388. All footnotes deleted.

†Michael C. Kaser is University Lecturer in Soviet Economics, University of Oxford and Fellow of St. Antony's College. His publications include: *Comecon: Integration Problems of the Planned Economies* (1965), "The Organization of Soviet Industry and its effects on Decision Making" *Value and Plan* (1960) Gregory Grossman (ed.), and "Welfare Criteria in Soviet Planning," *Soviet Planning* (1964) Jane Degras (ed.).

of the Chairmanship of the Council of Ministers in October 1964. Finally, but perhaps most significantly, the new Administration has allowed the press much latitude in the criticism of economic policy. A Soviet economist's estimate that 20 per cent of the urban population were virtually unemployed recently gained world-wide attention, but many other past practices have come under fire. The article therefore concludes with a review of the industrial problems now publicly debated and of the new policies described by Brezhnev and Kosygin to the Central Committee of the Soviet Communist Party in March 1965.

Interpreting Liberman

A technique of news presentation which centres upon personalities has brought Liberman vastly more publicity in the Western than in the Eastern press. In direct proportion to Western attachment to the man himself, Soviet newspapers have striven to minimize personal authorship. Indeed, with broad acceptance of his proposals, Soviet press mention of his name has virtually disappeared. Liberman himself has deprecated his share in the movement and he may justifiably be considered to personify, rather than to lead, a group of industrial reformers whose ideas have been emerging in print over a decade. As an economist specializing in factory administration—he had published a book on the organization of engineering shops—he represented the twin streams of reform, academic economics and enterprise management. In the other planned economies of eastern Europe his profit and interest ideas had been still more prominently discussed, and bore little novelty by the time his famous *Pravda* article appeared on September 9, 1962.

Any analysis of that article must distinguish between the enterprise as a profit-maker (from which his proposals start) and the enterprise as a profit-taker (a concept he rejects). Liberman bases himself on the Marxian definition of socialist 'productive relations', which requires collective ownership of the means of production. The 'surplus value' created by 'socially necessary labour' (i.e. over and above the return to that labour in consumption goods and the replacement of means of production) is available for the accumulation of new means of production (Marx's 'extended' reproduction). The surplus value is a 'profit' to society, and only in the case of what Marx called 'simple reproduction'—when capital is solely replaced (gross investment thus equalling depreciation)—would no 'profit' arise. The form in which this profit is made is not implicitly prejudged either by Marx or by his Soviet followers. Indeed, Soviet economists make clear that they regard as purely formal the distinction between taxes on State enterprises and profits earned by such enterprises. It goes without saying that in such an economy the enterprise is the profit-maker, but the State (or society) is the profit-taker. Marx's analysis of the bourgeois State identified the capitalist as the profit-taker: not only did he see this income as derived by exploitation of the workers (whose efforts alone justify remuneration, under a labour theory of value), but in its disposition as strengthening capitalist accumulation.

If this analysis is carried to the case of a socialized economy, the possibility arises that a socialist enterprise may retain its profits to undertake socialist accumulation. This, of course, is the theoretical foundation of the Yugoslav system, but has been absent from Soviet practice since 1930. The director of a Soviet enterprise has been allowed to keep a small proportion of his profit for bonuses and amenities but hardly any for productive investment. Under the reforms now advocated profits would play a larger role as material incentives, but would remain preponderantly subject to allocation by higher authority.

The many industrial managers who support the new ideas have no quarrel with the central planning of investment funds, but seek relief from the planners. Their part in the debate has been to protest against the multiplicity of vacillating instructions handed down to them: their hope is for a single profit target set for a full year—or still longer, In addition, profits are rightly seen as an index of saleability, and a parallel reform discussed below (the 'Bolshevichka-Mayak experiment') is intended to use them to match output more closely to the requirements of consumers.

Since Stalin's death, managers have had a taste of autonomy only under Bulganin's interregnum from 1955 to mid-1957. Other Administrations favoured more centralization: in 1953 Malenkov instituted tightened industrial control with 'overlord' Ministries; in 1957 Khrushchev transferred many of the central functions to regional bodies (*sovnarkhozy*) and from 1962 to 1964 tried to combine Moscow 'overlords' (in the form of State Committees for each industry) with consolidated regional authority. In 1962 also he called in the regional committees of the Communist Party to strengthen centripetal power.

The 'production principle' thus introduced for the Party was abandoned immediately after Khrushchev's departure, and the division of political supremacy has given new impetus to managerial claism. It is certainly significant that such a plea by the Director of the Moscow Electric Lamp Factory (to diminish the number of plan indicators and allow the enterprise frredom to negotiate certain of its own prices) cited 1956-7 as his factory's best period. 'Apart from declaratory affirmations,' he protested, 'practically nothing has been done.' A conference of economists in June this year complained that draft laws on the status of the enterprise and of the enterprise association ('*firm*') had been awaiting ratification for three years (reported in *Pravda* of June 23).

The Original Liberman Proposals

Neither of the two management techniques which combined to form the Liberman proposals of 1962—'plan indicators' and 'material incentives'—was new in itself.

An 'indicator' is the measure of conformity to a plan set by an upper echelon: in the case of a worker it is a 'labour-norm,' in that of an enterprise it is, in Nove's term, a 'success indicator.' The concept of 'material incentives' is simply payment by results. The 'indicator' has been a feature of Soviet planning since the first Five-Year Plan (1928–32), and 'material incentives' date from Stalin's denunciations of 'petty-bourgeois egalitarianism' in 1932 and, more sharply, from the Stakhanovism of 1936. The enterprise manager receives a supplement of about one-third of his salary if his enterprise meets one or more indicators, in the same way as, under piece-rates, a manual worker receives a bonus on completion of his work-norm.

The 1962 proposals were new in attaching the managerial premium to a new indicator—the profits earned in the enterprise—to supplant the many currently in use. The proposals formed part of the trend., now widely advocated, towards the replacement of physical controls by monetary instruments. Moreover, by relating profits to the enterprise holding of fixed assets, the reformers sought to counter the inefficient use of equipment, the unfustified applications for budget allocations, and the dispersal of capital resources which were the causes of the Soviet investment crisis of 1961–2. Most investment in State enterprises has been financed by central taxation as interest-free grants; the practice dates from the credit reform of 1930 and was not publicly questioned until 1954. There have since been many advocates of a system of bank finance—i.e. that investments should be paid for by repayable and interest-bearing loans. The present proposals, however, concern not only new capital but all existing assets, and are thus like the Yugoslav tax on fixed assets, enacted in 1954, and the East German, Hungarian, and Bulgarian practices introduced last year.

Liberman, a professor at Kharkov University, the original exponent of the new proposals, first advocated management reform nearly a decade ago when he suggested that the cost of production should be made the sole indicator for an enterprise. At about the same time he drew attention to the revision of price formation which goals in cost terms would require Liberman's cost indicator was adopted by the Soviet Government in 1960 (although in public its authorship went unremarked both in the U.S.S.R. and elsewhere), but a number of other indicators were retained as supplementary determinants of premia, doubtless because the authorities baulked at his second requirement of price reform. The 1960 change did, however, depose 'global output' as the chief, and often unique, indicator and those who were to be opponents of the profit principle began promoting experiments to find a substitute: the clothing and printing industries, for example, changed to a measure of something like 'value-added.'

Liberman's main contribution to the current theme of reform was presented to the Scientific Council of the U.S.S.R. Academy of Sciences in April 1962, and taken up enthusiastically by the chairman, Academician Nemchinov, as he revealed in *Pravda* of September 21. The Council approved it with some qualification and encouraged Liberman to write up his scheme for *Pravda*. Liberman's key idea in his own words, was to ensure that 'what is good for society is good for the enterprise'—a classic enough definition of the profit-motive in a capitalist society. Furthermore, a plan based upon the realistic appraisals and expectations of the enterprise director is likely to be a better one than a plan evolved by central direction or by any quasi-automatic procedure: Liberman therefore suggested an ingenious technique for profit to be planned by the enterprise itself. Such a plan would be made when the enterprise had received its production plan and concluded its contracts with suppliers and clients (for he did not, as already stressed, seek to dismantle centralized planning). The premium then paid at the end of the year would be that scheduled for the profit halfway between the planned and the actual figures. The enterprise would not—as had been standard practice in the past—'struggle for an "easy" plan . . . [Under the proposals] the enterprises themselves will seek supplementary tasks and will not "fight off" such assignments as they do now.' If the enterprise did not reach its goal, it would get the premium scheduled for its actual profit.

A number of contributors to the ensuing debate took issue with Liberman on the suitability of profits as an indicator when prices were not necessarily indicative of plan directives. Not only was this an old problem, but Liberman had of course long recognized it. At this juncture, his reply was that his scheme would encourage enterprise directors to press for rational prices—'at present, prices are quite a matter of indifference to the enterprise.' When wholesale prices were last revised in July 1955, under Bulganin's Administration, it had been intended that they should be realigned with costs (then seen exclusively as labour costs) on the eve of each Five-Year Plan. By 1960, however, the sixth Five-Year Plan had just been superseded by a Seven-Year Plan (1959–65) and it was decided to bring in a new list on January 1, 1963. As the Director of the Moscow Electric Lamp Factory recently complained, 'the general reform of wholesale prices and freight tariffs has been continually postponed, and it is doubtful whether it can be completed before 1966.' January 1966 has now been officially announced as the date of introducing new price lists, which promise, as is indicated below, to take some first steps towards reflecting other scarcities than labour (i.e. land and capital) and consumer utilities.

The Intermission in Public Debate

At the November 1962 plenary session of the Central Committee, Khrushchev introduced measures of centralization and Party control which ran counter to hopes for extending enterprise autonomy, and stated that judgment on a profit 'indicator' should be reserved until the Planning Commission had reported on their experimental application. In early 1963 a committee was set up to examine the proposals, but the promised recommendations never appeared. More significant than this official silence, however, was the introduction at the beginning of 1964 of 'value-added' as the plan 'indicator' for a number of consumer-goods industries, on the grounds of successful experimental use in the Tatar ASSR. The incompatibility of this 'indcator' with the profit instrument was soon voiced at senior level—by Malyshev, Deputy Director of the Central Statistical Administration and a long-standing proponent of price reform. The Chairman of the Tatar *Sovnarkhoz*, Tabeev, confirmed that the 'value-added indicator' excluded profit, and stated that profits were irrational in the existing state of price-fixing.

The practicability of a 'profit indicator' continued, however, to be a subject of discussion in the technical journals. A paper by Vaag and Zakharov suggested a specific rate of profit (20 per cent of the value of fixed assets) for Liberman's 'long-term norm'; this was criticized by Bachurin and Pervukhin, on the ground that Marxist value-theory required profit (surplus value) to be related to wage cost. Bachurin and Pervukhin wanted to adopt only those of Liberman's proposals which made little change in the existing system, namely, to link managerial premia to the fulfilment of the profit plan and to apply material incentives to an indicator of capital utilization. Another contribution suggested that a 'long-term norm' be set for wages: during the period for which the norm was set wage increases could only be paid for out of increments in factory productivity. This was to emerge in the 'Bolshevichka-Mayak experiment' the following year. The proposal has much in common with wage determination as practiced in Yugoslavia and advocated in the present Czechoslovak reform.

The Second Round of Debate

In March 1964 Nemchinov, without mentioning Liberman, argued for a 'system of central planning with enterprise autonomy' to counter 'spontaneous voluntarism in the links of the chain of socialist management'; reform should not replace but should implement 'the basic [central] directives on the national economic plan.' (After October

Brezhnev was to epitomize Khrushchev's agricultural policies as 'voluntarist,' but Nemchinov died before this vindication.)

In May, Liberman cleared the way for his own re-entry by a declaration of his Marxism, explicitly dissociating himself from those Western commentators who had suggested that his proposals embraced capitalism; in an interview reported in the Yugoslav newspaper *Borba*, July 9, 1964) he reiterated the Marxist character of his proposals, which he affirmed were again under active consideration.

In an article in *Pravda*, July 10, 1964, Academician Leontief reinstated the debate at the point where Khrushchev had left it in November 1962. He emphasized, as Khrushchev had done, that profit-taking under socialism was radically different from the process under capitalism and that material incentives could be based upon profit-making if this conduced to the more efficient use of resources. He placed the debate as much in the framework of the Sino-Soviet dispute ('the Peking leaders fiercely attack the principle of material incentives . . . [and] present this major feature of the economics of socialism as a retreat from Marxism, as evidence of bourgeois degeneration') as in competition with capitalism ('the bourgeois apologists, who seek to present the improvement of management as a return to capitalist principles . . . doubtless calculate that improvement in economic management will still further strengthen socialism's position').

On August 17 another Academician, Trapeznikov, publicly reopened the *Pravda* debate on profit as an enterprise indicator. In envisaging the accompaniments of profits as a success indicator by 'a few other quantity and quality indicators,' he did not go as far as Liberman; he stressed, of course, that 'in capitalist society, capital is a source of income and the interest on it is the capitalists' profit. . . In our country it has become an economic instrument to accelerate the circulation of funds.' Although he agreed that capital should no longer be doled out without charge, he would not accept 'long-term norms,' and thus conceded more central control over the enterprise. He claimed, in fact, that rapid technical progress would erode the rationality of any long-run norm, and thus he was ready to advocate flexible wholesale prices, partly to demote 'global output' as a plan indicator and partly to stimulate technical and qualitative progress in production.

The contributors who followed in the *Pravda* debate were all favourable to this sort of reform. In contrast to the first round of 1962, radical opposition was not expressed, although, in conversations in Moscow at the time, the present writer gained the impression that some senior officials in central departments remained strong opponents. Until Liberman himself took a hand in the debate, his name was not mentioned, although Leontief's contribution in *Pravda*, September 7, 1964, observed that 'a couple of years ago the proposition that profit, in certain defined conditions, should be used as the basic criteria for the operation of an enterprise encountered opposition "in principle". . . Now such voices are rarely to be heard.' It is significant that the other contributors represented the main spheres of interest in the debate. Trapeznikov and Leontief (and, earlier, Nemchinov) had represented the academic world. Two participants were selected from factory management, one from each major centre, namely, a senior official of the big Likhachev Motor Vehicle Works, Moscow, and the Director of the Leningrad Machine Tool Combine. The two other entrants in the debate came from the central administrative departments, one from each of the main lines of authority, namely from the *Sovnarkhoz* of the Russian Federation and from the U.S.S.R. Planning Commission. Liberman's own contribution on September 20 made a significant addition to his original ideas, and this explicitly as a result of the 1962 discussion. He proposed that the rate of profit should be attached not exclusively to the value of productive fixed assets but also to the size of the wage fund. He emphasized that the profit motive must be reflected in incentives throughout the enterprise if it were to eliminate thoroughly the conflict of interest 'with society, as represented by the State.' 'In the economic regions of the Russian Federation there are over 10,000 enterprise directors,' the *Sovnarkhoz* Chairman, Afanasev, had remarked. 'In the majority they are energetic, resolute and competent organizers of production'.

The consensus of opinion among participants on the eve of Khrushchev's fall was, first, that success indicators now operative should be reduced towards (though not necessarily to) a single index, since it was multiplicity which had caused conflict between State and enterprise interest; secondly, that the need to rationalize capital utilization was urgent. Profit per unit of productive outlay as an indicator satisfied both propositions, and difference of opinion was overt only on the phasing of the reform. The most cautious viewpoint in print was that of the representative of the Planning Commission who observed: 'Once the role of profits in material incentives has been strengthened, developments themselves will show which indicators need not be planned for enterprises.'

The Bolshevichka-Mayak Experiment

At the same time as the tacit decision to reopen the Liberman debate, a parallel experiment began in the linking of the supply of consumer goods to the pattern of demand. As has been pointed out earlier, the exposure of profits to prices dictated by the market (or to some other decentralized decision) was never at issue in the Liberman debates. Nor has it been in the Bolshevichka-Mayak experiment, which sought to adjust the assortment of goods to consumer preferences, at centrally fixed prices and within overall production limits set by current capacity. The Bolshevichka-Mayak experiment does not permit the expansion of plant to comply with consumers' preferences, unless that expansion is approved by the central authorities. Under the repressed inflation and low real incomes of Stalin's Five-Year Plans, consumers could choose only between buying up whatever was offered and hoarding cash—a practice defended in theory as Say's Law, whereby supply creates it own demand. In 1956, this policy was reversed: price and wage equilibrium was adjusted to allow aggregate supply slightly to exceed effective demand. To match this change, serious market research was begun, for which the academic break-through came in a symposium on consumer-goods supply and demand in *Ekonomicheskie nauki*, No. 5, 1963. Significantly, Kosygin's speech to the March 1965 Plenum of the Party Central Committee, released in *Planovoe Khozyaistvo* of April, ended with an assurance of the correlation of supply to consumer demand by what he termed 'a normal circulation of money in the country.'

The Bolshevichka-Mayak experiment falls into two parts—that introduced before the fall of Khrushchev, and that decreed in January 1965, which comprises an element of the Liberman scheme. On July 1, 1964, two unions of ready-made clothing enterprises—Bolshevichka in Moscow and Mayak in Gorky—were authorized to take orders direct from shops. Associations of this nature had begun three years previously in the footwear industry of Lvov (and had been given the title of 'Soviet firms'—*firmy*). The orders sent in by shops formed the plan indicator for the constituent enterprise, and target fulfilment was represented by the sales consequent on those orders. Incentives were provided not only for the technical and managerial staff (to whom plan-fulfilment premia have, as mentioned, long been paid) but also to all workers: such bonuses on completion of the sales plan were, moreover, at a very high level—40–50 per cent of basic wages, compared to the average of about 30 percent of salary for managers under the traditional schemes.

In January 1965, approximately 400 textile, clothing, leather, and footwear associations (all the clothing and footwear factories in Moscow, Leningrad, Kiev, Odessa, Kharkov, Lvov, Minsk, Vilnius, Riga, and Tallinn) were put on the Bolshevichka-Mayak system, to which was added one of Liberman's proposals. In the January experiment the plan indicators were jointly the sales plan (in relation to orders placed) and the profit plan. Because unsold stocks or returned *brak* (faulty goods) would count neither for the sales nor for the profit plan, the two indicators would normally move in harmony, and thus operate in the same way as the Liberman system.

The Key Debate over Qualitative Indicators

The Liberman debate in the press came to an abrupt halt in late September 1964. Towards the end of that month (reported as 'recently' in *Pravda*, October 2, 1964) Khrushchev addressed a meeting of plan officials and managerial representatives on the draft of the 1966–70 Five-Year Plan. In what was patently an abbreviated record of the speech, his sole reference to the debate was a cryptic demand for better 'qualitative indicators.' This term can best be explained by its definition in the Russian *Short Economic Dictionary*:

> Indicators which characterize the efficiency of use of an enterprise's productive capacity. They comprise indices of the use of fixed assets— of equipment or floor-space (e.g. the output of steel per square metre of open-hearth furnace, machine-tool productivity, wagon turnround time, etc.); indices of use of working capital (input of raw materials, fuel and electricity per unit of production); and norms of the output of finished production per unit of material (output of metal from ore, of oil from oilseed, etc.).

The phrase particularly needs explanation to the non-Soviet reader because, as is shown below, the management reformers in the U.S.S.R. use a similar term—'better-quality production'—to distinguish utility-oriented planning from the old *Tonnenideologie* (Ulbricht's word) of output for output's sake. To Khrushchev's audience the First Secretary's call for 'qualitative indicators' was, at worst, a demand for the maintenance of the existing system of a multitude of physical targets in terms of physical measures of capacity and input, and at best—because he used the plural— an indication that he was not prepared to introduce a single money target in terms of a money-valued inventory.

There were, moreover, other arguments in Khrushchev's speech which may well have stiffened the opposition of planning officials and industrial managers behind Kosygin, a former Gosplan chief and Finance Minister. In referring back the draft Plan for 1966–70, Khrushchev in effect disrupted the foreign-trade implications of the output targets and thereby all the corresponding plans within Comecon. Comecon negotiations on 1966–70 Plans had begun in October 1963 and the trade flows had been finalized in July 1964; its Executive was even in session in Moscow at the time of the October Plenum which ousted Khrushchev. Dissatisfaction with the lack of progress towards satisfying consumer demand (Kosygin was also a former Minister of Light Industry) and with agricultural policy (as Brezhnev was to demonstrate) may similarly have influenced economic policymakers against Khrushchev.

Criticism of the delay in introducing planning reform appeared in general terms immediately after the Plenum, and, within a month, discussion of Liberman's ideas was publicly resumed. In January, as mentioned, the profit element in programming was brought into the extension of the Bolshevichka experiment to 400 enterprises.

On January 1 another constituent of the Liberman scheme was authorized in a further experiment, namely the replacement of budget grants for investment by long-term credit. The experiment covers a wide range of industries and areas—chemical-engineering in the Volga *Sovnarkhoz*, mechanical engineering in the Central Black Earth *Sovnarkhoz*, furniture frame-making in Kirgizia, domestic refrigerators in Lithuania, etc. The profits tax is not to be levied until the loans have been repaid, so that in effect these plants will be able to devote all profits to debt amortization and service. It has not been suggested that these enterprises will be able to open new loans once the original loan has been repaid, and loans are only available from the Construction Bank if the object of the loan is approved in the investment plan. In pressing for the extension of an interest charge to all State enterprises, Alperovich, an economist in Rostov-on-Don, was able to cite wide support among his colleagues (he mentioned in particular Nemchinov, Vaag, Birman, Vinokur, Marinko, and Moshkin) and to quote the implementation of similar schemes in East Germany, Hungary, an Bulgaria. In fact, he went further than the east European experiments quoted and suggested that his proposed 'rental taxation of fixed assets' should replace both the profits and the turnover tax. Such a reform would be far-reaching: it would unify the present two-level price system (a lower level for producer's goods than for consumer's goods) and—if the relative prices of consumer's goods among themselves were unchanged—convert the margin between wholesale and retail prices into enterprise profit. Profits would thus become the index of the degree to which consumer preferences were being satisfied (at the prices put on them by the plan authorities) with the least diversion of resources from the investment programme.

A conference on plan indicators convened by the U.S.S.R. Academy of Sciences (reported in March) revealed the strength of those wishing for a compromise. The Chairman, L. Gatovsky, gave his view that in the long run profits would come to be the single indicator of enterprise operation, and that such profitability should be related to the enterprise's stock of fixed and working capital. In the immediate future, however, he felt that the demonstrably useless 'global output' targets should be replaced by 'qualitative indicators,' though of a more sophisticated sort ('value added' or 'the normative value of manufacture'). The Bolshevichka-Mayak scheme should, he believed, be eventually extended to producer's goods.

The conference proved to be as cautious as its chairman and recommended only further study.

A brown-coal mine near Lvov was reported at the end of May to have operated more efficiently in the first five months of the year with its plan indicators reduced to three than during the previous year, when it was given more than thirty. Two indicators were set by superior authorities— physical production and profit per ton (though not the profit rate on fixed assets)—and one by clients—ash content—as an indicator of quality.

The hesitancy with which the new ideas began to be put into practice in the first half of 1965 indicated the strength of the opposition, which was brought to a head in an article in *Voprosy ekonomiki*, No. 2, 1965, by Yuri Koldomasov, Director of the Material-Supply Department of Gosplan. Placed as the first article in the journal, it praised a number of 'initiatives' which were much in the spirit of former 'campaigns' and managerial methods, and concluded that 'the limitation of the number of indicators,' especially those on assortment, would hinder rather than foster development of the economy. In one sentence Koldomasov opposed the unification of indicators (Liberman) and the decentralization of 'assortment' planning (Bolshevichka-Mayak). In the following sentence, a reference to 'incentives to fulfil above all the targets for the global volume of industrial output' seemed to ignore all the demonstrations of that indicator's irrationality.

Opinion, among professional economists at least, seems to have strengthened behind the profit indicator at a conference convened by Moscow University (and attended by representatives from thirty others) in late June. The report in *Pravda* of June 23 said that they all

> . . . pointed out that the time had come . . . to renounce detailed planning from above, to curtail the number of indicators established for factories and thereby to create conditions for the operational independence of, and for the development of healthy business initiative in, the enterprise. Many of the economists believed that the moment was ripe for strengthening the function of profit in evaluating the activity of an enterprise, considering it as one of the main indicators.

The transition from a general view to that of 'many' on the profit indicator—also defined as 'the fundamental indicator for management,— implied majority agreement, while only a minority seemed to favour a capital charge ('some economists stressed that productive investment assets should be paid for').

A fortnight later, on July 10, Brezhnev announced that a meeting of the Central Committee was to be convened to discuss industrial reform, but gave no indication of the agenda, let alone of his own thinking.

The Issue of 'Unemployment'

A day or two before Brezhnev spoke, the monthly journal of the Institute of Economics appeared with an article which created, if anything, a greater international stir than had Liberman's article of 1962. Yefim Manevich, an economist long specialized on labour questions, estimated:

> At present the share of the population capable of work but not engaged in the social economy amounts in Moscow and Leningrad to 6 or 7 per cent, and in the U.S.S.R. on average to 20 percent; in Siberia it reaches 26 per cent and in some towns of that area even higher.

He followed with a table of towns in Novosibirsk *oblast* where, in 1962, the share of the active population occupied in 'housework or private gardening' varied from 10 per cent in the administrative centre to 39 per cent in a town 100 km. away. He stated that these were 'not only women fully or partially engaged in household activities, but also a significant number of young people and adult males.' Novosibirsk had in fact just been examined by sociologists from its university, the results appearing in the May 1965 journal of the U.S.S.R. Institute of Philosophy: the considerable unemployment found among school-leavers was attributed to the 'demographic echo' of the second World War. Between 1963 and 1965 the number of seventeen-year-olds in the city had risen by 60 per cent and of eighteen-year-olds by 70 percent. The educational reform of 1958—substantially shaped by Khrushchev himself, as his speeches then showed—had reduced the term of full secondary schooling and required university entrants to have two years' working experience. This increment in young job-seekers had come at a time when mechanization and automation were reducing the number of vacancies created per unit of new industrial capacity; Manevich added that more jobs would be available if reduction could be made in the 231 million work-days lost through machine breakdown and poor factory organization. The Novosibirsk study called attention to 'the abolition of the Ministry of Labour [in 1933] and the research institutes it ran, and the liquidation of research on labour organization and management.' Both the studies implied that the present situation required the reintroduction of labour exchanges and of unemployment benefit; the eventual devolution of recruitment authority to enterprises (resulting from a restriction if indicators to a profit or similar quota) would necessitate them all the more.

The Reappraisal of 'Dogmatic' Planning

The setting of the deadline of January 1966 for the wholesale price reform has already been mentioned. The aim of the new prices is to stimulate the production of 'goods of higher quality,' that is, by the relation of price to 'utility.' Because the reform does not affect retail prices, the 'utilities' in question are to be measured by machine productivity, or other technical parameters which can represent the value of the goods to the user. On the cost side, the extension of Marx's labour content of value to cover a charge for capital is implicit in the Liberman proposals as they have now evolved. The Secretary of the Party Committee in Stravropol *krai* has asked for a cadastral survey of the U.S.S.R. to permit the incorporation of differential rent into the calculation of agricultural profits. A corresponding call has appeared for the extractive industries (which are affected by the same sort of factors as farmland), and a specific scheme was put forward by K. Kuprinov, of the Research Institute of Gosplan, in March. For manufacturing and services, variations in location are partly accounted for in the zonal price structure, but the more strictly local problems—the equivalent of rateable valuations—are now being tackled by the so-called *'passportizatsia'* of urban districts.

Soon after Khrushchev's fall, the Director of the Vulkan Plant in Leningrad found an apposite term for the previous policy when he condemned the 'arithmetical approach' in price-fixing. For long, Soviet planners have abandoned their own freedom to choose between alternative uses of resources by conforming to what are now commonly called 'the planning rules.' They were partly driven to invent such rules because of lacunae in their economic analysis, which the new freedom to reformulate theory has now begun to fill. Indeed, as Andrew Shonfield has remarked, the Western capitalist economies have shown that they can do better than the preformance postulated by the 'rules.'

Kosygin has accepted the need for change. In a speech to the Central Committee in March he admitted that 'in taking decisions on many major problems we are often prisoners of canons we ourselves laid down.' An unsigned article in *Pravda*, April 29, 1965, drew together this policy with what may become the new empiricism in industry, agriculture, and science:

> The decisions of the October-November (1964) and March (1965) Plenum of the CC of the CPSU were of the greatest importance in realizing the Leninist direction of our Party. . . The Party decisively rejected subjectivism in politics, and voluntarism and administratization in the resolution of political and economic problems.

Stalin and Khrushchev laid down their 'canons' and their 'campaigns' as substitutes for rational decisions: will Kosygin and Brezhnev be powerful enough to be empirical?

PLANNING AND THE MARKET IN THE U.S.S.R.:
THE CURRENT SOVIET PLANNING REFORMS*
— · — · — · — · — · — · — · — · — · — · — ·

Abram Bergson

Recently announced decisions of the Soviet government to reform its planning system have been greeted in the West as a momentous international event. The changes being made are surely not quite as dramatic as this assumes, but the government is reorganizing, often in novel ways, its proverbially centralized arrangements for industrial planning, and it has good reason to do so.

Although some of the reforms are novel, one of them, concerning the administrative structure of industry, is hardly so. Prior to May, 1957, branch ministries were preeminent in industry, but Khrushchev at that time supplanted this traditional apparatus with one in which regional authorities became primary. Khrushchev acted with much fanfare, but his successors apparently have concluded that the branch-ministerial form of organization is superior, and no doubt with some basis, though Khrushchev may not always have been so "hare-brained" as charged. In any event, the government has now decreed reestablishment of the branch ministries. As the latest example of the familiar Soviet proclivity for bureaucratic reshuffling, this reversal is not without interest, but Western attention has properly been directed to other changes being made in industrial planning that are relatively novel.

Of the reforms in question, the chief were initiated at a meeting of the Central Committee of the Communist Party held during September 27–29, 1965. As elaborated in a report submitted to the Central Committee by Premier Alexsei N. Kosygin, and in the numerous, although not always revealing, decrees, instructions, and commentaries which (as is characteristic in the U.S.S.R.) followed immediately in the wake of the Central Committee action, the September, 1965, program is more complex than many reports might suggest.

To refer only to bare essentials, the agency at the lowest bureaucratic level in Soviet industry, and hence the one immediately in charge of operations, is the *predpriiatie*, or enterprise. This has been so whether branch-ministerial or regional agencies have been preeminent, and will still be so now that the branch-ministerial system is again the order of the day. Under centralized planning, enterprise management has not been

*Reprinted by permission of the author from Alexander Balinky, Abram Bergson, John N. Hazard, and Peter Wiles, *Planning and the Market in the U.S.S.R.: The 1960's* (New Brunswick: Rutgers University Press, 1967), pp. 43–64. All footnotes deleted.

subject to control from above to quite the minute degree often supposed, but its authority has been severely limited. Under the new program, such authority is to be expanded. This will occur through a reduction in the number of the enterprise's plan targets that must be approved by superior agencies, and also in other ways. Thus, in utilizing available wage funds, enterprise management previously was much constrained by targets for wage payments, for employment, and for average earnings for different categories of workers. Now management will be subject to only one such target, for total wages paid to all workers. Within the limits of the total fund assigned it, the management may employ labor as it wishes. Scales of basic wage rates for different categories of workers, however, will continue to be determined primarily by superior agencies.

Decisions on capital investments hitherto have been especially centralized, but through charges to profits and depreciation, each enterprise is now to establish a "fund for the growth of production," which it may use with some discretion to finance modernization, automation, and various other capital investment projects. Since, for industry generally, funds for the growth of production are expected to finance about 20 per cent of state capital investment in 1966, the additional authority gained at this point could be of some consequence.

Enterprise management is also to be allowed greater discretion in some other, related ways. Thus, it may now decide whether and to what extent piece (rather than time) work is to be employed in determining wages; it has more authority than before in respect to custom production, and so on.

Plan targets in the U.S.S.R. constitute at once standards of performance, "success criteria," for enterprise management, but necessarily not all targets can have equal weight. Interestingly, then, not only are targets approved by superior agencies being reduced in number; to some extent they are also being changed in character, and apparently also in their relative importance. Among other things, targets for output, including unfinished goods and stocks, which were previously stressed, are to give way to one for "realized production," or sales. Contrary to many reports, profits have long been calculated in the U.S.S.R. but now the target for profits is also to become an important test of performance.

Along with success criteria, changes are also being made in arrangements for managerial bonuses. These affect managerial behavior under Soviet socialism hardly less than elsewhere. Thus, bonuses, which hitherto have been based chiefly on performance relative to the plan target for output, are henceforth to depend primarily on performance relative to plan targets for sales and profits. Bonuses are to vary according to the degree of fulfillment of one of these two targets, but will be conditional on fulfillment of the other. The bonuses will also be conditional on satisfactory performance regarding other matters, such as the assortment of goods produced.

Then, too, such managerial bonuses, together with some premia for workers generally, are now to be paid out of a new "fund for material encouragement," which is to be maintained to a considerable extent through charges from profits. The charges are to vary according to an intricate system that is not easily summarized and that perhaps will not always be readily grasped by managerial personnel themselves. Suffice it to say that appropriations will depend not only on sales and profits, but on other indicators of performance, including "profitability," a Soviet euphemism for the rate of return on capital. Regarding sales and profits, what will count is performance relative not only to the plan but to pre-plan levels. The government is also establishing new arrangements for rewarding the introduction of new products, and hopes to heighten interest in satisfactory performance generally through diverse changes in procedures for financing of housing, nurseries, and the like, that are administered by the enterprise.

Last but not least, the changes in success criteria are to be accompanied by revisions in financial and price-fixing practices. According to a strange but long-standing policy, new capital hitherto has been made available to enterprises for the most part in the form of interest-free grants from the government budget. In future, however, enterprises will have to pay a charge out of their profits on their capital (typically 6 per cent). The enterprises will also have to finance their capital needs increasingly through repayable loans. A firm which enjoys an especially favorable position regarding natural resources may also be subjected to a fixed "rental" payment.

For the rest, the manner in which price-fixing practices will be changed is still under study. Apparently, industrial wholesale prices, which usually are fixed to allow a standard mark-up over average branch cost, but which for the most part have not been changed since July 1, 1955, are at long last to be up-dated. In the process, the prices presumably will also be altered to allow for the novel charges on capital and rental payments.

In advancing the new program, Kosygin was careful to explain that it will be implemented only in the course of time. Although the government has clearly committed itself to the reform, it apparently expects to review it as it is being put into practice. In fact, the new arrangements affecting enterprise autonomy, success criteria, and finance began to be introduced only in January, 1966, and at that time only for forty-three enterprises. In April, 1966, however, the new arrangements were extended to an additional two hundred enterprises, and Kosygin explained in his report to the twenty-third Party Congress that by the beginning of 1967 enterprises operating under the new reforms will employ one-third of all industrial workers. The reform in industrial prices, declaredly, is to be carried out in 1967 and 1968.

I have been referring to the reform program initiated by Kosygin at the Party Central Committee meeting of September, 1965. Prior to the Central Committee meeting, the government had already experimentally initiated changes in planning for consumer goods industries much like the changes now being instituted in industry generally. The experimental changes were first introduced in two clothing firms, the Bol'shevichka and Maiak, in the summer of 1964, and then, in 1965, were extended to several hundred enterprises producing clothing, shoes, leather, and textiles. Under this earlier experiment, procedures different from those being introduced under the September, 1965, program were sometimes employed. Among other things, the enterprises affected were given much discretion to determine the assortment of goods produced in response to orders received from wholesale and retail trade outlets. Often such enterprises also gained more authority in other spheres than is now being given industrial enterprises generally under Kosygin's later reform. Procedures employed under the experiment, however, varied in the course of time and between enterprises, and are in any event often difficult to judge from the incomplete information available. The experiment remains of interest because the government intends to continue it in operation, and probably will further broaden its scope while it reorganizes industry generally in accord with the reforms projected by Kosygin in September, 1965.

In sum, the Soviet government is scarcely dismantling wholesale its system of centralized industrial planning, as sometimes has been suggested in the West, but it is adapting this system measurably in the direction of decentralization and increased use of market-type controls. The adaptation, moreover, cannot be very palatable to a political group which has been bred ideologically to view market institutions as a source of anarchy, and is sensitive to the threat to their authoritarian rule and the bureaucratic status of superior personnel that is inherent in any consequential economic shifts in the direction now taken. Why is the government at long last initiating such changes?

The U.S.S.R., it has been reported, is "going through a crisis as profound, if not as eye-catching, as capitalism's crisis in the 1930's." This is hardly accurate, but the government is manifestly concerned about the onerous responsibilities which superior agencies in the bureaucratic structure must bear under centralized planning. Subject to approval at the highest level, such agencies must, among other things, determine in essentials the volume and direction of capital investment. They also have major responsibilites for the coordination of myriads of plan targets, and for the control of current factor inputs, especially of materials, fuel, power, and machinery that are required to implement the plan.

With such responsibilities the superior agencies understandably find it difficult to cope, and one must read partly in this light complaints that lately have become commonplace even in the U.S.S.R. such as this: "The basic flaw in planning and management was that every detail was supposed to be decided from the center and, since it was impossible to know the circumstances at each enterprise, the center proceeded from average conditions that did not exist in reality in any one enterprise, and added an approximate average rate of growth, which was low for some and intolerable for other enterprises."

Or this: "There are also irregularities in deliveries and incomplete deliveries; the grades, types and sizes of materials ordered are frequently replaced by other less economic ones. For example, the Ukraine Chief Supply and Marketing Administration sent the Novo-Kakhova Electrical Machinery Plant a large amount of 750 × 1,500 mm. sheet steel for dynamos instead of 860 × 1,720 mm. sheet; as a result the coefficient of use of the metal dropped by 23 per cent.

"Shortcomings in supply also affect the economics of enterprises. . . . At the Rostov Farm Machinery Plant, for example, there were approximately 11,000 substitutions of rolled metal shapes and dimensions in five years—that is, an average of seven substitutions a day; this resulted in an overexpenditure of more than 22,000 tons of metal. Frequently there are also huge losses from the low quality of products supplied, in particular cast parts."

Or this: "Because of the absence of equipment, there are now about 1.5 million square meters of deserted productive floor space. In the textile department of the Kursk Synthetic Fiber Kombinat more than 3,000 square meters of floor space have been empty since 1960. In the "Tadzhiktekstilmash' Factory around 5,000 square meters of productive floor space . . . have been idle for more than two years because of the lack of specialized equipment."

The government understandably is now seeking to lighten responsibilities of superior agencies. Since managers of enterprises have often complained of the "petty tutelage" to which they are subject, it is also hoped that the authority transferred to them will be exercised more effectively than it was by their superiors.

The government has no less reason to reform managerial success criteria, however, for within their limited sphere enterprise managers also act wastefully, and curiously they are even impelled to do so by the success criteria that have prevailed. Even with a "visible hand" replacing an "invisible" one, as it has turned out, what is good for the individual enterprise is by no means always good for the country.

Thus, the infamous "safety factor" which is also a familiar theme in the U.S.S.R.: enterprise managers of necessity are allowed to negotiate with superior agencies regarding their plan targets, and in doing so seek to limit their assignments. In this way they hope more easily to earn bonuses for plan fulfillment. To the same end, the managers also hesitate to overfulfill targets, for fear that subsequent goals will only be made higher.

In trying especially to fulfill the target for gross output, managers also often find it possible, and even expedient, to stress inordinately goods that bulk large physically. Alternatively, where gross output is calculated in value terms emphasis may be placed on products that have relatively high ruble prices, but such prices also have their limitations, so the resulting assortment again may be strange. Thus the unending reports of difficulties of the Soviet consumer in shopping for particular items: for example, in buying large-size boys' shoes, as distinct from small-size men's shoes; of shirt, as distinct from bandage, cloth; of small-size as distinct from large-size electric bulbs, and so on.

Almost inevitably shortcuts are also taken regarding quality: as in the Russian Soviet Federated Socialist Republic, where among products examined by inspectors of the Ministry of Trade in the first half of 1962, 32.7 per cent of the clothing articles, 25 per cent of the knitwear, and 32.6 per cent of the leather shoes were rejected or reclassified in a lower quality category; or in the Ukraine, where 20 to 25 per cent of the clothing and knitwear examined by the Ministry of Trade during 1963 had to be condemned as defective; or where a factory manufacturing tractor parts found it advantageous to overfulfill its output goal by 60 per cent while lowering the quality of its products and so reducing their useful life by 40 to 50 per cent. In order to fulfill the current target for output, managers also hesitate to introduce new products, and find it profitable to abuse their machinery. The list of managerial aberrations could easily be lengthened still further.

In the determination of wholesale prices for industrial goods, the rule has long been simply to cover anverage branch cost. Whereas a modest planned profit is also allowed, no charge has been included in cost for interest on fixed capital or rent for scarce resources. The rule nevertheless has often been honored in the breach, and sometimes the prices must be closer to scarcity values than they otherwise would be, but often too, they must have been even less so. Most importantly, as noted, prices generally have been left unchanged since the last major price reform of July, 1955. For this reason alone, prices must frequently differ far from costs as well as scarcity values generally.

As determined in these ways, ruble prices evidently bear the earmarks of obsolete doctrine, particularly the Marxian labor theory of value, as well as of cumbersome central planning. But the effect on the relation of prices to scarcity values is much the same in either case, and curiously the very divergencies from such values is itself a major reason why the task of superior agencies is so difficult. For such agencies to calculate in terms of such prices is not easy, but it is no easier for them to calculate otherwise. As indicated, the dubious prices have also been a source of distortion in the behavior of enterprise management and they only promise to become more so as far as sales and profits are to be cardinal success criteria. Regarding prices, too, therefore, there is both room and need for improvement, though the government has yet to commit itself on the precise changes that will be made. It is also seeking to make success criteria more valid by revising procedures for financing of capital investment.

These deficiencies in centralized planning are hardly new; they had already become manifest in the early Five-Year Plans under Stalin. Why is the government only now taking any consequential action to alleviate them? Reform might have been in order long ago, but it has become especially so lately because of the ever increasing complexity of the task with which the cumbersome system of industrial planning must grapple. In Western comment on the current Soviet economic scene, this trend is properly often referred to. The task is becoming more complex because of the continually growing number of industrial enterprises (recently 200,000 of "census" size), whose interrelationships must be planned; because of the ever increasing variety of commodities that such plants supply (according to a "complete" classification, an estimated 20 million items are now in production); and because of the ever more exacting requirements of modern technology.

The complexity is also greater because the government's own aim is no longer simply to produce steel and then more steel, as it was under Stalin. In his famous attack on Gosplan men in "steel blinkers," Khrushchev, of course, meant to urge not merely a greater use of plastics, but a more flexible outlook on alternative industrial branches generally. Despite their criticism of Khrushchev, his successors probably will hesitate to abandon altogether this particular policy. Moreover, the government, which in the face of crop shortages has been importing about 20 million tons of grain since mid-1963, is also more attentive to consumers than it was under Stalin. For the dictator, food shortages did not even preclude exports. And the task of directing economic activity has become the more intricate because, though still not affluent, the consumers themselves have become more choosy, as witness the quite new phenomenon in the U.S.S.R. of overstocks of consumer goods of less desirable sizes and styles.

If prevailing priorities reflect a greater awareness of alternatives, this must be owing partly to another development which has also been favorable to economic reform in other ways as well. The pretensions of poor Comrade Yaroshenko to the contrary notwithstanding, Stalin had held that "the directing bodies" must reserve for themselves consideration of the "rational organization of the productive forces, economic planning, etc." Hence, these vital topics could not be the subject matter of a "political economy of socialism" open to inquiry by economists generally. Yet the government has now found it expedient to allow economists generally to explore these very same questions. In doing so, the economists are even permitted to use forms of analysis, especially of a mathematical sort, formerly regarded as *bourgeois*, and so taboo.

The invigorated economics that has quickly emerged has itself been a factor in the equation indicating economic reform. Thus, much of the Soviet criticism of planning procedures that has been referred to is to be found in the writings of Soviet economists themselves. The reforms now being implemented, it has been reported, were largely shaped by the ideas of the Kharkov economist, Yevsei Liberman. In fact, many other Soviet economists have also contributed, but the U.S.S.R. too now has its influential "new economics," and the new reforms bear its stamp.

Scarcely less momentous than these developments, however, has been another: as reported, the rate of economic growth has declined, and markedly, according to both official Soviet and Western calculations, though the former as usual seem inflated:

TABLE 1
REAL NATIONAL INCOME,
AVERAGE ANNUAL PER CENT INCREASE

Years	Soviet Official Data	Western Data
1950–1958	10.9	7.0
1958–1959	7.5	4.2
1959–1960	7.7	4.9
1960–1961	6.8	6.8
1961–1962	5.7	4.3
1962–1963	4.1	2.6
1963–1964	9.0	7.2
1964–1965	6.0	3.0

Even the reduced rates are still respectable, but the decline must be disconcerting for proponents of a social system whose asserted economic superiority is held to be observable, above all, in its ability to generate rapid growth. And, still worse, the rival capitalist system in the West lately has itself shown unexpected capabilities in this regard, first in Western Europe and most recently even in the United States. To "overtake and surpass" the advanced capitalist countries economically can no longer seem the easy task that the ebullient Khrushchev assumed not so long ago.

By all accounts, economic growth has declined in the U.S.S.R. for diverse reasons, and among these some of the most important, such as those causing the continued stagnation in agriculture, are remote from deficiencies in industrial planning. By repairing these deficiencies, however, the government hopes to assure an increasingly effective use of productive factors in industry, and on this basis to offset more successfully retarding forces affecting the economy generally.

As Kosygin made clear in his September, 1965, report, the government seeks increased effectiveness in the use of all productive factors, but especially capital. Even when growth was rapid, it could be achieved only by a disproportionately rapid increase in the capital stock. Now that growth has slowed, the increase in capital stock has become inordinate. To continue to rely so heavily on capital inputs as a source of growth necessarily would mean that the share of total output going to current capital investment, which already may be one-third, must rise still higher. Only in this way could the government hope to find the wherewithal to assure a continuing increase in the capital stock more rapid than the increase in output. By implication, supplies of goods available to provide long-promised gains for consumers would likely be meager. Through improved planning procedures the government seeks to arrest the rise in capital coefficient which currently besets it, and so to limit the increases in the investment rate and encroachments on consumption that will be needed for future growth.

In reporting to the Party Central Committee in September, 1965, Kosygin expressed confidence that "with tireless work" the measures being undertaken would yield "beneficial results." Although he referred primarily to the reforms that he has proposed to the Central Committee, the government obviously is of the same view regarding the rearrangement that already had been made experimentally for consumer goods enterprises. How beneficial will the results be?

Under the reforms, the responsibilities of superior agencies will be somewhat diminished, but will still be onerous. Still, the experiment in consumer goods industries has, as reported, brought a marked improvement in quality and assortment in many enterprises, but this has often been achieved in the face of adverse profit margins which could be discouraging under other than experimental conditions. Difficulties have also been encountered in procuring through the still cumbersome supply system materials needed for an improved assortment. Under the September, 1965, reforms, appropriations to the enterprise's bonus fund are to depend partly on the projected improvement in its performance over the previous year, and the government hopes on this basis to weaken the "safety factor." Perhaps it will, but it remains to be seen to what extent, under the intricate incentive procedures being established, management will be interested in foregoing use of this device. Successes in this regard have been reported among the forty-three enterprises placed under the reforms in January, 1966, though one wonders again how typical such initial experiences will prove to be.

Under both the experiment in consumer goods industries and the September, 1965, reforms, the government also has reason to expect managerial performance to improve in other spheres, but here, too, difficulties have arisen wich may prove more than episodic: a wholesale oil supply base seeking to fulfill its target for sales compelled its customers, by the threat of fines, to fulfill their contracts, though as a result of operating economies the customers' requirements had declined; management's newly won discretion as to investment has been balked by difficulties in obtaining needed services of construction agencies; the enterprise autonomy generally is still constrained by red tape and improper encroachments of superior agencies.

When adversities have been encountered, the still dubious prices are sometimes a factor, and the projected reform in such prices should be to the good. But the principles to be observed in fixing the new prices are not yet settled, and even after such prices prevail, the bureaucratic reluctance to change them will still be deleterious.

In sum, time alone can tell what will be achieved, but even a proponent of Western market institutions may feel that resort to such arrangements in such a limited fashion in a strange environment is apt to yield only limited gains. By implication, the government may soon find the system of industrial planning again on its agenda, though in changed circumstances. Possibly it will refrain from further reforms but this would not be promising, and it would be no more so to abandon the reforms now in progress, though this, too, is possible.

The government is not promoting the use of mathematical economics and advanced computers, and some enthusiastic proponents of these tools have held that they will permit centralized planning to work after all, so that decentralization and market-type controls can be obviated. But the government thus far has properly been guided by a more responsible view that mathematical analysis and computers can be helpful, but are hardly a solution tothe problem of planning organization. In a complex modern economy, with myriads of unknowns to be determined, perfect computation is conceptually intriguing as the electronic analogue of the perfect competition of economic theory, but scarcely a practicality.

The government is not about to restore capitalism, and Soviet economists have rightly criticized commentators, both in China and the West, who have suggested as much, but it may not be easy to confine the market to limits now being observed. Another characterization of the current reforms also suggested, therefore, may not really be amiss: "creeping capitalism." It will be fascinating to see how in the years ahead the government grapples with its complex problem of planning organization.

SOVIET ECONOMIC PERFORMANCE AND REFORM: SOME PROBLEMS OF ANALYSIS AND PROGNOSIS*

(A Round-Table Discussion)†

This article is based on a recording of a three-hour discussion held at Columbia University on December 3, 1965. The participants were Abram Bergson, Alexander Erlich, Herbert S. Levine, G Warren Nutter, and Stanislaw Wellisz, with Henry L. Roberts as moderator.

Henry Roberts: In extending my invitation to this informal discussion, I remarked that for the layman at least, and possibly for the economist, there are a number of interesting questions to be explored with respect both to the performance of the Soviet economy and to our shifting appraisals of it.

In pursuance of this I suggest that we discuss today three or four related, though not identical, themes concerning the Soviet economy: its performance, the possibility and practicability of reforms, and also the question of our own appraisals of this economy—the means available to us, changes in our views over the last decade, and the prospects for useful prognostication.

The Kosygin Report

Abram Bergson: You have presented us with a formidable menu. Perhaps it would be desirable if I were to comment first on the much-discussed economic reforms dealt with in Kosygin's report to the Central Committee last September. We ought to try to reach an understanding first as to their nature. The reforms represent a significant change in the Soviet scene, but we clearly must dismiss some of the more dramatic interpretations that have been presented, such as those stressing the possibility

*Reprinted by permission from *Slavic Review* (June 1966), pp. 222–46.

†Dr. Henry Roberts is Professor of History, Columbia University and the editor of the *Slavic Review*.

Dr. G. Warren Nutter is Professor of Economics and Director of Office of Soviet Economic Research, University of Virginia. His publications include: *Growth of Industrial Production in the Soviet Union* (1962), and "The Effect of Economic Growth on Sino-Soviet Strategy" in David M. Abshire and Richard V. Allen (ed.) *National Security* (1963).

Dr. Stanislaw Wellisz is Professor of Economics, Columbia University. His publications include: *An Analysis of Soviet-Type Economy* (1963) and *The Economics of the Soviet Bloc* (1964).

that the Russians are now about to restore capitalism. This obviously is much too excited. Someone has said that the reforms represent creeping capitalism. This may be somewhat more appropriate.

The reforms are by no means radical. The government is not dismantling in any wholesale way the centralized system of planning; this will continue under the reforms Kosygin has described. Still, a number of novel changes are being made, and while we should not exaggerate their importance, we must not discount them altogether. A certain degree of decentralization is to take place under the reforms, and there are some changes being made in regard to incentive arrangements, accounting, and financial controls which would warrant our saying that the Russians are making a very cautious and limited step, let's say, in the direction of market socialism. It's not a dramatic step, but it still represents a new direction and poses interesting questions as to why the Russians are doing what they're doing, what the circumstances are that have at long last impelled them to take even this limited step, and what the possible consequences will be.

Herbert Levine: Abe has accurately described the general tenor of the reform. I think that I would emphasize the fact that Kosygin in his speech made it very clear that, as in the debate that followed the orignal popularization of the Liberman approach, the centralized nature of planning would be retained. The reforms as announced by Kosygin in September do differ from the Liberman proposals in that the role of profit incentives—that is, rewards to be paid according to profit and profitability—is not central in the reforms, although there are suggestions that in certain places much more attention will be paid to these criteria. The major reform is that the main objective for the industrial enterprise will be shifted from just quantity of output to volume of sales. Much of what was wrong with the previous incentive system lies in the fact that the Soviet enterprise has had no concern for the users of the products it produces. The change to volume of sales as the main indicator of success is intended to take account of this weakness; the hope is that this will aid substantially in improving the situation by making the producers much more concerned with the needs of those who use their products.

G. Warren Nutter: I think I agree with the appraisal as to what is being done, but it might be useful to draw some distinction between action—what is being done—and what is being talked about. It would seem to me that there are perhaps three convenient and rather normal groups into which you could put the Soviet economists. On the one end are the conservatives, who want to keep things pretty much as they are, or at least retain the quantitatively oriented system. On the other end are the radicals, at least radicals in the Russian context, those who want to move very boldly toward a price-oriented economy. In the middle I would put Liberman, as not quite willing to go all the way, wanting to pay his respects to the existing system but to patch it up a bit by introducing a little more emphasis on profits.

Bergson: Warren, whom would you classify as being much more radical than Liberman?

Nutter: Well, I would say Nemchinov and, in his own way, Kantorovich initially. And those like Vaag and Zakharov who argue for reform of the price sytem as a necessary beginning to moving toward a profit-guided economy.

Bergson: There is quite a range of opinion among the Soviet economists, but Liberman is probably well toward the left. I don't think there are many prominent economists who are further to the left than he. I agree, though, that the reform does not represent as large a step in the direction of decentralization and the use of market controls as Libermanism or Liberman's own views would have entailed. Actually it represents a smaller step in this direction than the experiments introduced in the consumer goods industries in the summer of 1964. But this could be a misleading comparison if it were left at that. The point is that Kosygin outlined a reform which is to apply to all industry—not only consumer goods industry but heavy industry. The experiment with several hundred light-industry enterprises apparently is continuing alongside the changes that Kosygin has initiated. So we should not think of these new reforms as necessarily representing a step back; the new reforms will be juxtaposed with the experiment.

Levine: If I may interject here. In the new statute on the Soviet enterprise, paragraph 30 says that those enterprises which produce consumer goods will organize production on the basis of orders from trade organizations and contracts concluded with them. Now it's much too early to draw conclusions, but it seems that, although the reform as a whole is less liberalizing than what was previously done in consumer goods, this paragraph might be interpreted to mean that they have in view extending the type of planning that was started in July 1964 to all consumer goods enterprises.

Bergson: Since this issue has been raised, it might be well to record that the precise nature of the reforms that are being introduced is not always clear. I do feel, though, that the burden of the evidence I've seen is that under the 1964 experiment in consumer goods the enterprise has more authority regarding the assortment of goods than the enterprise in heavy industry, say, will have under the reforms that Kosygin elaborated. Possibly the enterprise under the experiments initiated in 1964 will also have somewhat more authority in regard to prices than will be the case under the proposals that Kosygin has set forth for all of industry.

Roberts: In this connection Mr. Nutter earlier raised the question about the relation between discussion and deed.

Nutter: Whether or not Liberman is further to the left than the center, the discussion in the Soviet Union has ranged much more widely and has suggested much more fundamental kinds of reform than seem to be taking place. Now, I quite agree that it's virtually impossible to know precisely what's happening. We just have snatches of information and little teasing bits of pronouncements that suggest a change in one direction or the other. But from the whole atmosphere of what is happening I draw the conclusions, for the moment anyhow, that the leaders, the political leaders, are moving very cautiously and very slowly and have no immediate intention of making fundamental, radical changes in the economic system if they can possibly avoid it.

Alexander Erlich: I believe the main difference between this recent project of reform and the so-called decentralization of 1957 is that 1957 was not even a step toward decentralization. It was a sidestepping of the issue. It was a regionalization that shortened the distance between planning agencies and enterprise, but it didn't essentially modify the nature of the relationship. The autonomy of the enterprise was not increased at all, and while there were some gains due to this greater closeness, there were also some drawbacks which were later characterized in literature as "localist" tendencies. Moreover, under the ministerial system the enterprise at least knew whom it was dealing with, while under the subsequent system the enterprise was getting contradictory orders from different independent agencies.

Now we definitely have a step toward decentralization in the meaningful sense of the term. The number of success indicators is reduced, the plant can retain a much larger portion of the gross profit (that is, parts of net profit and amortization), and it is free to use it. Then we also have the introduction of some purely economic incentives to economize, like charges on fixed capital and a switch from outright grants to credit. I would also like at once to emphasize certain limitations, especially as compared to some earlier Soviet ideas. The late Academician Nemchinov, one of the leading mathematical economists, was, during the last year or two of his life, a very consistent advocate not only of more autonomy of enterprises but of actually scrapping the system of centralized allocation of resources and substituting for it some system of state-owned wholesale trade. In short, he was for creating a market of producer goods.

Prospects for Improvement

Stanislaw Wellisz: If I may, I would like to shift the focus of the discussion just a little and, rather than consider who favors what, start thinking of what it all means For purposes of convenience one can classify the kind of inefficiencies the Soviets are struggling with into "visible waste," resulting from lack of coordination—like somebody producing sewing machines which nobody wants to buy—and "invisible waste"—products that do find buyers but that are nonoptimal products, in the sense that one can, with the same factors of production, produce things that are more useful, however one wants to define usefulness. Now, it seems to me that this big change from gross output produced to salable output is mainly a measure to eliminate visible waste. It should improve coordination of flow. This does not necessarily mean it will reduce invisible waste. In consumer products there is more of a market; hence consumers are able to turn down goods or buy other goods, and they might even influence prices. But in the producer goods sector the choice of alternatives is limited, and as long as the price system does not respond to production decisions, just switching from gross output to salable output is not going to reduce this kind of waste.

To be sure, measures have been taken to increase efficiency and reduce invisible waste; these consist mainly in the very cautious move toward taking profits into account. Frankly, I have very great doubts as to the meaning of this because so long as the price system is rather arbitrary, profit maximization will not necessarily improve assortment from either the planning or the social point of view. The managers will now take profit maximization into account, but whether this will move them in the direction of a better or worse assortment from the social point of view is very difficult to say in advance.

There is another danger, too, one that is sometimes ignored, and that is that goods of an excessively high quality might be produced. Imagine for a moment that stainless steel gets priced in such a way that it is more profitable to produce stainless steel than ordinary steel. Then every enterprise producing steel will have an incentive to produce stainless steel, which then will be used in places where ordinary steel, which is cheaper, could do just as well. So there are dangers of arbitrary prices misallocating even in a market where there is no tremendous pressure to take whatever is produced.

Erlich: I am glad I yielded the floor to Stan, because he said very effectively quite a few of the things I would have said. I would like to mention one or two points in addition. First about the switch from gross value to value of realized production. I believe this eliminates some of the crude sort of waste. It is more difficult now to produce things nobody really wants or has any use for. But we have still to decide what kind of general situation prevails in the economy. If we have what is essentially a seller's market, chances are that some of the users will kick and be mad but will accept some of the second-rate stuff. Obviously they won't accept anything that is totally useless, which may be a step forward, but they will accept something which does not quite live up to specifications and does not quite meet their quality requirements. Here we are shifting from micro-economic problems to macroeconomic problems. I believe that in this respect the first part of Kosygin's speech was very revealing indeed.

Levine: I agree strongly with Alex's last comment that increasing the decision-making power of a purchaser to refuse to accept the output that is sent to him, which was intended to give him some countervailing market power over the producer, depends very much on the macro-pressure in the economy and the presence or absence of sellers' markets. As to the question that Stan raises about the fixity of prices and the usefulness of the volume of sales, I think it's interesting to note that through all the Soviet discussions, and through Kosygin's speech, there is, associated with this reform of concentrating on volume of sales, the indication that the producing enterprise will now be concerned with the needs of the purchasing enterprise and will try to develop new products, not now produced, that will be more useful to the purchasing enterprise.

Erlich: Could I say perhaps a word about price setting? First of all, the interesting thing is that while the reform is supposed to take place now, or is to be effective next year, the new prices won't be in operation until 1967–68. This creates some time lag. Then there is a question about the nature of these prices. Kosygin speaks of making prices correspond to the amounts of socially necessary labor. Also an article by Sitnin, who is chairman of the price committee, sounds as if he were for something crudely resembling average-cost pricing, because he takes very strong exception to the view that prices should be oriented to the costs of most expensive enterprises—presumably some sort of a rebuke to marginalists.

Extent of Decentralization

Bergson: There is a problem that arises in characterizing the possible impact of the reforms. In fact, we are not very clear about what the reforms are in respects that really matter. We come back again to ambiguities. It should be stressed again that the degree of decentralization of decision-making to the level of enterprise is rather limited. And actually, if one takes Kosygin at face value, the decentralization envisaged under his reforms occurs chiefly in a sphere rather different from the one that we've been talking about. It occurs primarily in regard to the staffing of labor, that is, determination of the volume and structure of employment within limits of the target for the wage bill. From Kosygin's report to the Central Committee you come away with the impression that the enterprise will gain authority chiefly in this area. I think it has become fairly clear that the consumer goods assortment as well as the assortment of goods produced by heavy industrial plants is still to be the subject of targets fixed by superior agencies. That is, there is at best only a limited decentralization in regard to assortment, and this occurs primarily in regard to the consumer goods industries affected by the experiment. My guess is that the crucial success criterion for management—I judge this partly from the experience under the experiment—will be the performance with regard to the target for realized sales and that the enterprise will be expected to conform to the plan in regard to other aspects such as the volume of profits that are earned, but that maximization of profits probably will not be the primary criterion.

Levine: To follow, in line with this discussion, the comments Abe made about the tasks that will be assigned centrally. In addition to the volume of sales, it is clear in Kosygin's speech that the assortment of output will also be confirmed from above. However, I find it interesting that he also says that, while at present the Soviet Union will still have to indicate from above the assortment of output, in time, when direct contracts between producing enterprises and consuming enterprises are more developed, the regime may feel it possible to withdraw its centralized target of assortment of output.

There is also an interesting comment toward the end of the speech that the combining of different enterprises within a branch of production into a production association, which will give them more scope to make their own decisions as to specialization among themselves, will make it possible to devolve more decision-making power to these production associations. One almost gets the feeling that this is, in Western terms, an attempt to push oligopolies in industry. Interestingly enough, there is in the West a well developed debate on the advantages and disadvantages of oligopolies —in which Professor Nutter has participated—and it seems to me that Kosygin is taking a position in this debate that the development of oligopolies is useful.

Piecemeal Reform?

Nutter: My comment is on the question of step-by-step reform and merely adds to the catalogue of problems we have been developing. Naturally, the reforms have to take place in a gradual way if they're going to take place at all, but I think we have to be on the alert for problems arising because this approach that they're taking may mean that the cure is worse than the disease. Let's just take one area—the experiment in producing to order in some parts of the consumer goods industries. Now, this sounds very good and makes pretty good sense if we think in the context of an economy we're accustomed to, but suppose that we start, as in Russia, with shoes, and you let the shoe factory produce to order. How many orders it gets presumably depends on how good a shoe it produces. Well, suppose that the shoe factory turns out very good shoes. The prices are fixed from above. Presumably its orders will increase. Now, if it has to meet its orders, it has to get leather to produce the shoes, but presumably the leather isn't produced to order—it's produced to plan. And so you face the dilemma that the factory that is producing bad shoes presumably will still get its leather, and the factory producing good shoes can't get the extra leather. The consumers cannot determine the price of leather, so shortages in good shoes will remain. There's a very grave question in my mind as to how possible it is to introduce these kinds of reforms piecemeal.

Bergson: Warren is pointing to a problem that is posed again and again in Western discussion of this question—whether you can reestablish a market economy piecemeal, step by step. Is it really feasible? I must say I share Warren's feeling that it may turn out to be rather difficult to do this. There are really two issues. One is a very speculative issue but a very basic one. Does one assume that if there were very substantial decentralization, efficiency would rise? This, of course, is fundamental to any discussion of the effect of piecemeal reform. I think there is a growing opinion among economists in the West that a market type of socialism would function more efficiently than a centralized one, at least if there were substantial decentralization, though some might argue that only going the whole way to restoration of private enterprise would do the job. But then, even if one accepts the view that a great deal of decentralization and a substantial reestablishment of market institutions would be efficient, there is a question as to whether one can approach this position by a series of small steps. There are obvious difficulties that arise, for example, if prices are fixed centrally and some decisions are decentralized but the prices don't reflect scarcity values; then the people who are making decisions down the line in response to the success criteria of the government may make the wrong decision. The East Europeans have, as usual, found an amusing way to describe the problem we are discussing. When I was in Eastern Europe last summer, one economist said, when I asked him how the experiments that have been initiated were working, "Well, it is like an experiment with automobile traffic in which you allow 90 percent of the traffic each way to move on the right, as is usual, and 10 percent of the traffic each way to move on the left."

Erlich: I suspect that Stan and I, as representatives of Eastern Europe in more than one sense, have probably similar views on this. Eastern Europe, particularly Poland and Czechoslovakia, have since 1956 provided examples of what happens if you decentralize on the installment plan. The development led in Poland to recentralization around 1959 and in Czechoslovakia to an even more critical situation around 1963, when there was an actual drop in industrial output. There is a large measure of agreement that this had something to do with partial decentralization. Partial decentralization may be a very difficult matter even if macroeconomically everything is OK, but in neither Poland nor Czechoslovakia was everything OK macroeconomically—in the middle of decentralization there was a very substantial upward spurt of investment, a very drastic shift to heavy industry, which sharpened the seller's market.

In all fairness I believe that this situation is not very likely to occur in the case of the Soviet Union, at least as far as the intentions of the administrators go. One of the most revealing observations in Kosygin's preamble is a clear-cut statement to the effect that the rate of investment should decline. He put it in a nicer way. He said the share of consumption in the national income must increase. But absolute investment would go up, and this might or might not open the door to a seller's market situation. No doubt, arithmetically it is true that you can have a slight absolute increase in investment and a declining rate of investment at the same time, but you can pretty easily overshoot this tolerable level. Complaints about increasing tension, about investment being undertaken on too broad a front and leading to excessively long gestation periods are not new. We heard them as early as December 1956, but later we got more of the same. Liberman made the point very clear in his November 21, 1965, article. He said you shouldn't worry if you have a situation in which the supply slightly outruns the demand for a time. This seems sensible enough. If you want to make decentralization operational, you have to create a little bit of slack in the economy, you have to take some tension out of the economy.

Levine: On this question that Warren raised about the piecemeal establishment of markets, there are two points I would like to add. First, in the current consumer goods experiment, both the shoe producer and the leather producer, or the garment producer and the cloth producer, are linked to consumer demand. Second, an economy is not totally interrelated in all of its sectors. To a certain extent you can isolate the consumer goods sector—from its beginning materials to its end products—from the producer goods sector. It has always seemed to me that the Soviet willingness to experiment in the consumer goods sector was not, as far as priorities are concerned, as crucial as was made out in the West. The objective was growth of the producer goods sector, and all that was needed was to constrain the diversion of resources to the consumer goods sector. Economically, it doesn't matter too much what the composition of output of the consumer goods sector is as long as the total is kept under control. And to the extent that you can isolate all the interrelated producers in the consumer goods sector, then this does not prove a major threat to the imposition of the dictatorship's priorities in the economy.

Rationale

Roberts: One thing that has struck me in the discussion thus far of the reforms, their purpose, the question of decentralization, of getting rid of certain waste, and so forth, is what seems to be the absence of the term

GNP—the global aggregate. Just where does this enter into the picture these days?

Bergson: It's not a switch. I think it's very much in the minds of the Soviet leaders, and it was certainly in Kosygin's mind when he introduced the reform. Indeed, he is very explicit on the subject of the rate of growth, and it's easy to believe that this was uppermost in his mind when he elaborated the reform. What is really in question is, I think, why the government has at long last taken even the limited steps it has in the direction of, let's say, decentralization and market socialism. This has been discussed over a period of years.

There are various reasons for this, I am sure. We have referred to a number of deficiencies the government wishes to remove. The first thing to observe is that these are not novel deficiencies. They have been a subject of complaint for years and years. When Joe Berliner interviewed refugees from Russia after the war, many of the things that the refugees discussed regarding the practices of enterprises and the like were things which are being discussed today. The deficiencies are not new, but there have been some changes which make the deficiencies more burdensome and less tolerable than they used to be. If we want to understand why the limited steps in a novel direction, one must bear in mind these changing circumstances.

I have in mind, for one thing, the familiar fact that the economy, which was always complex—and I think more complex than is often assumed— has become still more complex as a result of the steadily increasing number of enterprises that have to be coordinated with one another. Not only has the economy become more complex, but the government's own priorities have become more complex. While under Stalin the aim was essentially to produce steel and then more steel—that's an oversimplification, but a very illuminating one—the government has now discovered chemicals and plastics, and within the sphere of heavy industry it's now aware that it must often make choices. It cannot proceed along one groove, as it did in the past. Moreover, the government's priorities have become all the more complex because, for a variety of reasons, the government is more concerned with consumer demands than it used to be. This, I think, can be substantiated in many ways. I would take as one outstanding piece of evidence the willingness of the government to import grain in the face of shortages—certainly very much in contrast to the behavior under Stalin. To add to the dimensions of the problem, while the government has become somewhat more attentive to consumer demands, the consumers are becoming a little more affluent and a little more choosy. This makes them less willing to buy the wrong goods, goods of the wrong size and inferior quality, than they used to be. So you have the paradox of the appearance of excess stocks of goods in an economy of scarcity. This increase in complexity has been a very important factor impelling the government to seek ways of reducing the burden of decision making on superior agencies, to limit petty tutelage, to give enterprises a little more discretion, and to try to arrange controls which will make the enterprises more responsive to the government's wants and the consumers' wants than previously.

But I would add to this a further fact—a very familiar fact but I don't think it can be stressed too much—that the rate of growth, which was quite high for a period of years up to 1958, has declined. The Soviet government in the course of time became committed to the notion that rapid growth was the success criterion for the system as a whole, and, under the influence of this commitment and the rapid growth that was actually realized for a time, the government became very buoyant. Khrushchev in particular regularly issued challenges to the West—he would overtake us very quickly in one area or another. And then, as it turned out, the rate of growth slowed down, and in recent years it has really not been any higher than the American rate. It has fluctuated, but the average for a number of recent years has been just about that of the United States economy. This must be very disturbing to the Soviet government. I would list this, along with the difficulties with China, for example, as among the major problems that worry the Soviet government today, and I do feel that if the Soviet government has been impelled at long last to take even a limited step in the direction of decentralization and new types of institutions, the desire to reattain rapid growth, to assure again a superior performance of the Soviet economy, is one of the major considerations.

Roberts: A question of clarification on the matter of reattainment of rapid growth. Is this an attempt to get back to the old notion of growth as being the best measurement of success? Because that is in some contrast to the notions of complexity, of variety, of quality. It would seem perhaps that a new yardstick might have come into the picture.

Bergson: This is a very basic question, Henry. I feel that the government is unwilling to settle for a rate of growth which is just like a Western rate of growth and may be even inferior to the rates achieved in some Western countries. This is politically and ideologically very disturbing, and the government is committed somehow to raise the rate of growth. But I also agree that it has many conflicting aims now which pose a dilemma for it in the sense that it also is committed to do something more for consumers, not merely in assuring greater variety but also in raising levels.

Wellisz: Maybe there's another way of looking at this. It's really not in any way contradictory. Until the 1950's at least, the Soviet Union could achieve growth by tapping its under-used labor resources and accumulating capital. This method is less effective now because labor cannot be transferred so readily from the less productive areas, just because there's now a full equipment, so to speak, of capital. Now the question is how to use it more efficiently. So the focus has shifted from accumulation of capital to efficient use of capital.

Bergson: Stan, I still would put the matter in a somewhat different light. The government, I agree, previously relied very heavily on assuring growth through rapid increase in the capital stock. It also relied heavily on borrowing technology from the West. Now, for both these sources of growth the government's power to raise quickly the rate of investment was decisive. This assured rapid growth of the capital stock and also permitted the rapid introduction of Western technology. What has happened now— and it's a very basic factor—is that the capital stock has grown a good deal in relation to output. The Soviet economy is no longer primitive, but an economy with a lot of capital. It's terribly difficult to keep growing rapidly by the old methods because, if you wish to expand the capital stock, even at the old rate, this means a rising and very large share of the national income going to investment. It's all the more burdensome in a community where consumers are expecting improved living standards.

Levine: Let me say something concerning the reasons for the reform. I would add a slight variation on what Abe has said. I think also involved here is the success, if you will, of the type of centralized planning used in the past in leading to the present problem. Centralized planning was instituted in the Soviet Union as a method of bringing about not only growth of output but also development, in the sense of changing the structure of the Soviet economy. Soviet centralized planning concentrating on the growth in capital stock and the change and shifting of the labor force accomplished what it set out to do more or less by the mid-1950's. The structure of the Soviet economy, except in regard to the proportion of the labor force in agriculture, was by then, and is now, that of an industrialized economy. I would agree with Abe that they still are very much concerned with a rate of growth, but it's no longer that easy to get the desired rate. In the past their priorities were clear: they knew they had to develop the metals industry, fuels industries, the machinery industry. Now it's not so clear how to accomplish this growth. There are now other products that can do the job of steel. In order to make these decisions it is now much more necessary for the central leaders, for the planners, to get feedback of information from the economy, from the producing unit, about production alternatives. In order to get more efficiency from the economy, they have to pay much more attention to questions of decision making at the basic producing levels.

If we were all Marxists here, we would not be too worried about the situation. That is, we would not say that the past system was a failure. We could say proudly that the past system, in accomplishing what the Soviet leaders wanted, was by and large a success, but now there is a new stage of development.

Nutter: I want to take some exception to this characterization.

Penalties of Success?

Bergson: Warren, you don't feel that they're suffering from success?

Nutter: No. I would put it in a somewhat different way. I think that if, instead of being preoccupied with this job of building industry as fast as possible, they had been attending a bit more to these problems and deficiencies as they went along and attending to a little more development in other important areas of the economy, they wouldn't be faced with quite the crisis they are faced with at the moment. On this score I would put a little different emphasis from Abe's on what is in the background here. Of course, it's the problem of continuing accumulation of capital, but equally important is the fact that they have run out of the easy jobs. They now are faced with some of those tough jobs that they have not been willing to look at for so many years. They have an economy which is industralized, yes, but it doesn't have any roads. It has inadequate housing, and there are no services to speak of for consumers, and so on. To go back to Stan Wellisz's point about untapped labor, there is still untapped labor in a fundamental sense on the farm, but it's very difficult to tap because— well, where are you going to put these people? This is the problem they face in their cities, and they can't overcome it easily—making up for their lack of construction for so many years is an enormous job. I would hate to be in the position of having to face it, or the problem of building roads and everything else that's needed. All I'm saying is that I think the leaders chose the wrong objectives, the wrong way of doing it.

Wellisz: I want to agree with Warren in this matter. Leontief characterized the Russian system as the input-input system. Things go in and nothing comes out. Now, it is fine to say, we will build steel mills to build more steel mills to build more steel mills, but finally one reaches the point of what to do with all that steel. I don't believe that the way they tackled this was correct because they assumed that, once you build a heavy industrial base, then other things would follow easily, and they don't.

Levine: I wonder if I may interrupt. My point was not to make a judgment as to whether the Soviet leaders could have done what they wanted to do it a better way. That's an interesting argument that could occupy us for a long time. My point was that the way they did choose did accomplish their dominant priority.

Wellisz: I don't think any of us can be sure, but I would like to propose that instead of saying that the trouble now is that they have had so much success, the trouble is precisely the opposite. It is the combination of past mistakes: if you accumulate capital without much regard to efficiency, without much thought as to what it will be used for except for such things as war production—where they clearly were very successful—then a point comes where you face the crisis. Now that you have all the capital goods, what do you do next?

Erlich: I am not buying the idea of growth *versus* choice. I don't see why we are constrained to make this type of antinomy. A growth which implies very often the wrong choices, even if we moved far out toward our technological frontier, is a less efficient kind of growth than is possible. I find a good deal of attractiveness in Rosenstein-Rodan's notion of a big push in application to underdeveloped countries, but I believe that there is such a thing as an oversized push. You can speed too much, and not only by taking a very hard view of the needs of consumers. It can be shown that during the first Five-Year Plan—after all a very decisive period of time —they tried to grow faster than their capacity, or, more specifically, capacity of their capital goods sector, would allow. They landed in a series of disproportions which were important, and not just from the view of the Soviet consumers. Steel became a bottleneck for quite a while, and the rapidly expanded machine-building industry had to operate at less than full capacity. This was clearly a waste from the viewpoint of the planners' own objectives, and so was the tremendous lengthening of the average gestation period of investment which resulted from this hypertension.

They established a system which was never effective, but still it was less of a brake on further development than it is now. It was perhaps second best in the past, but it certainly isn't even the third best today. One of the characteristics of this system is that it is very difficult to shift gears, as they tried to do after 1959 with the switch from steel to chemicals. No doubt one should make allowance for the extravagance of Khrushchev. To paraphrase what Lenin said about fighting barbarism with barbaric means, one can say that Khrushchev was trying to fight Stalinist economics with Stalinist means. He was trying to make up some of the arrears too fast by trying to triple the output of mineral and chemical fertilizers within seven years while at the same time expanding at a very respectable rate most of the old lines. But he was right when he complained that in the planning apparatus there were strong built-in obstacles against giving more emphasis to chemical as against metallurgical equipment. The Soviet machine-building plants were pretty good at producing metallurgical equipment after having learned it the hard way. The switch to different types of equipment would mean a temporary drop in efficiency, greater difficulty in fulfillment and overfulfillment of plans; and this would penalize not only individual plants but also very powerful industries. As a very clever Soviet economist wrote some time ago, it is typical of the prevailing approach to technological progress that great improvements in steam locomotives were made at the time when steam locomotives were no longer needed. In short, they have been much better in continuing and improving the things they have than in switching to things they don't have.

Success or Crisis?

Bergson: I, too, feel that it's misleading to describe the Russians as suffering now from success, and I don't think that Herb would want to press this very hard. It is arguable at least that with other procedures, other techniques, they might have produced even more steel this year than they are now producing, so that even if you assume that this was the be-all and end-all of Soviet planning, it's not clear that their arrangements have been optimal. Beyond that, it's open to question whether, even if they wished to continue to produce more steel, they could proceed along the old lines with their presently developed economy and grow as they would like, but the fact is that their priorities have changed, and the task has become more complicated. At the same time they *are* suffering—I wouldn't say they're suffering from success, but from many things. And let's bear in mind, though we may not be able to explore this, that one of the things they're suffering from very much is agriculture, which we have passed by, but which really isn't easily understood in terms only of the factors we have been discussing. Warren spoke of the Russians as experiencing a "crisis" now, and this term has been used by other economists describing the current Soviet scene. While I agree that they're suffering, I do wonder about this term, too. I must say I speak without great conviction, because I have the feeling that it's going to be terribly difficult for the Russians to work out a solution for the problems they are dealing with. The present period is a rather serious period, maybe even a critical period for them. Still, "crisis" seems to me a bit strong. Even though I take exception to this, however, as I look about the Soviet scene and the East European scene, it's easy to feel that, even if "crisis" is inappropriate for the Russians, it perhaps begins to be appropriate for some East Europeans. I think especially for the Czechs, who have experienced a very low rate of growth lately. They seem to be somewhat shellshocked as a result. But their situation is worse, distinctly worse, than that of the Russians at the moment, and I would hesitate to characterize the Russian scene in these terms.

Nutter: I threw the word out, not meaning it in the sense of what we would consider a crisis in our economy, which would be a situation in which a sharp break took place, let's say, in consumer production, or we were worried about the continuation of the kind of system we have. But I think that from the Russian point of view this is a crisis. I would use that term. I, think they view it in that sense because all of the developments that they have come to take for granted are now being challenged, and they are facing extremely difficult problems of choice as to which way they will move—to the point of whether they will fundamentally change their economic system. And this is a very bitter pill to have to swallow. Let me put it in a little different light. You mentioned, Abe, in passing, Khrushchev's buoyancy in 1958, 1959, and 1960, when he was going to outproduce this and that and the other thing. There was a very real overconfidence on his part, and perhaps pride here went before a kind of fall. I believe he really thought that some of the agriculture problem was solved. He had his great harvest—and this had been his big talking point—and then in his great overconfidence he proceeded to do what I think triggered the difficulty. He overcommitted himself in the space and military field and went ahead with what would seem, looking back—we couldn't follow it closely then—a rather reckless expansion, and this gave him further success. He had sputniks in space, he could brag about being first. Confidence fed on itself, and great expectations arose at that time, at least in his mind. I don't know how deep or how far they went. But now, in quick order, these expectations have been, to say the least, disappointed, and disappointed in a rather dramatic way through a series of events, the worst of which was the agricultural crop failure. If I were in their shoes, I would think that this was a crisis for my system.

The Question of Incentives and Price Reform

Wellisz: I think it might be useful to take another look at the reforms, because I think what has been presented here is a picture of a rather fundamental difficulty. A third promised reform, increased incentives both to management and to labor, is probably easiest to dispose of in that it probably is not very significant. The idea that the enterprises will have some possibility of giving a profit incentive to workers, who will somehow share in the profits, so that profitable enterprises will pay better than unprofitable ones—that, in a mass production modern society, is probably not a very important factor. Indeed, it might become dangerous. It's not important because the individual worker doesn't have very much effect on the profitability of the enterprise, and the year-end bonus, which is now promised him, will certainly not affect his daily work very much. The only possible way it might affect him is the danger that being discharged from a profitable enterprise might mean a lack of earnings, because he might have to move to one which is less profitable and which therefore pays lower bonuses. This might improve labor discipline in the profitable firm, but by the same token it might worsen it in an unprofitable firm. If the firm is not profitable, the worker would have an incentive to leave it. He will not have much of an incentive to work better because his own work is not likely to increase the profitability of a firm very much. He would like to get out and move into a firm which is more profitable.

The best way a worker can improve his position is to move to an enterprise which is already profitable, or, if he is in one, to stay in it. So, as an over-all incentive, it's not very likely to work very well. Moreover, there is very great doubt that as an allocative device differentiation of wages according to earnings—between profitable and unprofitable enterprises —is a move in the right direction. I think Yugoslavia has trouble with workers' bonuses because basically what should matter in the determination of the wage, from the point of view of allocative efficiency, is the worker's marginal product and not whether the enterprise in which he happens to be is profitable or not.

I would like to say just a few words about the proposed price reform. In my opinion price reform in a planned system is a very difficult thing indeed, unless one wants to go all the way to a quasi-market mechanism, and there is no sign as far as I can see, at present at least, that this is what is intended. It's very difficult to imagine how a price reform will be instituted. I think it is a very naive view of reality to believe that everything can now be computed on computers. In a centralized economy, or indeed in any kind of economy, it's extremely difficult to feed into the machine meaningful coefficients for the whole country. So my personal feeling is that although it will be possible to eliminate some very gross errors in pricing—and I suspect very largely by copying prices in other countries where there is a market mechanism—the movement to an allocative mechanism where prices really will allocate and yet where there will be no market is most unlikely to occur.

The Capital-Output Ratio

Bergson: You know, Stan, you're raising the question again of the impact of the reform, and maybe we should consider this further. In thinking about this, I feel that one cannot stress too much the problem of capital accumulation, the rate of investment, and this problem now has to be interpreted in the light of the rising capital-output ratio, the increase in the amount of capital that's required to produce a unit of output. The crucial point is that it becomes more and more expensive in terms of capital to maintain a high rate of growth if the capital-output ratio is rising, and it means necessarily that if you want to achieve rapid growth you must be investing more and more of your output in capital accumulation in order to provide the capital to produce the rising output. When we consider that this rise in the capital-output ratio prevails in a context where the government, for one reason or another, has allowed a somewhat more permissive political atmosphere, and where it has aroused consumers' hopes again and again, I think that to do more for consumers is a cardinal element of the government's dilemma. A major concern under the reform is to economize on capital in relation to output, to arrest this increase in the capital-output ratio, and so allow a larger margin of the rising output than would otherwise be possible to go to consumers. What is hoped is that through rising efficiency it will be possible to reconcile these conflicting claims of growth and capital investment, on the one hand, and expanding consumption, on the other. Now, the question Stan has posed is: What is likely to be achieved in this respect? I suppose, if you look at the individual reforms, it has to be acknowledged that some of them bear more directly and some of them less directly on this question of economy of capital. The increased authority granted to the enterprise with regard to capital investment is going to be limited. The government obviously hopes for gains in a variety of ways, including a charge for capital. At long last the government has committed itself—though it's still very delicate about the language used—to include interest in price. I come back, though, to the point we made earlier, that the reforms represent generally only a limited change from the system that existed previously. It's difficult to see how the government can get a big bang out of this with regard to economy of capital. I don't see the reforms as arresting in any very large way the increase in the capital-output ratio and assuring rapid growth on the cheap.

Roberts: Can I interject a layman's question? Is this rising capital-output ratio a normal concomitant of the industrialization process, or is it the result of errors of allocation and planning?

Bergson: Well, Henry, if we consider, say, the United States experience as a standard, we did have a somewhat rising ratio in the latter part of the last century and, I suppose, into the earlier part of this century. This rise was arrested, and there was something of a decline for several decades, if you compare the late 1920's with the post-World War II period. Lately, I think, the ratio has not been changing appreciably. The Russian experience was very much in contrast to ours in that throughout the period of the plans, but certainly in the period beginning in the 1950's, there has been a sharp rise in the capital-output ratio. In order to achieve the growth that has been achieved the Soviet government has had to expand the capital stock much more. This was already true in the 1950's, when growth was rapid. It's still more true in the period since 1958, when growth has been slow. Now why this is so is a complex matter. I would say there are a number of factors. One of them is that the government has used a very high and rising rate of investment as an instrument to achieve growth. As a result, the capital stock has grown very rapidly in proportion to the labor force, and I would think that some kind of diminishing returns to capital has occurred. Very likely the factor of inefficiency is also to be reckoned with, and it seems to me Kosygin himself was talking in these terms when he referred to deficiencies in the planning system, the failure to use capital promptly, the long gestation period, and so on. I think it reflects a combination of things, but the fact is that it's rather deeply rooted in the Soviet system and represents a very dramatic difference between the Soviet and the United States growth process.

Innovation

Nutter: To put just a slightly different light on this and to go back to a point Herb raised much earlier. Fundamental here is the question whether anything they have done so far, anything they can do with the system as it exists, will bring about the kind of innovation that occurs in other economies. I'm amused at the love affair with computers, for instance, which I think is wearing off to some extent in the East European countries, although it's still fairly ardent. One raises a question of this sort: Could you ever expect a computer to discover a computer? This whole question of how the system is going to deal with innovation, or help to stimulate it, has simply not been faced. It's been discussed but it hasn't been faced at the top, and certainly none of these reforms seem to me to do very much to stimulate innovative activity.

Levine: If I may just follow that point, I think this is the key to Kosygin's thinking, at least: that what is necessary now to reverse the rising capital-output ratio is just this—technology, improvement in technology. As I understand it, this is what really accounts for the stopping of the rise in the capital-output ratio in the United States. So much of what they're talking about is an attempt to achieve increased technology. Whether it will work out or not is of course a moot question.

In addition, we haven't yet mentioned one of the major reforms, the change in the organization of administration in industry—from the regional organization that existed since 1957 back to the ministerial type of organization. At times in his speech Kosygin seemed to be referring to the regional form of organization as one of the important reasons why capital wasn't being used effectively. One of the major inefficiencies of the regional organization was the chaotic condition of materials allocation in industry. I have a feeling that this really played havoc with the introduction of new enterprises, especially in new fields such as the chemical industry. When a new enterprise was set up, there was the need to organize the supplies for it, but they were stuck with a regional organization that did not have the power to ensure these supplies, and to a great extent this new capital invested just languished and wasn't productive.

Wellisz: Something that puzzles me is that while a recurring theme in Kosygin's speech is the need to facilitate an introduction of new techniques, I don't really see what in those reforms will expedite the introduction of innovations. I wonder if Herb would like to comment on this.

Levine: First of all, these reforms are focused on volume of sales. They talk in terms of the user now having more power to demand better products, better machines, and the producer consequently being forces—since the volume of sales will be the major success indicator—to try to develop new machines. This may be just a pious hope, but I think that the return to the ministerial form of organization of economic administration is clearly connected with the implanting of advanced technology. With the return to the ministerial form, the research institutes will be in a better position to develop the scientific aspects of new technology, and the ministries, they hope, will have a better chance to force the application of this new technology.

Wellisz: But the assumption here is that high civil servants or high administrators are risk-takers. Every innovation involves risk, and my observation of administrative behavior—not so much in the Soviet Union as in other countries—is that administrators are not innovators. It's much easier to do the same thing that you did before than to risk a great deal by introducing something which might fail. Now I don't see anything in this system which permits enterprises to innovate and fail and be punished for it in a radical way.

Levine: As for the high administrator, there is, of course, the outstanding case of Mr. McNamara in the Department of Defense. If the Russians can get enough McNamaras, they may get some effective innovation from above.

Nutter: Even if the system did work to bring about a more efficient introduction of technology, it would seem to me that the fundamental area in which it would work would be in finding better ways of doing the same old thing. The really crucial question is, is there anything here in this system that will bring about, or stimulate, or force the finding of new things?

Wellisz: Of course, there is still the possibility of imitation. The advances in Western technology in the last twenty years have been much faster than in the previous twenty or even fifty.

Levine: Following what Stan has just said, it is perhaps too easy to say, as some Western economists do, that the Soviet Union has exhausted the possibilities of borrowing technology. However, it is perhaps true that they have exhausted, or pretty nearly exhausted, the possibility of adapting the easy technology and what there is now to borrow involves very difficult, advanced technology.

Erlich: I do believe one can say that they are now, on the whole, less backward—they have reduced the lag a little—but still there is obviously a substantial gap. However, they now have to switch at the expense of some high priority sectors. In the early 1930's they tried to make switches at the expense of sectors they considered, rightly or wrongly, quite expendable. They could expand investment by compressing consumption, for the planned consumption increases used to be just eyewash, or at least dummy plans which could be expanded and then contracted at will. Now it is not quite the same. Shall we push chemicals, say, at the expense of steel? Steel occupies a much more crucial position in the total setup and is a much more powerfully entrenched industry. They will certainly need plenty of steel anyhow, so every cutting and switching here meets more serious resistance.

Levine: I wonder if it's worth speculating here about a generational problem. I don't know very much about this, but it does seem to me that the Soviet managerial class at the present time may on the average be quite old. These are the people who came into high positions when they were fairly young, after the purges, at the end of the 1930's. They are now in their sixties and maybe older. Perhaps there will occur a discontinuity —the replacement of the present managerial groups by younger people, who might be more amenable to new things, although I agree that the institutional forms work against risk taking, but this is what they're trying to improve.

Nutter: We mustn't forget the importance of those institutional forms. It's true that there's still room for copying though not as much as before. But one of the essential characteristics of an innovative system such as ours is something they can't copy, and that's the flexibility of the system which allows it to adapt quickly to new technology. Now their problem, it seems to me, is as much this as any. Sure, the technology is there, but it changes quickly. Now when they go through the process of centralized decisions, of deciding to put in new technology, this is a big order. And once they do it, they commit themselves. The typical pattern has been that they're always just a little behind, and then when they come around to introducing something new, it also has to be on a fairly massive scale and they go slowly, and by the time they bring it in, there's something else new happening somewhere else. There is at the root this fundamental question whether they're building enough flexibility into the system so that it can really adapt quickly to change and utilize it.

The Question of Reducing Tautness

Erlich: What do we mean by centralized economy? An economy may be centralized in doing certain things, more than some of our Western economies are, more than the United States economy is, but it may allow for a great measure of decentralization in other things. I believe that this kind of generalized black-and-white formulation is one of the problems which has been harrying our profession in analysis of the Soviet economy. We have been arguing between a completely centralized economy and, at best, a Lange-Lerner kind of economy. Maybe there is something in between. Besides, the transition from the undesirable overcentralized economy to the much more desirable Lange-Lerner economy or to some kind of in-between economy cannot occur in one jump. This is a complicated problem. It involves several simultaneous operations, and one of the things I am so obsessive about is that of reducing the tension in the system, of shifting to a lower gear in terms of the rate of growth. Kosygin seems to recognize this in part when he talks of increasing the share of consumption, but I still am not sure how far he is prepared to go, particularly when we introduce a new and somewhat sinister note. There is still an area that can be either cut or expanded—the area of defense. The international situation is not the subject of our discussion here, but it is shaping up at the moment in a way not very conducive to relaxation. It may make the shift to a lower gear more difficult. If there isn't any shift to a lower gear, I suspect that the experience of Poland and Czechoslovakia might repeat itself: the greater freedom of managers to spend some of the retained profits might create an explosion of investment demands, with not enough capacity to meet this explosion. In such a case the old-timers would come out and say "I told you so" and try to switch back to centralization, which after all achieved actual or alleged successes for several decades.

Wellisz: I think what Warren said was that innovation, as general improved allocation, depends very strongly on the degree of flexibility of the economy. If in an economy conditions are rigid, then an innovator has great difficulty in innovating—by definition. Alex pointed out a very important factor in that rigidity: no matter what the administrative reforms are, if there are continuous shortages, if the economy is going full blast, then the rigidity remains. And this clearly is a great danger. There is the other danger, too. If the administrative reforms are made, the controls removed, and nothing much is done to replace them, then, even if you get flexibility, you get wrong results; and then, as you say, you reintroduce the same controls. I think the reforms do open up possibilities of improvement; they also open the possibility that things will go back to where they were.

Western Analysis of the Soviet Economy

Roberts: Could I toss one final, historian's question to you gentlemen. This is simply my impression that over the last decade, since, say, the mid-1950s, our picture of the Soviet economy seems to have changed enormously as contrasted to our impression at that time: of extremely rapid growth that, even if it slowed down, showed promise of continued fast expansion—and at a point when the American economy seemed not to be doing too well. As I recall, a great deal of the attention of American and other Western economists centered on this question of the Soviet economy overtaking and surpassing our own. It seems to me that the questions of interest in today's discussion have been quite other. This is obviously in part a reflection of changes in the performance of the Soviet economy since 1958 and also of changes in the performance of the American economy. But I would be most grateful for comments on this in your roles as economists who have been following this problem over a number of years.

Bergson: Henry, you were good enough to forewarn us that you would raise this question. Perhaps the first thing to say is that it is a little dangerous to try to characterize the opinion of the American students of the Soviet economy in any simple terms. I think there was some variation at different times. There were differences in degrees of optimism, differences in degrees of caution with which different people looked at the future. As I observe the scholarly scene, though, I would agree that generally there has been a perceptible change in outlook regarding Soviet economic prospects since, say, the mid-1950's or somewhat later. It is fair to say that the Western economists tend to be less "optimistic" and more "pessimistic" than they were in the 1950's in viewing the Soviet future. This is true of me, though even in the 1950's I think I was usually rather cautious about the Soviet outlook; and I believe it is also true of many colleagues.

Now why this should be so, why the outlook should have changed, is a matter which would require inquiry among the various people concerned into their reasons for shifting views in the course of time and in varying degrees.

But no doubt a very important factor often has been the accumulation of evidence regarding the performance of the Soviet economy, the slowdown in the rate of growth, the difficulties in agriculture, which were apparent long ago but which turned out to be even greater than was anticipated. I would include matters of this sort, and I would also include one other aspect.

A decisive factor in Soviet rapid growth has been the authoritarian control of the rate of investment. Given this, it was widely assumed that, if there were retarding factors in the growth of the Russian economy—such as diminishing returns, resource difficulties, agriculture, and so on—by exercise of this authoritarian control of the share of output going to capital, the government could offset the retarding factors and more or less assure whatever growth was sought. This was a fairly familiar view in the 1950's. It came out, I think, in the conference that I organized at Arden House in 1952. And I too was influenced by it in some degree. But as was not so clear previously, the Russians, in achieving their growth, have been relying on a growth of capital stock far more rapid than the growth of output, and so have been suffering from a rising capital-output ratio. Given this, the authoritarian control of the rate of investment is not such a simple way out, for this reason: given the rising capital-output ratio which the Russians have been experiencing, they actually have to raise the rate of investment even in order to maintain the old growth of the capital stock. A steadily increasing share of output has to go to the capital stock just to maintain the old growth, and this says nothing of the possibility of accelerating the growth of the capital stock in order to offset retarding forces, due to resource difficulties and the like. As I reflected on this—and I believe I still speak for many colleagues as well as myself—and on the fact that the capital stock had become rather big, I came in time to feel that the rising rate of investment did not provide the simple way out that was widely assumed in the 1950's might be open to the Russians. This did have a very perceptible impact on my thinking about the nature of the difficulties that Russians face, and if earlier I put this in the central place in my discussion, I have had in mind my own reaction to it. I do feel it's at the very heart of the Russian problem. In the course of time I have also come to feel that the rising rate of investment, as a way out for the Russians, has all the more limited possibilities because of the changed political atmosphere and the increasing commitment that has been made to consumers. In some degree this necessarily affects the government's freedom of action.

I do want to add, though, a word of caution. This is in order in the light of the performance of economists generally, and I don't speak of any one in particular. In appraising the Soviet prospects we are very often compelled to proceed without systematic projections. To some extent we have to play this matter by ear. I must say that even in the 1950's I was disturbed at the ease with which some analysts projected past lines on charts into the future, and I don't feel that even now we have the basis for very reliable projections into the future. This should be borne in mind. We have to be careful, too, not to be overwhelmed by what's happened during the last few years. If we erred previously in varying degrees on the side of optimism, we must be careful, since our projections are somewhat speculative, not to err in the other direction now.

Nutter: I think that all these elements undoubtedly played a role, and the last point needs underlining. I would emphasize that we have to be awfully careful in making any judgment on four or five years' experience. I don't know what's going to come out of all the stirring about that's going on in Russia at the moment. It could be that they will make some changes in the system which will bring them back to a higher rate of growth than they're now experiencing. In fact I would consider it rather remarkable if they stayed at the present rate. That's not a prediction, I'm just saying that I would be surprised if they did. We have to be extremely cautious in not jumping to the conclusion that simply because there's been this dip, and a very graphic one in the last few years, it ought to be projected forward. I prefer to rely on history. I am more and more impressed by the forces of history, and I am much more inclined to look at long periods—how systems have managed over the long haul—and this I term the cautious view. I'm sticking to it, while recognizing the pitfalls in that too. You cannot automatically project this kind of experience, but my feeling is that the good and the bad somehow tend to balance out, if we keep our perspective and don't jump overboard making a prediction on the basis of current events.

Erlich: I would also like to be autobiographical, as Abe was. It is slightly more difficult for me than in Abe's case because I have very few explicit statements to fall back upon. I have been keeping myself very safe in the Preobrazhenskii corner—or, a little more seriously, I didn't produce any estimates. But I was consuming them, and as long as I approved of them, I believe I shared responsibility for them. I would like to emphasize the fact that although none of us, to the best of my knowledge, predicted a sharp drop, some degree of leveling-off was anticipated by those who actually produced estimates. Fingers were put rather clearly on some key factors which caused the slowdown. There was a large degree of consensus that the big spurt in agriculture during the 1950's was a one-shot affair. Then, the idea about the tendency of the capital-output ratio to increase had been developed way back. Abe said it in his *Real National Income of Soviet Russia*. I found that Gregory Grossman made similar predictions in his Arden House Conference speech. I think that none of us was very much taken in by the Khrushchevian industrial reform of 1957. I recall that it was met with a lot of tongues in a lot of cheeks. But I'd say that all of us have learned during the last decade or so a lot of additional details about the inefficiencies of Soviet-type planning, very largely because they told us so. They had not been talking very much before, and I believe there are some inefficiencies which we could not simply have imagined while sitting back in our armchairs; but when we're being told these things with increasing frankness and incisiveness, something sinks in. On the whole, I don't think we have reason to be in a particularly self-castigating mood because I think that most factors which made for a slowdown were recognized properly although the degree of the slowdown undoubtedly was underestimated. I very strongly second the warning, voiced by Abe and supported by Warren, that we shouldn't commit the mistake in reverse and extrapolate uncritically from comparatively low rates of growth.

Levine: The point has been made that the decrease in the Soviet rate of growth is a compound both of long-range factors, the factors affecting capital, and also of some specific short-range factors, especially in the period, say, since 1958. A number of these short-range factors have already been mentioned, and they have been discussed quite extensively in the Western literature. I imagine this is what previous speakers had in mind when they warned about not making easy extrapolations into the future.

There is the question of the diversion of resources to the military. People around this table have taken different positions on the importance of this factor. Abe has written recently that he doesn't think this could account for very much and that the absolute amount of diversion of investable funds to the military doesn't loom large proportionally. Others have argued that while this may be the case, the specific factors (labor and capital) that have been transferred to the military and space programs are highly productive factors and that this has been costly to the civilian economy. There is also the decrease in the rate of growth in the labor force, accounted for by the thin generation resulting from the war and the effect of the decrease, for a time, of the length of the work week. And there have been other factors.

But if one is to look to the future, what can we extrapolate? I would agree that we should at least be prepared for some increase in the rate of growth in the Soviet economy over that of the immediate past five-year period. But as Abe said, there is a long-run development quite apart from the capital-output ratio, that is, the political attitude now developing in the Soviet Union as indicated by all the talk of increasing the role of the consumer. They seem now not to be willing just to go on raising the rate of investment at the expense of the Soviet consumer. On the other hand, when they talk about improving the situation for the Soviet consumer, they very frequently make the point that an incentive mechanism is involved, that it's not just a welfare question, that improving the material goods that to into the consumption patterns will give a positive incentive to Soviet workers to improve their productivity. What are some of the external effects of this increasing concern with the Soviet consumer? Might this work to limit the power of the dictatorship? Will it lead to a deterioration of the regime's power to control the economy? This, of course, is a speculative question. There is Professor Gerschenkron's interesting hypothesis that the rationale for the dictatorship is the forcing of sacrifices, that if the dictatorship is not forcing sacrifices, then its *raison d'être* disappears and it will fall. Will the reforms that are now being talked about erode the power of the dictatorship and the power of the party? What *is* the role of the party in a more decentralized economy? There is an interesting provision in the statute on the Soviet enterprise that states that all plan assignments are to be given to enterprises only by superior agencies. Is this a slap at the party? Is Kosygin really representing the economic managers and saying that the task of the party is not to interfere directly in the operation of the economy? If these things do develop, if there is an erosion of the power of the dictatorship—and I'm not one who subscribes strongly to this position—but if history does work out in this way, then the ability of the regime to maintain high levels of allocation of its economic resources to growth will of course be limited, and we might then expect the rate of growth to approach the rate of growth of a market economy.

Bergson: The hour is very late, but there is one aspect which I think should be mentioned before we close. The government faces a dilemma. There are conflicting claims which are terribly difficult for it to reconcile. It hopes by increasing productivity and efficiency of technological progress to assure greater harmony of these conflicting claims. We still have to bear in mind, though it's a rather somber note to sound at the end of our session, that one way out of such a situation is not the economic but the political, aiming by conduct abroad to create an atmosphere, or at least to acquiesce in the creation of an atmosphere, in which sacrifices at home are accepted more readily than they would be otherwise. As I look around the political scene, I feel that the Soviet government has been circumspect in the last year. It's been cautious and could not be viewed as exploiting in any great degree opportunities to create tension. Let's hope that continues, but we have to be aware that matters may change in this regard and that a change in political relations and foreign circumstances could possibly be a basis for a change in priorities.

REFLECTIONS ON SOVIET ECONOMIC REFORMS*
— · — · — · — · — · — · — · — · — · — · —

George R. Feiwel

For many years the Soviets were able to counteract the declining marginal productivity of investments and to evade marked deceleration in the industrial growth rate by relying heavily on a rapid and increasing rate of investment, mainly in heavy industry, assimilation of Western technology, and extensive use of labor and natural resources. Such a policy could not be depended on ad infinitum because it would require, *inter alia*, a steadily growing share of national income to be diverted from consumption to investment. Growing consumers' demand for improvement of cur-

*Reprinted by permission from *The Soviet Quest for Economic Efficiency* (New York: Frederick A. Praeger Inc. 1967), pp. 318–339.

rent consumption standards and the system's inability to raise them significantly, mainly because of the investment pattern, efficacy of the planning system, and policy commitments, have seriously affected productivity and had political and social repercussions. In the face of the economy's growing complexity, the system is unable to meet the proliferating priorities by applying the traditional growth and planning instruments. The system fails to generate the spirit of innovation in the enterprise and its immediate superiors. The center is unable to disseminate technical progress on a sufficient scale for shifting the parameters of the production functions to counteract violations of economic efficiency.

The reform attempts to foster efficiency as a significant additional source of growth. It is in the better utilization of available resources, more rational use of existing capacities, and better investment choices so as to get more and a better composition of output, that the approach to the problem by and large differs from past experience. It is in this connection that there seems to be some inherent inconsistency in the strategy chosen by the Brezhnev-Kosygin team, for improvements in allocative efficiency require choice criteria and parameters which would make such choices possible. The rethinking of the growth strategy would require some fusion of the Preobrazhensky-Bukharin approaches, perhaps with something like a set of Lange-Lerner Rules.

Gosplan's reported analysis of various variants of the present five-year plan is an indication that the question of the optimal share, composition, and limits of investment was given more comprehensive treatment. In defense of the investment program chosen for the current quinquennium, Gosplan specialists, L. Burovo and A. Osadko, advance that if a larger share of investment had been diverted to producer goods' industries, the resulting increases in wages and effective demand could not be satisfied by concomitant increases in the flow of consumer goods, with adverse effects on labor productivity. They argue that the share of investment in national income cannot be lower, and its basic composition cannot be altered, for this would result in deceleration of growth and unemployment. Underinvestment in consumer goods and agriculture would produce a slowdown in the rise of living standards. In addition a slackened investment pace would lower the productivity of the subsequent period.

Although much muddled thinking still prevails about the "iron law" of the preferential growth of sector A over B, its dogmatic interpretation was assailed. But it is not overly clear what is the official stand on this matter. Academician A. Arzumanyan attacked Stalin's "erroneous economic dogma" and criticized many Soviet economists who "divorce the law of preferential growth of production of the means of production from personal consumption in a socialist society and reduce this law to absurdity." There seems to be a weakening of the "law's" impact with its reinterpretation. It is realized that the growth of heavy industry "at forced rates above requirement" at a given moment results in inefficient application of capital and deceleration of national income. The rapprochement between the rates of growth of producer and consumer goods' industries is not considered as a "violation of the law." It is granted that the proportions between those sectors are fluid, depending, *inter alia*, on the extent of industrialization, production function, factor endowment, and productivity. Even if unanimity is not reached, the current thinking seems to reflect that at the present stage of industrialization the "pace setting" growth of sector A "can and should be accomplished not only and not so much by means of an increased allotment of investment as through the fuller and more efficient utilization of existing potential, fuel, materials, and labor resources."

Although in broad contours the general strategy as far as priority of sector A over B, with emphasis on heavy industry, is to be maintained, with resources channelled to those branches, the development of the previously underpriviliged sectors is to be accelerated mainly through better use of existing resources. The increased flow of output in sector B and agriculture is to be achieved not predominantly by reshuffling resources from A to B, but by raising the efficiency of the system, basically by reducing visible waste. Estimates show that increase of efficiency of fixed capital by only 1 per cent would augment industrial output by 3 billion r. Fixed capital is reported to be underutilized in almost all branches of industry by 20 to 30 percent. Frequently the constructions last two or three times as long as planned, the actual costs exceed planned costs by 50 to 100 per cent, and the mastering of capacities is delayed. According to the new five-year plan, capital in the majority of industries should be utilized from 96 to 100 per cent. The efficiency of capital will increase by 12 to 15 per cent. Since sizable new projects and extensive mechanization that will be introduced in this quinquennium will not be mastered until the 1970's, it is anticipated that the efficiency of investments will somewhat decline, but less than in the past.

In a larger perspective the reform could be viewed not only as a recognition, even if inarticulate, of the importance of the previous "nonpriority" sectors for enhancing productivity, more balanced development, and increasing the consumers' welfare, but also as an improvement in the planning system which would enhance efficiency and would not shift, or at least not to such an extent as before, the burden of all planning failures on the underprivileged sectors. Both at the planning and execution stages measures are sought to eliminate the major failures of the past. The consumer goods' product mix should be more sensitive to consumers' demand, although a radical change in marketing, production, and price determination will be required for considerable improvement. Also the response to demand would have to penetrate deeper; for otherwise it creates an artificial distinction between consumer and producer goods. How can a factory produce what the customer wants if it cannot obtain the required inputs, if they are subject to central allocation and their producer has an assured clientele, and if it cannot adapt its capacity to variations in demand?

There is little indication of pronounced reductions of macroeconomic hypertensions so as to allow for a breathing spell to shift to a lower, but perhaps more sustained, rate of growth. Stop gap measures were taken in agriculture, but no drastic changes are in sight. A real obstacle to the new currents is the increased commitment of resources to defense. Some, even if hesitant, steps are being taken to generate growth by a more appropriate composition of investment. But there are no distinct signs that a market solution, resembling the Yugoslav variety, will be adopted, at least in the near future. Of course, the scope and direction of the reform are contingent on the economy's performance.

An examination of the proposed changes reveals how conservative they are in relation to some views of the profit-oriented school and how far-reaching they are in relation to the existing system. In examining the reform it seems that a distinction should be drawn between rather radical changes in approach to economic problems and the potency of measures taken to produce the desired effect. The direction of the movement should not be identified with the workability of proposed arrangements. The direction may be salutary, whereas the working arrangements may be inadequate. Keeping in mind the shortcomings and inconsistencies of proposed measures and the totality of working arrangements to make them successful, it may be that the introduction of the measures per se is a drastic step forward that may contribute to finding *à tâtonnement* the adequate working arrangements which will offset the short comings and inconsistencies. For example, introduction of the capital charge will generally be an improvement even if its rate is not potent enough to constrain sufficiently abuses of capital, does not reflect opportunity cost of capital, cannot be applied as a test for selecting variants, and the valuation of assets is misleading. The sales index is generally superior to gross value as it shifts emphasis on realization, implying users' or consumers' approval. But if such approval hinges on the strength of a sellers' market, prevalence of central allocation of producer goods, and assignment of key assortment indexes with assured sales, fallacious prices and merchandising methods, etc., it cannot be overly significant. Profit as a measure of efficiency reflects composite performance and, depending on the method of calculation used, is much superior to the past performance criteria. But as prices do not reflect scarcities, and are irrational in terms of the planner's objectives, profit is an accounting rather than economic category, which plays little role in plan construction. Its application in plan execution may not only produce misleading, but also harmful, effects. At present profit is considered only as *one* of the performance criteria and it is not assigned a significant interbranch allocative role.

The likelihood of the scheme's success in eradicating present deficiencies and providing a vehicle for implementing ambitious goals can only be evaluated in terms of the scheme's logic and its internal consistency. Without attempting at this point an analysis of the coherence of the scheme, one is struck by the fact that the proposed price changes are virtually revisions to allow for interim changes of prices of factors and certain policy considerations, rather than a thorough reform of pricing methodology to arrive at, or approach, scarcity-opportunity-cost-efficiency prices for *economic* verification of production. The expected price revision should bring prices closer to average costs and substantially mitigate but not eradicate deficits. There is a discernible shift toward the price of production, with the significant divergence of widely differentiated profitability rates, and pronouncements that greater allowances are to be made for "user values." The price revision does not break away from tradition because it continues to focus on the financial, rather than economic, aspects of prices. In addition, it is recognized that prices should facilitate choice, perform an incentive function, distribute national income, etc., with the arising conflicts between functions often solved in favor of expediency. Actually the scheme is without a mechanism for successfully tackling the problem of relations between the central planner and plan executants. It lacks the assurance of faithful implementation of the planner's goals without explicit commands.

Today's influential officials reiterate that comprehensive central planning will be retained, prices will be fixed centrally, at least for the bulk of producer and consumer goods, and will not be allowed to fluctuate in response to market forces. The restoration of the market as a verifier of the plan is denounced. It is inconceivable to the planners to forgo price formation as a tool for controlling and influencing economic activity. Apart from the deeply ingrained fear of price fluctuations and spontaneity, there is apprehension of monopolistic practices, obsession with inflation, etc. The deputy chairman of Gosplan and chairman of the GICR (Gosplan's Interdepartmental Commission for Reforms) assailed a recent essay calling for intrabranch competition, complete freedom for enterprises to choose buyers and suppliers, price determination by mutual agreement, development of branches in response to market forces, with the plan merely coordinating interbranch activity.

Principally the conservatism of the reform is manifested in its attempt to herald the new with the old methods. Centrally imposed indexes are in many respects too restrictive and may produce results contrary to those intended.

For example, the restrictions on the wage fund are imposed to arrest "unplanned" increases in purchasing power and inflationary pressures. However, wage increases may be necessary for a swift adjustment of the production flow to demand. Restriction on flexible adaptation of output in itself contributes to inflation and produces maladjustments. Complaints are common that the gross value index is assigned to enterprises. On the face, the index is to be planned by the enterprise. However, since the wage fund is centrally assigned and since predominantly this fund is related to gross value, actually gross value is planned for the enterprise indirectly. In fact, when correcting the wage fund Gosbank requests evidence of the degree of fulfilment of this index. Consequently when the enterprise will strive to acquire a comfortable wage fund, the shortcomings generated by the gross value index will soon reappear.

Without repeating the colossal handicap of central allocation of materials and equipment as a source of inefficiency, contributing to sellers' market pressures, it should be remembered that it actually widens the gamut of central specification of assortment assignments. Central allocation also reduces the impact of the sales assignment because it provides assured customers. It reduces adaptability and maneuverability because even when output composition is altered to suit a buyer, the producer is expected to fulfil assortment assignments. Often output cannot be changed to suit buyers' needs for the required inputs were allocated beforehand and may be unsuitable for the altered requirements. The aim of cost minimization is impared by the restrictions on substitution of inputs.

To meet assigned profit and profitability the producer will tend to turn out a product mix with the most advantageous price cost ratio for him, producing output of highest profitability in descending order, subject to constraints. However, with the envisaged prices, the output may not be necessarily what the planner wants him to produce. Hence imposition of the assortment plan. The available evidence seems to point that by and large breakages of assortment plans do not mitigate shortages of producer goods in a sense that the resulting output weakens disproportions, even if it violates the plan.

In the consumer-oriented industry, there is an indication that if the present trend of direct ties continues, the output composition, subject to centrally imposed constraints, may eventually be patterned by consumers' preferences. However, price rigidity, limited supply flexibility, and bureaucratization of the price setting process may stultify the producers' response to consumers' demand. The reform is deficient in providing a mechanism of response and adjustment to such demand. Apart from the constraints and incentives for the supplier, the mechanism for transmitting consumers' signals is deficient, particularly in view of anachronistic merchandising methods, insufficient advertising, the embryonic stages of consumers' demand studies, etc. If the producer has not met given profit and profitability assignments. and the orders placed by trade specify low profitability commodities, he is forced to make package deals and foist on trade articles of high profitability together with its orders. There seems to be a dual problem here: The producer is motivated to produce goods for which there is excess supply and the trader's knowledge of the market often dictates him to request those of lower profitability for which there was demonstrated excess demand. Among the problems encountered here, are the deficiencies of prices and the market knowledge of the transmitter.

The approach persistently concentrates on the financial aspects of profit and other value categories, rather than viewing them from the allocative standpoint. Economic categories are often confused with financial instruments, e.g., the new prices envisage a profit which all suffice to pay the capital charge, rent, if any, and cover the desired level of decentralized funds. The interest rates will probably be differentiated according to the financial ability to bear the burden and the level will not conform to the marginal efficiency of capital in all uses. Financial manipulations for equalizing the conditions under which enterprises labor may often be a sort of subsidy perpetuating backwardness. There seems to prevail a belief that alterations in financial arrangements will produce significant improvements without fully grasping the concomitant measures without which the financial ones are doomed to impotency, or at best will serve as budgetary controls.

The state, as the sole owner of the means of production, determines the distribution of profit, the share it takes, and the destination of the remainder. It should be emphasized that the state maintains its *commanding post* not only in distribution between the enterprise and the budget, but also between the shares of profit destined to augment current personal income, housing and welfare measures, and the enterprise's development, considerably restricting the enterprise's maneuverability of resources. These are the crucial control weapons ensuring that the budget will be provided with sufficient revenue (especially worth noting here is the novel "free" remainder of profit), that current consumption will not be augmented at the expense of investment, and generally that the enterprise should not have enough funds to allow it to get out of hand. The strict control over decentralized funds is essential to the system. Yet such funds can hardly be called decentralized for the enterprise cannot decide at will in what manner they should be spent. The lack of autonomous disposal of funds circumscribes the scope of financial reforms.

As we know, three funds with delineated functions have been created, with profit as one of their sources and no ceiling on their increase. The superficial division between efficiency and growth as rather self-exclusive still prevails in the approach to the formation of the three funds from profit. It is indicated by the emphasis on the volume of sales, where increase of production is of paramount importance and on profit where increase of production is not particularly sought. It implies that increase in profit should be accomplished mainly by cost reduction. It is true that the second criterion, profitability, emphasizes all aspects of activity. By and large greater weight was assigned to the contribution based on profitability, although there are notable exceptions. It should be borne in mind that the emphasis on profitability may somewhat hamper ventures where the marginal rate of profitability would reduce the average, but still increase profit's size. Although understandable from the expediency angle, the validity of the assumption of linearity may be questioned. Are equiproportionate increases of decentralized funds appropriate in case of variable returns?

The reduction of normatives applied to plan overfulfilment in order to infuse enterprises with the spirit of taut planning does not seem to be overly effective because, *inter alia*, the increase of sales (profit) target relies on the level already achieved. With the widening of its horizon, the enterprise becomes understandably cautious when it realizes that its future decentralized funds may suffer from a rash increase of targets in a given year, for if this year's increase is large, next year's will have to be larger still, becoming more out of reach with a higher level attained. The problem could be solved by expansion, but, as we have seen, this *is* a centralized decision, curtailing the enterprise's long-range planning. Furthermore, the uncertainty of supply, the deeply rooted habits, the insecurity and caution of a transitional period, and the side conditions restricting premium distribution, contribute considerably to weaken the incentives for taut planning. It seems so far that the phenomena of considerable plan overfulfilment and underfulfilment as disturbances of the national plan are here to stay.

There seems to be a general awareness among Soviet economists that sizable material incentives at the start could give a vital impetus to the reform movement. The officials, however, particularly those associated with the MF (Ministry of Finance) and the Committee on Labor and Wages, "swear that the means are lacking and, therefore, to count on something large and tangible is impossible."

The experience of the first convertees will not be conclusive because, *inter alia*, the conditions under which they work and under which they were converted differ from those proposed by the reform. For example, normative setting starts with a set amount and then the normative is arrived at, instead of the other way around. The danger in converting the initial enterprises without changing their 1966 plans lies in that the normatives will be perpetuating the past inequality in tautness of plan assignments and other inequities and incongruities of past experience. It must be remembered that the provisional normatives established this year will undoubtedly serve as the starting point when, and if, group normatives are set.

In order for the DF (Development Fund) to perform its function it is, of course, not sufficient to appropriate funds for investment purposes, but the enterprise must be able to command the real resources. One of the primary objectives of the DF is to inject flexibility into the investment process, to widen bottlenecks, take advantage of quick returns, etc., requiring swift adaptation to changing conditions. However, as practice has shown, enterprises are required to include such investments in their plan, defeating the very purpose of the DF, for if those investments could have been foreseen, they could have been financed from central investment funds without resorting to the trouble of creating a decentralized fund. Mitigation of one of the major deficiencies of Soviet-type economies through decentralized investments has generally failed, as the Polish and Czechoslovak experience indicate, because decentralized investments competed for physical resources with the centralized, endangering the central investment plan. Therefore, the understandable reaction to control the pulse of decentralized investments. Frequent disproportions occur between the investment plan and the capacity of construction and building materials industries as a result of taut and "unscientific" investment plans. The lack of reserves in construction and the building materials industry contributes to stricter controls of decentralized investments. Another barrier imposed on the DF is that it generally cannot be used for substantial expansion, therefore, largely limiting the enterprise's function as an agent of economic change. However, with present prices, interest rates, and other choice criteria, it is doubtful whether decentralized investment choices will be efficient.

Alterations are made in the methods of financing centralized investments in cases of additions to existing plants or construction of new ones, with a maximum period of recoupment of five years. Apart from the fact that these measures do not seem to be well thought out, the recoupment period, the repayment period, and the efficiency of investments over their life span are badly confused. The much debated question of the efficacy of credit financing of investments brings to mind the obvious advantages of a businesslike approach when investments have to be repaid and interest charges borne. Although more detailed investigations of this phenomenon are required, it would probably be not too sweeping a statement to make that, within the context of the Soviet economy, there is no real economic compulstion to repay because the enterprise does not face bankruptcy or does not substantially carry the burden of direct economic responsibility for failure. Responsibility for repayment is further impaired by the large turnover of personnel. Similarly, the potency of the interest rate, a subject not devoid of controversy in our own economy, is a moot question, for generally it diminishes profitability only inconsequentially, and, in view of other accessory conditions imposed and the great benefits from virtually free expansions, further investigations are required to determine whether it is a significant constraint.

To arrest increases in the capital-output ratio, the Soviets propose to promote development by shifting the parameters of the production function, with sharp increases in the efficiency of production processes. It is questionable whether, in view of their failure to provide powerful incentives to create new productive resources and products and in the absence of conditions for over-all increases in efficiency, they can muster sufficient forces to accomplish these tasks.

In a market economy technical progress is encouraged by competition. Industrial research is undertaken for "aggressive purposes" in search of extraordinary profits and for "defensive purposes" in order not to lag behind rivals. Technical progress is also stimulated by imitation of firms other than immediate competitors and the promotional activity of capital goods industries. The reform does not seem to be equipped to generate the above, or at least not as strong forces. No palpable incentives have been developed to motivate research and investment. The fact that the majority of capital goods will still be centrally distributed will not release the sales effort in that industry, for even if it is evaluated on sales, the latter will be assured by central distribution.

One encouraging development should be noted in this context. The increasing involvement in foreign trade both inside and outside the bloc may eventually awaken a spark of competition and force the Soviet manager to produce cheaper and better. Some relaxation of the foreign trade "monopoly" may even be in sight. At this stage there appears to be no desire to extend consequentially the negligible private enterprise even in such areas as services and small-scale consumer goods' manufactures where private initiative would not encroach on the commanding outposts. Apart from ideological reasons, private entrepreneurship is probably feared on the grounds that it may subject state industry to a severe competitive test. Furthermore, once introduced, it may be difficult to check its infiltration.

Perhaps in a most fundamental sense one of the stumbling blocks of the reform is its failure to cope successfully with the problem of injecting the system with sufficiently powerful incentives for risk taking and deploying true enterpreneurial ability. So far the solutions sought by and large lack a developed mechanism of response and adjustment to economic stimuli, something like the *effort releasing* effect of the market. At best incentives are offered to execute the plan better, but no sufficient stimuli are created for managers to become agents of economic change in the Schumpeterian sense. There seems to be insufficient motivation for managers to develop and introduce new techniques, largely because, but not exclusively, there is no sufficient compensation to reward such action. In this sense the incentives concentrate, and here lies the improvement, on inducing managers to be more receptive to technical progress foisted on them from above, rather than becoming its initiators and creators of new. The system lacks the vehicles of continual change, those in search of entrepreneurial profit who have "the will and the action" to employ "means of production differently, more appropriately, more advantageously" to carry out new combinations. There is a manifest need for motivation to make new things happen, rather than at the very best to react to a changing environment.

With the shift of some prerogatives from the apparatus to the enterprise, the reform naturally focuses on the caliber of available managerial staff. As Professor Albert Hirschman pointed out "among the proximate causes of economic development, the supply of entrepreneurial and managerial abilities now occupies in official documents a position of preeminence at least equal to that of capital. There is a need for qualified personnel to carry out managerial functions in a businesslike manner and to exercise initiative and ingenuity within the boundaries drawn by the reform. There is a discernible shift to let managers manage and one of the perplexing problems is the shortage of those qualified to do so. For example, it was recently reported that in Moscow there are less than a dozen top managers with a university degree in finance, and, of course, the number of top managers with other university degrees is not too impressive either, with a majority of those with degrees molded in the technocratic tradition. However, it is possible that in view of the past financial training, the dearth of finance specialists in top positions may not prove to be such a disadvantage. The efforts to redesign the curriculum to train future managers and the mushrooming managerial training programs in enterprises are commendable. However there are signs that more often than not a new label is put on the traditional "tool box." A few pages describing the reform are usually added to the old textbooks whose context remains unaltered.

It should be noted that the lasting problem of the relationship between the manager and the Party is as acute as ever. In the past a *nomenklatura* list was issued, specifying the persons politically acceptable for certain jobs. In time the list grew from 400 to 8,000 positions. It is implied that those listed do not necessarily have the professional qualifications for the jobs for which they are politically acceptable. Recently Liberman urged dismantlement of this list, alluding to its impairment of the managerial situation.

Another development that will be interesting to watch will be the role of the Party cell within the enterprise. Will it be transformed into a countervailing force to the extended managerial prerogatives, and if so, to what extent? Simultaneously it is worth mentioning that the reform does not invigorate trade unions to protect the workers' interests, especially in view of possible unemployment. The present congress of trade unions seems to indicate that no steps were taken for trade unions to assume their real functions. There are no signs of a movement to workers' councils. But there is an awareness that the reform should also permeate labor relations.

As could be expected there are "psychological barriers" to the reform and vested interests that resist it, manifested primarily in the groups threatened by the reform. The usual pattern of resistance in this context is not outright opposition, but an attempt to limit the reform's application, and undermine its implementation on a wide scale. Of course, "the forces of habit rise up and bear witness against the embryonic project." There is conceivable opposition in the local Party organizations and upper echelons for fear of losing their hold over economic activity. Apart from the fact that many "traditional" bureaucrats may be displaced as they lack the new qualifications, at the enterprise level the old successful director may not fit into the new scheme of things as his qualifications and manner of doing things differ from what is now expected of him. In this context he too may have vested interests in opposing the reform.

If there is sufficient opposition, especially at the ministerial level and higher, this may prove to be a serious impediment halting the development of the reform. As has been pointed out by K. Galanshin at the Twenty-third Congress, the fact that decisions have been made and orders given is no assurance that they will be carried out. There are many such orders that await execution even though the deadlines have long since passed. The opposition can be detected in the GICR where—as Professor Liberman is reported to have remarked—"each department upholds its own viewpoint. This frequently results in compromises and half-baked decisions. The enterprises receive huge amounts of instructions and directives that, intentionally or otherwise, sometimes put a damper on creative searches." That the opposition is more than just speculation on our part is indicated by a refutation of a Gosplan official in charge of reform implementation of the rumors that the reform is only an experiment, and assurance that it is in full swing. Only particular solutions are at the experimental stage.

Ministerial opposition is reinforced by the slow adjustment of the ministries' work to new conditions. For example, their incentive system has not been revamped to accord with that of enterprises, provoking frequent clashes of interests, with the ministry usually carrying the day. In addition, although the number of plan assignments have been reduced, complaints are raised that the number of plan indexes on which the enterprise is required to report to its superiors and other statistical agencies grows daily. Whether from inertia or vested interests, there is every manifestation of the ministries' proposing to continue in the old pattern of things, paying lip service to reform implementation. But whether this is only a transitory phenomenon is a moot question.

It is difficult to speculate from an economist's vantage point to what extent a consensus was reached at the leadership level on the nature and direction of the reform, and what is the real attitude of influential Gosplan and other officials. In very broad outlines and at the cost of oversimplification, the political background to the reform seems to be one of dissent between basically two articulate groups; one favoring the continuing thaw and the other yearning for a return to the old proven ways of doing things. There is probably fear that liberalization of economic life may entail an inevitable *détente* in the political, social, and cultural spheres. There is a growing awareness of the need for a changed approach in economics. with an everpresent compulsion to retain full political control over public life. Reconciliation of the two seems improbable and it is possible that by allowing greater discretionary powers and freedom to the lower economic units, the Soviet monolith may find itself on the inexorable road to liberalization in other domains. On the other hand, it is possible that those who fear such liberalization may yet thwart the economic reform. Whether the conservatism in some circles may prove to be a serious impediment to the unfolding of the reform remains to be seen.

Notwithstanding changes in political attitude, the major pitfall of the proposed reform is its disregard of consistency in economic measures and policies. More concretely, they combine certain incompatible elements and expect a smooth interaction between them. They do not respect the internal logic between methods of calculation, prices and incentives. To implement the plan smoothly all elements should be consistent with each other. To achieve a given aim no alteration should be made in one element without tracing the repercussions in others. The other elements should be simultaneously adjusted to provide for unity in functioning.

When prices are irrational, activating economic incentives, stimulating choice to increase output of a more profitable product, may result in output that is less desirable since profit is not an economic category here. Since prices were not used for verifying optimality of production at the plan construction stage, they should not be activated for such a purpose during plan execution. Conflict between calculation at the planning stage *in natura* and execution by the means of value parameters generates a mechanism producing disparities unbalancing material balances. Consequently, an order specifying to the producer what to do is more in conformity with the logic of the system than activation of economic incentives to fulfil, say, the profit plan. Fulfilment of the latter depends on the relative ratios of prices which were not taken into account at the time of plan construction.

Since no attempts are made for producers' prices to equilibrate demand and supply, even at the time of their setting, and since excess demand pressures will be exerted for the bulk of key producer goods at those prices below clearing levels, physical allocation must necessarily remain and flourish. The scarce supply must be allocated to priority uses and its dissipation among others must be prevented. Not only will the supply be rationed, but, depending on the relative price-cost ratios for different products, the producer may seek to forego production of underpriced scarce products, and assignments *in natura* will proliferate to obtain the desired product mix.

The *conditio sine qua non* for successful decentralization is prices that approach scarcity with a degree of flexibility. It may be recalled that in the Lange prewar model the original price is of no great consequence, but its successive variations elicit economic response and the equilibrating process is put into motion. Then central allocation can be basically dispensed with. Pronounced divergence from clearing level prices would require an equilibrating mechanism to eradicate endogenously the disturbance. Although not devoid of shortcomings, price flexibility is probably the most efficient device for eradicating shortages, at least as long as it is not called upon to perform a structural change. Among other devices are variations of supply—either from a given capacity and/or from added capacity—and attempts to shift the parameters of demand function by income policy, substitutes, market promotion, etc. To be effective the variation of supply requires, *inter alia*, prompt transmittal of signals, the producer's ability to command real resources with the financial resources he can muster, the necessary economic motivation, and rules and criteria for achieving the process economically.

If shortages prevail without accompanying appropriate changes in below-equilibrium prices, or if expansion of supply is insufficient, the industrial buyer will press for administrative intervention to secure deficit supplies. Even without the central planner's intent, or irrespective of it, pressures will be activated to recentralize supply allocation. When recentralization gains momentum it will become a cumulative force as the past experience of half-measure reforms in Eastern Europe indicates.

It is futile and confusing to talk of centralization versus decentralization without clear recognition of the type of economic calculation to be used. Decentralization of economic decision-making is incompatible with a type of economic calculation that essentially uses physical units for plan construction. Decentralization, within the framework of a centrally planned socialist economy, requires a mechanism assuring successful and faithful implementation of the planner's targets essentially without commands. Such a mechanism presupposes the existence of market (or simulated) prices serving both the central planner and the firm's manager as tools for economic calculation and rational allocation of resources between alternative uses at all planning stages. Planning without a market mechanism is a costly and inefficient process. Detailed planning can hardly be substituted for a market mechanism as the Soviets have learned in the past. Probably abstinence from a market mechanism, or its mathematically contrived counterpart, will still impede efficiency even when enterprises will be endowed with greater independence.

As the reform movement gathers momentum, the nature, direction, speed, and consistency of measures taken become collectively a focal point. The first and rather obvious observation is that the evidence is yet to meager to hint at either success or failure. It is much too early to venture an opinion whether the reform is just a first step in a radical transformation of the Soviet economy, or simply a stop gap half-measure. In the first case, even without speculating on the leadership's intentions, it is quite possible that as the incompatibility of the measures taken will be revealed, the regime's leaders will push the reform to its logical conclusion by adopting a method of economic calculation more akin to decentralization at the execution level. They may seek a workable solution along the lines of Lange's prewar model of market socialism, or more likely, along those offered by planometrics, and Lange's last contribution comes to mind in this context. Or, there may be an about face, reverting to stricter centralization in view of the maladjustments created by allowing executants to calculate without providing them with meaningful value parameters for doing so. Here the development of computer techniques and network may prove advantageous in recentralization. Essentially, from here on there are only two ways the Soviets can go: forward or backward. But they certainly cannot rest on their laurels for the reform is either too much or too little.

The regime's leaders face formidable tasks and this may prove to be yet one of the most significant, fascinating, and challenging chapters in Soviet economic, social, and political development. The great determination with which the bureaucracy never rushes into anything new and the potent incentive to preserve the status quo and reduce the impact and nature of the reform are disquieting thoughts. However, the shadow cast over the reform movement by the might of vested interests that may retard its progress seems less dangerous when viewed in historical perspective. In final analysis one can only repeat after Lord Keynes:

> I am sure that the power of vested interests is vastly exaggerated compared with the gradual encroachment of ideas. Not, indeed, immedi-

ately, but after a certain interval; for in the field of economic and political philosophy there are not many who are influenced by new theories after they are twenty-five or thirty years of age, so that the ideas which civil servants and politicians and even agitators apply to current events are not likely to be the newest. But, soon or late, it is ideas, not vested interests, which are dangerous for good or evil.

CHANGES IN ECONOMIC THOUGHT*
— · — · — · — · — · — · — · — .

Alfred Zauberman

There is more than one reason why the first half century of Soviet economic thought, just coming to its close, should have its special fascination for a student. It represented a dramatic break with the Russian heritage in this field and thereby with the mainstream of post-Ricardian thought; it included the groping for a theoretical scaffolding suitable for a new social-economic system; the determination to build it upon a Marxian foundation; the search for a planning doctrine attuned to the kind of planning that was being empirically evolved with hardly any positive help from Marxian economics; more generally, the correlation of economic thought with the specific economic environment and the economic strategy pursued at different times. Here it is possible to deal with only a few of the many aspects which attract the student.

On the eve of the Revolution there were close links with western economic thought; one was the quest for some symbiosis of Marxian and Ricardian elements with contemporary trends in the West. This is true of both Tugan-Baranovsky and Struve, two eminent Russian economists. Struve in particular tended to look to Marx for a broad sociological background. For fundamental economic concepts he turned to Ricardo, and tried to combine this with rigorous analysis borrowed from the mathematicians and the Austrians. Complementarity of the labour theory of value and the marginal-utility theory was one of his principal tenets.[1] At the same time the irreconcilability of Ricardo with the Marxian propositions on 'socially necessary labour,' on value resting on the average labour content, was already recognised in Russian economics, especially—at the turn of the century—by the mathematician Dmitriev[2] (the matter was to become a major issue decades later). Moreover, 'subjectivist' tendencies were making a strong impact on Russian thinking in various areas of economics: an outstanding original Russian contribution was the pioneer-

---

*Reprinted by permission from *The Soviet Quest for Economic Efficiency* (New York: Frederick A. Praeger Inc. 1967), pp. 318–339.
[1]M. Tugan-Baranovsky, *Osnovy Politicheskoy Ekonomii* (Petrograd, 1915), p. 549.
[2]V. K. Dmitriev, *Ekonomicheskie Ocherki* (Moscow, 1898).

ing work on demand analysis published by Slutsky on the eve of the Revolution.[3]

Of great interest too is the strong impact made by the Marxian macroeconomic approach *as such* in directing pre-revolutionary thought towards problems of economic growth. It should be borne in mind that in the pre-Keynesian world Marx had a virtual monopoly as a source of inspiration for such an approach. His formulation of the growth model was taken up and extended at the turn of the century in Russian writing. The significance of the model was recognised by Tugan-Baranovsky (who, incidentally, deduced from it the rule of faster advance of the producer-goods sector as a condition of the growth of the system).

Naturally, the Bolshevik revolution tended to give a dominating position to Marxian teaching. To be sure, the retreat from War Communism and the subsequent experiment in mixed economy revived links with western economics. The work by Bazarov and Yushkov may be taken as characteristic for the epoch.[4] In the mid-twenties Bazarov designed a noteworthy scheme for a mixed system, a system with two sectors of which only one would obey strict rules of profitability: a considerable area of operation would be reserved for a market mechanism in the allocation of resources. In dealing with their efficient employment, Yushkov returned to the order of ideas of pre-1917 economics; his approach was marginalist par excellence, and with him economic calculation rested on opportunity costs. Moreover, except for the lack of rigour of his apparatus, his work contains in embryo a remarkable anticipation of the optimality concepts which were given formal shape only a decade later.

At the same time—during the twenties—the question of the scope for economic science under socialism, and indeed of its very *raison d'être*, was becoming the subject of a major controversy. This was related to the cardinal practical problem—the area of freedom of action for the planning State. In philosophical terms—the fashion at the time—it marked the battlefield of two camps, the 'teleologists' versus the 'geneticists.' The central question—often framed as that of the survival of economic law in post-capitalist society—was answered positively by those who argued that the plan should and could in essentials be derived from extrapolation of time series. This was the opinion of the chief protagonist of the genetic view, Bukharin.[5] (It has a close affinity with conceptions which were to obtain currency a quarter of a century later, when indicative planning

[3]E. Slutsky, 'Sulla teoria del bilancio del consumator', *Giornale degli Economisti*, no. 1, 1915. Cf. my 'Remarks on a Discovery in Soviet Economics', *Bulletin* of the Oxford University Institute of Statistics, no. 4, 1962.

[4]V. Bazarov, 'Printsipy postroienia perspektivnogo plana', *Planovoe Khoziaystvo*, no. 2, 1928; L. Yushkov, 'Osnovnoy vopros planovoy metodologii', *Vestnik Finansov*, no. 10, 1928.

[5]N. Bukharin, *Kritika Politicheskoy Platformy Oppozitsii* (Moscow, 1928).

was taken up in capitalist countries, and with the idea of a plan-prognosis which today has penetrated the theory of Soviet-type normative planning, with the probabilistic approach introduced by the mathematicians.) Others contended that, in the dialectical process of an economy's transformation from capitalism to socialism, the mode of operation of economic law would also be transformed, and economics would turn from a descriptive into a prescriptive discipline.[6] In the mid-twenties Preobrazhensky proclaimed that the beginning of disintegration of economic law had actually begun.[7] The teleological extremists insisted that socialism entailed the inexorable dissolution of economic law, spelling the doom of economics as an analytical science. This was the school that gained supremacy by the end of the twenties—on the threshold, that is, of the planning epoch.

Looking back we recognise this as the first instance of a process which was to be repeated in the history of Soviet thought—the process of its reacting to the requirements of economic life rather than shaping it. This is borne out by what happened in the theory of economic growth. Growth became *the* cardinal issue. Soviet official doctrine, invoking the authority of Marx and Lenin, adopted as the cornerstone of its growth strategy the well known principle of preferential development in the producer-good sectors. Decades later—in the sixties—the support of the classics for this proposition came to be questioned; and perhaps legitimately.[8] Moreover, a stricter analysis has brought out a host of assumptions which condition and circumscribe the universal validity of the principle. In particular it has been shown that the validity of the principle turns on the prevailing type of technical progress.[9] Some of the assumptions which rob the principle of generality were patently not realised either by Marx or by Lenin.

However, there is every reason to believe that the emphasis on producer goods was decisive for the vast expansion of the Soviet industrial potential. This is *a fortiori* tenable in respect of the Soviet reformulation of the precept that growth promotion must be centered on a few selected leading links. What on the face of it would seem to have been irrational growth for growth's sake was given its rationale in Soviet literature a quarter of a century later in the rigorous terms of the von Neumann model,[10] that is, a model in which consumption as such is to be minimised.

What would be unacceptable, however, is the postulate of growth being necessarily of a balanced kind. The fate of the Feldman model—now

[6]B. Khmelnitskaya, in *Ekonomicheskoe Obozrenie*, no. 3, 1925.
[7]E. Preobrazhensky, *Novaya Ekonomika* (Moscow, 1926. Engl. translation *The New Economics*, London, 1965).
[8]L. I. Dovgan, *O Tempakh Rosta Dvukh Podrazdelenii Obshchestvennogo Proizvodstva* (Moscow, 1965).
[9]O. Lange, *Teoria Reprodukcji i Akumulacji* (Warsaw, 1961).
[10]J. von Neumann, 'A Model of General Economic Equilibrium', Engl. translation in *Review of Economic Studies*, no. 33, 1945-46.

rescued from oblivion and famous—is illuminating. Persuasive in the logic of its growth mechanism—its affinity with Domar-Harrod has been shown by Domar himself—the model was out of tune with its epoch.[11] True, Feldman did not identify dynamic equilibrium with optimality of growth. In fact he did consider variants of unbalanced growth both for a steady and an accelerated pace, and he related them to the given conditions (structure of the economy, varying factor productivities, required consumption levels and so on). But whatever its merits, an analysis which presented a set of viable alternatives to the economic strategist disqualified itself at that particular time. It did so in any case by bringing into relief the constraints which circumscribe the planner's area of manoeuvre. This is true also of several other analyses produced at the time, for example Kondratiev's criticism of the first plan.[12] Strumilin, in his first attempts at plan construction in the twenties, inclined towards the non-equilibrium school; in the mid-thirties he produced a design for a 'national economy balance' which would form the basis of a long-range plan.[13] The idea was unacceptable to those responsible for economic strategy; today it can be seen that it was premature. *Planovoe Khoziaystvo*, which published the model, had to apologise editorially (1937, no. 4) for its blunder in printing a construct which was described as counter-revolutionary.

The question of timing also provides the explanation of the abandonment of the Soviet pioneering effort of the twenties in the field of industry (input-output) analysis.[14] Here again one of the handicaps was a (static) general equilibrium approach. The economic system could be viewed only as one of overall equilibrium. When Popov's remarkable attempt is thought of in these terms, one finds it less surprising that further work in this pioneering exploration was left to an economist abroad (W. Leontief): at the time it was evolved, it too was out of touch with the needs of its native land, for this was a period when efforts had to be concentrated on selected objectives. Theoretical economics could offer little help in this selection, indeed not even in its principles: growth promotion would have largely to rely on the arbitrary, more or less intuitive judgment of the policy makers. In fact, in a strikingly short time, Soviet practice designed its own very rough methods and crude instruments to operate the fairly primitive kind of planning and controls required in the given milieu with a given strategy. In such circumstances economics was perforce 'de-theorised.' Indeed it lost virtually all its theoretical content. This explains the poverty of

[11]G. A. Feldman, 'K teorii tempov narodnogo dokhoda', *Planovoe Khoziaystvo*, no. 11, 1928, and *ibid*, no. 12, 1929; E. Domar, *Essays in the Theory of Economic Growth* (New York, 1957).

[12]D. N. Kondratiev, 'Kriticheskie zametki o plane razvitiya narodnogo khoziaystva', *Planovoe Khoziaystvo*, no. 4, 1927.

[13]S. G. Strumilin, *Planovoe Khoziaystvo*, nos. 9–10, 1936.

[14]*Balans Narodnogo Khoziaystva SSR 1923–24* (Moscow, 1926).

Soviet economic thought precisely at a time when the economy itself was passing through a phase of spectacular change and advance.

Some time around the turn of the thirties the need for objective criteria in the calculations underlying the plan came to be increasingly felt, and this led to a renewal of theoretical reasoning.

Once again fundamental matters were debated within the familiar framework of the scope of economic laws under socialism. It was now acknowledged that 'objective necessity' existed in any social-economic system, and that it changed with changes in the system. Under socialism it would operate as a 'conscious necessity': the abolition of private ownership of the means of production and of entrepreneurship would make it objectively necessary to replace the forces of the market by planning, while scarcity of resources would make it imperative to adopt the socialist (as distinct from the communist) laws of distribution.[15] Broadly speaking, this would imply the use of economic calculus, that is, commodities would have to have a common measure of value. The question was, how was this to be done? In the forties, Voznesensky[16] answered this question by saying that in socialist society the price of a commodity is based on its value and hence on production costs: that value under socialism corresponded to the actual amount of social labour used up in production. And, typically, Voznesensky drew the conclusion which exploded his argument: the socialist state determines the prices in the interest of strengthening socialism. Voznesensky was unable to offer an answer to the problem he was able to pose: perhaps it was too early for an answer.

As the break-through phase of growth was coming to an end, the methods of running the economy had again to be re-adjusted. A search for more refined techniques began. While still lacking a clear theoretical basis, Soviet economics followed suit and gradually oriented itself towards the use of money as the measure of value.

The search for the correct method of pricing was reflected in the debate among the economists in the fifties, once again carried out in terms of the operational principle for the law of value under socialism. At one extreme the Strumilin school postulated a price strictly based on the Marxian variant of the labour theory of value; at the other the Vaag-Malyshev school argued in favour of the 'production price'—the *Produktionspreis* in Marx's analysis of the competitive capitalist market.[17]

[15]A. Leontiev, *Planovoe Khoziaystvo*, no. 6, 1947.

[16]N. Voznesensky, *The War Economy of the USSR* (Moscow, 1947).

[17]For Strumilin's view see in particular *Voprosy Ekonomiki*, no. 12, 1956, and *Planovoe Khoziaystvo*, no. 2, 1957. For Vaag's view see in particular *Voprosy Ekonomiki*, no. 8, 1957; no. 4, 1958; no. 9, 1958, p. 113; for Malyshev's *Voprosy Ekonomiki*, no. 3, 1957, and no. 9, 1958, and *Planovoe Khoziaystvo*, no. 7, 1957. Cf. my 'Law of Value and Price Formation', in G. Grossman, ed., *Value and Plan* (Berkeley, 1960).

Before the controversy could lead to any definitive conclusion, the limitation of its conceptual framework was revealed. Not surprisingly for an economy so strongly directed to expansion, the groping for an objective measure of value was expressed with particular strength, and at a fairly early stage, in the discussion of the relevance of the time factor in measuring values. Here the appearance, in the mid-forties, of Strumilin's celebrated paper on the measurement of investment efficiency—his argument related to depreciation of product over time due to rising factor productivity—was a milestone.[18] This method was later elaborated and, though rough, it contributed to the awareness of the acute and complex problem of efficiency.

While Soviet economic thinking gravitated increasingly towards the wider employment of money-term instruments as efficiency instruments, the problem of efficiency was not really understood. The point is that under a direct-centralist regime there is little harm from a non-efficiency price. It is only when an attempt is made to shift to the indirect variant of centralism, a variant under which the centre controls the economy by means of orders coded in prices of factors and goods, that the question of efficient steering with such instruments becomes crucial.

The growing maturity of the economy has accentuated the issue, and has turned Soviet thinking in this direction. Theoretical attitudes adopted for a phase of extensive growth have gradually outlived their usefulness. And reasoning confined to the use of the Marxian apparatus has been helpless where a framework for handling the efficient growth equilibrium was needed.

At this point Soviet economics began again, in many crucial fields, where it had left off at the beginning of the thirties. It has tried to avail itself of the advances which mathematics have made in the meantime in areas carrying a promise to the economic planner. Soviet economics has by now become ready to be 're-theorised.'

In the new climate it has turned in the first place to Leontief's input-output method, since this offered immediate help in imparting a general equilibrium approach to national planning as well as the use of powerful computational apparatus.[19] It was even more remarkable to find the roots of a mathematical formulation and solution of the more generalised problem of the optimal (efficient) equilibrium in Soviet work as early as the turn of the thirties. At the time its meaning escaped the attention of Soviet economists.

[18]G. Strumilin, 'Faktor vremeni v proektirovkakh kapitalnykh vlozhenii', *Izvestiya Akademii Nauk SSSR*, no. 3, 1946.
[19]W. W. Leontief, *The Structure of American Economy 1919–39* (second ed., New York, 1951).

In evolving the mathematical formulation, Kantorovich laid the foundation of programming theory, the discipline concerned with the theory of constrained maxima and minima. He did so in his construction of the comparatively simple, linear form. (Recently the claim has been advanced that he formulated, and even designed, as early as 1940, a computational method for a relatively general non-linear programme as well.)[20]

Programming is in substance the mathematical formulation of rational decision-making in pursuit of adopted goals. It is in this sense a theory of planning; significantly, its use in economic planning and control was stressed by Kantorovich in the very title of his pioneering 1939 paper: ever since the work of his school has been 'plan-oriented.'

Kantorovich's work brought into Soviet economics the idea of duality. As often happens with ideas of genius, once acclimatised they seem almost self-evident. The gist of his idea is that in every linear optimisation problem, the maximisation is tied to minimisation, and vice versa. The economic interpretation indicates that a set of 'objectively conditioned valuations' ('solving multipliers' in Kantorovich's original work) is inherent in the optimum solution, and this has a patent implication for pricing. Of special relevance for the habitual Soviet frame of economic thinking in these matters is the point incisively made by Baumol: 'the dual problem turns out to have an extremely illuminating economic interpretation which incidentally shows that old-fashioned marginal analysis is always implicitly involved in the search for an optimal solution of a linear programming problem.'[21] (I would add that at the same time the programming formulation is closer to reality than old-fashioned marginal analysis.) True, Kantorovich in his original work of 1939 did not provide a very effective computational method (that had to wait for the development of the simplex algorithm in the forties by Dantzig). But he did throw new light on pricing as related to efficient planning. His work, supported by a strong mathematical apparatus, was paralleled chronologically by Novozhilov's contribution[22]: a contribution also of signal importance though resting on purely logical argument or arithmetical example or simple algebra. (Years later Ragnar Frisch translated Novozhilov's formulation

[20]L. V. Kantorovich, *Matematicheskie Metody Organizatsii i Planirovaniya Proizvodstva* (Leningrad, 1939); its main impact on Soviet economic thinking dates from its republication in V. Nemchinov, ed., *Primenenie Matematiki v Ekonomicheskikh Issledovaniakh* (Moscow, 1959). L. V. Kantorovich, 'Ob odnom effektivnom metode resheniya nekotorykh klassov ekstremalnykh zadach', Academy of Sciences of the USSR, *Doklady*, 1940, vol. 28, no. 3.

[21]W. J. Baumol, *Economic Theory and Operations Analysis* (second ed., Englewood Cliffs, 1965), p. 103.

[22]V. V. Novozhilov, 'Metody nakhozhdeniya minimuma zatrat v sotsialisticheskom khoziaystve', Leningrad Industrial Institute, *Trudy*, no. 4, 1939.

of a principle of 'feedback' inter-relations into the language of modern programming theory.)

As one would only expect, ideas so utterly unfamiliar—indeed in ir-reconcilable conflict with the established way of thinking—met with determined opposition from Soviet economists. Novozhilov's point of departure was condemned as 'a non-historical concept of "maximum effect with minimum outlay,"' a concept long since unmasked in Marxian literature.' His approach to problems of productivity of capital and growth was dismissed as 'Keynesian.'

But these ideas could not be long suppressed. In the later fifties they came to the surface again and with greater strength; and once again they came under fire from the orthodox. Kantorovich's conceptions were by that time twenty years old, but only when decoded from mathematical into 'literary' terms was their message understood. His ideas, as well as Novozhilov's, were now lumped together and subjected to a barrage: both were reproached for being trapped by Say's concept of factors and of services rendered by capital, and for coming dangerously close to western marginalism. The inventor of programming had to resort for a time to Galileo's tactics. The criticism was correct in stressing the incompatibility of the new and the established ideas but it was anachronistic.

What is impressive is not the resistance to these novel ideas, natural as it was to the Soviet economist's orthodox mode of thinking, but rather the speed with which the opposition was overcome. Its defences, though rationalised in terms of Marxian theory, melted away as the gap between the approach dictated by the changed economic milieu and the traditional one yawned ever wider. (The late Nemchinov's contribution in promoting this process should not go unrecorded.)

The idiosyncratic attitude towards mathematics may still linger in the old school, but it is no longer of any consequence for contemporary thought. The help of mathematics in economic planning theory and practice is fully appreciated, both on the heuristic plane and on the plane of application. No Soviet economist now fears to resort to this help even where it patently compromises time-honoured conceptions. It is noteworthy that the process of reconciliation of thought and life coincided with the increasing practicability of the new ideas due to spectacular advances in computational technology as well as to an extension of frontiers of theoretical knowledge.

In this expansion certain trends are clearly discernible, a few of which will be mentioned here.

One is the continuous refinement of the new mathematical-economic apparatus, enhancing its usefulness in planning practice. One important direction of inquiry is shown in the attempt to introduce dynamic factors into the balance of the national economy by Konius, Smirnov, Dadayan, Dudkin, and others. Of exceptional importance is the work carried out in recent years by Kantorovich—in part jointly with Makarov—on the efficiency of long-range plan-programming.[23] It should be noted that problems of stage-by-stage optimisation—that is of what is technically labelled dynamic programming—have been for quite a time the area of an important and original Soviet work by the Pontriagin school.

At this point one may at least hint at the research in the field of information and control systems with an eye to the practical possibilities this promises to centralist planning resting on a network of high-powered computer stations. This school of thought looks for help to the theory of 'self-teaching' systems. Soviet theoretical achievement in systems of automatic optimisation is, thanks to Lerner, Feldbaum, and others, very strong indeed, and links up with the work of Pontriagin and his associates.

To put this in a broad frame, what is at present under intensive exploration in Soviet economics is optimal functioning of hierarchical, multi-grade economic systems. Here the mechanism of centralist steering is under theoretical scrutiny.

The investigation of the price structure has an obvious bearing on the practicability and efficiency, or otherwise, of a plan. In other words, it is of crucial significance for the guidance of a centrally planned economy under the regime of profit-maximisation. This has become of immediate practical interest since (again under the pressure of the growing complexity of economic life) ideas of profit-guidance were aired in connection with the reform of the Soviet economic machinery. Probably it is the theoretical clarification of the problem—the enlightenment due to the theory of optimisation—that accounts for the abandoning of the Liberman proposals.

When dynamics came to be tackled in a rigorous fashion the problem of planning for remote horizons was revealed as the crucial one. What is involved is the asymptotic behaviour of key variables, the feasible pace of economic growth, the effect of the choice of the optimality criterion on the construction of rational criteria for the plan-period, with due allowance for at least broadly stated goals beyond-the-horizon. Here, too, it is the Kantorovich school that has posed the decisive problems. Soviet thought has indeed moved full circle. From a broadly postulated equilibrium approach, via its emphatic and total rejection, it has returned to this approach but in a new, far more sophisticated form, revealing new aspects and offering new insights.

The matters now under discussion—in particular as related to opti-

---

[23]L. V. Kantorovich, V. M. Makarov, 'Optimalnie modeli perspektivnogo planirovaniya', in V. S. Nemchinov, ed., *Primenenie Matematiki v Ekonomicheskikh Issledovanyakh*, vol. 3, 1965.

mality criteria—touch upon certain paramount issues of social philosophy. To be sure, once the question of the optimality criteria has been raised as a technical one, the question of substance—that is, of the nature of a socialist society's objectives as well as the optimal means of achieving them— has almost inevitably become the subject of controversy in Soviet economics. Several Soviet students have attempted a technical statement of the objective function. Most recently Kantorovich has come forward with the striking proposition that, together with those elements which can be planned, socialist economics have to take spontaneous forces (*elementy stikhinosti*) into account as well, in particular the behaviour of the consumer and of the seeker of employment. Hence, he argues, workable models have to combine the plan-controls with the use of 'economic indicators' as parameters of control in the area of decentralised decision-making. In fact, among the new fields of economic enquiry, that of consumer's behaviour has been one to which the most intensive theoretical effort has been devoted.

The accent on these ingredients of the economy, on the implications of consumer's choice, is a *novum* with far-reaching social as well as economic implications. Both the change in the environment and changes in the economics of planning indicate a trend from what is usually described as 'resource planning' to 'demand planning,' with some consequential change of attitude towards consumer's preferences. As the 'zero-consumption' model of growth ('zero-consumption' in the technical sense) becomes obsolete and is discarded, attention is turned to demand analysis on both the theoretical and the practical level. Consequently maximising exclusively the 'objective' measure of output loses its rationale, and the 'subjective' aspect comes into the picture. Designing some social welfare function, measuring and weighing utilities, becomes a legitimate concern. Here, too, deeply ingrained thought habits have to be overcome. But Soviet welfare economics is being born—or rather reborn; a link-up with Slutsky of fifty years ago is being established (curiously enough after the Revolution he himself accepted the extinction of his approach under socialism as inexorable!).

Thus, again and again, Soviet economics has had to make readjustments, sometimes drastic. The student of Soviet economics has always been aware of its dogmatist inclinations, and there is little need to stress the tendency to proclaim rigid truths exempt from examination; to discover its ability to shed such dogmas in response to the needs of the time; its flexibility at critical points—and in this sense its pragmatism—thus comes as a certain surprise, not least to the writer of the present lines himself. But then to obtain a balanced view, one apparently needed half a century's perspective.

3. BANKING AND CREDIT REFORMS IN EASTERN EUROPE

*BANKING AND CREDIT IN THE FRAMEWORK OF NEW ECONOMIC POLICIES IN EASTERN EUROPE**
— · — · — · — · — · — · — · — · — · — · — ·

George Garvy

By this spring, all countries of Eastern Europe, except Rumania, had proclaimed their intention to undertake significant changes in their economies. Taken together, the reforms announced or already initiated amount to a considerable departure from the centrally-planned command economies that emerged in the Soviet Union with the first Five-Year Plan and in the other countries of Eastern Europe with the establishment of communist regimes from World War II. It would make an intriguing study of an intellectual revolution in the making to trace the way in which these changes crystallized and the uncertain progress of the reform until, with the Soviet Union finally joining the movement, it emerged as the most significant change to come out of Eastern Europe. The purpose of the present study is more limited; indeed, I intend merely to focus on those common features of the new economic policies which affect the future role of money, credit, and banking in Eastern Europe. This is no easy undertaking because, in spite of the general similarity of the underlying rationale, the actual implementation of the new policies follows somewhat different channels in the individual countries. While in the past it was adequate to discuss arrangements in the Soviet Union to identify the fundamental traits of the working of all centrally-directed economies of Eastern Europe, this is no longer possible; the new policies originated, and first acquired the right of citizenship, in the industrially more advanced countries on the Soviet Union's western border.

Profile of the Changes

It is by no means clear in what final guise and when the brave new world of the resolutions that have cascaded from the Communist Party congresses and "plenums" of the last two years will replace the centrally-planned economies in the various countries of Eastern Europe. Nor is it certain what range of macroeconomic decisions will remain the realm of national political bodies or multinational agreements (under the aegis of the *Comecon* or otherwise). But it is clear that many of the aspects of the new reforms involve a significant change in the role of credit and bank-

*Reprinted by permission from *Banca Nazionale del Lavoro Quarterly Review* (Sept. 1966), pp. 3–8 and 18–29 (excerpts). All footnotes deleted.

ing and considerable reliance on the cost of credit as a tool of economic policy. Taken together and pushed to their logical consequences, the new policies represent a decisive move toward the replacement of centrally-directed by socialist market economies. But the course of history is never straight and determined by logic; only the future will show how powerful economic logic is once the process of transformation has started.

What caused the change? No doubt, the verdict of history will encompass a wide range of economic, political, and sociological factors. But, looking at the economic scene alone, I believe that the death knell of the old system was not rung by its failure to achieve a satisfactory rate of growth. It is being changed not because of its failure to solve certain stubborn problems, such as the raising of productivity in agriculture; not because it was incapable of suppressing inflation; and certainly not because communist theoreticians have developed a superior alternative model. It became the victim of some modest success it achieved in increasing the flow of goods to consumers above the basic subsistence minimum. When consumers refused to buy inferior, unfashionable, or overpriced goods, unsalable goods piled up in distribution channels. A planner-directed economy had no mechanism for adjusting automatically to changes in consumer preferences. Something had to be done to prevent the immobilization of working capital in goods nobody wanted—to transmit signals from the consumer to the producer and make the producer respond to these signals. Other shortcomings of the system became exposed as foreign trade developed and as freer travel permitted wider comparison of economic performance, within as well as outside the Eastern bloc. Countries that before World War II engaged in a relatively open system of foreign trade and travel became more sharply aware of the cost, in opportunities foregone, of adhering to the rigid Soviet patterns of trade bilateralism and internal economic centralization.

And so the countries of Eastern Europe discovered a mechanism that would do the trick: the competitive market. This is not the place to reflect on the ideological hurdles that had to be overcome or to ponder over the sparring in theorietical journals about the compatibility of the new approach with the established doctrine. In some quarters the hope still lingers that powerful electronic computers will replace the all-knowing central planning agency and its holy spirit, the Central Committee of the Communist Party, in achieving an optimal allocation of resources and perhaps even a rational price system. Yet it is clear that decisive steps are now being taken toward a system that will rely on material incentives and rewards and on flexible prices, instead of on rigid and detailed production targets, directives, and administrative sanctions, and toward a system in which credit will play a significant role.

Behind the various organizational and procedural changes in the area of credit and financing lies the recognition that some economic principles, long regarded as applicable only to the capitalist system, are equally valid in the socialist economy. The allocative function of the market, the rationing function of prices, and the need for limitations on the power of the authorities to perpetuate disequilibrium situations are now being widely recognized.

The three Eastern European countries on the rim of the Western world—Poland, Czechoslovakia and Hungary—have pioneered in many ways in first removing the most obvious shortcomings of the centrally-directed system copied from the Soviet prototype and then developing the basic principles of a transition to a market socialism. Rumania, which in recent years has achieved a better rate of growth than the other countries of Eastern Europe and which has made good use of its substantial earnings of convertible currencies in developing its economic potential and raising the standard of living of its population, was for a while reluctant even to admit the need for a change. But by the spring of 1966 all the countries except Rumania had decided to embark on reforms, even Bulgaria, the least developed and smallest country of the group, which normally hews close to the policies of the Soviet Union.

The Soviet Union has tried for a long time to make all changes appear as merely improvements in the "steering of the economy" and to minimize the significance of its departures from the old methods. It is still the least ready to make bold changes, preferring to experiment cautiously with alternative methods applied to selected enterprises and, in some cases, making related experiments in the area of plant management, labor compensation, and the like. It commands a broader range of resources than its neighbors in Eastern Europe, and for a variety of reasons is not subject to the same pressures for change. And it has learned from bitter experience that mistakes made by a big, centralized country are usually also big and costly.

The political system based on the philosophy of historical materialism is patently unhistorical. Yugoslavia was a pathbreaker in replacing a Soviet-type economic system by a socialist market economy; yet reference to Yugoslavia is studiously avoided—particularly in the Soviet Union —by the proponents of the new reforms. Yugoslavia also exemplifies the kinds of resistance and difficulties that the reformers of the various countries are likely to encounter before the day is won—including sabotage and downright resistance from the entrenched bureaucracy, inability of local plant managers, reared on executing orders, to make independent decisions, and dislocations resulting from doing away with uneconomic production sustained by subsidies and artificial prices.

The changes contemplated in each country require important adaptation to be put into effect over a number of years, in practically all aspects of economic policy, lines of responsibility, and administrative arrangements. Specific time tables have been adopted in some countries, and everywhere important details, including many in the area of finance, still remain to be worked out. The basic decisions already made involve a radical break with much of what in the past was considered an organic part of a socialist economic system, but the difficulties that lie ahead in passing from a command to a demand economy are immense. They involve more than the achieving of adequate practical solutions to such questions, for instance, as how to shift to a system of equilibrium prices. Beyond the purely economic questions lies the problem of how to depolitize the operations of the economy so that the process of economic decision-making can follow its own laws, not party dictates, and how at the same time to preserve the control of the communist party.

The new policies generally involve a shift toward decentralization of planning, reduction in the number of physical plan targets, grossing up of the magnitudes determined and controlled from the center, and giving the management of individual plants greater flexibility in achieving the prescribed goals. Equally, if not more, significant is the tendency to place greater reliance on individual initiative, to depend on incentives instead of on orders from the center, to devise a system of "economic levers" that would act as an alternative to administrative intervention, and to replace the excessive range of physical indicators by the profit ratio as the single, or at least the main, success indicator. Under the new system of "steering the economy" the administrative emphasis is shifted from the ministries in charge of specific industries to aggregations of enterprises.

The reforms now being introduced involve significant changes in financial flows and in the role that credit, which is being elevated to the position of a key "economic lever," is expected to play in the economy. They will increase the role of banks (without significantly changing their character) in channeling (gross) investment funds and in financing the flow of goods through the economic system. A closely related change is a restructuring of the price system which, in addition to achieving other objectives, will recognize capital as a cost factor and introduce a charge for its use. As a logical extension, the financing of fixed investment is shifting from free and nonreturnable budgetary grants to a combination of bank loans and decentralized investment funds accumulated from enterprise profits. As a result, it may be expected that the proportion of national income redistributed through the budget will decline, and that the importance of decentralized investment funds and bank loans will increase in relation to the national product. Taken together, the reforms now

projected will not change the basic characteristics of Soviet-type economies—state ownership of the means of production and central planning
the main targets of economic activity—but they will narrow considerably
the gulf between command and market economies.

First Steps Toward Flexibility

The trend toward greater flexibility in the area of banking and credit
started in the middle fifties, after the death of Stalin and the insurrection-
ary events in Poland and Hungary. By the middle sixties, when broad
economic reforms were announced, the emphasis placed on detailed credit
planning had been considerably reduced, especially in Hungary and Poland, and credit administration had become more flexible. Some of the
greater flexibility had resulted from the enlargement of responsibility
given to, or initiative taken by, banking officials on the firing line who
were better acquainted with local needs and problems than planners at the
center. The ability of local banking officials to maneuver was, however,
rather narrowly circumscribed by the authorization to transfer limited
amounts of unused credit lines among areas, industries, and individual
enterprises. In the meantime, the basic objectives, principles, and methods
of credit administration remained very much intact. The banking structure, too, continued basically the same. In Czechoslovakia, the investment
bank was absorbed into the monobank and the activities of foreign trade
banks were generally expanded. By now, all countries of Eastern Europe
have separate Foreign Trade banks in charge of conducting all foreign
payments and credit operations. Credit policy remained essentially implementary, the bank officials merely verifying whether loan requests conformed with applicable rules, and not deciding whether the intended use
of credit was more profitable than an alternative use.

One of the steps toward greater flexibility in the use of short-term
credit took the form of "grossing up" the various authorized purposes for
which credit could be obtained under the financial plans (which specified
the amount that could be extended to each industry for each eligible purpose). Under the standard system these "objects of financing" had proliferated, but in the late fifties they began to be reduced; in Poland, for
example, their number was cut from 20 to 7, and in Rumania from more
than 13 to 8. Another innovation was to give local managers of monobank
offices greater authority in allocating credit funds and in transferring unutilized credit lines between enterprises of the same industry—with the
regional banking offices empowered to make similar adjustments among
credit quotas assigned to local offices. A further development was the
offering of more favorable terms to well run enterprises that showed ad-

equate or better-than-expected profits and otherwise met their targets well. Enterprises that experienced financial difficulties through no fault of their own—as a result of delayed payments by their customers or inability to complete production because of shortages of parts or for similar reasons—were given access to credit on favorable terms to replenish their balances (such as "liquidity credits" in Poland and East Germany).

It came to be no longer regarded as an overriding principle, except perhaps in the Soviet Union, that credit must be an exact counterpart of the movement of goods through production and distribution and that therefore all loans must be collateralized by real assets. Actually the principle had never been enforced literally—as was inevitable if the authorities were to avoid the chain reactions resulting from the failure of some enterprises to pay suppliers or workers. At first the problem was dealt with by permitting enterprises to obtain credit for purposes other than the traditional specific "objects of crediting," such as financing of inventories or of the collection float. These new types of credit were introduced under the headings "transitional," "special," "interim," and "extraordinary" loans; as a matter of fact, all four terms were simultaneously in use during the early fifties in Poland, where the standard system seems to have hit more snags than in any of the other countries. Subsequently the extension of loans for general working capital purposes, including the payment of wages, became more widespread; Poland pioneered in the introduction of such "production credits." A variant of this technique is "crediting of turnover," whereby the amount of credit extended is a fixed proportion of total output or sales, and no longer geared to seasonal peaks of inventories of specific raw materials or fuel. Finally, instead of extending credit to sellers to replenish working capital when customers delayed payments, loans began to be made directly to buyers to permit them to meet their payments on time. Indeed, one of the weaknesses of the old system was that it did not exert pressure on the debtor to discharge his obligations. Thus, without sacrifice of the claim to the superiority of socialist credit techniques, of which so much is made in the banking literature of Eastern Europe, the extension of credit to enterprises gradually came to be geared more to the borrowers' actual needs, conditions and prospects than to the execution of rigid plans passed down from the center. And the enterprises themselves were given a greater role in the framing of credit plans. The departures from rigid credit planning went furthest perhaps in Hungary, but in general credit plans acquired, at least outside the Soviet Union, the status of guidelines rather than of fixed targets.

Since the late fifties a steadily increasing amount of credit has become available to the population, largely through loans made by the savings bank system. The growth of output available for domestic use made it possible to do away with what was in effect the compulsory purchase of government savings bonds and to encourage the use of consumer credit which was introduced in the Soviet Union in 1959, but in some other countries earlier. On the other hand, various techniques, partly adaptations from the West, were developed to encourage savings and to link the availability of scarce goods, such as housing and cars, to the accumulation of substantial downpayments by the population. Various types of savings accounts were introduced to encourage savings for specific purposes and, conversely, loans became available to meet exceptional expenditures (such as weddings, funerals, removal to a new location). Other techniques include in some of the countries numbered accounts, preferential tax treatment of savings, and various transfer services to accommodate the holders of savings accounts.

Private and cooperative housing construction has received official encouragement in the form of long-term, low-interest loans; in some countries, notably Czechoslovakia and Poland, a significant proportion of new urban dwelling units came to be financed in this way, replacing the provision of staff housing by municipalities and factories or other employers. Credit availability to the private sector has been somewhat improved in recent years, particularly in Poland, Hungary, and East Germany, in order to stimulate the output of consumer goods, including items not normally produced by state factories, such as custom clothing and furniture, and to improve service available to consumers, including repair services. Similarly, lending to independent farmers was expanded, especially in Poland, where these farmers account for the overwhelming bulk of agricultural production, and in some countries also to workers on state farms and members of collective farms for carrying on their limited private farming activities. Even the Soviet Union, in a new departure, recently made loans available to members of collective and state farms for their private cattle raising.

During this period some liberalization occurred in the extension of medium-term credit, which in all the countries had been used as a means of stimulating small-scale mechanization and technological improvements. The terms of such loans were gradually made more favorable and their scope was later extended to include expanded production of mass consumption goods. Investment of this type continued to be hampered, however, by excessively rigid restrictions; new construction, for instance, was typically ruled out. Furthermore, there was usually difficulty in obtaining equipment for projects no included in overall economic plans. More basic, perhaps, was the reluctance to resort to credit financing for such purposes: why pay interest on a loan when a free grant could be obtained by having the project included in next year's economic plan?

Altogether, the various moves taken after the mid-1950's toward a more flexible use of credit resulted, at least in the smaller countries of Eastern Europe, in some loosening of the rigid standard system. But before the mid-1960's these measures did not succeed in making credit a means of achieving a better allocation of resources or of increasing the efficiency of the economic system as a whole.

The Emerging Use of Credit as a *Lever*

The elevation of credit to the status of an "economic lever," with a considerably increased role in the economy, occurred as part of the recent shift in the various countries of Eastern Europe toward a new "system of economic steering." The official resolutions and documents explaining the reasons for the changes, outlining the basic principles, and specifying the institutional implementation (also setting timetables for the change-over) make curious reading, both for their admissions and for their omissions. These documents have a good deal of explaining to do to a generation raised on the notion that "market" necessarily carries the adjective "anarchist" and that profits are identical with exploitation. In fact, the difficulty experienced by the communist countries in accepting the proposition that the role of interest is not necessarily linked to the capitalist method of production is matched only by that of some Western economists in viewing profit in a context broader than the capitalist economy.

The resolutions of the various communist party congresses defining the new policy, and the supporting speeches differ in the extent to which they try to make the new system appear to be a linear descendant of the precepts formulated by Marx and Lenin; and they differ in their persuasiveness in demonstrating the compatibility of a market adjustment process with central macroplanning. But all of them spell out in quite substantial detail what is to be done, why, and how. Our interest here is limited to the area of banking and credit, which is given considerable treatment in some countries (Poland and Hungary) and is touched on only slightly in others.

The new system of economic steering represents a decisive move away from central planning of production and distribution toward a socialist market economy guided by preferences of final users. It is a move away from detailed sets of targets and norms, handed down to production units by administrative organs, toward reliance on a flexible price system and the profit criterion to guide production and allocate resources, and toward the provision of material incentives as a means of achieving maximum effort.

The first step in moving toward the new system is the gearing of production to demand. This is to be done in several ways. Factories, at least in the consumer-goods area, will plan production in conformity with negotiated contracts or with orders actually received, in most cases directly, from retail outlets or industrial users. Management will be given greater scope for making production decisions. And its success will be judged not by its ability to hit detailed output targets, but by a small number of key indicators, among which the profit rate has a crucial role.

A related development is the creation of industry associations (in the Soviet Union the so-called "firms" represent a comparable move toward aggregation) thus introducing a major change in industrial organizations. These associations of enterprises—sometimes organized on a regional as well as on an industry basis—are designed to decentralize responsibility for production; professional managers and specialists in the associations work directly with enterprise management, thus reducing stifling central control and bureaucratic influence. Among other things, the associations will make possible a greater specialization of output and will place research and development activities and decisions on the use of amortization funds—hitherto made by industry ministries and other central administrative organizations—closer to the production process. In the Soviet Union these groupings are still in the experimental stage and of relatively limited significance. Elsewhere they already include most of the large enterprises and many of the smaller units; in East Germany, for instance, 1,800 enterprises, accounting for about two thirds of total industrial output, belong to 82 such industry associations.

The industry associations constitute and administer funds for capital investment and for supporting research and development, and also industrywide reserve funds for providing temporary financial assistance to their member enterprises in the form of short-term loans and loan guarantees. The associations have considerable latitude in selecting investment projects and in determining financing procedures. Their funds are constituted in part from credit made available by the banks. The establishment of these association funds represents, in effect, the creation of financial institutions for the servicing of specific industries, and thus introduces an entirely new element in the financial structure of communist countries. In addition to the financing provided through the associations, individual enterprises will use that part of profits which they can retain to aliment their development fund to finance their own investment projects (which normally will require approval by the planning authorities) and they will be free to undertake projects on their own responsibility if they can obtain bank financing for the purpose.

Another basic change is in the area of capital formation and cost accounting. Under the standard system, as was emphasized above, no charge was made for capital, on the theory it was public property; the result was misallocation and wasteful use of investment funds, as a larger investment per unit of output was not automatically reflected in higher costs. Another universal consequence was delay in completing construction projects. Now the principle is being introduced that producer prices must reflect the cost of capital. Interest is to be charged on both fixed and working capital; and to equalize the cost of new and existing fixed capital (the latter originally supplied on a grant basis), a charge is being imposed on the depreciated volume of capital assets in use. In effect, the capital-use charge means that some of the amounts previously transferred to the budget as enterprise profits will henceforth be paid by the enterprise under the heading of interest.

While the underlying principle of recognizing capital as a factor of cost now seems to have been accepted by all the countries of Eastern Europe, its practial application is likely to be gradual and to vary from country to country. In Hungary, a charge on investment capital (at the uniform rate of 5 per cent) was introduced in 1964; in Poland, specific details are now being worked out; and practical implementation of the principle is still being studied in East Germany, Czechoslovakia, and the Soviet Union. One major problem is that the introduction of a charge for capital will increase the number of enterprises operating at a loss. For the new system to fully justify itself, such units must either be made efficient or discontinued; the official comment accompanying the introduction of these measures apparently recognizes this.

While the changes with regard to industry organization, and in particular the operations of industry associations, require considerable modification of past credit policies and procedures, the most significant consequences for banking arise from the redirection of funds to finance investment and related shift of a large part of financing from a grant to a loan basis. Instead of being channeled almost exclusively through the budget, a significant part of the profits of state-owned enterprises will become available for decentralized investment (originally pioneered by Poland), either by the originating enterprise itself, or (as already mentioned), through industry associations or similar groupings.

The new policies will clearly produce significant changes in financial flows and in the allocation of real resources. With the reduction in the portion of investment funds channeled through the national budget, the budget will become more similar in scope to that of Western countries. Budgetary grants will continue to be made, not only for social overhead but also for such priority projects as new industries and major programs for the development of national resources, in some cases with provision for subsequent recoupment of at least part of the initial financing. But the great bulk of investment funds from the budget will be allocated to the State Bank or the Investment Bank (the respective roles of the two in making investment loans is still not clear for most countries) as a revolving loan fund.

The relatively small part of profits previously retained by individual enterprises (known in the Soviet Union as the "enterprise fund")—mainly to provide bonus payments to management and staff, either in cash or in the form of fringe benefits such as housing, vacation trips, nurseries—will be increased significantly. The precise way in which the proportion of profits retained is to be linked to economic performance—primarily the profit rate—differs from country to country, as does the distribution of this share among various uses. In the Soviet Union three different retained-profits funds will be constituted at each enterprise: one for paying cash bonuses to staff and management ("material stimulation"); one for fringe benefits, including construction of factory housing; and a "development fund" for research and investment. Similar arrangements are being introduced in the other countries, with perhaps greater emphasis on using profits for financing investment projects initiated by the enterprise (or group of enterprises) generating them.

The ultimate objective of the new arrangements is to achieve a more rational pattern of investment in productive capital and a reduction of the investment-output ratio. Financing of investment through repayable loans instead of grants, or from retained profits, which will for the first time become a significant source of investment funds, is counted on to achieve results that administrative decisions and detailed control could not deliver. It is expected to reduce the widely criticized waste of real resources and to cut down the prevalent and costly delays in the completion of new projects.

It is readily evident that the new system of investment financing will have important implications for the price system. All the countries are now engaged in revising their still administratively determined price structures, to make them reflect more closely all relevant factors of production and relative scarcities. In particular, prices of producer goods, artificially held down to stimulate investment, and prices received by the farm sector, kept low to favor industrialization, will tend to rise. The entire price structure of the Eastern European countries is likely to move closer to that of the Western world. This would probably lead to significant changes in the structure and direction of their foreign trade, as did similar changes mady by Yugoslavia in the course of recent years.

It is clear that the rise of credit financing of fixed investment and the development of industrywide associations importantly affect the role of the banking system. In several countries specific monobank offices have been put in charge of servicing the banking needs of associations and of centralizing and supervising the planning of their credit and currency requirements while actual operations remain in the hands of the local offices in whose territory the association members are located. A further step was taken by Czechoslovakia in 1965: the creation of special units within the monobank on the industrial rather than territorial principle to service one or several of the newly formed industry associations or the giant individual concerns. such as Bata and Skoda. East Germany has gone even further in this direction by creating, within the framework of its monobank (the Notenbank), specialized divisions (Industriebankfiliale) that service the credit needs of up to three industry associations. Obviously, credit needs differ greatly among industries and in accordance with specific conditions. The new method of crediting recognizes this and requires a more intimate and current knowledge of the technology, supply and demand conditions, and profitability of each unit than did the old system.

For the first time official banks will become involved in project appraisal and negotiations with prospective investors. Individual enterprises will have to justify the profitability of projects for which they require financing, and their willingness to commit their own funds will also become an important factor in the bank's decision to grant loans. With the passage of time the banks, in effect, will be administering a steadily growing revolving investment fund whose resources from loan amortization and interest payments will be supplemented by periodic appropriations from the budget. So long as they do not exceed the centrally accumulated funds available to them for investment lending, they will have considerable latitude in dealing with loan applications. A logical development would be the establishment of a separate national investment fund, completely bypassing the budget; suggestions along these lines have already been made at least in Poland.

The attempt to make credit an "economic lever" involves also a greater differentiation of interest rates on short-term working capital loans and a change in accounting arrangements whereby the cost of such credit directly enters into the determination of profits to be retained by the enterprise. The principle of uniform—and low (in the Soviet Union, mostly 1 or 2 per cent)—short-term rates that prevailed under the standard system began to break down in the mid-fifties, at least outside the Soviet Union, but differentiation tended to be based on the purpose of the loan rather than on the creditworthiness of the borrower, and to be used mainly to discourage loan delinquency and to subsidize socially desirable activities. Under the recent developments, the monobank has greater flexibility in its short-term crediting and is able to take the risk factor into consideration. And with interest expenditure entering into the determination of enterprise profits and management compensation, credit costs become an important influence on managerial decisions. Publications of the Eastern European countries are full of accounts of how the new policies have had the immediate effect of reducing plant inventories (not many months ago argued by plant managers to have been held at rockbottom levels)—just as the introduction of a charge on fixed capital suddenly revealed that factories could relinquish a considerable quantity of machinery and equipment kept as a safety margin as long as capital was a free good.

Clearly, under the new economic system credit policy is not to supplant planning, but is rather to permit a reduction of its scope and to increase its effectiveness and flexibility. The total volume of credit to be extended and the broad categories of its use will continue to be centrally planned in order to preserve monetary equilibrium. In the framework of the new policies, credit is to be regarded as a tauter string rather than as a looser leash, but it will be used in conjunction with a different set of objectives and criteria. The effectiveness of the new use of credit will depend on the success in actually shifting a considerable part of decision-making from central planners to enterprise managers.

These prospects are relevant to the question whether something identifiable as a "socialist monetary policy" is about to emerge. Even though an answer cannot yet be hazarded, it appears that the new developments are more likely to enhance the role of the monobank as a financial intermediary than to endow it with more attributes of a central bank in the Western sense. They will make the individual enterprise's access to credit increasingly dependent on its profitability, its financial position, and—indirectly at least—the quality of its management. Even significant steps toward some blend of centrally planned and market-oriented economies will not necessarily entail a basic change in the role of the banking system. The monobanker, permitted considerably more flexibility in dealing with microeconomic problems, will have an opportunity to become a more efficient commercial and investment banker, but there is no indication that he will be given wider responsibilities as a central banker.

4. ECONOMIC REFORMS IN POLAND

THE POLISH ECONOMY AFTER OCTOBER, 1956:
BACKGROUND AND OUTLOOK*

Alexander Erlich

The dramatic events of October 1956, which brought a shake-up in the leadership of the Polish Communist Party and of the Polish state have been often referred to as a "revolution," and there is little doubt that the use of this exalted term is not inappropriate. The "Polish October" came as a combined effect of the pressure from below and of the faltering at the top; it was born of a desire for total change in economic as well as in

*Reprinted by permission from *American Economic Review* (May 1959), pp. 94–112.

noneconomic spheres; lastly, and not unlike many revolutions of the past, its results, while significant enough, have fallen short of expectations aroused at the start. All this makes the discussion of recent Polish economic developments a challenging and at the same time a highly exacting task, particularly in view of the limitation of space. It is hoped, however, that even a quick thumbnail sketch may serve a useful purpose.

I. The Six Year Plan Period, 1950 to 1955

In order to understand the revolution, we have to take a look at the *ancien régime*. The Polish economy of the early fifties, governed by the "Six Year Plan of the Economic Development and Construction of the Foundations of Socialism, 1950 to 1955," displayed familiar characteristics of the Stalinist pattern and seemed to move inexorably toward complete adaptation to it in every important respect.

On institutional level, 99 per cent of the Polish industrial output in 1955 came from state-owned enterprises or state-controlled co-operatives.[1] In agriculture, the collectivized sector was slowly but steadily gaining ground: in June 1956, it covered 23 per cent of agricultural land, with nearly three-fifths of this area belonging to the state farms and the rest to the "production co-operatives" whose number had risen from 243 in December 1949, to 10,510 in September 1956.[2]

In the field of economic administration the centralist "command economy" reigned supreme. The managers were severely constrained in their decisions by the fact that resources (with labor as the most important exception) were allocated to them from above and that only minor variations in the product-mix were permitted with the fulfillment of global output target in gross value terms being the main objective and with bonuses for fulfillment or overfulfillment as the strongest pecuniary incentive to expand output. The price system while showing a measure of operativeness in consumer goods markets was largely nonfunctional as a vehicle of resource allocation. Moreover, although prices of goods were ostensibly related to average costs purporting to reflect the "socially necessary labor" (with no allowances for interest on capital or for scarcity rents in case of natural resources), they were subject to "deviations from value" such as turnover tax on consumers' goods and subsidies for producers' goods and were permitted to stay at levels at which demand would exceed supply.[3]

[1] *Rocznik Statystyczny 1957* (Warsaw, 1957), p. 61.

[2] *Ibid.,* pp. 124 and 138.

[3] A lucid description of the administrative setup of the Polish economy in the early fifties can be found in Thad P. Alton's *Polish Postwar Economy* (New York, 1955). For a full discussion of the Polish price system, cf. John M. Montias, "Price-setting Problems in the Polish Economy," *J.P.E.,* Dec., 1957, pp. 486–505, and his unpublished Ph.D. dissertation, "Producers' Prices in a Centralized Economy: the Polish Experience" (1958; on deposit at the Business Library of Columbia University).

The pattern of growth is illustrated by the tables in the Appendix. They show the index of national income advancing by 73 per cent between 1949 and 1955, the index of gross industrial output shooting far ahead and nearly trebling, with the index of engineering and metalworking moving much faster still, the index of industrial materials developing considerably slower, and the output of four grains being almost stagnant. The rate of net capital formation, finally, shows a steep rise from its initial level of 15 per cent and fluctuates between upper and lower limits of the 20 per cent range during the subsequent period. The statistical methods used in compiling these data contain a number of deficiencies which have been freely admitted by Polish economists during the last few years. They make it virtually certain that most of the indexes in question contain a substantial upward bias also after the inherent intractabilities of index numbers in a rapidly changing economy (the "Gerschenkron effect") have been allowed for, and that peculiarities of the Soviet-type pricing must have resulted in understatement of the rate of capital formation.[4] Yet there was no disposition on the part of critics to argue that a differently construed index would yield a substantially divergent pattern of development or that the scaled-down rate of growth would not be high by comparative standards.

It is not difficult to discover a large measure of interrelatedness between these three aspects of economic structure. Given a decision in favor of a rate of growth which would be very high when measured against the normal productive capacity and saving potential of the economy in question, it could certainly be argued that in conditions of the resulting stress and strain over-all controls aiming at manipulation of broad aggregates might be too blunt a tool to deal with specific bottleneck situations and to expedite the necessary shift of resources from one area to another.[5] It would be even less controversial (and it had been, indeed, standard prac-

[4]The major criticisms made in the discussion of the official index could be summed up as follows: (1) the so-called "1950 prices" were, in fact, only slightly refurbished 1937 prices which imparted an exaggeratedly high weight to the industrial products owing to the strong monopolistic elements in the prewar Polish industry; (2) new machinery and chemical products whose output was growing particularly fast were introduced into index at prices which, to cite a recognized authority, "were as a rule unduly high as compared with prices of other products" (H. Fiszel, *Prawo wartosci a problematyka cen w gospodarce socjalistycznej* [Warsaw, 1956], p. 179); (3) the development of interplant specialization and of subcontracting led to an increase in extent of double counting in the gross value index over the period under review; (4) no allowance was made for drastic deterioration in quality of consumers goods over the period under consideration; (5) virtual disappearance of private small-scale industry and of handicraft was reflected only to a very insignificant extent. It is not surprising, in view of all this, that the post 1956 statistical abstracts have quietly dropped the old gross value index of Polish industrial output while *Voprosy ekonomiki,* one of the leading Soviet economic periodicals, displayed it proudly as late as May, 1957.

[5]A similar argument emphasizing the similarities between the early stage of Soviet-type industrialization and the Western war economy was made by Oskar Lange in his Belgrade lectures, given in November, 1957, and published subsequently in Poland. Cf. his "Rola planowania w krajach socjalistycznych," *Sprawy miedzynarodowe,* Feb., 1958, pp. 21–24.

tice among Western students of the Soviet economy) to explain the turn-over tax as a convenient device for mopping up excess demand generated by a high-level investment expenditure whenever the voluntary propensity to save is low and could be made still lower as a result of high direct taxation; lastly, the collective farm system could be treated as a high-powered tax collection device. Yet while this reasoning can help toward understanding of important aspects of a Soviet-type economy, it certainly cannot carry us the whole way. There is a considerable distance between recognizing the need for selective direct controls and having the size and technological setup of individual plant laid down in the central plan or setting targets for sour pickles to be produced and amount of hares to be shot (to cite two instances which received a considerable amount of derisive publicity in early 1956). Nor would it be self-evident that the turn-over tax should be levied on consumers' goods only or that a broad measure of correspondence between prices of producers' goods and their marginal costs (with reasonable disregard of very short-term cost fluctuations) would not improve the rationality of investment decisions even under a system or priorities; and it would be far from obvious that the risks involved in compulsory collectivization would make it under all circumstances a game which was, on purely economic grounds, worth the candle. Moreover, the "very high rate of growth" was up to this point simply taken for granted. But if we decide to scrutinize the underlying decision, a new line of inquiry opens; and in pressing it further we shall do little more than follow up some of the points which have been made with considerable force by prominent Polish economists during the last several years.

The term "disproportions" has come to constitute one of the key words in the present Polish economic vocabulary. It was designed to describe not merely the general state of inflationary tension we just spoke about but also the whole set of underlying (or related) phenomena most of which could be easily gleaned by a quick glance at the figures of our tables. Disparities between rates of increase in total productive capacity and consumption levels, industry and agriculture, metal processing super-structure and raw material and fuel basis of the producers goods' sector, power requirements and power supplies—these were the most important cases in point.[6] It goes without saying that by labeling them as dispropor-

[6]The picture shown by Table 1 should be undoubtedly taken with a grain of salt. On the one hand, it would tend to overstate the extent of disparities since the upward bias in the official index of metal processing industries was (for reasons indicated in the footnote 4) much larger than in the basic materials' index. On the other hand, however, the comparison between the all-industrial index and the electric power index would not tell the whole story because industries which are the heaviest consumers of power (engineering, chemicals, quality steels) expanded much faster than others; and while the output of power more than doubled, the capacity of power plants increased by less than 60 per cent—a clear indication of the very high pressure under which these plants were operating.

tions Polish economists meant not merely to emphasize that some areas of the economy had been growing faster than others and that the fulfillment of plans had been uneven. Their point was that these divergencies when pushed as far as they actually had been were bound to cause loss of potential gains as well as actual waste in the faster advancing areas. The most clear-cut instances of such boomerang effect were frequent interruptions in the work of industrial plants as a result of power failures and low capacity utilization in greatly expanded machine building due to insufficient supplies of materials for processing. Other repercussions were less direct but by no means less important. Slow expansion in coal which had been for decades the strongest single earner of foreign exchange deprived the economy of some of the vitally needed imports of foreign capital goods and kept the domestic fuel supplies thinly spread. The inability of grain production to meet the mounting demand generated by the fast-growing urban centers or even to keep in step with the increase in total population enforced another cut in industrial imports for the sake of unanticipated increase in imports of food in order to soften the adverse impact of shortage of domestic supplies on the productivity of industrial labor.

The difficulties in the agricultural sphere which reached their climax in 1953 when the harvest of four grains declined to 10 million tons or 75 per cent of the average prewar level in the comparable territory[7] were due only in part to the low investment ration.[8] Seventy per cent of the total state investment went to the collectivized farming—an amount which was, according to virtually unanimous view of the Polish economists of the later period, less than adequate in order to make new productive units attain the hoped-for advantages of scale. Yet at the same time other factors making for low efficiency within the socialist sector were at work: poor quality of management and scarcity of labor in state farms, restiveness among the none-too-voluntary members of the "production co-operatives," shortage of livestock and crushing burden of the large-size and low-price compulsory deliveries in both. Yet the individual peasants who, it will be recalled, held more than three-quarters of the total agricultural area even at the peak of collectivization drive were not merely deprived almost entirely of investment allocation passing through state channels. They were effectively discouraged from undertaking any substantial investment on their own unless they desired to qualify as *kulaks* and be subjected to vengefully progressive taxation and prohibitively high rates

---

[7]*Maly Rocznik Statystyczny 1958* (Warsaw, 1958), p. 46.

[8]In order to get a clearer notion of the supply of capital goods to agriculture, it may be worth noting that the value of the output of agricultural machinery accounted in 1950 for one-half of 1 per cent of the total value of Polish producers' goods industry in the same year (*Zycie Gospodarcze,* Nov. 11, 1956), and that the small-scale industry and handicraft from which the prewar Polish peasants derived a large part of their equipment was reduced to utter insignificance by that time.

of compulsory deliveries. It was therefore only logical that, according to information released many years later, the estimated investment in peasant agriculture during 1951–53 ranged from 36 to 41 per cent of its 1949 volume—a situation which implied, to quote the same source, "not only a decline in agricultural production and decapitalization in the villages but also a reduction in the marketable share (the village was consuming instead of investing)."[9] Another by-product of this "class war" policy was the progressing fragmentation of farms, in spite of the rapid outflow of the surplus population to the cities. The percentage share of holdings above 5 hectare in the total number of farms declined by nearly 11 per cent between 1950 and 1954.[10] The implications of this state of affairs for the development of living standards in the cities were obvious; even the official real wage index which was published in early 1956 and immediately discarded for its evident upward bias, admitted a substantial drop in the real wages between 1950 and 1953.[11] In sum, the Polish agricultural planners seem to have fallen between two stools. They did not dare to collectivize all-out, which made their direct hold on agricultural marketable surplus rather tenuous. Yet they were eminently successful in weakening the peasants' stimulus to produce and in letting the urban workers bear the brunt of the resulting decline in consumption.

The limitations of space do not permit us to discuss in detail the impact of the prevailing price system and of the peculiarities of the planning methods on the over-all efficiency of the economy—a problem which received an extensive treatment in recent Polish literature.[12] I shall confine myself to a few remarks about their relevance for some of the disproportions mentioned above. The policy of below-equilibrium prices of raw materials was bound to stimulate their excessive use (to the extent that managers or lower level planners could exercise a certain choice), to encourage their careless handling and to give a wrong slant to technological progress. Material-saving innovations were neglected while laborsaving innovations were pushed, although the prevailing scarcity relationship would dictate the opposite—a point which had been made more than two years ago by Oskar Lange.[13] Another obvious source of waste consisted in the fact that the system of setting targets in gross value terms made it advantageous for the bonus-conscious managers to inflate the raw material content of their output as much as they could.

---

[9]A. Szerwentke, "Wykonanie 6-letniego planu inwestycyjnego—Proba oceny i wnioski," *Gospodarka Planowa,* Jan. 1957, p. 15.

[10]*Rocznik . . .*, p. 130.

[11]F. Blinowski, "O ksztaltowaniu sie stopy zyciowej w Planie Szescioletnim," *Nowe Drogi,* Feb., 1956, pp. 11–33.

[12]For an able summary, cf, the already quoted article by Montias.

[13]"O dorazny program gospodarczy," *Zycie Gospodarcze,* July 16, 1956.

The situation could be conveniently summed up in terms of the familiar Domar-Harrod formula, $r = s/v$ in conjunction with the Marxian two-department model ostensibly accepted as a theoretical underframe by Stalinist planners. The planned rate of increase in national income (r) during the Six Year Plan was 13.4 per cent per annum. Let us assume that incremental capital/output ratio (v) to be 2, which would be, if anything, too low, since almost a half of the total investment went into industry, and 85 per cent of this amount were allotted to producers' goods lines which were much more capital using than the rest. Accordingly the rate of net investments would have to be nearly 27 per cent—which is obviously very high for a country with low per capita income; attempts to impose it on the economy would generate powerful inflationary pressures and call for drastic measures of compulsory saving which would certainly be resisted one way or another. The picture gets darker if the Marxian model is brought in. It would then become evident that limits for increase in the share of investment in national income lie not only in the community's willingness to acquiesce to the required increase in the rate of nonconsumption but also in the capacity of investment goods industries which had not been geared to anything like the desired rate of expansion and which could be adapted to it only gradually. (The speed of this adaptation, it goes without saying, would be determined by the amount of annual gross investment which went until now to the "Department II" and is now allocated to the "Department I" as well as by the difference in capital requirements and in the length of gestation periods in both sectors.) Consequently, a bit of plain arithmetic should be sufficient to demonstrate that in the initial years there would be no increase in the rate of growth even in the most extreme case of allocation of the *whole* gross investment to the "Department I," and while later the positive effects of the relocation process[14] would begin to show (provided the society can take the sacrifices of the interim period), it is utterly fantastic to expect that national income could more than double within six years if any halfway plausible coefficients are assumed.[15]

This, to be sure, need not be the end of the story: the planners could try to do something to compress (v). This might imply some (or all) of the following: 1) use of highly noncapitalistic methods in lines where it is technologically feasible (the "dual economy" strategy); 2) increasing the degree of capacity utilization, whenever manpower is available; 3) cutting

---

[14] I am borrowing this expression from Adolph Lowe.

[15] It could, of course, be pointed out that the capital/output ratio might decline over time as a result of technological progress. But not every technological progress leads to a decline in capital/output ratio particularly when it is paralleled by a shift of investment toward more highly capital consuming lines of industrial production and when it occurs in a way which taxes the capacity of the economy to the limit—a point about which we shall have more to say presently.

down as far as possible on investment in lines which have particularly long gestation periods and high capital coefficients; 4) relying on foreign trade for some of the highly capitalistic items. In the case under consideration, the first possibility was out for ideological reasons (crusade against "small-scale capitalists"). Items two and three were actively tried, and item four was certainly strongly desired. But loading of additional (and highly unskilled) labor into existing capacity was followed by steep decline in marginal productivity of labor which (in conjunction with a rapidly swelling wage bill) fanned the inflationary pressure; moreover, the concomitant massive shift of population to the cities pushed up the demand for food and made the shortages of housing more acute. The economizing on outlays in power and coal affected adversely the operation of the economy as a whole and might very well have led, on balance, to a lower and not to a higher marginal efficiency of investment. With regard to foreign trade, finally, soaring domestic demand for coal and food (as well as under-investment in these lines) kept the export surpluses low and created a stimulus for costly autarky,[16] particularly since the countries of the Soviet bloc, Poland's chief trade partners, were operating, in varying degrees, under pressures of the same kind. To conclude: The attempts to get around the basic dilemma by cutting corners were successful only to a limited extent.[17]

At this point one could not help wondering about the motives for adopting a plan which was so obviously unrealistic. An analogy with the Soviet developments on the eve of the First Five Year Plan might help toward solution of this puzzle. Both in the Soviet and in the Polish case the period of relatively "cheap" (and highly successful) expansion which was based on full utilization of existing capacity and of eliminating bottlenecks due to the destruction and dislocation had been just brought to a close. The impending shift to full-scale investment offered the same fundamental choice: a moderate industrialization entailing a more or less

[16]The point about autarky as a price paid for excessive rate of investment was made most tellingly by Michal Kalecki in his article, "Czynniki okreslajace tempo wzrostu dochodu narodowego w gospodarce socjalistycznej," *Gospodarka Planowa,* Aug., 1958, pp. 1–5. Another way in which such a rate of investment pushes up the capital/output ratio consists, in his view, in lengthening of construction period of new plant as a result of shortage of technical organizational personnel. A glance at the Table 1 of our appendix suggests yet another example of the same kind. The unusually high share of "increase in stocks" in total investment reflects, as a fairly orthodox Polish economist put it recently, "a smaller degree of stabilization of the economic processes in a faster growing economy"—a rather conservative way of describing the waste which is due to difficulties in selling wretchedly poor products, on the one hand, and to the managers' propensity to hoard materials in view of uncertain nature of the supply flows in a shortage-ridden economy, on the other. Cf. M. Rakowski, "O tempie wzrostu gospodarki w planie perspektywicznym," *ibid.,* Oct., 1958, p. 31.

[17]To be sure, this "corner-cutting" was only in part a deliberate strategy; to a large extent it represented merely a way of plugging unexpected gaps which kept arising here and there as a result of general hypertension.

"peaceful coexistence" with the peasant suppliers of food, or a crash program calling for a noncompensated appropriation of a large part of agricultural surplus with the collectivization as chief vehicle of this appropriation. The natural proclivities of Polish Stalinists were no different from those of their Soviet mentors. They showed similar inclination to combine a romanticized view of potentialities of modern technology with abiding faith in their own ability to manipulate the rate of saving-investment within wide limits and to shorten the gestation period of new projects by stern command and fiery exhortation. Yet in the face of all this it is interesting to note that the Polish followers of Stalin had initially contemplated a much less extremist plan, even after having dutifully purged the deviationist Gomulka in the summer of 1948, and there is fairly conclusive evidence that the drastic revisions in the final draft were made on Soviet "friendly advice."[18] It would be not unreasonable to assume that the authors of the initial draft were aware at least of some of the differences between the Soviet and the Polish situation which were brought out with considerable force by the Polish economists of the post-October period. They must have realized that in case of Poland the cost of autarky and of an all-around development pattern would be bound to be much higher as a result of a more lopsided endowment with natural resources and of smaller size of the economy which made it impossible to achieve advantages of scale in a comparably large number of industries. They could hardly have been ignorant of the fact that Poland lacked virgin lands which would be put into use in order to compensate, at least in part, for the decline in agricultural output which was bound to occur in process of forced collectivization, and they had every reason to expect that the Polish peasants would put up an even more formidable resistance than their Soviet opposite numbers had done in the late twenties and early thirties. Under such conditions, the "big push" along the lines of the First Soviet Five Year Plan could be assumed to usher in a period not of relative stability but of mounting tensions. No doubt, Stalin's views as to the imminence of war must have been, particularly since Korea, a weighty factor behind the pressure for all-out increase in output of armaments and in related industries throughout the orbit, regardless of cost.[19] But the strategy of all-

[18]"It is being said and written that Comrade Minc [Minister of the Industry, and first Chairman of the State Commission for Economic Planning] was the author of the first version of the plan, of the good plan. Only later another plan was imposed whose author was not Minc. Who imposed it? The friends did." (Speech by B. Ruminski at the VIIIth plenum of the Central Committee of the Polish United Workers' [Communist] Party, *Nowe Drogi*, Oct., 1956, p. 70. The term "friends" represents usual tongue-in-cheek reference to the Soviet Union.) For a very helpful analysis of the two drafts, cf. Alton, *op. cit.*, pp. 116–117.

[19]According to S. Jedrychowski, the present chairman of the State Planning Commission, investment in the armament industries in the years 1951–55 absorbed 11 per cent of the total investment allocated to industry. Cf. "The Polish Economy since 1950," *U. N. Economic Bulletin for Europe*, Nov., 1957, p. 26.

around development at breakneck tempo might very well have been designed to serve more than one purpose. It was instrumental in making
Poland as well as other countries of the bloc dependent on the Soviet Union
for supply of materials which they needed, but utterly lacked, for carrying
through this pattern of growth. Besides, and no less important, it helped
to maintain the whole area in a state of high tension which prevented the
local regimes from losing their uncompromising rigidity and from backsliding into some kind of "right wing nationalism." The Polish economic
policies of the early fifties were effectively molded by these influences.
One might merely guess as to what the course of the events might have
been if the creator of the pattern had not passed away in March, 1953,
and if the deepening disproportions in Polish Stalinized economy had
not coincided with the beginnings of the Soviet "thaw."

II. Beginnings of the Polish "Thaw"

The developments of the period which followed Stalin's death brought
a measure of relaxation. There was a certain easing in taxes collected from
peasants and a reduction in rates of compulsory deliveries levied on the
poorest among them; moreover, use of outright pressure in promoting
the production co-operatives was officially deplored. The rate of investment
was reduced by several percentage points and the share going to agriculture rose from 8 per cent in 1953 to 11 per cent in 1954 and 14 per cent in
1955. Certain changes in the price structure took place; more specifically,
attempts were made to bring the prices of producers' goods into line with
costs. Yet all these policies were inconclusive, or worse. Increased allocations to agriculture went almost entirely to the socialist sector; in fact, the
year 1955 saw a resumption of the collectivization drive on a large scale.
Cuts of investment in heavy industry carried out across the board brought
to a halt some of the construction processes in the next-to-final stages.
Postponement of completion of the quality-steel Warszawa which led to
large underutilization of capacity in automobile factories was a particularly
drastic example of such parsimony which was as haplessly indiscriminat-
ing as the prodigality of the past. Rise in prices of producers' goods was
followed up by wage increases which recreated the deficits (although to a
somewhat attenuated degree) and thus negated the purpose of the reform.
Nor was this all. The mounting wave of wage increases caused strong inflationary pressure which the government was no longer able to tackle
with the old ruthlessness; it could no longer allow prices to surge ahead of
wages or take recourse to a monetary reform which would slash the purchasing power of peasant cash holdings by two-thirds, as it was done in
1950. The result was an inadequately repressed inflation with black market
prices soaring and upward pressure on money wages continuing relentlessly and with the dictatorial government half resisting, half yielding—

a policy which set the stage for the Poznan explosion of June 1956, and which paved the way to October.

III. October 1956, and After

It was shown in the earlier sections of this paper that the pattern which was imposed on the Polish economy of the early fifties reflected a remarkable unity of purpose on the part of its architects. The heretical ideas which began to bud shortly after Stalin's death and which surged to the fore three and a half years later represented an equally consistent and emphatic negation of this pattern. In refreshing distinction from the defenders of orthodoxy, the advocates of reform displayed a wide range of diverging views on a number of important subjects. But there seemed to be a solid area of agreement on fundamentals in the heady days of the "spring in October."

In the institutional sphere, there was a clear break with the Stalinist dogma of ever sharpening conflict between the socialist and nonsocialist components of the economy as well as with the supporting notion about the inherent inability of the small- and medium-size peasant farming to expand. Practically speaking, this meant abandonment of confiscatory taxation policies directed against private sector, as well as of drastic discrimination against it in the allocation of investment funds, and, most important of all, freedom to leave the collective farms.

In the field of economic administration, maintenance of central planning was overwhelmingly favored. Yet it was felt that its operation should be restricted to a relatively few decisions of broadly aggregative nature and to setting the output targets only for a limited number of key industries such as steel, machine building, and the like. Individual enterprises were to get more autonomy in their output and investment decisions which would now be taken with the active participation of the "workers' councils." The market was to receive more scope as the vehicle of allocation of resources and to serve as the only link between the urban and agricultural sector, with the compulsory deliveries to be abolished at the earliest possible date. A fundamental price reform, directed at making prices reflect relative scarcities, was put on the agenda.

On macroeconomic level, an equally radical reversal was envisaged. The planned rate of growth was to be scaled down and the disparity between increases in producers' goods and consumers' goods reduced, not merely as a temporary emergency measure, but as an inherent part of the new and more balanced development pattern. Concomitantly, the rate of investment was to be lowered and its allocation altered for years to come: agriculture had to increase its share at the expense of industry, and within the latter more weight was to be given to coal, power, and basic chemicals at the expense of steel and engineering.

Such were, in broad outline, the major objectives which could be distilled out of official statements and of innumerable articles by leading economists. What about their fulfillment?

A most fundamental change took place in the institutional sphere, with agriculture far in the lead. The number of collective farms fell by more than four-fifths within five months after October, and their share in total agricultural area shrank to 1.2 per cent by the end of June, 1957.[20] (The state farms were not affected by this upheaval, except for a very minor reduction in their total area resulting from the sale of several hundred thousand hectares of land to the peasants). In the urban sector, the effects of new policy were less dramatic but nevertheless pronounced. The number of private artisan shops leaped upward by more than 40 per cent from 1956 to 1957, thus exceeding substantially its 1949 level,[21] and the revenues of the whole nonsocialized urban sector more than doubled during the same year.[22] It should be remembered, however, that this was an increase from a very low level.

The overcentralized system of economic administration proved most impervious to the new ideas. The most palpable innovations included reductions in the number of indicators (i.e., output targets and technological norms) in annual economic plans, deductions for the "fund of the enterprise" from the earned profits, right of individual plants to carry out replacements and major repairs out of their own means or out of credits rather than rely on budgetary grants. In addition, the organization of the so-called "industrial associations" which is now in progress aims at strengthening the position of industries with regard to the central planning agencies. A very small number of enterprises has been chosen to experiment in new and less centralized ways of management. The workers' councils which sprang up spontaneously in a number of major factories in the pre-October months are now in existence in almost all large-scale enterprises. Yet their position was weakened last spring when they became part of a broader structure called "conferences on workers' self-government," containing, besides the spokesmen of the councils, also representatives of the Party and of Party-controlled unions. Moreover, as a prominent Polish economist put it recently in an informal conversation, those workers' councils which took their rights to participate in management seriously were quick to find out that there was very little left for them to manage because all crucial decisions continued to be made outside the enterprise, in spite of the minor relaxations noted above. The promises of abolition of compulsory deliveries were carried out only

[20]*Maly Rocznik* . . . , p. 45.
[21]*Ibid.*, p. 39.
[22]I. Chodak, "W sprawie roli i znaczenia gospodarki nieuspolecznionej w naszym systemie gospodarczym," *Gospodarka Planowa*, Jan., 1958, p. 16.

with regard to milk. A draft of price reform proposals containing an explicit (although none-too-consistent) recognition of the marginal-cost principle and of the importance of the rate of interest, was made public in December 1957, by the advisory Economic Council (another institution of the post-October vintage). But no action on it has yet been taken.

The changes in over-all output and investment targets found their reflection, first of all, in the new draft of the Five Year Plan for the years 1956–60, with the over-all rate of growth scaled down to 8 per cent per annum with the rate of investment being on the average about 20 per cent and with substantial changes in the distribution of investment as shown in Tables 3 and 4. The new approach found its expression in the annual plans and in their actual fulfillment. A glance at Table 1 shows that the 1957 rate of investment was the lowest since 1951 (with exception of year 1956, when mounting economic and social tensions enforced a last-minute cut in investment below the originally planned level). Also, the allocation of investment in the plan for that year is indicative of the new orientation: the share of the nonsocialized sector was to double and the appropriations for coal and power were to rise by 2 and 8 per cent, respectively, while the total volume of planned investment was expected to remain unchanged.[23] In addition, there was apparently a drastic reduction in the volume of investment in armament industries.

The possibilities of appraising the over-all performance of the new setup are seriously limited by the fact that it has been in operation no more than for two years out of which only 1957 has thus far been fully reported. During that year, as our Table 1 shows, the net domestic product increased by nearly 8 per cent. The gross industrial output is known to have increased by 9.4 per cent. The signal feature consisted in an unusually good performance of the agriculture which for the first time reached, and slightly exceeded, its prewar harvest on the comparable territory.[24] No less if no more significant were such unmistakable signs of agricultural revival as sharp increases in prices of land, horses, and constructional material and a considerable rise in peasant savings. Yet on the opposite side of the ledger there were the following developments.

Powerful inflationary pressures which had broken through in 1956 continued to mount during 1957: they were propelled by continuing wage increases and rise in earnings of the peasantry, with increasing savings being an important but less than sufficient offset. The money income of the population in 1957 is known to have increased by 22 per cent over 1956[25]

---

[23]A Szerwentke, "Plan inwestycyjny na rok 1947," *Gospodarka Planowa*, Feb., 1957, p. 10.

[24]*Maly Rocznik . . .*, p. 46.

[25]"Sytuacja gospodarcza kraju a zadania czwartego kwartalu" (editorial), *Gospodarka Planowa*, Oct., 1958, pp. 3–4.

while the output, as has been pointed out a while ago, increased much less. The attempts to stem the inflationary tide by stepping up imports of consumers' goods led to a growing deficit in the balance of trade which reached a record level of 119 million U.S. dollars in the first half of 1957.[26] According to the more recent information, the picture changed during the first eight months of 1958 when money wages were kept almost entirely stable while prices showed marked increases, primarily because of the switch to production of more expensive kinds of goods. In fact, for a number of consumers goods' industries this implied a switch from seller's market to buyer's market and a sharp increase in stocks. Such a development admittedly entailed a decline in real wages at least for some categories of workers. It is hard to say whether it will be possible for the Polish economic administration to hold out for long against the pressure for another round of wage increases. In other words, inflation is still lurking in the background, and this threat has been invoked more than once to justify the slow pace of economic decentralization—more specifically, to explain the postponement of price reform and the persistence of compulsory deliveries of grain and meat.

The rise of open as well as of the disguised nonagricultural unemployment began to cause concern in 1957. It represented a composite effect of several factors, such as economic decay of the small towns which had once been centers of small-scale industry and handicraft and which consequently suffered most in the period of ruthless drive against the "capitalist elements" in the pre-October period; difficulties in moving idle labor to the areas of labor scarcity owing to housing shortages in growing areas; interruptions in flow of raw materials and/or fuel supplies due to disproportions; reduction in labor requirements in new plants as they are beginning to "master the technique," to borrow a Soviet expression; near-constancy in the volume of state investment expenditures in the years 1953–57. According to official data, the number of registered unemployed attained its peak by the middle of 1957, when it reached the 100,000 mark and then declined abruptly.[27] The disguised unemployment is much larger and, apparently, more persistent. The official estimates for 1957 put it at 500,000 or roughly one-fifth of the total industrial labor force,[28] and Polish economists are outspoken in discussing its negative effects on incentives for efficient working and for continual improvement in technology.[29]

The enthusiasm of the October days has not been followed by the hoped-for break in the psychological attitude of workers. All defense

---

[26]"The Polish Economy . . .," p. 36.

[27]*U. N. Economic Survey of Europe in 1957* (Geneva, 1958), Chap. VII, p. 45.

[28]*Ibid.*, p. 48.

[29]Cf. M. Kabaj, "Problemy pelnego zatrudnienia (II)," *Zycie Gospodarcze*, June 20, 1958, p. 2.

mechanisms developed in response to the Stalin-type industrialization —high labor turnover, absenteeism, theft—continued to operate. Indeed, the weakening of the stick and lack of significant increase in the carrot led to further deterioration of labor discipline in the short run. The situation in the countryside where the changes were much more tangible was, as we saw, quite different. Yet the same peasants who stepped up their buying of land and their rate of saving showed reluctance to acquire large quantities of agricultural machinery and to engage in construction for productive rather than personal purposes—an attitude which reflected, in all likelihood, the lingering fears that the collectivization drive may get under way once again. It is possible, besides, that difficulties to sell larger amounts of agricultural equipment were due, in part, to the fact that the standard types of this equipment, produced in Poland, had been adapted for use in large-scale state farms and Machine-Tractor Stations rather than for the needs of medium-sized peasant holdings—a point which was made recently by Professor Galbraith.[30]

IV. Summary and Prospects

The Polish economy after October, 1956, has undoubtedly some substantial achievements to its credit: maintenance of over-all rates of growth on respectable levels, pronounced improvements in agriculture. It is equally plain that the present Five Year Plan is a much more realistic document than its predecessor. The 8 per cent rate of growth and the 20 per cent rate of investment, while quite high, pass the Domar-Harrod consistency test much more successfully—particularly if it is remembered that the producers' goods capacity was greatly expanded in the preceding period. Moreover, the allocation of planned investment, showing the marked shift of emphasis to basic chemicals and to coal, is much more in line with the structure of comparative advantages. The same holds for the so-called "perspective plan of fifteen years 1961–75," which shows an even lower rate of growth and somewhat higher rate of investment. More important is that also the annual plans adopted and carried out this far reflect this break with the old pattern.

But at the same time the Polish economy is continuing to pay for the extravagancies of the past. The inflationary pressure reflects another crisis of relocation, albeit with the opposite sign. It is easier to decompress the consumption than to increase the supply of consumers' goods just as it was simpler in the past to jack up the rate of planned accumulation than to adjust the capacity of the producers' goods industry to the required rate of expansion. The Polish economy experiences now, in different spots, shortages of capacity in capital-starved consumers' goods industries which

---

[30]*Journey to Poland and Yugoslavia* (Cambridge, 1958), p. 45.

sets limits to the increase of output also when the required raw materials are on hand. Inability to provide sufficient processing facilities for increased volume of foodstuffs coming from the villages or for imported cotton financed from the proceeds of American loans are cases in point.[31] Another disproportion is even more serious: The increase in inadequate supplies of power, fuel, and chemicals requires an expansion in lines which are among the heaviest capital users in the economy and whose gestation periods are the longest. An ominous interaction between these two sets of difficulties is at work. By lifting the lids on consumption and by reducing elements of outright compulsion in labor-management relationship, the administration helps to raise the domestic claims on resources which are needed for export purposes and can even cause a temporary decline in their total availability. It is certainly not accidental that the output of coal showed a slight drop in 1957 when the use of prisoners and army personnel in the mines was abandoned and the amount of overtime work sharply curtailed, and that the coal exports kept declining. (There was an improvement in 1958, however.) It was equally clear that the pressure of growing consumption on imports was difficult to reconcile with the task of securing supplies of foreign equipment needed for rapid expansion of the neglected and most promising sectors of basic industries.

It is certainly important to bear in mind a point that has been stressed time and time again in the recent literature: The Polish economy after 1956 could, in a sense, take advantage, not only from solid achievements of the previous period, but also from its miscalculations. The post-October planners had at their disposal an impressive tail-end of investment projects which had been started during the early years of the Six Year Plan and which, while not completed on schedule, were nevertheless more or less substantially advanced toward completion. To the extent that the current constructional work represented a continuation of these projects, its capital requirements could be kept relatively low. The importance of this argument should not be exaggerated, however. First of all, in an economy which embarks on a significant change in the direction of its development, some of the unfinished projects which reflected the priorities of the past would not necessarily be the most useful ones. Secondly, and more important, to the extent that such tail-ends could fit into new plans, they could compensate only in part for the decline in reserves which the planners of the earlier period had at their disposal and which they used to the hilt. The old method of expansion owed a lot to the possibility of crowding raw manpower of the surplus peasants into existing plant which

---

[31]A. Karpinski, *Zagadnienia socjalistycznej industrializacji Polski* (Warsaw, 1958), p. 20. The last point, needless to add, constitutes not a deprecation of American loans but an argument in favor of increase in their volume in order to enable the Polish economy to import adequate quantities of cotton and of cotton-processing machinery.

was, to a considerable extent, obsolete and undermaintained already at the beginning of the Six Year Plan. By now, this policy has exhausted its potentialities and could not be pressed forward without causing serious disruption at the industrial as well as the agricultural end. No doubt, as was shown in preceding section, substantial pockets of unemployment (open as well as disguised) are still present, although the incidence of this unemployment has now changed. But in order to deal with them, it would be necessary to do something about the shortage of housing in vast regions of the country as well as about shortages of raw material and (in spots) of productive capacity; and every determined move in that direction would inevitably require heavy capital outlays. Here again, a determined application of the "dual economy" strategy could help. But while the leaders of the post-October administration abandoned the Stalinist approach to this problem, they were not ready to move beyond a merely permissive attitude toward the activities of the private sector in the area of small-scale urban and agricultural economy, and remained apprehensive about its possible degeneration.

It might be objected that the situation may be hopeless but not serious, after all. As long as the total output is growing at a respectable rate and the investment keeps adding to capacity in a less lopsided way than before, the process of relocation will be over before long, and Poland will finally get on the escalator of balanced growth; in the meanwhile, a measure of repressed inflation is something to live with. The trouble consists in the possibility that some of the short-term troubles might grow more serious before the salutary long-term effects would set in.

The gap in the balance of trade can become even more disturbing, particularly if foreign loans should not be forthcoming in anything like an adequate volume. The paralyzing effect of inflationary pressures on attempts toward decentralization and price reform is bound to weaken the incentives for better allocation of resources and for their efficient use in a period when idle labor and capacity margins can no longer be counted on to soften the impact of the massive irrationalities of the bureaucratic planning and to prevent the capital/output-ratio from becoming too high. The unchanged attitude of industrial workers toward production remains a source of serious concern. While the situation in agriculture seems very much better in this respect and a certain "from Missouri" approach with regard to investment in productive facilities may give way if the fears of another collectivization wave will be effectively dissipated, major question marks still remain. It is hard to feel certain that before the relocation process will be successfully completed, the peasants will keep providing marketable surpluses sufficient to guarantee the steady growth in real wages and at the same time practice the necessary degree of wise restraint in spending or accept without serious resistance the appropriate

taxation policies. Last but not least, as long as disturbances and hitches
are likely to develop, there is always a chance that diehards of unrecon-
structed (or partially reconstructed) Stalinism may attempt to step in and
to turn the clock back. The Poles are reported to be saying, "How terrible
is the past that awaits us." We should hope that this would remain merely
a sad joke; but we cannot be entirely sure.

APPENDIX

TABLE 1
NATIONAL INCOME AND PRODUCT OF POLAND, 1949 TO 1957

	1949	1950	1951	1952	1953	1954	1955	1956	1957
1. Index (1949 = 100)*									
Net national product.......	100.0	115.1	123.7	131.4	145.1	160.4	173.5	188.2	203.3
Net national income	100.0	115.3	124.0	131.8	145.7	161.0	175.2	188.4	213.5
2. Breakdown by Use (Percent of Total income)†									
Consumption.................	84.4	79.3	79.7	77.2	72.1	76.8	77.8	79.8	78.7
Individual.................	79.3	74.5	74.4	72.5	67.9	72.2	72.2	74.5	73.8
Social.....................	5.1	4.8	5.3	4.7	4.2	4.6	5.6	5.3	4.9
Net investment	15.6	20.7	20.3	22.8	27.9	23.2	22.2	20.2	21.3
Accumulation:									
Net fixed investment........	11.4	13.4	13.8	15.5	16.7	16.1	15.4	14.6	13.7
Increase in stocks...........	4.2	7.3	6.5	7.3	11.2	7.1	6.8	5.6	7.6
Total	100.0	100.0	100.0	100.0	100.0	100.0	100.0	100.0	100.0

*Chain index: 1950 prices for 1949–55, 1956 prices for 1955–57.
† In 1956 prices.
SOURCE: *Maly Rocznik Statystyczny 1958*, pp. 14 and 17.

TABLE 2
GROSS INDUSTRIAL AND AGRICULTURAL OUTPUT, 1949 TO 1955*

	1955
All industry (1949 = 100)	270
Electric power	224
Mining.	130
Metallurgy	251
Engineering and metalworking	421
Chemicals	308
Textiles	204
Food processing	229

	1955
Total agricultural production (1949–50 = 100).	112
Gross plant production	108
Gross animal production	123

* In 1938 prices.
SOURCE: "The Polish Economy Since 1950," *U.N. Economic Bulletin for Europe*, November, 1957, pp. 28 and 44.

TABLE 3
PERCENTAGE DISTRIBUTION OF GROSS FIXED INVESTMENT BEFORE AND AFTER 1956

	1950–55 Actual	1956–60 Planned
Industry	46.3	39.7
Construction	3.5	2.7
Agriculture	9.6	18.4
Forestry	0.4	0.5
Transportation and communication	12.2	9.2
Trade	3.5	2.6
Local government	3.2	3.1
Housing	10.4	16.2
Culture and social welfare	5.3	6.1
Administration and other	5.6	1.5
Total	100.0	100.0

SOURCES: 1950–55, A. Szerwentke, "Wykonanie . . . ," page 15; 1956–60, K. Secomski, "Z problematyki planu 5-letniego," *Gospodarka Planowa*, September, 1957, p. 7.

TABLE 4
PERCENTAGE DISTRIBUTION OF INVESTMENT IN INDUSTRY BEFORE AND AFTER 1956

	1950–55 Actual	1956–60 Planned
All industry	100.0	100.0
Fuel	18.0	21.9
Electric power	9.7	13.1
Metallurgy	20.9	13.1
Engineering	17.4	8.3
Basic chemicals	12.5	13.1
Building materials	5.8	8.8
Textile industry	3.7 ⎫	
Food processing	5.9 ⎬	12.3
Other light industry	1.8 ⎭	

SOURCE: A. Karpinski, *Zagadnienia socjalistycznej industrializacji Polski* (Warsaw, 1958), pp. 74 and 79–80.

PROPOSALS FOR CHANGE: THE MODEL DISCUSSION
AND AFTERTHOUGHTS*

— · — · — · — · — · — · — · — · — · — · — · — ·

George R. Feiwel

The discussion on the model was concerned with changes in the system of planning and administration of the economy within the framework of a socialist system. The proposals were considered only as technical variants of the socialist system taken as given. In his recent appraisal of the development of economic thought in post-war Poland, Lange referred to the discussion as "a revitalization of Marxist economic thought" and described it in these terms:

> To the forefront came such problems as centralization and decentralization of decision in administrating the socialist economy, democratization of administration through the workers' councils, the role, on the one hand, of economic instruments, and on the other, of administrative means in managing the economy, the role of economic incentives, the principles of price formation, the problem of market equilibrium, etc. In Poland these problems were dubbed the *economic model*. The discussion which developed was termed the discussion on the model.

Among the debaters, the extremists, so called value-men, believed that the panacea lay in restoration of the market mechanism functioning within the socialist system. Kurowski, "the angry young man" among Polish economists, postulated that the firm should have absolute freedom in choosing what and how much to produce and set prices on its products according to the law of demand and supply operating in the market. This precept should apply to manufacturers of both producer and consumer goods. Furthermore, although the enterprises should remain socialized their ownership should pass from the state to the collective of workers. The firms' sole goal should be maximization of profit. A share of profit should be divided among the workers employed. The foreign trade monopoly should be abolished and firms should decide on the import and export of goods. A central currency fund should be established where the exporters would exchange the foreign currency obtained for their products and the importers would buy this currency at its market price.

Kurowski limited the role of the central plan to forecasting and coordinating the general trend of development in the economy. He envisaged that central authorities would correct market maladjustments. To perform these functions the planner would use mainly monetary policy as a mitigating device. Furthermore the power of the planner with regards to division of national income between consumption and accumulation

*Reprinted by permission from *The Economics of a Socialist Enterprise* (New York: Frederick A. Praeger Inc., 1965), pp. 17–25. All footnotes deleted.

would be strongly curtailed by extending co-decision privileges to representatives of the working class. Such co-decision would involve struggle between the two forces and counteract the recurrence of low consumption levels. The central planner's investment program should be limited to building new enterprises. Prices of investment goods should be determined by market mechanism and investment decisions made on the basis of such prices. Investment funds should bear interest and the rate should result from the supply and demand for capital and the policy of the central planner.

Few economists advocated restoration of a free price mechanism and complete decentralization of decision making. They rather leaned towards a model in which the main macro-decisions would be taken by a central authority with prices, at least for the most important products, set centrally, a few directives sent down from top to bottom, and mainly economic incentives used in the process encouraging initiative and improving speed of adjustment and transmission of information. Within defined limits, economic choice would be left to management of enterprises. Economic calculation would become a tool of both management and planning authorities.

The *differentia specifica* of the so-called decentralized model is that it assumes many levels of decision making, whereas the strictly centralized model assumes several organizational levels, all essential decisions are made at the top. Recently Zielinski suggested that complete decentralization, with the planner retaining supreme power in constructing the plan, would mean governing the *executing* apparatus exclusively by means of parameters. Complete centralization would mean governing the executing apparatus by non-parametric means (commands). The various degrees of decentralization would depend on the role performed by parametric versus non-parametric means. Without detracting from the planner's essential powers, Lange conceives transformation of a centralized model into a decentralized one by means of setting up such goals and incentives for the lower levels that the result of their activity should conform to the planner's preferences; in other words, that in a decentralized model the lower echelons should autonomously execute the tasks previously foisted on them in a centralized model.

Brus produced a comprehensive literature on the concept of a decentralized model within the framework of the present political regime. He appears to have come close to embodying the prevailing opinion among the majority of Polish academic economists. At the expense of oversimplification we have adopted it as a frame of reference.

In this model the central planner is assigned the task of building the NEP on the basis of "economic and social rationality." The implication is that the plan should reflect Party preferences. In this respect there is no essential difference between the centralized and decentralized models. The same decision maker is responsible for the major economic decisions in both models. The central plan would still embrace the major problems: the rate of growth, production, national income and its distribution for accumulation and consumption, the division of accumulation for investments and increase of working capital, determination of the industries' development, localization of investments, distribution of consumption among collective goods and individual consumption designating changes in the income structure of individual branches of industry and localities, specification of the production structure (in branches of industry and on territorial basis), designation of major assortments in physical units, manpower and labor productivity, and the magnitude and structure of foreign trade.

But, whereas in a centralized model the plan formulated centrally reaches all units of economic activity, in a decentralized model "the national economic plan ceases to be a central sun whose rays-directives must reach all units." According to Brus, in a decentralized model, the central planner decides directly in the following instances.

1. In the field of national income the planner defines a) labor's share in national income and the wage structure b) the respective shares of the firms' profits designated for centralized and decentralized funds, and c) distribution of centralized funds among collective goods and accumulation.

2. It is up to the planner to choose the basic composition of investments, allocating the central investment fund among the various branches of industry, to determine the size and capacity of plants, and decide on investment criteria and methods, without necessarily deciding directly about particulars.

3. Prices should be centrally established as parameters for enterprises. But when the market is competitive and firms cannot fix monopolistic prices, and when the state does not intend to influence the buyer or seller by means of prices, prices may be formed on the market.

In this decentralized model all remaining economic decisions are to be made directly at the enterprise level. Initially the enterprise is endowed by the state with fixed and working capital. It autonomously organizes the production processes, chooses the size and composition of output, methods and factors of production to be used to minimize costs. It plays an active role as buyer and seller of goods. It chooses its sources of supply and channels of distribution. The firm decides on the division of profit remaining at its disposal and on the investments from its own funds and/or bank loans. When investments have been decided centrally and are financed from centralized funds, the enterprise should be allowed to decide on methods for their execution. Finally the enterprise decides on its internal organization, system of wages and premiums within the framework of centrally established regulations.

In a centralized model where economic decisions are made outside the firm, only production may be maximized since labor and material inputs are predetermined in both physical and monetary units. But when the methods and composition of output are decided by the enterprise, the use of output criteria as a measure of performance cannot suffice. Profit, being a synthetic yardstick, is then the best performance criterion. Hence the firm's main decisions would be geared to profit maximization. The profit criterion is usually identified with activating economic incentives, "a situation stimulating people to realize a predetermined goal of economic activity." The supposition is that when profit grows the enterprise improves its financial situation with respect to further expansion, improvement of working conditions, and increase in premiums. Conversely, when profit decreases the firm may encounter financial difficulties encroaching on expansion and the size of premiums.

Attacking profit sharing or premiums based on profit, Professor Kalecki questioned the practicality of substituting, even to a certain extent, economic incentives for central planning of production. He pointed out that if an enterprise is badly managed and profits suffer there should be no reason for increasing the premiums. But if technically inferior equipment causes high costs and low profits, why should the employees be penalized? Secondly, Kalecki argues, the quantitative effect of the share in profits is limited by the fact that income from it cannot constitute a substantial part of remuneration. But if the share in profit is not substantial, both as an absolute amount and in relation to basic pay, it would have only a negligible effect as an incentive. Profit is not only a function of the volume of production, but primarily reduction of costs. Kalecki fears that firms would tend to reduce costs instead of increasing production. He recognizes that in some cases it may be desirable but the result might be a complete failure from the overall viewpoint. As an example he offers the detriment to society arising from a substitution of materials and machinery for labor in case of an oversupply of labor. He fears that the desire to reduce labor costs may cause unemployment rather than increase of per capita income.

At the beginning of 1957 the SCEP was abolished and a new planning body organized under the name of Planning Commission of the Council of Ministers (PC), with S. Jedrychowski as its chairman. The PC's personnel was reduced and stress was laid on long range planning and use of economic analysis in the planning process. A month after taking office Jedrychowski described the new economic patterns:

We are now going through a period of transformation and shaping of our economic model . . . directed towards decentralization and democratization, towards organization of workers' councils, towards autonomy for enterprises and economic autonomy for the People's Councils. The economic model must take shape in practice. No ready-made theoretical conception, no cut and dried patterns or formulas can provide the details for this economic model which is to take shape in practice on the basis of our own specific conditions.

He considered a diminished rate of forced industrialization as a political, economic, and social necessity stemming from the need for a more rapid and immediate rise in the standard of living. To fulfil these promises the economic policy of the state would have to undergo drastic changes:

In which direction will these amendments go? In the direction of increasing individual consumption, of limiting capital investments, of lessening the burden of defence expenditures on the national income; in the direction of revising the production plans for mining . . . the plans for the metallurgical industry, and so forth; in the direction of changes in the principles of foreign trade and the balance of payments.

He explicitly stated that the basic plan indexes—the wage fund, the investment fund, exports, imports, accumulation of enterprises, and their contributions to the state budget—will have to be in the nature of directives. Central allocation of materials should be curtailed and the quantity of assortments planned centrally for key industries should be reduced to allow firms some freedom in producing certain assortments according to buyers' requirements. The discretionary powers should be wider for consumer than producer goods industries. But:

Central economic administration should not order enterprises about and deluge them with trifles and paperwork. It should coordinate the work of firms, control their activity and help them to attain the best economic and production results.

During the spring of 1957 a commission of the Economic Council considered the proposals for change and produced a set of theses. The document was a compromise of divergent views and lacks cohesion and clarity. Nevertheless it is important since it was to guide the state in initiating changes. The salient points raised by the *Theses* were:

1. The crucial industrial investments should be decided centrally on the basis of analysis of their relative efficiency and guided by the growth rates in the long range plans. Such investments should be financed by interest bearing non-repayable credits. The firms should be free to allocate depreciation and repair funds to investments or repairs. However, central authorities may limit enterprise investments in part or in full by freezing the funds.

2. The central industrial plan should differentiate between value of marketable output and value added, identifying quantities of basic raw materials and semifabricates.

3. The establishment of assortment indexes for individual firms should be the exception rather than the rule. It should be applied to distinctly deficit goods. Specifically it should be reverted to when sale is subject entirely to rationing and /or material inputs are rationed.

4. Central establishment of wage funds for enterprises should be retained. Under no circumstances should the balancing of income and expenditures of the population be impaired.

5. Enterprises' activity should be directed by their own plans, coordinated with the NEP. The principle of profitability should be the guide and economic incentives the rule. Whenever directives supplement incentives they must be observed. The former should never contravene the latter. Gross value of output should be abandoned as the main criterion for evaluating performance.

6. Relations between firms and their supervisory units should be specified, delineating the supervisors' prerogatives beyond which the firm is an autonomous economic unit. The firm should be allowed to invest from its own funds from depreciation write-offs, profit, or bank loans. It may plan its production basing it on an evaluation of procurement and marketing possibilities, subject to directives received. It may conduct transactions of procurement and sale directly with other producers or trade centrals. It must divide the wage fund according to collective agreements. It is authorized to apportion the part of profit remaining at its disposal as it sees fit. The workers' council and the director who manages the firm and is responsible for its activity to the state are the authorities of the enterprise.

7. The incentive system should be independent of tasks set in the output plan. Incentives should be tied in with profit adjusted for results independent of the firm's activity, e.g., increase in prices, etc. Premium funds should be stabilized for a period of a few years to exert a long run influence. The magnitude of the wage fund prescribed for the firm should not be set as heretofore in relation to gross output but in relation to value added. Within the frame of legal regulations governing the wage fund, the firms are authorized to dispose of it autonomously.

8. In view of the foregoing, an improved price system must depart radically from the prevailing accidental price relations. Price formation must consider actual economic conditions in a given production and exchange sphere. The different price levels for producer and consumer goods should be abandoned since they distort calculation and proportions in the division of national income. The state should definitely control prices, either directly by establishing prices or indirectly by influencing production and the market. The price reform of producer goods should be based on a calculation of genuine costs of production, the level and relations of world prices for goods subject to foreign trade, and ensure

profitability to producers. Prices of consumer goods should ensure equilibrium on the consumer market and assure the interests of consumers.

Although a relatively wide decentralization is advocated by the *Theses*, central planning as a *conditio sine qua non* for the economy's development is emphatically reasserted. This was not a very "dangerous" document. But the main changes it proposed were not implemented. Presumably they did not meet with the blessings of the Party. The discussion on the model was only an outward demonstration of a desire for change. The real decisions were made by the Party.

POLAND'S LASTING PREDICAMENTS AND SEARCH FOR REMEDIES: THE ECONOMICS OF HALF-MEASURE REFORMS*
— · — · — · — · — · — · — · — · — · — · — ·

George R. Feiwel

Enhancing the role of economic incentives, adoption of performance criteria steering enterprises in the desired direction, and furnishing firms with meaningful value parameters are among the foremost conditions for decentralizing economic activity. But such action can be successful only if the internal strife between incentives, performance criteria, and prices is eliminated and these components *integrated to function consistently.* However, the present system is not a coherent whole. Dr. Stefan Jedrychowski, the Chairman of Polish Planning Commission, said recently:

> I cannot agree with those comrades who do not perceive that there is a central concept in our economic incentive policy. Such a fundamental concept exists and aims at making these incentives dependent on synthetic performance criteria.

Unfortunately I will have to classify myself in the ranks of those "nonperceptive comrades." It seems to me that a fundamental distinction must be drawn between the source or basis for the formation of premium funds and the conditions for the distribution of premiums from these funds. The receipt of premiums hinges on production plan fulfilment. Consequently management does not face the problem of maximizing a single variable (profit) but joint value of two or more variables (output and conditions for special premiums) which may drive management's efforts into opposite directions. Since the size of the wage fund is geared to the value of output, the crucial significance of the latter is further enhanced. It is reinforced by the political pressures for production plan overfulfilment due to a deeply

*Reprinted by permission from *The Economics of a Socialist Enterprise* (New York: Frederick A. Praeger Inc., 1965), pp. 34, 194–196, 266–83. All footnotes deleted.

rooted belief that this is the most important target. The history of the Polish incentive system indicates that in practice one magnitude assumes the predominant role as the basic target, with the other targets playing second fiddle. Until very recently such a magnitude was gross value of output.

But increase of production is not by itself a sufficient test of rational allocation of resources. It is a fundamental proposition of the theory of the firm that optimum allocation of production factors requires that, *ceteris paribus*, in every case the value of the marginal product should equal the marginal (opportunity) cost of each factor in all its alternative uses. Quantitative increase of production as the main target motivates an augmentation of output at almost any cost as long as the increase is a positive magnitude. Within the capacity and resources at its disposal, management will strive to expand production even should the cost of the increase diminish the profit attained reducing the premium fund. It will do so because it is more advantageous to form a smaller premium fund which will be activated than a larger one from which premiums will not be distributed. The increase of production is often attained by deteriorating quality, manipulating assortments, inflating value of goods in process, undue development of subcontracting (not dictated by the benefits flowing from a division of labor and specialization), negligence in maintenance of capital equipment, storming, waste of materials and unwillingness to introduce technical progress and new product lines if they unduly disrupt the current production flow.

The present system of price formation rests on the computation of average costs of production for a given branch of industry plus a small percentage of profit computed on cost. Since any element of cost is deemed "price determining," it will enhance the cost and "value" of production and with a given rate of profit will increase the amount of "profit." Theoretically the value of output and the size of the wage fund will increase if the enterprise would produce the most material intensive products, given a uniform rate of profit on all products, or would produce goods where a minimum of value should be added on premises. Under these circumstances maximization of output will produce higher profit even without real cost reduction. Needless to say, in its pursuance of this course the enterprise is constrained by the availability of materials, possibilities of subcontracting, directives as to the assortment plan, and its technological processes. We can conceive, as indeed the information at our disposal suggests, that as a rule the enterprise will first produce the most material intensive commodities, and then by force of necessity, reconcile itself to production of less material intensive goods in a descending order on its scale of possibilities.

But since the rate of profit differs on particular goods, another variable enters the calculation. Should the rate of profit be relatively low on a material intensive product and high on a labor intensive one a balance must be struck. In case of a uniform rate of profit the higher the cost the higher the absolute profit and the higher the value of output. However, with a differentiated rate of profit the value of output may rise whereas profits may fall as a result of changes in the assortment plan. It is not important for management to increase profit alone but to augment profit in conjunction with fulfilling the production plan, in other words, to maximize the premiums ensuing from a maximization of the joint value of profit and output plan. Generally the highest possible value of production is best achieved with material intensive output and extensive subcontracting, whereas the improvement of profitability is most easily accomplished by manipulating the assortment so as to produce a profitable product mix which may or may not be most material intensive. Since the benefits derived from overfulfilment of the production plan generally outweigh those flowing from high profits, should a conflict arise between the two, the assortment will be juggled in favor of the former.

By retaining output maximization as a most important parameter of managerial action the state did not eradicate from management the desire for minimal plans. The weak incentive prompting increase of plan indexes by firms must fail, as it does since its benefits are incommensurate with the penalties for underfulfilling the plan. That our conclusions are not farfetched is substantiated by Vice-Premier Woniolka's bitter comment:

> The following situation is still universal: During the year enterprise A increased production by 20 per cent reduced costs, reduced labor inputs but fulfilled the yearly plan by only 98 per cent. Enterprise B increased production by only 2 per cent, exceeded the wage fund, cost plan, but fulfilled the plan by 102 per cent. Common sense tells us that better results were achieved by factory A. Yet all splendor will descend on factory B. Because—it fulfilled the plan. . . .

The desire for lower targets which may be easily met brings about understatement of production capacity by firms, creating a situation where the central planner does not possess the necessary information for plan construction. Investments are pursued for expansion of capacity, while existing plants are underutilized. Uneven overfulfilment of plans, often caused by some enterprises being less successful in concealing capacity than others, creates perturbing bottlenecks in material supply, hoarding of materials, work stoppages, loss of potential output, irregular flow of production, overtime, and great waste in the process of procurement and distribution of goods. Overfulfilment of the plan has become a fetish. It is not generally grasped that premiums are actually paid for deficient planning rather than efficient performance as only a slack plan can be greatly overfulfilled. One cannot help but agree with Jedrychowski that "from the point of view of the national economy and individual enterprises it would be much better to have realistic but high plans and overfulfil them to a smaller degree than to greatly overfulfil slack plans."

The performance criteria used are hardly correct for evaluating enterprises. Gross value of output may indicate spurious results, as we have already pointed out, since it does not disclose the contribution of a firm to the national product (value added) and could be augmented simply by juggling assortments and subcontracting. Moreover, reckoning unsold output contributes to an abstraction of the producer from the needs of the market as goods are not produced to satisfy buyers' requirements but for the plan. Production is disrupted since the industrial buyers receive unsuitable or low quality materials. The buyer cannot oppose the seller's deterioration of quality and nonadherence to the order since the producer dominates the market and only buyers compete to seize the limited supplies. Given the general scarcity of materials and the desire to fulfil the plan at almost any cost, the producer accumulates whatever supplies he can. In some firms stocks of materials mount, whereas total depletion and unavailability cause others to cease operations temporarily. Procurement difficulties bring about socialist graft. Barter of materials is common. The procurement market unduly absorbs and wastes resources.

Mindful of pressures on the consumer market, the state has placed observance of the wage fund limits on a pedestal as a performance criterion. Due to the pressures within the enterprise to expand the size of the wage fund, its magnitude has become of paramount importance. The significance attached by the state to the wage fund necessitated finding adequate means for controlling its size and a relatively simple method of computation. Due to unremitting preoccupation with the repercussions on the consumer market, it resulted in complete disregard for administration of resources in the enterprise. As we know, the wage fund is simply related to the value of output, which is one of the crudest methods available. Without repeating the various methods of enhancing the value of output and enumerating the shift parameters of the production function, even in the simple case of a single product of one assortment, quality and specifications, a direct correlation between the size of the wage fund and the magnitudes of output could exist only if the labor intensity would not be subject to change, the structure and composition of the labor force would remain unaltered, and the remuneration of employees would be proportionate to labor productivity and would depend on nothing else. It is hardly necessary to add that these conditions are almost never satisfied. The oversimplified computation of the wage fund is highly inequitable and contributes to serious difficulties in some enterprises whereas others reap unwarranted benefits.

It seems that the use of gross value has yet another pitfall. At the present stage of its economic development Poland has a relative shortage of basic raw materials and in many instances depends on their import. To alleviate the balance of payments it could save on the use of imported materials and contract their import and by parsimony of domestic raw materials perhaps increase their export. With the present relatively abundant supply of labor it would generally be preferable to save materials and substitute labor for materials whenever economically justified. It goes without saying, that long run factors of growth and many other variables must be considered. Labor and materials could not be taken as homogeneous aggregates but the benefits accruing from substitution in every particular case would have to be analyzed. However, the system is directed mainly towards savings on labor costs. Waste of materials is largely condoned. The computation of the value of production and the wage fund related to it are de facto incentives for increasing the consumption of materials. The prevailing method of wage payments to production workers, the piece rate system, is uniformly directed towards augmenting output offering, in a sense, an incentive to the individual worker to substitute materials for labor.

There seems to be a contradiction between the price and incentive policies. As we know, the state lowers or increases prices of substitutable products to promote or restrain their use due to their relative abundance or scarcity. From the standpoint of profit maximization, the firm, subject to constraints, would endeavor to minimize costs but only if the ensuing benefits would be larger than those flowing from production plan fulfilment. However, for this purpose it is in the interests of the enterprise to use a more expensive raw material that may be less labor intensive to process. Indeed the larger the cost of materials the more expensive the product and the larger the value of output. In a sense, the firm's demand function for materials is often upward sloping largely influenced by performance criteria.

On January 1, 1964 the regulations governing the wage fund were altered embracing enterprises producing about half of the industrial output. The existing regulations were retained for extraction, metallurgy, food, and some branches of the light industry. The changes in the remaining industries were not far-reaching extending only to the automatic correction of the wage fund by the bank. Thus the initial wage fund granted an enterprise is still computed in relation to the planned gross value of output. But the firm cannot expect an augmentation of the fund in relation to overfulfilment of the output target. However, reduction of the wage fund by the bank in case of output plan underfulfilment has been retained.

The new system hinges on wage fund reserves formed by the ministries and associations to be distributed to enterprises that overfulfil the output targets of assortments "in short supply" that the planner wishes to promote (reserve B), and production for export (reserve A). When the firm exceeds its wage fund in any one period, the excess is deducted from the association's reserve B. However, this excess cannot exceed 20 per cent of reserve B. If it does the balance will be deducted from the ministry's reserve. Hence an alarm system has been incorporated notifying the superiors of wage fund excesses. It should be noted that the ministry and association should specify in which assortments over-fulfilment will be honored for wage fund adjustments to be calculated in relation to the products' labor intensity. The reserve may also be used by the superiors to supplement the wage fund of firms that have been assigned above plan targets.

Fick claims that the 1964 experience with the new wage fund system showed that although the enterprises subject to it remained within the limits of the planned fund, they overfulfilled their production targets by 2.3 per cent, indicating that overfulfilment of the production plan must not necessarily be accompanied by an increase in wages. However, the result hinges, *inter alia*, on the composition of output and substitution of materials for labor. But the reform was not mainly aimed at restricting the wage fund. Primarily the idea was to curtail inutile above plan produc-tion, secondly to enable overfulfilment of planned production in needed assortments, and thirdly to shift the responsibility for the wage fund from banks to the firms' supervisors. The 1964 experience in this sphere was not particularly encouraging. Obtaining additional funds from reserves was greatly bureaucratized. For example, the Ministry of Heavy Industry did not distribute reserves among its associations. The firms had to demand funds from the association, and after approval the request was forwarded to the ministry for further processing. Enterprises demanding additional funds received replies to their requests with two to three month delays, hence often too late to execute the above plan targets. The new system has not fostered a swift process of adaptation to changing requirements during plan realization. Associations blamed the trade centrals for not supplying them with lists of articles in short supply on the market. But the associations also fell short of expectations. As a rule, they did not assign their firms above plan targets for specific assortments. Wage fund reserves were distributed generally upon specific requests emanating from enterprises. Furthermore, although complaints were voiced that the total 330 million zl. reserve allowed to industry was a mere pittance, at the end of the third quarter there remained 155 million zl. undistributed.

Notwithstanding the above shortcomings the new wage fund system suffers from its relation to gross value, the difficulties of establishing and quantifying this relation, etc. Hence a search is presently continuing for a more meaningful yardstick, concentrating primarily on variants of value added.

To eliminate material inputs and intra-industry flows from influencing the size of the wage fund, it is proposed to depart from relating the wage fund to gross value of output, replacing it by a yardstick approximating the value added ($v + m$) by the enterprise. There are considerable difficulties in arriving at a workable definition of value added that could be applied for computing the wage fund in various industries. In the definition adopted by the CSO value added is reckoned as gross value of output at current prices, or (a) direct materials, (b) indirect materials, (c) fuels, (d) electric power, (e) services procured (f) depreciation, (g) direct labor, (h) indirect labor, (i) labor surcharges, (j) profit or loss, and (k) turnover tax or budget differences, less a, b, c, d, e, and f.

The problem whether output should be reckoned in transfer or factory prices must be faced when deciding on the use of value added as well. The irrationality of prices constrains the validity of this yardstick. Total output embraces products sold, changes in inventories of finished goods, work in process, and production designated for the firm's internal uses. Consequently no matter whether output has received the buyers' seal of approval, and with the prevailing difficult to detect juggling of work in process, output reported in value added can indicate a rate of increase larger than when reckoned in gross value. If the transfer price falls below cost the calculated value added may be negative and reported value added would decrease as output would increase.

The limited experience with value added confirms that to overfulfil the production plan material inputs are inflated at the planning stage resulting in lower value added targets, while at the executing stage value of materials is deflated reporting a larger value added. This would be of foremost interest in industries where bank correction of the wage fund is still in force. Similarly to gross value the use of value added induces assortment manipulations to satisfy the producer aiming at producing the most labor intensive output. But in view of material shortages this may be the lesser of the two evils. Although generally it would be preferable to induce replacement of labor for materials, whenever feasible, it does not necessarily follow that it would be efficient in all cases. Because of irrational prices computation of the rate of substitution in particular cases will be of little assistance in guiding decisions. In view of procurement difficulties firms have little control over the size of material costs and value added will fluctuate pending on the source and quality of materials the firm was able to procure. Hence hoarding of materials will still prevail.

In favoring labor intensive production value added may be an impediment for introducing technical progress. But in view of the present unwillingness towards the introduction of technical progress and the magnitude of malpractices generated by the present system, it would seem that the computation of output in terms of value added has much to recommend it. Although not grossly misled by material intensity, the correlation between the wage fund and value added is also a spurious one as it does not simply depend on labor input but, *inter alia,* on changes of differential rate of accumulation, prices, capital intensity, quality of material inputs, wage differentials, etc.

So far, with the notable exception of the clothing industry, application of value added is at the experimental stage. Two notable variants have been evolved to be adopted for particular industries during the years 1966 to 1970: standard labor costs (machine building, electrical, and transport equipment industries) and standard processing costs (the clothing, chemical, furniture, glass, sugar, food concentrates, fruit and vegetable, brewing, china, leather and shoes, apparel, fur, and insulating materials industries) with an altered version for metallurgy and building materials industries. The corresponding yardsticks in the extraction and electric power industries will be variants of physical units and those of the textile and paper industries will still be gross value in transfer prices.

Standard labor costs are reckoned on the basis of technological norms or past statistical data indicating labor input per unit of output multiplied by the standard wage. Hence the sole component of value added in this case is standard direct labor. The standard cost measure is impaired by the technocratic, as distinct from economic, approach to the problem. It disregards the substitution effect of the marginal productivity theory and market valuation. The standards are subject to distortions due to setting and verifying time norms for products, classifying and shifting labor from direct to indirect and vice versa, changing the product mix, converting work in process into whole units, and altering the extent of subcontracting. Moreover, standards will vary depending on their computation for all operations or identifiable cost centers, groups or individual products, all producers or individual firms. An additional problem is defining the qualifications needed to perform operations and wage differentials. Notwithstanding the foregoing, standards will be inaccurate in view of management's pressures to have them set at the highest possible level and revised only sporadically.

The components of the standard processing cost are: direct and indirect labor plus surcharges, indirect materials, fuel, electric power, depreciation, and services procured. Hence this variant of value added differs from gross value by excluding direct materials, profit, and turnover tax. The standard processing cost is computed on the average standards in a branch of industry. By its very nature standard processing cost suffers from shortcomings similar to those attributed to standard labor costs.

The report of a joint Party and government commission, headed by

F. Blinowski of the Central Committee's economic department, indicated that although the results of the clothing industry are rather favorable, standard processing cost is far from being an accurate yardstick for wage fund computation. Since the standard processing cost does not cover particular operations it is also vulnerable to subcontracting manipulations. It offers no inducement for savings of materials, does not encourage production of new goods and introduction of new processes, and is unsuitable for industries where preparation for production is labor consuming. Due to the differential rate of labor and other components in the standard processing costs in different enterprises and for different assortments, the computation of the wage fund may be inequitable. In view of the magnitude of indirect non-labor costs in some industries muddled by the process of allocation, the wage fund is related to elements that do not directly influence its size. For example, in one branch of the chemical industry the components of the experimental standard processing cost are: direct labor 27 per cent, overhead 26 per cent, and departmental costs 47 per cent. Furthermore the contemplated stability and data used for computing the standard processing cost are highly questionable. For example, the experiments in the pharmaceutical industry were based on 1962 cost computations. Hence the standard processing costs for many products are obsolete at their very inception. With the passage of time such a situation would be intensified making the standard less and less representative.

No matter what variants of value added will be applied within the next few years, according to the present forecasts they will serve only to measure output for calculating the wage fund and labor productivity. Gross value will still remain as the yardstick for planning output at all levels. Notwithstanding the optimistic pronouncements that the wage fund problem will be solved during the next five year plan (1966–70) through a systematic adaptation of yardsticks approximating value added, the present experiments are meeting with many difficulties in practice. The planning apparatus is not eager to abandon the routine entrenched gross value methods. This reluctance is reflected; *inter alia,* in the notorious non-execution and postponement of experimental adaptations of value added:

> The dominating role of gross value of production index creates simply too favorable and too long exploited possibilities to compensate for deficiencies in planning and administration of industry that everyone should be willing to give it up so easily.

In view of the prevailing juggling of assortments by producers resulting in intense shortages of certain products, the existing premium system in the heavy, chemical, light, and building materials industries was amended on January 1, 1964 by removing the condition of production plan fulfilment, replacing it with fulfilment of the output targets of specified assortments. A revised premium system was introduced in enterprises and associations effective July 1, 1964. Simultaneously a number of specialized premiums were discontinued and their funds directed towards the main premium fund. However, it should be noted that specialized premiums for technical progress, savings of fuels and materials, export activation, etc. have still been retained.

The two main characteristics of the new premium system are: 1) upper limit of the total premium fund allowed for that year transmitted as a plan directive, and 2) it is a mixed system employing both profit and execution of special tasks with a pronounced shift of importance to special tasks. The firm's total premium fund is divided by the association's director into three parts: 1) premium fund for managerial personnel (with individual premiums limited to 80 per cent of salary), 2) premium fund for engineering, technical, financial, and administrative personnel (with individual premiums limited to 50 per cent of salary), and 3) premium fund for white collar workers (with individual premiums limited to 25 per cent of salary). The parts so established are rigid and no funds can be transferred from one part to another. Parts 2 and 3 are further subdivided by the firm's director into funds for individual departments. The mainspring of the system is the assignment of tasks and the corresponding amount of premium granted for execution to particular organizational units within the firm. To prevent the frittering away of premiums a maximum of 5 tasks may be assigned to each unit. The execution of each task entitles the unit to receive a previously stipulated number of points. The total of all points granted for the execution of all tasks should equal 100 corresponding to the total premium fund allotted to that unit. The points for all tasks should be set so as to allow 65 (and in special cases 75) for the execution of planned tasks and the remainder for execution of the plan or overfulfilment of the planned ones.

The general conditions for distributing premiums to managerial personnel are fulfilment of the profit plan or fulfilment of the planned share of costs in sales revenue. The general task imposed on management in all enterprises is fulfilment of the production plan in stipulated assortments. A given number of points should be assigned for this task. The remaining tasks and corresponding points are assigned by the association's director. They may vary according to particular needs, e.g., introduction of new technical processes, decrease in stocks of materials, greater utilization of production capacity, etc. The premium fund for engineering and administrative personnel is subdivided into two parts. Payments from the first part are contingent on management's fulfilment of its tasks, whereas those of the second part are solely subject to fulfilment of those employee's individual tasks assigned to them by the director of the enterprise.

Finally the premium fund for white collar workers is entirely dependent on those employees' execution of tasks assigned to them by the firm's director.

To eradicate the existing contradiction the premium system in associations has been constructed along similar lines. The size of the premium fund is set by the minister and differentiated according to planned improvement in the production of desired assortments, increase in export production, assimilation of technical progress, use of capacity, increase in labor productivity, and profitability. As in the enterprises, the fund is divided into three parts and payment made according to points granted for execution of assigned tasks. The general tasks imposed on management of all associations are: introduction of new products into production and fulfilment of export orders. The minister assigns the remaining tasks, e.g., execution of given assortment orders, improvement of quality, improvement of profit, etc.

Although overshadowed, the profit criterion has been introduced in two steps. Firstly underfulfilment of the planned financial result will decrease the premium fund. When the planned financial result is fulfilled by only 95 per cent the premium fund cannot be activated. Secondly 30 percent of management's premium fund is intended for an annual premium paid out in half for fulfilling the planned financial result of the past year and the other half for taut planning of those results for the following year, improving them in comparison to the preceding year.

This construction is intended to counteract the firms' pressures for lower plans resulting from relating their premiums to plan fulfilment. Nevertheless the effectiveness of this tool is highly doubtful as the part of premium paid to a manager for taut planning amounts to a maximum of 15 per cent of his annual premium. Moreover, he is induced to be rather careful in profit planning as payment of the other 85 per cent of his premium is contingent on the fulfilment of the financial plan. Hence a tendency to lower the financial plan may be expected at the enterprise's level with little opposition at the association's level.

The construction of the system assumes that the firm's director will assign his subordinates tasks which will promote the execution of his own tasks assigned to him by the association. It is doubtful whether with the present quality of data at his disposal the director can successfully allocate tasks in such a manner. Moreover the system relies on subjective appraisals of the intensity of tasks. Should it prove in practice that the assigned tasks are not taut enough, the entire system will collapse and its premiums will be transformed into additions to salary.

The scant experience with the new premium system indicates that the tasks are not sufficiently differentiated according to specific conditions. As a rule, neither the ministries nor the associations have assigned above plan improvement of profit as a task to their subordinates, assuming that execution of the other tasks will improve the financial result. But practice indicates that execution of such tasks as overfulfilment of the plan of stipulated assortments, decrease in the use of certain materials, improvement in quality of output, etc. cannot always be equated with improvement of profit.

The elimination of profit as a performance criterion from a wide range of premium recipients is a move away from synthetic criteria. Essentially the new premium system boils down to a replacement of profit by several variable performance criteria directed towards particular work segments. This will threaten neglect of all tasks other than those rewarded by premiums.

Profit, by the very nature of its computation, embraces both revenue and costs and prima facie is a superior measure than gross value, value added, any specific tasks, or even cost reduction, as it reflects both costs and benefits and their mutual relationship. It is the only criterion that presents an over-all picture of the enterprise's or association's performance. Banned in the past as incompatible with socialism, profit is now gaining respectability and is recurrently advocated by economists as a superior performance criterion. Nevertheless in practice a distinct trend away from profit is observed. Indeed, the revision of the premium system seems to bear out the contention that the fallacy of the price system makes profit an inadequate performance criterion.

In fact profit is a purely accounting, as distinct from economic, category since prices do not reflect current economic scarcities. In view of the fundamental deficiency of the price system, the measure of profitability may not be considered a sufficient guide for the direction, expansion, or contraction of production. If production of low profitability or even deficit goods, e.g., children's shoes, is to be expanded in view of great shortages on the market, with the simultaneous abundance of highly profitable assortments, e.g., women's shoes, whether or not sold to the final consumer, the producer will naturally endeavor to produce the latter at the expense of the former, although it would be deemed that production of children's shoes is socially more desirable. Neither sales revenue nor costs are meaningful categories as both output and input prices are generally fallacious. Cost calculations are incomplete, methodologically deficient, and tendenciously distorted. Hence the residual profit cannot be more meaningful than the components that went into its determination. Prices and profit cannot guide enterprises in economic choice and it seems to follow from the very logic of the system that directives must instruct firms to produce more of one product and less of another, in our example children's and women's shoes. If the use of raw materials in short supply is to be curtailed, it must be conducted by fiat since the price ratios in the obsolete catalogs, even assuming that they were originally correct, no longer constitute indexes of economic choice. The fallacy of the price system nullifies any serious attempts at decentralization of economic decisions. If management cannot be guided by prices, maximization of profit may not be in the state's interest. If there is a serious chance that maximization of profit will be arbitrary and not in the general interest, profit cannot be used as a performance criterion. In such a case there is a necessity for a multitude of performance criteria which leads us right back into the present highly unsatisfactory situation.

Notwithstanding its shortcomings, the central planner basically distrusts profit as a performance criterion because it is a resultant of many variables. The direction and intensity of each variable may be different and their importance may not seem additive from the standpoint of the central planner's scale of preferences. The increase of profit that results from a decrease in total production costs without an augmentation in the value of output may be considered inferior to an increase in output with costs remaining unchanged. Furthermore it may be deemed that a reduction in material costs and equiproportional increase in labor costs, although neutralized in the computation of profit, may not be of the same order of magnitude. This is related to the material balances where every element enters into a separate central balance and even though equivalent in monetary terms is not substitutable without the central planner's decision. The guidance of the economy through material balances precludes acceptance of profit as the only performance criterion.

It is worth noting that the pronouncements at the IV Congress of the PUWP held in June, 1964, indicate an attempt at revitalizing the administrative apparatus by investing associations with greater powers. Economists and "captains of industry" have taken their cue from those promulgations and came up with a number of proposals to invigorate the associations.

Their starting point is a transformation of associations into "socialist combines" with enterprises as their component parts. The combines would be interested in their financial results (profit) and guided by economic calculation. But there would be no basic changes in price formation. The contention is that such an organization would allocate production more efficiently on the basis of specialization, improving the process of cooperation. The socialist combine should be development oriented. Its investments, largely financed from profits, would be more efficient since it will invest in the units which will produce highest returns. Moreover, the large combine is better suited to risk new ventures and develop foreign trade. The latter should be stimulated (and become more profitable) by allowing the combine to benefit from it financially.

The promoters of these changes argue that not only is a large organization more efficient and easier to control, but both domestically and abroad the future lies in large organizational units. Some Polish economists, however, take the "association campaign" with a grain of salt and see in it a manifestation of the tendency to curtail the enterprises, autonomy.

The financial system per se depends on the prevailing degree of decentralization and its changes are contingent on overhauling the administrative and planning systems. In view of the pronouncements at the IV Congress of the PUWP impending but not fundamental alterations of the financial system may be expected and are indeed augured by the work conducted at the MF, reported recently by the Vice-Minister. Indications are present that the future financial system (1966–70) will be shaped along these lines.

As a result of revitalizing the role of associations and enhancing their performance of the investment function in expanding existing firms, the funds for financing such investments should not be as heretofore drawn from budget subsidies but from a larger participation in enterprises' profits and depreciation. The possibility of charging interest on the enterprises' fixed assets is seriously contemplated, although the variants of solutions, repercussions on cost determination, determination of the objects (base) of interest levy, level and uniformity or differentiation of rates, and methods of computation, are still unsettled. Enterprises should be allowed a wider latitude in replacing and modernizing existing equipment. Their investment-repair fund should be discontinued. A special fund should be set up for repairs and the firm's investments should be financed largely from the development fund.

The development fund should be formed as heretofore from profit and be the source for financing investments and working capital. The enterprise should be allowed to benefit from larger investment funds when it reduces its working capital needs and vice versa. It is suggested to set up two bank accounts for this fund. In account A, funds from profit would be accumulated in a given year and the following year transferred to account B from which funds for working capital needs would be drawn first and the remainder allotted to investments. This procedure would afford the central planner and the firm a clear picture of the availability of funds for any given year. To induce economical expenditures from account B, its funds must be subject to an interest charge lower than that levied on bank loans. Bank loans will be available to supplement investment funds but the bank will have to be satisfied with the efficiency of the proposed investments.

It is suggested to do away with financial normatives of working capital. The required working capital should be financed in about 50 per cent by the enterprise's own funds and the remainder by bank loans. When, as a result of better performance or curtailment of investment expenditures, the enterprise augments its own working capital it could then repay the loans reducing the interest charges. When, as a result of deterioration in performance or hoarding of materials, the enterprise will be short of funds to cover its own working capital, it will have to supplement it with investment funds or seek additional loans with a higher interest rate, reimbursable immediately from the following year's working capital.

Such a system hinges on the bank's ability to evaluate the situation and perform the control function over financial activity at the lower echelons. It is doubtful whether with the tools at its disposal, the efficacy of economic parameters, and the quality of its personnel, the bank can apply economic criteria (which in themselves are of questionable validity) in evaluating efficiency. Another dilemma facing the initiators of the reform is that if the bank's control is effective it cramps and stifles managerial action, and if it is not, it does not serve the central planner faithfully.

The proposed changes seem to rely heavily on the interest rate as an incentive and constraint. Without detracting from the usefulness of such a tool when used consistently, coherently, and concordantly with other methods, the present limited and discordant experiences with it are not a good omen. It seems that change of the producers' market from sellers' to buyers', revitalization of other economic parameters, transformation of profit into an economic category, and strengthening its hold over management would be necessary conditions to assure the success of the financial scheme. Indeed:

> Our past experience indicates that narrowly conceived changes may be almost completely unavailing unless accompanied by other changes strictly connected with the former.

An awareness of the present shortcomings prevails and is echoed in Party pronouncements, the press, and economic literature. The continuing deliberations of special commissions and conferences studying planning methods, prices, performance criteria, industrial organization, and economic incentives indicate a prima facie desire to revamp the system. Nevertheless, perusal of the latest promulgations indicates that remedies are sought for specific ills and there is a lack of understanding of the interdependence of the system's components. There is still a widespread belief that the desired effects can be produced by half measures, whereas for efficient functioning the entire system must be integrated into a coherent whole. Doubtless the direction, speed, and magnitude of future changes will largely be determined by political forces which I do not feel competent to judge. However, no matter what the political trend, it seems that the leaders of the regime would be well advised to keep in mind these words of Probrazhensky, a great Soviet economist:

> . . . in our country where the centralized planned economy of the proletariat has been established, and the law of value has been limited or replaced by the planning principle, foresight and knowledge play an exceptional role as compared with the capitalist economy. Errors in foresight committed by our central leadership may have much heavier consequences than errors committed by managers of private enterprises where mistakes in one direction are often cancelled out by mistakes in the opposite direction according to the law of great numbers.

To counteract false judgment, improve knowledge, and enhance foresight leading to a better use of resources, the central planner needs more precise tools for plan construction and implementation. It is perhaps in this respect that a closer tie between economic theory and practice would be most desirable. Professor Brus, one of Poland's leading economists, said:

> For the last seven or eight years economics . . . is offered far more favorable conditions for development than before. The results . . . are evident: greater freedom in scientific research and confrontation of different views, strengthened Marxist socialist economic thought, and in certain fields and works serious creative enrichment of theory. . . Economics belongs, however, to the fields of knowledge which should not be satisfied with purely intellectual achievements. This is why it should not be surprising that at least some theoretical economists are convinced that their influence—in the broad sense—on reality is minimal, and, at any rate, incommensurate with the intellectual achievements and actual needs. It is possible that they are wrong, that they overestimate the real value of what they have to offer. . . However, if they are not wrong, conclusions must be reached rapidly and consistently for the point in question is not only, and not primarily, of importance to economists.

REFORMS IN POLAND*
·—·—·—·—·—·—·

Leon Smolinski

At last things have begun to move. We have finally broken out of the vicious circle of experiments, more experiments, and nothing but experiments!'' This reaction to the economic reforms announced last year in Poland sounded a note of impatience—as well it might. Discussion of a "New Economic Model" for Poland has been going on for years, but while the economists talked, the decision-makers were hardly listening.

*Reprinted by permission from *Problems of Communism*, July–August 1966, pp. 8–13. All footnotes deleted.

It took the initiatives of other bloc countries, as well as the serious malad-justments that developed in the Polish economy under the 1961–65 Five-Year Plan, to drive home to the politicians the necessity of remedying the deficiencies of the traditional planning system.

The new guidelines adopted in June 1965 by the Central Committee of the Polish United Workers' (Communist) Party aim at making the planning process "more scientific" and less arbitrary. Economic calculation of costs and profits is to play an increased role at all levels of decision-making, reserves will be built up, and some decisions on resource allocation will be decentralized. These changes are intended to improve the quality of output, raise productivity, and discourage the systematic production of unsalable goods. In broader terms, as Stefan Jedrychowski, Chairman of the State Planning Board, put it, "The interests of society as a whole, as expressed in the national plans, are to be geared more closely to those of enterprises and workers."

How is this to be accomplished?

Guidelines for Reform

The first question that arises when dealing with reforms in a centrally-planned economy is whether or not they promote decentralization. The Polish reforms do to the extent that various operational and planning decisions formerly made at the ministry level are now shifted to the so-called *Zjednoczenia*, or industrial associations, each of which is in charge of all enterprises belonging to a given branch of industry. These associations are to become autonomous, self-financed bodies with their own investment and incentive funds. Each of them will be responsible for the development of its particular industrial branch and will receive over-all output targets from the Planning Board and apportion them among the individual enterprises under its control.

The targets assigned to an individual enterprise are not significantly reduced in number, but their nature and order of priority are changed. Until now, the size of the bonus fund out of which incentive premiums were paid depended in practice mainly on the fulfilment of the output target, and output was measured in gross terms—*i.e.,* including the value of raw materials and semi-manufactured goods purchased from other enterprises. This practice gave rise to what one economist termed "the most serious illness afflicting our economic organism: the [managers'] preference for turning out products containing large amounts of materials purchased from outside . . . the race for, and waste of, the most expensive deficit materials." Such wasteful behavior, though harmful to the economy, was "rational" from the manager's viewpoint since it enabled his factory to meet its gross output target with a minimum effort of its own. To remedy the situation, the June 1965 guidelines called for gradual replacement of the gross output target by a measure of the value added by the enterprise.

More important is the fact that the output target, whether gross or net, is to lose its dominant position as the criterion of enterprise performance. Instead, the so-called profitability rate (defined as total profits earned before turnover tax, divided by total costs of production) is to become the main measure of industrial efficiency. Each enterprise will be assigned a planned target rate of profitability, which will presumably be set in advance for a number of years, and the degree to which this rate is fulfilled will determine the size of the enterprise's bonus fund. As actual profitability increases above the planned figure, allocations to the bonus fund are also increased, but somewhat less than proportionately according to a regression table especially designed to make it more advantageous for an enterprise to opt for a higher profitability target than to retain a lower target and overfulfill it. Unlike the reforms instituted in the USSR, however, those in Poland leave both employment and wage-fund targets still in force, seriously constricting the enterprise manager's freedom of maneuver.

The reforms also effect important changes—"a real revolution," according to one observer—in the methods of financing investment expenditures. Formerly, investment decisions were highly centralized, funds for new projects were provided as free grants, and no interest was charged on plant and equipment in operation. These practices encouraged wasteful and inefficient uses of capital, and the situation was getting increasingly out of hand. Delays in the construction of new plant were becoming longer, the volume of unfinished construction rising from 61 to 83 billion zlotys between 1961 and 1964, while planned additions to plant capacities in operation were only 60–70 percent achieved.

Three steps have now been taken to delegate some investment decisions to enterprise managers and to make the enterprises financially responsible for the consequences of these decisions. *First*, since January 1966, interest charges are being gradually introduced in cost accounting, starting initially only with industries which can afford to pay these charges out of profits. Unlike in Hungary, the interest rate is not to be uniform throughout the economy, but differentiated according to the industry.

Secondly, except for priority projects, bank credits replace free grants as the source of funds for financing new plant construction. Bank loans are repayable but interest-free; however, if the construction of new plant is not completed on schedule or the actual cost exceeds the planned level (which happens in Poland almost as a rule), interest will be charged on the excess cost. The extent of this change is indicated by the fact that 60 percent of all non-private investment is to be financed by bank loans during the 1966–70 period, as against only 5 percent during 1961–65.

Thirdly, investment decisions on such matters as modernization and replacement of worn-out machinery have been decentralized. The industrial associations and individual enterprises are given greater responsibility for such decisions and in turn will be expected to finance modernization and replacement projects largely out of their own retained profits and depreciation allowances.

Decisions on prices continue to be strictly centralized. As Planning Board Chairman Jedrychowski emphasized last February, "We are not moving in the direction of permitting free price formation. The state will continue to fix prices." The government's announced intention is to combine stability with flexibility in its pricing policies. The general level of consumer retail prices is to be kept stable, while individual price relationships within the aggregate will be flexible, subject to adjustment in response to changes in costs and the demand for particular goods. Flexibility is to be promoted, *inter alia*, by means of the so-called three-step pricing system, which was first introduced in 1959 for some consumer goods. Under this system, the basic price of a commodity is determined according to the long-run costs of production. In order, however, to encourage the introduction of new products and models—a notoriously difficult problem in Soviet-type economies—a somewhat higher provisional price, allowing for some extranormal profit, is permitted during the initial period of production of a new commodity while it is in high demand. Then, as the scale of output increases and unit cost declines, the price is reduced to the basic level covering only long-run average costs. Finally, as the commodity goes out of fashion, remaining stocks are disposed of at prices below cost, the losses from such sales being defrayed out of a "risk fund" built up by the allocation of a part (58 percent on average) of the producers' initial extranormal profits. In 1965, such three-step price levels were fixed for only about 10 percent of all new products, but the system is now to be applied on a wider scale.

As early as 1956, the principle that "industry should produce only to meet orders by trade agencies" was formulated in Poland, and experiments were begun, seven years in advance of the Soviet Union, with "direct links" whereby enterprises manufacture product assortments ordered directly by the trade agencies rather than by the central authorities. These experiments are now to be expanded, and the number of products whose output is centrally planned will be reduced.

Despite general agreement that the existing relative prices of producers' goods fail to balance supply and demand, no broad price reform in this sector is contemplated during the remainder of the 1960's, although adjustments are envisaged in the prices of some types of machinery and equipment. To get away from the irrationalities of domestic prices in one especially vital area, additional reforms are being effected in enterprises producing primarily or exclusively for export. From the start of this year, their output is being valued at world market prices (expressed in so-called "foreign-exchange zlotys"), and they are required to maximize profits measured in these terms. With these new success indicators, what is profitable for an enterprise should also be good for Poland's balance of trade. Part of the profits from foreign sales of an enterprise's products are to be allocated to its bonus fund: the more profitable these sales, the higher the bonuses. Conversely, complaints and returns of merchandise by foreign customers will operate to reduce the bonus fund.

Perhaps the most significant reform of all is the directive calling for the creation of adequate "reserves" at various levels of decision-making. As conceived here, "reserves" embrace much more than just inventories of finished goods and materials. They are also to include a financial reserve fund (possibly 10 to 15 percent of planned investment expenditures); reserves of foreign exchange which would act as a shock absorber in case of unexpected changes in world market prices; reserves of skilled manpower; and even reserves of physical production capacities in plant and equipment. As a Polish commentator observed, "A few years ago, keeping unused capacities in reserve was still considered a mortal sin"; now it is to become standard practice.

This innovation amounts, in fact, to a repudiation of the traditional principle of taut planning in Soviet-type economies, where output targets were regularly set somewhat in excess of the enterprises' combined capacity to meet them with available inputs. It also reflects growing recognition that even the best-laid plans are merely forecasts which may have to be rapidly revised in the light of such factors as technical progress, fluctuations in world markets (on which Poland is increasingly dependent), crop failures, and even the whims of fashion. In short, the planners now recognize explicitly the simple truth that the future is uncertain. As one writer commented in advance of the 1965 reform guidelines:

> For years we have overestimated the importance of plans, attributing to them the power to eliminate any accidental events, to almost faultlessly determine developmental trends. The creation of reserves and, by the same token, recognition of uncertainty . . . [are symptomatic of] a defetishization of plans.

Prospects for Effectiveness

All in all, the Polish economic reforms are more hesitant and less far-reaching than those enacted in Czechoslovakia and Hungary. In fact, they hardly add up to the long-desired "New Economic Model" for Poland insofar as this implied a comprehensive set of mutually consistent incentives, prices and institutions. While each of the reform measures, taken separately, seems to represent a step in the right direction, most of them do not appear to go far enough to have the hoped-for effects. In economic policy, two half-measures do not necessarily add up to one success. Nor are all the goals of the reforms entirely consistent with one another or with the means envisaged for attaining them.

The two cornerstones of the reforms are (a) the adoption of profitability as the main indicator of enterprise performance; and (b) the introduction of repayable investment loans and interest charges on capital. The effectiveness of the first, however, is likely to be reduced by the fact that while an enterprise will be expected to achieve a certain rate of profitability, it will continue to be saddled with other assigned targets that may enter into conflict with the profitability objective. Furthermore, profits will still be computed in terms of irrational prices, and profit maximization under such conditions may well lead to misallocations of resources. As for the second, it is certainly a fact that the former method of rationing out capital free of charge to all users was wasteful. Under the new scheme, however, some enterprises will pay higher interest charges than others, while some will not pay any. Moreover, priority projects will continue to be financed by free grants rather than by bank loans, representing a political infraction of the economic discipline otherwise emphasized by the guidelines.

Another obstacle to the efficacy of the reforms is the fact that although some relatively minor limitations on the managers' freedom of action are removed, the basic ones are left intact. In a 1964 survey of 354 factory managers, 85 percent of the respondents singled out the system of centralized allocation of material supplies as the most serious impediment to efficient enterprise operations; yet this institution remains intact. How then can the manager avail himself of his newly-acquired freedom to spend part of the enterprise's investment fund the way he sees fit, to replace equipment at the time he chooses, and to gear product assortment more closely to consumer demand? To the extent that such decisions involve changes in the planned allocation of material supplies, they will still have to be authorized by the central authorities, and this has always involved long delays.

Furthermore, a sellers' market, of which the rationing of key producer goods is merely an extreme symptom, continues to prevail in many branches of Polish industry. This absence of effective competition among sellers seems likely to reduce the effectiveness of the incentives now offered.

In the final analysis, moreover, the best plans are only as good as the people in charge of their implementation. In Poland, an attempt is being made to graft economic innovations onto the traditional institutional framework, with all its ingrained bureaucratic inertia. But, to quote a Polish proverb, "pears will not grow on willow-trees." An interesting survey published in a Warsaw journal last year found that in five East-Central European countries sociopolitical institutions uniformly lagged behind governmental policies of economic liberalization and decentralization, thereby setting effective limits to the success of these policies. In each of the countries examined, the respondents queried in the survey expressed the opinion that the main stumbling blocks to the implementation of projected economic reforms were "the traditional bureaucratic style of work" and the inadequate preparation of those newly entrusted with responsibility in making economic decisions.

The effectiveness of decentralization depends not so much on the smaller number of decisions reserved to the central authorities as on the manner in which these decisions are made and enforced. Suppose that the central authorities now make only a few decisions each year concerning an enterprise but procrastinate so that each of these decisions reaches the enterprise a few months behind schedule. The enterprise will then continue to be effectively paralyzed, and "decentralization" will not work. The actual habits of the Polish planning authorities under the old system do not augur well in this respect. Annual output targets tended to reach the enterprises six to nine months *after* the beginning of the year, resulting in what one critic described as "an *ex post* rather than *ex-ante* system of planning."

There is nothing in the new guidelines to prevent the continuation of such malpractices. Neither the rights nor the obligations of the higher economic authorities vis-à-vis individual enterprises have been spelled out. In practice, the former have the rights, and the latter the obligations. No penalties have been provided for errors or delays on the part of the planners. Characteristically enough, as late as November 1965, five months after the Central Committee's adoption of the guidelines, it was reported that "no enterprise has yet received any binding instructions concerning its new success indicators and the consequences of the new model for it. The new guidelines have not yet been translated into the enterprises' language." And the plans for 1966 were still being prepared by the old methods.

The choice of the *Zjednoczenia*, or industrial associations, to become the mainstays of the new planning pyramid is not very felicitous. These agencies had already been in operation for years, albeit with more restricted rights, and were unenthusiastically described in Polish economic literature as mere "transmission belts" or "mail boxes" for commands issued by the ministries and reports sent in by enterprises. Even in this modest role they seemingly failed, as evidenced by the following assessment:

> The *Zjednoczenia* poorly transmit success indicators, are incapable of economic forecasts and ignorant of the enterprises' actual capacities. . . They do not assist enterprises which seek higher targets, and sometimes they squarely oppose such requests.

Moreover, the associations shirked risk, lacked drive, and were often accused of wearing departmental blinders. Now these bureaucratic-minded agencies are being placed in charge of streamlining Polish industry. They hardly seem fit to assume the responsible tasks of socialist entrepreneurs.

Who, then, *is* ready to assume these tasks? In the earlier-cited survey of East-Central European countries, planning officials in Czechoslovakia—a more industrially advanced country than Poland—were asked who could play the role of socialist entrepreneurs in their decentralized economy. The answer was: "There are none qualified—and that's bad." One explanation advanced by the survey author was that in Soviet-type economies enterprise managers are still not allowed to perform the typical entrepreneurial functions of risk-bearing, or deciding what to produce and at what price to sell. Another, related reason is that, at least in Poland, many factory managers, even if assigned such functions, might not be willing or able to exercise them adequately. In the late 1950's, only 23 percent of Polish factory managers had higher education, and four out of ten had nothing more than grade-school education. By 1964, the situation had improved significantly, suggesting that the chances for decentralization to work are relatively better now than before. Nevertheless, even today less than 50 percent of enterprise head managers and only two out of ten chief accountants are graduates of higher educational establishments. while three out of ten chief engineers still lack engineering education.

Polish managers are said to approach the reforms "with cautious enthusiasm." Caution actually seems to overshadow enthusiasm, and the implantation of the new guidelines promises to involve a long and painful learning process. Nevertheless this process itself, with its new emphasis on economic rationality, the defetishization of growth for growth's sake, and the search for efficiency, may have useful side-effects. In Adam Sarapata's words, "a factory produces more than goods alone; it also produces social relations, attitudes, opinions. . ." Effects in these areas may in the long run be more vital than the economic fruits of reform.

An interesting question arises in this connection concerning the future role of the party. In Poland as elsewhere in the Soviet bloc, the party apparatus has developed more and more into a machine for mobilizing national resources and generating economic growth, tasks in which it used to excel. Now, however, the emphasis is shifting from the mobilization of resources to their intensive utilization, from growth to efficiency, from carrying out commands to forecasting market demands. To the proud slogan "There is no fortress which the Bolsheviks will not storm!" the current reforms seem to add a postscript, "Yes, but at what cost?" The traditional attitude that a target must be met, almost regardless of its economic, social and human cost, is changing. Targets are to be defetishized, and planning is to become more scientific.

In this changing situation, scientists, economists, market researchers, and such appear likely to gain in importance as compared with the party apparatchiks. The bureaucrats' resistance to the reforms may therefore reflect their vested interest as much as it does mere inertia. Can the party's *machine à gouverner* assume the functions of a machine for profit-making? The job seems to call for Communist professionals rather than professional Communists, but it is still the latter who keep crowding the corridors of power.

5. ECONOMIC REFORMS IN CZECHOSLOVAKIA

*CZECHOSLOVAKIA'S NEW ECONOMIC MODEL**
— · — · — · — · — · — · — · — · — · — · — · — · —

Harry G. Shaffer†

After the Communist takeover in 1948, Czechoslovakia's political and economic system was patterned on that of the Soviets and its government became as Stalinist as any in the Soviet bloc. Political and cultural control by the Stalinist party apparatus was complete; five-year plans gave priority to heavy industry at the expense of the agricultural and the consumer goods sectors; and central planning authorities left few economic details to be decided at lower echelons of the economic machinery.

Even after Khrushchev's denunciation of Stalin at the 20th CPSU Congress in 1956, Czechoslovak party leaders embarked upon the Kremlin-ordained course of destalinization with utmost reluctance and with correspondingly little effect. Long after the body of Stalin had been removed from its place of honor in the Lenin Mausoleum in Moscow's Red Square, and long after other Soviet bloc countries had demolished the outward vestiges of the personality cult, Stalin's 50-foot statue continued to tower over Czechoslovakia's capital. It was not removed until October 1962.

It is true that throughout the 1950's the centralized Czechoslovak command economy experienced considerable growth—largely because

Reprinted by permission from *Problems of Communism* (Sept.–Oct. 1965), pp. 31–40. All footnotes deleted.

†Dr. Harry G. Shaffer is Associate Professor of Economics, University of Kansas. His publications include: *The Soviet System* (ed. 1965), *The Soviet Economy* (ed. 1963, and the *Communist World* (ed. in print).

of the forced expansion of heavy industry. Yet it is questionable whether even this specious form of economic growth, achieved by sacrificing quality of production and consumer interests, took place because or in spite of the centralized planning apparatus. In any case, the growth rate of Czechoslovakia's industrial output and national income, averaging about 11 and 7 percent respectively between 1957 and 1960, began to drop in the 1960's; both were negative in 1963.

A Background of Economic Ills

Of all the Communist countries, Czechoslovakia has had the longest tradition of capitalist democracy, and it entered the era of "dictatorship of the proletariat" at a considerably higher stage of industrialization than any of the others. Yet in 1963 Czechoslovakia became the only industrialized country in the entire world to register a decrease in industrial output, national income and real wages.

In addition, the goods that were produced were of such inferior quality that the value of rejects reached 1.5 billion Kcs in 1963; during the first seven months of 1964 defects in industrial projects cost the country 365 million Kcs. So serious has this problem become that Czechoslovak observers openly admit that "quality has become the foremost concern of the party and the economic authorities." Newspaper reports, radio broadcasts, countless complaints from dissatisfied customers and official statements testify to the fact that the difficulties in quality control persist. In February 1964, for instance, show windows in the East Bohemian town of Hradec Kralove displayed in "one of the most effective forms of the struggle against rejects . . . an electric shaver which did not shave, an iron which did not iron, a cooker which did not cook, and pen knives which did not cut." In 1964, too, a shoe factory in Slovakia turned out shoes whose soles fell off after only a few days of wear, although the shoes retailed for 105 crowns a pair. Defective coolers used in agricultural cooperatives caused milk losses "amounting to hundreds of thousands of liters every month." And the Elektrosvit factory in Nove Zamky, Slovakia, which had been granted the "Red Flag" award "in recognition of its splendid results in the fourth quarter of 1963, "the next year sent 500 refrigerators to Brno, all of which, on close inspection, proved to be defective.

As almost everywhere in the Communist world, concentration on capital goods production brought in its wake a great housing shortage, especially in the industrial centers. In Czechoslovakia, almost one third of all families are reported to have less than eight square meters (about 80 square feet) of floor space available per person, and a pool of 1,800 young couples in the 20–23 year age group, taken in several large cities, revealed that 60 percent of the newly-weds live with the parents of one of the spouses.

The supplies of some food items (especially meat and meat products) improved considerably in the early months of 1964, eliminating some of the previous shortages, but many other consumer goods such as beer, mineral water, canned condensed milk, transistor radios, silicon raincoats, and some electrical appliances failed to meet demand. A Czechoslovak writer vividly depicted the trials and tribulations of the Czechoslovak consumer in the Prague literary journal, *Literarni noviny*:

> I fear becoming so used to daily calamities that I will consider it an unusual and happy occasion when there are available in places where they should be batteries, transistors, buttermilk, red beets, upholstered chairs, white lead for paint, reserved train tickets, nylon shirts, fountain pen refills and recording tape. . . .

While there is a pronounced shortage of many consumer goods, the economy continues to produce many "unmarketable" commodities. In 1963, total inventories increased by 7 billion Kcs, and the total value of unsalable inventories is estimated to approximate one fourth of the country's national income.

To alleviate such discrepancies, the regime changed prices of consumer goods several times in 1964, raising the prices of goods in short supply and lowering the prices of products that were not taken off the market in sufficient quantities to clear the shelves. Since price increases of some goods were at least partially offset by price decreases of others, it would be impossible, without statistical computation, to evaluate the overall effect on the Czechoslovak consumer. However, a series of drastic changes decreed early in 1964 provided a definite indication that living standards in Czechoslovakia (although generally considered still the highest in the Communist world) left much to be desired. In an unusual radio and television appearance on February 7, Premier Jozef Lenart announced an upward "adjustment" of rents, hitherto subsidized by the state, "to cover approximately the costs of operation, particularly maintenance and repairs"; the imposition of a progressive tax on pensions of more than 700 Kcs per month; the introduction of small charges for drugs and some school supplies heretofore given out free of charge; and an increase in the prices of formerly subsidized meals for workers served in factory cafeterias.

These measures are a part of the effort of the regime to make the country live within its means; they are, moreover, an expression of the awareness that artificially maintained low prices (or high incomes) can lead to shortages and disproportions without raising overall living standards. As one Czechoslovak commentator put it:

> We must take into consideration the old, well-known truth that we can only parcel out what there is to be parcelled out. . . . Even the best possible government cannot distribute what it does not have.

In addition to all its other economic woes, Czechoslovakia has been suffering from a severe labor shortage. Early in 1963, in fact, the regime termed it the underlying reason for the abandonment of the 1961–65 plan. By late summer 1964, there were at least 50,000 job vacancies in a country whose population numbers around 14 million.

In an effort to combat the labor shortage, the government last year decided to import a few thousand badly needed coal miners from Poland and to reintroduce small-scale private enterprise, primarily in the service trades, to tap the two million pensioners, the unemployed housewives and those members of the present labor force who are willing to engage in after-hours work. The importation of foreign workers has of course the disadvantage of increasing the number of consumers as it increases the number of producers, and it has therefore not been attempted on a large scale in Czechoslovakia. At the same time, the opening of certain service trades to private enterprise has met with rather limited success. Deterred by red tape, high license fees and the requirement to submit to supervision by a socialist enterprise, very few individuals in Czechoslovakia seem to have taken advantage of the opportunity so far, although the first partial re-privatization decree has been on the books for more than a year. In any case, since Czechoslovakia already has one of the world's highest labor-participation rates, efforts directed at a *more effective* utilization of the *present* labor force appear more promising. Towards this end, the government in 1964 started shutting down all unprofitable productive capacity; introduced special financial incentives to lure workers into such sectors as agriculture, mining and building, where the labor shortage is especially pronounced; reduced by more than 37,000 the country's administrative apparatus, and offered special premiums and awards to collectives, groups or workers and even individuals who succeed in reducing the working force of an economic unit while still fulfilling the output quotas.

The Search for a Cure

The economy of any country may be adversely affected by events that lie beyond the control of the government. At least two such events (a political crisis and a natural calamity) left their imprint on Czechoslovakia in the early 1960's. First, the Sino-Soviet split resulted in a sharp and sudden drop of Czechoslovakia's trade with China, depriving the former of a supplier of food and raw materials and a not-too-demanding customer of machinery and equipment. Secondly, the severe drought of 1962 played a major role in the agricultural debacle of that year, which, compounded by the savage 1962–63 winter that temporarily interrupted transportation, was bound to leave its mark on industrial production in 1963.

Yet, however damaging these events may have been, Czechoslovak officials have not blamed them exclusively for the difficulties that have beset the economy. They have noted instead many symptoms of a lingering disease and they have applied, in piecemeal fashion, spot remedies to provide temporary relief. Most economists, however, and even key party officials soon agreed that a radical cure was needed to restore the economy to a healthy condition.

Even though Czechoslovakia's economic problems are manifold, the economists are convinced that one single systemic defect—*detailed economic planning from the center*—is at the root of the trouble, and that only the elimination of the existing planning structure will provide a fundamental cure. They advocate, therefore, a decentralization of economic decision-making, emphasis on material incentives and strong reliance on the forces of supply and demand as the principal measures necessary for a successful recovery.

Attempts to institute such reform are not entirely new in Czechoslovakia's post-1948 history. As far back as 1957, the party Central Committee had decided that central management of "fundamental matters" ought to be combined with extended rights and responsibilities of plant managers in "current matters" and that more emphasis should be placed on material incentives. On April 1, 1958, certain economic reforms were in fact, introduced; these, however, are recognized today as "halfhearted" and "rather shy steps in the direction of economically sound management of the economy" and as an ineffective "compromise solution."

When the 1961 plan was underfulfilled, the party first placed the blame on the decentralization measures of the 1958 reforms and, reversing its former positions, asked for the "strengthening of central management." But subsequently, the 12th Czechoslovak Party Congress (December 1962) decided that henceforth all proposed economic measures must be carefully examined and subjected to public discussion. Thus an atmosphere was created in which progressive thought could flourish, allowing the debate to swing once again in the direction of greater economic decentralization. For the following two years, first timidly and then ever more frankly, the shortcomings of the prevailing system of management and planning were discussed and analyzed, and eventually there emerged a plan for a "New Economic Model."

Winds of Reason

In February 1963, Radoslav Selucky, a young Leningrad-trained ecomomist, launched the first major attack against the "cult of the plan." He soon found rapidly spreading support among reform-minded intellectuals. Although the opposition of the conservative officialdom, including party leader Antonin Novotny, remained strong, a conference of leading Czechoslovak economists in October 1963 openly discussed the country's economic ills and made strong recommendations for abandonment of the rigid system of centralized planning, urging in its stead increased dependence on market forces in economic management. By the year's end the discussion had spread from scientific conferences and technical journals to daily newspapers and cultural and political periodicals. It soon became apparent that those who advocated a "fundamental change" in the system were gradually gaining the upper hand.

In the summer of 1964, the editors of *Pravnik* (the publication of the Law Institute of the Czechoslovak Academy of Sciences) sent a questionnaire to leading economists and lawyers asking them for their views on the "proper" system of management of the national economy. Not one single voice among those who replied defended the system of central planning under which, ever since 1948, the Czechoslovak regime had tried to determine everything from the output of hydroelectric power and steel to the production of toothpaste, ice cream and engineering graduates. By 1965, university professors no longer hesitated to criticize publicly the "Stalinist model" of economic centralism and to denounce as a mistake the copying of the pre-Khrushchev Soviet system of management in a highly developed country like Czechoslovakia.

Arguments in many respects similar to those propounded in the USSR by Yevsei G. Liberman have been advanced in speech after speech and in article after article by the Czechoslovak reformers. As long as quantitative output is ordained from above and remains the primary achievement indicator, the argument goes, is it any wonder that managers and workers alike tend to disregard product quality and consumer demand, "stubbornly continuing . . . to produce useless goods?" Is it any wonder that productive capacity is concealed to secure easily attainable targets; that it often becomes "more important to fake the fulfillment of a task than to make a real effort to achieve socially desirable results;" that machinery and equipment (allocated free of charge by the state) are hoarded irrespective of immediate usefulness; and that technical innovation is considered an unwise risk which, if successful, would only bring higher output quotas for the subsequent year? All in all, the economists believe, the prevailing system of management has failed to correlate the interests of individual enterprises and their employees with those of society.

Since quantitative output has proved to be inadequate as an index of efficiency, planners in several Communist countries of Eastern Europe have been experimenting with different success indicators. Expedients, such as bonuses paid for increasing labor productivity, for introducing innovations, for improving quality and for saving on scarce inputs have been tested, but all of these measures have merely further complicated the already cumbersome planning apparatus. (In Czechoslovakia, not long ago, the case of a director was reported who had to fulfill 17 indices to quality for a bonus.) Today, the progressive economists are convinced that there is only one index that would suitably measure performance and at the same time coordinate the interests of workers and directors with those of society at large: profit.

If profit is to perform these functions, enterprises must be free to seek it without interference from centralized controls over details of production. They must be allowed to decide for themselves what goods to produce and where to sell them, what inputs to use and where to purchase them, how many workers to hire and how much to pay them, what share of total net profits to distribute among employees and what share to set aside for investments intended to increase future income. To the extent to which enterprises are not free to make such decisions, to that extent profit loses its value as a meaningful measuring rod of enterprise efficiency and to that extent also the profit motive is weakened as an effective incentive towards efficient and socially desirable performance. Hence, almost by definition, the utilization of profit and of the profit motive must go hand in hand with economic decentralization and with a considerable extension of the influence of market forces over economic decision-making.

The blame for the lack of success of the 1958 decentralization measures in Czechoslovakia is now placed primarily on the failure to make profit the basic index and to link the material interest of the enterprise with it. This shortcoming of the 1958 reform (apparently resulting from an ideological aversion to what then was held to be too "capitalistic" an approach) is not to be repeated in the mid-1960's. Although the details of the proposed changes have been sharply debated, Czechoslovak reformers are in general agreement that profit and the profit motive must be given a meaningful place within the framework of the socialist economy. It is also generally understood that the proposed reform will entail a diminution of the central planning organs' economic powers and a simultaneous transfer of such powers to the lower echelons in the productive process and, in the final analysis, to the consumer.

The New Economic Model

On October 17, 1964, *Rude pravo* published in a 12,000 word article the "Draft Principles for the Perfection of the System of Planned Management of the National Economy." The document had been approved in September by the Presidium of the Communist Party Central Committee and generally conforms in its thrust to the ideas publicized during previous months by a number of economists in particular by Ota Sik, head of the Economic Institute of the Academy of Sciences and member of the party Central Committee. In essence, the "Draft Principles" envisage the scrapping of detailed economic planning from the center and propose to substitute for it the mechanism of a market economy operating within the framework of a broad overall social plan.

After the Presidium's preliminary approval, the "Draft Principles" were returned to the Central Committee's Economic Commission for further study. To the surprise of some observers who expected that the dogmatists within the party would assert at that stage their opposition to the proposals, the Commission proposed no alterations beyond emphasizing the need for a more consistent elaboration of questions related to prices, levies, credits and the status of the central organs. The Central Committee plenum, held, after one postponement, at the end of January 1965, then followed suit by issuing a resolution that approved the New Economic Model without substantial change.

After proclaiming that the existing system of detailed planning at the center had "fulfilled its historic mission" (the "Draft Prinicples" had characterized it as "unwieldy, bureaucratic, and obsolete"), the CC resolution proceeded to outline the new approach to economic planning and management as follows.

Greater Authority for Enterprises. The function of central economic planners is to be reduced to the laying down of "the basic proportions of production . . . and distribution." Central planning bodies and central control agencies are to concentrate their efforts on broad, long-term planning; on such important, fundamental questions as price, wage and incentive policies, and the balanced economic development of individual regions; and on the control of situations presenting "the gravest danger" of "antisocial trends" (such as, presumably, could arise if large production units were left free to exploit their monopoly status without restrictions from above). The actual management and initiative in the productive process is to be left "as much as possible" to the basic economic units or their joint organizations. Enterprises, in other words, will be free to decide by themselves or in conjunction with other enterprises all economic details within the limits of the broad outlines laid down at the center.

Profits. From their total revenues, or "gross income," enterprises are to defray direct costs of production (including expenditures for raw materials, parts, transportation, and interest on bank loans) and their "obligations to society" (*i.e.,* interest and installment payments on state investments in the enterprise and contributions to the state budget). The remainder is then to be used by the enterprise for distribution among workers and managerial personnel and for investments in the enterprise itself to enhance future income.

From the part of enterprise income set aside for the remuneration of employees, basic wages will be paid out first in accordance with the overall wage policy laid down by the central planning authorities. The rest, under a kind of profit-sharing system, will be distributed among workers (and managers) at the discretion of the economic unit, presumably in the form of incentive payments and bonuses for especially deserving employees. In regard to basic wages, the plan calls for the discontinuation of leveling policies, so that henceforth acquisition of greater skills and preparation and training for more important and more responsible positions should be more adequately rewarded. In this manner, a worker's income is to be related to his own qualifications and performance as well as to the economic achievements of his "intra-enterprise unit" and of his enterprise as a whole. Since enterprise profitability is assumed to result from both efficiency in production (low production costs) and concentration on quality and assortment reflective of consumer demand (salability), a direct link is thus presumably established between the interests of individual workers, economic enterprises, and society at large.

Investment. In the sphere of investment, too, the central organs are to lay down only the overall policy: they are to decide upon "the basic orientation of investment policy, the big development programs, and the conditions and criteria for the effectiveness of sector investments." Otherwise, guided by considerations of profitability, enterprises will be responsible for their own investments. They will finance them out of their own funds or through bank loans. Contrary to prevailing practice, all debts will have to be repaid with interest, out of future earnings.

Prices. If the market mechanism (rather than an all-wise planner) is to allocate resources so as to meet consumer demand, arbitrarily set prices must be replaced by prices which reflect relative scarcity. The party leadership, however, is unwilling to let prices fluctuate freely, in accordance with the market forces of supply and demand. The new economic model calls therefore for three types of prices: fixed, "limited," and free. Raw materials and all basic products such as coal, electricity, steel, wheat, etc., will carry fixed prices set at the center, but, similar to the price reforms instituted in East Germany in April and July 1964, costs and demand are to be given due consideration and prices are to be changed whenever changed conditions indicate the necessity for such action. "Limited" prices, apparently applicable to a wide variety of commodities, will be permitted to fluctuate within prescribed limits. Fee prices, affecting initially only a small sector of the consumer goods industry, will be left to respond, without limitation, to the forces of supply and demand.

Enterprise Combinations. Structurally, the new economic model provides for horizontal integration of enterprises through the formation of "trusts" and for vertical integration via "concerns." While the offices of the trusts and concerns will clearly represent the highest agency still directly concerned with the financial management enterprises, a precise delimitation of authority within the integrated units remains to be defined.

Foreign Trade. The foreign trade mechanism is also to be "liberalized." To motivate domestic enteprises to sell abroad, they are to have the right to keep a part of the foreign currencies they have earned. On the other hand, they will also be relatively free to purchase their supplies abroad if foreign producers can deliver them more cheaply than domestic suppliers.

Schedule of Implementation. The reformers have cautioned again and again that the major changes they advocate could not be put into effect at once. While the "Draft Principles" clearly stated that "the Central Committee can no longer wait" to *start* the introduction of the new measures, there is clear cognizance that the new system must be introduced gradually. The year 1965 is to be a period of experimentation during which some of the principles of the reform are to be tested in selected enterprises. In 1966, the "basic principles of the new system" are to be implemented in the "main branches" of the economy, even if details will still remain to be worked out later.

Isolated experiments with economic decentralization involving the utilization of profit and of the profit motive were actually started early in 1964. In January 1965, the testing went into full swing. During the first half of the month, selected enterprises in the consumer goods industries began to experiment with entirely uncontrolled prices, and it was announced that a freer system of prices (limited prices in state-owned factories, free prices in cooperative enterprises) would be tested in an entire production sector: the furniture industry.

Ideological Justification. In the Communist world outlook, Marx is not merely the John Locke and the Adam Smith of socialist political and economic thought; he is viewed more in the way in which Christ is looked upon by Christianity. Hence, to be acceptable, such far-reaching changes in the system of planning and management as are incorporated in the New Economic Model first had to be justified in terms of Marxist ideology. The economic reformers have therefore consistently denied that they were "revisionists," and they refer to their experiments with various aspects of a market economy as "creative Marxism." In a hundred different ways during the past two years they have expounded the view that "in the process of the regeneration of creative Marxist thinking . . . economic theory has gradually disposed of the supposition that socialism will always continue operating under one and the same model of management," and they have attacked as "ideological prejudice" the notion that socialist production cannot be regulated by the market. Finally, since planning has always been held to be the backbone of an economy structured along Marxist-Leninist lines, they keep insisting that the proposed new system "will not mean less planning but better planning" and that "the effectiveness of central management will be increased by its being relieved of the task of making decisions in questions which, by their very nature, should be reserved for the enterprises. . . ."

Conclusion

The system of detailed economic planning from the center, which may have certain merits if used to speed up the development of a backward country, has been imposed for a decade-and-a-half upon Czechoslovakia, the industrially most advanced state in Eastern Europe. Now, at long last, economic necessity and a powerful intellectual effort by a new breed of Communist-trained economists have, at least for the time being, convinced a somewhat reluctant party leadership that complete economic control from the center is not necessarily the epitome of economic wisdom. But how well the reformers will succeed when their New Economic Model is put to the test of life is a wide open question. Few will doubt that there are very serious difficulties ahead, stemming partly from imperfections of the new scheme dictated by the necessity of political compromise, and partly from the necessarily slow pace of changing the practices and overcoming the attitudes established during long years of economic controls from the top.

To mention just a few of the more obvious problems: The party leadership will surely not be induced for some time to come to go very far in releasing price formation from central control. To the extent that prices will remain centrally determined, they will reflect, in some measure at least, the preferences of the planners rather than those of the consumers; and to that same extent, profit will fail to function as a fully meaningful measure of economic efficiency. Similar defects will result if a policy of rigid wage control from the center is maintained. Other problems are likely to arise in the wake of the prospective industrial amalgamations. It is true that these may help reduce costs of production in certain cases, but they will also tend to create monopolies which, under a reasonably free price system, would find it profitable to restrain production and maintain high prices. In other words, here is another possible inducement to the government to exercise price control.

One more problem must not be mentioned—one that may, indeed, turn out to be the most serious the economists and the government will face: the shortage of trained and experienced and enterprising managerial personnel. During fifteen years of detailed economic planning from the center, the regime had little use for the skilled managerial resources the country had developed prior to 1948, nor did it see any need to train new ones. Apart from the party's established personnel policy, which rewarded political conformity and neglected skill and ability, the highly centralized system of detailed planning could virtually dispense with managers in the true meaning of the word. What it needed, and what it promoted, was political bureaucrats who could take orders and then gladly pass them on. But the New Economic Model is predicated on skillful and *enter-*

prising management, in other words, on enterprise directors who not only are adequately trained, but who also have a personal stake in the fulfilment of their task; in short, men who can act as entrepreneurs in the best sense of the word. Unfortunately, the government's effort to overcome the scarcity of managerial personnel by training more capable individuals for managerial positions is handicapped by the continuing requirement that, as Novotny phrased it in his last New Year's message, "capable and *politically conscious* individuals be appointed to leading posts." Nevertheless, the trend appears to be in the direction of greater emphasis on qualifications and less emphasis on "political maturity."

All this is not to say that the outlook for the New Economic Model is altogether bleak; with time many of the present difficulties could be overcome. The big question is whether the party leaders who still hold the reins of power will be willing to relax their grip sufficiently to permit the advantages of the proposed reforms to take full effect. Yet, whether it likes the new course or not, the regime itself is in large measure dependent on the reforms' success. The only alternative is a regression to the old system of management, which has proven inadequate, and further economic failures, which even a totalitarian Communist government can politically ill afford in Eastern Europe today. Viewed objectively then, the New Economic Model bears the promise of desirable ends to the party leadership itself; and to the country at large it opens up the possibility not only of material betterment, but also of a more humane and more democratic socialism. For everyone concerned, the stakes are clearly high.

PROBLEMS OF TRANSITION TO THE "NEW MODEL" IN CZECHOSLOVAKIA*[1]

— · — · — · — · — · — · — · — · — · — · — · — ·

Vaclav Holesovsky†

The fascinating spectacle of East European command economies being prepared for demolition has evoked rather stereotyped interpretations. The imminent, or not so imminent, transitions to "new economic models" have been thought of as transitions toward "market socialism," as "borrowing a leaf from the book of capitalism" and even as a step in the gradual convergence of socialism and capitalism. Obviously, the "need for . . . tidier semantics" in this field has not diminished since Alexander Gerschenkron mentioned it in 1960.

*Reprinted by permission from *ASTE Bulletin* (Fall 1966), pp. 2–9. All footnotes deleted.

†Dr. Vaclav Holesovsky is Associate Professor of Economics, University of Massachusetts. He is a co-author of *National Income and Product in Czechoslovakia, 1947, 1948, and 1955–56* (1962).

[1]Paper presented at the Third Congress of the Czechoslovak Society of Arts and Sciences in America, Inc., Columbia University, New York, September 3–4, 1966.

I don't want to open a debate on terminology here; but I do want to stake out, very briefly, the boundary of my talk against the domain of the theory and practice of socialism. It seems to me that a socialist economy, in the sense of a "free association of producers"—to use the broad but unequivocal definition of Marx—has as yet existed nowhere, and that, therefore, discussion of changes in Soviet-type economies in terms of different types of socialism or different proportions of socialsm and capitalism are likely to lead to a theoretical dead end. A more fruitful approach is to view the Soviet-type economies as one peculiar historical and geographical species of the large genus Capitalism. To call the Soviet system —as Alfred Meyer did—"U.S.S.R., Incorporated" is more than a *bon mot* of a political scientist. It also serves, in my opinion, as a remarkably adequate rendition of a social and economic truth. To take one aspect: the "profit motive" was never absent from Soviet-type economies. The "system's directors"—like those of a badly run diversified corporation— merely lost track of the real cost and profitability of various lines of production, with the consequences that could be expected.

I shall resist the temptation to elaborate further on the parallelism between the corporate form and state capitalism. I merely want to suggest the usefulness of considering the incipient reforms in East Europe not as a transformation of economic systems in the sense of great socioeconomic formations, but in terms of radical changes in quasicorporate management methods.

Seen in this light, the crisis of the classic Soviet-type economic organization is nothing but a crisis of management of several company towns of country-size dimensions. The reforms, planned or implemented, resemble very much attempts to refloat a company which was beginning to go under in market competition, the professional economists playing the role of management consultants and the managers halfheartedly doing what they are being told.

As a matter of fact, the reforms have not been adopted primarily under the pressure of endogenous forces—as one would expect in a true mutation of an economic system—but directly under the pressure of international economic competition. By competition I do not refer to the content in economic athletics between "socialism" and "capitalism," in the Khrushchovian sense of a parallel race of growth rates, moon shots, ICBM's and milk consumption, but the hard competition of merchandise against merchandise on the world market, including its Soviet-bloc and Western portions. I propose that internal reforms have been the direct consequence of strains and dislocations in the intrabloc foreign trade, of the crisis of bilateralism among Soviet-bloc countries. The crisis is the outcome of a stage of economic development which has come to an end.

Putting it very schematically, the time has passed when the more advanced industrialized countries processed raw materials for their less-developed partners into industrial equipment and were paid for the job in raw materials and foodstuffs for their own use. The less-developed countries have begun to use the accumulated industrial equipment to absorb their raw materials themselves, gaining an interest in exporting their own wares, losing interest in articles previously imported, and losing the ability to export agricultural produce just when the need has become most pressing. The more advanced industrial countries of the bloc found themselves saddled with an economic structure and a composition of output geared to the preceding stage of initial industrialization of their partners. The advanced members of the bloc were thus forced to try to adjust to an entirely new situation in foreign demand and supply, which also meant entering Western markets more than marginally and competing with Western articles on the Soviet-bloc market. But which way to turn; how to succeed—the existing system of economic signals could not provide an answer. This explains the search for economic criteria to orient production and for flexibility in decision-making to make response to these economic criteria possible. It is hardly an accident that, roughly speaking, the degree of urgency of reform in the different countries of the bloc corresponds to their degree of industrialization. East Germany and Czechoslovakia lead the movement, followed closely by Hungary and trailed by the rest, including the Soviet Union. It should be noted that the most advanced countries, Czechoslovakia and East Germany, were also the countries hardest hit by the crisis of trade relations, both suffering an absolute decline in production during the early 'sixties.

All this is not to deny or underestimate the importance of purely internal factors, such as the pressure of competing claims upon the national product, which moves the governments to search for more efficient ways of raising output. However, judging by the record, the predominance of internal factors over foreign trade pressures seems to allow for far more procrastination with reforms than is the case where external factors predominate.

After this panoramic view, I shall concentrate on the problems of the transition to the "new model," as exemplified primarily by Czechoslovakia, reducing the number of flashbacks into the pre-reform past to a necessary minimum. The most striking feature of the transitional stage is a dizzy accumulation of paradoxes. Here is a sample of contradictions inherent in the effort at reform, some apparent, some real.

1. The interconnection of elements and functions in the economy being what it is, the reshaping of the economic organization with the intended scope and depth cannot be gradual. Yet, the measures are too complex and

the preparatory labors too time-consuming to make a change-over at one stroke conceivable.

2. Market relationships and the system of pecuniary incentives cannot take hold and would actually make matters worse, as long as relative prices are kept at existing ratios, divorced from actual cost-and-demand conditions. But market prices seem unobtainable without first having a market to determine them.

3. The crisis of growth rates and productivity has been to a large extent due to flouting the principle of complementarity between economic branches. Since these disproportions had been caused by central commands, they have to be corrected by central commands in order to prepare the ground for changes in the microsystem of management which will have to come later. On the other hand, without functioning market signals centralized corrective decisions are as much subject to errors of "subjectivism" and arbitrariness as the decisions of the past which are to be corrected.

4. The decentralization is to be implemented through central organs, in a sort of "cold process" in which increased autonomy and decision-making power are being foisted by unwilling bureaucrats upon equally unwilling managers who seem, on the whole, non too enchanted by the prospect.

However, having mentioned these paradoxes and vicious circles, I should add that none of them presents really insuperable difficulties; they do not, in my estimation, condemn the reforms to failure a priori. Contradictions which implicate the political future of the system present a different set of problems which I have reserved for the conclusion.

1. Taking first the apparent paradox of the impossibility and the necessity of introducing all changes simultaneously: it has been solved by deciding to introduce a core package of operational changes on one date, that of January 1, 1967, to see what problems will automatically take care of themselves and to give individual firms a chance to make their adjustment by sensitive and differentiated treatment. It is to the credit of economist-consultants that they have convinced the political leadership of the need for radical measures, the futility of prolonged piecemeal testing in partial so-called experiments, and the inapplicability of gradualism. The course of the year 1966 has confirmed that there cannot be a stable middle ground where a command economy could incorporate isolated elements of market behavior and incentives. This is merely a repetition of lessons learned from the years following the 1958–59 reforms. These lessons are that partial reforms under unrelieved conditions of excess demand and fixed prices, alias repressed inflation, inevitably invite back-

sliding to a full command system. Relaxing the centralized system of material supplies and reducing the number of obligatory output quotas lead firms to cut down on the quantity of their supplies, whereupon frustrated customer-enterprises require intervention from above. A recentralization of planning—initiated from below—is the end-result. Similarly, letting the volume of sales and net revenues play a decisive incentive role in a world of crazy prices will lead to changes in output composition compared to which physical command planning will appear as a model of rationality.

The lack of understanding of these interdependencies has caused un-necessary disappointments for enterprises eager to start playing according to new rules. Formally, fininical incentives (in the form of enterprise per-sonnel sharing in the financial results) have been in force since the beginning of the current year. However, the "branch trust" organs supervising—and, in reality, closely running whole economic branches since the middle of 1965 ("vyrobne hospodarske jednotky" and their "odborova reditelstvi") apparently took care of defining financial obliga-tions of enterprises in a way which amounts to the old planning of profits from above and leaves little at the firm's free disposal. The "branch trusts" have imposed new graduated tax rates ("odvody z hrubeho duchodu") on the enterprise sector so as to soak up 1) the equivalent of the old "profit tax" ("odvody ze zisku"), as well as 2) a good portion of additional enterprise earnings; i.e., the equivalent of the old tax on above-plan profits, whatever the source of the extra earnings—windfall or genuine managerial merit.

The backsliding—due to the hurry of reformers to have at least some halfway measures enacted in 1966—was taken as a bad omen by enter-prise managers. The high-handed manner in which enterprises saw them-selves treated by the new "branch trust" authorities and by the govern-ment (in addition to the above, all liquid working capital previously owned by the enterprises was confiscated, and enterprises were forced to turn to bank credit as the only source of liquidity; at the last minute, enter-prises were unexpectedly informed that, in 1965, 15 percent of their in-vestments would have to be financed from their own earnings)—all this during the din of reform talk on the expanded rights of enterprises— served to contribute to an atmosphere of uncertainty and reinforce ingrained managerial cynicism. However, in my opinion, the course of economic events up to the end of 1966 should be written off as a poor source of enlightenment on the reform's merits and prospects.

2. The capstone measure which is rightly expected to test the viability of the model and put life into all other measures is the price reform. It has been feverishly worked upon since February and is to be introduced

in January 1967. The paradox of having to create a full set of market prices without a market and without direct knowledge of existing demand and supply functions was bypassed in the only possible way: by not trying to solve it in one fell swoop.

The new wholesale prices are supposed to give the economy only a rough but consistent set of approximations of average-cost prices, built up from existing labor-cost relations, existing depreciation allowances, and with a profit markup calculated according to a uniform rule: as a sum of a certain percentage on fixed capital stock and a smaller percentage on the labor cost. This is a price type which East European economists call the "double-channel price," although officially it has been presented as an approximation to the "production-price" formula. Even though it is open to serious theoretical criticism, the great advance it brings is to provide a consistent rule for price construction so that the resulting set of prices may be regarded and used as a coherent system. Only then will the forces of demand and supply be given free play and allowed to correct these calculated prices in the market place, pushing and nudging them toward equilibrium levels with the help of price agencies acting in the spirit of Oskar Lange's Central Planning Board. This feat of preparing a coherent set of prices via laboratory computation—a goal vainly striven for in all the previous price adjustments in the bloc countires—has been made possible by advanced mathematical methods of the input-output type. It is a measure of the path that Czechslovakia traversed within the past year or two to recall that the application of these methods was considered an economic "science fiction" as recently as 1963.

In theory, it is conceivable to make the passage from a command system to a market economy by letting only supply and demand directly determine the corresponding set of rational market prices. This might be practicable if the necessary price adjustments were small, as they were assumed to be in Lange's model, taking over after a well-functioning private capitalism. However, the distance of existing relative price levels from any set of prices calculated according to a consistent formula has been shown to be so enormous that a direct transition under the power of market forces alone would be bound to end in a chaotic crisscross of feedback sequences and with a degree of uncertainty, which it is hard to imagine a real market handling successfully. In this way, mathematics and computers are expected to do the worst part of the job for the market and thus to remove the greatest obstacle to reform. It was this question of price adjustment which, originally, made me doubt the very possibility of effective reforms.

3. Now for the paradox of great structural corrections having to take precedence over the new model. Under closer examination, this turns out to be a false issue. Actually, it is one of the last defensive positions to which

the routed adherents of the old system like to cling. It starts from the premise of a new large discontinuity being required in the allocation of investment resources. It proceeds to the second premise—"Large discontinuities have always been effected by central command." Conclusion: "Control command has to take care of them again." One of the fieriest critics of this strain of thought, Joseph Goldman, has convincingly disputed the need and advisability of a new investment cycle—"Big leaps belong in the gym" and argued that structural corrections require, first of all, correction in the structure of output from the existing capital stock and consolidation of its efficient use, rather than new massive infusion of investments—all of which presupposes economic signals and mechanisms obtainable only through the new market model. To paraphrase Samuelson's aphorism on the stock exchange—central planners cannot know more than the market would because they don't know anything. The only restructuring central planners may be capable of is the crude method of imitating the structural trends in Western advanced industrial economies, which can work only with a lag, without proper accounts of domestic resource endowment and without taking advantage of international specialization. For optimal changes in the macrostructure, in other words, the microstructure of prices and firm behavior, as anticipated in the new model, is a prerequisite.

4. Finally, there is the paradox of having to rely on old personnel, steeped in the old ways and methods, to implement the new. Observers of the changes under discussion—most of those in the West and many of the Czech ones—have had something to say about the constraints imposed upon the reforms by the human element: by the absence of the entrepreneurial talent and the sticky presence of the planner-bureaucrat, governmental bureaucrat, manager-bureaucrat. This way of reasoning is appealing because it seems so self-evident, but I wonder if it is not too facile. We may be committing an error analogous to the Stalinist attribution of undesirable behavior to the "remnants of capitalist thinking in people's heads," while the actual cause lay with contemporaneous institutions. What I am trying to suggest is that we may not know how much business talent, initiative, entrepreneurial creativity and general adaptability there is, as long as the institutional and legal framework isn't suitably changed.

It can be objected that it is the very institutional and legal framework of the new model which is being worked out by the central bureaucracy—a perfect case of the "goat appointed gardener." There is much to support this view. The "branch trust" organization of 1965 certainly is not designed to promote autonomy of enterprises, direct links between producers and customers, or expansion of the range of real alternatives in managerial decisions. It betrays the old striving for uniformity and comprehensiveness in organization, and it has already succeeded—e.g., by an effective territorial cartellization of trade—in thwarting some local initiative in buying and marketing. It is also known that the "dark forces" of the past are quietly sabotaging the spirit of reforms by slipping the leaders their own ideas "behind the back of the theoretical front" of the economists. Although these facts bode ill for a smooth and conflictless passage to the new model, it is possible that their significance may be reduced within the first years of its practice run. Schematically—the managerial strata may develop enough energy to become an effective counterweight to the now frightening power of "branch trusts" directorates; in time, central planners may learn—as they must—a new metier of econometric forecasting and generalized market research and lose the taste for operational interference with economic units; and the political leaders may remain sufficiently open-minded to listen to their consultant economists and trim the economic organization to the needs of a managed but competitive market economy. With respect to the "human element" as well, I would, therefore, discount this year as a source of decisive signs for predicting the future.

Czech economists like to make a clear distinction between the transitional reforms of the years 1966–67 and what they call the "target-" or "final-shape solution" (*cilove reseni*), which they tend to place in the early 'seventies. They have also consistently warned against great expectations of early results and steeled themselves and the public for retarding frictions and conflicts during the period of transition. This testifies to their acute awareness of social realities. It also gives the reforms their open-end character and stresses their learning-process aspects, both in their implementation and in theorizing about them. This is why—while keeping a certain amount of skepticism in reserve—I am inclined to believe in the ultimate success of the reforms as intended by the reformers.

The bitter irony which the reformers reserve for the dogmas of the past; the readiness to learn, to revise, to absorb Western thought; the liveliness and openness of polemics—this makes up the climate of the theoretical level and in current commentaries of the press. It seems, therefore, fair to give our criticism of weak points in the theories of reform a subordinate place. It is, for instance, rather disappointing to learn that the price reform stopped short of immediately abolishing the turnover tax. There was no extra work involved. It is perhaps understandable that fiscal authorities should have insisted on its preservation, but one had been led to expect a more than sporadic comprehension of the distorting effects of the tax in the pricing process, even after the reduction of its total volume and the introduction of a uniform rate. Since the distortion affects mainly the relative cost of labor, the tolerance of the turnover tax has probably something to do with the reluctance to treat wage rates as an integral part of the price system and to blur the boundary between the category "wage" and "share in the national dividend." Indeed, what amounts to the "share in the national dividend" (in A. Lerner's sense) is being used, in the reform scheme, as a source of incentives for management and employees alike.

Other weak spots concern the lack of theory behind the determination of the level of "capital charges," to be paid by firms from their "gross revenue," and the level of bank-credit interest rates, which again may be connected with the widespread resistance, even on the part of the most open minds, to marginalist thinking. However, an intensive study—and also independent rediscovery—of economic problems has been going on for several years now. The progress from Ota Sik's opening salvos, still heavy with a deposit of dogmatism, to the writings of economists who dominate the scene at present, is striking. There is a good chance they will discover their weak spots in due time themselves and adjust their advice to the political executive accordingly.

In the most general sense, the educational process implies a profound change in the concept of the economic sphere. Command systems deal with the social and economic universe as if it were a piece of physical machinery; ideally, they reduce the field of autonomous alternatives to zero; they coordinate activity of the system's components from the center, keeping them in a state of externality to each other. Upward flow of information concerns the execution of commands, not back talk. The new model preaches a concept of dialectical unity between plan and market. The market is to make rational planning possible, and a rational plan is to make the market efficient. This is a reversal, as systems' analysts might call it, from a formalist design to a heuristic design. In a heuristic model the system is operated by general rules, with a wide range of potential alternatives, with ample room for the uncertain and the unpredictable, coordination being assured by a hierarchy of feedbacks between relatively autonomous components and the center, and the interrelated components themselves. Presumably, such a qualitative reversal is bound to have political implications, which brings me to my concluding remarks.

Most economists writing on reform problems have preferred to keep to themselves what they might think of the political implications of the new model. Some, however, have boldly spoken of political democratization, of humanist planning, etc. The totalitarian concept of enforced social harmony has been flatly rejected by others. "We assume," say Ruchotnik and Kyn, analyzing the problem of social preference systems and politics, "that social interest can be derived from individual interests via a process of their continuous open confrontation." There is only a short step from this formulation of principle to working it out in terms of freedom of association, necessity of social conflict, right to strike, etc., as was done recently by Dr. Jovan Djorjevic, a leading Yugoslav lawyer. Such statements lead to a problem: How dependably does political pluralism follow from a market-dominated economic model?

It seems to me not inconceivable that the totalitarian regime may be able to absorb the changes in the economic model without altering the essential features of political controls.

As far as freedom of expression is concerned, the experiences to date show that it is *not* indivisible. The totalitarian state is able to relax its prohibitions in some areas and for some people—those whose brains it needs —while keeping them in force elsewhere. Even in China the latest "cultural revolution" appears to have stopped at the doorsteps of scientists. Official policies symbolized by the names Sinyavski and Daniel, Havemann and Mikhailov have been entirely compatible with freed economic discussion and economic reforms (if they were not, indeed, their logical accompaniment). Also, the discussion of economics may be suppressed once the new principles are irreversibly adopted. What seems an authentic product of free speech in the mid-sixties may petrify into a new dogma later. The possibility of such a process can already be discerned in the divorce between the new vocabulary and facts. Thus, even though economists may be playing a role similar to that of republican lawyers in the French Ancien Regime, they are in no position to turn political potentialities into reality. They need their "peuple de Paris."

As far as freedom of association and of social action is concerned, the new economic model need not shake the political essentials either. Consumer sovereignty on consumers' goods market, better assortment and per capita consumption of products may strengthen the loyalty of workers and citizens to the regime (see Germany in the late 'thirties or Peronist Argentina). It is possible to make the population richer, yet not more free. The regime may strike a new balance in the combination of areas under the rule of contractual law, and others under the rule of command.

However, the transition to the new model does necessarily bring with it shifts in the relative position of social groups, instruments of control, and in the relative importance of the rule of law compared to the arbitrariness of police methods—as Leonard Shapiro so gently explained in his open letter to Premier Kosygin. And it is the shock of these shifts which may bring into motion a new social dynamics transcending the totalitarian setup. In one word, too much depends on too many noneconomic variables, of which we know very little as yet, to permit dependable political predictions. Still, from the point of view of democratic values, there is definitely reason for guarded optimism and hope—none of them, however, a respectable scientific category.

MARKET SOCIALISM: THE CASE OF CZECHOSLOVAKIA*

Jan M. Michal†

I. A Perspective

Market socialism has become an accepted economic term ever since the late Oskar Lange published *The Economic Theory of Socialism* in the thirties. However, Lange's "economic theory of socialism" has remained a mere blueprint. The Communist countries, after nationalizing a vast majority of the means of production, resorted to a quite different economic system, under which most of the market functions were replaced by central command authorizing what to produce and how to produce it. Consistency between the centrally fixed pattern of output and "administratively determined" pattern of demand was supposed to be secured by a system of material balances in physical or gross value terms. Needless to say, such balancing between output and use in a mere technological sense has created severe economic disequilibria. When some of the Communist countries decided to reintroduce the market functions to a significant extent, they had to start from these disequilibria. This, together with some important ideological and institutional obstacles, may help to explain the difficulties of transition as well as the substantial differences of the actual "market socialism" systems of today from the prewar Lange model.

Yugoslavia was the first Communist country to make widespread use of the markets as an alternative to detailed central command. From the purely economic point of view, it is rather surprising. Yugoslavia is one of the least developed Communist countries in Europe. Many economists would argue that at a low stage of development there is a case for deliberate deviation from partial market equilibria in order to speed up "unbalanced" growth, to realize important external economies, and also to create a more acceptable distributive justice. Furthermore, the task of the planners to coordinate the outputs and inputs centrally is less formidable if the country still has a relatively simple pattern of production and consumption.

The switch in Yugoslavia's economic system in the early fifties was caused mainly by a change in the socio-political set-up after Tito had broken off with the Stalinist Communism. The recent economic reforms in Central and Eastern Europe had been primarily induced by *economic* considerations. In the sixties, Czechoslovakia, East Germany, Hungary, and Bulgaria have gravitated towards "market socialism" more than the other COMECON countries. The first three of these countries are highly industrial areas with diversified output and consumption, and all four of these

*All footnotes deleted.

†Dr. Jan M. Michal is Associate Professor of Economics, State University of New York at Binghamton. His publications include: *Postwar Economic Systems* (1946) and *Central Planning in Czechoslovakia* (1961).

countries depend heavily on foreign trade. Obviously, the tendency to discard a substantial part of central command in favor of "planning by economic means" has been a function of the level of industrialization, on the one hand, and of the dependence of foreign trade, on the other. This is in line with economic analysis. In a highly industrial country which produces approximately one and a half million different kinds of products, with further millions of specifications by size, technical properties, etc., it is extremely difficult for the planners to secure a reasonable consistency between output and use. As a result, large unsaleable inventories of some products accumulate, while chronic shortages of many other products exist. In addition to this visible waste of resources other serious misallocations occur. Goods are being produced which are less desirable under a given set of preferences and a given distribution of income, whereas the production of most desirable goods is being neglected. In the domestic economy, this "invisible" waste of resources is concealed behind the lack of selection, artificial pricing, and inflation. Final consumers buy low-quality, undesirable products simply because they have no better use for their money incomes. Intermediate consumers buy inefficient inputs because of their artificially low price. For instance, under the old system, fixed capital was provided virtually free of charge to the socialized enterprises. In the foreign trade sector, the situation is different. Even the planned economies have to face the world market preferences and prices. The inability of the central planners to produce at low cost and to adjust flexibly the pattern of output to the pattern of demand for exports resulted in painful losses in foreign trade.

These basic weaknesses in central planning seem to have caused most serious economic troubles, and have been most candidly acknowledged, in Czechoslovakia. This may be the reason why the Czechoslovak economic reforms are most penetrating. Furthermore, they have not been presented piecemeal, but as a rather comprehensive "New Economic Model." After some hesitation, the new system began to be put into practice on a limited scale in 1966, and has been generally applied as of January 1967. The substitution of the markets for central command is now at fuller swing in Czechoslovakia than in other COMECON countries. And yet, the Czechoslovak economy remains very "socialist": a greater portion of the means of production remains nationalized or collectivized than, for instance, in East Germany; private enterprise in Czechoslovakia is still rather negligible in comparison to Yugoslavia. For all these reasons, Czechoslovakia lends itself very well for a case study of "market socialism."

II. Czechoslovakia's "New Economic Model"

My discussion of the new economic system in Czechoslovakia will rely in principle on "The Basic Ordinance Concerning the Planned Management of National Economy" of December 1966. This law, which was enforced as of January 1, 1967, regulates the operation of the State-owned enterprises in industry, construction, and domestic and foreign trade; and it regulates the economic activities of local governments (the so-called National Committees). The application of the market system in agriculture, banking, and other sectors has been, or will be, determined by additional laws. However, the Basic Ordinance is sufficiently illuminating as to the nature of the new economic system.

The main characteristic of the new system is the decentralization of most economic decisions concerning production and consumption. The number of commodities, the production of which is being determined by central planners in physical units or in gross value terms, has been reduced from approximately 2,000 under the old system to 12 under the new system. The Basic Ordiance emphasizes that even these production tasks will be eliminated later if "the enterprises behave in a normal way" (probably, if they do not misuse their monopolistic or monopsonistic power). In the future, the central directives should be limited to some research tasks, to investments financed from the State budget, to the economic development of backward regions, and to defense. Otherwise, the production decisions would be up to the managers and to the trusts of the socialist enterprises. The managers would also decide what input mix to use, but there would be certain "limits." These direct controls of intermediate consumption will apply, for instance, to the inputs subsidized by the Government, and to some basic commodities, such as wood, etc. In addition, individual Government departments (ministries) and local Governments may impose extraordinary production tasks and additional limits on the use of commodities; however, if the enterprises can prove that this has caused them financial losses, they can claim damage.

In principle, the socialist managers will have a substantial freedom to decide what and to whom to sell, and what and from whom to buy, in response to financial incentives. However, these incentives differ somewhat from those in a private enterprise market economy.

The first important difference is the substitution of the concept of "gross income" for an explicit profit motive. "Gross income" is actually a misnomer. It is not a gross revenue. It is defined as the gross money revenue from all sales by the enterprise *after* (a) deducting the cost of materials and services supplied by other enterprises, (b) deducting the turnover tax on products, (c) deducting the proceeds of the resales, if any, of previously purchased raw materials or of fixed capital assets, (d) after adjustment for the change in inventories of products, (e) after deducting the contributions to the trusts of enterprises (the so-called "odborová ředitelství"), (f) after adding (price) subsidies from the State budget.

Except for (e) and (f) the gross income would resemble the Western concept of value added. But the price subsidies are still very important in

Czechoslovakia. In 1967 they are expected to amount to as much as 1/5 of the anticipated aggregate "gross income." As long as this is so, gross income cannot be really compared to value added.

The enterprise has to pay a complex set of charges (the so-called "odvody") on its gross income. In industry and construction the charges are as follows:

1. *"Basic funds" charge.* This is actually a charge on fixed capital. It is an important innovation in the Czechoslovak socialist economy. Hitherto a great part of the fixed capital was provided free by the State.

2. *Charge on inventories.*

3. *Amortization charge.* This is a temporary payment of depreciation charges to the State so that the enterprises that in the past obtained large amounts of free fixed capital do not have an undue cost advantage over enterprises which are at present enlarging and paying for their fixed capital stock.

4. *Charge on "land taken away from agricultural use."* This is obviously a substitute for rent.

5. *The so-called "stabilization charge."* This is a combination of a tax on the wage bill and a very heavy extra tax on the increase in labor employment. It is perhaps the most curious and most distorting construct among all the charges on gross income, and I shall discuss it in some detail.

6. *The charge on "gross income."* This is also a misnomer, for the charge is not paid on total gross income, but only on a residual after deduction of the charges on fixed capital, inventories, and some other contributions. It is basically a combination of a tax on net revenue and an additional tax on the wage bill. The rate is flat—18%. The non-progressibility of this tax safeguards the incentive of the sum of the net revenue of the enterprise and the wage bill. The central authorities seem to have some doubts about the economic effects of the "gross income" charge. They have reserved for themselves the right to replace it by a 32 per cent tax on profit plus a 15 per cent tax on the "workers fund" as described below.

After having paid all the charges and obligations, the enterprise can allocate the residual of "gross income" to its funds: the reserve fund, the fund for cultural and social projects, the investment fund, and especially the "workers fund." It is out of this last-mentioned fund that premiums are paid to management and workers if the allocation to the fund exceeds the total of fixed-rate wages.

One would expect enterprises operating under the new economic system to tend to maximize the workers fund; if the managers had a sufficiently long time horizon, they would, of course, try to strike a balance between allocations to the workers fund and to the investment and reserve funds. The authors of the model seem to suspect (and probably with right) that the managers would be mostly interested in very short-term profits and short-term bonuses. Therefore, a special directive has been issued forcing the enterprise to make some minimum allocations to the reserve and the investment funds.

One can ask why the Czechoslovak model uses the concept of gross income and the various "charges" instead of relying on profit-maximizing, with profit-sharing for the workers. A part of the answer may lie in an ideological distaste for the term "profit." Economically speaking, the explanation can probably be found in the official description of the various charges as "economic instruments of planning." The discriminatory rates of charges are supposed to be the necessary tools for planners to influence the market process. The authors of the model probably did not realize that they can enforce their preferences through other means, such as other taxes, selective monetary controls, etc.

If the charges on capital, land, and labor were of a parametric, non-progressive nature, and if they brought the cost of the factors approximately to the clearing levels, the concept of the "gross income," combined with the "charges," would not in itself put the socialist enterprise in a position dramatically different from that of a non-monopsonistic, profit-maximizing firm in any market economy. But the charges are discriminatory in an economically dubious way. Above all, the "stabilization charge" is progressive and creates a discontinuous supply function of labor.

This can be demonstrated easily in a diagram (see Figure 1) if we accept some simplifications—which, however, do not change the basic argument. We shall assume that the average wage and the number of work hours per capita are constant so that we can plot on the horizontal axis the number of workers, and the wage bill (they move in a parallel direction). On the vertical axis we shall measure the marginal revenue product of labor (MRP), and the marginal wage cost per capita after the stabilization charge (MFC), both in monetary units (Czechoslovak korunas—abbreviation Kčs). The downward-sloping part of the MRP curve constitutes the short-run demand curve for labor for a profit-maximizing competitive firm.

Suppose this is approximately true also for the two socialist enterprises in Czechoslovakia under the new market system which we will compare. We shall assume that they employ homogeneous labor (inasmuch as this homogeneity assumption could hold for two industries, our analysis could also be applied to the problems of allocation of labor between two small, non-monopsonistic industries). We shall also assume that both enterprises can hire any number of workers within the relevant range of output at a given basic wage rate so that the supply curve of labor (MFC_L curve) *before* the incidence of the stabilization charge can be represented as a horizontal line. The basic wage rate is, however, below macro-equilibrium, so that there is a tendency towards aggregate overemployment. Finally, we shall assume that both enterprises face an identical MRP_L curve.

FIGURE 1

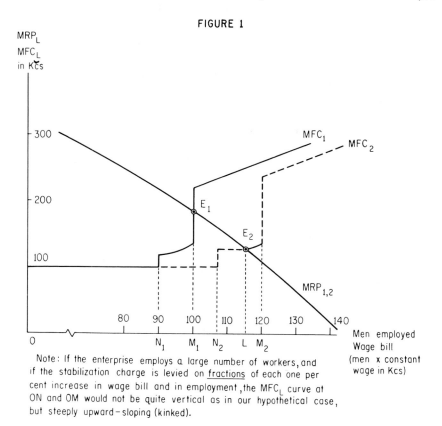

Note: If the enterprise employs a large number of workers, and if the stabilization charge is levied on <u>fractions</u> of each one per cent increase in wage bill and in employment, the MFC$_L$ curve at ON and OM would not be quite vertical as in our hypothetical case, but steeply upward-sloping (kinked).

Yet, there is one important difference between the two: Enterprise No. 1 operated last year at a much lower level of employment than enterprise No. 2. Assuming the identical MRP curve, this was, naturally, a disequilibrium situation on the micro-level. Enterprise No. 1 was, other things being equal, more profitable than enterprise No. 2 because of the higher revenue product per unit of labor (the return on capital was not important under the old central planning from the point of view of the enterprise because most of the fixed capital was provided by the Government free of charge). There was, in fact, a wide spread in profitability between industries (and probably even a greater spread between individual enterprises) under the old system in Czechoslovakia. Therefore, the assumption of an initial great difference in MRP of labor between two enterprises is quite realistic. One of the goals of the new market system is simply to correct past severe misallocations of labor—and of other economic resources.

Let us examine whether, and to what extent, the stabilization charge may defeat this goal.

The stabilization charge consists of two parts:

1. It includes a *tax on the wage bill in excess* of "nine-tenths of the average wage of last year, times the number of currently employed workers." Under our assumption of a constant average wage, the incidence of this tax begins simply at nine-tenths of last year's employment. Its basic rate is 30 per cent of the amount exceeding nine-tenths of last year's wage bill, but for every one per cent decrease in employment in comparison with last year, the rate is reduced by 0.3 per cent. Thus, the incidence is 27 per cent of the "excess" wage bill if employment is reduced by one-tenth, and increases to 30 per cent of the "excess" bill at and beyond the employment level of last year.

2. The stabilization charge also includes a *tax on increase in employment* over the last year. The rate is 1 per cent of the *total* wage bill for every one per cent increase in employment.

The result of the whole stabilization charge is a sudden jump in the marginal cost of labor as seen by the charge-paying enterprise when the wage bill reaches nine-tenths of last year's level, and another jump when employment reaches the level of last year. This is represented in our diagram (see Figure 1) by the vertical portions of the MFC_L curves at ON_1, ON_2, and again at OM_1, OM_2. Our two enterprises face two different MFC_L curves only because their employment levels were different last year. If they tend to maximize net revenue, enterprise No. 1 should employ OM of workers, and enterprise No. 2, OL of workers. Consequently, in our diagram, the marginal revenue product of labor in enterprise No. 1, M_1E_1, would still be much higher than MRP_L in enterprise No. 2, LE_2. The misallocation of labor has not been sufficiently corrected. It would be possible to increase the total output without any increase in the new (slightly reduced) aggregate employment by transferring labor from enterprise No. 2 to enterprise No. 1. The stabilization charge which discriminates against employment-expanding in favor of employment-contracting industries prevents such an efficient allocation of labor.

The discontinuous character of the MFC function, due to the rates of the two taxes which constitute the "stabilization charge," can cause much economic harm. For instance, suppose that foreign demand for, and the export price of, the product of enterprise (industry) No. 1 goes up. (I have chosen this example because an increase in domestic demand may not be easily translated into a higher domestic price in view of the rather inflexible system of domestic prices as we will discuss). The MRP_1 would go up relative to MRP_2. It would be to the benefit of the national economy to increase the output and exports of product 1 relative to product 2. An undistorted market mechanism would normally respond in this direction. But a Czechoslovak socialist enterprise (whether the producing unit or the export company) may not respond at all to increasing (or falling) demand if the new MRP curve still intersects the MFC curve within its vertical portion.

What could possibly be the reasons for such a distorting tax?

As the name suggests, the authors of the "stabilization charge" probably wanted to counteract the existing tendencies toward aggregate over-employment and the inflationary pressures resulting from over-employment and from wage increases. The danger of inflation is, in fact, very great in Czechoslovakia, as I shall argue when discussing the transitional difficulties of the new system. However, if the purpose of the stabilization charge is to reduce aggregate employment in order to combat inflation, this can be achieved without severe infringement on allocational efficiency by a high *flat* tax on wage bill which would shift up the labor (MFC) curve without discontinuities, rather than by the present clumsy construct.

It is interesting to note that, according to the first reports on the operation of the new system in the first half of 1967, the aggregate over-employment has not been noticeably reduced (although it has become more difficult for old people, especially women, to find employment in certain areas), and in several industrial sectors wage bills have continued to rise faster than productivity of labor. One of the possible explanations of the ineffectiveness of the stabilization charge may be the economically irrational behavior of some socialist managers. They may not realize that, in order to maximize net revenue (and thus the allocations to "funds"), they should equate MRP to MFC, or they may not dare to reduce inefficient employment in line with this rule. Another possible explanation is that the new, higher wholesale prices, as we will discuss, may have shifted the MRP_L curves in some enterprises so high that they intersect the MFC_L curves at a level of employment above that of 1966. If this is so, the stabilization charge, while obstructing improvements in allocational efficiency on the micro level, fails to achieve even its basic anti-inflationary goal.

In contrast to the "stabilization charge," the charges on capital are non-progressive, but discriminatory. The basic funds (fixed capital) charge in industry is usually 6%; in trade, 3%; and there is no charge on fixed assets for the purification of water or air or for the safeguarding of the health of workers. This charge should not be confused with the capital charge in the Western sense. In addition to the "basic funds charge," the enterprise also has to pay interest on bank loans, usually 6%. Thus, the cost of bank-financed fixed capital is 12%. The basic charge on inventories is only 2%; but again one has to add interest on bank loans, or "opportunity cost" in case of self-financing by the enterprise, to obtain the actual cost of working capital.

Aside from the concept of "gross income" and the various charges, the new Czechoslovak system differs from a typical market economy also in its system of prices. Usually, flexible prices are supposed to serve as signals between producers and consumers. Originally, price flexibility was referred to as the "ultimate target" in Czechoslovakia, too. Recent official statements indicate that most prices will continue to be centrally determined and inflexible for a long period of time. Is it possible for any market economy to operate in the framework of a rather rigid price system? Some economists who analyzed the new Czechoslovak system consider the inflexibility of prices to be its important weakness. However, it is to be borne in mind that even in a Western private-enterprise market economy many important prices are far from freely fluctuating. In large-scale oligopolistic industries such as steel, automobiles, some chemicals, etc., administered prices are usually revised only after a long period of time. Most wages are subject to tariff agreements, and special "prices" such as the rate of interest, or the exchange rate, are subject to control by Government agencies. Even in the framework of non-flexible prices there is some room for bringing the pattern of output closer to pattern of intermediate and final demand. Instead of price changes, the shrinking inventories of goods facing a rising demand, and the accumulating inventories of less demanded goods, may signal the changing preferences of the buyers to the producers. On the other hand, there is no perfect or even imperfect, substitute for price flexibility to send signals from the producers to the users about changing cost conditions. (This kind of "signal" can easily be misused for monopolistic price increases.) What seems to me to be an even more important requirement than the "right degree" of price flexibility is the initial set of mutually consistent prices which would not deviate explosively from the pattern of relative cost and from the pattern of acceptable preferences. I shall discuss this problem in the next section.

The new Czechoslovak system differs also in many other ways from Western market economies. Instead of discussing these other important differences, such as the activities of State-owned banks, the operations of State monopolies for exports and imports, and the manner of appointing the socialist managers, it seems to be useful to devote a part of the limited space of this article to some prerequisites for the new system to be viable.

III. Some Necessary Conditions for the New System

Initial Price Reform. The most basic prerequisite for operation of the socialist markets is the initial price reform. During the 18 years of central planning in Czechoslovakia relative prices have been fixed largely without regard to relative cost and, on the wholesale level, almost completely disregarding the pattern of demand for consumer goods. Retail prices of consumer goods were supposed to be brought to clearing levels by excise taxes, the so-called turn-over tax, with rates varying from zero per cent to 892 per cent of the wholesale price. I shall not attempt to inquire into the failure of even this extremely discriminatory turnover tax in securing partial equilibria in the consumer goods markets, but shall concentrate on the main obstacle to the new allocational system: the irrational structure of whole-sale prices applied to transactions between socialist enterprises. Prices of material inputs and outputs have been fixed in such an inconsistent way that some enterprises, although efficient from the viewpoint of preferences of the planners, suffered continuous losses and had to be subsidized, where-as some inefficient enterprises easily realized relatively large profits. The wholesale price reform of 1964 has been reported to have reduced the spread of profit as per cent of total "cost" from +27.8 per cent to −11.7 per cent, to +6 per cent to −0.9 per cent. However, the "cost" under the old definition excluded the cost of fixed capital. If one allows for the capital cost, and the varying intensity of capital inputs, the profitability of most enterprises in Czechoslovakia under the 1964 wholesale prices would probably be negative, and the differences in profitability very substantial.

The price reform which was enforced, together with the new economic system, on January 1, 1967 had to fulfil two objectives: to raise the whole-sale price *level* sufficiently to leave the enterprises with a positive net revenue (after the payment of all "charges") as a sufficient inducement to produce; and to bring the *structure* of wholesale prices more in line with the structure of cost and with the pattern of (still regulated) demand. The market could not take care of such a tremendous restructuring of whole-sale prices. Quoting Professor Holesovsky:

> The distance of existing relative price levels from any set of prices calculated according to a consistent formula has been shown to be so enor-mous that a direct transition under the power of market forces alone would be bound to end in a chaotic crisscross of feedback sequences with a degree of uncertainty which it is hard to imagine a real market han-dling successfully.

For several years, the problem of how to calculate the initial consistent set of relative wholesale prices was debated in Czechoslovakia. Some economists argued in favor of determining a consistent price structure with the help of mathematical methods and input-output analysis. Others argued that the technical coefficients reflect the undesirable technical re-tardation under the old central planning and the past misallocations. Furthermore, the size of input-output tables was probably considered in-sufficient to solve the interlocking prices of many hundreds of thousands of products. The Czechoslovak Government announced in September 1966 that the initial price structure "will be calculated on the basis of indices of 25 thousand world market prices." What these indices really indicate are not relative "world prices," but the prices of groups of products as realized in actual Czechoslovak exports and imports, after adjustment for transportation costs and tariffs, and after discounting the differences in payments.

It is not quite clear whether the price reform of January 1967 was really based on the imitation of foreign trade prices, or on the domestic cost calculations, or a combination of the two. Recent references to "25 thousand group prices" leads me to believe that, in principle, the Government decision to imitate the foreign trade price structure has been carried out. In a big country, or in any country with highly specialized exports and imports of only a few kinds of commodities, an imposition of foreign prices on the domestic economy would be a situation in which the tail wags the dog. In a small country which depends heavily on very diversified exports and imports, the proposition is not quite so nonsensical. However, the necessary conditions for the relative foreign trade prices to approximate partial equilibria in domestic markets are: a free foreign trade, and a very high price elasticity of demand for both exports and imports. Under these assumptions, surpluses and shortages in domestic markets could be taken care of by exports and imports without leading to disruptive price swings. But these conditions are far from existing in Czechoslovakia today: a great part of her exports are differentiated products which face a price-inelastic demand, and free trade is not yet in sight.

Before it has been possible to make a market test of how far the new relative wholesale prices remained from partial domestic equilibria, the central price control, instead of being relaxed, has been strengthened. It has been argued that the restructuring of wholesale prices through 25,000 indices had not been detailed enough. Around each of the 25,000 prices of groups of commodities, the old price relations for individual products continue to exist. According to Vladislav Knobloch, as long as a more detailed price reform is still pending, it is impossible to free the prices on the wholesale level. This also is the reason, according to Knobloch, why the retail prices have not yet been reformed in such manner as to somewhat equalize the incidence of turn-over tax on various consumer goods. With the turn-over tax still so extremely uneven, the consumer demand has only little impact on the pattern of output, and the new system is, of course, far from being optimal from the consumers' point of view.

The average level of wholesale prices has been raised by 25 per cent, but even this substantial increase (with the inadequate restructuring of prices) has not been sufficient to avoid the necessity of very sizeable price subsidies under the new system. The problem of pricing is still far from being solved. The Czechoslovak experience of the difficult transition to socialist markets shows how intractable the correction of the price structure may become once the pattern of prices has been allowed to deviate tremendously from the pattern of cost and of demand.

Avoidance of Severe Inflationary Pressures. The second necessary condition for an acceptable operation of socialist markets is the avoidance of severe inflationary pressures on the macro-level. Even this is not easy to achieve in view of the present over-employment, of the excess of purchasing power (suppressed inflation), and of the probably large size of income multiplier due to a probably low marginal propensity to save. The propensity to save has been undermined by two post-war currency reforms which confiscated a large part of personal savings.

Caution Against Harmful Monopolistic Powers. The third necessary condition is to prevent potentially strong monopolistic powers from being exercised in a harmful manner. The organization of industries, with associations (výrobní hospodářské jednotky) and trusts (odborová ředitelství) of enterprises, creates quasi-monopolies. It remains to be seen whether these associations and trusts will encourage the enterprises to stand on their own feet, or whether they will become vehicles for monopolistic collusion. The possibility of exposing domestic producers to competition from imports has also been much discussed in Czechoslovakia. But the possibility of an efficient foreign competition is limited because of Czechoslovakia's balance-of-payments difficulties in relation to the developed Western countries. A hard-currency foreign loan would enhance the prospects to overcome this and other difficulties of transition, but such a loan can hardly be expected under the present political circumstances. The exercise of strong monopolistic powers could become a further obstacle on the way to a more flexible price system. But even in the framework of essentially rigid prices, such power could have harmful effects (for instance lower quality of products for which the consumers could not find an alternative source of supply).

A severe constraint on the operation of market forces in Czechoslovakia are the heavy long-term export commitments to the USSR and other COMECON countries. It may be rather difficult to bring compulsory export (and some import) targets in physical terms in line with the decentralized decisions of the producers and of the export-import companies, based on financial incentives.

Cooperation. The cooperation of the human element is, of course, also a fundamental presupposition of success of "market socialism." The behavior of socialist managers will be of special importance. Some of the old managers may be so used to obey orders, and so ignorant about the operation of the markets, that they cannot be expected to behave rationally under the new system. It may take some time before a new generation of managers takes over. The workers and the consumers, too, may have to learn how to live with greater freedom and greater risk in a market economy.

Decentralization of Economic Power. Last but not least, a market economy presupposes a genuine decentralization of economic power. It remains to be seen whether the Communist Party, the Communist Government and the central planners will be ready to accept a sufficient degree of such decentralization.

IV. What Kind of Economic Success?

If, despite some theoretical weaknesses of the new model, despite the great transitional difficulties, and despite the possible political opposition and sabotage, the new economic system in Czechoslovakia proves to be operational, what kind of economic success is it likely to achieve?

Since actual sales, rather than fulfilment of gross production targets, will now be important for realizing the premium, the enterprises will be induced to slash the output of rejects and of unsaleable low-quality products, and to adjust the pattern of production to demand, however distorted. In the sector of domestic intermediate consumption the number of bottlenecks will probably go down. The pattern of that portion of national product which will be earmarked on the macro-level for domestic final consumption will probably be more in line with consumers' choices (still subject to distortions through turn-over tax). In the export industries, the pattern of output will also probably be more flexibly adjusted to the changing pattern of foreign demand because of the new economic link between the funds-maximizing domestic producers and the funds-maximizing foreign trade companies. This will tend to improve Czechoslovakia's terms of trade, especially in relation to the market economies.

Beside optimum sales, the cost economy is another side of the tendency of the enterprises to maximize the workers' fund within given constraints. This will probably lead the enterprises to make the input mix more efficient and to apply modern technology, unless they can prosper financially in the shelter of their monopolistic power without really trying.

The relatively greatest improvement of allocational efficiency through the market forces can be expected in the static sense. Special measures would probably be necessary to enhance very long-term projects and external economies, and to prevent external diseconomies. But an improved static efficiency is, at the present stage, the most important prerequisite to sustain economic growth in Czechoslovakia. The relatively rapid growth in the 'fifties has been engineered by a reckless mobilization of resources. In Professor Šik's terminology, it was an "extensive" growth. Once the bearable limit of the mobilization of labor and of the investment rate has been reached, the main hope of maintaining a reasonably high rate of growth lies in increased productivity of capital and labor. In fact, the acid test of the new system will be whether or not it can secure lower incremental capital-output and labor-output ratios. During the great change of economic structure in the transitional period, the rate of growth may, of course, slow temporarily down, and the incremental K/O ratio and possibly also the incremental L/O ratio may temporarily go up. It will be necessary to wait for several years before one can attempt to assess the growth performance of the new market socialism in Czechoslovakia.

The new system will naturally also have its drawbacks—for instance, a possibly serious frictional and technological unemployment, especially during the transitional period; and a tendency towards price increases. Yet, the potential economic advantages seem to outweigh the possible disadvantages. *Market socialism* in Czechoslovakia is a very interesting economic experiment to watch.

THE CZECHOSLOVAK ECONOMIC REFORMS IN
PERSPECTIVE
— · — · — · — · — · — · — · — · — · — · — · —

John M. Montias†

The economic reforms promulgated in Czechoslovakia in 1966 and 1967 were shaped by the apparent failure of the experiment in economic decentralization initiated in 1958–1959 and by the unprecedented deterioration in the performance of the Czechoslovak economy that set in after 1961.

Two basic disequilibria precipitated the crisis that led to the slowdown in growth of the first half of the 1960's: 1) an increasingly severe balance of payments problem, and 2) an inability to reconcile the total volume of investment outlays with the capacity of the construction sector and of the machine-building industry. The roots of the external difficulties, as we shall see presently, can be traced to the Party's development strategy in the decade following the Communist takeover of 1948; the internal disequilibrium resulted from a flagrant overcommitment of resources in the Third Five-year Plan, which was scheduled to last from 1961 to 1965 but which had to be abandoned as early as mid-1962. The collectivization of agriculture and the decentralization of the economy that was attempted from 1959 to 1961 aggravated the structural maladjustments to which the economy was already subject.

The strategic decisions adopted by the Party between 1948 and 1951 reoriented Czechoslovak industry away from its traditional concentration on consumer-goods industries in order to create an 'arsenal' for the develop-

†Dr. John M. Montias is Professor of Economics and Director of Graduate Studies in Economics, Yale University. Publications include: *Institutional Changes in the Postwar Economy of Poland*, with W. T. Stankiewicz (1951), *Central Planning in Poland* (1962), *Economic Development of Communist Rumania* (in print).

ment needs of the Socialist bloc, particularly of its less developed members. Heavy industry was also assigned the task of delivering a substantial portion of the military hardware required by the less industrialized economies, especially during the Korean War.

The overwhelming concentration of development efforts on heavy industry and the reorientation of Czechoslovak foreign trade toward the Communist bloc where the demand for consumer goods was relatively restricted led to a drastic change in the structure of Czechoslovak exports. From 37 percent of total exports in 1937, the share of consumer goods dropped to 12.2 percent in 1953. Exports of textiles, leather goods, and paper products accounted for a much smaller share of output than before World War II. Starved of investment funds, light industry fell behind in the international competitive struggle for lower costs and more attractive designs. Many of its skilled workers were drawn into better paid occupations in heavy industry. For many years the lack of contact with customers in the West prevented designers from keeping up with the latest trends and fashions; in the meantime, Belgian, Scandinavian and even Japanese firms producing porcelain, glassware and other traditional Czechoslovak exports, pushed ahead, thanks to their more imaginative and up-to-date designs, more reliable delivery schedules, and generally superior quality.

The first crisis in Czechoslovakia's foreign trade occurred after Stalin's death when the New Course inaugurated in each of the East European economies and the sudden termination of the Korean War created conditions unfavorable to Czechoslovak heavy industrial exports. A Czech economist complained soon afterwards that, "as a result of the lack of coordination of post-1953 policies, the Czechoslovak economy, which had been built up as the machine works of the socialist camp, suddenly found itself faced by the curtailment of its market."[1] Starting in 1955, COMECON, which was supposed to promote specialization in the bloc, disappointed Czechoslovakia's hopes: the less developed countries kept on expanding their own machine-building industries, often in parallel with existing capacities in the more developed economies. But even among such market opportunities as remained open to her, Czechoslovakia's formerly dominant position as a purveyor of machinery and armaments to the communist states was never restored. In recent years she has lost a good deal of ground to competition within the bloc, chiefly on the part of East Germany, but also to competition from western Europe. The deterioration in Czechoslovakia's competitive position may be attributed partly to shortcomings in the *model,* which failed to generate sufficient technical progress to meet the requirements of foreign customers for modern highly productive equipment, and partly to the hand-to-mouth existence she had to lead

---

[1] *Politická ekonomie*, No. 4, 1956, p. 241.

to pay for her imported raw materials and foodstuffs. This harsh constraint caused her to export an excessive share of her best machinery output, to the detriment of her domestic replacement needs, as a result of which her equipment, particularly in light industry, became increasingly obsolete. Balance of payments problems also prevented her from improving the quality of some of her products by importing the necessary ingredients.

The delicately poised equilibrium of the Czechoslovak balance of payments was seriously upset, from 1959 on, by a number of factors. The imported food bill went up unexpectedly when domestic farm production fell short of target, due to a combination of poor weather and inefficient management of the collectivized and state farms that now occupy over 90 percent of the country's arable area. Gross agricultural output rose by 2 percent in 1960, stayed at the previous year's level in 1961, then fell by 6 percent in 1962—compared to the 4.4 percent average yearly growth envisaged in the Third Five-year Plan. Secondly, trade with China unexpectedly collapsed, leaving the Czechs with cancelled orders on hand, some of them for equipment tailored to specifications that could not be marketed elsewhere. In 1961 alone, exports to China fell from $110 million to $34 million, that is from 5.7 to 1.7 percent of Czech exports.[2] To replace the cancelled deliveries of raw materials and foodstuffs that were slated to come from China, Czechoslovakia had to expend $56 million in 1961 alone on "capitalist markets." Only a fraction of the specialized machinery and equipment ordered by China, found an outlet in other foreign markets. Some of it could not even be used in Czechoslovakia and had to be scrapped. This was the case, for instance, for certain types of hydraulic equipment designed according to Chinese specifications.[3]

Finally, the balance of payments has been burdened with large credits to underdeveloped countries and to Cuba, some of which it appears, were not repaid on time. The Third Five-year Plan called for a doubling of trade with this group of countries, whose share of trade with the capitalist world was scheduled to rise to 43 percent. From 1953 to 1961, Czechoslovakia extended trade and investment credits to countries of Africa, Asia, and Latin America amounting to at least $330 million. This figure probably understates the real amount, since, these loans being unpopular, the Party is reluctant to reveal their full extent.

The combined effect of these adverse elements on the balance of payments was to turn a surplus on trade account with capitalist countries of $50 to $60 million a year, which normally served to settle Czechoslovakia's expenditures for transportation and other charges in the West, into a deficit of about $20 million. In the meantime, Czechoslovakia's noncon-

[2]*Statistická ročenka CSSR 1962,* p. 353.
[3]*Statistická ročenka CSSR 1962,* p. 353; *Fakty-Argumenty,* No. 16, (1963), p. 16; and interview material.

vertible surplus with the Communist bloc, including China, declined from about $100 million to less than $50 million in 1961. The combined surplus with both blocs of countries was raised substantially in 1962 (to about $200 million), but this was achieved at the cost of reducing essential imports and forcing exports of machinery and equipment to the detriment of domestic needs. As a result, many plants had to operate below capacity for lack of imported raw materials. A rough estimate made at the end of 1962 was that about one-fourth of the capacity of the machine-building industry was unutilized because of the "lack of harmony between capacity and the production programme."[4] On the export side, 'there were periods during which foreign trade took away practically the entire production [of an industry] and exported it, without conception or design, in order to ease the trade balance.'[5] Not only machines were pre-empted for export but also consumer goods for which there was a strong demand on the domestic market; this led to an increasing disparity between the kind of consumer goods offered for retail sale and the structure of consumers' preferences, reflected in the appearance of queues outside shops selling goods in demand, while other, less desirable goods, accumulated as surplus inventories.[6]

The improvisations of these crisis years, the frantic endeavors to "salvage the plans," the indiscriminate measures to redress the balance of payments—all would seem to testify to the shoddy design and construction of the Third Five-year Plan. Yet there is evidence that the technicians who drew it up put more time and effort into the job, and were more systematic in searching for internally consistent solutions, than at the time the First- and Second-year Plans had been hastily pasted together. The institutional reforms that were the indispensable accompaniment of the new plan were more radical than anything that had been tried hitherto. Nevertheless, most of this zeal was in vain because the plan was drafted under intolerable constraints. The ratio of investments to national income—the so-called "rate of accumulation"—was set too high; the agricultural targets, based on a very optimistic assessment of the benefits conferred by collectivization, were completely out of line with past experience; the approved policy of forcing machine exports—if necessary by crediting barely solvent customers—was bound to overtax the balance of payments. Whatever the merits or demerits of the original draft plan—from which the 1959 directives to enterprises for elaborating *their* five-year plans were derived—it could not resist the additional pressures of the new assignments that were tacked on to it in the course of the next year and a half.

One important reason for the planners' sanguine expectations was the

[4]Z. Vergner in *Plánované hospodářství*, No. 11, 1962, p. 4.
[5]J. Macek in *Plánované hospodářství*, No. 12, 1962, p. 56.
[6]*Rudé právo*, January 9, 1963, p. 3.

very satisfactory performance of the economy from 1957 to 1960, or what appeared to be a very satisfactory performance at the time, with national income, according to the official index, rising at a steady 7 to 8 percent a year, the gross output of industry climbing at 11 percent per year, and even agricultural output expanding at the slower but still relatively rapid pace of 2 to 4 percent annually.

Very few officials had any inkling that these achievements rested on an exceedingly fragile basis: most of them believed that, with certain modifications, the old planning methods would generate satisfactory rates of growth at least for the duration of the next five-year plan. The events of 1961–62 came as an unwelcome surprise. The explanation most frequently given for this inability to predict the slowdown is that the economy's 'reserves' had been suddenly and unexpectedly exhausted. Enterprises, ever since they had been nationalized, had planned with room to spare, but each year they had been forced by higher authorities to cut their safety margins; eventually, they were assigned tasks that could not normally be fulfilled.

In the new planning system introduced in 1958–59, long-range planning was scheduled to play a major role. Henceforth, the yearly plans were supposed to be derived more or less mechanically from the longer-range plan, with such minor adjustments as circumstances might dictate.

A major distinguishing feature of the refurbished system was a new complex of incentives, calculated to induce enterprises to volunteer more challenging "counter-plans" than the directives handed down by their superior authorities. Enterprises received 'normatives of personal stimulation' and 'normatives of enterprise stimulation', which were supposed to stimulate enterprise managers to 'uncover reserves' in the directives and submit 'mobilizing plans'. For example, the system of normatives of personal stimulation that governed the relation between increases in the average wages paid by the enterprise and its gains in labor productivity provided that if the enterprise volunteered higher labor-productivity increases than the directive called for, it should be allowed to raise wages according to a higher ratio than if it had committed itself only to fulfilling the directive. The same principle operated in the normative of enterprise stimulation that determined the share of profits that an enterprise could retain for increasing its working capital and for its decentralized investments.

It should be stressed that the new incentive scheme was fashioned in virtual isolation from the revision of prices for producer goods. The 1958 revision fixed prices for the next six years at levels more or less closely adhering to the production costs that had prevailed in 1956–1957, in keeping with the traditional price-setting pattern in vogue at the time in the Soviet-type economies.

The undermining of the new reform started from the top. The decentralization was incompatible with the authorities' predilection for taut, pace-forcing plans. The Third Five-year Plan directives issued in September 1959 had called for an overall increase of 50 percent in the gross value of industrial output from 1960 to 1965, which was to be achieved mainly by virtue of a 40 percent rise in labor productivity. The ministries, on the basis of their enterprises' proposals, drafted plans which, cumulatively, provided for increases of 56 percent in output and 41.3 percent in labor productivity over the same period. These counter-plans were not as 'mobilizing', however, as the government had expected. Only a minority of enterprises volunteered higher labor-productivity targets than those they had received in the directives.[7] The draft plans of the ministries violated the instructions issued by the Planning Commission which stipulated that at least 50 percent of any increase in output above the directives should be covered by higher labor productivity. The Planning Commission ratifies the 56 percent increase for industry proposed by the ministries, but proceeded to 'correct' the labor-productivity targets in the ministerial drafts so that they finally averaged out to a 43 percent rise, which just met requirements. This 43 percent target was promulgated in the Third Five-year Plan.

The central authorities also complained that the ministries' demands for raw materials were greatly in excess of the limits prescribed in the directives, and these requests also had to be cut down to size. Enterprises were indeed willing to produce more than they were asked to, but only if they could have larger inputs.

The normatives were ineffective in coaxing out 'reserves' because enterprises had too much to lose and too little to gain by raising their ministry's bids: the normatives were not sufficiently differentiated to reward commitments made above the preliminary directives. Most enterprises preferred not to stake their chances on a mobilizing plan when they could do almost as well by overshooting the initial targets, without the unpleasant risk of not meeting the plan and losing the right to the bonus altogether. Most enterprising managers also learned that it did not pay to submit mobilizing plans which the ministry could use to justify still higher final assignments. Finally, the enterprises were discouraged from taking far-reaching measures for improving efficiency that might pay off only on future years because the long-term normatives, in violation of the basic law on the reforms, were 'adjusted' for each plan-year on the basis of the current year's results.

The conflict between over-ambitious targets and the orderly conduct of the decentralization was nowhere more apparent than in the difficulties

---

[7]See, for instance, *Plánované hospodářství*, No. 11, 1961, p. 1021.

caused by decentralized investments. These were by no means negligible; in the Third Five-year Plan they represented over 50 percent of total investments, a significantly larger proportion than prevailed in Poland, for example, in 1957-58 at the peak of the decentralization campaign. Unfortunately, the centralized programme was already so ambitious, it absorbed such a large part of the capacity of the construction industry, that there was just no room for all the decentralized investments that enterprises could finance with the funds left at their disposal: there was not only a shortage of building workers, but also insufficient facilities for designing investment projects or for supervising their execution. Building materials were also in scarce supply. At first, until about the middle of 1961, enterprises had the upper hand and succeeded in deflecting resources from centralized projects to carry out their own plans. Later on, the authorities interfered to make sure that centralized projects were given full priority. By late 1961 all sorts of regulations had been promulgated, subverting the original principles under which investments had been decentralized. The distinction between centralized and decentralized investments was formally abolished in the Plan for 1963.

In 1962, according to Finance Minister Duriš, only 106 out of 161 centralized construction projects schedules for completion during the year were actually completed. The record was worse still for decentralized projects. Work on projects that were not completed, for lack of materials, machines, or manpower, continued at snail's pace; investment resources were thus frozen for long periods; it was mainly due to these delays that the average gestation of investments turned out to be about twice as long as had been envisaged in the plan.[8]

Once the Five-year Plan was abandoned, a spate of post-mortem articles appeared in the Czech press, many of which were unusually perceptive and convincing. They gave cause for wondering where all these intelligent kibitzers had been when the initial mistakes in formulating the plan were made and why they did not draw their conclusions *ante morbidi mortem*. The salient points they brought out about the concepts and implementation of the 1959 decentralization, which received a good part of the official censure for the failure of the plan, will now be summarized.

1. The Five-year and longer plans had not provided a stable enough framework for the yearly plans, so that neither ministries nor enterprises had a clear view of the future development of their sector. Frequent changes in the plans upset the long-term normatives, whose effectiveness, in the circumstances was, to say the least, problematical.

2. The new incentive system had not succeeded in eradicating various

---

[8]*Rudé právo*, 25 January 1963; *Plánované hospodářství*, No. 12, 1962, p. 5; No. 2, 1963, p. 23.

malpractices on the part of the management. Managers still concealed 'reserves' in the plans; they applied their initiative and energy to fulfilling their gross-output targets, with the knowledge that their supervisors at higher echelons 'closed their eyes to any abuses so long as they fulfilled this plan.' [9] The quarter-by-quarter variations in the output of enterprises were judged to be at least partly 'speculative'; by this was meant that managers, angling for soft plans for the coming year, reduced their current output in the quarter when these plans were being laid in order to conceal capacity reserves and to give their superiors a lower base on which to peg the enterprises' output tasks for the plan-year; they then more than made up for the shortfall by 'storming' in the last quarter of the year (which often consisted simply in delivering goods formerly stashed away in the form of supposedly unfinished inventories). Producers performed least well in meeting their contractual obligations to 'non-market consumers' (i.e. to other enterprises in industry and construction) because they knew that these deliveries were less closely checked than sales of end-products to the export market and to the trade network for consumer goods.

One critic was candid enough to point out that it was not always the fault of managers when they followed these devious paths; managers put in padded requests for materials because their confidence in the stability of supply plans had been shaken in the past. It was up to the authorities to draft internally consistent plans; as it was, managers were reluctant to inform their employees about the unrealistic plans they had received from above 'for fear that the workers might become irritated'.[10]

3. Despite all entreaties from superior authorities, ministerial officials kept on representing the narrow interests of their sectors instead of considering the interests of society as a whole, as these interests were interpreted by the Party. Though they might themselves be prone to act correctly in matters directly under their jurisdiction, officials often hesitated to intervene operationally to curb enterprises and productive economic units scheming to promote their local interests in unjustifiable ways. This passive attitude was motivated by the laudable but misplaced intention of preserving the reinforced authority of lower organs in the spirit of the reform.[11]

4. Suppliers did not know their clients' real needs. They often crossed off requests when it was already too late for their customers to get supplies from other sources.

5. When suppliers and their clients could not solve their differences by

---

[9]O. Bača, 'Zvýšit autoritu státního plánu' (To increase the authority of the state plan), *Hospodářské noviny,* No. 51–52, pp. 1,4.
[10]*Ibid.*, p. 1.
[11]B. Kratochivíl, 'Zabránit překračování mzdových fondů' (To prevent excess disbursements of wage funds), *Finance a úvěr,* No. 6, 1962, p. 322.

direct negotiations, conflicts were 'kicked upstairs' to the Ministry where they took a long time to be settled—when they did not have to be referred to top officials in the Planning Commission. Often, by the time conflicts were resolved, the plans had already been approved and changes had to be made to accommodate petitioners. Ministries were so deluged with these routine conflicts that they had no time to work on the development problems of their sectors, which should have been their main preoccupation according to the principles of the reform. There were also occasions when conflicts between enterprises or between the Planning Commission and the Ministries were not resolved at the highest level and were kicked back to lower echelons, under the delusion that somehow things would work themselves out below. Such practices undermined the confidence of subordinates in their superiors. The unquestioning acceptance of impossible tasks by underlings, who then proceeded calmly to ignore the plan, only made things worse.[12] Officials who concealed true conditions from their superiors in order to 'look good' were also to blame.

6. Officials in the ministries and even in the Planning Commission were labouring under the misconception that the decentralization reforms had done away with the necessity for the top-level coordination of supply and demand, since consumers were now in direct contact with their suppliers; this misconception had led to the slackening of control over procurement activities and material-technical norms. It was inadmissible that norms should be left to the discretion of enterprises, as had too often been the case in recent years.

7. The upshot of all the malfunctions listed so far was that yearly plans lost a part, or all, of their operational significance: "Some officials keep the state plan in their drawers: they use the plan for negotiations with higher-ups, but on the way down they work with their so-called operative plans."[13] In other words, the plans were no longer a blueprint to be executed but a front behind which officials managed their sector on a day-to-day basis. In this, and in most other respects, the 1958–1959 reforms had not brought about any improvement over the previous centralized system.

The critics, as we have just seen, spotted many weaknesses of the reforms, but they glossed over one of its most serious shortcomings: the failure to devise a new price system that would have reinforced the new incentive scheme and caused producers to turn out the right sorts of goods in the quantities demanded. As it was prices, set at average production costs, exclusive of capital charges on rents, were totally divorced from

---

[12]On the other hand, it was also wrong for managers of enterprises to tell their staff that the plans could not be fulfilled. This sort of talk 'spreads mistrust of Party and government decisions and saps the authority of the plans'. V. Šterba in *Hospodářské noviny*, No. 10, 1962, p. 1.

[13]Bača, *op. cit.*, p. 1.

considerations of demand, so that enterprises seeking to maximize profits, were induced to produce an assortment out of harmony with the demand of their customers and to use relatively inefficient combination of inputs to produce their output—judging at least by economy-wide standards. (They could of course continue to sell their inferior assortment as long as a sellers' market prevailed.) Among the few economists who perceived that the failure of the decentralization was bound up with the deficiencies of the price system was Otakar Šik, the head of the Economic Institute of the Academy of Sciences, who was to become the principal architect of the 1966–1967 reforms.

By mid-1963, a number of palliative measures had been worked out to deal with the worsening economic situation. The Planning Commission was encouraged to use its operative authority to check disproportions as soon as they arose. Responsibility for balancing and distributing a number of goods recently planned by enterprise was handed back to the ministries. The nomenclature for balancing and distributing essential materials at the Planning Commission and ministerial levels was widened and made more detailed, thus leaving less scope for arbitrary decisions by marketing organizations and enterprises formerly charged with distributing their own products. Norms of material consumption were again set and supervised centrally. The normatives of enterprise stimulation, which determined the size of the employees' bonus fund, were subjected to stiffer controls, in particular by the imposition of an absolute limit on the bonus funds.[14]

These various measures represented a decisive retreat from the principles of the 1959 reforms. They inaugurated a trend back to centralized management, which left enterprise managers less autonomy and scope for initiative than at any time during the previous decade.

This swing back to centralization called forth some of the malfunctions that prompted a loosening of central controls in 1958–1959. Experience has shown that when the planners seek to embrace too many activities, they fail to keep them in their grasp. "Spontaneous" activities go on at lower levels, without regard to approved programmes, because the plans are too inaccurate to regulate the detailed operations of producers.

It is interesting to note in this connection that there are also forces making for re-centralization in a partially decentralized system. In part, these forces stem from the upper echelons of the administration, intent on neutralizing the negative effects of uncoordinated decisions taken at lower echelons,[15] and in part from the enterprises themselves, which are constantly appealing to superior authorities against adverse decisions on the

[14]*Finance a úvěr*, No. 1, 1963, pp. 25–26.
[15]On similar centripetal forces in the Soviet economy, see G. Grossman, "The Structure and Organization of the Soviet Economy," *Slavic Review*, No. 2, 1962.

part of their suppliers or of their functional organizations. The dynamics of a bureaucratic organization kept under political pressure are such as to cause a larger share of these detailed questions to be referred all the way to an ultimate decision-making authority. In short, *the natural equilibrium of a command economy tends to be repelled by both extremes of centralization and of decentralization.*

Whether or not the defects of the 1959 reforms outweighed their advantages, one lesson may clearly be drawn from the fiasco of 1961 to 1963: a complex system of new institutions cannot be successfully introduced when plans are overstrained. The programme of centralized investments for the Third Five-year Plan should have been kept down when the plan was originally drafted to leave room for the maximum volume of decentralized investments that might reasonably have been expected. If the actual financial resources of enterprises had turned out to be too small to sustain this maximum volume of investments, it would always have been possible to tack on less essential projects, already prepared but so far held in reserves, to the original programme of centralized investments.

But this type of traditional strategy would have no appeal for the tradition-bound planners in the party apparatus, who continued to operate as if their plans were immune to the vagaries of chance. The prescriptive nature of the plans, backed up by the sanction of law reinforced their mental prejudice against programmes providing for alternative courses of action to meet a variety of contingencies, even though unpredictable changes in foreign trade conditions and in the demand of private consumers, as well as the sudden mutations brought about by technical progress, all speak in favor of such a probabilistic approach.

For political reasons that are still partially obscure, the top leaders of the Czechoslovak Communist Party, who had deplored the "weakening of central direction" inherent in the decentralization of 1958–1960 and blamed it in large measure for the failure of the Third Five-year Plan in 1962,[16] permitted a resumption of the "discussion on the economic model" in 1962 and eventually endorsed a new set of reforms that called for even more radical departures from the old centralized model than its predecessor.

For the first time since the institution of comprehensive central planning in Czechoslovakia in 1948, the notion of a market for producer goods where supply and demand relations influenced by prices might operate, was explicitly recognized. Prices of certain products were to be freed from all central controls as soon as the reforms were introduced. The range of freely priced goods was to be gradually enlarged. Simultaneously, the

---

[16]See in particular President Novotný's speech at the Twelfth Congress of the Czechoslovak Communist Party in *XII Sjezd KSČ* (Prague, 1962) pp. 12–14.

incentive system for enterprise managers was, at least on paper, completely divorced from performance relative to plan and was linked to the 'disposable net revenue of the enterprise', a concept closely related to profits after taxes.[17]

In this brief survey of the recent reforms, which can only be fully and objectively appraised after two or three more years of experience will have elapsed, I shall focus on a narrow range of problems revolving around the price mechanism, the nature of the newly created 'markets', and the legacies of the old centralized allocation system.[18]

Even before the general revision of producer prices introduced in January 1967, the prices of certain goods were freed from all controls. For a fairly wide range of goods 'limits' were centrally imposed. Table 1 shows

TABLE 1

	Fixed Prices	Subject to Upper Limits	Subject to Upper & Lower Limits	Free Prices
Total industrial output	64.0	14.7	14.1	7.2
Ministry of Fuels	96.2	3.6	0.2	—
Ministry of Metallurgy	83.2	12.2	1.2	3.4
Ministry of Chemical Industry	61.0	14.0	17.0	8.0
Ministry of Heavy Machine-Building	6.0	64.8	28.4	0.0
Ministry of General Machine-Building	35.0	26.1	29.5	9.4
Ministry of Consumer-Goods Industry	65.2	0.6	19.3	14.9
Ministry of Food Industry	93.6	0.2	3.3	2.9

SOURCE: *Hospodářské noviny*, No. 39, (1966), p. 3.

the share of industrial output in various branches subject to fixed prices and limits, together with the share of output for which enterprises may set prices without centralized approval.

For the most part, prices subject ot limits were set by enterprises at, or very close to, the sanctioned upper bound.[19]

[17]Cf. the excellent discussion in Václav Holešovský's "Financial Aspects of the Czechoslovak Economic Reform" paper prepared for the Workshop in Money and Finance in Communist Countries, University of California, Berkeley, (December 1966), pp. 7–13.

[18]For other facets of the Czechoslovak reforms see the papers by V. Holešovský and J. Michal in this volume and Holešovskýs "Financial Aspects of the Czechoslovak Reform," cited above.

[19]See the comments in Source to table above.

In 1967 the range of consumer goods whose transfer prices had been set free or subject to limits was severely curtailed. The share of consumer goods output with free or limited transfer prices declined from 20–25 percent in 1956 to 13 percent in 1967.[20] The context of this retrogression to central price controls suggests that the authorities are unwilling to allow inflationary pressures to burst into the open in a situation where demand still exceeds supply for a wide variety of goods.

The price reform of January 1967 set 'coefficients of price changes' for about 25,000 commodity groups, on the basis of which the industrial ministries were to determine the prices—fixed, limited, or free—for all the goods produced under their jurisdiction.[21] In the initial stage prices for individual items will be increased or reduced by the average coefficient for the commodity group. Eventually, however, prices are to be calculated by the ministry for each separate item in such a way as to eliminate unjustified disparities between prices and production costs that would be likely to arise from the across-the-board application of the group coefficients.[22]

The principles for setting the new level of prices for producer goods differed from those applied in prior revisions (e.g., those of 1958 and 1964) mainly in the provision of special charges on wages and capital assets over and above standard production costs. The latter consisted, as before, of wages, costs of materials and services purchased from other enterprises, and depreciation. But in addition each producer good was to generate "surplus value" in proportion to its unit wage costs and to the capital invested in the industry. Thus prices were to be set high enough, on average, to cover a gross profit allowance, equal to 12 percent of total wages and salaries, plus employer's contributions to social insurance equal to 10 percent of the wage bill, and charges on capital equal to 6 percent of the depreciated capital assets and "circulating funds"—inventories and other working capital—of producing enterprises.

The new price level for producer goods was approximately 24 percent higher than the old. As usual in the postwar price revisions of the Soviet-type economies, industries with slowly growing or stagnant labor productivity such as mining and building materials exhibited the greatest price increases, while industries with rapidly growing productivity, such as machine-building and food processing exhibited a decline in prices.[23]

---

[20]*Hospodářské noviny*, No. 4 (1967), p. 3. Note that these transfer prices apply to transactions between socialized enterprises and are detached from retail prices, which are subject to even more rigid controls.

[21]The reason given for the inclusion of all three categories of prices in the new price lists is that it was not yet certain to which category any given commodity group might eventually be assigned. (*Hospodářské noviny*, No. 44, (1966), p. 1.

[22]*Ibid.* and *Hospodářské noviny*, No. 4 (1967), p. 3.

[23]*Hospodářské noviny*, No. 43, (1966), p. 4.

Two fundamental questions about the new price system call for an answer:

1. Are the new prices likely to equate supply and demand for individual producer goods? and

2. Will they prod enterprise managers to input and output decisions consonant with the allocation policies the government wishes to pursue?

I see no reason why one should expect the new administered prices to achieve either of these objectives. Prices of producer goods are still supply-determined. They are bound up with production costs that reflect inefficient input-output relations at a time when the central planners wish to correct these relations and deploy resources to achieve a more "intensive" development. The allowances for interest charges in the gross profits of enterprises are arbitrarily determined, without relation to the scarcity value of capital in the Czechoslovak economy.[24] The surcharge on the wage bill, which is also part of gross profits, can only be justified economically if it is assumed that the money wages paid by enterprises do not reflect the full costs borne by the economy when labor is hired from the countryside, owing perhaps to the higher social and cultural expenditures that the state metes out to urban residents. But whatever the general validity of this surcharge its actual magnitude is as arbitrary as the interest levied on capital.

The main point I wish to make, though, is that even if prices did reflect the scarcity relations of 1967. they still would not emit the proper signals for managers to correct the present misallocation of resources. They would, in fact, cause this misallocation to be impacted, insofar as managers, sensitized to profit incentives, were led to resist central directives conflicting with the dictates of profit maximization.

All my strictures so far apply to "average enterprises," faced by prices covering their production costs plus standard gross profit margins. As we shall see below, the concentration of enterprises has now proceeded so far that there is unlikely to be a wide range of production costs among enterprises in any one industry, except perhaps between enterprises located in the Czech lands and in Slovakia. Insofar as these cost disparities do persist, the various authorities supervising the activities of enterprises— from the ministry down to the association—will be seized with requests for subsidies from high-cost producers or at least for dispensations from paying interest and other charges to the treasury. To cut costs and economize on resources the authority ultimately responsible for making decisions in this domain should act to close down hopelessly inefficient enter-

---

[24]It is my guess that the six percent charge underestimates the true scarcity of capital services in the Czechoslovak economy.

prises. (Here at least the signals emitted by the costs-price system should be in general conformity with the policy of "intensive development" pursued by the state.) It is by no means certain, however, that the correct responses will be forthcoming. The associations in recent practice, have tended to redistribute profits and losses among their constituent enterprises, too often without regard to considerations of efficiency. Similarly, at higher levels there has been marked reluctance to curtail the output of exporting enterprises, even though their production costs were significantly in excess of the effective price obtained by multiplying the foreign price by a uniform exchange rate and adding to it a standard export bonus for the industry.[25] Here the conflict is between 'export requirements' as they appear in the Planning Commission's physical balances and the results of economic calculations. Since neither the balances nor the calculations are reliable instruments for measuring relative scarcities, and comparing the efficiency of alternative solutions, there can be no unequivocal resolution to this conflict.

Although there is a deplorable lack in official writings and speeches of serious comparisons with the previous reform, one important lesson at least was learned from its failure: this time, all investments, whatever their source of finance, will be coordinated and controlled from above. The framers of the new system are not counting on any spontaneous reconciliation of supply and demand for investment resources by way of voluntary agreements between investors and contractors, a method which, when tried out in 1960 and 1961, had led to the proliferation of small projects to the detriment of priority investments. By such centralized controls, the reformers may also be hoping to avoid the inflation-generating disequilibria between aggregate supply and demand that have plagued Yugoslavia for years.[26]

In general, investments are the type of resource-allocating decision that best qualify for a certain measure of central control and coordination, since at least the major projects are likely to generate externalities and economies of scale and to be subject to indivisibilities that would be incompatible with the efficient operation of a fully decentralized system.

The present reform continues the trend started in 1958 towards the concentration of productive capacities in fewer enterprises, each of which will be entrusted with the monopoly management of an entire sector. Out of 1,417 national enterprises in existence previously, the 1958 reform had

---

[25] *Hospodářské noviny*, No. 51–52, (1966), p. 3.

[26] Note, however, that the Fourth Five-year Plan (1966–1970) is still said to be 'unbalanced'. If so, the planners may have repeated the mistakes made in carrying out the 1958–1959 reforms. Unbalanced plans create disproportions which usually manifest themselves in inflationary pressures, materials shortages, etc. These in turn make it necessary for the central planners to intervene directly 'to put things right', thus undermining one of the primary principles of the decentralization.

created 383 'productive economic units', made up of 316 leading enterprises and 67 associations of smaller, scattered enterprises. In 1965 the number of leading enterprises was reduced to 100. Only four national enterprises are left in the steel industry and five in chemicals, compared to the earlier total of 36 in the two industries.[27]

Each sector (*obor*) is now organized as a 'productive economic unit', consisting either of several enterprises with equivalent status, or of a leading enterprise together with its auxiliary enterprises. In both cases research and development facilities, as well as other functional departments necessary to plan and to operate the sector in the most comprehensive manner, are incorporated into the unit. To direct the productive economic unit, sector administrations have been set up as an intermediate echelon between ministries and enterprises. (This echelon, incidentally, had been abolished in 1958). For the first time, however, the sector administration will itself be on cost accounting, and its personnel will be remunerated according to the financial results of its ward enterprises. The administrations that have already been established in some industries are said to be working closely with their ministries and with the Central Committee of the Party itself to prepare the long-term plans for their sector. If, as seems likely, the real locus of power in deciding the production profile of a sector is going to reside in these intermediate agencies, the enlarged enterprises themselves, let alone the plants which were formerly enterprises on their own account but have now been merged into larger units, may not have so much more leeway to conduct their business according to conditions in the field than they had in the past.

On September 23, 1965 the *Compendium of Laws* of the Czechoslovak Socialist Republic published a Government Declaration, dated August 25, 1965, which served as the legal framework of the reform. Quotations from the text are given at some length below, partly for the intrinsic interest of the Declaration, but also because it represents a fine example of the type of official communist pronouncement that can be given almost any operational content, depending on who happens to be in charge of carrying out its provisions.

One of the first questions anyone might wish to ask about the reform is whether the administrative machinery for commanding and controlling the economy will be dismantled and, if so, whether it will be replaced by a system of coordination through markets, financial levels, and other indirect pressures. The official announcement, as the following extracts testify, provides no clear-cut answer to this question.

> The chief instruments to ensure planned development are, on the one hand, compulsory tasks, binding limits, and guiding plan indicators, and, on the other, economic instruments.

[27]*Rudé právo*, June 2, 1965.

Compulsory tasks may include:

State scientific and technical assignments

Specifically listed investments

Export tasks and specific deliveries of goods important for the development of external relations and for the fulfillment of international obligations

Tasks concerning the training of cadres

Specific production tasks

Defense tasks

Tasks relating to the development of Slovakia and of individual regions.

Binding limits may be set for:

The volume of investments in a sector and the total volume of investments not specifically listed; the volume of construction carried out by construction enterprises.

Non-investment expenditures by centrally directed budgetary organizations for science and research.

Total commodity imports as well as the import of specifically listed goods important for the development of the economy.

The number of persons employed, wherever this may be essential for ensuring the proportional development of the economy.

The wage fund, as well as other indicators, in organizations where the development of wages is not guided by economic instruments.

The consumption of certain materials of electric energy.

Binding tasks and limits are set in the long-term plan. As "need arises," they may be specified in greater detail in the current plans, along with "additional tasks and limits."

Tasks and limits are assigned to central organs and to national committees, which in turn may ensure their fulfillment either by economic instruments or by issuing binding tasks and limits to their subordinate organizations. Central organs and national committees may widen the scope of the binding tasks and limits set by the government in the long-term or in the short-term plan only exceptionally, in cases where they are imposing extraordinary tasks. . . . . Binding tasks may be set only for the production of especially important concretely defined goods, and this only in specified quantities.

Exceptionally, a specific task may be set for the production of a larger group of commodities, in cases where:

(a) objective conditions limit the effectiveness of economic instruments;

(b) the effectiveness of economic instruments and market relations cannot be relied on (deliveries for export, for the internal market, for specifically listed investment projects, etc.).[28]

[28]These provisions allow for the stipulation both of specific targets and of gross output, since the latter may be interpreted as a target for a 'larger group of commodities'. Otakar Šik, in a lecture in West Berlin on the impending reforms, had stated that enterprises would receive only 'guiding figures' (*Orientation Ziffern*) for their production programme, not binding targets (*Frankfurter Allgemeine Zeitung*, 15 March 1965).

> Economic administrative organs will analyze deviations between the actual economic performance and the guiding indicators of the state plan and on this basis arrive at conclusions concerning the use of economic instruments and the application of measures involving the utilization of reserves, imports, and investments . . . If the deviations in question significantly threaten the fulfillment of the basic tasks of the state plan, the government will stipulate additional binding tasks and limits or will instruct central organs and national committees to safeguard the proportions of the state plan by assigning extraordinary tasks, and this in cases where the use of economic instruments would not be effective.

On the economic instruments themselves, the Government Declaration has this to say:

> The organs of the economic administration are obliged to employ economic instruments in such a way as to create a material incentive for enterprises to improve and to expand production, to adapt it flexibly to the needs of society, and to increase labour productivity on the basis of the systematic use of new technology.

The long-term instruments include schedules of percentage deductions from "gross income," interest charges on capital assets, and the variable proportion of depreciation allowances left at the disposal of the enterprise. Short-term instruments also comprise a whole gamut of indirect controls and financial inducements, including prices, utility tariffs, wage scales, labor-productivity norms, working-capital and investment credits, loans in foreign currency, specific subsidies, and the share of certain sector-wide investments that must be financed by contributions from the enterprise.

To make sure that enterprises, after meeting all their obligations from their gross income, will not distribute too large a share of the remainder to their workers, steeply progressive additional deductions will have to be paid to central organs, in accordance with the discrepancy between average wages paid and some basic average wage established for the enterprise.

One of the most positive sides of the new reform, compared to the previous experiment, is the severance of incentives from performance according to plan. Whatever limitations may be imposed on the distribution of residual profits to employees, their volume at least will not have any relation to a plan magnitude; it is not to be subject to *ex ante* bargaining with superior authorities.

With the exception of specific improvements, such as I have just mentioned, the framework of the reform, as laid out in the Government Declaration of August 25, seems so loose that it can accommodate anything from a regulated market system to a tightly centralized set-up such as was in operation in 1963. Who, if not the central planners themselves, is to judge whether deviations from the plan 'significantly threaten the fulfillment of the plan', or whether special circumstances make it necessary to widen the scope of compulsory directives? Will they not be free to manipulate the economic instruments to force enterprises to comply with their detailed directives? In what way has the state really restricted its power of interfering in the routine affairs of producers?

On the whole the impression remains that the Party has committed itself to very little. If it wishes to hamper the decentralization, it can restrict the scope of free prices to insignificant commodities, set narrow limits that will in effect rig prices wherever flexibility has been provided for, and use the sector administrations and the national Bank as transmission belts for central directives. By these and other devices the Party could conceivably preserve the essentials of the old command economy.

Recent pronouncements are beginning to throw light on the intentions of Party leaders. In December 1966 the Declaration of August 25, 1965 was "brought up to date," and an official commentary on the reformed planning system was published as a supplement to the economic weekly of the Central Committee of the Party.[29] This commentary is somewhat more precise than the Declaration in stipulating situations in which specific tasks and limits may be imposed by higher authorities. It also describes certain cases where enterprises may claim damages for having to carry out tasks tending to disrupt their financial program. From the summary it gives of the instructions issued by the Planning Commission for 1967, which only lays down twelve binding targets and a small number of limits, it would seem that the highest planning authorities, at least for the present, are intent on respecting the spirit and the principles of the reforms. One will have to wait a year or two to see whether they will also be willing to countenance the deviations from their guidelines that are certain to arise if the reins on producers are significantly loosened.

The "highest planning authorities" of course need not have identical views on the reform. Some, like Premier Josef Lenart, probably want a thorough overhaul of the system. Lenart's fellow members of the Party Presidium, and above all President Novotný himself, may be going along with the reform as a necessary evil. It may be significant, in connection with the attitude of Presidium members to the reform, that one of the initial impulses for change in the system came from the Soviet Union itself when Khruschev threw his support behind proposals for decentralization at the time of his visit to Prague in August 1964.

Several ministers in charge of industrial branches are reputed to be against decentralization, as are many influential officials of the Planning Commission, although it is also limited that there has been a change of heart on the part of some of these functionaries, especially among those responsible for price formation.

[29]*Hospodářské noviny*, No. 1, 1967.

Many economic administrators, unable to envisage the workings of a decentralized system, are reluctant to embark on fundamental changes without years of preparation and study. They hamstring the reform more by their inertia than by their outright opposition. A strong current against the reform emanates from Party officials in the provincial National Committees, who foresee that their power will be curtailed if enterprises are cut adrift from administrative regulation. District Party secretaries represent an important minority in the Central Committee of the Party; together with various conservative allies, they are said to form a strong enough opposition to block any proposals for the creation of a market-type economy. At present it seems unlikely that there will be significant changes in personnel at any level; this is liable to frustrate the intentions behind the new model. If, as is rumored, those in charge of its operation are the very people who were most strongly opposed to its introduction, the scheme will be undermined from within.

Enterprise directors are not all happy about the prospects for reform either. Many directors who were getting large bonuses under the old system without really exerting themselves are worried about the uncertainties of the future; some who banked their career on their Party connections and on their understanding of the rules of the game in a command economy know they will be at a relative disadvantage when it comes to competing with professionals with the education and the experience necessary for running a firm according to business principles. Many rank-and-file workers, insofar as they care at all about the reforms, are apprehensive of greater wage differentiation, which might leave them at least relatively worse off than before. The Slovak communists want more administrative autonomy but fear that the new stress of profit criteria will work to the disadvantage of Slovakia, where industrial investments have been located, irrespective of "rentability," for the sake of industrializing this less developed part of the country.[30]

It is manifest then that there is no unanimity in any quarter for a radical change in the system. Yet "informed public opinion," the crystallized consensus of numerous dispersed but influential individuals in all regions and in all walks of life, seems to desire such a change devoutly. Their scattered forces will have to wage an uphill fight to overcome the resistance of those who stand to lose by the reform, and who are, for the

---

[30]During the central committee debates in January 1965 that preceded the adoption of the Party resolutions of the reforms, M. Sobolčik, one of the top officials in the Slovak Communist Party, pointed out that many chemical plants in Slovakia, which had been working at a profit, could not pay the interest charges at the full rate on their capital assets without suffering losses; several months later, it was announced that the charge would be reduced to 2 percent for less developed areas, including Slovakia (*Figyelö,* June 9, 1965).

most part, in a better position to mobilize forces within the present political system to support their opposition than they are to defend it.

Like the progress of the threatening army of Fortinbras which precipitates the action in *Hamlet,* the performance of the Czechoslovak economy forms the background against which the contending forces are playing out their struggle. A further deterioration of the economic situation might well impel the final dénouement of Czechoslovakia's institutional crisis. However, there has been an upturn since 1965. Gross industrial output, the economic indicator the party leaders are most concerned about, has again been rising at an annual rate in excess of 5 percent. This improvement, most Czechoslovak economists would agree has little to do with the reforms but stems chiefly from the fact that a number of investment projects launched during the great investment drive of 1959 to 1962 are now coming to fruition. If the economy can sustain a rate of industrial growth of this magnitude, and if the most pressing problems of the country's balance of payments can somehow be palliated, the pressure for institutional reform will almost certainly abate. After 1968, however, the investment trough of 1963 to 1965 will begin to depress output, and there may be some lean years in the offing. If the reforms are emasculated in the next year or two, the pressures favoring radical reforms may build up again before the end of the decade.

In the meantime, a compromise system incorporating a fairly wide measure of decentralization, new profit incentives, and a *mélange* of administered and market prices has been launched, the implementation of which deserves careful and objective examination in the coming years. My guess at this juncture is that the new system will be helpful in reviving initiative and accelerating innovation at the enterprise level which, if nothing else, should contribute to the improvement of the competitive position of Czechoslovak products on external markets. But I doubt whether the new arrangements are capable of supplying the signals and incentives that would cause enterprise managers to make the decisions required to put the economy on an efficient growth path.

6. ECONOMIC REFORMS IN HUNGARY

HUNGARY: IRON OUT OF WOOD*
— · — · — · — · — · — · — · — ·

Joseph Held†

The new economic reform program adopted in Hungary is characterized by greater zeal, higher ambitions, wilder expectations—and more

*Reprinted by permission from *Problems of Communism* (Nov.–Dec. 1966), pp. 37–43. All footnotes deleted.
†Dr. Joseph Held is Assistant Professor of Hungarian Studies, Rutgers University.

double-talk—than any of its counterparts in Eastern Europe. At a plenary session of the Central Committee of the Hungarian Socialist Workers' Party on May 25–27, 1966, the long-awaited system of reforms was finally accepted. According to the official announcement, the most important changes gradually to be introduced between now and 1968 are: 1) a new type of planning that will give greater independence to directors of enterprises; 2) greater freedom of the market through deference to the "spontaneous" workings of the laws of supply and demand; 3) a new system of prices and wages, based on the coordination of national interests with those of individual enterprises; and 4) greater emphasis on the development of agriculture.

A great deal of cautious planning and debate preceded the adoption of the reforms. The significance attached to the program was exemplified in the comment of one participant in the discussions, József Bognár, who stated that "the proposals represent the most important changes in the history of socialist economy since the introduction of socialist relations of ownership." By no means was there universal enthusiasm, however; during the protracted discussions, the proposals encountered resistance from diverse elements in the party. The old guard saw the reforms as a repudiation of the cherished ideal of a centrally-controlled economy, the basis of the party's monopoly of political power. On the other hand, some of the reform-minded party members were fearful that the admission of total failure of the old methods would produce such a sharp reaction that the new mechanism would represent a step backward to "capitalism."

Yet there was hardly any choice. As early as 1963, it had become painfully clear even to the hard-core Stalinists that the system was bankrupt. In 1964 the *coup de grâce* to Stalinist methods was administered by Iván T. Berend, a historian of economics, in a short book with a long title that created immediate controversy.

The appearance of this book in itself reflected the greater freedom of expression that the Kádár regime had cautiously extended to Hungary's intellectuals. Disregarding ideological myths and fallacies, the study succeeded in indicting the economic policy of the party during the Rákosi era. The author demonstrated—supporting his arguments with documents from the party archives(!)—that the nation's economy had been systematically ruined by dilettantes after the Communist conquest of power in 1948. He maintained that during the entire Rákosi era, waste, deception, incompetence and terror had characterized the process of economic policymaking as well as the direction of the political life of the country. He showed, in fact, that the entire mechanism of the planned economy had broken down by the time the Rákosi-Gerö clique fell from power. Although he did not do so, he might have added the same about the political mechanism, as the events of 1956 strikingly demonstrated.

It is hardly likely that this book could have appeared without the permission of the party authorities, the more so since Berend had been expounding his ideas for some time before the study was published. Probably the intention was to show that the present leadership was thoroughly fed up with continuous obstruction by hard-core Stalinists. The study also served as a starting point for the actual introduction of reform plans. At the same time, in order to show how much times had changed, the regime invited economic experts and "other leading citizens" to participate in preliminary discussion of the reform.

The need for reform was manifest in virtually every sector of the economic system. Hungary's chronic problems were in many respects even more critical than those of the other East European countries. In the wake of the 1956 revolution, the Kádár regime had pursued a relentlessly Stalinist course, relying for its economic survival on credits extended by its "socialist" partners. Collectivization of agriculture had been pressed to completion in 1960–61, but agricultural production continued to lag. Rural living conditions were so miserable that there was a steady exodus of farm labor to the cities, siphoning off the youngest and most vigorous members of the collectives. Even so, there were not enough workers to meet the demand for skilled labor in the factories, reflecting in part a long and steady decline in Hungary's birth rate. The consequence of these and other factors was virtual stagnation in the overall growth rate of the economy. Though there were some improvements in the living conditions of the population during the early 1960's, they were so slow in coming that there was perceptible unrest in both the urban and rural areas. Finally, serious problems arose out of the fact that Hungary's exports had been subsidized throughout most of its "socialist" history; the deficit in foreign trade had steadily increased in the decade up to 1964, leading to the weakening of the *forint*. It was clear that—even without prodding from neighbor regimes—the Hungarian party had to do something to change the situation.

From the start, however, the leaders faced a fundamental dilemma. The problem was not unique; it was—and still is—shared by all Communist-controlled governments of Eastern Europe. If the rigidly-controlled, inflexible economic system was to be replaced by a more efficient one, by a system able to respond to the growing complexities of society, then the parties had to consider delegating greater authority in the economic decision-making process to non-party experts and managers. Yet economic life is hard, if not impossible, to separate from political life; the next logical step would be decentralization of the monopoly of political power. Communists, who take pride in their correct understanding of history, could hardly overlook the many examples from its pages of groups who first gained economic independence and then began to demand a greater voice in the political life of their countries.

This dilemma made itself felt throughout the discussion and formulation of the reform program. Fear of losing its monopoly of power prevented the Kádár regime from accepting the logical conclusions of its own reasoning.

Planning: Old and New

During the Rakosi era the economic plans provided gross output targets for every single enterprise and collective farm, large and small alike. The main task of the managers and chairmen of these units was to follow central directives. Since the managers received bonuses and recognition only if they reached their targets irrespective of any other consideration, they had no interest in improving the quality of production. The orders of the central organs were often unreasonable, failing to take into account special conditions at the enterprise level and forcing managers to indulge in fraud, deception and misrepresentation. Many managers juggled with statistics to show a high level of accomplishment when their factories actually produced substandard goods; in fact, a high volume of production usually meant a large number of unsalable items. Thus the interests of the firms often ran contrary to the interests of the economy as a whole. Relations between managers and the government deteriorated to such an extent that it was not unusual for directors to be threatened with jail if their production fell behind targets.

The error of the regime was one common to all dictatorships. By insisting upon close conformity with central directives, the party eliminated individual initiative of the "right" kind—though there was plenty of initiative for deception—both within and outside its ranks. Such an economic system was suited only to the rigid conditions that prevailed in Hungary, was well as in the rest of Eastern Europe, during the Stalin era. Accordingly, the realization that the methods no longer sufficed prompted the Kadár regime to end centralized, detailed planning.

According to initial explanations of the reform, the central plan would henceforth contain only a few guidelines indicating the long-range objectives of the economy. Instead of being assigned compulsory targets, enterprises would simply be informed of the amount of money they would be expected to contribute to the national budget; any profits remaining to them would be used at their own discretion. Managers would have the task of making short-range plans for their firms, coordinating them with the broad guidelines set forth by the central planners. The most important concern of the managers would be to increase the *profitability* of their production. They would be expected to pay close attention to the market, and they would have to be flexible in their plans.

These stipulations seemed to hold the promise of a significant move toward a more rational system. Yet the degree of independence they appeared to grant to enterprise managers became one of the major issues generating alarm within the party (as it turned out, without justification). A number of party economists argued that if managers were left free to set their own plans, they would be sorely tempted to ignore national interest, just as they had proved soft in resisting erroneous directives during the era of the "personality cult." They would, it was held, promote "anarchy of the market" by following the path of least resistance to the pockets of their customers. In the face of these objections, the architects of the reform found it necessary to clarify just how much—*i.e.,* little— freedom *was* being granted to enterprises, as well as how much reliance was actually being placed on the market.

It fell to Ottó Gadó, a member of the Central Planning Bureau, to explain

> . . . the independence of enterprises is not one of our goals. . . Enterprise independence means, instead, that firms have their own fields of responsibility. Central directives—and there will be cases when direct orders must be given to firms—will be stricter than before.

Another spokesman asserted:

> The firms will not be independent, but they will have to pay close attention to "spontaneous" economic forces as well as to central direc- tives; in this way central directives will be more efficient.

Considering the fact that the distribution of industrial supplies is to remain centralized, and that priority projects will undoubtedly be favored by the central planners, it seems patently clear that the authority of managers will not be greatly increased. Apparently the main objective of the reform is not to make enterprise-government relationships more rational but to make central direction of the economy more effective. It is true that managers will have greater leeway in implementing central directives, and that central planners will probably be more restricted in issuing direct orders to firms. Yet while this may be an improvement over the old system, it does not amount to decentralization of the economic process. And since the "remainder" of the enterprise's profits depends ultimately on the planners, the latter will remain in control as before.

The role to be assigned to the "market" was another issue that needed clarification. In a statement reporting on the proceedings of the plenary session of May 25–27, the party economist György Varga noted:

> The socialist market is an organized one. This means that all the tools by which the state can exert its influence over both the market and enterprises will be retained by the state.

Varga then reported that new commercial companies would be established by the party to act as middlemen between the firms and the "market."

Added to other restrictions, this plan underscores the fact that enterprises will have very little independence, since the "market" will not represent a regulating mechanism in the true sense of the term. The market will be a new intermediary in the chain of command, its regulation remaining in the hands of the *apparat.* In certain cases it will be used to transmit the orders of the party to the firms. Therefore, it is clearly not a new form in the economic mechanism.

Price Reforms

In a lecture to the 1966 session of the Hungarian Economic Society, József Bognar announced:

> We are introducing an economic system that will make comparison between activities in different sectors of the economy possible, one that will promote rational economic activity.

The real basis of such a rational comparison would be a price system corresponding to prices on the world market. But prices have long been arbitrarily determined in Hungary, and the habit of control does not die quickly. Settling on a course of reform must have been a difficult task; but in the end the party came up with the answer. The basic element involved in pricing was not to be changed: prices were to include, as before, the cost of "social investment." The fact that the system which resulted is no less arbitrary than the old one did not disturb the reformers.

As a first step, radical price increases were ordered in some of the most important categories of foodstuffs. Together with wage increases for certain categories of workers, higher taxes were declared on higher-than-average-income pensioners.

It seems likely that the leaders had several goals in mind when deciding on these rather unpopular steps. It was evident that the party hoped to stimulate production of the most important foodstuffs by increasing wholesale prices paid for them. It is also probable that an important idea behind the increases was to limit consumption of meat and dairy products, since these are increasingly becoming the mainstay of Hungary's exports to the West.

Price increases were only one part of the reform program. In order to establish a balance between the rather conflicting goals of stability and flexibility, three categories of consumer prices were introduced. In the first category prices were to remain fixed; in the second, maximum-minimum limits were to be established; while in the third, prices were to remain free to follow market fluctuations. In its anxiety to maintain the stability of the price system, however, the regime decided to include the great majority of consumer products in the first two categories. Thus the prices of most foodstuffs, clothing, and building material for private use, to mention only the most important items in the average Hungarian's budget, continue under the control of the central government, and there will be relatively little opportunity to determine the real value of goods on the basis of the market mechanism.

Another important segment of the price structure comprises industrial prices. Formerly industrial prices, like consumer prices, were determined arbitrarily. In some of the most important categories of producers' goods, enormous subsidies were given to firms that were unable to operate profitably, especially in the sector of basic industrial raw materials. Increasing these prices therefore became imperative in order to set the producers on their own feet. But the dilemma was that if prices of basic industrial raw materials were raised, this might start an inflationary chain reaction which the regime could not afford. Therefore, the central planners resorted to a partial increase of raw material prices, while at the same time they continued—and intended to keep on—subsidizing the producers of these materials.

A "New" Investment Policy

The most important aspect of the reform of investment policy is that, while managers will decide on short-term investment expenditures or on replacement of depreciated machinery, control over long-term investments and priority projects will be left to the central planners. It is hoped that by gaining control over at least part of their profits, directors will be forced to organize production in their factories along more rational lines.

It is also expected that banks will take on a larger role in financing short-term investments for enterprises by acquiring the right to formulate their own credit policies. Their major consideration in weighing credit requests will be the profitability rate expected from the proposed investments.

In order to propose rational investments, however, the directors will have to know their expected profit rate; in other words, they must know the *actual* value of goods produced in their factories, on the one hand, and market conditions on the other. According to the reform, they will be empowered to spend part of their depreciation fund for market research; they will also be expected to establish close connections with their customers. But the market will not be a freely operating mechanism, and through the fixed-price category the government will again be in a position to assign "real values" to goods. The proposed profitability rates will thus depend on what the party deems acceptable and desirable for its own goals.

Interest rates, which according to the reforms should serve as a stimulant for greater profitability, will reflect instead priority assignments.

In short, the reforms have not yet succeeded in providing sufficiently

new motives for rational activity at the enterprise level. Since the reforms
will be combined with severe restrictions on the buying power of the
general population in order to avoid sudden scarcities of consumer goods,
little incentive will be left for greater profitability. It seems rather strange
that the regime should try to disprove the old Hungarian proverb that
"one cannot make an iron ring out of wood." Yet granting that its intentions are sincere, the regime has chosen an odd way of going about the
rationalization of the economic mechanism. Certainly, it is rather difficult to discover the "free play" of economic forces in this system.

Agriculture

One of the brighter aspects of the reform program may be discovered
in the party's new approach to agriculture. Through the aforementioned
price increases of last December, the first halting steps were taken to
channel needed funds to the collectivized farms. Compulsory production
targets were also abolished, and the government began encouraging
greater initiative on the part of managers of agricultural units.

But the measures go only halfway; here again commitments to
ideology have prevented the party from following up its own lead. Despite
all the talk about individual initiative, the party has retained its monopoly
over purchasing and distributing agricultural products. There will be
little added motivation for collectives and individual peasants to produce
more if they have to sell their output at prices that depend on the
planners.

On the other hand, further hopeful changes are being contemplated—
some of them revolutionary when compared with the party's past approach.
For instance, the economist Imre Tar has recommended that a new
system of plot-distribution be introduced. He suggested that able and
willing peasant families should be given more than the customary single
private plot, and that they should be supplied with small agricultural
machinery, seeds and chemicals. It is true that these proposals have not
yet been accepted, but the fact that they could even be voiced gives hope
for a further relaxation of the tight control that the party has exercised
over agriculture in the past eighteen years.

There is a further problem, however, that cannot be easily solved.
Since last December, there has been seething antagonism between the
urban and rural populations. City-dwellers have resented the increase
of food prices, regarding it as an effort to placate the peasantry at their
expense. The trouble is that the party cannot really divert significant
funds from the national budget in the interest of any segment of society
without injuring the rest. Thus the situation harbors a potential source
of trouble for the future.

In plain fact, the years of neglect of agriculture during the Rákosi era cannot be canceled out in a short time. The lack of agricultural machinery and chemical fertilizers throughout the period only begins to tell the story of that neglect. Rural roads, communications, railways, electrical-power needs and public health were also assigned lowest priority in national planning. Consequently, when the Kádár regime talks of increasing incentives for the collectives, it deals only with the most visible and immediate part of the problem.

The party knows that if it really wanted to improve Hungarian agriculture, it would have to embark on a program that would demand most of the funds available for the entire economy at its present level. It would have to begin building roads, modernizing railroad transportation, supplying refrigerated boxcars for perishable foodstuffs, improving storage facilities, and creating a whole new packing industry. It would also have to end insecurity in the countryside by proving its willingness to leave the private plots alone and to permit the peasantry to sell their produce on the open market.

At the present time, however, the party has neither the funds to embark on such a complete reorganization of agriculture, nor the willingness to discard old ideological clichés. The reforms represent an attempt to bridge the gap of the next few years, in the hope that meantime something might happen to solve an insoluble problem. Price increases of foodstuffs, while they may facilitate higher production in certain categories, cannot be substitutes for "changing the thinking-cap"—the fundamental step that is so badly needed in the Hungarian economy.

There is little doubt that the Hungarian Communists are moving in a vicious circle, inherited in large part from the unfortunate period of the "personality cult." Common sense and the logic of events compel them to seek a way out of the mess of a bankrupt economic system; on the other hand, they are unwilling to consider the necessary concomitant of genuine economic health—*i.e.,* decentralization of their monopoly of political power. They are not alone in this dilemma, as is evident from the doubts that other Eastern European governments have shown in introducing reform programs.

Manifestly, rationalization of the economic system is closely connected with the problem of democratization of the political life of the region. In Hungary, as in most of Eastern Europe, there is little in the current atmosphere to indicate that the party is willing to cross this historic barrier. Memories of Imre Nagy's innovations and their results are still too strong among most of the party membership to permit a smooth transition towards democracy.

The question whether the Hungarian economy will work better as a result of the reform program cannot be answered with any assurance. The most that can be hoped for, under present circumstances, is that *attitudes*, if not conditions, may change as a result of the reforms. As it is, the economy faces a long uphill fight before there will be any meaningful improvement in the living conditions of the Hungarian people.

MR. KADAR'S ALBATROSS*

Failed revolutions are nothing new in Hungarian history. But that was not why the tenth anniversary on October 23rd of the most recent of these was ignored inside Hungary. The present government had nothing to celebrate, and those who had at least something to commemorate knew better than to try. Hungary's brave October revolution has officially become a non-event and that, in a sense, is a measure of its failure. But its influence persists—not, most emphatically, as an inspiration to the Hungarians to try again, but as a barrier between most of them and their rulers. It is, to mix the metaphor, the invisible albatross round Mr. Kadar's neck.

On the face of it, the regime is increasingly giving the Hungarians more and more of what they want. Budapest's restaurants are full of people; its shops are full of food, clothes, furniture, transistors and television sets—and they are being bought, not just window-shopped. More and more people are buying their own flats; more and more are becoming car-owners. And yet behind all the evidence of growing material prosperity a basic mutual mistrust lies heavily between most people and the regime; it inhibits the regime from trying to put itself across more frankly and prevents people from giving it the benefit of any doubt.

The higher prices announced last January, together with some pension and wage increases, are a case in point. The government had a sound enough justification for them. But it chose to make the worst possible impression by officially denying that any increases were contemplated only a few weeks before they were in fact announced. The subsequent involved explanations by government spokesmen that what people lost on the swings they would surely make up on the roundabouts did not stop the grumbling or silence the alarmist rumours; they merely provided a field day for the Budapest wits. Mr. Kadar is said to have regretted afterwards that he did not handle the matter more openly.

*Reprinted by permission from *The Economist* (Oct. 29, 1966), pp. 454, 457, and (Dec. 10, 1966), p. 1127.

The government's nervous mistrust has been sharpened by the unexpected increase last year in the number of defections by Hungarians visiting western countries. The actual number involved is said not to have been large (less than a thousand) but the quality, in terms of intellectual training and professional skill, was high. The government was given a sharp jolt—in particular Mr. Kadar himself, who had always argued firmly and courageously in favour of a liberal policy on visits abroad. This policy has not been reversed this year; in fact there is believed to have been little, if any, drop in the total of Hungarians going west. But the numbers have been made up more of dependable groups than unpredictable individuals; and the regulations governing visits abroad have been tightened up. Writers, who had come to take their annual trip westward for granted, have found it harder to go west this year. The reason in their case is obscure; it may be due to the regime's general nervousness in this tenth anniversary year.

One reason for last year's defections was the worsening in the international situation, which made people feel that if they returned to Hungary they might get cooped up there for years. But by far the chief reason was the fear that they would lose their comparative affluence under the economic reforms that were then already being foreshadowed; they could feel far more certain of a rising standard of living if they stayed in the West where (especially in western Germany) their professional qualifications would command top salaries. Stuck with a government that commands scant respect or loyalty, individual Hungarians tend, if they get the chance, to go all out for their own and their children's prospects.

To be fair, the Hungarian public's profound mistrust of economic change is a problem that any government, communist or capitalist, would have to contend with. Hungary has had more than its fair share of economic crises and devaluations, with the result that the built-in reaction of the individual Hungarian to any government-engineered economic "reform" is that he is bound to end up worse off than before. The economic reform is not due to be introduced until January 1968. But Mr. Kadar is already having to deny rumours about price increases connected with it. His denials would, of course, carry more weight if the government had dealt more frankly with this year's increases.

The much-maligned economic reform is in principle a sensible attempt to rescue the economy from the dead hand of the planners along the lines of the reforms being introduced in Czechoslovakia and elsewhere. The Hungarians may be better off than they were, but the regime now accepts the view, which the experts have been trying to put across for years, that in the long run a healthy and expanding economy depends on substituting indirect controls and strong financial incentives for the sluggish, misguided and often plain stupid operations of central planning. Preparations are going ahead. The price increases in food, transport and fuel being introduced at intervals throughout this year are designed to clear away some of the anomalies and distortions that might obstruct the reform. In this year's economic plan the number of indices governing each enterprise's activities have been considerably curtailed. A number of firms, most of them manufacturing largely for export, are experimenting with various forms of self-management.

The party finally committed itself to reform in May, when the central committee passed a resolution which set forth at length the principles upon which the economic changes are to be based. At the moment nobody really knows precisely how these principles are to be put into practice. Innumerable experts and commissions are working overtime to try to find out. The hope is that the answers will all emerge by the middle of next year so that individual enterprises will have six months in which to prepare themselves for a more decentralised system.

Just how decentralised remains, understandably enough, rather vague. For instance, the party resolution commits itself to the three-tier price system favoured by the Czechs, but gives no indication of how large each of the three price categories (fixed; fixed within limits; and free) will be. Unofficial estimates of the proportion of free prices, which will not include basic foodstuffs, range between 30 and 50 per cent; even the lower figure is about twice what the Czechs have in mind. On the other hand, although commentators claim that the state will be responsible only for major investments under the reform, the party resolution betrays considerable reluctance to let control over investment slip too far out of the central planners' hands. One suspects there may still be quite a lively tug-of-war between the distinguished economists, whose brain-child the reform really is, and the more conservative members of the party hierarchy.

One point about the reform that does already emerge clearly is that there is to be no attempt to sell it to the workers by incorporating in it a measure of workers' self-management on the Jugoslav model. (Workers' self-management was among the original demands of the revolutionaries ten years ago.) Instead there is a good deal of rather vague talk about enlarging the role of the trade unions; and in fact the unions have recently been relieved of some of their routine chores in connection with administering the welfare services—presumably to clear the decks for developing other activities. The manager, however, is to be unmistakably the boss in his own factory; and one of the major questions facing the reformers is whether they can find enough men with enough of the right qualifications to run the factories successfully. Some people think the financial rewards of factory management should be sharply stepped up at once; on the whole, ordinary factory managers are not among those who can afford to have their own villa on Lake Balaton.

Inevitably the reform is causing considerable perturbation inside the party. Party members have perforce got accustomed to the idea that they do not have a prescriptive right to all the good jobs; for some years the regime has been firmly weeding out completely unqualified party hacks from responsible posts. But the new decentralised economic administration seems, to the bureaucratically minded party functionary, to contain all kinds of dire threats to the authority of the party in general and himself in particular. The party resolution of last May declared that the party's "leading and guiding role" would inevitably assert itself, and in the next breath stated categorically that "under no circumstances" must party organisations directly control economic bodies. It is all very confusing.

The Hungarian communists are not of course the only ones to be faced with this problem. But the leadership lacks the buoyant self-confidence of, say, the Jugoslavs; and most of the rank and file, especially in the provinces, completely lack either the ability or the imagination to rethink the party's role. When the party was re-formed after the revolution ten years ago, it naturally did not attract a very high calibre of recruit. Mr. Kadar remarked rather revealingly in a recent speech that what they would like was a situation in which there were few people inside the party whom they would like to see outside, and a great many outside whom they would be glad to have inside. Whatever one makes of the implications of that statement, the approach of the party congress, due at the end of next month, is probably regarded with some foreboding, especially by the rank and file. For at this rather critical time Mr. Kadar seems bound to make the best possible use of what party material he has—and that may well mean some changes, if not right at the top, at any rate further down the party hierachy.

Mr. Kadar himself seems pretty unbudgeable. He stands in the centre of the party, rebuffing the reactionaries and curbing the progressives. He is identified with the economic reform and therefore must pacify those who prophesy that it will end by fatally undermining the whole edifice of tight party control. (One way of doing this may be the current freeze on the general liberalisation programme.) On the other hand he must be encouraged by the knowledge that the party's future lies with the younger, more technocratically minded leaders who understand that the one really vital need in Hungary is to modernise the economy.

Mr. Kadar has the great advantage of being accepted by the Hungarian people as the best party leader they have. There is nothing at all positive about his popularity; nor is there about his famous slogan "he who is not against us is with us." He has to lead the country through a tricky period of economic change with a suspicious party behind him, and before him a public that is not only suspicious but apathetic. Unlike Mr Gomulka in Poland, he cannot try to whip up popular support by beating the anti-German drum, because the Hungarians do not feel all that strongly about the Germans. For obvious reasons (and with the country still garrisoned by Russian troops) he cannot, unlike Rumania's Mr Ceausescu, beat the nationalist drum. He has to remember, moreover, that the one thing that really rouses all Hungarians is the alleged treatment of the Hungarian minority in Transylvania.

Until the economic reform is safely launched, the regime will probably be content to let the process of liberalisation more or less go on marking time, although it will continue to do what it feels it safely can to lessen the gap between rulers and ruled. With significant timing, the central committee published, a few days before October 23rd, proposals for giving voters a more genuine choice of candidates at parliamentary elections. The effect of gestures like this and of the passage of time remains to be seen. Meanwhile, Mr. Kadar has no choice but to soldier on.

Facing both ways

Mr. Kadar tries hard to be all things to all men. He has been trying for years with a fair degree of success. He has turned himself into the virtually indispensable linkman between the Hungarian communist party and the population, both of whom are prepared to trust him as far as they trust anyone. The delegates, who watched him perform yet again at last week's Hungarian party congress in Budapest, may have been too familiar with the act to react strongly. But as a tight-rope act it was a remarkable performance; Mr. Kadar is likely to find it increasingly difficult to give satisfaction both as a party leader and a national leader if he really means to make a success of the economic reform due to be inaugurated in January 1968.

Mr. Kadar's problem is that he has to preserve the "leading role" of a party which is not really up to leading anyone anywhere—let alone in a distinctly unorthodox and adventurous direction. He and his colleagues told the congress frankly that there was a good deal of opposition to their cautious moves towards a more liberal regime as well as to the new economic course. They had been accused of falling down on their revolutionary ideals, and had been obliged to deal sternly with a number of recalcitrants; a few had even been expelled from the party.

It is one thing, however, to weed out the active opponents of a policy; it is quite another to make the rest of the party positively helpful in carrying it out. Mr. Kadar evidently realises that an essential preliminary is to remove party members' fears that if the economic decentralisation, which is an integral part of the reform, is really carried through, they will lose power and prestige and be thrust into a back seat. But in their efforts to do this at the congress, Mr. Kadar and his colleagues tied themselves into the most extraordinary knots; again and again they threw a sop to the anxious party members in one sentence, only to qualify it or snatch it away entirely in the next. One can detect a constant struggle between their anxiety to boost party morale—and how could this boosting be avoided at a party conference?—and their anxiety not to have the reform sabotaged by reactionary or plain stupid party members.

When the delegates got home they will not have found it easy to explain at all clearly how the leadership sees the new relationship between the local party organisations and the decentralised factory administration. One has the cloudy impression that the local organisations have been given (or may think they have been given) more of a green light to interfere in industrial affairs than is good for economic efficiency. The leaders may hope to counterbalance this by strengthening internal party discipline, punishing party members who abuse their powers and generally making the cadres more worthy of their responsibilities. Mr. Kadar made it clear that the aim is not to make the party much larger—membership now stands at just over 580,000—but to turn it into a real élite with the benevolent support (or at least acquiescence) of the rest of the country.

One instrument by which it is hoped to get the "broad masses" involved in the country's economic progress is the trade union movement. Several speakers referred to the new and more important role that was being worked out for the unions; Mr. Sandor Gaspar, who is head of the central trade union council, referred cryptically but tinglingly to the "socialist character" of the trades unions which "is only now beginning to unfold, in all its magnificence and with all its anxieties." How much of real substance there is in all this remains to be seen; it may be little more than window-dressing.

In his final speech Mr. Kadar upheld—although not without considerable shilly-shallying—his policy of not making party membership an essential qualification for holding top jobs. He must stick to this policy if the economic reform is to suceed and if he is to retain what popularity he has in the country as a whole. But some delegates will have found it a jarring note to sound at the end of a party congress; they may have remembered that one of the 40-odd resolutions which they had just approved criticised those who belittle political training and automatically give preference to educational and professional qualifications. But, then, that was typical of last week's proceedings; you had to listen to all the contradictory statements and then make up your own mind what to believe.

7. ECONOMIC REFORMS IN EAST GERMANY

THE NEW ECONOMIC SYSTEM:
*THE ROLE OF TECHNOCRATS IN THE DDR**
— · — · — · — · — · — · — · — · — · — ·

Thomas A. Baylis†

A recurring theme of political speculation from Saint-Simon onward has been the possibility of joining industrial and technological skill to political power; the suggestion has been that an age moulded by scientific and industrial revolution might see fit to grant political authority to the elite making that revolution. No group has been more diligent in trying to fit such a hypothesis to empirical reality than writers on the Soviet Union and Eastern Europe. There the very orientation of the regimes towards rapid industralisation and technical modernisation has made plausible the proposition that an élite of scientists, planners, managers, and engineers might successfully challenge the ill-trained party bureaucrats and professional revolutionaries originally in power. With the change in leadership personnel, so the argument proceeds, we may also expect changes in policy, from heavy-handed bureaucratism and emphasis on both internal and external class struggle, to economic pragmatism directed towards technical, and with it societal, rationalisation.

The assumption of power by the ex-engineers Brezhnev and Kosygin in the USSR, and that country's somewhat hesitant turn towards Liberman-inspired economic reforms, have given this argument new interest. My purpose here is to examine the evidence for a similar, and perhaps more pronounced, development in East Germany. There, a steady increase in the representation of highly-trained planning, managerial, and other technically or scientifically oriented officials in the higher party and state organs was followed in 1963 by the introduction of a broad set of economic reform measures known as the New Economic System (*Das neue ökonomische System der Planung und Leitung der Volkswirtschaft*—NÖSPL. The New Economic System became, and has remained, the centre of the SED's attention; except for the customary imprecations against the "fascists" and "militarists" in West Germany, public life and party propaganda in the DDR have been dominated by its demands. The hypothesis presents itself that a technocratic élite has indeed quietly taken power and has been translating its group interests into policy. It is the validity of this proposition I wish to examine here.

First it is necessary to clarify the meaning of the term "technocrat."

*Reprinted by permission from *Survey* (Oct. 1966), pp. 139–152. All footnotes deleted.
†Dr. Thomas A. Baylis teaches political science at the University of California, Berkeley. He is presently working on a study of intelligentsia in East Germany.

No argument assuming a rigid dichotomy between technical experts and "the party" in East European countries deserves serious attention, for the simple reason that virtually all leading technical officials are party members, often with long experience in organisational or agitational work, while an increasing number of leading party functionaries have had at least some technical training. The distinction I shall draw will be a more narrow, essentially functional one. Those whose training and experience have been primarily in technical, scientific, or economic fields, and whose present responsibilities lie in one of these areas, will be labelled "technocrats"; those whose training, experience, and present functions lie primarily in party organisation, agitprop, security, or other fields will be labelled, somewhat crudely, the apparatchiki. It is well to remember, however, that *both* groups are composed of loyal party members who have been thoroughly schooled in the principles of Marxism-Leninism and who deeply resent this sort of classification as overlooking, among other things, the essential dialectical unity of the political and economic spheres in a socialist society.

Classified according to their present functions (see Table 1), the

TABLE 1

COMPOSITION OF SED CENTRAL COMMITTEE AFTER 3RD, 4TH, 5TH AND 6TH
PARTY CONGRESSES, ACCORDING TO PRESENT FUNCTION

	1950 %	1954 %	1958 %	1963 %
Agitprop-culture-education	10.0	14.1	14.2	17.7
State functionaries	25.0	19.6	18.9	14.9
Mass organisations	13.8	12.5	10.8	8.8
Party bureaucracy	32.5	17.2	25.0	21.0
Workers	3.8	5.5	1.4	1.1
Economic functionaries	15.0	31.3	29.8	36.5

representation of economic functionaries among Central Committee members and candidates has increased from 15 per cent after the third party congress (1950) to 36.5 per cent after the sixth (1963). What is at least equally important, however, is the character of these functionaries. Most of those so classified in 1950 were in fact long-time party members without technical training, pressed into service as planners, economic ministers, factory managers and the like, in an era when political loyalty was more important to the regime than specialised expertise. Of those classed as technical functionaries in 1963, however, the majority have university or technical school diplomas; at least fourteen have the doctorate. The proportion of university graduates among the candidates is particularly high, and a large number of both candidates and full members are actively engaged in production or research, rather than belonging to the economic bureaucracy.

For the top members of the party, it is well to make the first distinction more explicit. Particularly among the older generation, many leading technocrats were in fact old party members whose technical careers date only from after the war, and who acquired their expertise, and often with it a rational economic outlook, on the job. The prototype of this sort of functionary was Bruno Leuschner, Chairman of the State Planning Commission from 1952 to 1961. Trained in sales work, Leuschner joined the German Communist Party in 1931, and spent the Hitler years in underground work in a series of prisons and concentration camps. Only after the war did he turn to economic affairs, first as Central Committee secretary and in 1947 as director of the planning division in the provisional East German government. The younger generation of technocrats have more often climbed to prominence on a series of economic and technical rungs; their political work has always been secondary. Erich Apel, Chairman of the Planning Commission from 1963 until his suicide in December of last year, is perhaps an extreme example of this type. While Leuschner was sitting in Mauthausen, Apel was at work on German rockets at Peenemünde; captured and exported to Russia, where he worked as an engineer, he returned to the DDR in 1952 to become Deputy Minister of Machine Building, and joined the SED only in 1957. Some of the younger functionaries (e.g. Mittag and Jarowinsky) have been educated and lived their entire adult lives under communism, and thus are without any attachment to the revolutionary and underground struggles of the past. They are the purer technocrats, and as a group are probably lower on ideological identification—but also on political skills and interest—than the older men. We shall see, however, that the differences between them are probably less important than their affinities.

The record of East German politics since at least 1956 is one of continuing conflict, sometimes latent, sometimes overt, between policies justified by the requirements of ideology or politics, and others answering to the demands of economic rationality. With few exceptions, politics emerged victorious from each of these encounters until the adoption of the New Economic System at the sixth congress. Then the situation becomes more blurred: the NES itself becomes the ground on which the struggle continues. The suicide of Erich Apel is a benchmark of this struggle.

The prehistory of the NES really begins with the 1956 heresy of the economist Fritz Behrens. Taking advantage of the relative intellectual freedom that flourished in the DDR that year, Behrens put forward a series of proposals which, while similar in some respects to those made by

Liberman and parts of the New Economic System itself, went beyond the detailing of economic reforms (e.g. decentralisation, price reform, use of profitability criteria) to their underlying political and ideological implications. He saw a "contradiction . . . between the form of state direction of the economy and the *content* of the quickly developing economic substructure," suggested that the state ought to begin withering away, and urged greater play for the "spontaneity" of the working masses. The implicit conflict between economic rationalisation and highly centralised political control thus emerged openly, as the regime was quick to recognise. Behrens was charged with "underestimating the significance of political power for the working class," ignoring the "leading role of the party," and minimising the menace of imperialist saboteurs. Not the withering away, but the consolidation (*Festigung*) of the socialist state was necessary at the present historical stage. After months of extravagent and bitter attacks on his "revisionism," Behrens in 1958—and again in 1960—performed the obligatory self-criticism.

One of Behrens' harshest critics in the massive campaign launched against his ideas was Fred Oelssner, a leading party ideologist who had turned his attention to economic problems; it was his class at the Institute of Economic Sciences that was reportedly the centre for the diffusion of the "revisionist" ideas of Behrens and several colleagues. However, it was quite clear that Oelssner shared Behrens' premise that DDR planning could not afford to ignore objective "economic laws," even when they appeared to contradict political imperatives. This view predominated in the DDR's powerful Economic Council, created in April 1957 as the central body for economic decision-making. The Council was headed by Leuschner and included in its membership Oelssner, two other old party functionaries turned economic specialists, Fritz Selbmann and Heinrich Rau, the head of the agricultural commission Paul Scholz, and the Finance Minister Willy Rumpf; Heinrich Ziller, the Central Committee's secretary for economic policy, while not a formal member, shared their pragmatic orientation. This orientation led some of the Council's members to increasingly open confrontations with Ulbricht: Oelssner and Scholz proposed following the Polish example and dissolving unprofitable collective farms, while Selbmann and Oelssner opposed Ulbricht's plan to imitate the decentralisation measures undertaken by Khrushchev in the Soviet Union.

The opposition of what came to be called the "managerialists" coincided with an unsuccessful attempt by the chief of cadres Karl Schirdewan and the State Security Minister Ernst Wollweber to replace Ulbricht, an undertaking which culminated in their own removal at the thirty-fifth Central Committee plenum in February 1958. Only Ziller, who committed suicide before the plenum, has been directly identified as one of the *frondeurs*, but Oelssner was accused of supporting them and removed from the Politburo, while Selbmann was fired as Deputy Premier. The latter bore the brunt of the attack on those accused of adopting a "Western managerial ideology." "For Fritz Selbmann," one party critic declared, "the new era is not socialism and communism, but the new technology and atomic power." Other presumed "managerialists," like Rau and Scholz, were not punished, but at the next party congress numerous economic officials, most notably the high planning official Grete Wittkowski, were removed from the Central Committee or demoted, and economic functionaries were purged in the party organisations of seven of the DDR's fifteen regions.

Following the purges, Ulbricht was able to implement his own economic reorganisation on the Soviet model. The central economic ministries were dissolved, certain planning functions were assigned to regional bodies, and power at the centre was concentrated in the Planning Commission under Leuschner, who, though he had sympathised with the outlook of the "managerialists," had avoided lending them open support. The focus of the SED's economic policy became the *ökonomische Hauptaufgabe*: overtaking the Federal Republic in per capita consumption of "all" important foods and commodities by 1961. This programme, with its initial emphasis on the expansion of consumer goods production, housing, and the like, followed a similar pronouncement by Khrushchev in the USSR, and was accompanied by new pressures for recognition of the DDR and the neutralisation of West Berlin. Ulbricht hoped to establish the legitimacy and viability of the DDR by increasing its attractiveness while liquidating the Western "show-window" within it.

Achieving the *ökonomische Hauptaufgabe* would have been problematic in the best of circumstances. In early 1960, however, Ulbricht decided to complete the collectivisation of the countryside, and forced the remaining one-half of the country's agricultural acreage into the "socialist sector" in the astonishingly short time of three months. Circumstantial evidence, as well as economic logic, suggests that collectivisation was carried out only in the teeth of opposition from the Planning Commission and Minister-President Grotewohl. Immediately before the collectivisation drive, several agricultural officials, regional party secretaries, and Grotewohl himself, had renounced the use of force in bringing farmers into the collectives. At the eighth Central Committee plenum, summoned only towards the close of the drive, the Planning Commission official Wunderlich and the party secretary of the Magdeburg district Pisnik both expressed their surprise at developments. Since Pisnik was a candidate member of the Politburo, it may well be that even this body was not consulted before the campaign was initiated. In any case, forced collectivisation upset the delicate balance of the economy and provoked a sudden growth of the refugee stream which was stopped only by the building of the Berlin wall.

The primacy of politics over economic rationality enjoyed still another triumph in the year of the Wall. In order to free the DDR from dependence on trade with West Germany, *Aktion Störfreimachung* was initiated; the attempt was made to put into production thousands of items previously imported, and to convert East German facilities to the utilisation of materials from the Soviet Union and Eastern Eruope. Once again, this unrealistic attempt at partial autarky was opposed by leading planning and factory officials. In July 1961 Leuschner left the Planning Commission to become "coordinator" of the entire economy and subsequently DDR delegate to Comecon. Later events strongly suggest that he was kicked upstairs, probably for opposing *Störfreimachung*. His functions as Planning Commission head were divided between two veteran apparatchiki without technical experience, Alfred Neumann and Karl Mewis—the latter notorious for his leading role in the collectivisation drive. The plan worked out under Leuschner's direction was rejected because it took too little account of the demands of *Störfreimachung*: the "wanderers between two worlds" in economic posts, said Mewis, would have to change their ways. Neumann added a criticism of the "confused leadership principles" of the old Commission. Only a year later, however, *Aktion Störfreimachung* was quietly dropped; six months after that, so was Mewis.

In the critical decisions of the 1956–1963 period, then, political considerations consistently triumphed over economic ones. It would be an error, however, to regard these years as ones of complete impotence for the technocrats. Their numbers in prominent positions in party and state increased; even when the Planning Commission was divided and placed under the leadership of political functionaries, the advisers and staff immediately below them remained largely unchanged. In these years demands for technological rationalisation crept increasingly into party propaganda; and the very fact that the crucial issues we have discussed could be formulated as a choice between political and technocratic alternatives testifies to the growing influence of the second perspective. Perhaps unconsciously, the ground was being prepared for the New Economic System.

What seems to have led to the actual introduction of the System was the convergence of practical problems with the discussion of new ideas and with changes in personnel, although it is difficult to assign to each the exact weight it deserves. The death of *Störfreimachung* may be taken as symbolic of a recognition on the part of the SED leaders of the failure of previous economic policy. Total growth had slowed, investment had fallen drastically behind plan figures, and the DDR suffered from serious economic disproportions. In mid-1962 Erich Apel moved to the Council of Ministers, and Günter Mittag, who had already expressed unconventional ideas concerning the usefulness of market devices in a planned economy, became Central Committee economic secretary. It seems probable that these, together with Leuschner, were in a particularly favourable position to promote measures of economic rationalisation, given the evident failure of Mewis and Neumann. The publication of Liberman's "Profit-Plan-Premium" in the DDR towards the end of September prompted a discussion among DDR economists encouraged by Ulbricht himself. It is noteworthy that one of Liberman's most enthusiastic advocates was the ex-"revisionist" Behrens. By November, the draft programme of the SED was ready, containing important elements of the NES. The essentials of the System were spelled out at the sixth party congress in January, and after some months of further discussion and a giant conference of managers and economic functionaries in June, the Council of Ministers published a lengthy set of directives putting the NES in relatively definitive form. The emphasis and details of the System, however, have fluctuated considerably in the ensuing years.

Official East German descriptions of the NES begin (and often end) with a series of highly generalised slogans. Since the NES has itself become a kind of reigning domestic ideology in the DDR, little is proposed or carried out in the economy that is not claimed to belong to it. Nevertheless, it is possible to identify the general orientations, organisational changes, and some of the specific economic reforms that constitute it.

Perhaps most important is the insistence that in the present stage of the DDR's development the critical problem of socialism is an economic one, which must be solved by economic means: "It is an irrefutable truth that the most effective political argument in the long run is the economic facts that the workers of our republic create in tireless labour", Mittag has written. Ulbricht has adopted the slogan of "thinking economically" as the desideratum for DDR citizens; others speak of 'rationalisation' and "leadership on the basis of economic principles." What must be promoted is the "scientific-technical revolution," which represents a *qualitative* change in the forces of production fully possible only under socialism. Its success entails a struggle against "bureaucratism" and "administering" in favour of "scientific leadership," increased responsibilities for lower-echelon economic officials, and "creative" worker participation in production and planning decisions. The chief mechanisms of rationalisation are to be the "economic levers," i.e., interlocking incentives intended to maximise efficiency, quality, and quantity of output. These are to be based on the "material interestedness" of workers and functionaries, for (in a slogan that seems to stand Adam Smith on his head) "what profits the society must also profit the individual factory and the workers in it." The principal lever consistent with the need for making planning simpler and more flexible and production more efficient is *profit*, though there are numerous others.

The basis of the reorganisation of party and state organs is the "production principle," which is intended to allow "all questions to be decided . . . where they can best be resolved." More specifically, it means organisation divided along vertical, functional lines rather than territorially, with a concomitant delegation of responsiblities away from the central organs to those "closer to production." This, it is held, will strengthen "democratic centralism," not weaken it, because it frees the central authorities from the burden of trivial details and permits them to concentrate on the more basic problems and long-run perspectives (another much-invoked slogan) of the economy. Beneath the National Economic Council (*Volkswirtschaftsrat*) authority is divided among over 80 "socialist concerns" (VVBs), each of which bears responsibility for the plants of a particular branch of the economy. The NES converted the VVBs into "economic" (rather than "administrative") organs, with profit and loss accounting and major responsibility for investments, sales, planning, and the distribution of incentives. The general directors of the VVBs, according to Ulbricht, are the key figures of the New Economic System. Nevertheless, the NES also provides for increased responsibility for the individual plant (VEB) managers.

Party organisation has also been reformed in accordance with the production principle and also, in part, with Khrushchev's reorganisation of the CPSU. Bureaus of industry and building and for agriculture (under Mittag and Gerhard Grüneberg) were formed at the Politburo level, and imitated on the district and local levels; these were given direction of the basic party organisations in the VVBs, factories, collective farms, etc. The effect of this is to put the party secretaries in these economic units under the authority of technically-oriented party leaders; they are instructed to concentrate their efforts on promoting the principles of the NES. Thus the potential frictions and rivalries between economic and party functionaries are to be transformed into cooperation based on mutual interests and goals.

The most significant of the specific NES reforms is undoubtedly the revision of the prices of DDR goods to correspond with their actual costs of production (or "the socially necessary expenditure of labour," as it is officially put, in accordance with Marxist theory). Such a reform was indispensable in order to make the economic levers of profit and cost effective in maximising efficiency. As before, however, prices are fixed by the state; no flexibility, i.e. direct responsiveness to supply and demand as proposed for some prices earlier by Behrens, is permitted. Thus the revision of prices, while initially carried out in three stages to end in 1966, is expected to be a continuing process. The revaluing of existing capital and of its depreciation rates, along with the *Produktionsfondsabgabe*, which amounts to an interest charge on that capital, similarly have the purpose of producing comparable cost structures throught DDR industry and thus making the profit criterion usable.

"In principle," new investment is to be financed out of the profits of the VVB and the individual VEB itself, or else from credit extended by the state bank and expected to be repaid from future profits. Since the regime is far from ready to relinquish its control over investment emphases, however, state subsidisation remains extensive, all major investment decisions must have central approval, and profit not devoted to approved purposes is skimmed off, as before, by the government. Special funds are at the disposal of the VVB director for investment in new technology and for instituting premiums as incentives for fulfilling the particular needs of his industry. "Performance-determined" wages and premiums are regarded as the principal economic levers spurring on the individual; while nothing new for the East German worker, they are now being extended to the higher economic functionaries, including the VVB directors.

Although the New Economic System falls short of adopting the more radical proposals of Liberman and Behrens, and has recently been outstripped by the Czechoslovak and perhaps the Hungarian and Bulgarian reforms, at the time of its initiation it gave the DDR the most liberal economic programme of the Soviet bloc. It represented an unmistakable triumph for the technocratic wing of the SED, and an unwelcome innovation for its bureaucrats. The very introduction of the system at the sixth congress was coupled with a thinly-veiled threat against the apparatchiki: Ulbricht remarked that even those party functionaries who had performed faithfully in the past would have to be removed if they did not acquire some technical education and adjust themselves to the requirements of the System. A year later he repeated his warning, noting that some had failed to abandon outdated work habits and to overcome antiquated conceptions of economic problems. While few ventured to oppose the NES openly, the complaints of the DDR press and of high party officials make it evident that many resisted its implementation in practice, or expected its effect to be only nominal, permitting the continuance of the traditional modes of bureaucratic party control. Meanwhile, Apel and Mittag were becoming its chief propagandists, bringing out a series of books and numerous articles justifying and elaborating its proposals.

It must be understood that from the outset the New Economic

System was considerably more than a set of economic reforms; it soon came to acquire something of the status of an official domestic ideology, and became the focal point of party activity and organisation. As ideology, it sought to enlist the adherence of the DDR citizen to a "revolutionary" programme of change, seizing the new in technology and science for the purpose of developing a genuinely new society of unprecedented material well-being. The virtues of this approach for the DDR are apparent: it counters the appeal of the West German *Wirtschaftswunder*, presents an attractive set of material goals to a population still largely hostile or indifferent to formal Marxism-Leninism, appeals to the interests of the growing, important class of engineers and managers, and partakes of the universal appeal of the scientific and modern, while also seeming consistent with the Marxian Utopia.

The result of turning the NES into ideology has been a blurring of the economic and the political in the DDR. Party members are urged to press the cause of economic rationalisation as part of their political duties, while failures in economic performance are laid to the "ideological" omissions of state functionaries. Much of the accompanying propaganda has stressed the need for party officials to qualify themselves technically; almost as frequently, though with less success, economic functionaries have been urged to exert "political" leadership. It may be supposed that leading technocrats utilise this ambiguity to press economic reforms in political guises. But there is also persuasive evidence that the apparatchiki have in considerable measure adapted their own work methods to the vocabulary of the New Economic System, and under its banner continued substantial interference with economic rationalisation. The struggle between technocrats and apparatchiki, then, continues, but has moved *within* the ample framework of the New Economic System.

Two symbolic figures here are Günter Mittag and Alfred Neumann. Mittag is head of the Central Committee's bureau for industry and building, holds a doctorate in economics, and with Apel's death probably may be called the DDR's leading technocrat. One of his principal functions, however, has been to explicate the role of the *party* in the NES. He has repeatedly exhorted it to assert leadership in the promotion of economic rationalisation, where necessary even against the will of economic functionaries who for one reason or another are reluctant to accept innovations. In one characteristic passage he argues:

> . . . a very important side of the *political-ideological work* of the party organisations consists of patiently analysing mistakes, eliminating their causes, and helping people step by step to *develop an economic way of thinking* and to learn to *observe the requirements of objective economic laws* in all their activity, and thus to wage a determined struggle for the implementation of the decisions of our party.

This view of the role of the party must be coupled with his observation elsewhere that "the class struggle in the German Democratic Republic is carried out today above all in the field of production." For Mittag, the party is to become the helpmeet of the New Economic System.

Alfred Neumann, by contrast, is an old communist apparatchik who has since 1961 headed the important National Economic Council, a body responsible for short-term planning and for the direction and coordination of the VVBs. A reading of his speech at the seventh plenum of the Central Committee (December 1964) will reveal his essentially bureaucratic mentality in collision with the New Economic System: detailed reports on all possible subjects are repeatedly demanded, and the creation of several new and probably redundant economic bodies announced. The work of the Economic Council has been frequently criticised as a result— Ulbricht once accused it of "bureaucratic perfectionism" and complained that preparing its reports kept technical specialists "bound for weeks to their desks." For Neumann and those like him, the NES represents one of the periodic organisational shakeups of the communist bureaucracy, not a "revolution;" its instruments merely change the form, but not the extent, of apparatchik dominance.

It is too early to judge whether the conception of Mittag or of Neumann has triumphed. Some retrenchment apparently set in by the seventh plenum, when Central Committee speakers once more emphasised the "territorial principle" of party organisation alongside the NES-oriented "production principle." Kurt Hager, Central Committee secretary for ideology, complained that while, earlier, economic questions had been neglected in favour of more general political propaganda, now ideological work had been pushed partially into the background. The increasing importance accorded his ideological commission and the commission for party and organisation questions was probably intended as a counterweight to the influence of the bureaus for industry and for agriculture.

The NES may have suffered much more profound a blow with the suicide of Erich Apel at the end of November 1965. The immediate impetus to this act was given by the signing of a long-term trade agreement between the DDR and the Soviet Union, providing for the exchange of some 60 milliard marks worth of goods in the next five years. Reports circulating in the West claim that the agreement forces the DDR to accept prices below the world market level for some of its exports and to pay excessively high prices for Soviet imports; even without open price discrimination, however, the agreement ties over 50 per cent of DDR trade to a country in many respects on an inferior technological level. Apel, it is said, wished to transfer much of the DDR's trade westward, and felt the agreement would greatly damage the potential of the NES; he fought a long battle with Ulbricht over the issue, who contended that political necessities demanded the signing of the agreement.

Whatever the truth of these reports, and of the less credible and more sensational ones that proliferated in the days after Apel's death, the official account—that Apel had suffered a nervous breakdown owing to overwork—also has much to recommend it. The transition to the New Economic System brought with it strains and confusions that kept him habitually working into the early morning hours. The reorganisation of party and production produced conflicts over spheres of responsibility, for example, between the VVBs and VEBs; some VVBs took advantage of their new powers to further their own narrowly-conceived self-interest at the expense of the whole economy, while others fell considerably below planned output; the planning process became so snarled that the perspective plan, originally intended to cover the years 1964–1970, is only now being submitted for discussion; finally, certain major economic results, notably the productivity of new investment and the growth in national income, have proved disappointing.

All these problems were brought up at the eleventh plenum (15–19 December 1965), meeting less than two weeks after Apel's death. While Apel was not criticised directly, the State Planning Commission was, for falling behind in the adoption of modern planning methods and particularly for failing to resist the "frequently unreal" demands of individual branches of the economy in favour of the more general interests of society; the Chairman of the Commission had the duty above all of maintaining "balance" in the economy. Ulbricht showed himself particularly concerned over the lag in national income growth, and demanded the steering of investments into areas which would improve it. Since the NES was intended in part to shift emphasis from purely quantitative to qualitative economic development, this lag should not have been terribly surprising; Ulbricht's complaint seems to indicate he is reluctant to accept all of the system's implications.

Nevertheless, he proclaimed 1966 as the beginning of its "second stage." This second stage will include the completion of the price reform, the partial introduction of the *Produktionsfondsabgabe*, and strengthened emphasis on the financing of investment in the VVBs from their own profits and borrowed funds. All these are important components of genuine rationalisation, although they do not go beyond what had been laid out earlier. The emphasis in Ulbricht's speech on VVB "egoism" might seem to suggest a curtailment of the prerogatives of their general directors, and some Western observers have so interpreted it. In fact the responsibilities of the directors are claimed to have been expanded, and indeed may have been, particularly in the planning process.

The abolition of Neumann's National Economic Council as "superfluous" points in this direction; it was criticised for overproduction of paperwork and for trying to decide all questions itself. The nine new industrial ministries replacing it, together with the new Planning Commission, are expected to employ fewer officials than the Council and the old Commission; this may be illusory, but of the new ministers, only two (Neumann and Fritz Scharfenstein) are apparatchiki; the other seven are managers or economic experts. Apel's successor as chief of the strengthened Planning Commission is Gerhard Schürer, a 45-year-old technocrat with long planning experience in both party and state organs. The day of the technocrat in East Germany is far from over.

In fact, what has emerged from the eleventh plemun is a Council of Ministers—and here, according to Ulbricht, will major economic decisions increasingly be made—dominated by economic officials. Not all, to be sure, may be identified as technocrats: Rauchfuss, Wyschofsky, Schürer, Balkow, and Zimmermann are; Ewald and Scholz are agricultural experts, Rumpf is an old communist who has been Finance Minister for many years, and Max Sefrin is Health Minister. Neumann, now Minister for Material Economy, is a member, and the chairman and Premier is Willi Stoph, an apparatchik with some economic experience who has often been regarded, without much evidence, as a relative "liberal."

The membership of the Council is particularly interesting in contrast to the composition of the SED Politburo, which remains dominated by apparatchiki, if not Stalinists. None of the twelve full members of the Politburo, and only two of its seven candidates, Mittag and Werner Jarowinsky, may be regarded as full-blown technocrats. Three other canidates, Gerhard Grünberg, Ewald, and Margarete Müller, have their principal responsibilities in agriculture, but have not been known to align themselves with the technocrats. Of the full members, only Neumann performs primarily economic functions.

The peculiar division of labour between the "political" Politburo and the "economic" Council of Ministers may be seen as reflecting the present unstable equilibrium of East German politics. In a crisis, the apparatchiki are in a position to enforce political requirements at the expense of economic ones; the signing of the new trade agreement is testimony to the ultimate primacy of the former. Moreover, given the present structure and balance of forces, the apparatchiki should be able to control the choice of Ulbricht's successor when the dictator retires or dies. At the same time they are publicly committed to an ideology of modernised production which lends legitimacy rather to the technocrats than to themselves. In spite of the undisguised Stalinism that characterised the pronouncements on cultural policy at the eleventh plenum, there was no basic tampering with the New Economic System. Even the apparatchiki appear to recognise that at its present stage of development the DDR can do neither without its technocrats nor without their economic reforms. It is further noteworthy that the ages of the full members of the Politburo range from 52 to 73 and average over 60; the technocrats on the Council of Ministers and Politburo range from 37 to 57 and average 44.

The question remains whether the technocrats have the will as well as the ability to assume political power. Here it is well to recall the caution with which I began: there are no pure technocrats or pure apparatchiki. In many respects the two groups share more in terms of training and outlook than the foregoing analysis may imply. Moreover, within each group divisions on other lines may sometimes be as acute as those between the two. There is also some tendency for the technocrats to regard politics as the special province of the apparatchiki, just as their own province is the economic sphere.

The history I have recounted demonstrates, however, that if the technocrats are to achieve their economic purposes they cannot remain aloof from politics or avoid some challenge to the apparatchik's pre-eminence. The years since 1956 have witnessed a steady expansion of their numbers and their influence on policy. It would be foolish to expect the technocrats to seize power in a spectacular *coup d'état*. But through the continuing quiet expansion of their presence and their influence, and without the abandonment of the forms or the vocabulary of Marxism-Leninism, they may one day become the effective ruling élite of the DDR.

ECONOMIC REFORMS IN EAST GERMANY*
— · — · — · — · — · — · — · — · — · —

Dorothy Miller and Harry G. Trend†

Economic reform is the order of the day in Eastern Europe. With the possible exception of Albania, every country in the area is currently considering a general overhaul of its planning and management system, and some are already experimenting with various phases of the contemplated reforms. In these experiments, East Germany is a trailblazer.

Before turning to the particulars of the reform measures in the GDR (German Democratic Republic), it may be useful to give an account of the economic factors which during the late 1950's and early 1960's characterized all of the economies of the Soviet bloc and which in turn awakened the current "cost consciousness" and desire for reform.

Declining economic growth rates occurred in Eastern Europe soon after the Communist regimes had harnessed their unused resources. As the decline continued, it became apparent that the initial beneficial effects on growth resulting from a release of underemployed rural and in some

*Reprinted by permission from *Problems of Communism*. (March–April 1966), pp. 29–36. All footnotes deleted.

†Miss Dorothy Miller is an analyst of East German affairs at Radio Free Europe, Munich. Dr. Harry G. Trend is an advisor on economic affairs at the same organization.

cases industrial labor, and from improved utilization of existing production facilities, were nonrecurrent. In time, fewer uncommitted reserves could be found to sustain growth rates comparable to those achieved during the early years of Communist rule. For long periods, these countries followed the policy of underinvesting in agriculture, housing, and the consumer economy, permitting these capital-starved sectors to deteriorate. Similarly, they neglected investments in research and development and chose to live on the technological and scientific inheritance of the past. In short, the Communist regimes concentrated their investments in areas with good prospects for success. But since all segments of even Communist-run economies are interrelated, the continued decline in productivity of the neglected sectors has acted as a brake on the entire economy, forcing the realization that the high rates of industrial growth in the early years were largely gained at the expense of potentially higher long-range growth.

Furthermore, the desire to push growth rates at all cost has encouraged the Communist planners to overtax existing resources. Rarely has provision been made for breakdowns or unforeseen contingencies. Thus production setbacks in one sector have frequently spread, through a domino effect, to other sectors.

In the first decade of Communist rule in Eastern Europe this over-extension was further stimulated by the policy of autarkic development adopted throughout the area. As long as the policy of economic self-sufficiency prevailed, inefficiencies remained obscured because their effects were redistributed within each country. Once, however, the first efforts were made to introduce international specialization within the bloc, comparative costs became an important factor. This is what happened in the early 1960's when the Soviet Union tried to induce Comecon to establish a supranational planning agency for the bloc. In the ensuing arguments about who should specialize in producing what, it was quickly realized that there was no valid basis, supported by economically meaningful comparative prices, for conducting studies on relative efficiency in Eastern Europe. It is indeed reasonable to assume that these discussions gave an early impetus to the economic reforms now in progress. Moreover, the eventual collapse of the attempts to introduce bloc-wide planning and multilateral trade relations in Eastern Europe strengthened the need for expanding trade with the West and thus further contributed to rising cost-consciousness.

But even more important as a stimulus to the new quest for efficiency was the pervasive internal economic deterioration throughout the bloc, marked not only by continuing shortages of key commodities and industrial bottlenecks, necessitating a constant resetting of targets, but by mounting inventories of unsalable goods. As long as the minimum needs of the population remained unsatisfied and an artificially-created demand for investment goods prevailed, almost any product, no matter how shoddy, could be sold. But when, at the end of the 1950's, the consumers had acquired sufficient purchasing power to exercise a degree of choice, the burgeoning warehouses of rejected goods became symbols of the bankruptcy of Stalinist command-planning. The established system of economic management stood exposed as a travesty of reason—and as a political liability to boot.

Factors Peculiar to East Germany

In varying degrees the economic conditions outlined above were typical of all the Comecon countries before the onset of the current reforms. The economy of the GDR, however, evidenced a number of peculiar characteristics which need to be spelled out if East Germany's lead in the reform movement and its particular approach to economic reform are to be properly understood. A brief enumeration of some of these special aspects of the GDR economy follows.

1. The East German economy is the most industrialized in Eastern Europe. As such it has lacked—since the repair of war damages—some of the systemic conditions that favored protracted rapid growth in the less developed economies of the bloc. This explains in part why next to Czechoslovakia—the other relatively highly developed country of Eastern Europe—the GDR since 1963 has experienced the most serious drop in the rate of economic growth in the area.

2. East Germany has experienced the most severe labor shortage in the Soviet bloc. Only the building of the Berlin wall in 1961 stopped the massive exodus of skilled labor and highly trained technicians to West Germany, forcibly stabilizing the labor force. Concern with labor efficiency was thus an early phenomenon in the GDR.

3. Unlike other East European countries, the GDR was required to pay heavy reparations to the Soviet Union. Paradoxically, perhaps, this burden stimulated growth rates in the 1950's and also obviated temporarily the need to pay any serious attention to quality and assortment in consumer goods production. Eventually, however, the excess purchasing power of the East German workers producing goods for delivery to the USSR, combined with unsatisfied domestic needs, put the East Berlin planners under heavy pressure to pay more heed to consumer preferences—and to problems of economic management.

4. East Germany's dependence on foreign trade (it is a heavy importer of raw materials and agricultural products, and an exporter of finished goods) along with its exposure to Western markets has encouraged cost consciousness and a desire for more efficient management methods.

5. Proximity to the German Federal Republic has forced the East Germans to make continuous comparisons of economic accomplishments on the two sides of the border and to reexamine their own system of management.

6. One of the institutional peculiarities of the GDR, unparalleled elsewhere in Eastern Europe, has been the wide variety of ownership forms both in industry and in agriculture. In the industrial sphere, the GDR has had the standard socialized enterprise, the semistateowned or state-participating enterprise (prevalent in consumer goods production) and the privately-owned enterprise. The coexistence of these three types of ownership has made it necessary to develop a new coordinating organization, the product group, which could cover all three institutional forms. Similarly in agriculture there have been three forms or degrees, of collective ownership, and the GDR leaders are using the current reforms as an instrument to further collectivization of the least "socialized" farms, the so-called LPG Type 1.

7. Successful implementation of the current reforms is predicated on the highly developed labor discipline in East Germany, which is unique in East-Central Europe. This inheritance of the traditional conscientious German attitude to work allows the East German planners to expect uncommon sensitivity to problems of efficiency. There is, in addition, the tradition of good management and high regard for skill, all of which foster respect for a well-run, well-organized enterprise.

8. The East German Communist Party (SED) has shown little tolerance for dissent within its ranks; it is probably the most authoritarian— or disciplined—of all bloc parties. This characteristic helps to explain the relative lack of opposition to the new economic model and hence the rapidity with which the party has been able to get the economic reform program underway.

9. Finally, one should mention Walter Ulbricht's unusual sensitivity to developments in the Soviet bloc; in the past this sixth sense often made it possible for him to be the first on any new bandwagon no matter how inconsistent his attitude might appear. When all members of the bloc began considering economic reforms, Ulbricht once again sensed which way the wind was blowing and—seizing the initiative—provided the GDR with an early lead in the economic reform movement.

Substance of the Reforms

Although a small number of experiments in economic management were conducted early in 1963, the general reform blueprint, entitled "Guidelines on the New Economic System of Planning and Managing the Economy," did not appear until July of that year. The report, which had been adopted by the Council of Ministers, gave immediate attention to industrial price reforms. Under its terms, a strict accounting system was to be introduced as a prelude to the establishment of new industrial prices which would cover "costs." Enterprises were to operate without direct state subsidy and become financially self-sufficient.

The first price modifications, affecting industrial raw material and semi-finished product prices, went into effect in April 1964. Further adjustments were to be completed in a series of stages by January 1966. On the basis of this new price structure, prices of finished goods would then be revised.

The new element in the revised price structure is the inclusion of all "costs." Currently, "costs" are largely influenced by administratively fixed prices of production resources, such as labor. Since these prices as well as the prices of semi-manufactured goods are centrally determined, the market forces of supply and demand have only a slight direct effect on final prices. Therefore, most prices will continue to be rigid. However, a few economic organizations are now experimentally participating in the price-setting process, which may signal the first move toward greater price flexibility.

Since the recent organizational changes, the various Associations of State Enterprises (VVBs) have become the new centers of economic power. This power has devolved to them from the industrial departments of the National Economic Council and the State Planning Commission. At the same time, the VVB has become the master of a large number of state-owned industrial enterprises (VEB). In effect, the VVB has been the beneficiary of a two-directional shift of decision-making power—downward from the central agencies and upward from the VEB. However, some enterprises are still directly responsible to the industrial departments of the National Economic Council, while others are subject to the local control of the Bezirk economic councils.

As a means of coordinating all enterprises along horizontal lines, legally independent product-groups, which include all types of enterprise—socialized, semisocialized and private—have been created. These are also responsible to the VVBs. It appears that the product-groups are becoming a merging device, enhancing the power of the VVBs.

Furthermore, certain limited experiments with indirect economic controls have been undertaken. They include the application of a selective credit policy by banks which follow commercial banking practices; a reduction of the use of state subsidies; the employment of a system of differentiated interest charges on capital funds; a revaluation of assets and the application of a system of differentiated depreciation rates; and a revision of the wage and premium systems, tying them to enterprise earnings so as to make possible the use of profit as a measure of economic performance. An expanded use of contracts, based on a new contract law, to facilitate interorganizational economic relations (replacing the directive-oriented system), is also envisaged, as well as the development of closer ties between production and distribution activities and eventually a more flexible price system.

Beginning in the spring of 1965, experiments with a "self-contained" system of economic levers followed earlier tests with only one or two of the economic instruments mentioned above. A broad application of this system is to be introduced in 1966.

Thus far the East Germans still rely heavily on the application of strict direct controls with supporting information from the new financial and accounting systems; they appear likely to continue keeping firm central control of the price mechanism for a long time to come.

The new reforms have largely eliminated direct state budgetary supports. A new system of financial assistance, directed by the VVBs, has replaced the old state subsidies. The VVBs now redistribute pooled profits as well as funds provided by banks through repayable credits. The VEBs and VVBs must also finance a larger part of their investments from their own resources. Investment grants by the state are to be limited largely to those industries which expand more rapidly than they can accumulate funds or obtain bank credits.

To a lesser extent these economic reforms have also been applied to the non-industrial production and the "non-productive" sectors of the economy, such as agriculture, building and construction, and foreign and domestic trade. Agricultural enterprises are being affected only slowly. The main reform features include measures to expand coordination between the less collectivized farms, to increase the employment of commercial contracts, particularly between the state procurement and purchasing enterprises (VEABs) and agricultural collectives, and between banks and agricultural collectives.

Although the building and construction industry was not specifically referred to in the "Guidelines," some reorganization in the industry took place during the latter part of 1964. By 1966, a new system of contruction-contracting should be fully implemented. New relations between investing enterprises, the general contractors, and the subcontracting and supplying enterprises are being established. In this field, too, commercial contracts will be the key instruments for defining mutual obligations and responsibilities.

The domestic and foreign trade networks are also being reformed. In both cases, attempts are being made to bring the producer closer to the distributor and the consumer. New marketing methods and commercial contracts are being gradually introduced, particularly in domestic trade. The old production system, based on centrally guaranteed orders, is being relinquished. Wholesalers will place purchase orders with manufacturers on the basis of market research data and information from retail distributors. An element of respect for consumer preference will thus have been introduced.

In the field of international trade, the foreign trade enterprise (AHU) will now be supervised by both the Foreign Trade Ministry and the production enterprise organizations (the VVBs and VEBs) under an arrangement of "co-responsibility." This measure represents the first dilution of the sacred principle of "state trade monopoly."

The new reforms also affect local governments, which will enjoy new powers of taxation and expenditure as well as generally enlarged financial authority.

In addition to the reforms discussed above, a number of other measures have been announced for the future. The schedule is very sketchy, but it does show that the implementation of the reform blueprint is expected to stretch over a period of years.

Impact of the Reforms

It may be permissible, even at this early date, to discuss some of the possible effects of the East German reform program. In so far as economic results are concerned, the Pankow regime has already pointed out marked improvements in the growth rate. This trend may continue, but little useful speculation about long-term prospects can be undertaken at this stage. Institutionally, the most important change is the new strengthening of the authority of the State Enterprise Associations (VVBs) and the State Owned Enterprises (the VEBs). As a result, a new type of "property right" is emerging, buttressed by new principles in Contract Law. Property may now be viewed as having two major aspects: ownership and management. As far as ownership rights are concerned, little change can be expected. The state will continue to be the owner of the major means of production, actually or nominally. This is an ideological minimum of socialism. The major change is the separation of ownership from management—a development similar to that long witnessed in the West—which is the result of the abandonment of much managerial authority by the central state organs in favor of local economic organs. The power to manage, of course, remains circumscribed by the regulations laid down by the political authority.

The shift of the spotlight to the managers of the VVBs and the VEBs immediately raises a question about the background and affiliation of these technocrats. Frequently, such a shift of authority is described in terms of a struggle for control between two antagonistic groups: the party functionaries and the technocrat-managers. However, there is no reason to rule out the possibility of a symbiotic relationship between them. As long as political organs can influence the economic environment within which an economic organization must operate, there will be a need for a politically-oriented leader in every economic organization who will be able to bring about favorable changes in the political environment, and thereby help to assure the economic success of the technocrat-managerial group. By the same token, if the success of a political leader depends on economic results, he will require the cooperation of the technocrat-manager. It is therefore conceivable that political-managerial teams may move together up and down the ladder of success. The state, operating through the party, will in any case continue controlling the teams, rewarding the more successful politico-techno-managerial groups by placing them in preferential positions with the concomitant emoluments, and penalizing failures.

The managers, under the new system, will have to adjust their behavior to conform to the new instruments of control rather than to the old central directives. For example, under the old system, bonuses were paid for quantitative overfulfillment of the plan. With this kind of an incentive, the managers usually sought to establish the lowest possible quota in order to assure the largest overfulfillment and, hence, the largest bonus. Under the new system, prices of raw materials are being set below the level that market forces would dictate. This means that some kind of administrative allocation of raw materials is necessary. At the established prices, these raw materials will be in short supply and, as in a war economy, become a sort of currency in barter transactions between enterprises. Similarly, under a system of administered prices, an enterprise might produce goods of different degrees of scarcity relative to demand. Under such circumstances, the enterprise manager would favor the practice of tie-in sales, selling desirable and scarce goods only if the buyer also purchases goods in lesser demand. These are hypothetical examples of how the reformed GDR economy might operate under the new rules.

Operational changes will influence many financial relationships within a State Enterprise Association (VVB). Previously, state subsidies were granted from general funds to a particular enterprise. It was thus not very obvious that taxes levied on successful enterprises were used to subsidize the inefficient firms. Under the new arrangement, profits within a particular VVB will be redistributed to the enterprises which suffer losses. The more profitable enterprises will readily see that their gains are being reallocated to inefficient operations, and certainly they will resent it. In the future, this will undoubtedly be one of the major sources of tension between the enterprises of a particular VVB.

Another significant change effected by the new economic reforms concerns the role of central planning and the central planners. The party leaders have traditionally visualized themselves as the architects of a perfectly symmetrical organic economic mechanism. In practice, all planning was reduced to a series of successive improvisations. Even today, the party leadership attempts to maintain the fiction of an omniscient planning system, with only "minor" aspects of the planning function devolving upon the VVBs and VEBs. Actually, however, the leaders have recognized the limitations of the planning process, and they are now moving in effect toward merely indicative planning at the central level. The increasingly rapid technological changes experienced in what is called the "second technological revolution" will underscore the need for flexibility at the levels where operational decisions are made. They will also further illuminate the limitations of total central planning.

There is increasing evidence that the East German regime is moving the current reforms toward further socialization of the only partially socialized sectors of industry and agriculture. Semi-state and privately owned industrial enterprises are being slowly nudged into more socialized units by various organizational and economic strategems. In effect, the horizontal product-group system, which covers enterprises of all types of ownership is bringing about increased socialization. Since it is under the leadership of the VVBs or VEBs, the product-group tends to favor the sponsoring organization and its affiliates. In practice, then, the less socialized enterprises will either tie themselves closely to the sponsoring body or will have to be satisfied to produce less profitable items. In either case, the disappearance of the less socialized organizations as independent entities is assured. Increasing state investment in the semi-state enterprises also dilutes the private element. Similarly bank credit and other financial instruments are being employed to weaken the private sector by systematically discriminating against it.

In agriculture, the same policies are being followed to hasten the conversion of the LPGs I and II into the completely collectivized LPGs III. For example, cooperating LPGs I are entitled to more favorable credit terms usually reserved to LPGs III. Farm equipment and machinery denied to the individual LPG I is made available to cooperating LPGs along with building materials, fodder and fertilizers. All of these measures are designed to raise the level of socialization in successive stages.

The material-incentive aspect of the economic reforms will no doubt modify income distribution and the shares of social and individual consumption. Income differences will widen, and with this, class differences and associated problems could become intensified. Furthermore, with greater emphasis on measuring labor costs more accurately, one might expect that the financing of a major proportion of thus far centrally-financed social consumption will be shifted to specific enterprises and to individual workers. The latter, for example, may be required to pay a larger part of their housing expenditures. This and similar measures would be designed to adjust the enterprise's direct labor costs to their real value and to force each firm to be more economical in the use of labor by making labor costs, now covered by budgetary expenditures, a part of the production costs of the individual enterprise. The shift in the burden of expenditures, a part of the production costs of the individual enterprise. The shift in the burden of expenditures will mean a reversal of the current tendency toward increasing the socialization of consumption, thereby orienting distribution toward the individual.

The effort to increase the cost consciousness of all economic organizations is likely to lead in time to a re-evaluation of the economic rationality of East Germany's relations to COMECON and the rest of the world. Ulbricht himself has recognized this as a necessary follow-up to the introduction of the new system of economic management. However, the GDR's ability to participate increasingly in the worldwide international division of labor depends not only on East German willingness and political good will abroad but also on the extent to which the country will be able to adjust its production to world requirements.

Since the above article was written, the Eleventh SED Central Committee Plenum was held between December 15 and 18, 1965. In a keynote speech, Walter Ulbricht strongly reinforced the trends in economic reform set in motion in 1963. Some of the major changes produced by the plenum are the following: (1) Organizational—(a) dissolution of the National Economic Council; (b) creation of nine industrial ministries; (c) establishment of a Central Auditing Commission; (d) a further expansion of the powers of the VVBs and enterprises. 2) Substantive—(a) more flexible prices; (b) introduction of interest on capital; (c) direct contracts between East German enterprises and firms in both East and West; (d) further reinforcement of self-financing of investment by the VVBs and VEBs) (e) revision of the method of agricultural price formation to assure self-financing of investments.

The powers of the abolished National Economic Council were redistributed between the new economic ministries, the VVBs and enterprises. The ministries are given minimal control over the operational activities of the VVBs and enterprises; hence the VVB has been the major recipient of additional economic power. The VVBs, however, lost their auditing functions, which were handed to the new Central Auditing Commission. Under this new arrangement, the VVBs will be less able to manipulate funds contrary to the established general rules.

Dissatisfaction with the degree of price flexibility, even after the series of industrial price reforms, was clearly expressed by Ulbricht as well as others at the plenum. These statements were preceded by a series of articles appearing in the economic weekly *Wirtschaft* urging a discussion of alternative theories of price formation. Other inadequacies of the reform program were also discussed. All in all, the plenum and the current discussions by professional economists presage further progress toward economic reform in East Germany.

8. ECONOMIC REFORMS IN BULGARIA

REFORMS IN BULGARIA*
— · — · — · — · — · — ·

J. F. Brown†

On December 4, 1965, the Bulgarian Communist Party daily, *Rabotnichesko delo,* published the party Politburo's long-awaited "Theses" on economic reform. The program that was outlined indicated that Bulgaria was intent on a comprehensive overhaul of its entire system of economic planning and management. Though more cautious in important respects than the various reforms underway in Yugoslavia, East Germany, Czechoslovakia, and Hungary, the Bulgarian program was just as dramatic in its impact—especially in the light of certain national conditions and characteristics.

Indeed, it was rather surprising that Bulgaria should have embarked upon a serious economic reform at all. In the past the regime, led by Todor Zhivkov, had been perhaps the most timid and unimaginative, not to say dogmatic, in the whole of Eastern Europe. Moreover, the Bulgarian economy was still largely undeveloped; as a consequence, it had been able to maintain an impressive rate of growth and was still on the wave of an investment boom. All these factors could have been expected to militate against a reform involving a large measure of decentralization.

Elsewhere in Eastern Europe, conditions were different. Two of the pioneers of economic reform, the German Democratic Republic and Czechoslovakia, had highly developed and complex economies, which quite clearly had outgrown the "Stalinist" system of planning. To a lesser degree, Poland and Hungary were in a similar position. Yugoslavia—the real trail-blazer in economic reform—was, it is true, a relatively undeveloped country. But the Yugoslav reforms were the offshoot of an ideological deviation long considered anathema by the rest of Eastern Europe; moreover, from an economic point of view, the results of the Yugoslav experiments were not so strikingly successful as to invite imitation.

Bulgaria and Rumania alone, then, remained in a category that could be considered more "suited" (or less ill-suited) to the classical Communist system of planning and management, since their low-key economies had not yet suffered the acute growing pains of the more advanced countries. Rumania's prudently conservative leaders seemed content, for their part, to stick with the old system until such time as it should become a victim of the law of diminishing returns. Bulgaria's leaders, however, apparently

*Reprinted by permission from *Problems of Communism*. May–June 1966, pp. 17–21. All footnotes deleted.
†J. F. Brown, a specialist on East European Affairs with the research department of Radio Free Europe, is the author of *The New Eastern Europe* (1966).

decided that weaknesses in the national economy were already serious enough to warrant action. For while great quantitative progress had been achieved in heavy industrial production, the country's very success in this respect had led to failures in others. The performance in agriculture had been depressingly poor, causing an unhealthy imbalance in the national income. And in all sectors of the economy qualitative factors—the quality of goods, rentability, costing, accurate pricing, etc.—had been neglected. Inefficiency and cumbersome planning at every level were creating problems which largely offset the achievement of a high rate of growth, and the strain of maintaining this high rate was in turn aggravating the weaknesses and contradictions inherent in the economic system.

The economic discussions conducted in the Soviet Union, sparked by Professor Yevsei Liberman's now famous article of September 1962, convinced the Bulgarian leaders that economic reform was not only pressing but also permissible. (In a period of changing relations between the East European countries and Moscow, Bulgaria has remained a model satellite, and had the Soviet Union not made it clear that she too was contemplating economic reforms, it is very doubtful whether the Bulgarians would have taken up the issue.)

At the Eighth BCP Congress in November 1962, a resolution was passed accepting in principle the need to reform the planning and management system, to increase workers' participation in the drawing up and implementation of plans, and to augment material incentives throughout the economy. The following May, a Central Committee plenum confirmed these decisions and announced some "ground work" moves, including the merging of certain industrial enterprises and the reorganization of economic administration in the country's 27 okrugs, or districts.

The decisions of this plenum attracted little attention at the time; they seemed to signify no breakthrough in official economic thinking. What did attract attention, however, was the initiation—also in May—of a series of discussions on economic reform in *Novo vreme,* the theoretical monthly of the Bulgarian Party Central Committee. The fact that *Novo vreme* was carrying the series was a sure sign that the party was preparing its own cadres for something new and big.

Over a period of months the discussions picked up in excitement, and by November they had become quite startling. In that month an article by Professor Angel Miloshevski proposed nothing less than the complete adoption of the Yugoslav workers' council system. Even more important was Professor Petko Kunin's article in the December issue. A rehabilitated follower of Traicho Kostov, Kunin was considered one of Bulgaria's outstanding economists. His comprehensive article amounted to a plea that all enterprises become financially self-supporting and autonomous vis-à-vis the state. He advocated a new system of planning and accounting that would allow for genuine competition between enterprises, for the "most rational and economic use" of fixed and working capital funds and of the labor force, and for profits and profit-sharing, to be used as "stimulating devices." Profits, Kunin argued, should determine the remuneration of managers and should be the main source for increases in wage payments. To the more dogmatic of the party cadres, this must have sounded very much like creeping capitalism, but Kunin argued that his proposals were essentially socialist and that "the approach to communism, the transition to this high form of society, demands bold ideas, bold steps, well thought out, realistically and skillfully applied."

In January 1964 it was made known that experiments somewhat along the lines suggested by Professor Kunin were already being carried out at the "Liliana Dimitrova" textile plant in Sofia. The innovations involved "non-state financing" and a system of remuneration and premiums based on profit. The first results were said to be very encouraging: By this time the regime had evidently made up its own mind on what the reform was to comprise. In the same first month of the new year, the party Politburo and the Council of Ministers announced what they called "basic principles" of the new system and decreed that these should be tried out experimentally in a number of enterprises, beginning on April 1, 1964. During the rest of the year a total of 50 enterprises, mainly industrial, began working under the new system, or at least parts of it. Collective farms in four of Bulgaria's administrative districts also operated under new principles. In 1965 the experiments were widely extended. By the end of the year the new system was being used in enterprises employing some 33.5 percent of the total number of industrial workers in Bulgaria and contributing 44 percent of the total industrial production.

Of no little irritation to students of the Bulgarian scene, in the two years which elapsed between official approval of the principles of reform (January 1964) and the publication of the reform "Theses" (December 1965), no official information was given out to describe the experiments being made, although the Bulgarian press regularly carried reports of progress. No one knew, therefore, exactly what the "new principles" were. The regime's reticence was of course understandable. This was a trial-and-error period, a time of empirical experiment, the first in Bulgaria for over a generation. Only after thorough experimentation could the regime feel confident enough to commit itself publicly to a coherent reform.

While outside observers faced an official blanket of silence, they could form some idea of the lines the reform was taking from various proposals, ideas and reports appearing in the press. The most stimulating article in this respect was a piece by Ivan Mironov in the May 1964 issue of *Ikonomicheska misal* dealing mainly with the issue of self-financing and autonomy for enterprises. Since the article appeared only one month after experiments at the factory level were supposed to begin, it could be assumed that the ideas contained in it were a fairly accurate reflection of what the regime had in mind in this area (an assumption finally proven correct when the "Theses" were published over 18 months later). Mironov advocated that wages and capital accumulation be tied to the profit level of individual enterprises. He also proposed that each enterprise be subject to a property tax and an interest rate on fixed and circulating capital, and that there be depreciation rates accurately reflecting wear-and-tear and obsolescence.

For the workers Mironov saw a considerably increased role, remarking: "When the accumulations of the enterprise and a considerable part of the wages depend on the size of the profit, the workers cannot be indifferent to the problems of management and the result of the work of the enterprise." The Politburo's "Theses" in December 1965 took some steps in this direction, establishing production committees designed to give the workers a greater say in planning, in income distribution, and even in "the selection of the management cadres." Of course, these provisions fell far short of Professor Miloshevski's proposals for the introduction of the Yugoslav workers' councils system. But if the regime leaders ever even toyed with such an idea—a rather doubtful assumption—they had thought better of it by the time they came to publish their official proposals.

If, on the workers' councils, the regime showed its conservatism, on another issue it moved, in the course of the almost two years of experimentation, to a more liberal position than it had apparently first envisaged. In an interview granted to a Yugoslav reporter in October 1964, Grisha Filipov, a vice-chairman of the Bulgarian State Planning Committee had spoken out adamantly against any form of free prices. The market, said Filopov, "can establish neither prices nor production, for this leads to disorganization. They will remain established strictly according to plan." Yet the official Politburo "Theses" of last December allowed for both a variable and a free price category, similar to the Czechoslovak model.

It was probably hesitation over how "liberal" or "conservative" to be on such issues, as well as the desire to give the experiments a thorough trial, that caused the Bulgarians to delay the publication of their officially approved plan. An official announcement had been expected early in 1965. In July 1965 Premier Zhivkov told a group of Austrian journalists that the official "Theses" would be published in about a month, *i.e.,* in August. There was, therefore, a definite delay for which differences of opinion on "how far to go" could well have been mainly responsible. Economists themselves seem to have been seriously divided on the question, and it is noteworthy that Professor Eugeni Mateev—a minister without portfolio in the cabinet, a first-rate economist, and the man who initiated the series of discussions in *Novo vreme* in May 1963—was described by Zhivkov as being "against the [new] system." Mateev is no dogmatist, and it may be that he regards the application of a rather advanced system of reform to a relatively primitive economy as being dangerously premature. He may agree with the point Filipov, himself a trained economist, was trying to make: that a great degree of centralized control was still necessary.

If some trained economists considered the reform too liberal, it can well be imagined what many party apparatchiks thought of it. "Stalinist" opposition to reform of all kinds in Bulgaria had been very strong since 1956 and had been responsible for frustrating more than one promising development. It is understandable then, that the fundamental changes involved in any radical economic reform would arouse the strongest apprehensions in the party.

Yet the leadership was able to play an important card: by conducting preliminary experiments, it could argue that the proof of the pudding was in the eating. It brought forward statistics—perhaps accurate, certainly politic—to show that in the first half of 1965 the growth of industrial production in those enterprises operating under the new system averaged 15.6 percent, as compared to only 11.5 percent for those still operating under the old system.

With the publication of the "Theses" last December, everybody finally got a chance to see what the new system was all about. Its reformist character was based on the following general principles: considerable decentralization of economic decision-making, with major responsibility assigned to the so-called industrial association, or trust (see further); increased use of the profit motive; a system of wages tied to production results; "ful use" of economic levers, including profit, prices, credit interest and taxes.

On decentralization, the Bulgarian "Theses" followed the pattern set by the East German, Czechoslovak, Polish and Soviet reforms. The economic associations, or trusts, are to be the new centers of power and will largely determine the degree of autonomy which individual enterprises will enjoy. Only in Yugoslavia, and possibly also in Hungary, will individual enterprises escape this control at the association level. In Bulgaria, as in all East European countries, the business of the associations and of the individual enterprises will be conducted on the basis of contracts. Priority in contracts is to be given to commodities listed in the centrally-fixed plan, and not all contracts will be officially approved. "Free contracting" will be allowed in the light of production possibilities and according to market needs. The degree of freedom which this new contracting system will allow will, of course, depend on the size of the priority list fixed by the central authorities. At least at first it will probably be large.

The decentralization reform reflects the government's obvious intention to shift part of the task of handling investments off its own shoulders and onto the enterprises. The responsibilities thus transferred are to be financed by the enterprises out of their own funds and through repayable bank credits. Within the enterprises—and here again Bulgaria conforms to the general pattern—a number of special investment funds are to be created; these include a development and technical improvement fund (the amound to be determined as a percentage of capital funds), a new products fund, a social-cultural fund, and a wage reserve fund. The development and technical improvement fund will be used to finance capital investments and capital repairs. Resources from this fund can be used to finance the development of new products. Its amount will be a fixed percentage of total production costs. The percentage of the enterprises' contribution to the social-cultural fund will be fixed by the state.

The amount of the enterprise's contribution to the wage reserve fund will be a fixed percentage of the total wage fund. Under the new system, wages will be made up of two components: the guaranteed portion (easily the biggest), and the incentive portion, which will, of course, vary. Here the Bulgarian system is very much like the Czechoslovak—but unlike the Soviet, Polish and East German, where the state still centrally fixes the overall level of each enterprise's wage fund.

It is generally recognized that the kind of price formation policy followed is one of the most important indications of the degree of economic freedom in any economy. Measured by this yardstick, the Bulgarian reform is a relatively advanced one. Like the programs adopted in Czechoslovakia and proposed in Hungary, it will have a three-price system of categories—fixed, variable, and free. The prices of basic production goods and the most important consumer goods will be fixed by the state. On other goods there will be fixed maximum and minimum prices or in some cases a fixed maximum only. A last category of goods, composed mainly of seasonal and locally-produced items, will be priced freely. One may assume, though, that this last category will be small.

To sum up, it is fair to describe several features of the new Bulgarian system as "liberal" or "advanced." Other features—in particular the scheme for more participation by workers in decision-making—can be termed "liberal" by Bulgarian standards, though timid and orthodox compared to Yugoslavia's reforms.

Finally, the program has its conservative aspects. While the Bulgarian leaders have shown their determination to ensure a more flexible and responsible economic system, they have also taken precautions to see that the trend toward greater freedom will not get out of hand. Thus a large number of controls have been retained by the regime. As the "Theses" themselves say, the state will carry out "a uniform policy in the spheres of technical programming, capital investment, foreign trade, prices, remuneration of labor, and finance." Central planning continues to be the backbone of the whole system, and unlike the proposed Hungarian model, which foresees the complete abandonment of compulsory, centrally-directed indices, the Bulgarian program simply stipulates a reduction. The obligatory indices that will remain include: the volume of basic production in real terms; the limit on capital investment; the limit for basic raw materials; and foreign currency limits for imports and exports. If all these controls are brought fully into play, the centralizing features carried over from the old system might well negate the effectiveness of liberal innovations. Perhaps the Bulgarian leaders have acted wisely here by taking into account the still undeveloped state of their economy and keeping all these controls within reach; more probably they have acted out of the chronic timidity that has characterized them in the past. Whatever the reason, if controls are applied indiscriminately as soon as the slightest disequilibriums occur, then the new system will be virtually strangled at birth.

Time will tell. Experiments with the new system are continuing in 1966, and in 1967 fullscale implementation is to take place "along basic lines in the whole national economy," including agriculture and even local government. It will be about another two years, therefore, before the system can be appraised realistically. In the meantime one can only follow its fortune through press reports, comparing its progress with that of the Czechoslovak system, which it most closely resembles. That one of the most backward countries in Eastern Europe has adopted a system similar to that of one of the most advanced countries is an intriguing coincidence. It will be instructive to follow the extent to which each country allows itself, or is allowed, to benefit from the reform.

9. RUMANIA: POLITICAL RADICALISM AND ECONOMIC TRADITIONALISM

RUMANIA: THE FRUITS OF AUTONOMY*
— · — · — · — · — · — · — · — · — · — ·

George Gross†

A future Toynbee, looking at the 1960's, may well conclude that the central event of the current decade was the disintegration of the Soviet empire. This historic development is already well under way, deriving its principal momentum from the great schism between Moscow and Peking. But Soviet hegemony in Eastern Europe is also fragmenting, though less abruptly, and this process is bound to continue.

*Reprinted by permission from *Problems of Communism* (Jan.–Feb. 1966), pp. 16–27. All footnotes deleted.

†George Ross is a pseudonym of an eminent student of Rumanian affairs who has recently returned from an extended visit to Rumania. He has chosen to remain anonymous in order to protect some of his contacts in that country.

Stalin's concept of a monolithic bloc, with Moscow as its Third Rome, was already thoroughly shaken by the rise of nationalism in Yugoslavia, Poland, and Hungary during the preceding decade. In the case of Yugoslavia, this challenge was successful, and the first "national Communist" state was born. Next came Albania, which made a decisive break in 1961, although it chose not to look westward because of its traditional antipathy toward Yugoslavia.

More recently, Rumania has gradually but surely asserted its independence from Moscow. When, on April 22, 1964, the Central Committee of the Rumanian Communist Party (RCP) adopted its declaration on party and state relations, and when the Soviet Union failed either to prevent or to respond effectively to this act, a new form of independent national communism came into being. What follows is an account of how and why this has been accomplished, and what this accomplishment means.

The Roots of Alienation

When reports of Rumania's controversy with the Soviet Union over economic problems first appeared in the Western press in 1963, many observers were surprised, if not skeptical. Rumania had long been regarded as one of Moscow's most docile "satellites." After all, it was noted, most of its leaders had occupied influential posts ever since communism gained power in Rumania and had long been identified with Soviet interests.

Acutally, unmistakable signs of friction between Bucharest and Moscow had appeared earlier. The clearest instance was the plenum of the RCP Central Committee in November–December 1961. The plenum's main purpose was to review—and rewrite—the history of the RCP in a manner which was strongly nationalistic and, implicitly, anti-Soviet. The tone of the debate suggested that the speakers were concerned not just with past grudges against the USSR, but with current disputes.

In his speech to the plenum, the then Chairman of the State Planning Committee, Gheorge Gaston Marin, put his finger on a specific source of discord: he criticized certain "erroneous theories" which would deny each socialized country the right to build its own heavy industry and which "present in a distorted fashion the principles of specialization and cooperation within the framework of the socialist international division of labor." This was a clear attack on Soviet proposals, then under consideration, for the economic integration of the countries belonging to the Council for Mutual Economic Aid (usually referred to in the West as Comecon), the Communist counterpart of the West European Common Market.

In trying to work out the precise order and interrelation of Rumania's early moves away from Moscow, a Western observer has few hard facts to go on. Essentially he is faced with a choice between two theories. The most common explanation holds that a conflict of economic interests was at the root of it all, and that the other facets of Rumania's independent stand were added on, willy-nilly, as the economic controversy progressed. In point of time, this would place the beginning of Rumanian-Soviet differences as far back as 1961, or perhaps even the late 1950's when Rumania evidently encountered some opposition from Moscow in drawing up its national economic plan for 1960–65.

However, there is weightier evidence that the roots go deeper, and that the defiance of Moscow on economic matters was but the opening shot in a more ambitious campaign. The events which will be reviewed strongly indicate a coordinated and preconceived effort to gain independence of action on a broad front—political as well as economic. This conclusion also finds some support in the history of the RCP.

Although their regime was a creature of the Soviet postwar occupation, and though they shared in this creation, the RCP leaders grouped around Gheorghiu-Dej, the late party First Secretary and President of Rumania, were not "Moscow men" but home-grown Communists, veterans of the Communist underground inside the country. As the Soviet Army approached Rumania, Dej and his closest associates were serving political sentences in Rumanian jails, and unlike the Rumanian Communist émigrés in Moscow headed by Ana Pauker, who were little more than stooges of Stalin, Dej's group had slight contact with or guidance from Moscow. In fact, they soon found themselves in a political struggle with the Moscovites. In April 1944, they succeeded in ousting the then leader of the RCP, Stefan Foris, who by their account was "a traitor" "imposed" on the party by Stalin. (Rumanian officials claim that the purge of Foris was carried out without Moscow's knowledge.) The next round, however, went to the Pauker group of Moscovites. With the backing of Stalin, these "foreign elements" suceeded in "usurping" dominant posts in the party leadership in September 1944. Even though Dej became and remained leader of the party in the period that followed, it was only in 1952, when Pauker and her associates were purged, that the native Rumanian group gained full control.

If this official Rumanian account of the early postwar struggle for the party leadership is accurate—and it probably is substantially so—Dej and his associates must have long harbored a sense of resentment and even alienation vis-à-vis the Soviet Union. The bitterness of subsequent attacks (in 1964) by Rumanian leaders on Soviet economic exploitation of Rumania in the 1940's and 1950's suggests that this, too, was an early source of alienation. Thus, it seems entirely possible that, at some time during the latter half of the 1950's, after they had consolidated their internal position by expelling the Moscovites, the Dej group gradually came to the conclusion that they should strike out on their own once certain preconditions were met and a suitable opportunity arose.

Such circumstances were not long in coming. The most important precondition was the withdrawal of Soviet troops from Rumania, which occurred in 1958. Secondly, the Rumanian leaders needed to establish a firm economic base elsewhere in order to lessen their material dependence on the Soviet Union. They proceeded to do just that—though other purely economic conditions were also involved—by rapidly expanding Rumania's trade with Western Europe. Finally, the opportunity came when the simmering differences between Moscow and Peking evolved, in the early 1960's, into a deep and irrevocable split. This was indeed a windfall for Bucharest, as it afforded ideal terrain for political maneuver against the weakened center of world communism.

The Economic Issues

Perhaps the basic and most conspicuous expression of Rumania's resurgent nationalism has been Bucharest's insistence on pursuing an independent economic policy involving full industrial exploitation of the country's raw materials, development of a diversified modern industry, and heavy reliance on Western technology and trade to accomplish these goals. This policy has conflicted with the Soviet campaign, launched in 1961–62, to strengthen Comecon organizationally and to deepen the "socialist international division of labor." Moscow conceived of these schemes as a means of strengthening its political control over the East European members of Comecon by binding them to the USSR economically. The "have" countries of Comecon, such as East Germany, Poland, Czechoslovakia and Hungary, have nevertheless favored the Soviet plans as a means of raising industrial efficiency and meeting their agricultural deficits. Rumania, on the other hand, regards them as an encroachment on national sovereignty and as a device to make Rumania a permanent food and raw material base for the more developed Comecon countries.

The concrete issues over which Moscow and Bucharest have disagreed can be briefly put as follows:

1. Rumania has rejected Soviet proposals that it cut back plans for developing industries which Moscow thought were inefficient or duplicated industries elsewhere in Comecon. It has also rejected the related Soviet proposal that Rumania concentrate its resources in agriculture and in industries which fit in with bloc-wide needs.

2. Rumania has refused to alter its "food-for-industries" trade pattern with the West in order to bail out the food and raw-material deficits of the industralized members of Comecon.

3. Given these substantive differences with the majority of Comecon members, Rumania has understandably opposed schemes to empower Comecon central organs (such as the supranational planning agency proposed by Khrushchev) to prescribe the economic policies of individual members by majority rule. It has likewise rejected other forms of co-operation between two or more Comecon members—such as jointly-owned enterprises or interstate economic complexes—which would infringe on national ownership or control.

After bubbling near the surface for a year or so, these divergencies came to a head at a session of the Comecon Executive Committee which met in Moscow in February 1963. Rumania's permanent representative, Vice-Premier Alexandru Birladeanu, flatly affirmed Rumania's opposition to Moscow's integration schemes and refused to budge from this position. The RCP Central Committee promptly convened a plenum on March 5–8 to throw its weight behind the policy voiced by Birladeanu. It pointedly declared that the principal means of developing the division of labor was "the coordination of *national* economic plans" based on "*respect for national independence and sovereignty, complete equal rights, comradely mutual aid and reciprocal advantage.*" (Emphasis added.)

By this act, Rumania passed the first significant milestone of its campaign to gain national independence. To drive the point home, the RCP leaders held a series of closed meetings throughout the country to explain their new policy. The discussions at these meetings, as at the plenum, were emotionally nationalistic and pointedly critical of Soviet policies.

There followed several months of diplomatic exchanges in which Moscow attempted to pressure the Rumanians into line, but without success. When a second denouement was reached at the summit meeting of Comecon party and government heads in Moscow on July 24–26, 1963, it was Khrushchev, not Gheorghiu-Dej, who backed down. Khrushchev's plan for a central planning agency was quietly buried, and the Rumanians were told that Comecon would take no steps affecting the Rumanian economy without their consent. However, the *modus vivendi* was little more than an agreement to disagree. Gheorghiu-Dej restated Rumania's determination to stick by its economic policies, while Khrushchev, Ulbricht, and others cautioned that Comecon would proceed to carry out various forms of bilateral and multilateral economic integration—without Rumania, if need be.

Although the controversy over Comecon integration has since undergone little change, the showdown at the July 1963 conference had significant and far-reaching consequences. For the Soviet Union, it meant the collapse of its scheme for a closely integrated economic structure in the Comecon area. Moscow's political hold, both present and potential, over Eastern Europe was weakened accordingly.

For the other Comecon members (excluding Rumania), the Rumanian monkey wrench meant that they would have to look for alternative solutions of their economic problems. Some of them, inspired no doubt by Rumania's successful formula, have already shown signs of seeking increased economic ties with the West as a long-term remedy.

As for Rumania, the conference has led to its increasing alienation from Comecon in a practical as well as formal sense. In 1963–64, the USSR set up a new network of bilateral economic cooperation commissions with Hungary, Czechoslovakia, Poland and Bulgaria (a similar agreement had been concluded earlier with East Germany). A parallel accord between the USSR and Rumania was not signed until September 1965, and its practical significance remains in doubt. Moreover, the idea of bilateral and multilateral specialization and joint-ownership ventures has been gaining increasing currency among the other East European members of Comecon. Several such groupings have been formed for the metallurgical, ball-bearing, and fertilizer industries, but Rumania is not a participant.

Perhaps more importantly, the victory the Rumanians won at the Moscow conference undoubtedly encouraged them to become even bolder in their quest for national identity. There independent attitude rapidly infected other facets of their relations with the Soviet Union in the months that followed.

Finally, the issues left unresolved by the 1963 *modus vivendi* continued to exacerbate Rumania's relations with the Soviet Union and the other East European countries. During the latter half of 1963, the Rumanian press published a series of thinly veiled polemics against the Soviet position. By the spring of 1964, these jibs escalated into open and direct attacks.

Bucharest Vis-à-vis Moscow and Peking

While the controversy within Comecon gathered steam in early 1963, Bucharest began unfolding a policy of non-involvement, or quasineutrality, in the Sino-Soviet dispute. This neutral posture is "quasi" in the sense that the Rumanian policy of positive coexistence with the West is diametrically opposed to the militant views of the Chinese Communists. However, it is very real as regards the dispute itself, which is basically a power contest between Communist Rumania's traditional master and the new Communist center in Asia.

Rumania has manifested its neutral posture in several ways. For one thing it has doggedly refrained from any sweeping public condemnation of Communist China. Since the beginning of 1963, it is true, Rumanian spokesmen have voiced some criticism of Peking, but these have been perfunctory and concerned with specific Chinese policies (*e.g.*, towards the test-ban treaty and general disarmament, which the Rumanians favor). In contrast to the torrent of condemnation which has poured forth from Moscow and its supporters, there have been no Rumanian speeches, editorials, or Central Committee resolutions directed against the Chinese. Also, Rumania has generally ignored the polemical broadsides issuing from both Moscow and Peking or, when it has chosen to acknowledge them, has given them equal space in the Rumanian press.

Actions as well as words have underscored Rumania's policy of neutrality. The first such action was an indirect rebuff to Soviet efforts to isolate the Chinese and their friends: the Rumanian Ambassador to Albania, who had been withdrawn along with other East European chiefs of mission in late 1961 following the break between Moscow and Tirana, was returned to his post in March 1963. Next, Gheorghiu-Dej studiously avoided attending a series of informal meetings at which Moscow sought to rally bloc support against Communist China. Dej neglected to put in an appearance at the SED (East German) Party Congress in January 1963; he boycotted the meeting of Comecon party chiefs held on the occasion of Ulbricht's 70th birthday in June 1963; he deliberately scheduled the April 1964 plenum of the RCP Central Committee so as to underscore his absence from a similar gathering for Khrushchev's 70th birthday festivities; and he failed to show up at the first meeting of Comecon party leaders with the new Soviet leadership in November 1964, shortly following Khrushchev's removal.

Finally, Rumania has on two occasions intervened on its own initiative in the Sino-Soviet dispute in an apparent effort to mediate. The first attempt was made by Premier Ion Gheorghe Maurer in March 1964 when he held talks with Mao in Peking and then met with Khrushchev on his way home. This intervention was reportedly prompted by Moscow's decision (postponed for six weeks because of the Rumanian intervention) to publish the February 14 report of the CPSU Secretary Mikhail Suslov violently attacking Peking. The second effort was an equally futile proposal that the Soviet, Chinese and Rumanian parties issue a tripartite appeal for Communist unity (drafted by the Rumanians).

Rumania's course vis-à-vis Moscow and Peking is a classic example of a small country exploiting a power conflict between two large rivals to serve its own interests. Indeed, the Sino-Soviet conflict has been the key factor in Rumania's assertion of independence from Moscow. With consummate timing and political sense, the Rumanian leaders have successfully exploited the conflict to show that they need not dance to the Soviet tune and to proclaim their right to act independently in pursuit of their own rather than Soviet national interests.

Declaration of Independence

The decisive step in Rumania's drive for independence was the issuance of the April 22, 1964, Declaration of the RCP Central Committee. Adopted at the conclusion of an expanded plenum of unprecedented dura-tion (April 15–22), this document was—and is—in fact a proclamation of Rumania's right to national autonomy and equality in the Communist world.

On Comecon, the declaration amplified the standard Rumanian arguments against economic integration, explicitly rejecting measures "such as a joint plan and a single planning body for all member states, interstate technical-production mergers of branches of industry," and other joint ventures. Such "suprastate" schemes, it maintained, "would turn sovereignty into a notion devoid of any content." As a counter to integration, the declaration elaborated upon Maurer's proposal of November 1963 to expand Comecon to include all 14 socialist states and asserted Rumania'a "steadfast" determination to strengthen cooperation with "all socialist countries"—an implicit but clear defiance of Moscow's excommunication of Albania. It also justified Rumanian policies and initiatives for developing trade relations with the West.

Turning to the Sino-Soviet conflict, the declaration condemned Mos-cow and Peking with equal force for carrying on public polemics and for dragging "almost all" other parties into the quarrel. It appealed to the Soviet and Chinese parties to make "all efforts to bar the road to schism," and called on all Communist parties to cease polemics and begin consulta-tions looking to a new world Communist conference to reestablish unity. The conference must include "all" parties, since the inclusion of only "a part" of the parties would be "against the cause of unity and would lead to the aggravation of the situation, to the isolation of some fraternal parties, and to the consecration of a schism in the world Communist and workers' movement." Moscow was clearly the target of this sally as the declaration's point of departure was the Soviet proposal to organize a conference as a "collective rebuff by Marxist-Leninist parties" to Com-munist China.

By far the most significant and novel feature of the declaration—indeed, its primary message—was the repeated affirmation of the need, in all—and not just economic—relations between Communist states, to respect the "basic principles" of equality and national sovereignty, and the explicit denial of the right of any party or state to be the center of communism. This thesis was developed as follows:

Basic Principles. The principles of "national independence and sovereignty, equal rights, mutual advantage, comradely assistance, non-interference in internal affairs, observance of territorial integrity, socialist internationalism . . . form the immutable law . . . of the entire world socialist system" and the "only" basis of unity.

Joint Formulation of General Line. Concerning "fundamental" problems common to all socialist states, joint positions should be reached, but only through mutual consultations and joint formulation of statements and "not by the stipulation of no-alternative solutions by some sort of superstate [*i.e.,* Soviet] authority." When agreement cannot be reached on basic matters of common interest, they should be put aside, and such differences should not be allowed to lead to "discriminatory" measures.

Polycentrism and Self-Determination. The "general laws" of building socialism are applied to "concrete conditions of great diversity, in keeping with the level or stage of development of each socialist country and its historical peculiarities." Strict observance of equal rights, of non-interference, and of "each party's exclusive right to solve its own political problems" is essential to unity and the resolution of disputes. "It is the exclusive right of each party independently to work out its political line, its concrete objectives, and the ways and means of achieving them."

Rejection of Central Soviet Authority. Given this "diversity . . . , there are not and cannot be any no-alternative pattern and recipes; no one can decide what is and what is not correct for other countries and parties." There are not and cannot be a "parent" party and a "son" party, a "superior" and a "subordinate" party. No party has a "privileged position, or can impose its line and opinions on other parties."

All in all, the Rumanian party's declaration probably represents the most forthright and thoroughly reasoned rejection of Soviet supremacy ever made by an ostensible supporter of the USSR. By this act, Rumania has in fact staked out a claim to have its cake and eat it, too. It has served notice that whatever the outcome of the Sino-Soviet conflict, Rumania will take its own independent course. If the unity of the socialist camp is restored, it must be based on a "diverse" association of equal Communist states, with no supreme "center." If Moscow and Peking irrevocably split, Rumania will stick to its policy of good relations with all Communist states and will not be obligated to join either side.

Aftermath of the Declaration

Khrushchev's reaction to the Rumanian declaration must have been seething rage. But he probably received an even greater shock when, several weeks later, the Rumanian Communist leaders launched a campaign to explain the document to the Rumanian people. Though never publicized in the Rumanian press, indoctrination meetings were held at virtually every place of work. Speakers at these meetings condemned Soviet domination and economic exploitation in explicit and outspoken terms. Moscow was accused of draining Rumania of its resources through the SOVROM joint stock companies, of exacting twenty times too much for war reparations, and of selling goods to Rumania at inflated prices. The Soviet proposals in regard to Comecon were of course another object of attack. Khrushchev himself was criticized in the strongest terms. According to an account given this writer by a participant, one speaker accused the Soviet leader of having attempted to overthrow the Dej regime by soliciting—unsuccessfully—the support of malcontents within the RWP. Another speaker charged that Soviet agents had tried to penetrate the Rumanian police and army.

The obvious purpose of the indoctrination campaign was to drive home the fact that Rumania had cut its ties of dependence on the Soviet Union and to rally public support for this new course. There is no question that the campaign was successful. Participants in the meetings (which sometimes lasted as long as ten hours) were stunned at the revelations they heard, but the general public response was strongly enthusiastic.

How Moscow reacted to all this is not entirely clear. For one thing, however, it apparently sought to pressure Rumania indirectly through neighboring Hungary. The Hungarian Government had for some time been conducting a quiet diplomatic and propaganda campaign accusing Rumania of suppressing the Hungarian minority of Transylvania. Then, in the late spring and early summer of 1964, scattered demonstrations against the Rumanian Government were staged by Hungarians in northern Transylvania. According to some Rumanian sources, supported by other collateral evidence, the demonstrations were instigated by Budapest with Moscow's secret connivance.

Meanwhile, Bucharest and Moscow engaged in a short but extremely sharp exchange of polemics. A culminating point was reached in mid-June when the Rumanian journal *Viata Economica* (Economic Life) published a violent diatribe against Soviet proposals for the establishment of "interstate economic complexes," in particular, a proposal advanced by a Soviet economist (E. B. Valev) to establish such a complex on the lower Danube. Intimating that this scheme was inspired by the Soviet government, the journal charged that it was nothing less than a "plan for the violation of the territorial integrity of Rumania, for the dismemberment of its national and state unity." At this point, following an apparent warning from Khrushchev conveyed to Dej through Tito (the latter two met hurriedly on June 22), the Rumanians decided to seek a cooling-off period, and Maurer was sent to Moscow to confer with Khrushchev in early July. The meeting was not entirely amicable because Maurer reportedly told the Soviet leaders that while Rumania did not wish to worsen its relations with the Soviet Union, it insisted on Soviet acceptance of the fact of its independence. However, the two leaders did agree to bring an end to open polemics between the two countries. Rumania also resumed publication of the Moscow-controlled international Communist journal, *Problems of Peace and Socialism*, which it had suspended in May.

This easing of tensions did not last long, however. After months of vacillation, Moscow formally proposed on July 30, 1964, that a preliminary conference of 26 Communist parties meet in Moscow on December 15 to prepare the way for a world conference with the obvious purpose of ex-communicating Communist China. Three days earlier, Moscow's trouble shooter, CPSU Secretary Nikolai Podgorny, had paid a hurried call to Gheorghiu-Dej at the latter's summer home on the Black Sea in an effort to persuade the Rumanians to go along with the proposal. At some point— whether during Dej's meeting the Podgorny or at a later time is not clear —the Rumanians formally rejected the invitation.

Partly because of this action, the Soviet leaders postponed the pre-paratory conference until March 1, 1965, and renewed their efforts to persuade the Rumanians and other racalcitrants to attend by calling the conference a "consultative" meeting and limiting its scope of action. But this did not sway the Rumanians. Publicly they continued their purposeful silence on the Sino-Soviet dispute and on the March 1 conference itself. Privately they reiterated their opposition to any conference designed to excommunicate the Chinese (knowing that they themselves could also become the eventual target of a Moscow-directed campaign against na-tionalism) and their refusal to be bound by the decisions of such a confer-ence. Thus, when the "consultative" meeting finally convened last March, Rumania alone among the countries of the Warsaw Pact and Comecon was conspicuously absent.

The Spread of Discord

In the meantime, Rumanian opposition to Soviet domination of the international Communist movement had been spreading to other areas. In September 1964 Rumania reneged on a promise it had made just two months before and again suspended publication of the Rumanian-language version of *Problems of Peace and Socialism*. (This publication has since been permitted to reappear but is subject to Rumanian censorship.) Next, at a conference of the World Federation of Trade Unions (WFTU) in Budapest on October 19–24, 1964, the Rumanian delegate openly opposed Soviet control of this front organization. The performance was repeated shortly thereafter at meetings of two other front organizations—the International Students' Union (IUS) and the International Federation of Democratic Women. Rumanian spokesmen charged that the Soviet-dom-inated leaderships of both these organizations had violated the "equal rights—sovereignty and autonomy of member organizations," and they argued that the practice of imposing decisions on all members by majority vote should give way to unanimity rule.

There have even been signs that Bucharest's independent attitude has touched on the most sensitive nerve of all in its relations with Moscow—its commitment to the Warsaw Pact. By a decree of October 31, 1964, Rumania reduced the term of service of army conscripts from 24 to 16 months, the shortest term of service in any Warsaw Pact country. This action was almost certainly taken unilaterally, and whether or not it had an important effect on bloc military capabilities, it was a breach of discipline which Moscow must have found intolerable. At about this time (from October 23 to November 3) the Soviet Commander of Warsaw Pact forces, Marshal A. A. Grechko, was on an official visit to Rumania, and the atmosphere between him and his hosts was reported as distinctly cool, apparently because of Rumania's unilateral action.

Discord was also reported to have developed between the Rumanian and Soviet representatives at the Warsaw Pact conference held in January 1965. Though lacking confirmation, these reports lent substance by certain facts: the Bucharest press made no comment on the meeting; the Rumanian representatives, headed by Gheorghiu-Dej, left Warsaw immediately after the conference closed; and they made the pointed gesture of inviting the ambassadors of Albania, Communist China, and North Korea to greet them both on their departure from Bucharest and on their return home from Warsaw.

There is no reason to believe that Rumania would contemplate so drastic a step as a sudden withdrawal from the Warsaw Pact since this could well trigger a dangerous Soviet response. It is , however, quite likely that the Rumanians, like the French in NATO (but under quite different circumstances), have balked at accepting certain organizational arrangements which they maintain would be an infringement on their country's sovereignty.

Bridges to the West

Rumania's drive for independence has, of course, had it greatest impact on relations with the USSR, but it has also involved the development of closer ties with the West. This is indeed almost an automatic corollary in view of Rumania's need for moral and material support against pressures from the ex-imperial power to the East, as well as the country's traditional ties with the West, particularly Western Europe.

The development of closer economic relations has been by far the more important component of this gradual shift to the West. Indeed, as observed earlier, it was an important precondition for the reorientation of Rumania's foreign relations. The dynamics of this development can be seen in Table 1.

TABLE 1
GEOGRAPHIC DISTRIBUTION OF
RUMANIAN FOREIGN TRADE

Free World		"Sino-Soviet Bloc" *	USSR
1955	20%	80%	69%
1958	25%	75%	50%
1964	33%	67%	41%

*Excludes Yugoslavia

An even more telling indicator is the fact that whereas, in 1957, 84 percent of Rumania's imports of industrial equipment came from Communist countries, particularly the USSR, the larger part of these imports now comes from the West.

West European countries—*i.e.*, West Germany, Italy, England, and France, in that order—claim the bulk of Rumania's trade with the non-Communist world. West European exports to Rumania consist almost entirely of industrial plant and equipment essential to Rumania's industrialization. In exchange, Rumania sends food and raw materials, particularly petroleum and wood products.

This policy has led to sharp disagreement between Rumania and the already industrialized countries of Eastern Europe—particularly East Germany, Czechoslovakia, and Hungary—which would like to dispose of more of their industrial output on the Rumanian market in exchange for food and raw material, in which they have deficits. Rumania has successfully resisted pressures from these countries by arguing that their industrial goods are of inferior quality, and that this trade pattern would retard Rumania's industrialization.

The RCP's April 1964 Declaration defended Rumania's trade ties with the West by saying that they are "an extremely important means of advancing peaceful coexistence." Premier Maurer reportedly put the case more bluntly when he was said to have asked: "Why should we send corn to Poland so that Poland can fatten its pigs to buy machinery from the West, when we can sell our corn to the West and buy the machinery we need ourselves?"

Because of its earlier, more restrictive policies toward trade with Eastern Europe, the United States has been slow in entering the picture. However, a development of potentially great importance occurred when United States Undersecretary of State Averell Harriman and Vice-Premier Gheorghe Gaston Marin held talks in Washington in May-June 1964 on economic and other matters. The principal economic results of these discussions were as follows:

1. The United States agreed to establish a general licensing procedure under which most commodities may be exported to Rumania without requiring individual export licenses.

2. The United States agreed to grant export licenses for a number of particular industrial facilities in which the Rumanian delegation expressed special interest.

3. Under a presidential decision made in June 1964, the United States agreed that its Export-Import Bank could grant guarantees for medium-term commercial credits used to finance the purchase of industrial goods.

4. Rumania agreed to guarantees guarding against the re-export of United States goods and technology without the prior consent of the U.S. Government and providing for the protection of industrial property rights.

All of the provisions listed above have since been acted upon.

In addition, the Washingtion talks produced two principal results of political rather than economic significance. The two countries agreed to elevate their diplomatic missions from legations to embassies, and Rumania reaffirmed its intention to permit the emigration of Rumanians with close relatives living in the United States. According to Washington sources, some hundreds of such persons, including dual nationals and their families, have come to the United States over the past two years.

Rumania's independent course has in fact had an ever-widening effect on its political relations with the West. One evidence of this is the fact that the Rumanian interpretation of "peaceful coexistence" has generally been much more positive than the Soviet, as well as largely devoid of the strident anti-Western formulas and threats which Moscow uses to balance its peaceful protestations.

A particularly striking example is the statement by Premier Maurer quoted in a box on the page opposite. This statement illustrates, in doctrinal language, the basic Rumanian attitude toward relations with the West and the relative position of this attitude in the Communist policy spectrum. It differs from the Soviet position on coexistence in rejecting the contention that there can be no coexistence of ideas. It stands still farther apart from the militant Chinese position which denies the possibility of any form of positive cooperation with the Western "imperialist" powers.

Rumania's moderate viewpoint has made itself manifest in the stance taken by Bucharest on specific East-West issues. The Cuban missile crisis of October 1962 provides a critical example. In its public posture, Rumania echoed the Soviet Union initially in condemning the US naval blockade, but in much less strident tones and with considerable hesitancy and caution. The main emphasis of its official pronouncements was placed on the need for "wisdom" and "negotiations" in resolving the crisis.

Rumanian-Cuban relations, moreover, have since cooled. Trade between the two countries dropped from $20 million in 1963 to $6 million (all Rumanian exports) in 1964. And in 1965 Cuba angrily withdrew all its students from Rumania when the authorities did not let them stage anti-American demonstrations.

Vietnam offers a more current example. While the Rumanian government does not approve of US military actions against North Vietnam and has made this position clear, there have been a number of indications that its only real concern is that the cold-war atmosphere generated by the crisis will limit its maneuverability both within the Communist world and in its relations with the West. On many counts—*e.g.,* relatively mild press reaction, less frequent official criticism, and containment of threatened student demonstrations against the US Embassy—Rumania's reaction to Vietnam has been the most restrained among all the Communist countries. Bucharest has also refrained from material support to North Vietnam: trade between the two countries amounted to only $3.6 million in 1964, a considerable drop from the 1963 level of $10.8 million. Rumania seems torn between keeping the way clear for expanding economic and other relations with the US and fulfilling an obligation to North Viet-Nam, a fellow Communist state with which, however, it has few common interests. Its restraint suggests that the first consideration is perhaps uppermost in Bucharest's mind.

Since 1963, Rumania has also taken several actions with the United Nations demonstrating its intent to pursue an independent foreign policy. The Rumanian delegation has broken ranks with the Soviet Union in three resolutions presented to the General Assembly. At the UN Conference on Trade and Development in 1964, the Rumanians voted against the Soviet bloc on a number of resolutions.

Perhaps most significant are the numerous steps Rumania has taken to strengthen its bilateral political ties with Western powers. These include the Gaston Marin mission to the United States in May-June 1964, the visit of Premier Maurer to France in July 1964, and to Austria in November 1965, First Vice-Premier Gheorghe Apostol's tour of Austria in the same month, several trips by Vice-Premier Gogo Radulescu to Italy, and delegations headed by Vice-Premier Birladeanu to Japan in 1963 and France in late 1964. Though most of these missions were primarily of an economic nature, the Rumanian leaders were undoubtedly aware of the political and psychological importance of establishing high-level contacts with the leaders of the West.

Impact on the Home Front

A review of Rumania's independent course would be incomplete without a brief look at its impact on the domestic scene. Most directly, it has given rise to a wide-ranging campaign to de-emphasize Soviet cultural and political influence and refurbish Rumanian traditions.

The first step was to purge Rumanian historiography of pro-Soviet distortions of the recent past. The initial guidelines were set by the November-December 1961 plenum of the RCP Central Committee, which rewrote the party's history so as to stress the leading role of the Rumanian Communists—as opposed to the Soviet Army—in overthrowing the pro-Nazi Antonescu regime in August 1944. More recently, Rumanian historians have rehabilitated a number of past political leaders who championed Rumanian national interests. They have also rebuffed Hungarian claims regarding Transylvania and have even made tentative moves to resurrect Rumania's historical claim to Bessarabia, occupied by the USSR in 1939.

Another important step was the abolition of compulsory Russian-language studies in the elementary-secondary school system, beginning with the 1963–64 school year. Simultaneously, the influential "Maxim Gorki" Russian Language Institute was abolished, and Bucharest's sole Russian-language bookstore was closed.

Rumania also has sharply curtailed Soviet cultural and informational activities. *Timpuri noi,* the Rumanian-language version of the Soviet foreign affairs journal *Novoe vremia,* was abolished in the fall of 1963 and replaced by *Lumea,* a largely Westward-looking Rumanian foreign affairs weekly. The Institute of Rumanian-Soviet Studies was closed shortly thereafter, and the Rumania-USSR Friendship Society, ARLUS, which was once a dominant force in Rumanian cultural life, has gradually been reduced to a mere shred of its former influence. Soviet movies, plays, and musical offerings run a poor second to Western performances in Bucharest. Cultural presentations officially sponsored by Western countries frequently receive top billing over Soviet events. And "Soviet-Rumanian Friendship Month," which for 16 years was celebrated with lavish demonstrations of cultural solidarity, was abolished in 1964.

At the same time, there has been a remarkable new emphasis on Rumanian national traditions, often with anti-Soviet overtones. This applies to the widest variety of fields: history, social sciences, literature, the Rumanian alphabet, even names of streets and commercial establishments. In all of this, the party leaders have sought to rally popular support and reinforce their independent activities abroad by showing that they are Rumanians first, Communists second, and definitely not Soviet pawns.

While Bucharest's new independence in foreign policy has been duly noted abroad, many Western observers cling to an image of the Rumanian leaders as unyielding practitioners of Stalinism at home. This image oversimplifies the present situation in Rumania and obscures significant changes in the direction of internal reform over the past several years.

To begin with, there have been important changes in the party leadership in keeping with Rumania's increasing independence and stress on economic growth. A significant development has been the rise to key positions of a group of "technocrats," valued more for their skills than for their party lineage. Similarly, on the mass level, the party has made vigorous efforts to broaden its base of support. Searching for a national consensus, the party has adopted a line which in effect recognizes that "those who aren't against us are with us."

The pattern of change appears with particular clarity in the key domain of state security policy. In 1964 the regime completed the release of virtually all political prisoners, numbering more than 11,000. This dramatic action has been reinforced by a decrease in the arbitrary use of police powers, a relaxation of other security controls and a purge of top-level officials of the *Securitate,* the secret police.

Nowhere, perhaps, has the change been greater—yet so little appreciated abroad— than in Rumanian intellectual life. In literature, this transformation has proceeded along several interlocking fronts: the rehabilitation of Rumanian writers of the monarchist period who once were blacklisted; an energetic campaign to reopen the doors to modern Western literature, including the works of authors diametrically opposed to socialist realism; and a direct and concentrated attack on socialist-realist restrictions as applied to living Rumanian authors. Directed largely by the party itself, these efforts reached a climax at a conference of the Writers' Union in February 1965, when the reactionary leadership of the Union was ousted.

There have been related developments in other areas of Rumanian intellectual life—in music, art, science and scholarship. Perhaps most important, news from Western sources has become far more accessible to the Rumanian public. Jamming of foreign radio broadcasts has ceased, non-Communist newspapers are available to the public (though still in limited quantities), and the press has adopted a policy of more objective and extensive reporting of events in the non-Communist world.

These and other reforms have been prompted by good and compelling internal reasons, for they represent a policy more closely attuned to the wishes and needs of the people. But they are also closely related to Rumanian foreign policy moves. By "standing up to the Russians," the Rumanian leaders have won greatly increased respect and support from the public. Thus armed, they doubtless feel more confident of their ability to introduce domestic reforms without running undue risks. Furthermore, having cast off the protective mantle of the USSR, which in years past was the essence of the regime's power, the Rumanian leaders must now base their power increasingly on popular support. This in turn means that they are under greater pressure to meet popular aspirations for a freer and more affluent life.

The Road Ahead

The death last March of Gheorghe Gheorgiu-Dej marked the end of one era in Rumanian politics and the beginning of another. All subsequent signs, however, point to the continuation and further development of the policies of independence and gradual liberalization charted during the last several years of Dej's leadership. Dej's successors—Party Secretary-General Nicolae Ceausescu, Premier Ion Gheorghe Maurer, and President Chivu Stoica—were all closely associated with him and his policies. Their activities and statements since Dej's death have clearly attested to their support of these policies and their determination to carry them forward. This was fully demonstrated at the Ninth Congress of the RCP last July, which squarely reaffirmed Rumania's intent to adhere to its independent course. Other recent indications—to cite just a few—have been Bucharest's continued nonalignment with Moscow in the dispute with Peking, open Rumanian opposition to Soviet pressure at a meeting of the WFTU last October, and relative forbearance on Viet-Nam. As recently as November 7, Secretary-General Ceausescu and President Maurer took the unprecedented step of deliberately boycotting the October Revolution anniversary festivities at the Soviet Embassy in Bucharest.

There are also compelling reasons for the new leadership to hew to Rumania's charted course. The independence drive has progressed so far that it would be virtually impossible—even if the new leaders were so inclined—to turn back the clock without causing deep divisions within the party and the public at large. And there are strong motives, as pointed out above, for continuing the process of internal reform.

Rumania's independent course has already produced significant results in the world arena. It has directly weakened Soviet hegemony in Eastern Europe in a geopolitical sense. It has blocked economic integration within Comecon, which from Moscow's viewpoint was a device to shore up Soviet political control of Eastern Europe. And it has given a powerful positive impetus to the spread of polycentrism elsewhere in the Communist world, especially in Eastern Europe.

In elaboration of this last point, we must recall the earlier outbreaks of independent nationalism in this region. Yugoslavia and Albania successfully broke away from Soviet domination, but only at the cost of violent economic retribution and with the aid of geography. Hungary tried it, only to be crushed by Soviet armed force, while the Polish October soon lost its vigor. Rumania, on the other hand, has shown that it is possible to gain independence under unfavorable geographic conditions without provoking either ruinous intervention or economic blockade. Deft maneuvering, courageous diplomacy, and skillful timing have been the essential ingredients of this achievement. At no point has the provocation been so great as to bring an overwhelming response from the great power to the East; at no point has Moscow's response been sufficiently strong to alter Rumania's course. The lesson this holds for other East European countries is abundantly clear.

*ASPECTS OF RUMANIAN INDUSTRIALIZATION STRATEGY AND PLANNING**

— · — · — · — · — · — · — · — · — · — ·

John M. Montias

The industrialization strategy of the Communist regime is most clearly expressed in the investment programs of the Five-Year Plans. Judging by the composition of these programs, particularly by the consistently high proportion of total investments allotted to heavy industry, we may affirm that the same broad goals have been pursued throughout the postwar period. We may detect a greater emphasis in recent years on industrial diversification, to create what the Rumanians call a "complex, many-sided and equilibrated economy"; but it may be argued that this autarkic trend is appropriate to a later stage in the country's development in the framework of the same over-all strategy, since the economy is now less pressed to build up a small number of export industries to finance large purchases of equipment in addition to meeting raw-material requirements (as it was in the early 1950's). The wider range of manufactures available for export also makes it easier to practice diversification.

The investment program also gives expression to the systematic policy of building plants on the basis of the latest world technology, no matter how capital-intensive it happens to be. This policy conflicts with the aim of providing as many peasants as possible with job opportunities in the cities, an aim that apparently fits on a lower rung of the planners' priority scale. As we have seen, the concentration of investments in industries that were capital-intensive to start with and that were slated to become even more capital-intensive as a result of these technologically advanced investments has led to a growing divergence between the modern, capital-intensive plants of heavy industry and traditional, labor-intensive, manufactures in light industry. Nevertheless, it would be premature at the present state of our knowledge to criticize the Rumanians for their technological fetishism. We have no way to judge, looking in from the outside, whether new plants in high-priority sectors, especially when they are built from

*Reprinted by permission of M.I.T. Press from *Economic Development of Communist Rumania* (Cambridge: M.I.T. Press), (in print), excerpts pp. 232–246. All footnotes deleted.

imported components or based on foreign known-how, come in packages whose factor proportions are more or less fixed by the existing technology or whether real alternatives exist of utilizing unskilled labor from low-priority sectors to economize on capital outlays in the "progressive" sectors. It is possible that the excess labor tied down in light industry or in agriculture (due to the lack of capital in these sectors) is poorly suited to work in heavy industry: female textile workers and sheep herders may have a very low opportunity cost in terms of the capital that they could replace in the metallurgical or machine-building industries.

Collectivization of the farm sector under state tutelage was another option taken by the ruling party that was both an end in itself and a means to other ends. From 1958 to 1962 collectivization helped to raise the share of produce marketed outside the state sector. It would seem also that it facilitated the imposition of direct controls over production, particularly to promote the expansion of technical crops, instead of allowing the output decisions of farms to be guided by the price system.

If we can make the simplifying assumption that the planners' goals and priorities were more or less the same throughout the postwar period, what can we say about the tactics that were employed to realize these objectives? Did similar problems evoke the same responses when they recurred, or were the planners eclectic in their improvisations? I think that a stable pattern of responses to changing circumstances can be made out.

The long-term plans, which were always framed with an optimistic outlook, demanded a strenuous investment effort each year if they were to be fulfilled even in their broad outline. How high a level the planners set for state investments depended on three basic factors:

1. The political climate of the moment. (In 1953–1954 and in 1956–1957, for instance, an unsettled and menacing political situation dictated retrenchments in the investment program for the benefit of consumers.)

2. The state of the balance of payments. (In 1955, in spite of more favorable political circumstances, investments remained sluggish, because there was insufficient foreign exchange left, after meeting external obligations and the minimum raw-material purchases needed to keep industry operating at or near capacity levels, to import a large volume of machinery and equipment. Domestic machinery production, which was still specialized in a small number of lines, could not satisfy the demand that would have been generated by a larger level of investments. In addition, the shortage of foreign exchange made it necessary to export lumber and cement that would otherwise have been consumed by the construction industry.)

3. The prospects for the forthcoming harvest and, more specifically, for state procurements of foodstuffs. The state fund for agricultural prod-

ucts is the main source of consumer goods that can be used to absorb the wages and salaries paid out by the investment sectors, including construction enterprises and the machine-building industry. A poor harvest and a depleted state fund, coupled with a high level of investments, tend to disturb the macroeconomic balance of the economy. A symptom of this disequilibrium is likely to be an excess of currency in circulation and rising prices on the peasant market. It also poses a balance-of-payments problem, which cuts down on the opportunities of using imports to absorb the additional purchasing power released by investments.

These were the factors directly determining the level of investments; others exerted an *indirect* influence through the balance of payments. The stagnation of petroleum output and the conservation of timber, for instance, both had a depressing effect on investments by depriving the economy of foreign exchange earnings that could have been used to buy investment goods or that would have made it possible to reduce food exports, which in turn would have allowed more domestic resources to be channeled into capital accumulation.

When I claim that planners "responded" to a variety of circumstances, I imply, of course, that they had a choice, that their decisions were not just a mechanical adjustment to changing constraints. The balance-of-payments crisis brought on by the liquidation of Soviet-Rumanian companies and by the repayment of old debts need not have inhibited investments, if the authorities had resolved a force a decline in individual consumption. In order to ram through this policy in the face of potential popular unrest, more resources would have had to be devoted to "ideological persuasion" and to the "repression of hostile elements." Stalin in the past, and Chinese and Albanian Communist leaders more recently, have demonstrated that a pliant population can, within certain limits, be coerced into sacrificing consumption. But such a Draconian policy has been eschewed by the Rumanian Party, at least in recent years. Nevertheless, it must be recognized that once they had made the major political decision to maintain minimum living standards and, if at all possible, to improve them from year to year, the planners were fairly restricted in the range of their responses.

In pursuing its investment strategy, Rumania, like the other industrializing members of CMEA, had a signal advantage over most underdeveloped countries in the rest of the world: it could translate any surpluses of primary goods it could spare from domestic consumption into imports of capital goods at constant terms of trade (determined, after a varying lag, by world price relations). Since "world prices" in use on the CMEA market tended to understate the relative scarcity of raw materials and foodstuffs relative to manufactures, primary commodities tended to be in short supply in CMEA. Hence the Rumanians faced a perfectly elastic demand for their corn, meat, timber, and petroleum exports. It so happened also that these exportables could be marketed in Western Europe at constant prices, at least for the quantities Rumania could supply. In contrast with such nations as India and Pakistan, which are said to face an inelastic demand for their staple exports and may on occasion suffer from the inability to convert their potential saving into capital formation (except by lavishing labor on projects that could more efficiently be carried out with imported machinery), Rumania had considerable freedom in choosing whether to import capital goods or to use domestic capacities to produce them. This leeway must have raised the marginal efficiency of investment, compared to what it would have been without this extra degree of freedom.

The next question I should like to speculate on is whether Rumania's conflict with Comecon was an "objective" concomitant of the strategy and tactics adopted by its leadership or whether it was the product of "subjective" elements of discord on both sides.

Some light may be shed on this question by comparing Rumania's policies with the policies of its fellow members of CMEA.

We conclude from the analysis of our sample of CMEA members that countries running a deficit in raw materials and foodstuffs with CMEA, such as Poland, Hungary, and Czechoslovakia, were forced to trade closely with those among their Comecon partners that were still willing to take machinery and consumer goods in exchange for raw materials and foodstuffs. The pressure on each country to reduce to a minimum its deficit in raw materials and foodstuffs with CMEA compelled the more developed countries, which suffered from an over-all deficit in these two groups, to shunt most of their supplies of these goods to the CMEA market. The exportable surpluses of raw materials and foodstuffs that they had left after meeting their import requirements from CMEA were not sufficient to purchase from the West any substantial proportion of their total imports of machinery or consumer goods. Bulgaria and Rumania, the least developed members of CMEA with the exception of Mongolia, were in a position, by contrast, to buy large amounts of machinery from the West because 1) they disposed of sufficient supplies of raw materials and foodstuffs to generate a surplus in these groups with CMEA and still have enough left over to pay for their imports of "soft" goods outside the Communist trade area, and 2) they received credits from the West (after 1960) to reinforce their earnings of foreign exchange in Western markets.

The question may be raised as to why the more developed countries did not cut back their imports of machinery and consumer goods *from* CMEA. The answer is that they were forced to buy large amounts of these "soft" goods from the newly industrialized members of the bloc if they wished to sell them more of these goods than they bought from them. Bulgaria, for example, would not buy nearly as much machinery from Czechoslovakia and Hungary if these two partners did not agree to buy machinery from her in return as part payment for these purchases. Only after meeting these "tied-sales" conditions were the more industralized partners permitted to buy "hard" goods to fulfill their more urgent needs.

In the past ten years politics have determined how each country's potential share in trade with the West has been utilized. In 1958 Rumania and Bulgaria were both capable of buying a substantial share of their machinery requirements in Western Europe because they already disposed of surpluses in hard goods with CMEA that they could shunt to the West, but political conditions were not yet ripe for them to do so. At that time, Poland, which received substantial credits from the West in 1958, had the means and enough political autonomy to buy a fairly large proportion of her machinery imports from outside CMEA. In 1959–1960 the Rumanians chose to draw on their political power to shift trade toward the West. Bulgaria followed suit around 1963 when political circumstances became favorable. When Poland's deficit in raw-materials trade with CMEA deepened and she began to accumulate a surplus in over-all trade with the West instead of a deficit, she lost some of her old margin in hard currency and was forced to reorient her purchases of manufactures toward CMEA sources.

The Soviet Union, which runs a large surplus in hard goods with the rest of CMEA and buys an above-average proportion of her machinery imports in the West, and East Germany, whose trade pattern is exactly the opposite, would, I believe, both conform to this same pattern although I cannot document this as precisely as for the other five countries.

A consequence of the logic of the trade relations I have described is that as Rumania and Bulgaria continue to industrialize they may *in the long run* tighten up, rather than loosen further, their trade links with CMEA. This is so for two interrelated reasons: first, as their raw material requirements and as their consumption of domestically produced food keep on rising, they will become increasingly dependent on the Soviet Union, *qua* supplier of these goods; second, they will soon be generating a trade surplus in consumer goods and machinery, for the disposal of which they will have to look to their fellow members of CMEA, and again especially to the Soviet Union, the sole remaining country willing to barter materials for manufactures. This retrogression can only be forestalled if the Balkan countries of CMEA can secure outlets for their manufactures in the West. Credits, of course, would help to tie the trade of these countries to the West, but in the long run these loans will have to be repaid, at least in part, in the form of manufactures, if they are not to impose an intolerable burden on the balance of payments of the recipients. It is too early to say whether the present *détente* between Eastern and Western Europe will proceed far enough in the next few years to allow this new pattern of trade to emerge.

The question that poses itself is whether an expansion based on the creation of productive facilities essentially similar to those already in existence in the more advanced nations can go on for a long period without running into some of the difficulties that have recently beset the more industrially mature nations of CMEA. Now it is true that Rumania's industry and her other modern sectors have a long way to go before they exhaust the reservoir of labor power still waiting to be drained in her collectivized agriculture. It is still a relatively simple matter for the Rumanian planners to draw off the additional manpower they need in other sectors by substituting modest amounts of capital for the prospective migrants from the countryside. The cost of doing so is limited to the provision of standard equipment for farms, including trucks, mechanical sowers, pickers, automatic balers, and harvesters, and the construction of modest housing facilities, hospitals, and schools to accommodate the new entrants into the urban labor force. The age structure of the Rumanian farm population is much more favorable than it is in the developed socialist countries. It is still possible to invest resources in the agricultural sector with a relatively high pay-off, especially if the institutional framework of agriculture can be reshaped so as to provide the collective farmers with incentives that seem to be lacking at the present time.

The more immediate problem that Rumania will face in her transition to a mature industrial economy lies in the industrial sphere. Her first phase of industrialization encompassed mainly the reproduction of technologies mastered before, during, or shortly after World War II in the Soviet Union, East Germany, and Czechoslovakia. In the second phase, from 1958 to 1965, Rumania drew on the most recent technologies of these same nations together with some of the more up-to-date achievements of Western Europe. Except in the manufacture of oil-drilling equipment, where Rumanian engineers were responsible for a number of innovations, Rumania's scientific contribution was small, consisting mainly in the adaptation of foreign processes to local conditions. One may wonder how competitive Rumania's industrial products will be on the world market—especially in the West—if they remain the outcome of processes mastered a few years beforehand in the scientifically more advanced countries. This relative backwardness can be overcome only if strong inducements are provided within the enterprise to develop new processes or to introduce technical improvements wherever they may originate. Rumania will soon resemble Hungary and Czechoslovakia, industrial countries with a very narrow resource base, which have had considerable difficulty shifting from an "extensive" to an "intensive" type of growth chiefly because of the inflexibility of the centralized economic systems they have been saddled with for so many years. It is hard to escape the impression that Rumania also will eventually have to abandon the system that has successfully carried the economy through the first stages of industrialization and devise some sort of market mechanism to guide enterprise managers toward the more sophisticated decisions necessary in an industrially complex economy.

10. A SUMMARY LOOK AT REFORMS

*THOSE ECONOMIC REFORMS BEHIND THE IRON CURTAIN: AN INTERVIEW WITH PROFESSORS ABRAM BERGSON, JOHN M. MONTIAS, AND ARTHUR SMITHIES**

Q: Gentlemen, for the last four or five years we have been hearing a good deal about "basic" and "revolutionary" reforms in the way the Soviet Union and the nations of Eastern Europe manage their economies. Some commentators in the West—and even some Communists—see the reforms as marking the first step away from Communist planning. In point of fact, how basic are these changes?

Bergson: While it is true that the reforms have often been discussed in what, to me, are excessively dramatic terms, they certainly represent a significant development. There has been—or is now taking place—a very pronounced shift in the nature of the planning systems of Eastern Europe and Russia. True, the changes are of a different order in different countries. But speaking broadly, the centralized and bureaucratic system of planning that came into being under Stalin is now giving way to planning that emphasizes much more decentralized decision making and market institutions.

Q. Do you believe the reforms will have far-reaching significance, Prof. Montias?

Montias: In theory, perhaps. I should say that the changes are potentially revolutionary in the freedom and permissiveness that is being built into the new planning machinery. But we still have to see how they will be implemented. Three or four years from now we shall know just how revolutionary the changes prove in practice because it is only then that we shall know the extent to which the spirit of the reforms has in fact been carried out and the planners have actually permitted people to exercise these freedoms. We may find that the reforms are more revolutionary in theory than in practice.

*Reprinted by permission from *Challenge*, May–June 1967, pp. 18–23.

Dr. Arthur Smithies is Nathaniel Ropes Professor of Political Economy, Harvard University. His publications include: *The Budgeting Process in the United States* (1955) and *Readings in Fiscal Policy*, edited with J. K. Butters (1955).

Bergson: I agree that this is a necessary caution. At the same time, I think it would be wrong to speak of the reforms as existing only on paper. It is true that in some cases the reforms have yet to be implemented. In Hungary, for example, the basic change—and it is supposedly a very sweeping one—is to come in 1968. In Czechoslovakia the reforms, however, are now in the process of being implemented. As for the Russians, they began initiating rather modest reforms in their planning system some time ago and the tempo of change has accelerated quite markedly in the last two years. It is very much in motion today. Still, I don't want to suggest that all is now clear, and Montias is certainly right to remind us that there is still possibility of a slip between the cup and the lip.

Smithies: It seems to me that we need a clearer description of what we mean by market socialism and decentralization in these countries. Under the traditional Stalinist system, both the production targets and the techniques for meeting these targets were prescribed from the top. Well, decentralization could mean that the central authorities still fix production targets but that in administering the plan the managers of enterprise are given some freedom in purchasing factors of production, making profits, and so forth. Or decentralization could mean something quite different. It could mean that the central authorities do not fix targets but let production emerge pretty much from the decisions of the decentralized economy. Which is it?

Montias: That's just the trouble. There is no clear blueprint for the reforms anywhere in Eastern Europe. The permissiveness of the reforms lies in this: as much as possible, enterprises will be guided by financial incentives and not by central command. But even in theory there is an extremely important restraint to this. In Czechoslovakia, for example, only a small fraction of total output—estimated at around seven per cent—will have prices freely set in negotiations between suppliers and buyers. The other 93 per cent remains centralized. And even where prices are not centralized, it isn't as though the planners had abjured central controls for all time. Central controls always remain as a standby to be reintroduced whenever the planners deem it necessary. In fact, this is precisely what happened in Czechoslovakia during the early Sixties. Although few Westerners were aware of it at the time, the Czech government in 1958–59 embarked upon some quite far-reaching reforms. They created new enterprise and personal incentives, and, even more important, put these incentives on a long-term basis so that individual plants and their managers could hope to benefit when they introduced innovations and improvements with long-term pay-offs. Well, the reforms fell apart, chiefly because ministry officials in effect sabotaged the system by diverting income from profitable enterprises to inefficient enterprises, thereby scuttling the whole incentive system. By 1963, they had been completely abandoned and central controls had been re-established. The same thing can happen again.

Bergson: The central authorities in the East European countries have obviously not abdicated their final authority to intervene with controls of a more traditional sort if they should not be pleased with the progress achieved under the reforms. What is significant, I think, is that for the first time they are committed to working arrangements under which they hope they will *not* have to intervene, at least not to the degree that they did before.

Smithies: I'd still like to know what *kind* of market socialism and decentralization they are working toward.

Bergson: Perhaps the best way to answer you is to describe what they are moving away from. Under Stalin, the Russians had a centralized system of planning. Inputs and outputs of production units (factories, farms, etc.) were determined by superior agencies in a bureaucratic structure and imposed through physical commands. Although centralization was not complete even then, I think the system under Stalin was more highly centralized than any that has ever existed in a modern economy, not excepting Germany under Hitler. Now I distinguish this kind of economic system from market socialism under which the production units are allowed great autonomy in determining their own inputs and outputs. True, the planning authorities may still direct the activity of factory managers, but *in principle* they limit their interference to *indirect* market controls—manipulation of prices, creation of proper incentives and the like. For the present, this is an ideal that you do not often find in practice. But I do think that the Communist economies are moving toward this ideal. Under the reforms, time and again the authorities are reducing the number of planned targets to which the subordinate production units must conform. And they are also relying more heavily than before on monetary and financial incentives to "guide" rather than command the production units to move in the desired direction.

Smithies: How conscious is this movement? Is there, for example, a coherent blueprint of market socialism, such as the Polish economist Oskar Lange worked out in theory?

Bergson: Only in the broadest sense. The Communist authorities have in the past been notably empirical in determining the organization of their planning system. As a young colleague of mine has said, they have been planning without theory for decades, and this is still largely true even though there is more theory today than there was in the past—and even though they are being advised by more sophisticated economists than used to be the case. We should still be careful not to think of them as trying to implement any specific theoretical model.

Montias: I would very much agree with that. The Oskar Lange model of market socialism (which is based mainly on the use of flexible prices to guide production and consumption by industrial producers) is certainly *not* the blueprint under which the reforms are being carried out in Poland or anywhere else.

Toward Market Socialism?

Q. What about Yugoslavia? Does the Yugoslav experience provide the planners of the other Communist countries with a model of the kind of market socialism they are aiming for?

Montias: It certainly provides *us* with a standard of comparison in considering how far the rest of Eastern Europe still has to go. When the Yugoslavs embarked on decentralization in 1953, they dismantled the planning commission, abolished completely all target setting and materials allocation, and for seven years did not even draw up any materials balances. That is what I call a revolutionary change! Compared to this performance, the changes elsewhere in Eastern Europe don't seem quite as dramatic, although I completely agree with Prof. Bergson that the direction is there. But it is still a very cautious movement.

Bergson: I agree that nowhere in Eastern Europe have the reforms gone quite as far in the direction of market socialism as in Yugoslavia. But the reform movement is still in process. Even in Yugoslavia the government vacillated, and it was only in the course of time that we began to see a really sharp move toward the essential realization of market socialism. And if the Czech and Hungarian reforms don't quite measure up to the Yugoslav standard, they do involve very substantial changes from the system that existed before. It is the Russians and the Poles who are proceeding with the greatest caution. In the case of the Russians, this is perhaps partly because Kosygin and Brezhnev accused Khrushchev of being hairbrained, and they may wish to project a suitable image of responsibility. But even here, the changes that have taken place, while comparatively modest, represent a significant departure from the Stalinist system which had, after all, prevailed with little change for much longer than in any other Communist country.

Q. Apart from Yugoslavia which countries have gone furthest in the direction of market socialism?

Montias: One could draw up a scale starting with the least developed country, Albania, which has undergone virtually no change. Then would come Rumania, where virtually no change has taken place internally, but where, in the field of foreign trade, enterprises have been allowed to participate with the Ministry of Foreign Trade in making contracts with foreign firms. That is at least a step toward decentralization of decision making in one area. Then, we have Bulgaria, which has been moving further, though I think the changes here are rather formalistic. Next comes Poland. Then, somewhere between Poland and Hungary, comes the Soviet Union. And finally we have Hungary, Czechoslovakia and East Germany, where the reforms are most advanced. This lineup makes a rather interesting pattern.

Bergson: Yes. The reform movement seems to be most vigorous in the more developed of the Eastern European Communist countries, and less vigorous elsewhere.

Q. How do you explain this?

Bergson: Well, the Stalinist type of centralized planning is probably most appropriate—if indeed it is appropriate at all—for the less developed Communist countries. It is true that the cumbersome bureaucratic controls that are an integral part of the Stalinist system proved costly everywhere they were applied. But I suspect that they have been especially costly to the more advanced and complex economies, such as, say Czechoslovakia.

Smithies: I think we may get a clearer answer to this question if we look at those sectors of the economy that the authorities have been most willing to decentralize. Am I correct in assuming that decentralization has gone much farther in the consumer goods sector than in heavy industry?

Montias: Yes, that's true both in the Soviet Union and in Eastern Europe, and it is true with respect to price fixing, central target setting and the choice that producers have of varying their output mix.

Smithies: How about foreign trade?

Montias: There has been a decided effort to bring exporters out of the isolation in which they have been for so many years. But at the same time there has been very little decentralization of imports.

Smithies: So it is fair to say that decentralization is primarily concentrated in the domestic consumer goods sector. This would, of course, be more substantial in the more industrialized countries. There is not much decentralization in the heavy goods area, and only limited decentralization in the foreign trade area. In other words, the reforms have been limited to those sectors the authorities consider less essential, at least as far as economic growth is concerned.

Bergson: That is not quite correct. Even with respect to heavy industry, there have been—or are in the process of being introduced—definite reductions in the number of planned targets and important changes in managerial controls. This is true in Russia. It is true in Czechoslovakia. And it will be true in Hungary, too, once the reforms are implemented.

Smithies: To the extent that decentralization *is* becoming more widespread in Communist countries, I would imagine it is resulting in greater emphasis on fiscal and monetary policy. Take Yugoslavia. I remember having a Yugoslav student in my course a number of years ago. I was lecturing on wage-price inflation, the difficulty of controlling it, and all that. For a long time I was sure he had come here to gather anticapitalist propaganda to take back home with him. But, no, I discovered that Yugoslavia was encountering the same kinds of wage-price inflation that we were. He had come here to find out how we coped with the problem rather than to see what was wrong with us.

Montias: To the extent that decentralization gives the individual enterprise greater control over wage expenditures that are not properly coordinated with investment expenditures, it may give rise to inflationary pressures. Whenever this has happened—in Yugoslavia, for example, or in Czechoslovakia during the early 1960's when some abortive reforms were carried out—there has been a countertrend toward centralization. Indeed, there are central planners who favor the reimposition of controls over enterprises in times of inflation to prevent excessive liquidity from being released.

Q This raises a rather basic question. From what you say it would seem that the authorities have been most cautious, indeed almost reluctant, to initiate the reforms. Yet they have taken the first steps. What made them do it?

Bergson: This a big question, to which there are a variety of answers. The London *Economist* said in a recent issue that the economies of Eastern Europe and Russia are now experiencing a crisis which, while not as eye-catching, is as profound as was the Great Depression in the West during the Thirties. That is overstating the situation. But there is no question that many Communist economies are experiencing economic difficulties and that the reforms represent an attempt, in part, to meet these difficulties.

Deficiencies in Planning

Q. Is this obviously true in the case of Russia?

Bergson: Even the casual reader of the Soviet press and journals is made aware of how inefficiently the centralized type of planning system has been functioning. One can readily compile quite a list of what have become almost classical deficiencies of the old system. The overburdened superior agencies which act arbitrarily; the manager of a production unit who responds to defective success criteria and refuses to innovate and increase efficiency so that he can more easily win a bonus for overfulfilling a planned target; the manager who produces defective goods or goods of the wrong assortment because bonuses are awarded primarily in terms of aggregate output.

Q. But these are long-standing problems. Why have they led to reforms now?

Bergson: It is true that there were reports of deficiencies of this sort in the Soviet press under Stalin as long ago as the Thirties. There are several factors to explain why the government has, at long last, decided to do something about them. First, the Soviet economy is getting more complicated and, therefore, more difficult to administer under the Stalinist-type apparatus. There are other factors. I would give a fair amount of weight to the change in economic theory. Under Stalin, economics was a dismal discipline, indeed. Stalin felt that economists should limit their activities to descriptions of what they observed, with perhaps an occasional polemic against fallen idols who had been purged. Very rarely was the economist expected to participate in what Stalin called "decision making undertaken by the higher authorities." Well, this situation has changed very rapidly. In a very short period a kind of "new economics" has emerged, often making use of previously taboo types of Western theory. This has no doubt led to greater Russian understanding of the weaknesses of the old system while helping them to formulate alternative policies.

Listening to Economists

Q. But why should they be listening to economists now when they weren't listening to them 10 years ago?

Bergson: Without pretending that it is the whole story, I do feel that the Soviet Union's growing economic difficulties have played a very important part. Let me just mention one most significant symptom of these difficulties—the decline in the Soviet growth rate. Between 1950 and 1958 Soviet GNP was probably growing at around seven per cent a year. While the government claimed even a better performance, seven per cent is certainly impressive. Well, the rate of growth has fallen to an average of perhaps five per cent a year. This is still respectable, but it is no longer a superrate, and the government is much concerned about this, especially since the Russians tend to think that the rationale of their system rests on its ability to grow rapidly.

Q. How about Eastern Europe? Has poor economic performance stimulated reforms there, too?

Montias: Very definitely, but this works both ways. Very fast-growing countries like Rumania and Bulgaria show relatively little interest in reform. It's not just that they are simpler economies. They are also—at least for the time being—more successful economies.

Bergson: Don't you think that they are more successful partly because they are less complex?

Montias: That is probably true. When you ask the Rumanians, for example, why they don't undertake sweeping reforms like their Czech and Hungarian colleagues, they answer: "You don't throw away the sheep's fleece because there is a flea in it." The defects that Prof. Bergson has mentioned for the Soviet Union have cropped up in all the East European countries. But countries with lagging economies are more prone to embark on reforms than others. Poland is a particularly interesting case. Here is a country with a strong tradition of high-quality economic thinking. After all, it produced Oskar Lange, whose model of decentralized decision making has had considerable influence, at least on other economists. And yet the government, so far, has rejected Lange's teachings. The reason for this is not just dogmatism. The fact is that Poland is in a somewhat less advanced stage of development and therefore is still performing fairly well under the old system. It has not yet encountered those difficulties of technological innovation that led Czechoslovakia and East Germany to embark on reforms.

Are We Moving to the Left?

Q. Prof. Smithies, it is often said that while the Communist countries are moving in the direction of capitalism, many Western countries have moved in the socialist direction since the end of World War II. Do you agree?

Smithies: No. My impression is not that we have moved in their direction, but that they have tended to move in our direction. A few years ago, it is true, many economists were bemused by the idea of indicative planning. The idea was that you prepared something like a central plan, announced it, and by the mere fact of announcing it were able to put it into effect without controls. Businesses, unions and other sectors of the economy would act accordingly. The leading example is provided by the French, although the British have done the same thing with their Neddy experiment. I rather doubt whether this kind of planning has amounted to nearly as much as its advocates have thought. Some effects of indicative planning may be self-validating, but I am inclined to think that other forces have prevailed. What do you do when you find, as in France, that carrying out the plan produces inflation and threatens your external trading position? What you do, and what France has done, is to let the plan go. As far as the under-developed countries are concerned, the recent misfortunes of India have demonstrated that attempts to apply some Russian methods of physical planning without Russia's bureaucratic apparatus simply won't work. And I predict that if India has effective government in the next few years, there will again be a retreat from attempts at physical planning. The fact remains that the success stories of the postwar period—Japan, Germany and the U.S.—have not relied on either physical or indicative planning.

Q. By the same reasoning, since the "success stories" of the Communist world are currently among the simpler and more Stalinist economies, do you feel that we shall see a return to the old system? In other words, are the reforms here to stay?

Bergson: I think it would be very difficult to return completely to the old, bureaucratic, Stalinist system. Even if the reforms prove unsuccessful, the authorities are more likely to experiment further than to return to the old system. This is certainly true of the Soviet Union, where there has been much talk recently about going further.

Q. Prof. Montias, do you think the reforms will last?

Montias: It is still too early to tell. But in Czechoslovakia at least there are some trends that are ominously reminiscent of what happened in 1961 and 1962 when an earlier reform movement collapsed. Eugene Loebl, president of the Bank of Slovakia and a very important figure in Czech reforms (he spent a number of years in prison before he was released in the early Sixties), has stated that the Ministries are once again taking funds from profitable enterprises and redistributing them to those that have sustained losses. This, as he points out, is a sure way of undermining incentives either to increase profits or cut losses. Moreover, the same personnel who administered the old system are implementing the reforms. The one exception is the Prime Minister, Josef Lenárt, and he is a very strong advocate of decentralization. But he is apparently a minority of one in the Politburo and is surrounded by tough, old-line Stalinists. True, the cultural and political atmosphere is more favorable today. But if the political situation deteriorates, there is no reason that I can see why there should not be a retrogression to the Stalinist system.

Q. But, on balance, you think it more probable that the reforms are here to stay?

Montias: In advanced countries like Czechoslovakia and Hungary, yes. Here the economic situation is so serious that reforms must take place if these countries are to retain, or, in the case of Czechoslovakia, recover, some of their lost markets.

Q. Assume the reforms are here to stay, at least in the more advanced countries. Do you think they will actually improve economic performance?

Bergson: Although the overall impact may not be very great in countries like the Soviet Union, I do feel that some of the changes will make Communist economies more rational. But the reforms have also created some difficulties. The new incentive system, for example, places a greater emphasis on profits. But many managers are finding that what is most profitable for the producer is not always what consumers most want to buy. Or take another example. The authorities have given factories funds for investment in automation and new machinery. But factory managers complain that they often cannot get machinery or construction firms to fill their orders and thus let them implement the new spending authority they have presumably acquired. These problems will not be easy to iron out.

Montias: I think the reforms will have a rather smaller impact on growth than many other current developments—such things as the expansion of trade, the integration of the region under COMECON, the exhaustion of natural resources, and so on. These trends are quite independent of the reforms and will occur with or without them. What is true is that if economic conditions deteriorate, the reforms will get a quite disproportionate share of the blame, as happened in Czechoslovakia in 1963.

Q. What are the political implications of the reforms? Will they tend toward greater democracy in the Communist bloc?

Bergson: The reforms have certainly contributed toward greater permissiveness, although it is highly unlikely that they will lead to any radical political change. Many of those who oppose reform do so largely for political reasons: they fear that it will weaken the power of the central authorities and ultimately of the party. The reforms are also contributing to the erosion of Marxist dogma, a process that has now been going on for quite some time. Here is an example of what I mean. Under the reforms, Soviet prices will for the first time be adjusted in such a way as to allow for a return on capital. Furthermore, the government is to charge interest for the finance capital it makes available. Now, this move clearly represents a sharp break with the labor theory of value and for this reason had been resisted for decades. But the Soviet government has finally recognized that an economic condition, scarcity of capital, has to be given priority over dogma. In this way, the pragmatism of the reforms is contributing to loosening the grip of Marxist dogma.

Smithies: I would agree that, to the extent that the reforms lead to a weakening of the central oligarchy, they are clearly to our interest. That is why more general Communist recognition of the inefficiency of the centralized system that brought about the reforms in the first place should be welcomed by the West.

Montias: I should like to add that in the foreign trade area, the reforms will also lead to more direct contacts with Western enterprises, since all business contacts will no longer be channeled through the government. It will therefore be possible to establish much broader contacts, and these new personal and business ties should make for greater understanding in general. Mind you, I am not one of those who thinks that trade is the solution to all international problems. Nazi Germany and the rest of Europe did a lot of trade before the war, but this did not prevent the war.

Nationalism and Reforms

Q. How about nationalism? Do you think that the reforms are helping to loosen the ties between the Soviet Union and the other Eastern European countries?

Bergson: Not really. The process of breaking away from Soviet hegemony antedates the reforms, and I think it is shaped by other forces, notably the split between Russia and China. But it is true that the Eastern European countries are using their new autonomy to enact more radical economic reforms than those in the Soviet Union.

Montias: They may go further, but they are not in conflict with Soviet policy. Some people even suspect that the Soviet Union is using the reforms in Eastern Europe as a kind of experimental testing ground to see how far she herself should eventually go. There may, of course, be a conflict of interest in the foreign trade area, for once enterprises are free to look around for sources of supplies and markets, they may look more to the West and less to the Soviet Union. But all this is highly speculative.

Q. Since there is general agreement that the reforms are in the West's interest, what can we do to encourage them?

Smithies: One thing we can do is to expand East-West trade. It seems to me, as it did to many of us in Washington at the time these restrictions were first imposed in the late Forties, that extreme restrictions on East-West trade do not serve our interest. It is decidedly to our advantage to have rising standards of living in Communist countries. Austerity, on the other hand, fosters the kind of political system we are not in favor of. Of course, it remains to be seen whether we can have the same kind of

trading relations with Communist countries as we do with private economies. Nor is it yet clear that foreign trade will be decentralized to the same
extent as other sectors of the economy.

Bergson: I see a real opportunity here. Communist restrictions on East-
West trade have certainly proved very costly, more for them than for us.
The reforms should make the authorities more interested in exploring
profitable trading opportunities. Of course, if there is to be much more
trade, there will also have to be more cooperation on the Western side
than there has been up to now.

Montias: I think we need to be very pragmatic here. It all depends on what
we want, what they do, and what advantages we expect to gain. Thus it
would certainly be a mistake to liberalize trade with those countries that
decentralize, but not with those countries that retain the old centralized
system. There are countries like Rumania which are not going to decentralize to any extent but with whom we might still find it very profitable
to trade for both economic *and* political reasons. We must not be dogmatic.

Q. Apart from trade, what can we do?

Montias: It is possible that some of the Eastern European countries say
Czechoslovakia or Hungary, might follow Yugoslavia and allow direct
investment by Western private enterprise. This might take the form of
joint partnerships between large Western companies and Eastern manufacturers and could be profitable for both parties. For the country involved it would be a means of obtaining technical know-how. From the
point of view of the Western firm, it is a way of taking advantage of the
low labor costs of Eastern Europe. Since there is nothing that Western
businessmen hate more than the red tape connected with centralized
planning, decentralization would favor this development.

Smithies: But when all is said and done, I don't think that anything that
we do will have any effect on the reform movement one way or the other.
The trend is at work, and we can't do much to either accelerate or retard
it.

Q. Thank you, gentlemen.

*ECONOMIC REFORMS IN COMMUNIST COUNTRIES**

Alexander Erlich

   In view of some very sweeping pronouncements that have been made
about the meaning of recent economic reforms in the Soviet Union and in

*Reprinted by permission from *Dissent* (May–June 1967), pp. 311–319.

Eastern Europe, it seems appropriate to begin by baldly stating my view as to what these reforms do *not* mean. They most definitely do *not* herald the restoration of capitalism in any form or shape; nor do they constitute a retreat toward the "mixed economy" of the Soviet NEP of the twenties or to a very similar system which was in existence throughout Eastern Europe during the late forties. Yet while the scope of these developments is much more limited than is frequently assumed, they are certainly important enough to merit our attention.

I. The Reforms in Outline

The proximate purpose of the changes in the system of economic administration which have recently been introduced in the Soviet Union and in most of Eastern Europe consists in enlarging the autonomy of the individual enterprises within the framework of centrally planned and predominantly collectivistic economies. To put the same thing somewhat differently, these changes attempt to bring about a shift in emphasis from administrative direct controls to pecuniary inducements as the guiding force behind the managerial activities. The specific devices used to achieve these objectives vary significantly from country to country, both in points of detail and in over-all degree of consistency and determination. But all of them share certain distinctive features:

1. Under the established system, the enterprise manager was confronted with a large array of planned indicators which were handed down to him from above and which determined the size and the composition of the output as well as the way of producing it; they also decisively, although indirectly, influenced the level of his own rewards. Now the number of these indicators will be sharply curtailed, and the most important of them—the *gross* value of output produced by the given enterprise—will be abandoned in favor of the total value of output actually sold or of some kind of index of the total *net* value accruing within the enterprise.

2. The standing of profitability among the planned indicators will be enhanced and the stimulus to raise it powerfully strengthened as the bonuses of the managers will be more closely linked to the level of profits earned and as enterprises will be allowed to retain and to reinvest a much higher share of their profits and depreciation allowances than exist now. (This particular category of changes is most frequently associated with the name of the Soviet economist Evsei Liberman.)

3. There will be a pronounced shift from outright grants to long-term repayable credits as the chief method of supplying investible resources to enterprises, and an interest-like charge on the use of fixed capital assets will be imposed (until now there was only a purely nominal charge on short-term bank credits).

4. An extensive price reform will be carried out in order to make relative prices correspond more closely to what is called in official parlance the relative amounts of the "socially necessary labor" expended in the production of goods.

5. There will be a stepping-up in the process of amalgamation of individual enterprises (most of them of a single-plant type) into broader organizational units ("firms" or "associations") which could relieve the central authorities of the tasks of intra-industrial co-ordination.

6. The direct contractual supplier-customers relationships between enterprises in interlinked industries are to increase in scope.

II. The Underlying Motives

The typical weaknesses of the Stalinist planning system have been so often stated and restated during the last decade in the East as well as in the West that they can be summed up in a near-telegraphic style:

1. The Soviet and East European planners lacked proper criteria for rational allocation of scarce resources. Neither did they have a meaningful and operative price system that could inform men in charge at various levels of economic administration about comparative advantages of different product mixes and factor combinations that lie within the range of choices open to the economy.

2. The far-reaching centralization of decision-making, in face of the stupendous multitude and complexity of the choices to be made, has caused the solutions to be slow in coming and not infrequently lacked in mutual consistency, not to speak of optimality (in the sense of extracting the greatest output of the desired composition from the given amount of productive resources). While a delegation of authority in matters of detail to the lower echelons helped to avert chaos, it still left the superior agencies with backbreaking tasks of evaluation and reconciliation of competing claims from below.

3. Some of the built-in incentives of the lower echelon men have been operating at cross purposes with the intentions of the central planners. The literature on the subject is replete with references to the "cat-and-mouse" game between managers and planning authorities, with the first lobbying for easy output targets and ample capital allocations, and the latter pushing for the opposite. Also, the perverse inclination to maximize rather than minimize the use of expensive raw materials as a result of output targets being formulated in terms of gross value or of weight has been widely commented upon; and it was pointed out that the same target-setting procedures made it possible for individual managers to earn a bonus for successful execution of the plan by including in their outputs goods which were actually not wanted but which happened to be relatively easy to produce.

4. Last but not least, attention has been repeatedly drawn to impediments against steady and rapid diffusion of technological innovations, except when they seem truly striking and/or when an area of particularly high priority is involved. Such impediments, it was stressed, were bound to arise at different levels of the administrative hierarchy; they reflected the central planners' desire to reduce the number of decisions they had to make, and the managers' fear of a temporary slowdown in operation in the wake of technological change-over, with underfulfillment of the output plans and a loss of the bonus as an inevitable concomitant.

It is generally agreed that all these inefficiencies are more critical now than they were in the formative period of the economies in question; the gaps left by mistakes in planning are now harder to fill. The reasons are manifold:

1. The steadily growing size and complexity of the economies causes the slapdash nature of decision-making to be more wasteful than before.

2. Transition from the "extensive" to the "intensive" stage of economic development is in full swing. Large labor reserves due to open or "disguised" unemployment are either exhausted or significantly reduced; the same is true of underutilized high-quality natural resources; rapid urbanization and improvement in skills set off the "revolution of rising expectations" whose demands can be ignored only at an increasingly high cost in terms of efficiency and socio-political stability.

In such a situation, it is no longer sufficient to clamp down a very high rate of investment on the economy and to make it stick by hook or crook. A dramatic change in efficiency of resource utilization and in the quality of decision-making becomes imperative in order to prevent the rate of economic growth from slackening as it did in most of the Soviet-bloc countries during the sixties. Nor is it surprising that Czechoslovakia —for which these considerations have acquired particular urgency and which experienced not merely a slowdown in her rate of growth but an actual drop in her national income in 1963—is at present in the forefront of the reform drive; her strong dependence on exports of high-quality manufacturing goods to Western markets is an added stimulus for moving rapidly in this direction.

It is likewise understandable that Rumania—with her vast manpower reserves still untapped, but above all with excellent prospects for further developments of her oil-based industries—can ride high by combining tight-fisted Stalinist methods of planning with an aggressive utilization of the good old "law of comparative advantage": she makes the most of the blessing conferred upon her by nature and unabashedly pushes the sales of oil and oil products in Western markets at the expense of much less remunerative trade with her Comecon associates.

3. The reduction of the technological lag makes it increasingly un-realistic to assume that a bold forward stride in adopting advanced foreign technology would more often than not represent a substantial improve-ment over the previous state of affairs even though the underlying invest-ment decisions had been made in a "blunderbuss" fashion and based on unreliable cost estimates. On the other hand, whenever new technological frontiers do come within sight or when old substitution possibilities appear in a new light as a result of shifts in relative costs, it is, at least in one important respect, more difficult to make the switch than it was in the past because this entails not sacrificing "expendable" mass con-sumption and sucking in unemployed labor, but slowing down the develop-ment of powerful and well-entrenched high-priority industries. Chemicals and oil vs. steel and coal are good examples.

4. According to a view shared by many non-Communist economists in the West, the Stalinist methods during the early period were not merely less harmful than now but positively advantageous in an important sense. Given the imperative need for rapid growth, the argument goes, a wide measure of centralized control and interference with the market was indispensable. Inflationary pressures which were bound to develop could not but strain the efficacy of the price mechanism and generate specific shortages that could not be adequately dealt with by across-the-board measures of monetary and fiscal policy. Rapid and drastic shifts in the composition of the output and in the level of technology called for delib-erate synchronization and coordination of major investment decisions affecting large and interrelated areas of the economy. In this connection, Oskar Lange's comparison with the "war economy" situation in the Western countries was often invoked; and it was pointed out that after the economy had been fundamentally restructured and made more com-plex, the advantages of the "warlike" methods would be increasingly dwarfed by their shortcomings. Yet while the reasoning is undoubtedly suggestive, it calls for strong qualifications:

> (a) Even in a "war economy" situation the tendency to concentrate the decision-making powers at the top can overreach itself and prove partly self-defeating: low priority and/or low-shortage areas should be allowed to shift for themselves, and some interdependencies are less stringent, and less crucial for the whole economy than others. Lenin was very candid in admitting by 1921 that the economic centralization during the years of "war communism" had gone far beyond the call of duty. His Soviet and East European followers are gradually beginning to con-cede that much also with regard to the early industrialization plans in their countries.
>
> (b) Disregard of, and interference with, the price mechanism can be pushed too far also within the context of the high-pressure-growth strat-egy. For example, the policy of keeping prices of producers' goods ar-tificially low in the face of an escalating demand for them made little

sense. The unwillingness to use the rate of interest or some workable substitute for it was likewise unfortunate: in view of the pressing need for quick and cumulative output increases, the Soviet-type economies would have been well served by a rationing device which could eliminate slowly maturing investment processes unless they promise strikingly high returns in the future, and forcibly remind the constructors that time is money.

(c) Most importantly, we are not obliged to follow the Eastern and Western neo-Hegelians in accepting the actually adopted growth strategy as an inexorable must. In terms of our analogy, not all wars are alike, and men in charge do have in most cases at least some possibility to exercise options between more or less limited war objectives, more or less unrestrained methods of warfare, smaller or larger numbers of enemies to be fought at the same time. This is, if anything, still more true when the "war objective" is socio-economic modernization of a country. Indeed, it stands to reason that if sacrifices imposed on the people of the Soviet Union and of Eastern Europe during the initial period of Stalinist planning had been less harsh, and if the planned rate of growth as well as the investment targets had been more consistent with the actual size and structure of the productive capacity of the countries in question, a more balanced and an ultimately larger expansion of effective economic potential might have resulted.

No doubt, the growth performance of the Soviet-type economies in the past has been remarkable by comparative standards, and development strategies suggested by various "deviators" from the Stalinist line would have had their share of tensions and risks. But if the above-indicated considerations are plausible, impressive results could have been achieved at a smaller cost in human welfare and without generating, on anything like a comparable scale, whole clusters of institutional and behavioral patterns which were bound to become increasingly counterproductive and to develop a formidable staying power after the circumstances had changed.

III. The Prospects

The over-all philosophy behind the reforms as seen by their leading intellectual protagonists was effectively summed up by Liberman:

> The system of centralized planning will be merely strengthened when we will free it of clogging detail. Only then will centralized planning be able to concentrate on providing a scientific basis for the rate and proportions of economic growth, on matters of technological policy, on the system of prices, public finance, and on optimal relationships between consumption and accumulation. . . . Some economists hope that miscalculation and mistakes under maximally centralized planning can be avoided by creating a vast network of computing centers, by combining them into one system and by subordinating them to a sort of operational electronic Gosplan. Yet it seems highly dubious whether it is possible to manage from one center (even if fully equipped by modern electronics) a complex organism such as a modern national economy. I have no great faith in a push-button economy. (Interview in *Komsomol'skaia Pravda*, April 24, 1966.)

As the earlier paragraphs indicate, I am in general agreement with this attitude. To put the same point negatively, and to restate what has been said at the outset, I find it very difficult to take declarations about impending "restoration of capitalism" in the Soviet Union and Eastern Europe seriously, no matter whether such statements originate in the U.S. or in China. Also, the much more sophisticated view, according to which the devolution of authority to individual enterprises will tend to reproduce some typical weaknesses of the atomistic market economy in a non-capitalist setting, seems unjustified.[1] Under the new system the central planning authorities will remain in charge of distributing the large bulk of investible resources over the major segments of the economy in conformity with the long-range development plans; they will be directly controlling monumental investment projects of country-wide importance; and they will obviously have a much more than adequate power to intervene whenever a profit-and-loss calculation of an individual manager or of an industrial branch directorate should be seriously deficient in accounting for all positive or negative external effects of the productive activities of the respective enterprises and industries. The trouble with the recent reforms is not that they go too far from the standpoint of rational socialist policy, but that they do not go far enough, and that the pace of change is likely to be halting and uneven. Here are, in all brevity, some of the reasons for apprehension:

1. The reforms as they stand now left a number of unresolved questions which can give rise to difficulties:

(a) While the number of planned indicators is now reduced, there are still quite a few of them left around. It is far from clear how the enterprise manager is supposed to act if the stipulations based on diverse indicators will turn out to be mutually inconsistent, and who is going to adjudicate the conflict. On the face of it, this holds true to a much attenuated extent, if at all, for the Czechoslovak reform which has only a few centrally fixed targets for directorates of industrial branch units rather than for individual enterprises, and which provides for compensating any economic losses caused to the enterprise by such fixed targets. Yet it should be kept in mind that these changes (as well as the less radical changes envisioned in other Soviet-bloc countries) are supposed to be carried out gradually through 1968; hence their immediate impact is not likely to be significant.

[1] For reasons which should be readily understandable to the readers of *Dissent*, I would not call the Soviet-type setting socialist. To put it in a nutshell, to Social Democrats like myself, a large measure of public ownership is a necessary but not a sufficient condition for considering a society socialist: and it hardly needs emphasizing that the second crucial component, i.e., a consistently democratic political framework, has been conspicuously absent in the Soviet Union and in Eastern European "people's democracies," although the oppressiveness of the dictatorial one-party rule has undoubtedly abated during the post-Stalin era.

(b) Greater latitude in spending retained parts of the enterprise's gross profits constitutes a clear gain in overall efficiency provided that managers are able to get what they actually want; this, however, presupposes a much greater degree of flexibility on the supply side than the Soviet-type economies have known thus far. It would surely be rash to expect that the reforms as such will significantly ease the "seller's market" situation prevailing in these economies, unless the planners will be reconciled to introduce an element of slack in the system by paring down their overall plans. (For a very clear recognition of the point, see Liberman's article in *Pravda* of November 21, 1965.) I shall have more to say about it presently.

(c) As was repeatedly pointed out, the enhanced standing of the profit criterion can improve efficiency only if the prices of goods and factors of production will be reflecting the underlying scarcities; otherwise individual managers might, in response to faulty price signals, economize on factors which are relatively abundant, and show excessive largesse in use of the short-supply items. Yet the outlines of the impending price reforms are still, in most cases, fairly vague. It is not known what ground rules for the price determination will be adopted (the average cost seems a more likely candidate than marginal cost, in spite of the justified preference of the leading theoretical economists of the area for the latter), nor how often the prices will be revised in response to changes in supply-and-demand conditions, and who will do the revising. On the last-mentioned point, the Czechoslovak reform is more explicit than all others. It envisages three basic categories of prices: centrally fixed prices for 64 per cent of the industrial output, flexible prices with centrally determined upper limits (or in some cases upper and lower limits) for 29 per cent, and fully flexible prices for the remaining 7 per cent. Yet the dangers of excessive rigidity in the first group and of oligopolistic manipulation in the second cannot be discounted; moreover, the final outcome of the new policy will decisively depend on the spirit in which it will be carried out by the powers-that-be, a point to which I shall return.

(d) Assuming that the profit criterion will be rigorously enforced, it is quite possible that the workers whose contribution to the output is very low will be dismissed—a situation which would bring relief in the labor-shortage economy of Czechoslovakia, but which could generate some unemployment in all other countries. On principle, quite a few of the discharged workers could be quickly and usefully reabsorbed by a labor-intensive and largely private small-scale manufacturing, construction, and trade. But chances of substantial expansion of such a sector are dim, for reasons which are, in major part, political and ideological.

2. The macro-economic setting within which the reforms operate is not too propitious. No doubt, the recently released Soviet Five-Year Plan is more moderate and less "voluntaristic" in its planned growth rate and investment targets than its Stalinist and Khrushchevian predecessors; the same is true of the Czechoslovak, Hungarian, and Polish Five-Year Plans. All of them, nevertheless, are still quite ambitious, and they seem to operate on the implicit assumption that the recent reforms will bring

about a quick and substantial improvement in over-all efficiency. (It might be worth noting, incidentally, that although Kosygin in his September, 1965, report envisaged an increase in the share of consumption in the national income, the draft of the Five-Year Plan adopted by the Twenty-third Congress of the CPSU six months later did not bear him out.) Should the fulfillment of these plans fall significantly short of expectations, tendencies toward recentralization will be strengthened. Moreover, the international situation as it appears now is not conducive to the relaxation of pressures on the economy, to say the very least.

3. The unusually frank discussion which preceded and followed the recent changes in the Soviet Union and in Eastern Europe has confirmed that influential elements within the existing political and administrative setup are still clinging to methods of the Stalinist command economy and are doing their level best to make the reforms a dead letter in a variety of ways:

There is evidence that Stalinist administrators in several East European countries managed to subvert the previous attempts to promote industrial associations and to transform these organizations into additional devices for the central planners' control over individual enterprises.

Some of the more nimble defenders of the old creed have been trying to steal a march on their adversaries in the prestigious area of the mushrooming mathematical economics by advocating extensive use of electronic computer techniques as a substitute for economic decentralization rather than as an important complement to it. (It might be added that none of the leading Soviet and East Eruopean linear programmers and input-output analysts was taken in by this maneuver.)

While the position of the enterprises with regard to the central authorities has been strengthened, the dice are still heavily loaded in favor of the latter: this holds true (for the duration of the transitional period, at least) also for Czechoslovakia. The consequences of this situation were succinctly stated by Liberman in his already quoted interview:

> One can easily visualize the possibility that a ministry through some of its representatives will try to intervene administratively in matters in which it is not supposed to intervene. Such an administrator who does not want to part with his old habits would harm the cause of economic reconstruction. A clash could ensue. The enterprise may be objectively right, and the representative of the industry not. But for the manager of the enterprise it will be hard to get embroiled every time in a conflict with the ministry he is subordinated to.

Last, and most important: should the difficulties outlined in the preceding paragraphs materialize on a significant scale, the "centralizers" could be relied on to use them in order to turn the clock back as they did in Poland in the late fifties and in Czechoslovakia in the early sixties. In other words, the cycle of reform and counter-reform may well be resumed unless some major external or internal developments of a non-economic nature should make this somewhat tame prediction look either unduly cautious or excessively optimistic.

ECONOMIC REFORMS: A BALANCE SHEET*

Gregory Grossman

The year 1965—like 1953 and 1956—was a memorable landmark in the postwar history of Communist Europe: it was The Year of Economic Reform. Anticipated quietly by East Germany in 1963—and, of course, by Yugoslavia a decade earlier—nearly all the countries of Eastern Europe succumbed within a span of twelve months, one after the other, like so many dominoes, to the winds of economic change: Czechoslovakia in January 1965, Poland in July, the Soviet Union in September, Hungary in November, and Bulgaria in early December. Just a fortnight before the year ran out, East Germany tinkered further with its "New Economic System." And as though to ensure its reformist lead on its neighbors to the east and north, Yugoslavia took another long forward step in July 1965. Only internally rigid Rumania, still too successful with Stalinist economic methods to fully realize their defects, and tiny Albania, defiant in Balkan manner behind its Chinese wall, have so far escaped the epidemic of economic reform.

The East German "New Economic System" is the sole reform system functioning at this time. In all the other cases the reforms have proceeded no farther than stated intentions on the part of the ruling regimes, or at best some preliminary steps in the promised direction. The next two to three years will test each regime's capacity and resolution to do the job. How far and how fast the reforms will eventually go is still largely a matter of conjecture—fascinating conjecture, given the welter of economic, political, ideological, and international factors impinging on their progress. We shall take a brief look at some of these factors in the present essay. But from the outset we must recognize that if each country's announcement of an economic reform represents the end of one era of political struggles and doctrinal debates, it also marks the beginning of a new era that will produce clashes no less intense. In what follows we are concerned with the USSR and other Soviet-type economies, and only incidentally with Yugoslavia.

*Reprinted by permission from *Problems of Communism* (Nov.-Dec. 1966), pp. 43–55. All footnotes deleted.

Problems and Causes

The readers of this journal—and especially of the series of articles on "Economics and Politics" in its recent issues—need hardly be reminded of the main problems associated with the traditional Soviet-type "command" economy, and hence of the considerations that have prompted some sort of reform in all the countries in question. Very poor articulation of demand and supply; accumulation of unwanted goods; highly wasteful use of resources in production; a relatively low share of the national product going to the consumer and, within the limits of this share, poor attention to his interests; generally low quality of products, which among other things affects the competitiveness of exports on the world market; undistinguished performance of the agricultural sector: these are some of the well-known "static" defects of the Soviet-type economy. On the "dynamic" side, we note considerable declines in the traditionally high rates of growth in all the countries in question after the turn of the decade; corresponding declines in annual rates of increase of labor productivity and consumption levels; disappointing—though in themselves often quite respectable—rates of technological progress, in part owing to opposition to innovation from below; falling increments in product per unit of investment, and so forth.

Underlying these negative phenomena are such institutional causes as overcentralization of decisions and correspondingly overextended lines of communication; exceedingly complicated administrative structures; primitive methods of planning; reliance on crude physical indicators; information that is at once excessive in volume and poorly adapted to sophisticated decision-making; faulty signals, chiefly owing to irrational pricing practices; a rigid system of materials allocation; suppression of initiative and impairment or misplacement of incentives; political interference at all levels of the economy; dogmatically rooted impediments, such as evidenced in pricing principles and in the opposition to virtually any private enterprise, even where it would be clearly beneficial to economic performance. These causes, no less than their effects, are well known both to outside students of the Soviet economic system and to domestic critics.

Yet the picture must not be painted in unduly dark tones. With some notable exceptions—such as the total halt in Czechoslovakia's growth-rate in 1962–1964, and the chronic ills of agriculture in most of the countries—the European Communist economies are continuing to grow at respectable rates, albeit less rapidly than before. Consumption levels are continuing to rise, and technological standards are advancing. The point is that these increases are inadequate from the standpoint of both the regimes and their populations. At the same time, it would be shortsighted to see the case for reforms as resting on economic grounds alone. There is little doubt that at this juncture in history the pressure for reform in Communist countries is rooted not only in economic expectations but also in political and moral aspirations. The *decentralization* of the economic structure is undoubtedly favored by some of its partisans as a step toward the eventual *democratization* of political and social life, as well as for its economic benefits.

External Influences

A number of forces from the outside world have also given a push to the reform movement.

The importance of the Yugoslav example—"socialist" and Marxist, but with a fundamentally different institutional system—can hardly be exaggerated. However wanting Yugoslav reality may be in relation to its own ideal or to the more advanced and sophisticated economies of the industrial West, its strengths often lie precisely where the major weaknesses of the Soviet-type economies and societies are to be found. Its market mechanism permits the suppleness and the dispersed initiative that the command economy lacks. There is greater acceptance of small-scale private enterprise. Its system of workers' self-government strives at that measure of industrial democracy which is conspicuously lacking in other countries proclaiming themselves to be socialist. Nor has Yugoslavia had to pay a price for these advantages in terms of economic growth, for its growth rate compares favorably with those of its more orthodox neighbors. Last but not least, Yugoslavia's economic reforms have been accompanied by some (if so far quite limited) liberalization and democratization in the cultural and political spheres. The party's role in society has become more circumscribed. In sum, by its mere existence Yugoslavia serves as an example of a workable, and in many respects attractive, form of socialist economy and society.

If the capitalist economies of the West do not represent an alternative for the Soviet-type countries in the same sense in which Yugoslavia does, they nonetheless provide forceful examples of technological modernity and consumer well-being that are not lost on either the regimes or the populations of Eastern Europe. At the same time, Western economics—especially that part of it which concerns itself with the maximization of social objectives through rational resource utilization—has made a profound impact on at least a part of the economics profession in the Communist countries. Being largely apolitical, this body of Western economics is in principle easily transferable into a socialist context, where it has a high potential impact because of its profound implications for rationalizing, planning and management. Moreover, its arrival in the East tends to de-ideologize and de-dogmatize the Communist political economy, thus smoothing the way for pragmatically-motivated institutional changes.

Lastly, the importance of foreign trade in preparing the ground for the reforms must not be underrated. All the European Communist countries have continuously faced serious shortages of foreign exchange, and for all of them, except the Soviet Union, rapid industrialization without relatively large importations of goods—whether raw materials of highly fabricated goods (especially machinery), or both, depending on the particular country—is impossible. Extensive credits are difficult for them to obtain. Thus, they must export on a large scale, both to the East and to the West. In doing so they submit their goods to a severe competitive test in terms of quality and technological modernity; and their economic institutions undergo a similar test in terms of adaptability to changing external conditions and overall effectiveness. Frequently they have found both their goods and their institutions to be seriously wanting on these scores. In all the countries, with the exception of the USSR, a major argument for thoroughgoing economic reform has been the need to render their economies more effective in both the "capitalist" and the "socialist" world markets.

But the influence of foreign trade on reformist thinking does not stop here. The "socialist world market," in which the European Communist countries transact about two-thirds of their external trade, is after all a *market*. As such, it has served as a school, and a very compelling one at that, in which the logic of market relations among *socialist* entities was inevitably learned by the regimes in question. Among other things, they learned in this school that rational economic decisions cannot be based on irrational price structures, and that every resource use has its opportunity cost—elementary verities of economics that all too often have been overlooked by Communist leaders and planners when not subjected to the discipline of the external market and the relentless need to earn foreign exchange.

Furthermore, a country which desperately needs to earn foreign exchange soon begins to think of it as a main objective of economic policy. Because foreign exchange is a relatively simple, quantifiable, and even almost unidimensional criterion of national-economic success (compared, say, to such domestic objectives as industrialization or the improvement in living standards), it can be easily incorporated into formal theories or mathematical expressions that purport to specify the conditions of efficient resource allocation. One thousand more dollars (or marks, or pounds, or even foreign-trade rubles) is always better than one thousand less when foreign exchange is desperately scarce, and therefore a pattern of resource use that earns the extra thousand is clearly better than one that does not. From this point on the rational economic calculus can take over. Hence, the chronic shortage of foreign exchange was a kind of blessing in the guise of a crisis—at least in the sense of opening the door to the intrusion of rational methods into Communist political economy and to the slow exit of scholasticism and dogma. This is just what has been happening in Eastern Europe since the mid-1950's, when formal theories of "foreign trade efficiency" began to make their appearance. There is thus a direct intellectual link between the primitive formulas for foreign-exchange maximization that appeared in Hungary in 1954 and the elaborate theoretical and philosophical underpinning of that country's far-reaching economic reform a decade later.

The Reform Proposals

Since the syndrome of economic malfunctioning is largely the same in all Soviet-type countries, it is not surprising that the remedial measures proposed by the current reforms consist of essentially the same ingredients, though often mixed in different proportions. To indicate the main ingredients we can do no better than to reproduce a list that was prepared by the research staff of the United Nations Economic Commission for Europe:

(i) Broad directives seeking to improve central planning techniques, requiring, in particular, greater reliance on the medium and long-term plans which are regarded as devices for achieving greater stability in the conditions under which enterprises operate;

(ii) Changes and reductions in the centrally planned targets that are mandatory for the enterprise, together with greater emphasis on gross income (*i.e.,* net value added), profit, and rate of profitability as criteria for judging the enterprise's success;

(iii) The expansion of decentralized investment funds available to enterprises and the larger economic units, and a greater use of bank credits;

(iv) The introduction of a capital charge on the fixed assets of enterprises, which will play an increasingly important role in transferring a proportion of profits to the budget;

(v) A strengthening of economic incentives (amounting in some cases to changes in the wage system) by establishing closer ties between the remuneration of employees and the enterprise's performance;

(vi) The promotion of direct contracts between economic units which, in contrast with the old system, are no longer conceived simply as instruments for the implementation of national plans, but rather as a means of guiding the plan itself;

(vii) Price reforms, which include changes in the determination of prices and in the price structure;

(viii) The concentration of industrial enterprises into larger units (sometimes accounting for a whole branch of industry), . . . [having] administrative responsibilities but being called upon to operate to a greater extent as economically accountable organizations;

(ix) The streamlining of the administrative apparatus responsible for the management of industry, and/or various administrative changes having more specific objectives.

The basic thrust of all the reforms is in the direction of decentralization, which is natural considering that the ills of the traditional system have been largely ills of overcentralization. But the various reforms differ greatly in the extent and comprehensiveness of the decentralizing measures. On this more presently. One feature should be noted here, however. In all the reforms except the most conservative, the Soviet, and the most daring, the Hungarian, the decentralization is in large measure not to the level of the individual enterprise but to that of the newly-created (or strengthened) "associations" into which the enterprises of whole industries have been or are being combined (see item viii above). This is important.

One reason given for creating powerful "branch associations" is that they can take over much of the burden of *centralized* planning, coordination, and management from the national planning agencies, and thus allow the latter to concentrate on broader and more basic problems. The associations are closer to the enterprises and can plan and manage them more effectively than can the top planners. The second reason for emphasizing the associations is that they have some distinct advantages over enterprises in terms of economies of scale: ensuring large production runs where possible, centralizing research for the industry, standardizing technology and design, dealing with foreign buyers. We may add a third reason: it is easier for central authorities to maintain economic and political vigilance over 100-odd associations than over thousands of enterprises, especially if some devolution of decision-making power is to take place.

But what remains unclear in all reforms that place heavy emphasis on the branch associations—including the East German case where the new system has been in effect for several years—is how the coordination between branches is to be achieved without depriving the associations of their autonomy. If the reforms stop short of creating a workable market mechanism, there is always the danger of either permitting the associations to develop into autarkic empires, with consequent loss of efficiency and progressivity, or, to avoid these defects, backsliding into the old-style command economy by recentralizing to the top level. On the other hand, should a market mechanism be introduced, the socialist country would enter the new era with a structure of supermonopolies, with all that again implies for efficiency and progressivity. Of course, insofar as the associations will be marketing abroad, they will be in salutary competition with foreign producers. But their domestic markets are likely to remain well protected, if only because foreign exchange shortages—which are sure to persist for a long time yet—will forestall active competition on the side of imports.

It is also necessary to take note of what the announced reforms are *not* to change—even on paper, let alone in the process of their realization:

1. They assuredly are not intended to overturn the political monopoly of the party, the exclusive power of the regime, the basic commitment to a socialist system, or the proclaimed advance towards full communism and further rapid industrialization.

2. The reforms do not challenge the principle of central planning of all the important "proportions" of the economy and of its speed and direction of development. Even should some of the reforms go so far as to establish socialist market systems, they will continue to be subject to comprehensive national planning and central control and regulation.

3. Moreover, there is little indication that the resources of each country will cease to be under great pressure. While the national plans in the future may be less ambitious—not to say fanciful—than in the past, they will most likely continue to call for the highest degree of resource utilization. A corollary is that sellers' markets are likely to persist.

4. Because of this, and because of fear of inflation and uncontrolled redistribution of income, prices on all or nearly all important producer goods are likely to remain under control for some time. (We shall return to the question of prices at a later point in this essay).

5. The physical allocation (rationing) of producer goods (materials and equipment) continues in all the countries, and—in part because of points 3 and 4 above—is likely to continue for some time. There is talk, even in the USSR, of eventually abolishing materials allocation and going over to "wholesale trade" in producer goods, and the talk itself represents a significant change. But for some time it is likely to remain talk.

6. The functionaries of both the government and the party on levels above the enterprise remain largely the same, although they may change offices and "hats." And their mental habits remain the same. This is surely one of the more important reasons to expect a conservative bias in the implementation of the reforms.

7. The principle of "one-man" management in the enterprise is not being significantly diluted, and the manager is still accountable only upward, not downward. In other words, the Yugoslav institution of "workers' self-management" is not being adopted. This is not an oversight; rather, it is a deliberate decision, common to all the regimes in question, to retain political as well as economic power where it now resides. More on this below.

8. Lastly, so far the institutional reforms have touched agriculture only marginally if at all, although in some of the countries (especially the USSR and Hungary) additional resources in the form of higher prices

and larger capital allocations have been channeled into the agricultural sector with the aim of improving its performance.

The Line-up of Forces

The question of economic reform has been one of the most intense political issues to arise in Eastern Europe in the last several years. It has been as widely debated in professional journals, in the daily and specialized press, in academic forums, and in high councils, as any economic measure in any part of the world in recent history. It has profoundly divided the economic profession (though not in equal measure in different countries), and it could not help but cause deep division within the leaderships as well. Yet we know relatively little of the *political* side of the coin.

We do know that some of the most ardent advocates of reform—that is, of *some* reform of a decentralizing and rationalizing nature—have been academic economists (including those affiliated with research institutes) rather than the economic experts involved in actual planning or administration. But we also know that there have been, and continue to be, great differences in approach and opinion within the profession, ranging from preference for relatively mild tinkering with prices and organizational structures to advocacy of a socialist market economy that is highly decentralized, at least for current production decisions and a portion of investment. Academic economists—some of them young and quite mathematically (or at least "Western") oriented in their economics—seem to have played an especially significant role in working out the blueprints of the two most far-reaching reforms, those of Czechoslovakia and Hungary. In the Soviet Union, where the generational pattern was more severely imposed by the preceding decades of Stalinism, the division among economists has been in good measure along age lines. But even there, some of the abler and more vocal pre-reform leaders belonged to a venerable generation: the late V. Nemchinov, V. Novozhilov, A. Vainshtein, and (the somewhat younger) Ye. Liberman.

Much of the discussion among economists has been characterized by polemical intensity, which is not unusual for economic debates conducted in the shadow of political and ideological authority. The would-be reformers show a missionary zeal that is compounded of deep dissatisfaction with the *status quo* and faith in newly-discovered (or resuscitated) economic truths. Their opponents have reacted to the challenge of their traditional axioms and habitual modes of thinking with predictable immoderation. Such, however, is the sweep of economic reformism in Eastern Europe (except in Rumania and Albania) that the Stalinist model seems to be no longer *openly* defended.

We know from their writings and from other evidence that some of the managers have been pro-reform, or at least in favor of lightening the weight of the superordinate bureaucracy and doing away with some of the irrationalities and inefficiencies of the existing system. But it would be overly hasty to assume that the vast majority of managers were in favor of the reforms, let alone of thoroughgoing decentralization. After all, the managers of today are the ones who succeeded under the old system by virtue of appropriate abilities or right connections. They are part of the Communist "establishment." Must we assume that they would overwhelmingly favor a change in the rules of the game?

What the man in the street or at the workbench has thought of the reforms while they were being debated in the press, after their announcement, and during the initial phases of their implementation, we simply do not know. Some may welcome the reforms for their promise of higher living standards. But many may fear for their jobs. In countries—notably Czechoslovakia—where, for incentive purposes, greater wage differentials have been advocated by the proponents of reform, the average (or below average) man may well feel apprehension. But we might also guess that having seen many a reform under the Communist regime in the past, the average citizen is prone to take an agnostic if not a cynical view.

Information on this score is fragmentary, but it seems that the chief opponents of the reform, and the chief obstructionists to their successful implementation at this stage, are to be found in the intermediate and upper layers of the party and government bureaucracy. The reasons, no doubt, are complex: fear of losing position or status, fear of opening a Pandora's box, ideological rigidity, and so forth.

Comparisons and Contrasts

Since the reforms in the individual countries have already been discussed in separate articles of the present series, we shall restrict ourselves here to pointing out the considerable range in the degree of "reformism" that the various measures—or, at this point more correctly, their language—represent. The most conservative, those of Poland and the USSR, bear a resemblance which seems to derive as much from shared caution or indecision as from anything else. Since the Polish reform was only recently discussed at some length in this journal by Professor Smolinski, we shall concentrate here on the Soviet reform as an example of a conservative measure.

The Soviet reform consists of two distinct, if interrelated, parts: 1) the abolition of Khrushchev's *sovnarkhozy* (regional economic councils) and the reestablishment of "branch" ministries on the pre-1957 model; and 2) the reform "proper," which amounts to some vertical decentralization, together with related measures in the realms of prices, incentives, and management.

The reversion to a ministerial organization—a move of some significance but not of central importance for our present discussion—was carried out immediately upon its enactment in early October 1965, even without waiting for the end of the plan year. This haste is rather difficult to
understand; it must have caused considerable confusion for a while.

The Soviet reform "proper" is being put into effect much more slowly,
and by stages. It is to be fully implemented only after the revision of the
price structure in completed—supposedly by 1967–68. The main features
of the reform are:

1. replacement of the "gross value of output" target by the "value of
sales" target as the chief success indicator for enterprises;

2. an enhanced role for profit as a criterion of successful operation,
although at this point it is unclear to what extent it will challenge the
primacy of the sales target in this regard;

3. a reduction, but apparently not a drastic one, in the number of
physical production targets;

4. somewhat more freedom for management in the selection of inputs (labor, materials, equipment) and in inventory holdings;

5. the shift of production planning toward more reliance on mutual
orders among enterprises (so-called "direct links");

6. greater freedom for industrial enterprises to decide their own investment and to finance it from internal funds or bank credit, rather than from
budgetary allocations;

7. financing of some *new* projects by bank credit rather than budgetary
allocations;

8. charging of interest (though not under this name) for all the capital
invested in an enterprise;

9. use of a part of the profit earned by an enterprise for bonuses to its
management and staff, linking the bonuses to the amount of profit earned.

Many of these measures—particularly those giving management
somewhat greater leeway as well as a financial inducement to economize—
are so commonsensical that one wonders why it took 35 years to introduce
them. The substitution of the sales target for the gross output target will
presumably eliminate or reduce the ridiculous but not infrequent situation
of enterprises producing utterly unsalable goods. (On the other hand, it
may in some cases only enhance the producers' efforts to pass on their low-
quality wares). Perhaps the most reformist of the features is the granting
of considerable autonomy to enterprises in the realm of investment,
especially for modernization and rationalization. By 1967, a quarter of
gross fixed investment in industry will supposedly have been "decentralized" in this fashion. The catch here, however, is whether the enterprises
will be able to obtain the necessary materials and equipment, which

continue to be tightly rationed, and whether they will have the requisite incentives to undertake the investment. Moreover, the economic rationale of decentralized investments, even if profit-motivated, remains under a cloud until the price structure is rationalized.

The Soviet reform is qualified here as a conservative one because it retains 1) most of the physical production targets, and 2) the rigid system of materials allocation. Both of these holdovers from the past will present serious handicaps to attempts by enterprises to adjust production to demand and to select economical input mixes, even if the role of the profits target under the new system is less equivocal than it seems to be. Lastly, the same functionaries staff the new ministries and bureaus, and complaints are already being voiced in the Soviet press that the bureaucracy refuses to give up its habitual modes of operation.

Some 700 industrial enterprises were converted to the "new system" by mid-1966. It was said in March that by the beginning of 1967 one-third of all industrial workers would be brought under the system, though it is not clear whether the conversion of enterprises implies adoption of all or only some of the above-enumerated changes. The crucial test will come, however, in regard to the revision of the price structure. It is here that much of the current discussion and struggle is centered. Should the price revision follow orthodox lines—eliminating most subsidies but paying little heed to the equilibration of demand and supply—as now seems likely, then (as we shall presently argue) it will be very difficult, even with the best will in the world, to get rid of materials allocation and physical production targets, with the result that no major decentralization can take place.

At the other extreme of the spectrum are the Czechoslovak and Hungarian reforms. The former entered its first phase of implementation at the beginning of 1966; the latter is about to be launched. In both cases, the accompanying rhetoric is more impressive than the institutional reforms themselves. In Czechoslovakia—where growth had ground to a halt and other economic difficulties were pressing—the dominant tone of published *economic* opinion swung from deep orthodoxy to extreme liberalism (in the Communist context) within a matter of months during 1963–64. In Hungary economic opinion shifted more slowly and over a longer period, but by now has arrived at a frontier of liberalism similar to the Czech.

The current rhetoric in these two countries consists of scorn for orthodox, Soviet-type economic insitutions (though with a bow to their contribution to "extensive" growth in the early postwar period) and lavish praise for the market mechanism, profit-making, and competition. To be sure, the profit-making and competition are of the socialist variety, and the market is to be a handmaiden of the national plan. But nonetheless it is hard to believe that statements like "the market is the final touchstone of the social usefulness of expended labor," or the "uniform and single criterion [for economic decision] is profit," emanate from Communist economists writing in official publications. The infatuation with the market—now evident among economists all over Eastern Europe and in the USSR, as well as in the two countries mentioned—may be an understandable and even salutary reaction to its former dogmatic rejection; yet this optimism will doubtless be followed in time by a swing towards the center, when it is realized that the market raises its own difficult problems.

The actual reform measures adopted in Czechoslovakia and Hungary do not fully share the economists' infatuation with the market. These reforms—though far-reaching in comparison to the system they aim to supersede—are much more cautious and compromise-ridden. The *leitmotif* is of course decentralization. We have already noted the agglomeration of Czechoslovak industry into 100-odd concerns and trusts, leaving little prospect for domestic competition. Physical production targets are not entirely eliminated; they remain (in Czechoslovakia) for several dozen commodities of key importance, such as items for which there are definite export commitments. Insofar as this writer is able to discover, the rationing of some scarce producer goods is likely to continue into the near future. Lastly, most producer-goods prices are to be either fixed or subject to ceilings (which amounts to the same thing, since pressure on them is likely to be upward.)

The formal introduction of the Czech reform began almost a year ago, and some useful lessons are already discernible. One of the most significant lessons is that the reforms are destined to have rough sledding, just as they have had even in the far less radical Soviet case. Usually blame is attached to deliberate sabotage or resistance on the part of the hostile and entrenched bureaucracy. (Similar charges have been continually made in Yugoslavia, culminating in the purge of Rankovic and his associates in mid-1966) Quite possibly, this is where most of the blame belongs. Yet, we should also realize that decentralized decision-making simply cannot do a proper job when the signals (prices) are still faulty and the economy is still ridden with scarcities. Under such conditions there may be very good social reasons to keep close rein on the enterprises and the trusts. And a way to discredit the reform would be to decentralize too fast, before prices were properly revised.

Pricing Problems

It is often said in relation to the East European reforms that their success is predicated on the establishment of *rational* price structures. This is not quite correct, if in this context "rational prices" mean what they usually mean to economists: namely, a set of prices which—together with appropriate managerial rules and incentives, and in the light of society's resources and technological knowledge—will maximize some kind of index of social welfare. Of course, in an authoritarian society this index is largely defined, if only implicitly, in an authoritarian way.

Needless to say, prices in no actual economy are "rational" in this theoretical sense. An economy can function quite well, albeit at less than 100 percent theoretical efficiency, if the actual prices deviate moderately from the theoretical norm; and many do. To be sure, the price structures of the Communist economies probably deviate more than "moderately" from the theoretical norm. If the efficiency of the economies is to be raised substantially, the price structures will have to be revised to conform more closely to a rational norm—even though complete coincidence is not to be expected.

What is meant by the reforms succeeding, however, is usually something else; namely, that the decentralizing and initiative-stimulating measures survive an initial test period, and that the economy performs in a reasonably satisfactory fashion there-after. Insofar as prices are concerned, the crux here is that the price structure should not be such as to force major recentralization of economic decisions, and this is achieved by the use of equilibrium prices. By "equilibrium prices" we mean prices which serve to equate demand and supply for each individual commodity, service, or resource. In the abstract model of a perfectly efficient economy, rational prices are also equilibrium prices. But in practice they are not the same, as attested to by every market economy without price control.

To see why equilibrium prices come close to being a necessary condition for the success of the reforms—in the sense in which we have just interpreted "success"—we need only inquire what will happen if the Soviet-type economies are organizationally decentralized, but prices are fixed at levels substantially deviating from equilibrium levels. Since these economies are likely to be experiencing high overall demand in relation to their productive capacity, *i.e.*, inflationary pressure, the fixed prices soon become too low to equate demand and supply. (As we shall presently see, a main reason for price fixing is precisely to resist inflationary pressure.) For the sake of simplicity, let us focus on producer-goods prices at wholesale.

Because prices are too low and demand exceeds supply, all important goods must be allocated (rationed) to reserve them for higher priority purposes, as indeed will continue to be the case under the reforms. As a result, enterprises are severely constrained in their efforts to maximize profits by using the best (*i.e.*, cheapest) combinations of inputs, and one of the chief aims of the reforms is thereby already frustrated.

Moreover, to allocate materials effectively the authorities must take care that the expected supplies are forthcoming. Yet the fixed prices may render the production of some goods unprofitable. Hence, there will be a strong temptation on the authorities' part to keep direct control of production, which means to assign physical production targets to enterprises. (If instead prices should be manipulated to elicit the requisite supplies, which is what the market mechanism would call for, then the objective of a stable price level would be endangered and the specter of inflation would loom larger). But physical production targets have a well-known tendency to proliferate—and before long most important decisions in the economy are recentralized. Even if a reform had gone so far as to establish a market mechanism, the retention of tight materials allocation and other physical controls would tend to undermine the "market" progressively, until finally the command economy was reestablished.

Furthermore, the complex and arduous process of price-fixing in itself strengthens the hand of the bureaucracy, diverts the attention and efforts of enterprises away from production and selling, and retards the de-politicization of economic life (which is one of the desirable corollaries of the market). Even *with* more or less equilibrium prices, the authorities and the bureaucrats might not wish to relinquish materials allocation, either because they want to hold on to their power or because they fear (in part justifiably) that the market alone will not be able to ensure the satisfaction of national priorities. But *without* equilibrium prices, there is little chance that materials allocation will be dismantled.

Thus, equilibrium prices are a necessary—or almost necessary—condition of the success of the decentralizing reforms. Yet, it does not seem that in any of the countries in question the impending price revision will result in bringing wholesale prices of producer goods to equilibrium levels, or at least in leaving them there for a critically lengthy period of time. First, as we have noted, in all cases price revisions will hardly depart from the traditional principle of *fixed* prices. Second, while lip service is often given to the equilibration of demand and supply through prices—especially in the case of Czech, Hungarian and (more recently) East German materials—the more concrete and authoritative statements offer little hope on this score. Rather, the usual formulation is that "prices must be fixed for all important commodities that are still in short supply," which is to say that prices are to be fixed at below-equilibrium levels. Third, in any case it is very hard to compute in advance what the equilibrium level of any price will be while all prices are changing at the same time (and the ground rules of economic behavior as well!). And those prices that are set too low are likely to be kept there as the authorities strain to hold the general price line. Which brings us to the fourth point. While much lip service is also paid to some minimal price flexibility, the arduous-ness of price calculation, the complexity of the procedure, the desire to hold the line against inflation, and the "politics" of the matter—all these considerations rather suggest that once prices are revised they will tend to remain fixed for lengthy periods. Which is to say that even if producer-goods prices start at or near equilibrium levels, they are not likely to stay there very long as supply-demand conditions change.

But why fix producer goods prices? Why not let them fluctuate freely? The reasons are many. The ideologically conservative are repelled by the idea of the "chaos" of freely fluctuating prices under socialism. The top leaders and planners are reluctant to forswear what will become in the process of the reforms a most important instrument of control over the economy. (We may recall here, for example, the danger of monopoly inherent in the newly formed or strengthened "associations.") Bureaucrats do not wish to deprive themselves of their functions, power, and jobs. Some managers may fear the uncertainty that would accompany freely moving prices. It must be noted that price uncertainty is now much more unsettling to enterprises than before, given the enhanced role of profit as a success indicator, as a source of personal income for management and staff, and as the chief determinant of internal investment funds.

Still another major reason for opting for fixed prices is the fear of inflation. Communist governments have always been sensitive on this issue, although—or because—their record on this score is none too strong. There is a good deal of validity to the fear of inflation at the present juncture. Reforms or no, the pressure of overall demand on resources is likely to continue to be strong. In the labor-short countries (Hungary, Czechoslovakia, and East Germany), the tightness of the labor market will continue to put upward pressure on labor costs. In the labor-surplus countries, rural-urban migration will continue to be rapid, continuing to swell money incomes. Relative wages and other incomes may have to be readjusted— for this is one of the rationalizing aspects of the reforms—but the days when it was politically possible to readjust relative incomes by pushing some *money* incomes down are long gone in the countries in question. Thus, the danger of cost inflation by dint of an upward drift in wages and other incomes casts a long shadow on the reforms, even allowing for their expected boost to efficiency. Not surprisingly, wage and salary rates remain generally under central control in all the reforms. But control of wage rates and even of total wage payments is not enough because of the profit-sharing features of the reforms. Hence, there is also an argument for simultaneously fixing prices. The effects of an inflation of producer-goods prices (in the socialist sector) would be serious, even in the socialist economy, and especially after the reforms. It might lead, *via* a "cost push," to inflation of consumer-goods prices, with likely negative political effects. It might also bring about an undesired redistribution of income *via* the profit-sharing schemes. And it would likely distort the direction of investment to the extent that investment is now decentralized.

As we have just noted, wage and salary *rates* will, as a rule, continue to be centrally set under all the reforms in question. However, as a means of checking inflation this control is imperfect, since the central authorities cannot oversee the classification of each employee, a matter which remains dependent in party on individual bargaining between employee and employer. Thus there is reason to limit or restrain the total outpayment of wages and salaries by each enterprise. The reforms provide a range of techniques. In the more conservative reforms, such as the Soviet, the old practice of assigning a maximum wage fund to each enterprise is preserved, although the fund is no longer to be broken down into subdivisions for specific categories of workers and employees. At the other extreme, in Czechoslovakia, there is apparently no such limit on each enterprise, but wages are taxed (*via* a tax on so-called gross income) and a new "stabilization payment" is being introduced, which is a 30-percent tax on wage payments above a stipulated minimum.

In sum, the need for rigid physical controls would be lessened, price flexibility would more likely be allowed, and hence the decentralizing reforms would be more likely to succeed, if the overall pressure on resources—which is to say, the ambitiousness of the national plans and goals of the countries in question—were to be restrained. To some extent the ambitiousness of the national goals is a delayed response to the long-repressed material aspirations of the population. But the pressure on resources also derives in large measure from more traditional Communist objectives—rapid industrialization, military power, *etc.* In this regard it is worth noting that an improvement in the international climate might well have a significant effect both directly and indirectly on the course of the reforms.

The Question of Viability

How viable are these reforms on purely economic grounds? It has already been noted that the "blueprints" of the reforms vary considerably along the scale of liberalization in terms of the decentralization of production and investment decisions—but that everywhere prices and wage rates are to remain under rather tight control, and that (most significantly) materials allocation is to be continued. Clearly the more conservative reforms, especially the Soviet and Polish, fall far short of envisioning anything like a functioning socialist market economy. The Czechoslovak and Hungarian blueprints, in both language and design, come much closer to instituting a market mechanism, at least for current production decisions.

We must bear in mind that the *implementation* of every reform, however liberal or conservative on paper, is likely to suffer from a conservative bias. This is so because, first, the detailed implementation is inevitably in the hands of the bureaucracy and party *apparat*—that is, largely in the hands of the reforms' opponents. But, secondly, there are also good "objective" reasons for the bias. In the course of implementation there will be innumerable specific, detailed problems to be resolved. They will mostly be problems of coordinating separate activities and ensuring harmony between the dispersed decisions and the national goals. As a rule, such specific problems can be resolved only by centralizing certain particular decisions and actions, not by leaving them to be handled at the enterprise level.

Thus, the implementation of the reforms is likely to fall short of the decentralizing reach of their blueprints. Will the resultant half-way or quarter-way solutions be viable? One wonders. If the market mechanism is not strongly enough established—and most of the reforms do not even intend to establish it—then the burden of coordination along the millions of economic decisions and activities will largely remain with the central authorities. To do this job—and to protect its own positions—the bureaucracy is likely to resume the process of centralization. In this it will be strongly abetted by the persistence of materials allocation and by the fear of inflation, as has already been argued. Moreover, the partial decentralization of investment in the absence of a suitable price system may well channel resources into directions that the central authorities deplore and that they will therefore attempt to thwart by administrative means. In general, effective decentralization in a centrally-administered economy can take place only when carried out on a very broad front all at once, which requires intervention from higher quarters and calls for big political battles. Centralization, however, can and often does proceed in little steps, virtually unnoticed but important in aggregate impact.

Of course, many of the sensible features of the present reforms are likely to survive the recentralizing process. Such measures as the substitution of the sales target for the gross output target, the charging of interest and economic rent, a moderate amount of profit-sharing, need not fall victim to recentralization.

To sum up, the more conservative reforms involve relatively little liberalization to begin with, and to the extent that they do, they are soon likely to begin drifting back towards the *status quo ante* (at least in the absence of additional broad decentralizing measures). The countries with more liberal reforms are also likely to experience recentralizing tendencies soon after the new institutions make their appearance. But here—which is to say, primarily in Hungary and Czechoslovakia—the repudiation of the old system has gone so far that the result is more likely to be a lengthy epoch of drift rather than a substantial reversion to the former extremely centralized setup—unless, of course, more resolute liberalization is decreed from above to establish a viable, market-bound alternative to the command economy.

It should be noted that the chances of such resolute liberalization do not seem to be high for the foreseeable future. No doubt voices will continue to be raised in favor of a fuller role for the market mechanism. The struggles and debates will go on. But, by having gone as far as it has already, "by consenting to reform the old bankrupt planning system, the regime hopes to gain a new lease on life, not to abdicate." Economic liberalization is pregnant with political risks—the more liberalization, the higher the risks—and the first imperative of each regime is to retain power, not to endanger it for the sake of better economic performance. In this it has the more-than-willing support of the bureaucracy and the *apparat*. On the other hand, it would be foolhardy to exclude altogether the prospect of "marketization" of the present command economies. Yugoslavia has accomplished a form of it, although under very specific conditions. The Soviet world is in flux and ferment; the chain of surprises has not yet come to an end. There may be a lesson in the fact that few competent observers would have predicted three or four years ago that the cautious Czechoslovak and Hungarian regimes were about to sanction their economic reforms, even if only on paper.

Political Implications

What, then, of the future? We noted at the start that economic decentralization should not be confused with socio-political democratization. True, in all East European countries the launching of the reforms was preceded by a remarkable broadening of the limits of economic discussion. Some extension of the bounds of permissible discussion also occurred in other social sciences (sociology and law) and in cultural affairs. Yet the launching of the reforms themselves need not at all imply further liberalization in the intellectual and cultural spheres. Indeed, the opposite may happen, should the regimes feel that the potentially centrifugal effect of the economic reforms ought to be contained by stricter ideological and social controls: or should bargains be struck between various factions in the leadership, in the sense that the "price" of economic liberalization becomes retrenchment on other fronts. Such seems to have been the case in the USSR, as evidenced by the divergent lines laid down at the 23rd Party Congress (March 1966), where the economic reforms of the preceding autumn were reaffirmed, together with a distinct hardening of ideological and cultural positions. A similar trend has also been evident in Hungary. Nor need we expect that the purely economic successes of the reforms—if they materialize—must perforce increase freedom and democratize political life in the Communist countries. Greater economic freedom for managers is not yet political freedom for everyone, and improvement in material conditions of life can come without the multi-party ballot.

It would be convenient to leave the argument at this point, but much too easy. For one thing, a successful decentralization of the economy—should it occur despite the various handicaps that have been outlined above—would tend to change the role of the party in society. Today, the lower and intermediate party levels owe their functions and powers in the economy precisely to the failure of economic institutions. So far, these levels of the *apparat* have had a job to do because of inadequate incentives, improper signals, imperfect coordination within the economy, conflicting goals and standards, shortages of all sorts, and other functional defects. In all such cases the party has had to step in to keep the wheels of the economy turning. But if the economic mechanism itself is so improved as to provide adequate and proper signals, incentives, and coordination, then most of the party's economic functions at the intermediate and lower levels disappear. The basic question of what role the party is playing in society, already looming on the horizon, will become even more apt and timely. Will the parties in the other Communist countries be prepared to restrict their day-to-day economic roles as the Yugoslav party has done?

Seen otherwise, the political implications of the reforms depend largely on the extent to which economic decentralization survives the initial test—about which we have already expressed considerable doubt—and proves capable of creating alternate nodes of power that in some measure escape the full control of the regime. The great autonomy of enterprises (or "associations") creates some measure of power that—almost by definition—is not under the close control of the party leaders. But whether this can contribute to the growth of meaningful political pluralism remains to be seen. On the other hand, enterprise autonomy may stimulate the appearance of labor organizations such as workers' councils (as distinct from the regime-controlled trade unions) with which to confront management "from below." Any such institutions would be potentially significant sources of power in that they would be relatively independent not only of management but of the existing political authority. Enterprise autonomy is conducive to labor autonomy, and it is the latter that poses by far the greater challenge to the existing order. Could the conservative opposition to economic reform be motivated in part by fear of this possibility? If so, the Yugoslav experience with workers' "self-management" offers nothing to allay the conservatives' apprehensions.

That the present European Communist regimes (except Yugoslavia) have little liking for autonomous workers' councils is clear. Where such councils arose spontaneously—in Poland and Hungary in 1956—they were quickly suppressed or subverted after the new regimes re-established internal control. They are most conspicuously absent from all the blueprints of economic reform, although some token gestures are made in the direction of worker participation in decisions at the enterprise level. Yet it is hard to believe that in time the issue of autonomous workers' councils and meaningful workers' "self-management" will not come to the forefront. When it arises, it will be inevitably linked with the issue of more meaningful enterprise autonomy, for without the latter, workers' councils or "self-management" lack substance. And at that juncture the political implications of economic reform will become much more profound than now.

ECONOMIC REFORM IN EASTERN EUROPE AND THE USSR: COMMENT*

— · — · — · — · — · — · — · — · — · — .

Abram Bergson

What is market socialism? Just how does it differ from the alternative form of socialist planning with which it is usually contrasted, centralized planning? Our speakers refer to these concepts without much elaboration. Since the two kinds of socialist planning systems have been construed somewhat variously, perhaps I should explain that I think of market socialism as differing from centralized planning chiefly in respect to procedures used for determining inputs and outputs of production units. If I may quote from a recently published essay of mine ("Market Socialism Revisited," *Journal of Political Economy,* October 1967, p. 432), " . . . under centralized planning such inputs and outputs typically are controlled to a marked degree by superior agencies in a bureaucratic structure through use of extra-market devices, such as physical quotas. Under market socialism, determination of factor inputs and outputs typically is left to authorities immediately in charge of production units, though superior agencies may still exercise much influence through manipulation of prices and other financial instruments."

To this I would now add that where prices and other financial instruments are used by superior agencies to control production units, market socialism also presupposes that these instruments not be highly discriminatory. The difference between market socialism and centralized planning would seem to narrow if, for example, superior agencies, while abstaining from imposing quotas on material inputs to different production units, should still charge such units very different prices for the same material.

All of this, I believe, conforms to the most usual understanding, but note that centralized planning and market socialism are considered here

*Reprinted by permission of the author and publisher from *American Economic Review*, Proceedings, May, 1968.

to represent a dichotomy, though decentralization and use of financial instruments may, of course, vary within each category. Professor Campbell,[1] however, apparently prefers to think of the two systems as polar opposites. He is certainly free to do so, but he refers to a particular case which he considers as falling under neither centralist planning nor market socialism as usually understood: essentially important responsibilities are borne neither by bureaucratic agencies at a high level nor by production units, but by intermediate organizations, say, "cartels" of firms in a particular branch. It should be observed, therefore, that in his famous Competitive Solution, Oskar Lange provided long ago for dual authorities of much the same sort as Campbell envisages: on the one hand, socialist firms responsible for current operations of individual plants; on the other hand, industry authorities in charge of large investments, especially introduction of new plants. Lange's Competitive Solution, of course, is usually considered as the outstanding theoretic example of market socialism.

Under the reforms in progress, how are the planning systems that are emerging in the USSR, Czechoslovakia and Yugoslavia to be characterized in terms of the two kinds of socialist planning as these are understood here? As Professor Ward makes clear, the Yugoslav planning system has been more complex than is often supposed, but I don't think he would object if I held that, even prior to recent reforms it approached, if it did not actually exemplify, market socialism. The latest reforms apparently are intended to result in a still greater reliance on market-like procedures.

Before the current reforms, centralized planning, of course, prevailed in both the USSR and Czechoslovakia. While I have differed somewhat from Professor Campbell terminologically, I can only endorse his account of the reform in progress in the Soviet Union. This is to say that the changes being made are not nearly as dramatic as has been widely reported. The revisions are modest on paper and apparently more so in parctice. As I see it, therefore, the Soviet system that is emerging is still a form of centralized planning. Within this category, however, a perceptible shift is occurring toward market-like arrangements, and so also toward market socialism.

As described by Professor Staller, the current reform in Czechoslovakia is decidedly bolder than that of the USSR. Perhaps the Czechs at long last are in a meaningful sense abandoning centralist planning for market socialism. Before we can properly interpret the Czech reform,

---

[1]*Editor's note.* Professor Bergson refers here to the illuminating papers by Professors Robert Campbell on Soviet economic reforms, George Staller on Czechoslovak economic reforms, and Benjamin Ward on Yugoslav economic reforms which appeared in *American Economic Review*, Proceedings, May, 1968. These papers were unfortunately received too late to be included in this edition of the Reader.

however, we must have further information on aspects that are not yet entirely clear. For example, as Professor George Feiwel has stressed in a Harvard seminar talk and as Professor Staller also points out, the new prices that are being fixed will hardly be at clearing levels. To what extent will the rationing that must often result involve the continued imposition of quotas?

Will the market-like procedures that are being introduced in the three countries prove a permanent feature? What are the prospects that they will be resorted to, if anything, on an increasing scale in the future? Campbell cautiously suggests that in the USSR the most likely eventuality may be the cartellized type of planning system already mentioned. Staller does not commit himself on the prospects in Czechoslovakia. Ward is uncertain whether the latest changes in Yugoslavia will be sustainable, though he nowhere suggests that any major reversion to centralized extra-market procedures is in prospect.

For my part, I join with those who consider that there is an economic case for a shift from centralized planning to some form of market socialism in the USSR, to refer to the country that I know best. The case is admittedly rather theoretic, and not exactly conclusive. Thus, how the Russians might fare economically under market socialism must be judged chiefly from analyses of notably abstract blueprints, including the Competitive Solution. As was brought out long ago and as further inquiry seems only to underline (see my article, previously cited), an attempt to apply such a blueprint could encounter decided difficulties. For the USSR, the difficulties during a transition period might be the greater so far as the resource allocation patterns and prices inherited from centralized planning must often diverge widely from the equilibrium values that have to be sought.

The economic merit of market socialism may also be seen in the light of the experience of Yugoslavia, but I doubt if I am alone in feeling that the available evidence on this experience is difficult to interpret; available evidence, that is, which includes many Yugoslav claims of success, many Yugoslav admissions of wholesale maladjustments and distortions, and the fact that the government itself finds it expedient to launch reorganization after reorganization.

Nevertheless, centralized planning in the USSR is by all accounts notably inefficient. The Russians should be able to improve their performance to some degree by shifting to market socialism. I for one doubt that the advent of the electronic computer will much alter this equation in favor of centralized planning in the visible future. For familiar reasons, including the ever-growing complexity of the economy, the trend may well be the reverse.

The prospects for market socialism in the Soviet Union, however, must also turn on how those in power there might respond to the economic case for it. We must consider, therefore, that while Soviet economics has as reported progressed much since Stalin it still has its limitations. Moreover, among persons bred on Marxian ideology, resort to market-like procedures can scarcely be appealing in any event. Such ideology, however, has been eroding, and in part with the progress of economics. As Ward rightly stresses, Communist authorities everywhere are also sensitive to the loss of power and status that market-like arrangements threaten. To this rule, the Soviet authorities are no exception. Here perhaps the Yugoslav experience is instructive but, as described by Ward, it cannot be very reassuring to communist rulers elsewhere. On the other hand, among some sophisticated proponents of reform such a change probably is valued for liberalizing political repercussions no less than for economic gains that are anticipated.

In summary, the most likely prospect in the USSR, I feel, is still further resort to market-like arrangements, but this is not at all certain, and we cannot rule out altogether reversals, or perhaps even the emergence of some cyclical pattern in which centralized and market-like arrangements simply alternate with each other without there being any very marked trend one way or the other. Such an eventuality is not entirely remote in circumstances such as those in question where there are conflicting goals, initial knowledge of the merits of alternatives is limited, trial-and-error is unavoidable, and because of the very complexity of things it is difficult to learn from experience. Indeed, though the causes must often be somewhat other than these, cyclical patterns of reorganization are not at all unknown in the annals of bureaucracy, including that of the USSR. The recent shifts between ministries and regional authorities are the most outstanding, but not by any means the only example. But intriguing as it is, this possibility could easily be overstressed and I do not wish to do more than bring it to attention.